WORLD TRIBUNAL
ON IF

D0800735

DOURO-DUMMER
PUBLIC LIBRARY

WORLD TRIBUNAL ON IRAQ

Making the Case Against War

edited by Müge Gürsoy Sökmen
introductions by Arundhati Roy and Richard Falk

OLIVE
BRANCH
PRESS

An imprint of Interlink Publishing Group, Inc.
www.interlinkbooks.com

First published in 2008 by

OLIVE BRANCH PRESS
An imprint of Interlink Publishing Group, Inc.
46 Crosby Street, Northampton, Massachusetts 01060
www.interlinkbooks.com

Library of Congress Cataloging-in-Publication Data
Irak dünya mahkemesi. English.
The world tribunal on Iraq : making the case against war / edited by Müge Gürsoy Sökmen ; with
introductions by Arundhati Roy and Richard Falk.—1st American ed.
p. cm.
Includes bibliographical references and index.
Translation of: Irak dünya mahkemes—CIP data view.
ISBN 978-1-56656-683-4 (pbk.)
1. Iraq War, 2003—Moral and ethical aspects. 2. United States—Armed Forces. 3. Great Britain—
Armed Forces. 4. Iraq War, 2003—Atrocities. 5. Iraq—Colonization. 6. Torture--Iraq.
7. Insurgency—Iraq. I. Sökmen, Müge Gürsoy. II. Title.
DS69.76.I4665 2007
956.7044'3—dc22
2007006861

Cover image: Tens of thousands of demonstrators crowd central Barcelona, Spain, Saturday, Feb 15,
2003 in a large anti-war demonstration to protest against possible military action against Iraq.
(© AP Photo/El Periodico de Catalunya, Albert Beltran)

Printed and bound in the United States of America

To request our complete 40-page full-color catalog, please call us toll free at
1-800-238-LINK, visit our website at www.interlinkbooks.com, or write to
Interlink Publishing, 46 Crosby Street, Northampton, MA 01060
e-mail: info@interlinkbooks.com

Contents

Preface

The World Tribunal on Iraq (WTI) was a collective effort involving hundreds of people from all over the world, most of them never having met in person. About twenty sessions were held in various cities of the world (see page 512), focusing on different aspects of the war on Iraq. The findings of these sessions were incorporated into a culminating session held in Istanbul on 23–27 June 2005. This book consists of the proceedings of that session.

The war on Iraq was waged despite the unprecedented global opposition, which was manifested even before the war began. When the war started, the antiwar movement did not yield and retreat; the protests against the war and the occupation continued.

Inspired by the Bertrand Russell Tribunal of the Vietnam War era, WTI aimed to record not only the crimes against the Iraqi people, but also crimes committed against humanity and against all other inhabitants of this planet. These records had to be kept, as a means of resistance to those forces that render our world unlivable, which invalidate all values that humanity has struggled to build, and usurp our hopes for the future. The records had to be kept because the US and its allies, who waged a war of aggression mobilizing everything at their disposal including lies and coercion, would not hesitate to rewrite history. Theirs would be a history of victors based on forgetting, one that would erase from view the history of the dissent.

When initiating the WTI process, we knew that the antiwar movement was not homogeneous; everybody had different reasons to oppose this war. The starting group included renowned experts in international law, people who worked for the United Nations on varying levels, peace activists, philosophers, political scientists, conscientious objectors, alterglobalization activists, and others with diverse identifications.

Some of us believed that it would suffice to improve the existing international institutions and international law; some of us believed that those should be abolished altogether; some of us defined ourselves as world citizens; some of us gave precedence to national, regional, or ethnic identities. But our common aim brought us together to work through our differences (for information on the preparation process of the WTI, see "WTI as an Alternative," in the sixth session). It was clear that we needed to raise our voices, to resist, and to find creative ways of resistance in order to reclaim our future, in order for the world even to have a future. It was also clear that we needed to work as hard as and be as creative as the enemies of humanity.

The process of preparing the tribunal was as important for us as its end result. We did our best to organize non-hierarchically in a horizontal network, and to include, rather than silence or exclude, debates and divergent views. We are left far behind our dreams, and have made many mistakes to draw lessons from, but at least we accomplished what may be called an "experimental assertion": working together as a global subject, leaving a record for history, bringing together material that can be used in appeals to the ICC or the UN, or as legitimate grounds for conscientious objection, and creating a spark of hope for future collective work.

The Culminating Istanbul Session of the World Tribunal on Iraq consisted of presentations of documents and analyses regarding the various aspects of the war by a Panel of Advocates who addressed the general public and a Jury of Conscience that brought together people representing the conscience of the world. The sessions lasted three days and were divided into three main parts: "Bearers of the Responsibility of the War," "The Concrete Details of the War and Occupation," and "The Effects of the War on the Future of Our World." At the end of the three days, the Jury of Conscience (see page 559 for their bios) convened to issue a preliminary statement, and then worked via the internet for the following weeks to produce the more detailed statement that you can find at the end of this book.

We have not included in the book photographs of the horrific details of war. As we know, such details distance the viewer from the sight, leading to the illusion that those who suffer such wrongs are far away from one's self. Instead we wanted to say: we are all Iraqis, what they suffer is what we suffer, or may suffer tomorrow. Not only their land, but ours too, is subject to nuclear pollution that cannot be undone for hundreds of years to come. Our hopes for finding peaceful alternatives to settle conflicts are also shattered, our future also darkened.

This documentary book is the result of the labor and support of hundreds of people who volunteered their efforts throughout the process:

Experts in law, politics, history, ecology, toxicology, archeology, economy, sociology, and philosophy who generously shared their knowledge; lawyers who worked for months to prepare the framework for prosecution; facilitators who took part in various stages of the process, trying to unite differing orientations toward a common aim and to resolve conflicts arising from differing views; translators; volunteers who ensured the smooth running of the sessions; individual funders who made it possible for many people to travel from different parts of the world; institutions and establishments who allowed us to use their resources; and most of all, antiwar dissidents from Iraq, who trusted us, acknowledged our legitimacy, and endured various difficulties to participate in our session.

Our conditions of working together render it unnecessary for anyone to thank anyone else, because all who contributed to WTI did so because they wanted to and because they cared about the result. So rather than a situation where some can thank others, we have one where people have empowered and given confidence to each other.

We believe that the culminating session in Istanbul is only a beginning. Now the task is to disseminate these findings as widely as possible, and to make sure that whoever wishes to use this material can do so. We all have worked hard in this process, but unfortunately we still have a lot to do, because the US and its allies increasingly continue their attacks. And there is no force that we can trust to stop these attacks, except for the global subject who says "no." This book is published with the hope that we will continue to answer pessimism of the mind with the optimism of the will and never cease our collective resistance.

—Müge Gürsoy Sökmen

Opening Speeches

Opening Speech of the Spokesperson of the Jury of Conscience

Arundhati Roy

This is the culminating session of the World Tribunal on Iraq. It is of particular significance that it is being held here in Turkey, where the United States used Turkish air bases to launch numerous bombing missions to degrade Iraq's defenses before the March 2003 invasion and has sought and continues to seek political support from the Turkish government, which it regards as an ally. All this was done in the face of enormous popular opposition by the Turkish people. As a spokesperson for the Jury of Conscience, it would make me uneasy if I did not mention that the government of India is also, like the government of Turkey, positioning itself as a "ally" of the United States in its economic policies and the so-called war on terror.

The testimonies at the previous sessions of the World Tribunal on Iraq in Brussels and New York have demonstrated that even those of us who have tried to follow the war in Iraq closely are not aware of a fraction of the horrors that have been unleashed in Iraq.

The Jury of Conscience at this tribunal is not here to deliver a simple verdict of guilty or not guilty against the United States and its allies. We are here to examine a vast spectrum of evidence about the motivations and consequences of the US invasion and occupation, evidence that has been deliberately marginalized or suppressed. Every aspect of the war will be examined—its legality, the role of international institutions and major corporations in the occupation; the role of the media, the impact of weapons such as depleted uranium munitions, napalm, and cluster bombs, the use of and legitimation of torture, the ecological impacts of the war, the responsibility of Arab governments, the impact of Iraq's occupation on Palestine, and the history of US and British military interventions in Iraq. This tribunal is an attempt to correct the record. To document the history of the war not from the point of view of the victors but of the temporarily—and I repeat the word temporarily—vanquished.

Before the testimonies begin, I would like to briefly address as straightforwardly as I can a few questions that have been raised about this tribunal.

The first is that this tribunal is a kangaroo court. That it represents only one point of view. That it is a prosecution without a defense. That the verdict is a foregone conclusion.

Now this view seems to suggest a touching concern that in this harsh world, the views of the US government and the so-called coalition of the willing headed by President George Bush and Prime Minister Tony Blair have somehow gone unrepresented. That the World Tribunal on Iraq isn't aware of the arguments in support of the war and is unwilling to consider the point of view of the invaders. If in the era of the multinational corporate media and embedded journalism anybody can seriously hold this view, then we truly do live in the Age of Irony, in an age when satire has become meaningless because real life is more satirical than satire can ever be.

Let me say categorically that this tribunal is the defense. It is an act of resistance in itself. It is a defense mounted against one of the most cowardly wars ever fought in history, a war in which international institutions were used to force a country to disarm and then stood by while it was attacked with a greater array of weapons than has ever been used in the history of war.

Second, this tribunal is not in any way a defense of Saddam Hussein. His crimes against Iraqis, Kurds, Iranians, Kuwaitis, and others cannot be written off in the process of bringing to light Iraq's more recent and still-unfolding tragedy. However, we must not forget that when Saddam Hussein was committing his worst crimes, the US government was supporting him politically and materially. When he was gassing Kurdish people, the US government financed him, armed him, and stood by silently.

Saddam Hussein is being tried as a war criminal even as we speak. But what about those who helped to install him in power, who armed him, who supported him—and who are now setting up a tribunal to try him and absolve themselves completely? And what about other friends of the United States in the region that have suppressed Kurdish people's and other people's rights, including the government of Turkey?

There are remarkable people gathered here who, in the face of this relentless and brutal aggression and propaganda, have doggedly worked to compile a comprehensive spectrum of evidence and information that should serve as a weapon in the hands of those who wish to participate in the resistance against the occupation of Iraq. It should become a weapon in the hands of soldiers in the United States, the United Kingdom, Italy,

Australia, and elsewhere who do not wish to fight, who do not wish to lay down their lives—or to take the lives of others—for a pack of lies. It should become a weapon in the hands of journalists, writers, poets, singers, teachers, plumbers, taxi drivers, car mechanics, painters, lawyers—anybody who wishes to participate in the resistance.

The evidence collated in this tribunal should, for instance, be used by the International Criminal Court (whose jurisdiction the United States does not recognize) to try as war criminals George Bush, Tony Blair, John Howard, Silvio Berlusconi, and all those government officials, army generals, and corporate CEOs who participated in this war and now profit from it.

The assault on Iraq is an assault on all of us: on our dignity, our intelligence, and our future.

We recognize that the judgment of the World Tribunal on Iraq is not binding in international law. However, our ambitions far surpass that. The World Tribunal on Iraq places its faith in the consciences of millions of people across the world who do not wish to stand by and watch while the people of Iraq are being slaughtered, subjugated, and humiliated.

Opening Speech on Behalf of the Panel of Advocates
Richard Falk

Let me express at the outset, on behalf of the Panel of Advocates, our profound gratitude to the conveners of this Istanbul session of the World Tribunal on Iraq (WTI) for their exceptional effort, and at the same time acknowledge the extraordinary contributions of the twenty earlier sessions of the WTI that have produced invaluable testimony and results that have increased awareness the world over of the criminality of the Iraq war. This unprecedented process of truth-telling about an ongoing war has produced what can best be described as "a tribunal movement" of which this Istanbul session is the culminating phase to date of this process.

The World Tribunal on Iraq (WTI) is remarkable for two principal reasons: WTI bears witness to the depth and persistence of the popular mobilization of people throughout the world in opposition to the Iraq war. Such a mobilization against a particular war has never occurred before on such a scale. It started with the massive street demonstrations before the war on February 15, 2003, in which some 11 million people took part in 80 countries and more than 600 urban communities. The WTI gives a continuing legal, moral, and political expression to this antiwar opposition which itself has entered a new phase: an insurgent war of liberation being waged in resistance to the illegal occupation of the country by the greatest military power in the history of the world. In this struggle, the Iraqi people are being denied their fundamental rights of self-determination, first by aggression and then by a cruel and criminal dynamic occupation.

The second reason for claiming historical significance on behalf of WTI relates to this initiative of, by, and for citizens to hold leaders accountable for severe violations of international law, especially in relation to matters of war and peace. It is not that this is an entirely new idea. The first such effort was inspired by the eminent British philosopher Bertrand Russell, who convened such a tribunal back in 1967 to assess the legal responsibility of the United States and its leaders for the Vietnam War. It gathered testimony and documented the massive abuses of Vietnamese sovereignty by a devastating war that took millions of innocent Vietnamese lives. Above all, this citizens' tribunal was a cry of anguish intended to break the wall of silence behind which the crimes associated with the

Vietnam War were daily committed. The Russell Tribunal in turn led to the formation of the Permanent People's Tribunal, located in Rome, operating since 1976 to reinforce the claims of international law by filling in the gaps where governments and even the United Nations are unable and unwilling to act, or even to speak. The WTI continues and extends this tradition of refusing to be silent or to be silenced. It accepts as a responsibility of democracy the obligation of citizens to insist on the relevance and applicability of international law to every use of force. This insistence includes a demand for criminal accountability whenever a government disavows its commitment to respect international law. It is primarily to honor this commitment to uphold international law that this tribunal has been organized, and its mission is to confirm the truth of the allegation directed at the United States and the United Kingdom, while also extending to all governments that support directly or indirectly the Iraq war.

We should be aware that such a commitment by the WTI is part of a longer journey of international law that has evolved by stages that can be identified.

The initial stage was to create in some authoritative way the norms of law, morality, and politics associated with the prohibition of wars of aggression. The legal culmination of this process occurred in 1928 when leading states, including the United States and the UK, ratified without qualification the General Treaty for the Renunciation of War as an instrument of national policy, also known as the Kellogg-Briand Pact.

This was followed by a second stage that attached criminal consequences to the violation of this norm, prohibiting aggressive war through establishing accountability. The criminal trial of German and Japanese leaders after World War II, the Nuremberg Judgment issued in 1945, was a milestone in this process. The judgment declared: "To initiate a war of aggression... is not only an international crime, it is the supreme international crime differing only from other war crimes in that it contains within itself the accumulated evil of the whole." And although Nuremberg was flawed by being an example of "victors' justice," the American prosecutor, Justice Robert Jackson, made what has been described as the Nuremberg Promise in his closing statement: "If certain acts in violation of treaties are crimes, they are crimes whether the United States does them or Germany does them, and we are not prepared to lay down a rule of criminal conduct against others which we would not be willing to have invoked against us." This promise has been broken, but such behavior is not acceptable, and we are gathered in part to insist even now on the promise that every state will pay the consequences if it wages a war of aggression.

This treaty pledge to renounce aggressive war informed the United Nations Charter. The Charter imposes a core obligation on members to refrain from the use of force in international relations except in circumstances of self-defense strictly defined and under the authority of the Security Council. It also, in a spirit relevant to the WTI, confirmed in its opening words that it is the peoples of the world and not the governments or even the UN that have been entrusted with the ultimate responsibility for upholding this renunciation of war: "We the peoples of the United Nations determined to save succeeding generations from the scourge of war..." that set forth the duties of states in the UN Charter. This tribunal is dedicated to precisely this undertaking as a matter of law, as an imperative of morality and human rights, and as an engagement with the politics of global justice.

Of course, this tribunal does not pretend to be a normal court of law with powers of enforcement. At the same time, it is acting on behalf of the peoples of the world to uphold respect for international law. When governments and the UN are silent, and fail to protect victims of aggression, tribunals of concerned citizens possess a law-making authority. Their unique contribution is to tell the truth as powerfully and fully as possible, and by such truthfulness to activate the conscience of humanity to resist. The US government told a pack of lies in its feeble attempt to find a legal justification for the invasion of Iraq. The WTI will expose these lies by presenting evidence and testimony. The task of exposing lies and confirming truth has become easier as a result of the release of the Downing Street memos. These official documents show that British and American officials understood fully that the Iraq war was unlawful, and not only did they go ahead, but they fabricated evidence to build a completely dishonest legal case. Neither governments, nor the UN, nor most of the media will tell this story of deception, destruction, and criminality. It is the mission of the WTI, building on the efforts of the 20 or so earlier citizens' tribunals, to tell this story and to appeal to the peoples of the world to join with the people of Iraq in opposing aggression against

Iraq. The tribunal is formed on the basis of a Panel of Advocates and a Jury of Conscience. The Panel will present the evidence and the Jury will draw legal, moral, and political conclusions and offer recommendations. The pledge of advocates and jurors is to act in an honest, nonpartisan, independent, and objective spirit to follow the evidence wherever it leads.

This tribunal differs from a normal court of law in the following main respects:

—it is an organ of civil society, not of the state;

—its essential purpose is to confirm the truth, not to discover it;

—its jurors are dedicated, informed, and committed citizens of the world, not neutral and indifferent individuals of the community;

—its advocates are knowledgeable, wise, and decent, but not legally trained specialists;

—its trust for the future is not based on violence and police, but on conscience, political struggle, and public opinion.

Nevertheless, we claim for this tribunal the authority to declare the law and to impose its judgment and to hope—hope that a demonstration of this criminality will not fall on deaf ears, but will awaken and exercise the peoples of the world to intensify their resistance to America's plans for world domination and stand in solidarity with the Iraqi people.

We need to realize that the Iraq war is the eye of a larger global storm. The storm expresses the fury of this American project to dominate the world by force of arms, to exploit the peoples of the world through the medium of economic globalization, and to administer its idea of security from its Washington headquarters. This project of world empire hides its true colors beneath the banner of anti-terrorism. It justifies every abuse by pointing to the 9/11 attacks. These attacks, even if they are what is claimed, do not justify aggression against states or the torture of individuals. We should remember that the imperial brain trust said before 9/11 that only "a new Pearl Harbor" would produce the political climate needed to achieve global hegemony. And they got a new Pearl Harbor— or did they? Read David Griffin's *The New Pearl Harbor*[1] and you will never be able to take 9/11 at face value in the future. The conveners of the WTI are mindful of this wider context of the Iraq war.

It should also be observed that Turkey is an appropriate site for this culminating session of the WTI, remembering that earlier sessions of the WTI in all regions of the world have gathered evidence of the illegality of the Iraq war and the criminal policies and practices that have been associated with its conduct. To begin with, Turkey stands at the crossroads between the old European geopolitical core and the Third World periphery. Earlier Russell, PPT initiatives were European. Now the moral, political, and legal platform is moving away from the Christian West. It was Turkey's proudest moment when its parliament refused the request of the US government to mount the invasion of Iraq from Turkish territory; this represented an expression of an increasingly robust democratic process here in Turkey. Turkey is also a natural site for the tribunal because it is an important neighbor of Iraq, and suffers a variety of bad consequences from the war and the turmoil in the region that has resulted. And further, the Turkish government has been complicit with the Iraq war, as well as with the preceding period of sanctions, by allowing its territory to be used for a strategic base that has been extensively used for the bombing of Iraq ever since 1990. It is a purpose of this tribunal to show that such complicity engages legal responsibility for Turkey, and for other governments in the region that support directly or indirectly such aggressive war making.

A special concern of the WTI is to take sharp issue with American claims of "exception" whether based on an alleged freedom to wage war anywhere on the planet as a result of the 9/11 attacks or securing an exemption for itself in relation to the basic obligation to uphold international law. The pernicious American exceptionalism contradicts completely the role played by the United States in seeking to promote the rule of law, the Nuremberg approach, and the UN Charter after 1945. The claim of exception moves in two directions: it operates, first of all, as an explicit effort to exempt American leaders from individual accountability for violating international law, specifically in relation to the recently established International Criminal Court; and secondly, in relation to the lawless barbarism of the detention of alleged terrorist and insurgency suspects being held in such notorious outposts of torture and official evil as Abu Ghraib prison in Iraq and Camp X-Ray at Guantánamo. This tribunal stands against such outrageous claims of exception, and operates beneath the jurisprudential principle that no government or leader is above the law and that every government and leader is criminally accountable for failures to uphold international law. If governments and the UN are unwilling to pass judgment, it is up to initiatives by citizens of the world to perform this sacred duty. The WTI has been formed against the background of these essential beliefs.

It should also be understood that the WTI views the Iraq war as part of this wider assault by the United States and the UK against wider prospects for a just world order. These prospects depend upon respecting the sovereign rights of all states, of working to achieve human rights, including economic, social, and cultural rights for all peoples, and to struggle on behalf of a humane world order, including a far more equitable world economy that is indispensable for achieving a sustainable world peace.

There was a start in this direction made during the 1990s, although amid an array of contradictions. But it is worth noting these progressive moves that have been stymied by the wars of aggression launched by the United States by relying upon the pretext of a war against terrorism. It is worth observing because it is important to revive these moves toward humane global governance based on the principles of global justice:

—the spread of democracy, and especially the rise of global civil society and of global social movements in the areas of environment, human rights, women, and peace;

—the increased support for human rights by civil society actors and governments around the world;

—the attention given to the remembrance and partial erasure of historic grievances toward indigenous peoples on all continents, toward the victims of forced labor, including so-called comfort women during World War II, toward the descendants of slavery;

—and most of all, the revival of Nuremberg ideas about criminal accountability, challenging impunity—the Chilean dictator Pinochet was indicted by Spain and detained by Britain; the UN-established tribunals to prosecute those responsible for ethnic cleansing and crimes against humanity in former Yugoslavia and for genocide in Rwanda; and over the objections of the leading states, the ICC was brought into existence due to the active coalition of hundreds of NGOs working together with dozens of governments dedicated to establishing a framework for applying international criminal law.

Such positive steps have been derailed, at least temporarily, by the firestorm released in the world by the US government since the 9/11 attacks. This tribunal hopes that truth-telling with respect to Iraq will also revive the emergent normative revolution of the 1990s, making us move again in the Puerto Allegro direction of insisting that "another world is possible," and adding "if possible, it is necessary," and with this affirmation the WTI will not only stimulate resistance to oppression and solidarity with victims, but will revive the vision of the 1990s that can be best summarized as the cause of "moral globalization."

First Session

The Role of International Law and Institutions

The Illegality of Preventive Attack and Unilateral Use of Force

Phil Shiner

In this paper I wish to address three issues:

Whether the Iraq war was a "crime of aggression" (which is the "worst of crimes");

Whether the way in which the war was conducted involved the commission of "war crimes" and;

Whether the subsequent occupation of Iraq involved, and continues to involve, the commission of "war crimes," "crimes against humanity," and other illegal acts.

However, before addressing these themes, I wish to put these matters in the context of a changing international legal order.

There is no doubt that the world has changed post-9/11. And no doubt too that international law has been central to that change. Much of the debate about the wars in Afghanistan and Iraq, and the so-called war on terror, revolves around questions of legality. It is plain that the neocons and Bush and Blair wish to restructure international law[1] to make it weaker but more flexible, and less concerned with the peaceful resolution of disputes. Who can counter this fundamental challenge to all those who are concerned with peace, and that international law should underpin and support an absolute legal commitment by all member states that the use of force is, and should remain as, the option of last resort?[2] It is my view that the World Tribunal on Iraq should have this fundamental ideological struggle in its sights. It can make those responsible for the Iraq war accountable, and it can be part of a global struggle in response to the Bush/Blair agenda on international law.[3]

The Crime of Aggression

International law is surprisingly clear and easy to understand on whether the Iraq war was lawful. First, war was abolished by the adoption of the UN Charter in 1947. Thereafter, contracting states entered into a compact. In return for giving up their right to wage war each vested the right to use force in the collective security provisions of Chapter VII of the

UN Charter. Second, Article 2 (4) of the UN Charter provides that

> All members shall refrain in their international relations from the threat
> or use of force against the territorial integrity or political independence
> of any state, or any other manner inconsistent with the Purposes of
> the United Nations.

This has been described by the International Court of Justice as a peremptory norm of International Law, from which states cannot derogate.[4] Thus, the effect of Articles 2 (3) and (4) is that the use of force can only be justified as expressly provided under the Charter, and only in situations where it is consistent with the UN's purposes.[5] Third, there are two limited exceptions to the requirement not to use force. The first, enshrined in Article 51, preserves states' rights to self-defense. As this was not an exception relied upon by the US or UK I need not dwell on it.[6] The second is where the Security Council has authorized the use of force under Article 42 of the Charter. That is the only relevant debate here.

I can remind the Panel that a consensus of international lawyers did not accept that such an authorization existed here, or that the UK and US were entitled to revive Resolution 678 (November 1990) from the start of the first Gulf war. The UK and US argued that the wording of Resolution 1441 (8 November 2002) allowed them to rely on Security Council Resolution 678 as they were entitled to interpret Iraq's behavior post 1441 as constituting a further "material breach" of Resolution 678 (Article 1) in circumstances where Iraq had been given its "final opportunity" to disarm (Article 2) and was warned of the "serious consequences" of non-compliance (Article 13). This is referred to as the revival doctrine. Not surprisingly, that is not the way international law works post the UN Charter. If the Security Council wish to authorize force, they do so in clear terms, latterly using the phrase "all necessary means" or "all measures necessary."[7]

One example of that consensus is a letter from 16 international law professors and teachers from the UK, which made headline news on 7 March 2003. It warned that:

> Before military action can lawfully be undertaken against Iraq, the
> Security Council must have indicated its clearly expressed assent. It
> has not yet done so… A decision to undertake military action in Iraq

without proper Security Council authorisation will seriously undermine the international rule of law.[8]

What I have done is to footnote to this paper all the relevant legal material so that you, the Jury, may be satisfied that this war did not have legal authorization from the Security Council.[9] The Jury needs to address the consequences of this. If there was no Security Council authorization does it necessarily mean that the war was illegal? If it was illegal, was it automatically a "crime of aggression" and thus a "crime against peace"?

Professor Philippe Sands[10] tackled this question head on during an interview last Thursday for the Australian Broadcasting Corporation. He said: "… Most people now realise that the war on Iraq was illegal and under international law, an illegal war amounts to a crime of aggression."[11]

Others have said the same. Here is the 18 March 2003 resignation letter of Elizabeth Wilmshurst, deputy legal advisor to the Foreign Office, who resigned because she did not believe the war with Iraq was legal:

> I cannot in conscience go along with the advice … which asserts the legitimacy of military action without such a [Security Council] Resolution, particularly since an unlawful use of force on such a scale amounts to a crime of aggression…[12]

Over the last weekend the controversy over the legality of the war, at least from the UK government's perspective, has flared up again. This time the row focuses on a number of leaked and secret memoranda between UK government's members and top officials detailing what had been agreed between Tony Blair and President Bush and Condoleezza Rice as early as March 2002. In particular, the following needs some explanation, if the UK government are to continue to protest they went into Iraq because of the threat of WMD, rather than for regime change:

> We spent a long time at dinner on Iraq. It is clear that Bush is grateful for your [Blair] support and has registered that you are getting flak. I said that you would not budge in your support for regime change but you had to manage a press, a Parliament and a public opinion that was different from anything in the States. And you would not budge either in your insistence that, if we perused regime change, it must be very carefully done and produce the right result. Failure was not an option.[13]

Thus, we are dealing with the crime of aggression. And let us remind ourselves of the enormity of that crime. This is the opening speech of Mr. Justice Robert Jackson at the Nuremburg Tribunal:

> It is not necessary among the ruins of this ancient and beautiful city with untold members of its civilian inhabitants still buried under its rubble, to argue the proposition that to start or wage an aggressive war has the moral qualities of the worst of crimes.

In his opening speech, he also described aggressive war as "the greatest menace of our time," and made it clear that if international law "is to serve a useful purpose it must condemn aggression by any other nations, including those which sit here now in judgment." He also said:

> This trial represents mankind's desperate effort to apply the discipline of the law to statesmen who have used their powers of state to attack the foundations of the world's peace and commit aggressions against the right of their neighbors.[14]

Accountability for the Crime of Aggression and Proportionality

But how can the actions of the US and the UK in committing the worst of crimes be made accountable to international law, and specifically the International Criminal Court (ICC)?[15] There are two routes that the ICC prosecutor can take which would give him jurisdiction to examine the legality of the Iraq war notwithstanding that the US has de-ratified the ICC Statute, and that the ICC will not have jurisdiction over the "crime of aggression" until the necessary elements of crime have been agreed, which may not be for several years.

Here is how the first argument goes. If the coalition forces had used force against Iraq pursuant to Security Council Resolution, that Resolution would have set the parameters of the authorization both in dictating lawful military objectives, and over time.[16] The authorization would have been carefully targeted, using a phrase such as "all necessary measures" focused on the threat of WMD.[17] Accordingly, decisions about military objectives, and thus crucially, in considering whether the use of force as exercised constituted "war crimes," and judgments as to whether the force used was proportionate to those objectives should have been taken within the framework of a Security Council authorization tailored to eliminating the threat to international peace and security of Iraq's WMD. However, in the absence of such an authorization, and with the coalition's unstated objectives of regime change coming into play, these crucial decisions about military objectives and proportionality became very different. It is arguable, for instance, that using a "bunker buster" bomb on a restaurant in a civilian residential area cannot be justified on the ground that Saddam Hussein was believed to be dining there. It is arguable also that, leaving aside the inherently indiscriminatory nature of cluster munitions, if the military objective pursued was the threat of WMD it is hard to see how their use in urban and residential locations could be justified or proportionate.[18] Further, the British Armed Forces minister, Adam Ingram, declared during an interview with the BBC that cluster weapons had been used against concentrations of military equipment and Iraqi troops in and around built-up areas around Basra, Iraq's second largest city. For the US, General Myers confirmed that cluster munitions were used against "many" military assets in populated areas.[19]

These are important concerns which the ICC prosecutor must address, and he has been urged to do so in a report from eight leading international law professors submitted to the ICC prosecutor by Peacerights on 20 April 2004 following the London Tribunal which supports this inquiry.[20] This is how the report summarized the professors' concerns:

> d. Were methods of warfare or weapons systems used, or locations of attacks chosen, such that...
>
> Impermissible military objectives were excluded, for example, those concerned with "regime change" rather than the elimination of any existing WMD;
>
> The proportionality requirement was at all times respected and in particular all feasible precautions were taken to avoid and in any event minimise incidental loss of civilian life, injury to civilians and damage to civilian objects...

The second route into the examination of the crime of aggression is through joint criminal enterprise and the context of any ICC investigation. Again, this is a matter already put to the ICC prosecutor by the London Tribunal. The ICC has jurisdiction over individuals who are nationals of state parties and the UK ratified the ICC Statute on 4 October 2001.[21] In addition to those who perpetrated the crimes, the ICC also has jurisdiction over those who may have ordered, solicited, induced, aided or abetted, or otherwise assisted in their commission or attempted commission. So the relationship between the US and UK in the coalition does need to be determined, and questions answered as to the criminal responsibility of UK nationals of acts jointly committed with the US. In particular, did UK nationals have prior knowledge of any internationally wrongful acts?[22] The Peacerights Report records that the panel had concluded:

> The evidence presented (that UK commanders were informed by the US of their military activities, and the selection of targets, and that they were concerned about the use of cluster bombs) suggests that the UK did have knowledge of the circumstances of the internationally wrongful act. (para 3.8)

This leads us to the prospect of senior members of the UK government being criminally responsible before the ICC for the commission of international crimes through joint criminal activities with individuals from the US, and this takes us into the illegality of the war.

It seems clear that the US and UK governments—and thus senior members of both as individuals—acted with a common purpose in waging aggressive war against Iraq.[23]

In simple terms, it is not necessary here that the participation of UK nationals be an indispensable condition, or that the ICC prosecutor needs to be satisfied that the attacks or incidents would not have occurred at all without their participation. Instead, the question is: were the UK nationals at least a cog in the wheel of events? The London Tribunal members answered this question in the affirmative.[24]

Building on this, the concept of "joint criminal enterprise" is now well accepted in international criminal law and is particularly useful in examining issues of liability when one of the parties in the joint criminal enterprise goes beyond what was originally agreed, even if the other party did not have full knowledge of this, provided that the act was a necessary and foreseeable consequence of the agreed joint criminal enterprise. And of course, the joint criminal enterprise we are most concerned with here is that of waging aggressive war.[25]

It does, however, need to be stressed, as the London Tribunal did, that in examining these issues in the context of aggressive war, it is not that the ICC would be attempting to actually hold any person accountable for that crime, as it must be recalled that the elements of crime have not yet been agreed. Instead, "it would merely be reaching the view that the criminal enterprise of waging aggressive war had been committed as a preliminary circumstance to the prosecution of criminal acts over which it may exercise jurisdiction—namely, Crimes against Humanity and War Crimes."[26]

Other Issues of War Crimes and the Use of Force

In the above section I have touched upon issues concerning the use of an indiscriminate weapons system such as cluster munitions in residential areas[27]; the risk that impermissible military objectives related not to the threat of WMD might have led to war crimes being committed because attacks were not justified (according to military objective) or were disproportionate; and lastly, the link between the "crime of aggression" and joint criminal enterprise. These are three very important issues that I would invite the Panel to examine in detail and consider whether to refer these matters to the ICC. There are others arising from the use of force (rather than the occupation, which I deal with below). They all arise from the London Tribunal and thus, the Peacerights Report. I summarize them below with their references:

The use of UK bases for the launch of US air attacks involving cluster munitions, or otherwise (para 2.1.3).

Attacks on media outlets (paras 2.2.2, 2.2.3).

Attacks on civilians and civilian, not military, objectives (paras 2.2.4, 2.2.5, and 2.2.7).

Attacks, other than ones involving cluster munitions, which did not discriminate between civilians and combatants (para 2.2.5).

Deliberate targeting of civilian infrastructure and, in particular, electricity supplies (para 2.2.6).

I invite the Panel to explore seriously all the above.

The Illegality of the Occupation Policy

I do not intend to focus on whether the UN Security Council had the power to give the coalition forces the legal status of occupying powers, as it purported to do by Security Council Resolution 1483. Although we now see the use made of Security Council Resolutions to undermine and disengage fundamental human rights protections, it seems that, on balance, on the narrow question—was the UN Security Council entitled to give *de jure* authority to the UK and US as occupying powers—the answer remains, it was.[28]

Thus, the focus of this section is on the illegality of the policy and acts that took place in the occupation. I want to briefly explore two matters. Both involve US and UK troops. The first is deaths and torture in detention and the second, unlawful killings during policing operations.

Those here today will be aware of the abuses by US troops at Abu Ghraib prison. Who could forget the outrageous photographs of prisoners on a leash, being attacked by dogs or sexually humiliated? But how many are aware of more widespread and similar abuses by US troops at other facilities including Mosul and Camp Bucca?[29] And who knows how many other atrocities have been committed by US troops at other facilities. To make it clear that these are torture allegations I read below extracts from statements of two of my clients. First, an engineer aged 46:

> ... I saw a young man of 14 years of age bleeding from his anus and lying on the floor. He was Kurdish and his name was Hama. I heard the soldiers talking to each other about this guy; they mentioned that the reason for this bleeding was inserting a metal object in his anus. I suspected that this was caused by a sexual assault but could not confirm it.

Second, the statement of an agricultural engineer:

> They have shown me in that room photos of certain people whom I knew and I was asked to make certain confessions against them. Once they placed a detainee on a chair in front of me and asked me to say certain words that indicated that I had confessed against him. They brought a man I knew who was fully dressed with a can of Coke and some food in his hand, they pointed out that if I would confess I would be in pleasant status like that man. I insisted that I had nothing else to say and I was innocent. Then they advanced the chair I was sitting on very close to a wood fire that they lit which left burns on my leg [photographed]... They inserted some strange objects into my anus and asked me to take very humiliating positions while they messed with me and moved these objects in different directions. They were calling these positions some names, which I did not understand. They took many photos while I was in these positions, they were laughing and enjoying it. There was also a male and a female soldier who sat behind me; they were messing with each other. Their game was that the male soldier would aim at my injured and swollen leg with a piece of rock,

as soon as he hit his target and I scream of pain she would reward him by letting him kiss her or fondle her. The stronger my pain was and the louder my scream was, the more he would get from her.

We know now of the US efforts to redefine torture and, in particular, the memorandum of 1 August 2002, from Jay S. Bybee, head of the Justice Department Office of Legal Counsel, in which he wrote:

We conclude that for an act to constitute torture… it must inflict pain that is difficult to endure. Physical pain amounting to torture must be equivalent in intensity to the pain accompanying serious physical injury, such as organ failure, impairment of bodily functions or even death.[30]

We know also of the US interrogation techniques involving unusual methods designed not to leave marks.[31] What we do not seem to fully appreciate is how closely UK interrogation techniques resemble those of the US. This is not rhetoric. I am acting in three cases where UK troops have tortured Iraqi civilians to death, ten other torture in detention cases, and additionally for nine victims of abuse and torture at Camp Breadbasket.[32] The statements of these victims makes it clear that like the US, members of the UK armed forces engaged in practices of sexual humiliation and systematic humiliation of male Muslims, routinely using women to sexually excite male detainees, devised games and routines to humiliate and disorient detainees, used methods of abuse designed not to leave marks, and, in fact, did everything we now know US troops did save for the use of bright lights and loud music. To make this explicit, I read an extract from one of my client's witness statements from a successful High Court case of 14 December 2004. His name is Kifah Taha al-Mutari. He gives evidence about the death in detention of his colleague, Baha Mousa, as well as the torture that he suffered which led to acute kidney failure. He says:

Baha appeared to have much worse ill treatment than the others. Two or more soldiers would beat him at a time whereas the rest of us were beaten by one soldier. Baha may have been punished more than the others in an act of revenge. Baha's father, who witnessed the arrest, had informed the officer in charge that he had seen the soldiers stealing money from the hotel. Baha received much more beating than myself and the other detainees. He was not able to stand up and the soldiers continued beating him even while he was on the floor. The soldiers used particular sharp jabbing movements into the area beneath the ribs, which was particularly painful.

We all had another hood put on top of the first hood. We were given water by it being poured over the hood so that we had to lick droplets that seeped through the hood. Freezing water was poured on to us and this was very painful as the temperatures in detention were 40 degrees plus. We were given one meal a day consisting of rice with extremely spicy soup, which we could not eat. ...

Soldiers took turns in abusing us, at night the number of soldiers increased, sometimes to eight at a time. We were prevented from sleeping throughout the three days as soldiers introduced the "names game." Soldiers would mention some English names of stars or players[33] and request us to remember them, or we would be beaten severely.

One terrible game the soldiers played involved kickboxing. The soldiers would surround us and compete as to who could kick box one of us the furthest. The idea was to try and make us crash into the wall.

During the detention, Baha was taken into another room and he received more beatings in that room.

On the third night Baha was in a separate room and I could hear him moaning through the walls. He was saying that he was bleeding from his nose and that he was dying. I heard him say, "I am dying...blood.... blood..." I heard nothing further from him after that.

On the morning of the third night, the other detainees and I were woken up from the only two hours sleep we had been allowed in three days. One soldier asked us to dance like Michael Jackson.

Unfortunately, there is much more to come, and worse. In the Camp Breadbasket incident a court martial heard evidence to explain the background to the taking of 22 photographs, publicly available now,[34] of abuse and humiliation of Iraqi civilians. The UK government's position was that the victims of the abuse could not be found, and that what happened was that a few "rogue soldiers" took too seriously the order to "work hard" some Iraqi looters inside a food depot. One man was photographed strung up on the forks of a forklift truck. The evidence to the court martial was that soldiers had been playing around, and had moved him out of the sun, and it all got out of hand.

Before the court martial concluded, three victims asked my firm to act for them.[35] Their evidence, which they wanted to put to the court martial, was compelling and put a completely different light on events. This included that the victims had lawful authority to be in the camp, that the abuse included torture, that women and sexual humiliation were involved, that officers were involved, and that the camp was being used as a detention center. Further, the Iraqi photographed in the forklift truck had lawful authority to be at the camp and was being punished for refusing an order to sever the finger of a fellow Iraqi. When I tried to have the victims' evidence heard, the court martial decided to ignore it and the attorney general threatened me with contempt of court proceedings if I attempted to alert the public and media as to what had happened.[36]

Additionally, I have complained to the UK's attorney general that there is clear evidence that the UK had a systematic torture policy, which requires investigation.[37] The attorney general has refused to recognize the importance of the issue and refused an investigation.

Both the US and UK forces have been responsible for large numbers of civilians deaths while carrying out policing functions.[38] It is important to emphasize that there is a different set of legal rules during an occupation, as compared to a war, and both the US and UK were bound by Geneva Convention IV, which protects civilians.[39] Further, both had legal powers of policing through Security Council Resolution 1483 and the Coalition Provisional Authority (CPA). The CPA passed a huge amount of legislation during the period from 22 May 2003[40] to 28 June 2004[41] through 11 Regulations (R1-11), 97 Orders (O1-97), 14 Memoranda (M1-14), and 11 Public Notices (PN1-11). These included weapons control (M5, O3).

I have about thirty cases of deaths at the hands of UK troops during policing functions.[42] The following points can be made:

The soldiers killed civilians, some in their homes, while operating under rules of engagement, which should have been changed from the war to the different circumstances of the occupation.[43]

The soldiers appear not to have been trained in the basic elements of Iraqi civil society. For example, people were killed after the customary discharge of guns at funeral parties were mistaken for gun battles.

In virtually all cases, the commanding officer concluded on the basis of the soldiers' evidence only that there had been no breach of the rules of engagement (ROE), which remain secret.

That no soldier, let alone officer, has been charged with any of the detention incidents let alone these unlawful killing cases.

That there appears to be a large number of civilian deaths at the hands of UK troops during the period May 2003 to January 2004.

As for US troops' actions during the occupation, much of what they have done is hidden from view because of the role of the media.[44] I want to focus on events in Falluja to give some legal input before the witness evidence in tomorrow's fourth session. It seems from what we know that US troops engaged in acts of collective punishment toward the civilian population of Falluja from at least April 2004 onward. Some of the few eyewitness accounts that exist are now emerging. One of the few reporters to reach the city is American Dahr Jamail of the Inter Press Service. He interviewed a doctor who had filmed the testimony of a sixteen-year-old girl:

> She stayed for three days with the bodies of her family who were killed in her home. When the soldiers entered she was in her home with her father, mother, 12-year-old brother, and two sisters.
>
> She watched the soldiers enter and shoot her mother and father directly, without saying anything. They beat her two sisters, then shot them in the head. After this her brother was enraged and ran at the soldiers whilst shouting at them, so they shot him dead.

Another report comes from an aid convoy headed by Doctor Salem Ismael. He was in Falluja in February 2005. As well as delivering aid he photographed the dead, including children, and interviewed remaining residents. He reports: "The accounts I heard… will live with me forever. You may think you know what happened in Falluja, but the truth is worse than anything you could possibly have imagined."

Doctor Ismael relates the story of Hudda Fawzi Salam Issawi from Falluja:

> Five of us, including a 55-year-old neighbor, were trapped together in our house in Falluja when the siege began. On 9 November, American Marines came to our house. My father and the neighbour went to the door to meet them. We were not fighters. We thought we had nothing to fear. I ran into the kitchen to put on my veil, since men were going to enter our house and it would be wrong for them to see me with my hair uncovered. This saved my life. As my father and neighbour

approached the door, the Americans opened fire on them. They died instantly. Me and my 13-year-old brother hid in the kitchen behind the fridge. The soldiers came into the house and caught my oldest sister. They beat her. Then they shot her. But they did not see me. Soon they left, but not before they had destroyed our furniture and stolen the money from my father's pocket.[45]

Naomi Klein has also produced evidence about what she sees as the US forces laying siege to Falluja "in retaliation for the gruesome killings of four Blackwater employees."[46] She speaks of hundreds of civilians being killed during the siege in April 2004, and of a deliberate tactic of eliminating doctors, journalists, and clerics who focused public attention on civilian casualties previously.

All of the above acts are arguably "crimes against humanity," defined by section 7 of the ICC Statute as "murder" (Article 7 (1)(a)), "extermination" (Article 7 (1)(b)), or "other inhumane acts of a similar character intentionally causing great suffering or serious injury to [the] body or to mental or physical health" (Article 7 (1)(k)). Further, they may be "war crimes" defined by Article 8 of the ICC Statute as a "wilful killing" (Article 8 (2)(a)(i)), "wilfully causing great suffering, or serious injury to body or health" (Article 8 (2)(a)(iii)), or "intentionally directing attacks against a civilian population as such or against individual civilians not taking direct part in hostilities" (Article 8 (2)(b)(i)), or "intentionally launching an attack in the knowledge that such an attack will cause incidental loss of life or injury to civilians or damage to civilian objects or widespread, long-term and severe damage to the natural environment which would be clearly excessive in relation to the concrete and direct overall military advantage anticipated" (Article 8 (2)(b)(iv).

As for the latter, questions need to be addressed as to military objectives and proportionality. If the force used was "clearly excessive in relation to the concrete and direct overall military advantage anticipated" then it would be disproportionate and unlawful. However, it must be remembered that this was a lawful occupation authorized by Resolution 1483. In its recitals, this recognized "the specific authorities, responsibilities, and obligations under applicable international law of [both] states as occupying powers under unified command."[47] The UK and US had to respect Geneva Convention IV. Thus decisions about military objectives and proportionality cannot be approached as if this were a time of war. But even if they could, it is hard to see how the US could possibly justify these acts, if proven. Further, liability does not stop with the US. I have already set out the arguments about joint criminal enterprise and thus the responsibility of the UK for the acts of the US. Legally, these arguments as to joint responsibility are enhanced during the occupation. Not only were both states acting under *de jure* authority as occupying powers but they were also senior partners within the CPA and thus responsible for all the legislative and administrative functions I have noted above.[48] Thus, a legal analysis of the issue of accountability for incidents such as these from Falluja, which may involve "war crimes" and "crimes against humanity," must begin by recognizing, first, the lawful authority of the US and UK to both occupy and administer Iraq, and second, recognizing the protection of civilians through international humanitarian law, specifically Geneva Convention IV, and international human rights law, especially the International Covenant on Civil and Political Rights[49] and the ECHR. It is also critically important to appreciate that any proper accountability is entirely dependant upon a lawful independent investigation being conducted. That is the importance of the protection given to the Right to Life (ECHR, Art2; IICPR Art 6)[50] by the requirement to hold such an inquiry. For example, if states know at the outset that killings and torture during an occupation will be investigated independently then this knowledge should be reflected in improved training for armed forces and thus more human rights–compliant behavior. Further, the requirement for independence is not met by the military investigation. It is only when such an independent investigation unearths who is responsible that one gets to deal with questions as to who, if anyone, should be charged with "crimes against humanity" or "war crimes." Accordingly, one sees that it is pre-judging the issues arising from the incidents in Falluja to say that those responsible in a few incidents were acting within the rules of engagement and using proportionate force.

The US and UK should have been proceeding on the basis that a lawful approach to international humanitarian law and international human rights law relevant to the protection of civilians in an occupation would be expected of them and rigorously enforced by the international community through, for example, if appropriate, critical resolutions of the Security Council. But it is not too late for accountability, and this tribunal may be part of a future process that leads to it.

Conclusion

The Iraq war and occupation challenges us all to face the threat to international law by the actions of the US, UK, and other members of the coalition. We must be resolute in our determination to make international law stronger and more concerned with peace. There must be accountability for the dreadful numbers of Iraqi civilian casualties in this aggressive war and bearing in mind the use of indiscriminate methods of attack. There cannot be impunity for the acts of torture in detention—and in some cases deaths—nor the wanton killing of civilians during the occupation. Insofar as US and UK interrogation techniques violate Article 1 of the UN Convention on Torture,[51] it cannot be acceptable that there be impunity. Accountability—rather than impunity—rests on two building blocks:

That there be an independent investigation to establish who is responsible for what acts and how far up the chain of command should responsibility lie. That is the importance of the positive obligation of Article 3 of the ECHR, and thus the critical importance of UK cases that attempt to establish that the ECHR did apply during the occupation.[52]

That the ICC prosecutor fulfills its functions to make those responsible for these "war crimes" and "crimes against humanity" accountable through principles of individual criminal liability. In decisions over the next few months as to how, if at all, to investigate and prosecute these matters, it is important that he recognize the fundamental duty he has to uphold the rule of law.

The Conduct of the UN before and after the 2003 Invasion

Hans von Sponeck

In discussing UN involvement before and after the 2003 invasion of US, UK, and other coalition forces into Iraq, a clear distinction has to be made between the policy makers and the civil servants expected to carry out the policies, i.e., between member governments in the UN Security Council and the UN Secretariat.

If this is done, it quickly becomes clear that primary responsibility for the human catastrophe in Iraq lies with the political UN, with those member governments in the UN Security Council who had the power to make a difference. The failure of the Council to make a humanitarian, ethical, and legal difference is much more monumental than is commonly known. There is not only the betrayal of the Iraqi people but also the betrayal of the UN Charter and the betrayal of the international conscience.

Why is this so?

World leaders were hiding behind the curtain of the UN Security Council to premeditate their betrayal before and after the illegal war of 2003. There can be no more doubts, the facts are present, that the US and UK governments were actively pursuing regime change by force at a time when the world was made to believe that international law, peaceful solutions to the conflict, and the protection of the Iraqi people were part of the US and UK governments' approach. They were not. Once the asymmetrical war was over, it also became clear to the international public that those who carried out this war had reached higher heights of irresponsibility by fighting this war without a strategy for peace.

The objective was to maintain a stranglehold on Iraq. Means of "disarray" and "deception" were deployed to justify the end of "domination." Iraq's armed forces were sent home. Civil servants were retired without evidence of wrongdoing, simply because they had belonged to the Ba'ath Party. New laws, the Transition Authority laws (TAL), were introduced by decree. These laws tried to re-colonize Iraq economically and institutionally and create dependence even in such areas as agriculture by banning local seed stocks in favor of genetically modified seeds to be imported from the Unites States. The ensuing Iraqi opposition and chaos left the occupying powers stymied and bewildered.

How did the UN Security Council and the UN Secretariat react to these bilateral aberrations?

Over a decade, the UN Security Council condoned what two permanent members, the US and the UK, were doing to pursue, first, their Iraq containment policy and later their regime replacement agenda. This amounted to nothing less but the de facto bilateralization of the Security Council. The rhetoric of the Iraq debates in the Council showed that there was an abundance of awareness of the evolving humanitarian crisis in Iraq. At the same time there was a severe shortage of political will to take timely steps to redress this situation.

It was known to all members of the Security Council that the linkage between disarmament and comprehensive economic sanctions meant that the people of Iraq were made to pay a heavy price in terms of life and destitution for acts of their government. It was known to all members of the Security Council that the inadequacy of the Council's allocations for the oil-for-food program and the bureaucracy with which this humanitarian exemption was implemented worsened the chances of survival of many Iraqis. It was known to all members of the Security Council that the refusal by the Council to allow the transfer of cash to Iraq's central bank needed to run the nation, to pay for training, installation of equipment, and institution building, encouraged the government of Iraq to increase illegal means to obtain cash.

It was known to all members of the Security Council that the establishment of the two no-fly zones within Iraq had little to do with the protection of ethnic and religious groups but a lot to do with destabilization. All members of the Security Council were aware that following "Operation Desert Fox" in December 1998, the US and the UK governments, giving their pilots enlarged rules of engagement, used Iraqi airspace as training grounds, eventually in preparation for war. The Security Council had access to air-strike reports when such reports were prepared by the UN in Baghdad and therefore all members of the Security Council knew of the destruction of civilian life and property. Yet, the Security Council did not ever debate the legality of the no-fly zones to challenge two of its members that they maintained these zones without a UN mandate.

All this was known.

With rare exceptions, members of the Security Council allowed the Council to become a convenient tool for the pursuit of bilateral policies. There was ample experience in the Council concerning the danger of misuse of consensus resolutions as demonstrated by the handling of Resolutions 687 (1991) and 1284 (1999) by the United States and the UK governments. This did not deter members of the Council from going along with yet another consensus resolution, 1441 (2002). The likelihood of misuse by individual members of the Council of provisions such as "material breaches" and "serious consequences" to justify military invasion should have prevented the adoption of such a resolution.

The UN Secretariat acquiesced when the US and UK, two founding members of the UN, insisted in the Security Council on an economic sanctions regime that caused a human tragedy. The UN Secretariat remained mute when these same governments dropped out of the international community to unilaterally mount an illegal invasion into Iraq. The UN Secretariat did not react even at this critical time when the very foundation of the institution was threatened. Dr. Hans Blix, chief UN arms inspector, had reported progress in verifying Iraq's lack of WMD and was pleading for more time to complete the inspection process. The UN Secretariat should have used this to confront the two governments about their war plans but chose not to do so. Without protest, the UN Secretariat withdrew the UN arms inspectors in March 2003.

The UN Secretariat could not have prevented the long-planned decision to go to war. The sheer seriousness of the violation of international law by two member countries and the sidelining of a world body created to prevent wars represented a challenge for the UN civil service to show that, ultimately, conscience was superior to obedience.

Since the illegal invasion of Iraq, there has not been a debate in the Security Council about the fundamental disregard by the coalition forces of existing conventions created to ensure that the occupation armies act in accordance with the Hague and Geneva Conventions to which they are parties. Looting and burning of the national museum and the national library, the damaging of archeological sites, and the humiliating treatment of civilians by the US armed forces provoked no protest in the Security Council. The Security Council watched impotently when the soul and ethos of Iraq was attacked. The detention of political figures for indefinite periods and the unimaginable brutality and sadism with which detainees were treated not just in Abu Ghraib and Camp Bucca but also in other prisons were not subjects of Security Council concern. Carpet destruction of towns such as Falluja, Tel Afar, and al-Qaim did not ruffle the Security Council and lead to emergency meetings. There were no protests in the Council that CPA administrator Paul Bremer and other CPA officials represented an allegedly liberated and sovereign Iraq at major international meetings such as the World Economic Forum in Amman and the WTO in Geneva. The Security Council took no note that the assignment of a human rights rapporteur for Iraq was abruptly terminated by the UN Human Rights Commission in Geneva following the illegal war. The Security Council agreed in 2003 to the continuation of payments by the UN Compensation Commission even though it had earlier agreed to discontinue the entertainment of claims.

The Security Council did play an important role in the preparations for an interim Iraqi administration and elections but ultimately succumbed to US heavy-handedness in deciding the details of the process.

In the history books of the United Nations, the handling of the Iraq conflict by the Security Council will be recorded as a massive failure of oversight responsibility.

The history books should also record that the voice of the people replaced the UN Security Council as the international conscience. This voice must not relent in its demands that the US and UK governments, bilaterally, as national administrations, and multilaterally, as permanent members of the UN Security Council, are accountable to their people and to the world community for their wrongdoing against Iraq, before, during, and after the illegal war.

It is a crime in many countries to leave the scene of an accident without helping the victims. This also applies to the responsibility of the international community to help the Iraqi victims. Conscience, compassion and a sense of responsibility are powerful reasons to stay involved. There must be involvement at two levels: Iraq and UN reforms.

Political leaders urge that we should look forward. This we must. However, a look forward receives legitimacy only when it is linked to accountability for the past. This applies to nations, communities, individuals—to everyone, particularly to those in power. The forthcoming trial of Iraq's former President Saddam Hussein acknowledges his accountability for past crimes against his people. The same applies to crimes against humanity committed by those who maintained economic sanctions with total disregard for the human costs, who fought a silent war in the no-fly zones, who invaded Iraq, who abused, maimed, tortured, and killed its people. The dock of the courtroom for Iraq has to have more than one chair! Law and justice, need it be stressed, are not only for the losers.

There are thousands of unnamed Iraqi fathers, mothers, and children who are victims of the failure to prevent war and destruction in Iraq. Let them be the stark reminders of our responsibility to keep the debate alive at least until the terms of accountability are met.

In summary, Iraq remains "unfinished business" for the international peace movement and responsible citizens everywhere. The challenge is to address three major issues:

1. The United Nations has failed in preventing unjust economic sanctions, an illegal war, and carnage under occupation.

This means that in the short term, the peace movement must persevere in their demands that those responsible be brought to justice. It must not be forgotten that what was done in the name of "freedom," "democracy," and "human rights" represents a travesty of the meaning of "freedom," "democracy," and "human rights."

In the medium term, the peace movement must forcefully contribute to the debate on UN reforms to create a structure which is protected against misuse. This involves much more than the enlargement of the Security Council.

2. The international peace movement, too, has failed in preventing unjust economic sanctions and an illegal war.

In the short term, the peace movement should take this as an important opportunity to carry out a self-critical review of why this failure occurred and what factors contributed to this failure.

The dangers looming on the political and socioeconomic horizon are horrific. The reaction of the peace movement, in the medium term, must be to leave turf battles and institutional or personal ambitions behind to facilitate significantly better organized responses to international crises. Only combined commitment and a joint strategy offer a chance to make a difference.

3. As individuals who understand and cherish the ethos of the UN Charter, who believe in peace and justice for all, who are abhorred by what has happened in Iraq before, during, and after the illegal war, we must first and foremost work on ourselves to become equipped for the tasks ahead. Beyond this obligation, we have to remain, in the words of Dag Hammarskjoeld, the UN's second secretary-general, "conscious of the reality of evil and the tragedy of individual life, and conscious, too, of the demand that life be conducted with decency."

The History of US and UK Interventions in Iraq
Larry Everest

During the run-up to the invasion of Iraq, US government officials and establishment pundits turned into self-proclaimed Middle East historians, energetically exposing the record of Saddam Hussein's crimes—many real, some imagined. But mysteriously, these same experts studiously avoided examining the well-documented history of US and British actions—and crimes—against Iraq and its people.

As a result, most Americans (and no doubt many around the world) would be astounded to learn that Iraq was created in the interests of British imperialism, not the peoples living in the region; that when the Iraqi people rose to overthrow their hated pro-Western monarch, the self-proclaimed defenders of freedom and democracy in London and Washington responded not with joy, but with threats of war—even nuclear war.

Many would be shocked to learn that the US government helped bring the Hussein regime to power and was directly complicit in the very crimes for which it was indicted—the use of chemical weapons, aggression against neighboring countries, and atrocities against the Kurds. And they would be even more horrified to learn that the UN sanctions—unjustly spearheaded and maintained on Iraq by the US and the UK—resulted in more Iraqi deaths than anything attributed to Saddam Hussein—yes, even after the Hussein regime had complied with UN demands by—as the world now knows—destroying its chemical, biological, and nuclear weapons. Yet these are all well-documented historical facts, as I and others have detailed in our work.

So this morning, I'm honored to be contributing to the extremely urgent and timely work of the World Tribunal by offering a brief overview of the history of UK and US intervention in Iraq since World War I. It may be a "truism," but it's still true that we can't understand events today without understanding their development over time—i.e., history. Of course, there is a much more thorough discussion of this record in my book, *Oil, Power and Empire: Iraq and the US Global Agenda*.

The main themes that emerge from this history—which must be understood in the context of the global and regional agendas of the US and UK—are:

First, for at least 100 years, US and British actions in Iraq and the Persian Gulf have been guided not by the lofty concepts of freedom, democracy, self-determination, justice, human rights, and international law bandied about so freely by imperial officials and their media stenographers, but by cold-blooded and ruthless calculations of global empire, regional dominance, and control of Persian Gulf oil—specifically, suppressing revolutionary and nationalist struggles for self-determination, including just struggles for self-determination by the Palestinian and Kurdish peoples; preventing rival imperial powers—most recently the former Soviet Union—from gaining influence in the region; and building Israel into a sub-regional gendarme for imperial interests and control.

Second, in pursuit of these objectives, Washington and London have acted covertly and overtly, wielding the carrot of aid and the stick of military assault—installing and overthrowing governments, exerting economic, political, and military pressure, waging wars, even threatening the use of nuclear weapons—committing enormous crimes, staggering duplicity, unfathomable hypocrisy, and cold-blooded betrayal along the way.

Third, as a result, neither the UK nor the US have ever brought liberation to the peoples of Iraq or the Middle East, but have instead inflicted enormous suffering and perpetuated oppression. While deep national, social, and class divisions run through the societies of the Middle East, foreign imperialist domination—by the US in particular today— has been and remains the primary obstacle to justice and liberation.

Fourth, US/UK actions have brought neither peace nor stability, but spawned a deepening spiral of resistance, instability, intervention, and war. America's current so-called "war on terror" is in reality a war *of* terror against the peoples of the planet in service of greater and more dominant global empire—and its 2003 invasion and occupation of Iraq represents a further, horrific escalation of this deadly spiral of intervention—an arrogant, yet desperate, effort to forcefully resolve the growing contradictions that the imperial powers themselves have engendered in the region.

Finally, the history of US/UK intervention in Iraq and the region shows that grand ambitions of conquest and control are one thing; realizing them is quite another. Oppression breeds resistance, actions provoke reactions, and events often career beyond the control of their initiators in unexpected ways—as the resistance and struggle in Iraq once again demonstrates.

The Creation of Iraq

I want to illustrate these themes—including their continuity and evolution—by briefly examining the goals and results of US/UK actions in Iraq over several broad historical periods beginning with the aftermath of World War I.

In 1921, the country of Iraq was created, its first government chosen, and its future determined—not in Baghdad, but at a closed-door meeting of British officials and specialists in the Semiramis Hotel in Cairo. Two pro-British Iraqis were present.

When the British entered Baghdad in 1917, their commanding officer spoke words that sound eerily familiar today: "Our armies do not come into your cities and lands as conquerors or enemies, but as liberators." In reality, the British considered such declarations, never formalized in treaties or binding agreements, as empty promises to be discarded when they were no longer useful. As the head of English intelligence put it, "Luckily we have been very careful indeed to commit ourselves to nothing whatsoever."

In fact, the creation of Iraq was shaped not by the needs of the Iraqi people or principles of justice and self-determination, but by the interests and ambitions of British imperialism—to help ensure British control of the Middle East for its strategic location at the crossroads between Africa, Asia, and Europe, and its vast oil reserves. The British understood that petroleum was the lifeblood of modern empire—a crucial prop of global power and wealth on many levels: an essential economic input impacting production costs, profits, and competitive advantage; an instrument of rivalry whose control ensured leverage over other powers and the world economy; and a resource crucial for the projection of military power globally.

Take three crucial dimensions of British actions: the creation of Iraq by combining three demographically distinct administrative units of the Ottoman Empire: Basra in the Shia south, Baghdad in the Sunni center, and Mosul in the Kurdish north, without regard to the aspirations of their peoples; the drawing of borders to prevent Iraq from becoming a major power in the Persian Gulf; and the institutionalization of a pro-British ruling elite.

Consider Iraq's Kurds. They had been promised independence by the world's major powers after World War I. Yet their aspirations, like those of the Arabs, were betrayed and then suppressed for British imperial interests. The British wished to incorporate the former Ottoman province of Mosul, an area populated mainly by Kurds and Turkomans, into the new state because without the oil fields of Mosul and Kirkuk, the new state of Iraq would not be economically viable.

Britain had no desire to see a strong state arise in the midst of the world's greatest oil fields, so when, in 1922, British High Commissioner for Iraq Sir Percy Cox delineated the borders between Iraq, Saudi Arabia, and Kuwait with the stroke of his pen, he made sure to limit Iraq's access to the Persian Gulf: Kuwait, a much smaller country, was given a Gulf coastline line of 310 miles, while Iraq was given only 36 miles.

(Cox's borders would wreck havoc for decades to come. Iraq's claims on Kuwait and its desire for greater access to the gulf nearly led to conflicts with Britain and the US in 1958 and 1961. They contributed to tensions between Iran and Iraq during the 1970s and to Iraq's invasion of Iran in 1980. And they were a major reason for Iraq's August 1990 invasion of Kuwait, which triggered the US "Desert Storm" assault five-and-a-half months later.)

The British held this new country together by installing a brutal comprador monarchy backed by feudal and tribal elites of the Sunni Arab center, backed by British arms, to rule over the Shia south and the Kurdish north. This oppressive configuration was supported by London and Washington—most glaringly in the aftermath of the 1991 Gulf War—up until the 2003 overthrow of the Hussein regime. The point was to prevent the emergence of a Kurdish state, which could threaten the stability of Iran to the east and Turkey to the north, and to prevent the rise of Shia power. Prior to 1979, this could have destabilized the Shah's rule in Iran; after his fall it could have increased the regional influence of Iran's Islamic Republic. Today, the US occupation of Iraq has not resolved these deep ethnic and religious tensions; instead, they have the potential to help turn Washington's conquest into a quagmire.

This arrangement proved a nightmare for the masses of Iraqis. Wealth and power were concentrated in the hands of a tiny land-owning elite linked with the monarchy, while the vast majority of Iraqis toiled in desperate rural poverty as tenant farmers or landless peasants. Iraq's oil wealth remained in foreign hands, while the country remained poor and undeveloped. In 1952, 55 percent of all privately held land belonged to one percent of all landowners, just 2,480 families. Over 10 percent of greater Baghdad's population—some 92,000 people at the time—lived in shacks made from palm branches. Over 80 percent of Iraqis were illiterate; there was but one doctor for every 6,000 people. Opposition was met with violent state repression.

The sordid history of UK and US actions in Iraq included many imperial "firsts": In 1925, the British forced the new King Faisal to sign a 75-year concession granting the foreign-owned Iraq Petroleum Company (IPC) all rights to Iraq's oil, in return for modest royalties—but no ownership. The US got its first Middle East oil supplies and profits from Iraq, and the British–US-controlled IPC became a model for oil cartel operations in other Third World countries.

Iraq was one of the first colonies policed with air power, and the British developed a number of anti-personnel weapons for use in Iraq, including phosphorus bombs, war rockets, metal crowsfeet (to maim livestock), man-killing shrapnel, liquid fire, and delay-action bombs.

The Iraqi people never welcomed foreign conquerors—with flowers or sweets! Kurds in Iraq rose for self-rule in 1919, but this and subsequent revolts were crushed, including by the RAF bombing of Suleimanieh in 1924.

In June 1920, over 100,000 Shias, Arab nationalists (many who had been officers in Hussein's Arab army), and tribal leaders rose up against the British forces which had occupied Mesopotamia during World War I. British forces retaliated with a rampage—destroying, sometimes burning whole villages, and executing suspected rebels on the spot. The Iraqis fought so fiercely that British leaders demanded chemical weapons be used—shortly after their horrors had been graphically demonstrated in World War I.

The Royal Air Force didn't drop gas bombs on the Iraqis—only because they hadn't yet perfected the necessary technology—but British forces did bombard Shia rebels with poison-gas-filled artillery shells, and RAF conventional air assaults were murderous as well, as described by one wing commander: "Within forty-five minutes a full-size village can be practically wiped out and a third of its inhabitants killed or injured." In crushing this first anti-British revolt, between 6,000 and 9,000 Iraqis were killed by March 1921.

In 1932, Britain's League of Nations mandate ended and Iraq became formally independent, but London still effectively ruled. Its armed forces remained in Iraq to ensure the continuation of the monarchy, which was widely hated and rightly considered a tool of British interests.

1958 to 1979

After repeated failures, and great suffering and losses, on 14 July 1958, General Abdul Karim Qasim and the secret "Free Officers" group within the Iraqi military—with much popular support—overthrew the monarchy, seized power, and declared a republic. This opened a new chapter in Iraqi history—and in imperialist efforts—now spearheaded by the region's new dominant power, the US—to regain its control of Iraq, suppress radical Arab nationalism, protect foreign control of Middle East oil, and prevent the Soviet Union from moving into the region.

Today, George W. Bush and his cohorts claim that US actions have always been guided by "friendship" for the Iraqi people. Yet when the hated monarchy fell and a bit of popular democracy reared its head in the region, the US did not respond with joy—or flowers and sweets—but with military deployments—including nuclear weapons—threats of war, and covert operations which would ultimately bring Saddam Hussein to power.

In 1963, the US directly assisted the Ba'ath rise to power by supporting its coup against the republic and providing it with lists of suspected communists, left-leaning intellectuals, progressives, and radical nationalists. CIA-provided lists in hand, the Ba'ath then unleashed a reign of terror in which thousands were killed, including, according to one author, "people who represented the backbone of Iraqi society—lawyers, doctors, academics, and students—as well as workers, women, and children."

Washington then helped the Ba'ath consolidate undivided power—dispatching former Treasury Secretary Robert Anderson to Baghdad to supervise the operation in 1967—via a July 30, 1968, coup. Iraq's chief of military intelligence would later write, "for the 1968 coup you must look to Washington."

The US preferred Ba'ath rule to the prospect of millions of politically energized Iraqis taking Iraq in a more democratic, anti-imperialist, or revolutionary direction. Yet tensions would soon grow between Washington and Baghdad. In 1972, Iraq signed a fifteen-year friendship treaty with the Soviet Union and completed the nationalization of its oil industry. These actions embodied some of the key challenges to US Middle East hegemony in the late 1960s and early 1970s: the spread of Arab nationalism, expanding Soviet influence, and the nationalization of the region's petroleum industry.

So Ba'athist Iraq was becoming a problem, and the US would spend the next 30-plus years trying to subordinate it—sometimes with the carrot of aid and weapons, more often with the stick of force.

In 1972, Iraq's Kurds became Washington's weapon of choice. Iran and the US encouraged them to rise against Baghdad and provided millions of dollars in weapons, logistic support, and funds.

The US goal, however, was neither victory nor self-determination for Iraqi Kurds. According to CIA memos and cables, Kurds were seen as "a card to play" against Iraq, and "a uniquely useful tool for weakening [Iraq's] potential for international adventurism."

When US and Iranian goals were met, the Kurds were promptly—and without warning—abandoned. Deprived of support, Kurdish forces were quickly decimated by Iraq's military and between 150,000 and 300,000 Kurds were forced to flee into Iran. The US–Iranian covert campaign further poisoned relations between Baghdad and Iraq's Kurds. The Pike Commission concluded that if the US and the Shah hadn't encouraged the insurgency, the Kurds "may have reached an accommodation with the central government, thus gaining at least a measure of autonomy while avoiding further bloodshed. Instead, our clients [the Kurds] fought on, sustaining thousands of casualties and 200,000 refugees."

"Covert action," Henry Kissinger infamously remarked, "should not be confused with missionary work."

The 1980s—Iran–Iraq War

The 1980s have been a goldmine for US propagandists. During the buildup to the 2003 invasion, George W. Bush condemned Saddam Hussein for invading Iran, for accumulating weapons of mass destruction, and for using them against Iranian troops and Iraqi Kurds, "leaving the bodies of mothers huddled over their dead children," as he put it in his 2002 State of the Union message.

What Bush did not say, however, was that these crimes took place when Hussein's government was closer to Washington than ever before—or since—and the US directly facilitated every one.

The story of the 1980s, however, is much more than a chronicle of US hypocrisy. It is also the story of how Washington fueled the Iran–Iraq War and helped turn it into one of the longest and bloodiest conventional wars of the twentieth century. It's the story of mind-boggling and Machiavellian twists and turns in US policy—first supporting Iraq, then Iran, and then back to Iraq again. It is the story of how Washington—including Donald Rumsfeld, the man later put in charge of destroying Saddam's regime for the Bush II administration—helped Iraq obtain and use the very weapons of mass destruction that provided the alleged *casus belli* for war in 2003.

The abrupt reversal in US–Iraqi relations from antagonism in the 1970s to alliance in the 1980s was fueled by three seismic jolts to US power which occurred in rapid succession in 1979: the February revolution that toppled the pro-US Shah of Iran; the November seizure of the American Embassy in Tehran; and the Soviet invasion of neighboring Afghanistan in December.

Encouraging, then manipulating, the Iran–Iraq War was one facet of a multi-dimensioned and aggressive US response to these shocks, in order to protect pro-US Gulf sheikdoms and prevent the Soviet Union from turning regional turmoil into geopolitical gain.

There are numerous indications that the US encouraged Iraq to attack Iran, initially as a means of weakening the Islamic revolution and pressuring Iran to release US embassy personnel being held, but without fundamentally altering the Gulf balance of power.

However, when the tide of war turned in Iran's favor in 1982, President Reagan decided the US should do all it could to prevent Iraq from losing the war, and began providing Iraq with billions of dollars in credits, military intelligence and advice, and by encouraging third-country arms sales to Iraq.

The US and its European allies were directly complicit in many of Iraq's worst wartime atrocities, including its use of chemical weapons. For example, the *Washington Post* reported that Iraq used US intelligence to "calibrate attacks with mustard gas on Iranian ground troops." Iranian estimates of the dead and wounded from these gas attacks range between 50,000 and 100,000, including many civilians.

By the mid-1980s, US strategists were confronted with yet another twist: the possibility that Ayatollah Khomeini's death could open the door to increased Soviet influence in Tehran. As one internal memo put it, "Our tilt to Iraq was timely when Iraq was against the ropes and the Islamic revolution was on a roll. The time may now have to come to tilt back."

The nefarious, soon infamous, and ultimately failed "arms for hostages" plan was born; the US would supply Iran with arms and military intelligence in return for the release of American hostages held in Lebanon, and more fundamentally, the possibility of a US geopolitical coup in Tehran.

US maneuvers contributed mightily to the war's murderous toll. "Doling out tactical data to both sides put the agency in the position of engineering a stalemate," Bob Woodward wrote in *Veil*, his study of CIA covert operations in the 1980s. "This was no mere abstraction. The war was a bloody one... almost a million had been killed, wounded or captured on both sides. This was not a game in an operations center. It was slaughter."

And what of Washington's support for Kurdish rights? Throughout the 1980s, it supported Baghdad's attacks on the Kurds and steadfastly opposed recognizing their basic rights, let alone self-determination. After the 1987–1988 Anfal offensive, Baghdad was not punished by Washington, which still hoped Iraq could become a loyal ally in the region, it was rewarded with increases in US aid and trade.

In the end, neither Iran nor Iraq would win a clear victory, but the suffering was enormous on both sides. Conservative estimates place the death toll at 367,000—262,000 Iranians and 105,000 Iraqis. An estimated 700,000 were injured or wounded on both sides, bringing the total casualty figure to over one million.

Despite the voluminous record of US complicity in these horrors, one can be sure that when Saddam is put on trial for his role in these crimes, he won't be allowed to call co-conspirators, like Donald Rumsfeld and other Reagan-era officials, as witnesses.

The 1990s—Desert Storm and Sanctions

The tortured twists and turns of US policy during the Iran–Iraq War were Machiavellian to be sure, but they also reflected the profound difficulties the American empire confronted in controlling a volatile region halfway around the globe. For all Washington's machinations, it still didn't have a firm grip on either Iran, Iraq, or the Persian Gulf region.

This was brought home in dramatic fashion in the early morning hours of August 2, 1990, when six elite Iraqi Republican Guard divisions crossed into Kuwait heading south, and quickly seized the capital. Overnight, Baghdad was transformed from a sometime US ally into its main enemy in the region, beginning a confrontation that led to two wars and a decade of murderous sanctions, and that continues, albeit in a different form, to this day.

It is important to note, first, that while Iraq's brutal seizure of Kuwait may have been a surprise, it was not a bolt from the blue, coming without provocation or warning. In large part, it grew out of the destruction and tensions spawned by the eight-year Iran–Iraq War. And US officials even gave a direct "green light" to Saddam's invasion.

Most importantly, US war aims were never limited to expelling Iraq from Kuwait and restoring the status quo ante; instead, coming as the then Soviet Union spiraled into collapse, and no longer constrained by the existence of a nuclear-armed superpower as it had been in the region and globally, the 1991 Gulf War represented a radical escalation of US intervention in the region and an attempt to usher in a "new world order" of unfettered US dominance. These objectives demanded crushing Iraq as a regional power and forcefully demonstrating US military power to the world.

The Pentagon bragged that Desert Storm was "a defining event in US global leadership." National Security Advisor Brent Scowcroft saw it as "the bridge between the Cold War and the post-Cold War eras." Bush said the Vietnam syndrome "had been put to rest and American credibility restored." Washington's objectives demanded war, not peace, and a brutal, devastating war at that. "We have to have a war," George H.W. Bush secretly told his war cabinet.

The last thing the US wanted was for Iraq to negotiate its way out of Kuwait with its military intact; war would also send a much clearer message of US power and will than simply pressuring Iraq into withdrawing. Between Iraq's August 1990 invasion and the end of the war in late February 1991, the US rejected or sabotaged at least eleven different peace proposals from a variety of countries. Bush I was literally "jubilant" when negotiations collapsed (for example during a 9 January 1991 meeting in Geneva between Secretary of State Baker and Iraqi Foreign Minister Tariq Aziz) and enraged when it seemed they might succeed (as on 30 January 1991, when Baker and Soviet Foreign Minister Bessmertnykh issued a joint statement calling for a cease-fire provided Iraq agreed to leave Kuwait).

Bush and Scowcroft wrote that they viewed the UN Security Council as its primary vehicle for building a coalition against Iraq and for giving Desert Storm a veil of legitimacy. As Scowcroft put it, "Building an international response led us immediately to the United Nations, which could provide a cloak of acceptability to our efforts and mobilize world opinion behind the principles we wished to project."

US imperialism's objective of crushing Iraq as a regional power and demonstrating the US's might dictated an extremely brutal military strategy. The Defense Department estimated the dead in this 43-day war at 100,000 Iraqi soldiers killed and 300,000 wounded; it never provided an accounting of Iraqi civilian casualties. In 1991, Census Bureau demographer Beth Osborne Daponte estimated that 158,000 Iraqis were killed in the war and its immediate aftermath. One can add to this toll the Iraqis killed in the war's aftermath after heeding George H.W. Bush's February 15, 1991, call to rise against the Hussein regime, only to be slaughtered when the US decided it preferred Hussein's regime to upheaval from below and the possible fragmentation of Iraq. Estimates of the dead in the rebellions in the Shia south and the Kurdish north range from 20,000 to 100,000.

88,500 tons of bombs were dropped on Iraq, the explosive equivalent of six Hiroshimas. But they were not only dropped on Iraq's military, but on its economic and social infrastructure as well—the foundations of civilian life. Coalition bombs and missiles destroyed eleven of Iraq's twenty power-generating stations and damaged another six. By the war's end, Iraq's electrical generation had been slashed by 96 percent and reduced to 1920 levels. Without electricity, water could not be pumped, sewage could not be treated, and hospitals could not function. This directly contravened Article 54 of the Geneva Convention, which prohibits attacks on essential civilian facilities including "drinking water supplies and irrigation works." Thus, the US bombing campaign constituted a war crime that would contribute to the deaths of hundreds of thousands of Iraqis in the decade after the war.

The US never stopped waging war against Iraq even after the 1991 Gulf War formally ended. The US and UK have systematically lied about the decade of the 1990s and in particular the nature, terms, and purpose of UN sanctions, sanctions which have been responsible for staggering levels of death and suffering inflicted on the Iraqi people.

US officials propagated three main myths about sanctions. First, that their purpose was simply to compel Iraq to abide by UN resolutions and disarm. Second, that they were aimed at Iraq's rulers, not its people. Third, that they were continued because Iraq did not comply with UN resolutions. Washington's line has been that it would have gladly lifted sanctions if only Hussein had complied with UN demands. Iraq instead "answered a decade of UN demands with a decade of defiance," according to George W. Bush.

This official storyline stands reality on its head. UN resolutions became weapons in this ongoing conflict, even as they were being violated more frequently by Washington than by the Hussein regime. In fact, Baghdad complied with UN demands more than it defied them, including on arms inspections and disarmament. This compliance is the simple reason that no weapons of mass destruction were found in Iraq following the 2003 invasion. They were destroyed early in the 1990s—a fact the Bush II administration knew perfectly well.

The goal of sanctions was never merely to disarm Iraq; the policy of slaughter by sanction was designed to further US/UK imperial aims—to cripple Iraq by preventing it from rebuilding its industry, economy, and military; block other global rivals from making strategic inroads in Iraq; and make life so miserable that Iraqis would rise up (preferably via a military coup) and topple the Hussein regime—shoring up US regional control and demonstrating its power in the process.

No one knows precisely how many Iraqis died or were permanently injured as a result of the 1991 Gulf War and twelve years of sanctions. In 2002, the Iraqi government stated that 1.7 million children had died from disease or malnutrition since the imposition of sanctions in August 1990.

A 1999 survey by UNICEF and Iraq's Ministry of Health reported that had sanctions not been imposed and infant mortality trends during the 1980s continued through the 1990s, "there would have been half a million fewer deaths of children under-five in the country as a whole during the 8-year period 1991 to 1998." So roughly 5,000 Iraqi children under five were dying each month thanks to US actions—more than a World Trade Center catastrophe every 30 days.

In a 1999 analysis published in *Foreign Affairs*, "Sanctions of Mass Destruction," John and Carl Mueller concluded that all economic sanctions imposed after 1990, the most significant case being Iraq, "may have contributed to more deaths during the post-Cold War era than all weapons of mass destruction throughout history."

The New Millennium: Invasion, Conquest, Occupation

The Bush administration offered so many rationalizations for its 2003 invasion, from links to al-Qaeda to WMD to spreading democracy—that it was difficult to stay current with their "pretext du jour." None, however, explained why the US was hell-bent on war. But the sweep and enormity of its global and regional agendas did.

The swift and brutal stroke of war in 2003 was an attempt to resolve the Iraq "problem" that had plagued America's rulers throughout the 1990s. Its policy of punitive containment through sanctions, subversion, and military strikes was fraying, and the toll it was taking on Iraqis had become, in the words of former CIA analyst Kenneth Pollack, "a major irritant [in] U.S. relations with the Muslim world in general." Meanwhile, other powers had strengthened their ties with Iraq, and US power and "credibility" in the region were being challenged.

So the problem was not that Iraq "threatened its neighbors," as Bush II charged. The problem was that the Hussein regime's survival could "threaten" to erode US regional hegemony. If sanctions were lifted, US "credibility" could have been undercut. Baghdad might emerge with its regional ambitions intact and possibly enough oil wealth to pursue them. The US could end up with less control than before the 1991 war.

Yet the 2003 war was also a leap beyond past US interventions: it was fought in the context of a new overarching strategy and its objectives went well beyond previous stratagems of balancing Iran against Iraq, or maintaining the Middle East status quo. It represented a radical leap in direct US intervention, war, and colonization—as a key component of a sweeping new US global agenda of greater, more dominant empire.

A momentous shift in US global strategy, in the making for over a decade following the Soviet Union's collapse, was codified in a new National Security Strategy (NSS) on September 20, 2002. Its goal is "freedom"—that is, freedom for America's dominant corporate-political elite to impose its values, interests, and economic system on all others. It is an audacious declaration that the US aims to remain the world's sole imperial superpower for decades to come by preventing rivals from even emerging with overwhelming military superiority and the Orwellian doctrine of "preemptive self-defense"—i.e., striking potential rivals down before they can emerge.

This unbounded campaign to forcibly recast global political, military, and economic relations necessitates trampling on international law, casting aside global treaties, eviscerating international organizations, reordering traditional alliances, and reducing other world powers to clearly second-tier status. The national sovereignty of others is now conditional on US approval, while US sovereignty is absolute—unrestrained by treaty, alliance, or law.

The new strategy advocates greater freedom for US business and accelerated capitalist globalization—demanding that US capital have open access to key global markets and raw materials; that trade, investment, ownership, and political barriers standing in the way be broken down; that global trade and economic relations be restructured to reflect and perpetuate US dominance; and that conditions be created for the unchallenged exploitation of hundreds of millions of laboring people worldwide. Combined with the NSS's insistence on US military superiority and its right to use it to enforce "regime change," the document's economic principles can best be understood as capitalist globalization on US terms, carried out at gunpoint.

"They have ambitions of essentially reshuffling the whole deck, reordering the whole situation," as Bob Avakian puts it, "beginning with the strategic areas of Central and South Asia and the Middle East that are more immediately involved now—but, even beyond that, on a world scale. They've set themselves a very far-reaching agenda with gigantic implications." US strategists saw conquering Iraq as a key step in unfolding this broader agenda and facilitating a host of objectives in the Middle East and beyond: it would demonstrate US might and determination; it could initiate the political, economic, and social reordering of the entire Middle East; and it was part of an ensemble of actions undertaken to solidify US control of the entire arc from Afghanistan through Egypt.

These goals in turn were linked to a larger struggle for global energy supremacy and overall dominance. Most broadly, the 2003 invasion and occupation were designed to solidify American political/military domination of the energy heart of world—the Middle East/Central Asia region, and are part of broader efforts to secure control of global energy sources and use that control to ensure the smooth functioning of US capitalism, strengthen its competitive position in world markets, and increase US leverage against potential rivals.

For Bush and the advocates of greater American empire, war wasn't the last resort, it was the first, and a bridge to the brave new world they openly dreamed of creating. Thus, unlike the war of 1991, the war of 2003 would not seek to cripple Iraq while preserving Ba'ath rule: its aim was regime change and occupation; instead of refusing to march on Baghdad, the 2003 war began with one.

The US is attempting to cloak its imperial agenda in the rhetoric of democracy, yet it is clear from its plans for the "new" Iraq—the country's relationship to the UN, its new government, its military posture, its economic structure, its foreign policy, its educational system, and its political system—that the US is attempting to create a colonial client state which would more directly impose American authority over Iraq's people and resources and facilitate broader US objectives in the Middle East and Central Asia. In short, the Bush team's brand of "liberation" is merely 21st-century neo-colonialism.

In sum, the US is striving to leverage a historic window of military (and to a lesser degree economic and political) supremacy into all-around political, economic, and military dominance for the foreseeable future, and dealing with the many contradictions it faces at home and abroad. Half-way measures, negotiated solutions, and diplomatic settlements are anathema to this brutal campaign of radical transformation.

There are deep connections between Bush's international and domestic agendas, and I must call attention to the grave and real danger of a Christian fascist theocracy in the US—a development which would have horrendous consequences for the world's people.

All of this demands the most urgent global resistance, resistance that aims squarely at stopping the Bush regime in its tracks, and forcing it from power. As a new call from the Not in Our Name statement of conscience declares, "The World Cannot Wait—Drive Out the Bush Regime! ... It is our responsibility to stop the Bush regime from carrying out this disastrous course. We believe history will judge us sharply should we fail to act decisively."

I believe the World Tribunal on Iraq can and must play a vital role in this effort.

The Doctrine of Humanitarian Intervention and the Neocolonial Implications of Its Revival in Our Unipolar World

Jim Harding

Introduction

Where did the doctrine of humanitarian intervention (HI) come from, and does it really represent a new, more human-rights orientation to international politics in the wake of the supremacy of the America superpower? Does the revival of this doctrine signal a new potential for this liberal, corporate democracy to tackle the roots and consequences of terrorism and genocide? How is this doctrine actually reflected in the actions of NATO and the US in international affairs, and in the process, affecting the operations of the United Nations and international law? Specifically, is HI enhancing human rights and the international law that is aimed to protect these rights, including through peace and security?

What can we learn about the doctrine of HI, in terms of the advancement of peace and security and human rights, if we compare human casualties of the UN sanctions on Iraq (and the Gulf War and the US invasion and occupation of Iraq) with casualties from the authoritarian regime of Hussein, while remembering that it was the "coalition of the willing" that helped get Hussein into power, and backed him during some of his most "barbarous" years of rule?

And, finally, are there better explanations than HI for the US's urge toward unilateralism, such as its fairly long imperial history and the centrality of the military-industrial complex within its economy and culture? What does the US's planned weaponization of space, and the broader processes of corporate globalization, suggest about the pretenses of HI in a unipolar world?

1. The Doctrine of Humanitarian Intervention

The doctrine of humanitarian intervention (HI) has its roots in past policies of European states intervening in the Orient. Legal legitimacy was asserted from moral pronouncements, and the notion of "legitimate intervention" or the "right of intervention" was created. This "right" was advanced in some manner as justification for European interventions in

Greece, Syria, Crete, Bosnia-Herzegovina, Bulgaria, and Macedonia from 1826 to 1905.

According to the doctrine of HI evolving before WWI, sovereignty was confined because countries are members of a "community of nations." The doctrine came to imply "that whenever the 'human rights' of the population of a given state are violated by its very government, another state or group of states has the right to intervene in the name of the so-called 'international community.'"[1] This in turn evolved into the notion of "limited sovereignty," whereby the "international community" (which really meant Europe) could substitute "their own sovereignty for that of the state against which the intervention is directed." Accordingly, a minimum standard of religious freedom was guaranteed by Turkey, in its Treaty of Berlin with major European states in 1878. This made HI part of public law.

This legalistic reasoning, purportedly based on humanitarian motives, has to be squarely placed in the context of the imperial agenda of the European states at the time. Hans Kochler argues that HI was explicitly created "to provide a kind of moral justification for the repeated intervention of European powers on the territory of the Ottoman Empire." He notes that the intervening states were not disinterested parties, but had their own geopolitical goals. Furthermore, "in the course of their own colonial rule," they "violated each and every humanitarian principle they proclaimed." The rights of Christian minorities were asserted but no comparable standards of treatment were advanced for indigenous populations with differing cultural-religious beliefs. The double standard was "veiled" by Christian universalism and Eurocentric chauvinism, but normative principles were never clearly defined.

The roots of this Eurocentric-Christian "universalism" can be traced back to the Treaty of 1815, known as the Holy Alliance, whereby Austria, Prussia, and Russia accepted "the precepts of that Holy Religion, namely the precepts of Justice, Christian Charity and Peace." The rulers declared themselves to be members of the "same Christian nation." France and England soon joined the alliance, which equated the destiny of humanity with the Christian world. Hans Kochler concluded, "The doctrine of HI was the natural outflow of the European powers' tendency to camouflage imperialist interests with lofty religious 'precepts'…"

The doctrine was criticized for its lack of precision regarding what constitutes humanitarianism, as well as the inconsistent practices of colonial powers. It was seen to be a doctrine of double standards, with "human rights" as only an "accessory motive of intervention." The colonial powers decided the criteria for applying the doctrine and were also their own judges. There was no democratic division of power between the authority formulating these criteria and the one executing the intervention. It was therefore a "tool of power politics" which shielded the fundamental inequality between the European and colonial states as well as the authoritarian relationship between the rulers and their own "citizens."

If this all sounds strangely familiar, it should. The revival of the doctrine at the turn of this century is being touted by backers of the Bush Doctrine as a rebirth of moral consciousness in support of spreading democracy and human rights through regime change. But it could only have been revived in the context of the hegemonic politics in the world since the end of the Soviet Union. Though the revived doctrine incorporates "spreading democracy" into its rhetoric, the thinking and its application remain thoroughly pre- or un-democratic. The vision of humanitarianism is still clouded with ethnocentrism, though it is now more America-centric. And, while thinking about human rights has steadily evolved since WWII, there is still no international institutional legal structure giving global credibility to human rights accountability.

2. Humanitarian Intervention over Genocide

The revived doctrine continues to be advanced primarily in righteous terms. When pressed, today's defenders may justify HI as a way to stop or even prevent genocide. The editors of a volume of writers taking this position say, "… far more often than the world's political leaders currently acknowledge, HI can work, can save lives, can overcome the political obstacles it inevitably faces."[2] However, a look at the modern history of intervention over genocide will make us leery of such a claim.

Catastrophic, violent events like "genocide" have to be named and better understood to be controlled and prevented. (This is also true for "global warming.") Naming is part of creating collective memory and action, which is one thing the WTI was set up to do. Raphael Lemkin invented the term "genocide" in 1944 after what was inadequately named the "race murder" of one million Armenians in 1915, and the "Holocaust" of Hitler's Germany in WWII. Hitler is said to have commented that no one really remembered the slaughter of the Armenians, and even after the invention of the term "genocide" this is still somewhat true. Much work remains to be done to clear up the historical record of genocide without the prolongation of any double standards.[3]

The UN's Genocide Convention of 1948 is primarily associated with the European Holocaust. Genocide that occurred elsewhere against other peoples during WWII, including the nuclear extermination of the Japanese civilians at Hiroshima and Nagasaki, has to be fully brought into the record. The deceit and manipulation of concerns about genocide involved with the invasion and occupation of Iraq compels us to keep this re-examination wide open.[4]

It is vital to open up the book on the European Holocaust itself, to see genocide in its more multifaceted terms. Six million Jews were exterminated with the aid of racializing ideology. And so, too, were five million Poles, Roma, homosexuals, and political dissidents exterminated through other dehumanizing tactics. The Holocaust involved the manipulation of anti-Semitism, but it was also about establishing totalitarian political hegemony. We know that in other historical circumstances, such as with the Armenians in Turkey in 1915 or the Tutsi in Rwanda in 1994, genocide involved other inherently violent "racializing" notions. And the "Holocaust" can itself be used as a political football. It is probably no accident that Hitler's killing of "communists" and "socialists," some of whom were among the front-line of the anti-fascist resistance, got little or no mention as the Cold War with the Soviet Union took shape. As well, the Holocaust has acted as a political football in the conflict over Palestinian land rights and Israel's national security.

Furthermore, the UN Genocide Convention did not even mention military intervention, so the thinking and strategies for preventing genocide at the time was an "open book." In the Nuremberg and Tokyo trials that held fascism accountable for its crimes against humanity, there was a mixed message about genocide and HI. Though the US Bush administration tries to impose an analogy that its invasion and occupation of Iraq is like overthrowing Hitler's fascistic regime in order to liberate an oppressed people, there is a deeper, and quite reversed analogy. It was the aggression of Hitler against neighboring states, and not the genocide per se, that was the main basis of the post-war tribunal. So, to correct the analogy: the US aggression against Iraq, and its manipulation of "terrorism" (as well as the threat of WMD), makes the Bush's Doctrine reminiscent of Hitler's regime.[5]

If we trace actions against "genocide" from the origins of the term, we find a litany of evasions for imperial gain.[6] After it entered WWI, the US did not declare war on Turkey, even though Armenians were being slaughtered in the imploding Ottoman Empire. Furthermore, the US had no qualms about committing its own form of "high tech," racialized genocide, when it dropped the two atom bombs on Japanese civilians on the, now very suspect, pretence of ending WWII and saving American lives.[7]

In 1969, neither the UK nor the US opposed the repression of the Ibo people of Biafra by the Nigerian military state. In 1971, US President Nixon did not oppose the slaughter of the people of Bengali by Pakistan's military state. In 1972, perhaps as a precursor to the later Rwandan genocide, these Western, imperial powers invoked "sovereignty" as a reason to refrain from intervening to stop the Burundi Tutsi killing 100,000 Hutu people.

The US directly helped create the conditions for, and in turn helped to cover up, the third-largest genocide in modern history. Between 1975 and 1979, in the chaotic regional aftermath of the imperial wars on Vietnam (first by a US-backed France, and then after the defeat of France, by the US "going it alone"), two of seven million Cambodians were slaughtered by the Khmer Rouge. Even after a Vietnamese military intervention ended this "holocaust," for a decade the US and most of Europe continued to back Pol Pot, keeping his seat at the UN. With its own imperial presence in Southeast Asia since WWII, the US had no credibility to undertake any HI in Cambodia. The Nixon administration even considered using nuclear weapons on the country in its desperate attempt to contain the nationalist guerrilla resistance. The US's role in dislocating the region, and covering up the genocide in Cambodia, clearly constitute complicity in genocide.

In 1992, the US and Europe watched as the Bosnian Serbs attacked both Muslims and Croats. The US continued to support the arms embargo on the Muslims, possibly already seeding a "clash of civilization" and war on terrorism with al-Qaeda. NATO intervened in 1995. In 1999 NATO launched its bombing attack on the Serbian army in Kosovo. Some believe that this saved thousands of Albanians from "ethnic cleansing," while others believe this contributed to the cycle of violence that fueled ethnic cleansing. The implosion of Yugoslavia and the reasons for Western intervention in the aftermath of the Soviet empire, still require careful, critical analysis.

When you stand back from the charges and counter-charges of repression of minorities, including the Serbs in Kosovo, it seems undeniable that we have been witnessing the fragmentation of a multinational state experiment. As a Canadian, living in a multinational state facing fragmentation from US continental power, Quebec separatism and the continuing failure to create fundamental justice with First Nations and Metis peoples colonized by European expansion, I remind myself how quickly this other multinational experiment, Yugoslavia, imploded in the power plays after the end of the Cold War. These two cases, Yugoslavia and Canada, show that human rights not only intersect with sovereignty, but with globalization.

If we turn our attention to the Middle East we find a similar story. The US and many European states were arming Hussein's Iraq when it was repressing the Kurds in 1987–1988. In their desperation to find a "righteous" excuse for the invasion and occupation of Hussein's Iraq, defenders of the Bush Doctrine referred to the need to stop Hussein from continuing this inhumanity. Yet there is evidence that the hard-won US sanctions against trade with Hussein, sanctions that were initially opposed by the Reagan administration and US agricultural lobby stopped this form of repression.[8]

The US-UK "coalition" in Iraq has tried to re-script its invasion and occupation from being about WMD to being a means to save the repressed Kurds from the Sunni-dominated state under Hussein. But it is extremely naïve to think that the US and UK would have enforced "no-fly" zones in northern Iraq, and in the process develop an alliance with the Kurds of the region, were major oil and oil pipelines not in the area. Using the slaughter of the Kurds under Hussein as a rationalization for the US's geopolitical intervention in Iraq contributes to the obscuring of the roots of and strategies for the prevention of genocide. The 2003 war on Iraq challenges us all to disentangle the realities of "genocide" from the imperial manipulation of "genocide politics." With the revival of the doctrine of HI, a new strategy of imperial manipulation of "genocide politics" seemed to be in the works.

Finally, we come to the fourth-largest genocide of the modern world, the slaughtering of nearly one million Tutsi and moderate Hutu in Rwanda in 1994. The first thing to consider is why no HI occurred, when the number of victims greatly outstripped those from Bosnia, Serbia, and Kosovo combined. The old imperial power, France, actually armed and defended the Hutu-led regime that instigated the killing. Having no major geopolitical interest in the region, and with the debacles of the Somalia UN's HI fresh in mind,[9] the US chose to ignore all the warnings and pleas for help. This was not unlike what the US and my own country, Canada, did when the Jews were pleading, mostly in vein, for help and a more open immigration policy while being exterminated under Hitler's Germany.

3. Humanitarian Intervention in a Unipolar World

Has anything fundamental changed since Rwanda? Can NATO's bombing of Yugoslavia and Afghanistan, or the US invasion and occupation of Iraq be seen as small steps toward more principled and effective HI to stop genocide? To even attempt such an argument is to continue to ignore the larger and deeper historical situation.

The doctrine of HI was not revived to combat genocide. Rather, it arose due to the unipolar geopolitical situation that includes the interplay of the UN, NATO, and the American empire. In the short period since the implosion of the Soviet Union we have seen the workings of "internationalism" shift from the UN to NATO to US unilateralism. We saw such a shift in the locus of international action and attempted legitimacy from the 1991 UN-authorized war with Iraq over Kuwait, to the 1999 NATO war with Yugoslavia over Kosovo, which received after-the-fact legitimacy from the UN, to the 2001 NATO attack on Taliban-controlled Afghanistan, to the 2003 unilateral US invasion and occupation of Iraq which was not authorized by the UN or supported by NATO.

These international actions have all been justified in terms of HI, but this obscures the more fundamental reasons and implications. Post-1989 changes in NATO signaled the return of the neo-colonial doctrine of HI. The North Atlantic Treaty that formed NATO in April 1949 recognized the mandate of the UN. NATO was to be a regional defensive organization, paralleling the UN Charter's emphasis on the rights of collective self-defense. (Article 5 of NATO complements Article 51 of the Charter.) And NATO's mission supported the peaceful settlement of disputes through the international legality of the UN. (Art. 1 of NATO complemented Art. 2(4) of the Charter.)[10]

All this changed on the 50th anniversary of NATO. The Washington Declaration (WD) of April 1999 set the stage for NATO taking on an aggressive, international role. While the language of "self-defense" remained, it was surpassed by a new, broad approach to security, which included the possibility of conducting "crisis response operations." Such "response operations" were to be launched over security risks such as "terrorism," but also, more notably, over "disruption of the flow of vital resources" (par. 24). And this "management of crises through military operations" (par. 49) was now to be carried out "beyond the Allies' territory" (par. 52).

This set the stage for NATO's role in bombing Yugoslavia in 1991 and Afghanistan in 2001. Then, in the climate in the US after 9/11, these two rationales (terrorism and resources) became merged, which fit well with the Project for a New American Century (PNAC) doctrine brought into the White House and Pentagon with the election of the Bush–Cheney ticket.[11] However, deepening geopolitical contradictions between the US and EU within NATO and the UN kept NATO out of the invasion of Iraq in 2003, though NATO is playing a role in the occupation of Iraq.

The language of HI—affirming democracy, human rights, and the rule of law—was inserted into the WD. It included the phrase "we remain determined to stand firm against those who violate human rights" in addition to "those who wage war and conquer territory" (par. 7). There was no reference to human rights in the original NATO treaty.

After 1999 NATO no longer saw itself as subordinate to the principles of the UN Charter. As Kochler says, "By going beyond clearly defined cases of self-defence against armed aggression, NATO's new doctrine seriously undermines the UN Charter's principle of non-use of force and severely erodes the system of international law as represented by the UN as a universal organization."

These changes were made in NATO because the multinational nature of the UN did not allow for the desired unilateralism of the American empire and its allies. The single superpower "world order" clearly wanted to re-establish the right to wage war and to police the world for geopolitical and corporate interests. To do this the UN had to be manipulated or neutralized, both of which have occurred. The regional framework of

NATO was revamped into a vehicle of international intervention. After the 1999 WD, NATO became the contemporary "Holy Alliance," holding itself up to embody the future of civilization and humanity.

There, however, is reason for some hope for those wanting to adapt and reinvigorate international law in this unipolar world. Many of the undemocratic, imperial strategies in the post-Soviet world have already become transparent to the world's governments and citizenry. It's no accident that this citizen-based tribunal is focusing on Iraq, for the US invasion and occupation of Iraq has exposed many of the international contradictions of the post-Soviet world. As Kochler says, "Because of conflicting interests among the permanent members [of the UN], the constellation of 1990/1991 could not be repeated in the 1999 war against Yugoslavia or in the 2003 war against Iraq."

In the aftermath of the invasion and occupation of Iraq, and all the flip-flops—from WMD to regime change—to try to justify the aggression, the imperial agenda is pretty much revealed for everyone except those in the homeland who are in denial about America's own imperial history and/or still controlled by post-9/11 propaganda. As Kochler puts it, "If the practice of intervention defeats the very principles the doctrine is based upon, the whole concept becomes ambiguous and loses its morally convincing and legally binding nature."[12] This is happening quite quickly in an occupied Iraq. While regime change has allowed for the attempted re-colonization of the country as part of a neocolonial strategy for Eurasia,[13] the conflict is taking on characteristics that were tried and failed in Vietnam and throughout Latin America. US-trained counter-insurgency death squads may already be in the works.

4. The Not-So United Nations

The UN was on a slippery slope well before NATO's WD made the new geopolitical situation more dangerous. All the pious Western talk of HI was already ringing rather hollow in view of the huge humanitarian crisis caused in Iraq by big-power UN politics.

Prior to the 1991 Gulf War, where UN-sanctioned, US-led troops ousted Iraq's army from Kuwait, Iraq still had first-class medical facilities and services. This all changed after the UN Security Council (SC) imposed sanctions on a country and people already crippled by the Gulf war on top of the eight-year, US-backed war with Iran. By 1993,

UNICEF was reporting a resurgence of preventable diseases across Iraq.[14] The now exposed "oil for food" program established in 1995 by the UN didn't fundamentally alter the reality that the sanctions were consolidating Hussein's power while punishing the Iraqi people. In 1997, UNICEF reported that more than 1.2 million Iraqis, including 750,000 children under five, had died due to scarcity of food and medicine. In 1998 the WHO reported 5,000–6,000 children were dying monthly due to the sanctions. By that year the once modernizing country of Iraq had slipped to the 126th position of 174 countries on the UN's human development index.

It is hard not to think of this scale of preventable human death and suffering among the most vulnerable as itself a form of genocide. The contradiction between the Security Council (SC) that approved the sanctions, and the warnings by broader UN bodies (like UNICEF and the WHO) was already weakening the credibility of the UN prior to the crisis caused by the US's invasion of Iraq. The comparison in the attention given to the 3,000 victims of the 9/11 atrocity and the 1.2 million Iraqi victims of the war and sanctions pretty much exposes the ethical contradictions of those advocating HI by the West.

The UN functioned under greater duress after the fundamental changes to NATO reflected in the WD. The voting procedure of the SC (Art. 27 of Charter) was designed around post-WWII big-power politics. (The assumption at the time that we were entering a postcolonial world has since been proven shallow and very premature.) According to the UN Charter (Chap. VII), collective force could not be used specifically for human-rights enforcement, but was limited to threats to and breaches of peace and acts of aggression. The veto granted to the permanent members of the SC ensured that no action could be taken on behalf of the UN if it was seen to challenge any big power's sphere of influence. (The question of what constituted an "internal matter," however, remained contentious and confusing.) While action could be taken when there was no veto (as in Korea in 1950 and the 1991 Gulf War), the US and USSR had to act without international legitimacy when they engaged in any Cold War ventures.

This structure works very differently in the post-Soviet era. Even if the UN wanted to criticize NATO, the US, or other permanent members' unilateral actions as threats to peace and security, its hands are now tied. As Kochler says, "…no effective measure can be taken by the international community against a self-proclaimed HI by NATO—as long as its permanent members in the SC are determined to use their veto power." NATO's military intervention in Yugoslavia and Afghanistan was guaranteed impunity by the veto control of the UN SC by three of NATO's major members. And to complete the circle of neocolonial self-interest, it has been these permanent members of the SC in NATO who are "the most active sponsors of NATO's doctrine of "preventive crisis management" and of the "humanitarian use of force."

The manipulation of the UN structure by NATO and the American empire in a post-Soviet world shows how "HI has become one of the key terms to legitimize what otherwise would have to be called 'acts of aggression' or 'interference in internal affairs.'" While we should have compassion for UN Secretary-General Kofi Annan, for being at the apex of these international contradictions, he should also be held accountable for statements which can be taken to sideline the UN as the only rightful transnational system and which leave open the legitimacy of HI under existing international law.

In these unipolar circumstances, with the vacuum left within the UN-based system of international law, a new imperial order may continue to emerge. It will be an "Anglo-Saxon" imperial order, driven by the US and its military-industrial power, but with the backing and expertise of the British colonial heritage. And it is no accident that some of the main "liberal" and "left" apologists for the new imperial order, men like Ignatieff and Hitchens who I discuss below, live and think within the politics of fear in this Anglo-American axis.

The revival of HI as part of this neocolonial, Anglo-Saxon imperial order is not an anomaly. The desire of the PNAC-ers controlling the White House and Pentagon and of other "neocons" is to normalize a new double standard in international affairs, which will give impunity to the US and its allies. To do this the US has to stay as far away from the mechanisms of international law as possible, and refusing to join the International Criminal Court (ICC) is part of this self-protection. However, the fact that a justification for HI cannot be argued from the mandate of the International Court of Justice shows that the US is already on some slippery ground.[15]

The religious legitimacy claimed for the imperial uses of HI by European powers in the last century has now been complemented with a more secular "human rights" discourse. This more secular influence has mostly come from Blair and Britain. The older, more "mature" empire is, so to speak, coaching the new adolescent one. However, fundamentalist Protestant ideology and the post-9/11 "clash of civilizations," still operate in the US "homeland" in ways similar to how such nationalist religious ideology did within British colonialism during its heyday. The Indian Mutiny of 1847, sometimes known as the "first war of independence," functioned to self-justify more overt ("defensive") aggression by the British Empire in the Indian territories, something like how 9/11 seems to now be functioning for the American empire in its aggressive interventions in the Middle East and Eurasia.[16]

International law will have to be adapted and strengthened to help prevent the atrocities of a new imperial order. Peace will still have to be protected to enable justice (social development and human rights) to advance. And justice will have to be enhanced for peace to become more stable. For the most part, security will be derived from this protection of peace and enhancing of justice. And, of course, ecological sustainability will remain at the root of all this—of peace, justice, and security. Disrupting ecosystems through military-industrial aggression, and the draining of limited human and natural resources into the military-industrial complex, are both antithetical to worldwide human development in coexistence with nature. Intervening to force regime change, in the name of HI that cloaks neocolonial interests, contradicts and undermines this larger project of international law and global justice.

5. Anglo-Saxon Apologisms for Neocolonial Humanitarian Intervention

Since the invasion and occupation of Iraq is starting to look like a failed state in the making, Michael Ignatieff has put his defense of HI on the back burner. He may even be a little embarrassed about his past defense of "democratic" imperialism. In his most recent work he tries to re-frame the new geopolitical instability as "democracies defending themselves" against terror. He ends up defending what he calls the "lesser evil." In his earlier writing defending HI, sovereignty was to be sacrificed for human rights. Now, in his defense of democracy, human rights are to be sacrificed for the Security State. It is not surprising that his analysis leads him to consider "nihilism."

When civil rights are suspended in the homeland, as Ignatieff says must happen to "fight terrorism," Ignatieff says there remains "an obligation on government to justify such measures publicly, to submit them to judicial review, and to circumscribe them with sunset clauses…"[17] This "lesser evil," of course, assumes that decisions within an imperial America are going to be accountable to such democratic processes. As we shall see, this assumption is terribly naïve.

However, perhaps hoping his "liberal" pleas will be prescriptive to those running the Pentagon and White House, Ignatieff writes "actions which violate foundational commitments to justice and dignity—torture, illegal detention, unlawful assassination—should be beyond the pale." However, later in his analysis, he admits, "liberal democracies consistently overreact to terrorist threats." He acknowledges that the appeal to so-called majority interests in a democracy "has weakened liberal democracies." (There was an element of this appeal to a majority and scapegoating of minorities in Hitler's rise to power, and also in the Bush presidency.) And, perhaps in an attempt to balance and justify (salvage) his argument and externalize the blame for taking away human rights, he says, "Far from being an incidental menace, terrorism has warped democracies' institutional development, strengthening secret government at the expense of open adversarial review." Even a superficial scanning of American history will show that terrorism wasn't required for the growth of invisible government.[18]

Ignatieff continues his argument for the "lesser evil" by making abstract appeals to human rights and international law, as though this is going to fundamentally restrain the actions of imperial America while it is "defending its democracy." Without considering the implications of HI and the "lesser evil" he is advocating for the deterioration of international law, he writes, "International human rights conventions serve to remind democracies at war with terror that even their enemies have rights." But will they really do this in an increasingly unipolar world where unilateral actions can undermine these very norms and accountabilities?

Ignatieff belatedly comes to the matter of global justice. He admits that without "peaceful political means of redress" being available to the world's oppressed "violence will occur." He even says "a counter-terror strategy that fails to address injustice… cannot succeed by purely military means." But he makes this appeal for global justice after narrowly framing the "terrorist" question, assuming only righteous and defensive military and political actions will be taken by democracies, and then trying to justify undemocratic practices which he admits likely won't be checked within an over-reactive state. "Justice" is treated as secondary, as an afterthought.

Ignatieff gets himself deeper and deeper into an intellectual quagmire of his own making. The analysis is built upon one questionable assumption after another. In his earlier work, there was the assumption that the military interventions of NATO, or the US going it alone, were primarily humanitarian.[19] He asserts this without ever looking at the imperial roots of the very doctrine of HI that he has helped revive. Then, in his more recent work, there is the assumption that the curtailing of civil liberties in the homeland is being done strictly for defensive reasons, to protect democracy. Yet, there is much evidence that terrorism was more serious before than after 9/11, and that worldwide there are only a handful of casualties a day from terrorism compared to other much more serious forms of human violence, including forced poverty, controllable HIV, etc.[20] In spite of this, Ignatieff totally accepts the imperial framing of the new geopolitics as a "war on terror." He is trapped within the imperial paradigm. This leads him to have to argue that these aggressive and undemocratic actions will somehow be kept in check by the very international codes that are being undermined by the actions he advocates. This is a very sloppy, compartmentalized analysis.

Collapsing the new geopolitics into "liberal democracies fighting terrorism" leaves huge holes in analysis. For one thing, the US's actions under the Bush Doctrine are not the same as other liberal democracies' ways of handling terrorist threats to national security and public safety. The politics of fear and imperial designs interplay in the US to create a very different domestic dynamic. Simply put, under the present US regime the threat from terrorism is a huge political and ideological football.

More fundamental, human rights have to be placed within the larger context of social (distributive) justice. Concentrating on HI to shore up failed states, to protect human rights, without looking at how the processes of global injustice—neocolonialism and maldistribution of resources, etc.—undercut state stability is a little like taking in stray cats without having a spaying program.

Writer Christopher Hitchens has also played a major, though more journalistic, role in apologizing for the US's unilateral actions in Iraq. In several essays written prior to the March 2003 invasion, he is nothing short of brutal in his condemnations of the global antiwar movement growing at the time. His ideas are not as systematically argued as those of Ignatieff. It is Hitchens's righteous but apparently fragile ego, and his tendency to see those who disagree with him as the "enemy," which hold much of his writing together. This psychological substrata may even have made the righteous neocons with whom he is now more politically associated more attractive to him.

It is worth looking at this emotional undertone, for this may be more important, and make him more representative of others who defend US unilateralism, than the validity of the ideas themselves. For there is little doubt that the events around and after 9/11 shook Hitchens's capacity to create self-critical perspective.[21] This event also appears to have put the final nails in the coffin of his version of "socialism."

The Twin Towers were only ten blocks from his home. For Hitchens, after the attack, "Islamo-fascism" or "theocratic fascism" became the all-consuming objective enemy of all civilized and progressive people everywhere. In an essay called "Chew on This," Hitchens wrote of how on the morning of 11 September 2001, "I got a very early call from my wife, who was three hours ahead of me. She told me to turn on the TV… Everyone knows what I saw when I turned on the TV." He continues, "Now hear this. Ever since that morning, the United States has been at war with the forces of reaction. May I please entreat you to reread the preceding sentence? Or perhaps you will let me restate it for emphasis. The government and people of these United States are now at war with the forces of reaction."[22]

In a revealing, earlier essay entitled "Armchair General," Hitchens says that when he was traveling on the Afghan border "my wife was fighting her way across D.C., with the Pentagon in flames, to try to collect our daughter from a suddenly closed school, was attempting to deal with the possibility of anthrax in our mailbox, was reading up on the pros and cons of small-pox vaccinations, and was coping with the consequences of a Muslim copy-cat loony who's tried his hand as a suburban sniper."[23] While this was a frightening time, it is what Hitchens has done with his generalized fear that now requires our attention.

This personal identification with a total war on "reaction" perhaps became Hitchens's version of "jihad,"[24] although he is now being forced by events in Iraq to pull back from his initial militant defense of the Bush Doctrine. He called his compilation of essays written after 9/11 and before the invasion of Iraq by the qualified and even confusing title *A Long Short War: The Postponed Liberation of Iraq.*

9/11 appears to have pushed Hitchens over the deep end, where he lost his ability to critically analyze. Before the invasion of Iraq he wrote a passionate defense of "Regime Change." In another essay, "Prevention and Preemption," he argued that an invasion of Iraq wasn't aggression, and wasn't about "imperialism." Always writing with a righteous tone, he spends more time attacking his presentation of the position he opposes than he does exploring his own.

Just prior to March 2003, when in his own words he was "fighting to keep my nerve" to support Bush's invasion, he wrote an essay that he hoped would stand up posthumously, to the unpredictable unfolding events, as "arguments for war." This became the introduction to his short book on the war.[25] It is interesting that this essay begins by discussing Paul Wolfowitz speaking to a meeting of Arab Americans supporting regime change in Iraq. Hitchens is typically hypercritical of positions that deviate even slightly from his own ideas at the time. However, he paraphrases Wolfowitz in the most sympathetic manner, saying Wolfowitz "hinted that the administration could be made to care just as much about democracy and emancipation" as about Iraq's disarmament. I am not sure what Hitchens would now say, after the US tried to privatize the Iraqi economy prior to any processes of self-determination, twice refused to hold Iraqi elections called for by the UN, and controlled the timing of elections to shape what kind of regime change occurred.

6. Reality Testing Humanitarian Intervention

Ignatieff's "idealistic" neoliberal reasoning and Hitchens's cynical and demoralized polemics quickly collapsed under the test of events. With all the rhetoric about freedom, democracy, and humanitarianism coming from the White House, it might be confusing for Ignatieff and others who defend HI that, in its recent annual report, Amnesty International (AI) targets the US democracy for violating human rights, ignoring international law, and sending a "permissive signal to abusive governments."[26] In this report AI says that the US's thumbing "its nose at the rule of law and human rights… grants a license to others to commit abuse with impunity and audacity."

AI was also critical of the US for not calling a complete, independent inquiry into human rights abuses in Iraq, Afghanistan, and Guantánamo Bay, Cuba. Its report says, "Torture and ill treatment by the U.S.-led forces [in Iraq] were widely reported." Though in *The Lesser Evil* Ignatieff writes as though the Geneva Conventions will moderate US actions, AI found the US to be in contravention of the Geneva Convention for harsh interrogation practices, ghost detainees, and rendering detainees to countries where torture isn't outlawed.[27] The AI report says the "arbitrary and indefinite detention is in violation of international law" and will provoke "counter-terrorism."

It is not that surprising that rather than reflecting on his earlier role in reviving the neocolonial doctrine of HI, Ignatieff has moved on to another angle of neoliberal thought. While Bush Jr. was pronouncing that his "war on terror" would bring democracy to Iraq and the Middle East, US soldiers were using terror on Iraqis. While Bush was defending the US invasion of Iraq as HI, soldiers in Iraq were systematically violating international humanitarian law.

After completing its invasion of Iraq, the US set up a military prison in one of Hussein's most notorious prisons, Abu Ghraib. Thousands of prisoners were incarcerated after US forces, seemingly stunned by the depth of the insurgency, engaged in "increasingly random and panicky sweeps."[28] Families of detainees were not informed of the whereabouts of their kin. Prisoners were systematically humiliated and tortured to try to obtain information on the insurgency. This was officially sanctioned policy, going back to Bush's decision in 2001 to ignore the Geneva Conventions in his "war on terror" and in the U.S. prison in Guantánamo Bay, Cuba. US intelligence was bad before the invasion of Iraq, and it apparently has gone from bad to worse during the occupation. "Torture at Abu Ghraib was born of desperation cloaked as necessity."

In February 2004 the Red Cross reported serious violations of humanitarian law, and the next month a US military investigation of the 800th Military Police Brigade running the prison confirmed this. War trophies in the form of digital camera pictures of the inhuman practices used in the prison made their way onto American international media networks, and the cat was out of the bag. These horrendous, dehumanizing images likely put to rest any remaining propaganda value from the rhetoric of HI. While the official US position has been that there were a few rotten apples in the military that "betrayed American values," and some (female) soldiers have already been scapegoated, the documentation suggests these practices come right from the top.[29]

In its 2005 report AI also found the UN Commission on Human Rights to be lacking in holding the US and other member states accountable for these violations. The commission "has become a forum for horse-trading on human rights" according to the AI report. It has "dropped Iraq from scrutiny" and was weak-kneed on Chechnya, Nepal, and Zimbabwe, and "silent on Guantánamo Bay." Haiti and Congo were also earmarked.

AI called for "sober reappraisal" and "rapid and radical" reform of the UN human rights machinery. And the context of the impunity for these abuses must be part of such reappraisal. Ironically, the very doctrine of HI, including its rhetoric about human rights, contributes to this impunity and the weakening of the UN itself. AI and Human Rights Watch were both astute and principled advocates of human rights when they refused to support the HI smokescreen for the invasion of Iraq.

Ignatieff also needs to engage in some radical reappraisal. He seems to think that the abrogation of human rights and international law is necessary to get information to make citizens of democracies safe from terrorism. In other words he fundamentally accepts the public justification given for the contraventions of human rights conventions by the Bush regime. And yet various analyses of the use of torture suggest its true purpose is "to terrorize." It is, as Naomi Klein has put it, designed to break the will to resist—the individual prisoner's will and the collective will."[30] Torture is being used as counter-insurgency by the US occupying army in Iraq much along the lines it was used by the US-backed military regimes in El Salvador and other South and Central American countries. It's not so much a "means justifies the ends" argument, as suggested by Ignatieff, as a "means to create imperial ends" process.

7. Will There Be "Humanitarian Intervention" from Space?

The absurdity of the notion of HI being supported by writers such as Ignatieff and Hitchens is shown by carefully looking as what is propelling the American Empire at this time. The US does not want to police the world to create a Human Rights' World Order under international law, along the lines of Amnesty International. This is even clearer after the invasion and occupation of Iraq. No, the US primarily wants to police the world as a military-industrial complex (MIC).

One of Bush's three international actions laying the ground for Pax Americana and the Bush Doctrine was his withdrawal from the 30-year-old ABMT (Anti-Ballistic Missiles Treaty) that banned weapons in space. The other actions were to withdraw from the ICC process and to not endorse the Kyoto Protocol; and weapons in space, geopolitical control of oil, and impunity from international law pretty much sums up the priorities of the Bush regime.

Bush Jr. had already backed the missile defense system, which, in spite of all the scientific critiques of its technical impossibility, was very lucrative to his donor "defense" corporations. The weaponization of space has been part of the Bush doctrine since the small cadre of PNACers took control of the White House and Pentagon five years ago. Defense Secretary Donald Rumsfeld headed the Space Commission that in January 2001 concluded that the military should "insure that the President would have the option to deploy weapons in space."[31] This commission called for new "national security guidance and defense policy to direct development of doctrine, concept of operations and capabilities for space, including weapons systems that operate in space." It is important to remember that this was well before 9/11 and the ratcheting up of political and military rhetoric about preemptive war.

In 2002, after reviewing Rumsfeld's report, Bush Jr. pulled the US out of the ABMT. A 2002 Pentagon planning document had already set out two categories of planned space weapons. One, "space control," is about anti-satellite warfare, and the other, "space force application," is about space weapons to attack ground targets. Both are well underway, even though Congress, the media, and the American people have had no public debate on the development and deployment of such military technology. This says something about how "democracy" is done within American imperial politics. Perhaps it is time we made a distinction between "democracy by consent" and "democracy through fear."

In May 2005 the head of the Air Force requested official presidential approval to develop weapons in space. And as of mid-June 2005, Bush still had to give the official go ahead, but this will just be democratic optics.

The previous Clinton administration vetoed plans for space weapons. In 1996 his administration supported the use of space for spy satellites, arms control, and nonproliferation pacts. So, in this regard, the expected support by Bush of the Air Force's space weapons program is a major shift of policy. But we have to consider that this, too, may be more optics than substance, for the planning of weapons in space was well along when Bush Jr. became president.

The failure of each and every president to be completely "on side" with the imperial trajectory of the military-industrial complex (MIC) may be just a "bump in the road." It is now known that President JFK was not totally on side with the MIC, or with the CIA of his time, but that did not stop the imperial trajectory. There continues to be serious speculation that JFK's assassination may be related to something like an order to "stand down," which reduced his own security, and perhaps a wider plot that changed the course of American and world history. Regardless of what one thinks about this or any other so-called "conspiracy theory," new research and revelations about Pearl Harbor as well as 9/11 is making it more difficult to avoid hypothesizing that some form of "invisible government" is at play in the shadow of the US democracy.[32]

In April 2005, the Air Force launched XSS-II, a micro-satellite able to disrupt military reconnaissance and communication satellites of other countries. Another weapons program plans to use laser weapons to hit targets on earth, and a third plans to turn radio waves into weapons that could "toast" earthlings. The most astonishing program "aims to hurl cylinders of tungsten, titanium or uranium," to strike targets on earth at speeds over 7,000 mph "with the force of a small nuclear weapon." Showing how totally interlocked fundamentalist religion and militarist ideology have become in the new American Empire, this program is called "Rods from God."

The general who heads the Air Force Space Command is fittingly named General Lord (yes, this is true). He apparently takes his name and "Rods from God" very seriously. He recently told Congress that this is "the American way of fighting." For him "space superiority" is "freedom to attack as well as freedom from attack." There's little doubt how this "Lord on high" sees American dominance of space. For him "space is an American frontier," and space superiority "can be our destiny if we work hard at it and continue to aggressively follow that."

In April 2005 General Lord told Congress that the plans in the works would give the US the power to destroy missile bases and command centers "anywhere in the world." Around the same time the head of the US Strategic Command reiterated the same view at the Senate Armed Services nuclear forces subcommittee, saying space weaponry is being designed to enable an attack "very quickly, with short time lines… anyplace on the face of the earth." This strategy, called "Global Strike," would utilize a space plane with precision weapons, called the "common aero vehicle," which "could strike from half way around the world in 45 minutes." General Lord calls "this type of prompt global strike… a top priority for our space and missile force."

International opposition to Bush's weaponization of space is bound to grow as non-Americans continue to grasp the aggressive and undemocratic nature of this program. While we shouldn't rule out some Orwellian attempt to justify this in terms of HI, it pretty much exposes the nature of Bush's Pax Americana project. Domestic opposition, however, will be restricted by a "politics of fear" which blends American patriotism with the interests of the interwoven national-security state and military-industrial complex.

The US's weaponization of space would likely jump-start another dangerous and wasteful arms race. The short interlude between the Cold War's nuclear arms race and this new arms race, veiled in the rhetoric of "anti-terrorism" and "humanitarian intervention," could shrink from collective memory. The expanded militarization of the US and world economy would further undercut both social development and international law. Since withdrawing from the ABMT, the US has no technical treaty or laws banning it from putting non-WMD weapons in space. The attempt to obtain space superiority, however, totally undercuts international law and sustainable development. Space should be considered a "global commons," and treating this global commons as a means for global strike is, simply put, a perversion of fundamental ecological and democratic notions.

Global mental strife grows with each expansion of the scope of military technology on the planet. The prospects of having US weapons in space will be too frightening for some people to even want to imagine. Those unable to tolerate knowing of this threat to human sensibilities will become psychological castaways.

I grew up in Western Canada knowing that Strategic Air Command B52 bombers loaded with nuclear weapons were flying overhead toward the Arctic Circle and the Soviet Union. American missile-launching silos existed just south of the Canadian border in the northern States. This land-and-sky killing machine did not provide the basic security that children and youths require for healthy human development. Having US "death stars" going over us every ten minutes would further undermine the conditions required for human development worldwide.

The best way to resist and overcome such overwhelm is to better grasp the institutional dynamics that push us toward this more threatening future. The aftermath of the invasion, occupation, and insurgency in Iraq is a key "moment" in the imperial trajectory of the US over the last half-century. The US's planned weaponization of space comes in the wake of the failure of the missile defense system. After 22 years and spending nearly 100 billion, the Pentagon still lacks a system that can reliably detect and destroy a "threat." A similar fate will hopefully be in store for the weapons in space program.

In April 2005, an Air Force consultant told the US Council on Foreign Relations that "the big problem now is it's too expensive." Estimates of the cost of a space-based weapons system range from $220 billion to $1 trillion. The price of single weapons would massively escalate—for example, a space-laser weapon could cost $100 million compared to $600,000 for a Tomahawk missile. And past experience suggests that weapons' prices are underestimated in this mostly non-competitive market. The cost of the spy satellite program, Future Imagery Architecture, has already tripled, with less than promised results. The cost of a space technology for detecting "enemy launchings" has risen by two-and-a-half times.

These rising military costs are part of the trajectory of the American empire. They and the war on Iraq will continue to put pressure on the US economy. While the American taxpayer continues to be exploited for such militarization, without receiving even basic public services like universal healthcare, the "defense" industry continues to benefit and grow. This bastardization of Keynesian economics has a long heritage in the US, going back to fiscal and imperial strategies after WWII. The prospects of policing the world with a space-based global strike force could be very profitable for the chain of companies that constitute the MIC in the US.

With the US now losing ground from stiff competition from rising manufacturing giants such as China, the MIC becomes even more vital to its superiority and hegemony. The US now seems positioned to dominate the global arms trade. According to a PricewaterhouseCoopers report, US defense spending will equal the rest of the world's combined within a year.[33] The US "defense" budget was already at $417.4 billion by 2003, which was 46 percent of the global total. Less than 2 percent of this spending went outside the home market, and half of this (1 percent) went to the US's only major imperial military ally, the UK.

Furthermore, the expansion of NATO into the countries left by the implosion of the Soviet Union not only provides a new, lucrative market for the US MIC, it enables the US to spread its military muscle into these areas as part of its Eurasian geopolitical strategy. This immense control of the world's arms trade by the US MIC is bound to place pressure on European contractors and countries to cooperate more closely with Pax Americana ventures.

8. Unpacking Globalization and Humanitarian Intervention

Whether the American democracy is resilient enough to be able to stop this trajectory is, perhaps, the most pressing question. And Americans are in a real catch-22. America's unilateral aggressiveness comes from the two-sided isolationism of not wanting to know about its own imperial history, and not knowing how to engage with the larger world in a non-reactive, non-ethnocentric manner.

Humanity has nothing to gain from either form of isolationism. In the transitory period, where internationalism spreads and deepens in the US, communicative, cultural processes that bridge the US and the rest of the world need to be encouraged. Americans who do not like the directions of corporate American may not be able to easily reach out, and anti-Americanism will further impede this. Changing the lens on America, to see vibrant city-states rather than the expansionist empire, can help build this connectedness. New York, the location of 9/11, remains a vibrant multicultural international nexus of the arts and politics.

A failure to critically and empirically assess the realities of globalization is perhaps at the heart of the flawed thinking of the righteous humanitarian interventionists. Economic globalization, and the ascendancy of finance capital paralleling this after the capitalist crisis of the 1970s, may have peaked. The Bush Doctrine may even prove to have accelerated its decline. The "aura of inevitability" is starting to dissolve as countries like Malaysia, who went against IMF advice by imposing capital control and currency stabilization, have reversed course. Meanwhile, countries like Argentina that fully embraced the ideological framework of trade liberalization were plunged into deep economic and political crisis. It has been countries like India and China with state-led economic development that have benefited the most from market reform, while not having to embrace globalization ideology.[34]

The cracking open of the ideology of globalization reveals its assumptions. And these are similar assumptions to those that lie beneath the doctrine of HI. The main assumption is that the fundamental determinant of the civility of a society is economic, and that by creating a free-market economy, democracy and peace will flourish. Another is that there is a technocratic rationality that is universally applicable to accomplish this.

An important Canadian writer, John Ralston Saul, disputes both of these assumptions.[35] He argues that civil society doesn't derive from the market, but vice versa. The "civil" functioning of the market depends upon society's infrastructure, including public service institutions for the public good, and the technocratic foot soldiers of globalization continue to live in a deformed intellectual world shaped by their ahistorical, narrowly rationalist, and economistic thinking.

As in his other books, Saul asserts that we are citizens before we are consumers. He rejects the dogma that making the world's peoples into corporate consumers will spread democracy and domestic and international civility. He notes that some of the indicators of globalization are even fraudulent. Trade within multinational conglomerates, currency speculation, and corporate acquisitions and mergers are not indicators of wealth creation but of the creation of the wealthy. Some individuals may become billionaires, but the discrepancies between "haves" and "have-nots" continues to deepen, both domestically and internationally. The most effective HI would be into these global economic relations so that the global crisis of poverty, violence, and ecocide can begin to be reversed.

Furthermore, the near hegemony of the ideology of globalization in a unipolar world has directly contributed to the international crisis we now face. As the reviewer of Saul's book wrote: "that decision-makers in the West had an almost blind faith in the primacy of economic relations explains why they were unprepared for the devastating ethnic and religious conflicts and 'irregular warfare' that have broken out since the end of the Cold War."[36] The attempt by the US to privatize Iraq's economy, even before it had partial elections, and to impose corporate rule on this would-be oil and military client state, cannot be called by its name, so righteous sounding terms like "regime change" and "freedom and democracy" continue to be spouted.

There is no disputing we live in a more interdependent world. Communications, travel, trade, and multiculturalism are all at play in this. So, too, are ecological vulnerability and the globalization of disease—for example, the prediction of the next pandemic. In such circumstances it is simply foolish to throw down national borders in a frenzied rush for corporate greed. In the big picture, the defeat of the proposed Multilateral Agreement on Investment in 1998 may be more significant insofar as the future of corporate globalization than the 1999 bombing of Serbia by NATO.

Unbridled nationalism can create conflicts that are used to justify HI that veils other, deeper interests. However, the alternative to unbridled nationalism is not imperialist unilateralism and corporate multi-nationalism. These actually perpetuate each other. More beneficial is a "safe place for national identities." While we have yet to see whether the EU can provide a safe shelter for nationalism, while establishing standards for social and environmental policy, and democracy and human rights, some version of the nation-state will be required for both collective security and "democratic agency." And this will have to develop hand in hand with international law.

The US and its imperial legacy reflect a model of nationalism developed among Europe's states during the height of their colonial and imperial rule. So it is no wonder that the US is spearheading the revival of the doctrine of HI developed in this era. As the surviving superpower of the Cold War, the US now flaunts the export of democracy while, at the same time, acting outside of international and domestic law. It escalates a humanitarian crisis in the name of HI. Meanwhile, its internal democracy is one of the most manipulated and "bought" democracies on the planet. Only 24 percent of Americans actually voted for Bush Jr. for his second term. While one-third of the electorate don't identify with either of the big parties, they have no real place to put their votes. Voter participation is the lowest among the democracies. For the present, fundamental electoral reform will continue to be resisted by the corporations that try to rule America.[37]

The huge irony and most telling contradiction in all this is that while the US advances its own sovereignty, supposedly to defend itself by bringing democracy and human rights to oppressed people, sovereignty weakens abroad and democracy and human rights are under even greater threat in the American homeland. Surely this historical contradiction tells us that it is time to rally around another, non-imperial vision.

"The fate of Iraq is a sideshow, the terrorist threat is a red herring, and the radical Islamist's dream of a worldwide jihad against the west is a fantasy, but the attempt to revive Pax Americana is real."

—Gwynne Dyer, *Future: Tense: The Coming World Order?* (2004)

Empire's Law and Human Rights as Swords of Empire[1]

Amy Bartholomew

1. The Bush Doctrine and "Empire's Law"

The horror that is the United States' illegal war of aggression against Iraq—the act that the Nuremberg Tribunal, which was largely a creature of the United States, called the "*supreme* international crime"—is one that will make sure that the US "live[s] in infamy." This was recognized, not long ago, by Arthur Schlesinger Jr., a former advisor to the American Kennedy Administration. Schlesinger was also important for calling the Bush Doctrine that underpins the attack on Iraq "a fatal change in the foreign policy of the United States."[2]

Why is this considered a fatal course of events? I think there are four major reasons that stretch beyond the immediate horror, the literally "fatal" consequences that have been imposed on Iraqis by this illegal war:

First: the legitimacy of war as "an instrument of policy" was renounced shortly after World War I,[3] a prohibition that was entrenched with the signing of the United Nations' Charter. And yet, the Bush Doctrine explicitly reinstates and defends waging war as an instrument of American policy.

Second: The Bush Doctrine articulates the principle of "preventive" war—a principle that violates the heart of the UN Charter and international law, which requires armed attack, the reasonable anticipation of immediate armed attack,[4] or the decision of the Security Council that a threat to the peace is sufficiently grave as to require action to legitimize and render legal a military response.

Third: The US defends its right to decide upon and wage war *unilaterally*, again, explicitly violating both the letter and the spirit of the UN Charter.

But, even more important than these three immanent threats that are posed by the Bush Doctrine is the fact the Bush administration has not just set out a policy to break the law, to flout it—it does not, as some critics have maintained, simply attempt to act "lawlessly,"[5] which, of course, it surely does—but it also sets out *to define and to state* the law—to constitute it—unilaterally—monologically, as we might say. This fourth dimension of the Bush Doctrine poses a "revolutionary" challenge to the project of international law[6]: it is an "international constitutional moment" in which the American empire attempts to establish a new world order based on "absolute security" for itself.[7] It is important to grasp that it is not mere *lawlessness*, then, that lies at the core of the Bush Doctrine, but something much more threatening. It is an attempt to establish an order "whose law is not yet [entirely] visible."[8] The Bush Doctrine means that the "law" that will now rule the globe is "Empire's Law"—that is, a form of unilaterally constituted and imposed, illegitimate, unaccountable rule by a global power that attempts to perform the role of a global sovereign declaring itself to be "the exception."[9] With regard to aggressive war—to war as an instrument of policy—the threat is that the US is attempting to establish a new norm of preventive war which would be available, on its view, only to *itself* but from the point of view of legality, would be a norm recognized as available to *all*.[10] Either of these results is obviously ripe with draconian implications. With regard to legality, the threat is that the US treats law as merely a "derivative of the will of the sovereign"[11]—that is, itself, the global sovereign.

2. Who Defined and Who Supports the Bush Doctrine?

The Bush Doctrine goes back well before the *US National Security Strategy* of 2002, even though that is typically taken to be its first official articulation. Its chief architects were those associated with the Project for a New American Century who, long before 11 September 2001, made the case for American empire stalking the earth in the quest for a Pax Americana and an "empire's law"—a Lex Americana—to further that aim.

This is bad enough. But, what makes all of this even more troubling, is that it is *not only* the neoconservative hard-liners in and around the Bush administration who have pursued illegal aggressive war and run roughshod over international legality by justifying its evasions, exceptions, rejections, and instrumentalizations in this way. The Bush Administration was supported and encouraged by forces whom I will call the "human-rights hawks" who, drawing on the previous decade's innovations in legitimizing (if not legalizing) humanitarian intervention and "humanitarian wars," aimed, at least ostensibly, at the protection of peoples from massive abuses of human rights, supported this war on human rights as well as security grounds. This is as true of Tony Blair as it is of American liberal public intellectuals, like Michael Ignatieff and the majority of the Democrats in the American Congress.

The human-rights hawks gave sustenance early on to the aims of American empire as they articulated the case for a "humanitarian war" against Iraq, a theme that has now become more deeply imbricated within the Bush administration itself as it fights to "spread democracy and freedom across the world" and "end tyranny" through continuing war and occupation (both de jure and de facto). Espousing their humanitarian concern and their cosmopolitan moral solidarity, the human-rights hawks gave crucial support to the project both of undermining legitimate legality as a medium of regulation[12]—international and otherwise—and of turning it into "Empire's Law," a form of rule that is deeply at odds with the post–World War II project of globalizing its obverse, that is, "law's empire."

While the earlier post–World War II project of extending "*law's empire*" was responsible for developing regimes of human rights and international law and foreshadowing (albeit highly imperfectly) a future order of democratic cosmopolitan law, "Empire's Law" seeks precisely to derail that project and to do so unilaterally, brutally, and by the projection of military as well as economic and political power across the globe. Thus is a new phase in the American imperial project born.

It is, therefore, crucial to address the fact that the responsibility for the terrible destruction of Iraq and the brutal killing, torture, and insecurity of the Iraqi people is shared by these hawkish liberals and neoconservatives alike, for the former—the human-rights hawks—gave the Iraq war the ideological and moralistic justification that was required to gain, and especially, to sustain, support for it by the citizens of American empire, particularly as it became glaringly apparent that WMD were a conjured fantasy. Viewed as a war of liberation, the decimation of Iraq, the terrible disregard and squandering of life, culture, and resources, seemed to many in the liberal camp, at least for a while, to be "worth the price." And, the fact that it would be an American empire that would wage the war was not cause for concern for them. Michael Ignatieff, for example, one of the organic intellectuals of the war, famously maintained (and I quote) "the moral evaluation of Empire gets complicated when one of its benefits might be freedom of the oppressed." For Ignatieff, the "disagreeable reality" was not just that "*war* may be the only remedy" for cases like Iraq[13] but that the only *power* capable of addressing this reality was the American Empire, with its "general world duty."[14] According to Ignatieff, who spoke for the liberal hawks: "The case for Empire is that it has become, in a place like Iraq, the last hope for democracy and stability alike."[15]

How far liberal human-rights hawks have strayed from Arthur Schlesinger, Jr., who, it will be remembered, recognized in the Bush Doctrine "a fatal change in the foreign policy of the United States," likening it to Japanese imperialism prior to the end of World War II such that now it is the US that will "live in infamy"!

But it must not be thought that it is only liberals or neoconservatives who could possibly defend such a stance, who could possibly treat human rights as "swords of empire."[16] Consider for a moment the argument made by the British Marxist political theorist Norman Geras. Geras has chastised his progressive colleagues for failing to address the needs of strangers, which, he maintains, in the case of Iraq required military "regime change" in order to meet the demands of cosmopolitan moral solidarity.[17] He argued, in addition, that there is a "universal right to aid" and a "universal obligation" to meet it while insisting that those who opposed the war in terms of anti-imperialism, anti-Americanism, and anti-capitalism have failed to appreciate the "manifold practices of human evil" in places like Saddam's Iraq.[18] He concluded with a eulogy for the antiwar left: "So much for solidarity with the victims of oppression, for commitment to democratic values and basic human rights."[19]

But even if we accept the importance of showing cosmopolitan moral solidarity and confronting "manifold practices of human evil," as I think we must, one does not have to belabor the obvious: that with greater hindsight than these analyses could provide there is no plausible argument to be generated that this was, in fact, a humanitarian war. It is crystal clear that the war waged against Iraq was never a "humanitarian war," and neither has the occupation been a humanitarian or transformative one. But, it is even more important to insist that long before the war was launched against Iraq it was clear that neither its aims nor its most likely consequences were to be "humanitarian." Both the officially declared but illegal war and the occupation have been light-years away from the sort of liberal policing, rather than military, model that would have to animate any truly humanitarian intervention where, for example, the interveners would place civilian safety at least on par with their own and refuse to use indiscriminate weapons, including those that will surely decimate the environmental, genetic, and health future of Iraq (and likely its neighbors) for centuries, if not millennia, to come. All of this death, pain, and destruction unleashed ostensibly in the name of extending freedom, human rights, and liberation to the Iraqi people is enough thoroughly to discredit claims of humanitarianism.

The American empire's disregard for humanitarian concerns was as apparent then, at the outset, as was its disregard for international law, international institutions, the safety, security, and human rights of the Iraqi people, and global public opinion.[20] Rather, from Abu Ghraib to Kandahar, Baghdad to Guantánamo, the US is asserting the sharp edge of empire, governing so-called problem states[21] through military violence and what Amnesty International has called an "archipelago of prisons" around the world,[22] which, as critical commentators have emphasized, have more in common with concentration camps than they do with prisons, all while the US proclaims its moral and political superiority—and its 200-year-old constitution—as a justification for doing so.

Human-rights justifications are being used to install by these very means—"by fire and sword" as Jürgen Habermas has put it.[23] And this, of course, is a very *particular* conception of the rule of law, the rule of Empire's Law—a rule that has virtually nothing to do with democracy or with human rights—but which is aimed at the expansion by military domination of a neoliberal conception of good governance[24] based upon market capitalism. This is combined with the imposition of a political structure via a constitution that, far from extending political democracy to Iraq, seeks to extend "Empire's Law" over it, treating it as mere terrain to be conquered, to be enveloped within the imperium's thorny embrace, a "problem state" to be "pacified" while being "freed" only insofar as that freedom is in line with the values and interests of the Empire, and "democracy" is really the name for another client state.[25]

It is clear, therefore, that it was an egregiously irresponsible act for the "human-rights hawks" to support the war against Iraq. In supporting virtually unilateral war, the human-rights hawks, alongside their neoconservative counterparts, performatively justified future forms of unilateral war and rallied against global justice. The important consequence is: Those who gave intellectual and ideological support *should be held morally responsible* for the devastation of human rights and global justice, the destruction of Iraq and the wanton murder of Iraqis, as well as for the "moralization of politics" that has accompanied this war such that "Empire's Law" seeks to trump "law's empire" in an Alice in Wonderland sort of inversion of legality.[26] And, those ostensibly humanitarian warriors who had the political power to decide whether or not to breach international law both in terms of committing the crime of aggressive war and in terms of committing grave violations of international humanitarian law—Tony Blair for one—must be held *legally* as well as *politically* accountable alongside those at the pinnacle of the American empire who have aimed at the creation of a new world order through criminally culpable behavior.

3. Empire's Law or Law's Empire?

We would do well, under these conditions of the Bush Doctrine in general, and the aggressive war waged against Iraq in particular, to remember the words of the American chief prosecutor at the Nuremberg Tribunal. He (Associate US Supreme Court Justice Robert Jackson) said that the crime of aggression cannot be justified by any political or economic conditions. He went on to say that "if certain acts in violation of treaties are crimes they are crimes whether the United States does them or whether Germany does them, and we are not prepared to lay down a rule of criminal conduct against others which we would not be willing to have invoked against us."[27]

This statement by the chief prosecutor at the Nuremberg Tribunal expresses the most elementary principle of legal justice: that legitimate law must be universalistic, displaying equal recognition, equal applicability, and impartiality. In order to be legitimate, law must be judged to be *equally* good for all. And in the contemporary context, this judgment must issue from the perspective of each. But the Bush Doctrine violates all of these principles of legality. It has, in fact, definitively raised the question of whether international law is to remain a medium for the regulation of problems between states.[28] Is the global spread of "law's empire" in the post–World War II era now to be definitively replaced by "Empire's Law" by the only power capable of constituting such a wrongheaded global politics—the American empire? Will we accept the combined import of the Bush Doctrine and the war against Iraq? Will we accept that the American imperium holds *the right of empire* to rule, to run roughshod over its self-declared enemies, to act as a self-declared "trustee" of the interests of the world and to undermine international legality?[29]

Conclusion

No.

We, the people of the world, must demand that the perpetrators of the aggressive, illegal, immoral, and irrational war against and occupation of Iraq, who, at the same time, seek to undermine "law's empire" in favor of the *nonreciprocal right of American empire* be held responsible morally, politically, and legally for their aggressive war, for the war crimes they have committed, and for seeking to undermine the entire post–World War II order of international legality.

Jean-Paul Sartre perceptively recognized the importance of the norms of international legality when, in his inaugural statement to the Bertrand Russell War Crimes Tribunal convened during the Vietnam War, he argued both that Nuremberg represented victors' justice and that once the principle of legality was inscribed, due to its "implicit universality" it would become difficult for those powers to avoid its reach.[30] The Nuremberg Tribunal created an "ambiguous reality," he argued, in which an "embryo of a tradition," a precedent, was created that, while it was never extended after the tribunal to the victors, nevertheless "created a real gap in international affairs." That gap lay in the fact that no institution had been created to affirm the universality that lies at the principled heart of the Nuremberg Tribunal. But that gap "must be filled," he said. Sartre went on to argue that, where no official institution would do so, it was up to the people. And, most interestingly, he maintained that that tribunal should be aimed at making "everybody understand the necessity for international jurisdiction—which it has neither the means nor the ambition to replace and the essence of which would be to resuscitate the *jus contra bellum* [i.e., the rule against war], still born at Nuremberg, and to substitute legal, ethical laws for the law of the jungle."[31]

Sartre's perspective should inform our own. The struggle for legality and for legal responsibility must be viewed as *one* of our weapons against the Bush administration, against "Empire's Law," and against the "moralization of global politics," all of which lay behind the violations that the US war against Iraq perpetrates against humanity in general and against Iraq in particular.

But we must now recognize the constitutively unequal structure of relations implicit in American empire. If that is the case, if what we confront is an empire, we must ask the question: How can we hope to bring such an empire to account? Not much is clear about the answer to this question except for the overly general answer that we will require contestatory politics that are anti-empire in orientation, not just the politics of pursuing a return to legality, and certainly not just antiwar politics. Our politics must be oriented toward contesting the US's *imperial position*—whether it issues from Bush administration, the Project for a New American Century, the human-rights hawks, or some future "benevolent" US administration that may be expected to promote imperial versions of legality "led" by the US. Our project must be to support a *critical cosmopolitanism* that is aimed at contesting "the imperial power" in part, but only in part, through legal means. And this politics must develop a very sober analysis of the prospects of the project of legalization even while it demands it.[32] It must be a politics that publicizes the crimes of an "empire that is no longer concealed"[33] as it builds the case against it.

We must demand that the US pull out of Iraq now, respect the Iraqis' right to self-determination, and pay reparations.

We must demand that the US commit itself to international law and institutions.

We must demand that the perpetrators of aggressive war and war crimes be put on trial.

And, we demand that those who have supported this war assume political responsibility, along with their leaders, for the devastation they have wrought for humankind.

Finally, we must reject that empire's self-proclaimed right to rule and we must and will express that *rejection* through manifold acts of *resistance*.

Law's Empire and Empire's Lawlessness: Beyond the Anglo-American Law

Issa Shivji

Law's Empire"[1] has been irreversibly shattered by the empire's lawlessness, of which the invasion and occupation of Iraq is the highest and most cynical expression. The outrage created by the invasion cut across the globe as it hurt every human sensitivity. Thought was ridiculed, conscience was wounded, and traditions of humanity mocked.

There was a sense of despair and hopelessness. But the human spirit is indomitable. Millions, of all ages, marched the streets in 650 cities simultaneously, with one voice: "No Blood for Oil." In this the peoples of the world showed their common humanity bound by blood against imperial barbarism thirsty for oil.

For those of us who come from Africa, the hypocrisy and the double standards of the Western establishment are not new. We have gotten accustomed to it. Yet, barring intellectual skeptics and political opportunists, the admirers of, nay believers in, values of Enlightenment and the virtues of the rule of law have been many and not far between. The Nkrumahs and the Nyereres, the Mandelas and the Mondlanes were all steeped in Western liberal values and crafted the demands of their people's independence in the language of law and rights. When accused of liberalism by left students in the 1960s, the author of *Socialism and Self-reliance*, Julius Nyerere, quipped: "I am a bourgeois democrat at heart!"

The nationalist critique of the Western legal, moral, and political order, which, in any case, the African leaders adopted in their countries, was from within. It was a critique which highlighted the divergence between the ideal and the real, between theory and practice, between the desirable and the achievable. The fundamental premises of the Western legal thought and its world outlook, however, remained, by and large, unchallenged.

Some of us who adopted more radical approaches, albeit still within Western traditions, did not perhaps subscribe wholly to Thompson's thesis that the rule of law was an "unqualified good." Yet we, too, saw in bourgeois law and legality space for struggle to advance the social project of human liberation and emancipation. Law, we argued, was a terrain of struggle; that the rule of law, while expressing and reinforcing the rule of the bourgeoisie, did also represent the achievement of the working classes; that even though bourgeois democracy was a limited class project, it was an advance over authoritarian orders and ought to be defended. The legal discourse, whether liberal or radical, thus remained rooted in Western values, exalting the Law's Empire.

To be sure, in my part of the world, the law faculty and students went beyond the confines of legal discourse. The 1960s and '70s saw an upsurge in interdisciplinary approaches to law. We crafted new courses like "law and development," read theories of imperialism, and demonstrated against the war in Vietnam. Imperialism was on the defensive.

We studied history and political economy. We discovered and recorded the crimes of imperialism against our people. We came to know how our continent was depopulated and its social fabric devastated by the slave trade and then colonialism. We were enraged. We were equally enraged as we read how the industrial revolution in Britain was built on the backs of child labor, and American development rose from the genocide of the indigenous "Indian" population and the enslavement of our brothers and sisters. In disgust, we learned that while the pundits of capitalism glorified competition, the textile houses of Lancashire conspired to have the hands of Indian craftsmen chopped off so as to destroy India's textile industry. Although all this was history, we were outraged because imperialism continued to be with us and showed its most brutal and ugly face as it napalmed Vietnam. Apartheid South Africa, with the connivance of imperialism, armed RENAMO, creating havoc in the newly liberated Mozambique. American multinationals continued to rape the resources of then Zaire, now the Democratic Republic of Congo. In much of the rest of Africa, the Cold War continued to be fought by the superpowers through their proxies, leaving the dead, the maimed, and the malnourished in its wake.

Eventually the Lilliputian Vietnam demolished, morally and militarily, giant America. David defeated Goliath. The backward Portuguese empire collapsed. We were inspired. Imperialism was demoralized. Then came the restoration.

The Berlin Wall fell. Imperialism rode on the triumphalist wave to rehabilitate itself. Douglas Hurd, then the British secretary of state for foreign affairs, heaved a sigh of relief: "we are slowly putting behind us a period of history when the West was unable to express a legitimate interest in the developing world without being accused of 'neo-colonialism.'"[2] The moral rehabilitation of imperialism was first and foremost ideological, which in turn was constructed on neoliberal economic precepts—"free" market, privatization, liberalization, etc.—the so-called Washington Consensus. Human rights, NGOs, good governance, multiparty democracy, and the rule of law were all rolled together with privatization and liberalization, never mind that they were utterly incompatible.

The "new" comeback of the rule of law had little to do with the original Enlightenment values which underlay it. This time around it came as both a farce and a tragedy. Farce because the law was not being made by the representatives of the people. International Financial Institutions (IFIs) and their consultants dictated it. Tragedy because the national sovereignty won by the colonized people was all but lost except in name, and this time around, as John Pilger says somewhere, without a gunboat in sight. But guns were never out of sight. Witness Panama. Witness Sudan. Witness Somalia and Iraq and Iraq again.

Globalization, through the laws of privatization and liberalization, struck at the heart of the democratic legislative process. Then, lo and behold, came 9/11. Mr. Bush picked up his phone to receive pre-arranged messages of support from African leaders, one after another. Everyone was told to fall in line. "You are either with us or with terrorists." No African leader could dare say anything even remotely close to what the Iranian leader said: "We're neither with you nor with the terrorists!" Iran was promptly included in the axis of evil.

One after another, African countries enacted similar antiterrorism statutes, contrary to their own constitutions, which had provided a bill of rights. The antiterrorist laws made no pretence of the rule of law. Due process, integrity, and certainty of rules, open trials, principles of natural justice, and right of appeal were all dispensed with. The definitions of terrorism are so wide that these laws are worse then some of the draconian statutes legislated during the one-party authoritarian rule. Opposition to antiterrorist law was ruthlessly suppressed. In my country, the president devoted the whole of his monthly speech to reprimanding the opponents of the antiterrorist law.

If privatization laws stabbed the heart of the legislative process, the antiterrorism laws tore the artery of the judicial process. The rhetoric of the rule of law was exposed to be what it was—rhetoric. As elsewhere, the

Americans are now in the saddle, training our police in antiterrorism. They will soon establish a regional school to train spies, of course, to spy on us, the people: the supposed beneficiaries of human rights, due process, and the rule of law.

This is only a beginning, though. The trends are clear. On the west coast of Africa, the American multinationals are striking roots to control oil resources, while on the eastern board, from Djibouti to, eventually, perhaps, Zanzibar, the Marines are establishing military bases. Who rules Africa today?

One could provide multiple examples to prove the point. But it is not necessary. The point is that the empire's lawlessness does not lie simply in acting against the rule of law but in violating the underlying values which constitute the legitimacy of law. So what remains of the "majesty" of law?

The exercise of authority (coercion) without legitimacy (consensus) is part of the definition of fascism. If Iraq demonstrates anything clearly, it is that American imperialism is tending toward fascism. And when this fascism is combined with barbarism on the scale and cynicism witnessed in Iraq, the consequences for the whole of humanity are likely to be too devastating to contemplate.

What is then the role and responsibility of the intellectual in this situation? I want to suggest a few pointers.

First, I want to suggest that the empire's lawlessness in the sense described here can no longer be explained in terms of the divergence between the ideal and the real. It is no more a question of double standards or not matching deeds with words. Rather, the very "word" is wanting. The law and its premises, the liberal values underlying law, the Law's Empire itself needs to be interrogated and overturned. In other words, fascism is not an aberration, it is the logical consequence of imperialism, and when imperialism runs amok, you get "Iraq."

Second, whatever the achievements of Western bourgeois civilization, these are now exhausted. We are on the threshold of reconstructing a new civilization, a more universal, a more humane, civilization. And that cannot be done without defeating and destroying imperialism on all fronts. On the legal front, we have to *rethink* law and its future rather than simply talk in terms of remaking it. I do not know how, but I do know how not. We cannot continue to accept the value system underlying the Anglo-American law as unproblematic. The very premises of law need to be interrogated. We cannot continue accepting Western civilization's claim to universality. Its universalization owes much to the argument of force rather than the force of argument. We have to rediscover other civilizations and weave together a new tapestry borrowing from different cultures and peoples.

Third, this can only be done if we think globally and humanly. While, for a long time to come, we may still have to act locally, there is no reason why we cannot think globally, all the time. The massive antiwar demonstrations happening simultaneously on the same day are a pointer in this direction. The anti-globalization and anti-capitalist demonstrations at the conferences of the rich are another example of rethinking the very basis of the Western, imperial civilization.

Fourth, as always, we as intellectuals have to interrogate our own commitment. We cannot simply allow ourselves to be "embedded." In a message to the World Congress of Intellectuals, Albert Einstein said:

> We have learned that rational thinking does not suffice to solve the problems of our social life… We scientists, whose tragic destiny it has been to help make the methods of annihilation even more gruesome and more effective, must consider it our solemn and transcendent duty to do all in our power in preventing these weapons from being used for the brutal purpose for which they were invented. What task could possibly be more important to us? What social aim could be closer to our hearts?

Can we say the same? Before even some intellectuals as journalists embedded themselves in the military to *misreport* on the war, how many more intellectuals as scientists, as advisors and consultants and spokespersons and speechwriters, were embedded in the establishment, producing cluster bombs and justifying and rationalizing their use? And since the invasion, how many more are getting embedded in lending legitimacy to the so-called reconstruction—read, "continued occupation and exploitation."

Some forty years ago, Georg Lukács warned his fellow intellectuals of their responsibility. It is as relevant today as it was then. Let Lukács remind us of our responsibility in the present situation and our attitude towards imperialism:

This new stage in the development of imperialism will quite probably not be called fascism. And concealed behind the new nomenclature lies a new ideological problem: the 'hungry' imperialism of the German brought forth a nihilistic cynicism, which openly broke with all traditions of humanity. The fascist tendencies arising today in the U.S.A. work with the method of a nihilistic hypocrisy. They carry out the suppression and exploitation of the masses in the name of humanity and culture.

Let us look at an example. It was necessary for Hitler, supported by Gobineau and Chamberlain, to formulate a special theory of races in order to mobilize demagogically his masses for the extermination of democracy and progress, humanism and culture. The imperialists of the U.S.A. have it easier. They need only universalize and systematize their old practices concerning the Negroes. And since these practices have up to now been 'reconcilable' with the ideology portraying the U.S.A. as a champion of democracy and humanism, there can be no reason why such a Weltanschauung of nihilist hypocrisy could not arise there, which by demagogic means, could become dominant.

Has Georg Lukács been proved right after 40 years?

It behooves us not to let this pass. I believe it was Eisenhower who said: What is good for General Motors is good for America. Bush is saying: What is good for America is good for the whole world. We should say: Nothing is good enough unless it is good for the entire humanity.

Iraq continues to burn. Humanity has been a witness to unbelievable acts of barbarism, the despicable treatment of Iraqi prisoners by the American and British soldiers that we have graphically seen in our media being the latest. The occupation has dogmatically refused to live by the rule of law, having already mutilated the values underlying it.

Need I repeat: bourgeois civilization has virtually exhausted all its potential. We have to rethink. *A better world is indeed possible, but we will have to conceive an alternative world view.* Neoliberalism has utterly failed to provide such a world view and intellectuals who continue to pay it lip service can only do so at the expense of integrity and honesty.

The Violation of the Will of the Global Antiwar Movement as a Crime against Peace

Anthony Alessandrini

In my testimony today, I will attempt to prove that the will of the global antiwar movement, a will that has been clearly and repeatedly made manifest through demonstrations, declarations, petitions, statements, and acts, has been knowingly and purposely violated by the government of the United States and its allies through the perpetration of the war on Iraq and the continuing occupation. I call upon the Jury to recognize this violation as a blatant crime against peace. Furthermore, I call upon you all to recognize and repudiate this violation as what it is: an attempt by the perpetrators of this war to create and maintain a situation in which those millions of people throughout the world who stand in opposition to crimes against peace will be forced to remain effectively voiceless, without institutions that can represent, embody, and enforce their will. It is, in other words, a crucial part of a larger strategy to ensure silence and impunity about the crimes committed, and still being committed, in Iraq, and also to ensure impunity for all future crimes. In the name of the World Tribunal on Iraq, I ask you to render a decision that will help bring to an end this silence and impunity.

I want to begin by thanking the organizers of the Istanbul session for asking me to take charge of an impossible task: namely, acting as an advocate for the global antiwar movement. Why impossible? For one thing, there is not one single "antiwar movement" that speaks at all times and in all places with a single voice; there is, instead, an interconnected network of people's movements throughout the world that have joined together—that is, constituted themselves as a single movement at critical moments—in order to express an absolute opposition to the war against, and continuing occupation of, Iraq.

By joining together in this way, the antiwar movement has itself acted as an advocate on behalf of the people of Iraq. It has consistently expressed a refusal to allow the massive violations against the Iraqi people to be committed in their name, and it has expressed also its solidarity with the struggles of the people of Iraq against occupation and for true self-determination. Of the many examples that could be cited of this advocacy, let me present just one. In May 2003, members of a popular committee in Cochabamba, Bolivia, who have been part of a struggle against the Bechtel Corporation over the privatization of water in Bolivia, wrote an open letter to the people of Iraq. Noting that Bechtel had been awarded a contract by the US government to conduct the reconstruction of infrastructure in Iraq, the popular committee of Cochabamba warned of the abuses committed by Bechtel in Bolivia and declared: "We support you in any action to remove Bechtel from your country and to protect yourselves from the abuse they are likely to bring with them."[1] This is one small but moving example of the global antiwar movement's active advocacy on behalf of the people of Iraq. So in this sense, I stand before you as an advocate on behalf of these millions of other advocates, whose will has been systematically and knowingly ignored, thwarted, and, in many cases, violently suppressed by those who have perpetrated and supported this war.

The organizers of the World Tribunal on Iraq have grasped an important fact: this task, the task of advocating for the global antiwar movement, which might seem impossible, is at the same time absolutely necessary. I stand before you today, not as a lawyer, nor as an expert on international law or international institutions, but rather as a member of the antiwar movement. In this sense, I might have been seen as something more akin to a witness, one who would be testifying to the violations committed against the antiwar movement by the government of the United States and its allies. However, the organizers have taken the important step of including this testimony regarding the violation of the will of the antiwar movement as part of this larger opening session on violations against international institutions and international law. And so I will attempt to live up to my charge, which is not simply to act as a witness, but to actively advocate for the global antiwar movement. I am here to ask the members of the Jury of Conscience, my fellow advocates, and all of you gathered here today to join me in this act of advocating for the antiwar movement.

What does this mean in practice? Coming at the end of this session, after the members of the Jury and the audience have already heard a great deal of important testimony regarding the violations committed by the government of the United States and its allies against international institutions and international law, one of the claims that I will ask you to consider is that through its opposition to the war on Iraq, beginning with the unprecedented global demonstrations on 15 February 2003, the global antiwar movement has in fact constituted itself as an international institution, in a very particular sense of the term. For on that date, one month before the commencement of the attack on Iraq by the US government and its allies, this global movement, which is in fact multi-vocal, multilingual, and in every way multifarious, spoke with a single voice. Millions of people throughout the world, representing the goals and interests of millions more, spoke together, and in the hundreds of different languages that were heard that day, the antiwar movement constituted itself as an international institution designed to state a single word: "NO." No to war, no to occupation, no to injustice, no to the proposed attack on Iraq.

I wish to quote at length from my fellow World Tribunal on Iraq organizer Ayça Çubukçu, who presented important testimony regarding the violation of the global antiwar movement at the New York session of the WTI in May 2004. Together with Balam Kenter, she was also responsible for gathering these images of protests from around the world on 15 February 2003.[2] I present these images to the Jury and to the audience as just a few of the innumerable images and words that can be presented as clear evidence of the will of the global antiwar movement. To quote from Ayça Çubukçu:

> New York City: Five hundred thousand. London: seven hundred thousand. Barcelona: two million. Istanbul, Warsaw, Calcutta, Mexico City, San Francisco, Paris, Rome, Cairo… Millions of bodies around the world simultaneously took to the streets against the imminent war on Iraq… A scream of NO forms a cloud hanging over the earth.
>
> We who are here today come from this global anti-war movement. Although we cannot claim to represent it, we are empowered by it. We are not merely an abstract "world public opinion." February 15, 2003 as an expression of the global anti-war movement constituted an unprecedented opposition to war. Unprecedented in history in its scale, global depth, and simultaneity, but also because it was against a war that was yet to unfold….
>
> The first bombs dropped on Iraq violated not just the principles expressed textually in law, but also the principles constituted actively in people's protest against this war. The World Tribunal on Iraq emerges from the constitutional moment of the global anti-war

movement because there is no official institution of international law that can hold the US and its allies accountable. In 1967, the British philosopher Bertrand Russell and the French philosopher Jean-Paul Sartre inaugurated the Russell Tribunal, which was to investigate the allegations of war crimes by the US and its allies in Vietnam. In his speech, Sartre said: "We are perfectly aware that we have not been given a mandate by anyone; but we took the initiative to meet, and we also know that nobody could have given us a mandate. It is true that our Tribunal is not an institution. But it is not a substitute for any institution already in existence; it is, on the contrary, formed out of a void and for a real need."[3]

This quote from Sartre accurately represents the void from which the World Tribunal on Iraq has been called into being. But it also represents the void into which the global antiwar movement stepped on 15 February 2003. By clearly and publicly joining together to express its opposition to the war that was being threatened against the people of Iraq, the global antiwar movement in effect created an entirely new form of international institution. It is an institution that refuses to be institutionalized, refuses to be locked away, refuses to be confined, refuses to be declared out of bounds, and refuses both the torments of the prison camp or the insane asylum and the comforts of the corner office with a view. What the global antiwar movement instituted on 15 February 2003 is no more and no less than the demand for justice without borders, without boundaries, without limits. With the single word, "NO," this movement declared that the war against Iraq, which had not yet been launched, would be absolutely illegitimate, now and forever more. With the single word, "NO," this movement instituted, gave form and substance to, the promise of justice, which, in the words of Ayça Çubukçu, "belongs not to a state, the system of states or to its institutions, but to the people."[4]

The official response to this clear expression of the will of the global antiwar movement is best encapsulated by a retort given by President George W. Bush at a press conference held three days after the worldwide demonstrations of 15 February 2003. Asked by a reporter for his response to the huge numbers of people who had turned out to protest against the war, President Bush responded: "Size of protest—it's like deciding, well, I'm going to decide policy based upon a focus group. The role of a leader is to decide policy based upon the security, in this case, the security of the people."[5] Despite the fact that he invokes "the people"—in this case, of course, the people of the United States—Bush's statement is clear evidence of a knowing and purposeful intent to violate the will of the people of the world any time this will contradicts US government policy in any way.

By equating the will of the global antiwar movement with the opinions expressed by "focus groups"—that is, groups used by advertising agencies to help them decide how to best promote and sell cola, cars, and Hollywood movies—Bush makes it clear that he believes that the US government can ignore, suppress, and silence the "NO" that was declared on 15 February 2003, with no consequences, with complete impunity. I ask the members of the Jury to show him that he was mistaken, and to declare this violation of the will of the global antiwar movement to be a crime against peace, one for which President Bush and the other perpetrators of the war against Iraq must be held accountable.

It must be said that recognizing the violation of the will of the global antiwar movement as a crime against peace is only the first step in initiating the difficult work that lies ahead, which is to hold those who have committed this crime accountable for their actions. It is also to initiate a difficult investigation, looking at, among other things, the relationship between popular movements and international institutions, between people's initiatives and bodies of law, between the poets among us who demand: "Come and see the blood in the street!" and the lawyers and judges and scholars among us who painstakingly document and classify the crimes that spilled this blood into the streets, and who do the crucial work of locating the mechanisms for punishing and preventing such crimes. Where such mechanisms do not yet exist, we must call them into existence, and in this task, the poets and the judges must work together and learn from each other.

In conclusion, it may seem that I am asking you, members of the Jury, to do something quite obvious and straightforward. Millions of people around the world said no to this war; their will was not heeded by those who carried out this war; therefore, you are seemingly asked to simply take note of and deplore this obvious violation of their will. But by declaring in your findings, clearly and directly, that the violation of the will of the global antiwar movement constitutes a clear and punishable crime against peace, you are doing something absolutely crucial. You are declaring that the "NO" that was declared throughout the world on 15 February 2003, a "NO" that has been repeated innumerable times since then—not simply in the form of protests, but also in the form of letters, petitions, articles, statements, declarations, films, songs, poems, paintings, indeed in countless forms—this "NO" cannot be refused, cannot be rejected, cannot be silenced. You are confirming that the process that was instituted by the global antiwar movement through the declaration of that "NO" is one that continues to this day, and that the proceedings here in Istanbul are just one of the many outcomes of that initial act of refusal. You are declaring, clearly and resoundingly, that the "NO" of the global antiwar movement is one that makes this war, all wars of aggression, all occupations, absolutely illegitimate, now and forever. You are affirming that it should be the goal of all international institutions charged with achieving and maintaining justice and peace to represent, embody, and enforce the will of the global antiwar movement.

In short, by confirming that this violation of the will of the global antiwar movement by the perpetrators of this war is a crime against peace for which they must be held accountable, you will take the first step toward ending the state of silence and impunity that these perpetrators have attempted to impose upon us all. This will in turn be a crucial step toward reviving and strengthening the global antiwar movement, indeed all people's movements throughout the world. The perpetrators of this war know that the best way to silence the antiwar movement is to try to convince the millions of people who make up this movement that their voices can be ignored, suppressed, and silenced, and that their will can be violated, with no consequences, with complete impunity. We know also that the best way to strengthen the antiwar movement is to demand that this impunity be brought to an end, and that the violation of the will of the global antiwar movement be seen as what it is: a crime against peace. The promise of justice resides, as it always has, among the people of the world. I call upon the Jury and the members of the audience to join with the global antiwar movement to help institute this promise of justice, on behalf of the people of Iraq and on behalf of all victims of wars of aggression and of occupation.

——————— Second Session ———————

The Responsibility
of Governments

Turkey's Situation and Politics in the US's Assault on Iraq

Baskın Oran

First, I will try to summarize the course of events starting from before the assault of 20 March 2003 from the standpoint of Turkey, and then I will try to deduce theoretical conclusions from them.

The Course of Events

The United States referred itself to Turkey after having decided to attack Iraq with the claim that Iraq was involved in the events of 9/11 and was hiding weapons of mass destruction. It wanted to attack both from the south and from the north, using Turkish territory.

At that time in Turkey, AKP [Adelet ve Kalkinma Partisi][1] had just won the elections of 2 November 2002 and set up its government. It was left in a serious state of hesitation.

The Acceptance of the First Permit (6 February 2003)

In an environment where things were not as yet clear, a permit that seemed comparatively neutral was presented to the National Assembly. The permit, which foresaw the modernization of Turkish ports and airports to be able to receive American soldiers and military equipment, was accepted 308 to 193.

After this vote, the United States Navy arrived just outside Iskenderun and started to wait for the second permit to be able to send soldiers on land.

Economic Aid Negotiations

Right after this, negotiations began concerning the economic aid that would compensate Turkey for any damage received in case of assault. As stated, $6 billion would be given as a grant and $20 billion as credit.

The discussions got increasingly prolonged. They continued until the end of February. It even took nearly fifteen days just to discuss the tax on American equipment and the legal status of the 1,600 or so American technical personnel that would be coming.

The negotiations took so long that at the end of this period, the two countries put their cards on the table. The US said: "The bargain is over. If you don't make your decision about the free passage of soldiers, you will have to bear the consequences." Turkey asserted: "We won't have the permission if we can't have an accordance on the economic aid package." In the meantime, in the words of the US officials, Turkey was alerted "16 times" to the need of making a "final decision." This caused Prime Minister Abdullah Gul to say that "so much pressure is enough."

The Arguments of the Different Parties in Turkey

This pressure was not only coming from the United States, but also from the inside. The proponents of war, including important newspaper columnists and TUSIAD—the association of leading businessmen. In addition to these, certain members of the media had started to claim that Turkey needed to be reimbursed with the oil in Mosul, and that this was the right time for making this claim. We can summarize the claims made by this line of argument:

—"The economy will be destroyed if we don't help the United States."

—"If we help, we will gain a lot of money from the import-export trade and bids" (KOC [one of the largest conglomerate groups in Turkey] and TUSIAD).

—"This assault will bring democracy to Iraq."

—"Saddam, who has weapons of mass destruction and who has used them on his own people, has to be controlled."

—"Saddam is feeding terror; terror can hit anybody."

—"The allied nature of a geostrategic ally comes out in such situations."

—"When the assault takes place, we will also go into Iraq to avoid the creation of a Kurdish state."

—"Even if we don't give them the permission, the US will still attack."

—"We are not getting into war, we are just giving permission to pass."

The proponents of peace, including President Ahmet N. Sezer, opposed this line of argument with moral, religious, political, and legal claims.

Moral claims: "Turkey cannot take part in an illegal and immoral imperialist assault."

Religious claims: "We cannot give support to an assault on our Muslim brothers in Iraq."

Political claims: "Reinforcing United States hegemony in the Middle East will weaken Turkey and disturb its relations with its neighbors."

Legal claims: "The 92nd article of the Constitution seeks 'international legitimacy' for calling foreign soldiers to Turkey and for sending Turkish military forces outside the country. The use of force is legitimate in international law on just two conditions: Legitimate defense and a decision of the UN Security Council. Both are lacking in this case."

The Denial of the Second Permit (1 March 2003)

It was in this atmosphere that a second permit arrived at the National Assembly: "Permission for the foreign soldiers to arrive and for Turkey to send soldiers to Northern Iraq."

Alongside the large reaction in public opinion, CHP also opposed the permit. An important opposition also existed within the ranks of the AKP.

However, what was most important was that the following two facts were asserted in the regular meeting of the National Security Council on 31 January 2003:

1. Efforts for a peaceful solution should continue. The war is undesirable for the countries of the region.

2. International legitimacy and accordance are the main principles guiding Turkey's attitude.

Even more importantly, the National Security Council had only said the following on the subject in its last meeting before that of 1 March (28 May 2003): "In the context of the possible US intervention in Iraq, the conclusions reached in the negotiations made with the United States have been considered."

In the closed election, in which AKP left its group free, the permit was denied because it did not receive the needed majority vote.

Developments after the Denial

1. There were huge protests held against the United States and its proponents in the Turkish government. Such were the arguments heard:

—"The government is in a state of absolute confusion and indecision."

—"We have let them down. They will leave us in a difficult economic situation."

—"After the invasion, they won't let us sit at the table."

—"They will create a Kurdish state."

—"Because we did not join the process, now the Kurds are allied with the US. We could have been in their place."

2. Turkey's attitude changed suddenly. The General Staff asked for the permit to be reconsidered. "If we don't participate at all, it will be damaging for us. If we participate, our damages will be compensated and we will sit at the table. We should support those who are fighting," it claimed. This assertion was made after a group of Kurds burned a Turkish flag in Northern Iraq on 3 March. Baykal from CHP said, "We should have gotten ten thousand into Iraq."

3. Two developments followed after this: a) The US started renting storage areas and territory in different places within Turkey. b) The American equipment convoys which were until then not permitted to leave the port of Iskenderun started out for the Iraqi border. According to the affirmation of the General Staff, this was a result of the first permit, which had been accepted. Thus, a secret treaty (on 8 February?) had been made.

The Acceptance of the Third Permit (20 March 2003)
In an environment where the United States was demanding eleven air corridors and saying, "If you go into Northern Iraq, there could be confrontations between your troops and those of the Kurds and the United States. Your planes might get hit by accident," the third permit was accepted· "Six months of permission for Turkish forces to be sent to Northern Iraq and for foreign air forces to use Turkish airspace."

On the same day, the invasion started.

The Situation after the Invasion
1. The Kurds: The Kurds of Northern Iraq started to make threats: "Don't come in. We have given the peshmergas the command to strike."

2. The Turkish government: It was in panic. Prime Minister Gul: "We are in the coalition." Three Iraqi diplomats were deported for no reason (6 April).

3. EU: The EU officials that had thought of Turkey as the Trojan horse of the United States until the denial on 1 March, started, from the beginning of May on, in a chorus in which Verheugen took the lead, to argue that Turkey should be accepted into the EU because of its geostrategic importance. These affirmations would continue until the end of 2004.

4. US: Sends insults and asks for troops. After the event of "sacking,"[2] "Yes, we want Turkey to admit that it has made a mistake. If you don't respond to our demands, the PKK will become an even greater threat." And later on: "Send 11,000 soldiers. You have a duty to be in Baghdad. You should send them in order to serve as an example for other Muslim countries."

5. Turkey: Became more willing. Gul asserted that "a UN decision was not necessary in order to send troops (29 July). The transitional government can invite them." "The strategic interests of our country cannot be imprisoned in Anatolia." TOBB: "If the responsibility comes, we should not avoid it." Ozkok: "If you don't buy the ticket, you can't win in the lottery."[3]

The Acceptance of the Fourth Permit
The Turkish government authorizes sending troops to Iraq for the duration of one year; the US decides against using Turkish troops.

—The United States changes its mind. Powell: "This is a sensitive issue for the Turks." *Washington Post*: "The Turkish card is dangerous." C. Rice: "The Turkish troops are a sensitive issue." Rumsfeld: "Turkish soldiers might not come." Holbrooke: "Turkey should not send troops" (September–October). Bremer: "Turkey is an ex-colonial power."

In return for $8.5 billion in credit, Turkey should not enter; if they do, the credit will be withheld.

—The Kurds and Arabs are against Turkish intervention. Talabani: "Don't come, even if under the control of the US." Two Turkish trucks have been burned. The embassy has been shot (16 August). Al-Sadr: "We'll consider your troops invaders." The sheikhs: "We will behead the Turkish soldiers" (September).

—The Iraqis do not want the Turks. The mullahs: "The Turkish soldier is a target." The Turkmen: "Turkish troops should come only as the result of a UN decision." The Temporary Council: "We do not want them."

—Turkey: Erdogan: "We want to send troops." Gul: "The invading power has made demands on us. They should solve their own problems."

—The EU: "Turkey should join ranks with Europe."

—Turkey changes its mind. TUSIAD: "No troops should go without a UN decision." Gul: "We need the UN decision" (24 September). Finally: "We won't be using the authorization permit."

Saddam is caught.

From here, we jump to June 2005. Prime Minister Erdogan has gone to the United States. He has blamed the anti-American sentiment in Turkey on CHP. Before that, he had gone to Israel. He nearly apologized. Yet, he still did not agree to cut ties with Syria and Iran.

Evaluation of the Events
Certain questions:

Why was the first permit accepted?

1. Because an isolated Turkey had not found in itself the force to say no to a monopolizing power such as the United States.

2. Moreover, at this moment, Turkey owed much to the United States:

Materially: An internal debt of $100 billion, external debt of $150 billion. Turkey's relationship with the IMF is in the hands of the US. If the public debt/YIGSMH exceeds 60 percent, the country will not receive any more credit. In 2002, the debt was at 144 percent. Two very serious crises had broken out in 2001.

Spiritually: Ocalan had been handed in by the US in February 1999.

3. Turkey was very isolated in the region. Its relations with the Arabs and the EU were not good. It was facing the Armenian and Cyprus questions.

4. Most importantly, Turkey's fear of a Kurdish state had for a long time made it difficult to say no to the United States.

Also, there were some who wanted to take this as an opportunity to prevent the establishment of a Kurdish state.

Why were the negotiations prolonged after the first permit?

1. Probably not to get more money, but to gain time, with the hope that the matter might be solved through peaceful means. Because a war in the region would disturb all balances and might result in the creation of a Kurdish state.

2. The government had just been founded and it was totally lost as to what it should do. The public opinion was against the United States, while the business circles and mainstream media were for it.

What were the consequences of the prolonged negotiations?

1. The public opinion in Turkey became increasingly anti-American.

2. This anti-American attitude extended to worldwide public opinion. While France, Germany, and Russia were expressing their opposition to the United States, millions started to participate in the demonstrations of the world peace movement. In this atmosphere, Prime Minister Gul visited the countries of the Middle East and the European Union; he tried to create an atmosphere to avoid the assault on Iraq and to force Saddam into greater coalition with the weapons inspectors. Leaders of many countries came to Ankara.

3. The United States lost a significant amount of time. Its navy wandered around Iskenderun for weeks on end.

4. Turkey had a serious loss of prestige. In the foreign press, there were cartoons of a belly dancer dancing in front of American generals who put money in her bra. Turkey acquired the image of trying to sell itself for the greatest amount possible in order to permit the violation of another's territory.

Why was the second permit denied?

1. The cutting edge: It was well understood, especially by the military, that the United States did not want to see Turkish troops in Northern Iraq (Kurdish parts).

Accordingly, in a context in which the public opinion was opposed to taking military action, the General Staff was also not willing (according to the reports of 30 January and 28 February of the Security Council). To go in was very dangerous, and with the US on the opposing side, it was totally impossible.

The main objective was to prevent the Kurdish state. In Turkey's policies with regard to Iraq up to that day, the tactical objective had been to separate the PKK from Northern Iraq, while the strategic objective was to prevent the formation of the Kurdish state.

2. The chronic reason: Turkey did not want to upset borders and balances. We will come back to this point in the conclusion.

The Consequences of the Denial

1. The people loved their parliament. They acquired confidence as a nation.

2. A new square was added to the cartoon that appeared in the foreign press: The same belly dancer was throwing the American general down from the table with a movement of her hip. In yet another cartoon, the first square had Bush claiming "We want to see democracy in Iraq," the second square said "... but not in Turkey."

3. As we have also asserted earlier, the "Trojan horse" image of Turkey was over in the eyes of the EU.

4. The US reacted negatively to Turkey. The extremely fast acceptance of the first permit had given the impression that they could easily have their way, and the United States wanted to attack before summer and finish Iraq up.

Why were the third and fourth permits accepted?

1. The third permit: Because it was clear by then that the US would be attacking in any case. Moreover, saying no to everything the US asked for was not possible for an isolated Turkey. The alternative to not giving permission for the use of its territory became that of letting the US use its airspace.

2. The fourth permit: The US troops had met with great resistance in Iraq and they were in great need of military units for the Baghdad area. The Turkish government decided to send troops, but the US stepped back when the Kurds reacted strongly. As a consequence, the Turkish government affirmed that they would not use the permit authority.

Some Analyses

The question of Turkish participation in the invasion of Iraq should be analyzed from two main angles:

1. This subject should be assessed as a power struggle between two unequal parties:

a) A Hegemonic State (HS) (a state that dominates the world with its military, economy, and culture) that has a total monopoly on power in the region and in the world; and

b) on the other end of the scale, a Strategic Medium-Sized State (SMS) (one that, just because of its geography, can exert power disproportionate to its size, while also causing disproportionately large problems), which has no opportunity to use another power (such as the EU) as a medium of balance.

In principle, the SMS cannot deny all the demands of the HS. However, it can at least delay or soften the demands that touch upon its life interests. In this case, of an invasion that would put it in a most difficult position, it has let the HS use its airspace but not its territory. Because of this, it has caused great difficulty to the United States. It has caused it to have to strike from one front only, to strike a month late, and to find itself face to face with the world public opinion.

2. This subject should be assessed from the point of view of two characteristics of Turkey that are in nature contradictory to one another:

a) The fact that one of the two external political principles of Turkey is, as we have asserted before, the conservation of the status quo/legitimacy. (The other is Westernism.) This principle arises from the fact that Turkey is located in a very fragile geopolitical region, which dictates that both regional and international borders be conserved, because, if these are disturbed, the consequences could be terrible.)

This characteristic has influenced Turkey not to support the US assault in principle, in spite of all the pressures in the opposite direction.

b) The existence of a fear arising from problems that are entirely internal to Turkey: the fear of a Kurdish state. Turkey is scared that its own citizens of Kurdish origin would lean toward such a state if founded, because it knows that it cannot make its own Kurdish citizens happy.

Therefore, this characteristic has had the opposite effect to the former, pushing Turkey toward entering Northern Iraq in order to avoid the creation of a Kurdish state there.

Conclusions

The elements of these two main angles—the capacity of the SMS to stand up to the HS to a certain extent, the status quo/legitimacy question for the Turkish state, and the Turkish fear of a possible Kurdistan—when considered together, in a dialectical way, have caused Turkey not to participate actively in the US assault.

As will be remembered, the possibility that Turkey join the assault was on the agenda on two separate occasions.

a) While the second permit was being discussed (February 2003), such a participation did not occur, because the US did not want to alienate the Kurds, who were the only Iraqi people to help them in the invasion of Iraq. Thus, they prevented Turkey from entering Northern Iraq. Therefore, the Turkish problem of the Kurds has in this case prevented the country from getting into further problems.

b) When the US wanted to situate Turkish units around Baghdad (July–October), in addition to the opposition of the Kurds, the consistent and decided reaction of the Iraqi people to the invasion of the HS (the killing of truck drivers, the bombing of the embassy, different and continuing assaults, reactions from Sunnis and Shiites, etc.) prevented Turkey from getting into such an undertaking and being partners in crime with the United States in the invasion of Iraq.

That is to say, the great opposition to the US's immoral and illegal invasion prevented Turkey from actively participating in it.

Because of all these complex reasons, the AKP government has experienced many ups and downs. For, on the other side, there exists the fear of the HS and of a Kurdish state, along with the already mentioned issues of a fragile and complex geography, concerns with the status quo and legitimacy of the Turkish state, and the concrete reality of Iraqi resistance. In the final analysis, this indecision has been a "good indecision" for Turkey and for the world at large.

The Responsibility of Arab Governments in the War on Iraq

Khaled Fahmy

If the war on Iraq was conducted in spite of widespread popular opposition, and if one of its prime casualties was the United Nations and the principles of international law it represents, it should also be stressed that the war would not have been possible without the complicity of various Arab regimes and without the active involvement of many Arab governments in providing significant logistic, diplomatic, and intelligence support to the US war effort.

It may be useful at the outset to stress that the complicity of Arab regimes with the US dates to a long time before the war actually started and also to remind ourselves that the servile attitude of Arab regimes toward the US could easily be seen not only during this, the third Gulf war, but during the first and second ones as well. For it has to be remembered that soon after he seized power in Baghdad in 1979, Saddam launched a bloody war against Iran, a war that lasted for eight bloody years and in which more than one million people lost their lives. That war, the first Gulf war, was made possible by direct diplomatic and military assistance that Saddam got from the US and to a lesser extent from Europe. He was also assisted in this devastating war against Khomeini's Iran by many Arab regimes who felt directly threatened by Iran's Islamic revolution. These regimes agreed to lend diplomatic and financial assistance to Saddam in order to continue with what the murderous Ba'ath regime called "Qadisyyat Saddam," evoking the name of a seventh-century battle between Arabs against Persians. When toward the end of this war, details of the Anfal campaign in which Saddam attempted to eradicate the Kurdish population living in northern Iraq became known, a campaign characterized by mass summary executions and the mass disappearance of many tens of thousands of noncombatants, including large numbers of women and children, and sometimes the entire population of villages; the widespread use of chemical weapons; the wholesale destruction of some 2,000 villages, including homes, schools, mosques, and wells; the looting of civilian property; the arbitrary arrest and jailing in conditions of extreme deprivation of thousands of women, children, and elderly people; the forced displacement of hundreds of thousands of villagers; and the destruction of the rural Kurdish economy and infrastructure—when all of this horrible information came to be known, neither the US nor the Arab regimes heeded the calls of many human rights groups pleading with them to stop assisting Saddam's regime and to bring him to justice. Instead, they supplied him with weapons, cash, and manpower (there was reportedly around one million Egyptian agricultural workers in Iraq during the war with Iran, making it possible for the murderous regime to send millions of young men to their deaths while maintaining agricultural production.

This ability and willingness of the Arab regimes and the US to turn a blind eye to the atrocities that Saddam was committing against both his neighbors and his own population was repeated during the second Gulf war in 1990–1991, when he invaded Kuwait. As we know, this gamble backfired tragically when the US saw this move as dangerously jeopardizing its access to Middle Eastern oil. Rather than allowing Saddam to get away with the Kuwaiti oil fields he had captured, and in order to prevent him from seizing the Saudi oil fields on which he had his eyes, the US moved half a million troops halfway across the globe to prevent Saddam from fulfilling his desire to be a major player in the oil market. In their panic the Saudis were only too willing to allow the US to use their military airbases as a launching pad against Iraq. In return, and as a sign of their gratitude to the Americans for not heeding Saddam's offer to replace them as the main oil suppliers in the region, the Saudis continued to play their servile role of pumping more oil, thus controlling the international oil market. Other Arab countries actively participated in the war by providing troops in the hope that they would get rewarded by the US following the cessation of hostilities. Most notably, the Egyptians sent some 30,000 troops to the war zone and in return got half their external debt scrapped by the US and its Western allies.

It is important to mention this disgraceful record as it helps explain the reasons why Arab regimes reacted they way they did during this, the third Gulf war. Being without exception undemocratic governments with little or no local credibility, Arab regimes were terrified after it became clear that the Bush administration was intent on launching the war with or without a legal sanction. And when they realized that the war was not about finding WMD or freeing the Iraqi people from Saddam's yoke, but, rather, was about regime change and redrawing the map of the region, the

Arab regimes rushed to see how they could be of assistance to Washington in its bellicose stance. Fearful of domestic public opinion and the widespread regional antipathy against the war, however, the regimes could not be open about supporting the war. This is what explains the insidious, sinister ways in which they offered their assistance to Washington.

Outward expression of opposition to the war was simply not allowed in Saudi Arabia and in many other Arab states. In some other Arab capitals the governments orchestrated small, pathetic demonstrations to show that they too were against the war. In Egypt, however, developments took a more serious twist. Soon after the scale of antiwar demonstrations that took place on 15 February in Europe, the US, and elsewhere in the world became evident, the Egyptian government reluctantly allowed people to take to the streets on 19 March 2003. No sooner had people started gathering in downtown Cairo with slogans against the US and the war than these slogans quickly turned against Egyptian president Hosni Mubarak and his government. Alarmed at the spontaneity of the anti-government demonstrations, and perplexed by the ease with which the people associated the antiwar cause with the anti-government one, the security forces decided not to take any chances, poured thousands of anti-riot personnel in the streets of Cairo, effectively closing off the entire downtown area, and then launched a massive campaign of arrests. In the days and weeks following 19 March 2003, hundreds of people associated with the movement protesting the war on Iraq were detained, including lawyers, journalists, members of parliament, academics, and students. Some detainees were seriously injured during arrest; others were subjected to torture while in custody. Several detainees were denied medical care for broken bones, damaged eyes, and other severe injuries. Even after demonstrations subsided, reports of new arrests and new incidents of torture continued to filter in. The whereabouts of many detainees were unknown for a long time, but large numbers of detainees later revealed that they had been held in State Security Investigations facilities, paramilitary Central Security camps, and other facilities not considered legal places of detention under Egyptian law. At least four of the known detainees were children, three under age fifteen and one child aged sixteen, and have been held with adult detainees in violation of international and Egyptian law. At least one of the children is known to have been badly beaten in custody.

Besides suppressing antiwar demonstrations, many Arab regimes devised ingenious ways to lend a helping hand to the US's war in Iraq, a war, it has to be remembered, which was part of the so-called war on terror. This was most visible in Egypt, where there were repeated calls on the government to close off the Suez Canal to US warships heading to the war zone. In response, the Egyptian government cited the Constantinople Treaty of 1899 governing navigation in the Suez Canal and offered a very narrow reading of its obligations according to that treaty. When it came to other international statutes, however, the Egyptian government showed remarkable imagination and resourcefulness in its desire to help Washington conduct its war in Iraq, which, it has to be stressed, was sold to the American public as part of the war on terror.

The most significant assistance that the Egyptian regime and other Arab governments have been giving to the US in its war on terror was by engaging in the infamous practice of "extraordinary rendition" whereby "terror subjects" were regularly sent to be interrogated under torture not only to Syria, a so-called pariah state, but mostly to Egypt, Saudi Arabia, and Jordan, all close and strong allies of the US.

Egypt has received by far the largest number of these so-called rendered suspects. Since the mid-1990s, Egypt has received scores of alleged Islamist militants, who have faced torture and serious mistreatment there. Significantly, after 9/11 and more specifically after the war on Iraq, the United States has been sending "terror suspects" to Egypt and to other Arab countries for interrogation. The Egyptian government has held many of these suspects in prolonged incommunicado detention. In some cases, Egypt has refused to acknowledge the whereabouts of those persons, and even the fact that they were in custody, raising concerns that some of the suspects have been forcibly "disappeared." In spite of the fact that the US Department of State's human rights report on Egypt, published in February of this year, stated that "torture and abuse of detainees by police, security personnel, and prison guards remained common and persistent," the US has been regularly sending suspects to Egypt for interrogation. This practice, it has to be stressed, is a clear violation of the international law that prohibits extraditing or otherwise transferring persons to a country where they likely face torture. Bush defended this practice on 28 April 2005, without mentioning Egypt by name. "We operate within the law, and we send people to countries where they say they're not going to torture the people," he said. However, the Bush administration knows full well that Egypt tortures people in custody, and that its promises not to torture a given suspect are not worth the paper they're written on. By promoting renditions to places like Egypt, Washington also sends a message to other states, in effect saying, "we don't care how abusive you are." At the same time the Egyptian government has been emboldened by the abuses in Abu Ghraib and Guantánamo, which it saw as giving the green light to go ahead with widespread use of torture in its prisons.

What is even more intriguing is the impunity shown by Egypt when it engages in what has been defined as "reverse rendition," whereby Egyptian security forces are recorded to have abducted foreign nationals on Egyptian soil, detained them for a while, and then transported them to Guantánamo. At least one such case has been documented, that of a Yemeni opposition figure who was seeking asylum in Egypt.

These cynical acts, conducted in flagrant violation of international law, it has to be stressed, were not an aberration to otherwise legal, normal, and healthy relations between the US and its allies in the region. As Secretary of State Condoleezza Rice has admitted in a speech she delivered in Cairo a few days ago, the US foreign policy in the Middle East has been misguided for the past sixty years. The US, she said, has preferred stability over democracy in this part of the world and has sided with undemocratic regimes at the expense of pushing for more openness and democracy. What is astonishing about this remarkable confession is that sixty years is an amazingly long period of time. There has been ample opportunity during this long period for US officials to change their policy and conduct the necessary amendments to the way they deal with this important part of the world. The reason this did not happen was not because these aberrations were not obvious, but because the US has strategically decided to pursue its own interests of securing a steady and cheap supply of oil and of blindly assisting Israel in suppressing the Palestinians, robbing them of their land, denying them their history, and subjecting them to a cruel, inhuman occupation, the longest in modern history. The US has been successful in doing so for two generations because it has always managed to find or implant regimes that were willing to serve US interests at the expense of their own populations. The complicity of Arab regimes with the US in the war on Iraq is, therefore, not accidental, but a characteristic sign of the way the US has managed to control this part of the world for over half a century. It is a complicity that stands in sharp contrast to the honorable position taken by the Turkish parliament when it turned down a request by the US to use Turkish territory to open a second front in the north. The servile stance that nearly all Arab regimes assumed during the war, to say nothing of the diplomatic, logistic, and, most notably, intelligence assistance that they have actively given to the US, has not been lost on the Arab peoples. Tragically, the realization of the degree and extent of this complicity of corrupt local regimes with an imperious US was what prompted bin Laden and his deputy Ayman al-Zawahiri to plan and coordinate the 9/11 attacks. This complicity is also one of the main reasons behind the bloody resistance to the US occupation of Iraq. Without a radical revision of its policy that entails a questioning of the two main pillars of its Middle East policy, namely, securing a steady and cheap supply of oil and uncritically backing Israel in its suppression of the Palestinians and in denying them basic rights, the US will always have to depend on local tyrants who have the ability to suppress their own people and control the people's hostility to US policy. The longer the US takes to recognize this basic fact, the more difficult it will be to have true democracy in the region and the more likely it will be that in sixty years' time we will, once more, have to listen to a failed academic turned chief diplomat who claims that her country has given up the complicit relationship with local bullies. In the meantime, however, Arab peoples in Iraq and elsewhere will not simply wait till the US sees the folly of its ways, but will continue their struggle for peace and democracy.

The Responsibility of European Governments
Guglielmo Carchedi

The European governments bear responsibility for the war in Iraq on several grounds. To begin with, if the war against Iraq is illegal, as it is, then any kind of support by these governments, from active military involvement to logistic assistance and political backing, is also illegal. Secondly, they have propagated, and continue to propagate, the view of insurgency against the occupation forces purely as terrorism. This undermines those democratic political forces fighting for self-determination and independence and promoting those reactionary forces moved by religious fundamentalism and terrorism. Thirdly, they have responded to the current economic slide toward recession and crisis in the Western world with deregulation, privatization, flexibilization, and casualization of labor, and more generally with yet more neoliberal policies. These policies have hit both the working class and the lower middle classes and, lacking credible left-wing, anti-neoliberal policies and analyses, have plunged sectors of these classes into insecurity and misery. This has cleared the way for right-wing ideologies ranging from ideological support for the war to passive acceptance of it. This holds for all European governments, both Social Democrat and those openly right wing, irrespective of their political connotations and official positions.

But there are differences. These range between two contradictory positions. On the one hand, in line with US denunciations, military participation, and unconditional collaboration with the US have been motivated by the threat supposedly posed by Iraq's weapons of mass destruction. This is the case of the UK. Like the UK, many European governments have failed to listen to the voice of the peace movement, the biggest antiwar movement in history.

On the other, opposition and refusal to become militarily involved have been motivated by the illegality of the invasion according to both international law (the lack of a UN mandate) and to certain countries' national laws. France and Germany are the most prominent supporters of this position. Between these two positions many countries have chosen to steer a middle course, for example logistic support or relatively small military contingents. A case in point is Italy. The Berlusconi government has attempted to portray Italy's military support for the war, numbering 3,000 troops and the fourth military contingent, as a principled stand against terrorism while at the same time depicting it as an escort for humanitarian convoys. In reality, the Berlusconi government not only did not want to displease the Bush administration but also wants to secure a slice of the lucrative reconstruction contracts ($300 billion, according to a recent television report). It is not by chance that Italian troops are stationed in the region of Nasiriya, which is known for its rich oil fields.

The conflict of positions between interventionism and non-interventionism is obviously influenced by political and electoral considerations. Each government has its own short-term specific reasons. For example, the German Chancellor Schroeder managed to retain popular support, in spite of his unpopular economic policies, because he championed the widespread opposition to the war. Parallel considerations apply for France. But these short-term considerations should be placed within the frame of more permanent and general factors. Of major importance is the clash between an economic and military block already consolidated around the US and a handful of emergent competing blocks at different stages of their constitution and power. The European Union is the most dramatic example of this. Consequently, the relations between states are shaped by the relations among the blocks to which those states belong. It follows that the European states' and governments' stance vis-à-vis the war in Iraq is heavily influenced by their membership in, and by the specificity of their position within, the EU. Only the major players will be considered.

Let us begin with the UK. The British government has been the most determined and subservient supporter of Iraq's invasion and has sent sizable contingents. The reason for its involvement is Britain's traditional supine subordination to US foreign policy, in this particular case the acceptance of the thesis of the terrorist threat posed by Iraq's weapons of mass destruction (which as we know have never been found). The need to "export democracy" was also raised but only when it became clear that Iraq had no weapons of mass destruction. This had been made abundantly clear by the UN inspectors, but the UK, following the US, decided to ignore this evidence. In short, the UK government supinely reproduced all the themes of US war propaganda. The reason is that this attitude is an aspect of Britain's "special relationship" with the US, i.e., its role as the mediator of interests between the US and Europe as a means to increase its political influence with the US and thus within the EU. A disassociation from the Iraq war would have jeopardized this special relation, thus weakening the pillar upon which British foreign policy rests. It was not by chance that, already in 2003, Prime Minister Tony Blair mentioned that after the war with Iraq he would discuss with President Bush "how to get America and Europe working together as partners and not as rivals."

A further reason why it would have been extremely difficult for Britain not to participate actively in America's military adventures is the very close tie between the military-industrial complexes of the two countries. The UK is not only much more dependent on imports for its stock of conventional weapons than France and Germany, but also it imports no less than 82 percent of its weapons from the US. Thus, the British government's responsibility for its active participation in the invasion of Iraq has its roots in some very concrete, long-lasting economic and political interests of important sectors of the British ruling classes rather than in high moral reasons.

Poland, Australia, Italy, Spain—before Zapatero—and other nations have also sent contingents. Their responsibility is certainly not less because of the smaller number of their troops deployed in Iraq. Also, these countries' moves are dictated by the need not to displease the US as well as by political, and possibly economic, considerations. These considerations apply to the UK as well. But these countries' motives are more short-term. In fact, if the benefits start eroding, the pressure to withdraw mounts. Italy, Poland, the Netherlands, and Ukraine have all begun to withdraw their forces or have announced their plans to do so in the near future. For example, Berlusconi faces political elections in 2006 and his decision to commit troops in Iraq has never been popular in a country which has witnessed the largest antiwar demonstrations.

At the other end of the spectrum we find France, Germany, and Russia. These countries have not sent combat troops to Iraq and have voiced their opposition to a military solution of the Iraq question from the very beginning. Their argument has basically been that there has been no UN mandate for the invasion of Iraq. However, this is only a cloak covering the real motives. To begin with, Russia is well aware that the occupation of Iraq is just another step toward its encirclement by the US and its allies. This is why it was and still is opposed to US military intervention in Iraq (and possibly in Iran in the near future).

As for France and Germany, they bear their share of responsibility, even though they are not directly involved militarily. For example, the German government should have applied the German constitution, forbidding use of German airspace and of Allied military bases on German soil for the pursuance of wars of aggression. Such a course of action was not even contemplated by Chancellor Schroeder. Yet such a stance would have given a powerful boost to the antiwar movement both in Europe and in the US itself. On the contrary, Germany is freeing up US troops for the war against Iraq by taking responsibility for security in Afghanistan, and by agreeing to organize the protection of US bases in Germany. France, even if against military intervention, has given together with Germany and other countries political and logistic support to the war. Foreign Minister Dominique de Villepin replied to a question about permitting the coalition to use French airspace that it was a "custom" in alliances. In this way, these governments have made it easier for the US not only to wage its war against Iraq but also possibly to attack Syria and Iran.

France and Germany too are moved by reasons of internal politics. But here too there are more enduring forces at work. Basically, these two countries are the driving force behind the concept of the EU as a block able to compete on all fronts with the US. They realize full well that the war against Iraq cannot but strengthen the US and weaken the imperialist European project. They are thus the engine behind the formation of a truly independent foreign and security policy that is less and less dependent on US foreign policy and US military might. This includes the formation of a truly independent European army, which is already emerging. Independent foreign policy and military strength are an indispensable condition for the EU to defend its economic interests. Moreover, of all the European major arms producers, France and Germany are the countries which depend the least by far on foreign imports. This indicates that within Europe they are the most technologically advanced producers of weapons. The substitution of arms and technologies produced by the US for those produced by the EU would imply that the technologies adopted at the European level would be basically French and German. These are the countries which will profit the most from a further militarization of the EU and from its military independence. They are the countries which have the greatest interest in creating a military might consistent with its economic might and interest.

How does Iraq fit in all this? The invasion of Iraq is only one pawn in Bush's "infinite war," or "war on terrorism," whose real aim is not only to monopolize oil wells and oil routes and to continue Russia's encirclement, but also to weaken the role of the euro. To see this point, we must introduce the notion of seignorage. It is well known that US imports have not been balanced by US exports for a third of a century now, i.e., an inflow of real value (goods and services) is not counterbalanced by an outflow of real value but by paper money, which is worthless as long as it is not used to purchase real value. This is the case for the difference between US imports and US exports. It is made possible by the dollar's role as the international currency, both as a reserve currency and as a means of international payments. In other words, the dollars paid for US imports are not used by foreigners to purchase US goods and services but are kept as international reserves either as cash or used to purchase US government securities. This inflow of imports into the US, not being counterbalanced by an outflow of exports from the US as a consequence of the dollar's role as the international currency, is an appropriation of real value. This is the dollar's seignorage. Its dimension is indicated by the fact that 68 percent of the reserves held by foreign central banks are dollars or US government securities. But the euro in its short life has already become the second international currency and a very dangerous competitor for international seignorage.

The challenge by the euro would become even more dangerous if the oil-producing countries were to ask for euros instead of dollars for their oil exports. Before the invasion, many countries had expressed their intention to diversify their international reserves, i.e., to switch from the dollar to the euro, whose international value has been constantly rising relative to the dollar. Let's not forget that this was Saddam Hussein's stated intention. By monopolizing international oil fields, the US is imposing payments in dollars and thus weakening the role of the euro. The war against Iraq is thus at the same time a war against the euro. Moreover, foreign central banks usually use their dollars to purchase US government securities. These dollars thus re-enter the US and are then used by the government to commission weapons. Foreigners thus subsidize US production of weapons through US seignorage. Just as US military interventions are a challenge by the dollar to the euro, the euro is a challenge to the sustainability of continued US military interventions and might.

Thus, the stance of France and Germany on Iraq has precious little to do with moral and legal considerations. It has much more to do with the defense of the Euro against the dollar and with the possibility for the EU to develop its independent military arm. This development is inversely related to the weakening of US military might.

The above reveals the nature of the calls for the EU to start a sort of Marshall Plan for Iraq and in fact for the whole of the Middle East. It is held that the EU is an external power that has not compromised itself through the war and that, due to its traditions of friendship with the area, is truly interested in an independent development of Iraq. But rather than expressing a sense of responsibility for the future of the country, these calls hide the design to at least diminish the US hold on a vital source of energy and more generally to weaken US imperialism.

It would be a dangerous delusion to think that there is a European power possessed of great economic, political, military, and moral resources to be used in the interests and for the development of the disadvantaged regions of the world. Iraq is today a tragic example of this. The European governments' different degrees of military involvement and political support are a manifestation of different needs in terms of internal politics and of their different geopolitical and economic strategies. No doubt these same countries who have refused to intervene militarily would have pursued a different course if, as in the past, this would have been necessary for their Great Power strategies.

The Role of the "Coalition of the Willing" in the Violation of International Law and Universal Human Rights

Walden Bello

My brief here intends to outline and detail the specific charges against the "coalition of the willing" assembled by the United States government to support its aggression in Iraq. The case against the prime aggressor, the United States, has been laid out by other advocates. I will limit my statements to other members of the coalition, including the US's main partner, the government of the United Kingdom.

The responsibility of the coalition of the willing for the invasion, occupation, and destruction of Iraq is that of a willing accomplice. The degree of guilt of course varies, but all the 50 countries that make up this front stand collectively condemned for providing legitimacy to a fundamental violation of international law: the invasion of a sovereign country. Thus all governments participating in this formation must be held accountable and arraigned before the appropriate international legal bodies for prosecution, conviction, sentencing, and assessment of reparations to the Iraqi people.

Coalition of the Willing—What, Who, Why?

The "coalition of the willing" was announced by US Secretary of State Colin Powell shortly before the 20 March 2003 invasion, after the US decided not to push through the famous second resolution authorizing war in the United Nations Security Council. At its height in March 2004, the coalition had about 50 members, including the United States. Thirty-four of these had troops deployed in Iraq. Various factors—most prominently, armed attacks at home, the activities of the Iraqi resistance, political pressure from citizens, and international embarrassment—caused fifteen countries to withdraw troops as of March 2005. Currently, there are about 23,900 non-US coalition forces in Iraq, compared to the US contingent of about 130,000 troops.

What reasons did governments have for joining the coalition? These varied. Despite his coming from an ideological and political background different from US President George Bush's, Labor Prime Minister Tony Blair truly appeared to believe in externally imposed "regime change" in Iraq. Much more understandable was the support of Bush's ideological fellow travelers José Maria Aznar of Spain and Silvio Berlusconi of Italy, the latter of whom was notorious for having declared that "[T]he West will continue to conquer peoples, even if it means a confrontation with another civilization, Islam, firmly entrenched where it was 1,400 years ago."

For Japan and Korean governments, the rationale was obviously a quid pro quo for the US military umbrella in their countries. Most of the other governments were, as one commentator described it, a veritable "opera bouffe of tiny states" that were either strong-armed or bribed with promises of fat post-war contracts or economic aid by Washington.

The Coalition's Basic Function: Deodorizing an Illegitimate Act

Whatever were their intentions, the members of the coalition of the willing were used by the United States to provide legitimacy for the invasion and occupation of an independent country, thus making them accomplices in a massive violation of international law. Statements from members of the coalition backing the US invasion were widely propagated by Washington to defuse the criticism of its patently illegal action. A sample of the official statements of these governments circulated by Washington prior to and following the invasion reveal the extent to which they allowed the United States government to manipulate them to justify an illegal and unprovoked war. The statements came word-for-word from Washington's published rationale for the war:

> Saddam Hussein is a danger to law and peace. Hence the Netherlands gives political support to the action against Saddam Hussein which has been started. (Prime Minister Jan Peter Balkenende, 20 March 2003)
> The Philippines is part of the coalition of the willing... We are giving political and moral support for actions to rid Iraq of the weapons of mass destruction. We are part of a longstanding security alliance. We are part of the global coalition against terrorism. (President Gloria Macapagal Arroyo, 19 March 2003)
> At a time when diplomatic efforts have failed to resolve the Iraqi problem peacefully, I believe that action is inevitable to quickly remove weapons of mass destruction. Koreans tend to join forces when things get tough. (President Roh, 20 March 2003)

The cabinet sitting under the chairmanship of HE Yoweri Museveni, the president of Uganda, on 21 March 2003, decided to support the US-led coalition to disarm Iraq by force. The cabinet also decided that if need arises, Uganda will assist in any way possible. (Minister of Foreign Affairs James Wapakhabulo, 24 March 2003)

The responsibility falls exclusively on the Iraqi regime and its obstinacy in not complying with the resolutions of the United Nations for the last 12 years... On this difficult hour, Portugal reaffirms its support to his Allies, with whom it shares the values of Liberty and Democracy, and hopes that this operation will be as short as possible and that it will accomplish all its objectives. (Prime Minister José Manuel Durão Barroso, 20 March 2003)

Coalition Participation in the Occupation

The following 34 countries stand accused of active participation in the invasion and occupation of Iraq through the deployment of troops: Albania, Armenia, Australia, Azerbaijan, Bulgaria, Czech Republic, Denmark, Dominican Republic, El Salvador, Estonia, Georgia, Honduras, Hungary, Italy, Japan, Kazakhstan, Latvia, Lithuania, Moldova, Mongolia, the Netherlands, New Zealand, Nicaragua, Norway, Philippines, Poland, Portugal, Slovakia, South Korea, Spain, Thailand, Tonga, the United Kingdom, and Ukraine. Twenty-five of these thirty-four countries continue to maintain security forces in the country. Some of these countries, such as Spain and the Philippines, have now withdrawn their troops or police forces, and others, such as the Netherlands, Ukraine, Bulgaria, and Italy, have begun or announced the phased withdrawal of their contingents. All, however, should nevertheless be held accountable for having concretely assisted in the US occupation.

The following countries, while they did not deploy troops, are accused of complicity in the violation of the sovereignty and territorial integrity of Iraq by joining the coalition of the willing: Afghanistan, Angola, Colombia, Costa Rica, Eritrea, Ethiopia, Iceland, Kuwait, the Marshall Islands, Micronesia, Palau, Rwanda, Singapore, Solomon Islands, Uganda, and Uzbekistan.

Table 1: Troop Contingents in Iraq by Country of Origin, March 2004

Country	No. of Troops
United States	130,000
United Kingdom	9,000
Italy	3,000
Poland	2,460
Ukraine	1,600
Spain	1,300
Netherlands	1,100
Australia	800
Romania	700
Bulgaria	480
Thailand	440
Denmark	420
Honduras	368
El Salvador	361
Dominican Republic	302
Hungary	300
Japan	240
Norway	179
Mongolia	160
Azerbaijan	150
Portugal	128
Latvia	120
Lithuania	118
Slovakia	102
Czech Republic	80
Philippines	80
Albania	70
Georgia	70
New Zealand	61
Moldova	50
Tonga	40
Macedonia	37
Estonia	31
Kazakhstan	25

Source: "Coalition of the Willing," Perspectives on World History and Current Events, 19 June 2006.

Among the coalition members, the role and responsibility of the following must be highlighted: the United Kingdom, Italy, and Spain. The United Kingdom played a major role in the invasion, and together with Italy and Spain provided the leadership role in the coalition in the first months of the occupation. Since then this leadership has faltered: Spain broke ranks by withdrawing troops in February 2005, after the Madrid bombing, and the Berlusconi government in Italy has announced its plan to begin withdrawing troops beginning in September 2005, following the controversial killing of an Italian government agent by US soldiers at a checkpoint in March 2005.

Japan and South Korea's role and responsibility must also be singled out. The two countries gave an "Asian" face to the occupation, and with its 3,600 troops, South Korea today maintains the third-largest military presence in Iraq, after the United States and the United Kingdom.

The United Kingdom's Special Burden of Guilt

Aside from the United States, it is the government of the United Kingdom that clearly must bear the burden of guilt among the coalition of the willing. Since others in the panel of advocates are focusing on the United States, I will confine my comments to the United Kingdom.

Participating in the Planning of the War

The recently revealed Downing Street memos show that as early as April 2002, the Labor leadership was aware that 1) the Bush administration was keen to invade Iraq; 2) that it was determined to do this on the issue of Saddam's possession of weapons of mass destruction; and 3) that the evidence of Saddam's ability to develop weapons of mass destruction was tenuous. As one Foreign Office memo, dated 22 March 2002, addressed to Foreign Secretary Jack Straw put it, "The truth is that what has changed is not the pace of Saddam Hussein's WMD programs, but our tolerance of them post-11 September." It continued: "But even the best survey of WMD programs will not show much advance in recent years on the nuclear, missile, or CW/BW [chemical or biological weapons] fronts: the programs are extremely worrying but have not, as far as we know, been stepped up."

Despite the fragility of the evidence for the existence of weapons of mass destruction, however, Prime Minister Tony Blair beat the drums for war on the WMD argument. At around the same time that the Downing Street memos were questioning the WMD evidence, Blair told the House of Commons on 10 April 2002: "Saddam Hussein's regime is despicable, he is developing weapons of mass destruction, and we cannot leave him doing so unchecked."

On 24 September 2002, again contradicting the lack of evidence, he declared: "It [the intelligence service] concludes that Iraq has chemical and biological weapons, that Saddam has continued to produce them, that he has existing and active military plans for the use of chemical and biological weapons, which could be activated in 45 minutes, including [against] his own Shia population; and that he is actively trying to acquire nuclear weapons capability."

On 25 February 2003, in the lead-up to the invasion: "The intelligence is clear: [Saddam] continues to believe his WMD programme is essential both for internal repression and for external aggression." In the same speech, he asserted: "The biological agents we believe Iraq can produce include anthrax, botulinum, toxin, aflatoxin, and ricin. All eventually result in excruciatingly painful death."

Then on the very day of invasion, 20 March 2003, Blair said: "If the only means of achieving the disarmament of Iraq of weapons of mass destruction is the removal of the regime, then the removal of the regime has to be our objective."

It now appears that concerted effort by the Blair government to produce evidence of Iraq's possession of WMD led to the doctoring or, as the British Broadcasting Corporation report put it, the "sexing up" of the British intelligence services' 50-page dossier on Saddam's alleged WMD program released in September 2002. This dossier served as one of the key British government documents to make the case for war. Caught in the crossfire between pressure from the government and the slimness of the evidence, senior government scientist Dr. David Kelley, a former WMD inspector in Iraq, revealed to the press his strong doubts about the dossier's allegations, particularly the claim that Iraq could activate WMDs within 45 minutes. This apparently triggered government pressure on him that eventually led to his suicide in July 2003.

The Downing Street memos also indicate that even as the WMD evidence was thin or nonexistent, the Blair government was strongly for invading Iraq to institute "regime change," though that was not something it could trumpet publicly, for that would come across as advocating a clear breach of international law. Indeed, as early as March or April 2002, a time that the Blair government and the Bush administration say they were not engaged in war planning, they were already at an advanced stage in the process. While the British government was not convinced of the threat of WMD, the memos reveal that it shared the Bush administration's desire for regime change through military means.

One memo in mid-March 2002 details a letter from Christopher Meyer, then British ambassador to the United Nations, on a lunch discussion he had with then US Undersecretary of Defense Paul Wolfowitz. "We backed regime change," he wrote, "but the plan had to be clever and failure was not an option. It would be a tough sell for us domestically, and probably tougher elsewhere in Europe."

At the same time, British officials knew that regime change per se could not be invoked as an objective for invasion. As an 8 March 2002 memo sketching out options for dealing with Iraq noted, "an invasion for the purpose of regime change has no basis under international law." The dilemma and the solution to it was stated over two weeks later by Foreign Secretary Jack Straw: "Regime change per se is no justification for military action; it could form part of any strategy, but not a goal," he said. "Elimination of Iraq's WMD capacity has to be the goal." Not surprisingly, the Blair government embarked on a course of manufacturing a nonexistent threat, culminating in the infamous 25 September 2002 dossier that became the key document propagated by Washington and London to justify the impending invasion of Iraq.

When all is said and done, it is clear that it was mainly Tony Blair, against the wishes of the vast majority of the British people and a significant section of his party, that brought the United Kingdom to the war. Why? Some commentators say that he really did believe in the morality of externally imposed regime change, which makes him, like Bush, a very dangerous man indeed. Others would discount morality and say that Blair was in fact motivated by cold realpolitik. My sense is that, along with a warped morality, this is a likely motivation: that is, the desire to put the British government at the center of global power alongside the United States. As he once asserted, "It's my job to protect and project British power."

Carrying Out the War

In addition to its role in planning the war, the British government's conduct of the war in Iraq clearly reveals its disregard for international law and universally recognized human rights.

The invasion of the country was preceded by a bombing campaign that began approximately ten months before, in May 2002. Jets of the Royal Air Force joined United States Air Force jets in what were called "spikes of activity" designed to goad the Saddam Hussein regime into retaliating and thus providing the pretext for war. These actions, which were justified by US officials such as Allied Commander General Tommy Franks as necessary to "degrade" Iraq's air defenses, were not authorized by any United Nations resolution. Indeed, as the leaked Downing Street memos reveal, the British Foreign Office provided a legal opinion in March 2002—two months before the intensification of the bombing—that asserted that allied aircraft were legally entitled to patrol the no-fly zones over the north and south of Iraq only to deter attacks by Saddam's forces on the Kurdish and Shia populations and had no authority to put pressure of any kind on the regime. This illegal activity was further intensified at the end of August 2002, following a meeting of the US National Security Council in which its purpose was revealed to be that of making Iraq's air defenses as weak as possible for a possible invasion.

Since the invasion took place, Britain has sent some 65,000 troops, or almost a third of the armed forces, to participate in an illegal war unauthorized by the United Nations. About 8,761 were stationed there as of March 2005.

The main assignment for the British troops was to secure the southern sector, notably the city of Basra. That campaign was marked by the deaths of scores of Iraqi civilians. Some of the deaths were caused by the use of cluster bombs, known to be deadly to civilian populations. Although officials at the British Ministry of Defense initially pledged not to use the weapons "in and around Basra," Human Rights Watch documented several strikes using cluster munitions in the neighborhoods of that city. At the height of military operations in March and April 2003, British forces used 70 air-launched and 2,100 ground-launched cluster munitions, containing 113,190 submunitions. Total US and British use came to 13,000 cluster munitions and 2 million submunitions in that period.

Human Rights Watch also accused British military authorities of failing to secure large caches of abandoned Iraqi Army weapons, resulting in civilians being killed or wounded. Basra's al-Jumhuriyya Hospital was receiving five victims of unsecured ordnance a day, leading Human Rights Watch Executive Director Kenneth Roth to declare: "Britain failed in its duty as an occupying power to provide security to local civilians. Its inability or unwillingness to secure abandoned weapons made a dangerous situation even more dangerous."

Foreign occupation invites systematic abuses of human rights. This has been the case of the US occupation in central and northern Iraq. Abu Ghraib prison has become a synonym for violations of the Geneva Convention, torture as a policy, and systematic sexual abuse, while the American retaking of Falluja in November–December 2004 has become a contemporary version of the implementation of the harsh Roman order "Carthago delenda est" ("Carthage must be destroyed").

The British occupation of the Basra and southern Iraq, while being less in the glare of publicity than the US occupation, has also been marked by violations of basic human rights. One year of occupation yielded numerous cases of the killing and wounding of civilians by British troops. Amnesty International reports that as of early March 2004, British authorities admitted that UK forces had been involved in the killing of 37 civilians. They acknowledged, however, that the figure was not comprehensive. In a number of cases investigated by Amnesty, "UK soldiers opened fire and killed Iraqi civilians in circumstances where [there] was apparently no threat of death or serious injury to themselves or others." Amnesty found that the British Royal Military Police (RMP) was "highly secretive and… provided families with little or no information about the progress or conclusions of investigations." Moreover, the process of gaining reparations by families of victims was grossly inadequate, plagued by inconsistencies, over-bureaucratic, and practically inaccessible to poor Iraqis.

Torture and sexual abuse of prisoners have been another black mark on the British occupation. In January 2005, photos were released in the national press depicting torture and systematic abuse of Iraqis by soldiers belonging to the first battalion of the Royal Regiment of Fusiliers. As described in one report, "One of the photographs showed a grimacing Iraqi civilian bound tightly in an army cargo net being suspended from a forklift truck driven by a British soldier. A second depicted a soldier dressed in shorts and a T-shirt standing on the bound and tied body of an Iraqi civilian. Other pictures showed two naked Iraqi men being forced to simulate anal sex and two Iraqis forced to simulate oral sex."

The soldiers were court-martialed, leading to a jail sentence and expulsion from the army of some of them. There was a grave miscarriage of justice at the trial, however, since evidence from the victims was not allowed in court, which could have led to harsher sentences or the implication of many more soldiers, including higher-ups. The evidence included that of the Iraqi in the forklift incident, Hassan Abdul-Hussein, who said that he was tied and strung up when he refused to sever another Iraqi's finger with a knife. Why was the evidence inadmissible? The honorable Phil Shiner, who is also part of this panel of advocates, has claimed that the purpose was, as in the case of the abuses at Abu Ghraib, damage limitation: "Here there is the clearest evidence that the military are incapable of prosecuting and investigating themselves. If they are allowed to, all we get is a whitewash and a few bad apples thrown to the dogs. Clearly, here something as gone badly wrong, officers were involved and a whole lot of people were abused."

With British soldiers themselves participating in the abuse of civilians, it is not surprising that they failed to provide security, as they were required to by international law. Like other parts of the country, Basra and other sites in southern Iraq have witnessed "scores, possibly hundreds, of people... deliberately killed by individuals or armed groups for political reasons, including for perceived moral infractions such as selling or buying alcohol." However, virtually no investigation or prosecution of these killings had occurred as of early 2004. Thus Amnesty considered the UK military authorities as in breach of its international obligations under Article 27 of the Fourth Geneva Convention, which mandates the UK as an occupying power to provide protection for Iraqis, especially from threats and acts of violence.

With the occupation provoking the rise of an armed resistance in 2003 and 2004, British troops were dragged in to support US military operations in central Iraq. The most notorious instance of indirect British support for US efforts to crush the Iraqi people's resistance took place in November 2004, when the 850-strong Black Watch Regiment was moved from southern Iraq to the Babil Province, south of Baghdad. The redeployment followed a request from US military authorities who wanted to use the US military units freed up for the assault on the city of Falluja that was to be launched after the US elections. The move provoked former British Foreign Minister Robin Cook to speak about "the suspicion that we sent a third of the British army to Iraq not in pursuit of our own national interest but in support of the White House's political agenda. This latest twist to the tale confirms the perception that it is Washington that calls the shots and Britain that jumps to attention. It is equally obvious that the request was the product of US politics." The ensuing US assault on Falluja was marked by hundreds of civilian deaths, thousands of people injured, routine violations of human rights by American soldiers such as the killing of wounded prisoners, and massive destruction of property. By redeploying British troops to release American soldiers for the savage attack, Mr. Blair's government must take some responsibility for the ensuing war crimes.

Conclusion and Recommendations

The record of the coalition of the willing in Iraq is a sordid and sorry one. The coalition tried to do the impossible: provide legitimacy to a glaring and unjustifiable violation of international law—the invasion of Iraq—an act that must rank as low in terms of ignominy and infamy as the Nazi invasion of Poland in 1939. The 50 members of the coalition of the willing have performed for the US today what the Romanian, Hungarian, and Italian fascist states did for Nazi Germany in the latter's aggressive and brutal conquest of Eastern Europe during World War II. Thus the coalition must be seen as complicit not only in the violation of Iraqi sovereignty but also in the systematic violation of human rights, political rights, and economic rights that is the main feature of the US and British occupation of that country today.

Among coalition members, the role of the government of the United Kingdom must be especially condemned. The Blair government's role cannot be reduced to that of being a reluctant partner of the Bush administration. It cannot be reduced to that of a supporter that merely provides convenient cover for the aggressor. The Blair government actively participated in the preparations and conduct of the war. It committed a third of the British army to the invasion and occupation, and went to war willingly—gleefully, some would say, in the case of Prime Minister Blair.

Mr. Blair's behavior went beyond that of a cheerleader to that of being one of the main apologists for the war, trying to convince the world that an immoral and illegal act was a moral one. Like Bush and like Hitler, he is, as we said earlier, a dangerous man.

Harsh censure by this body must be meted out to all members of the coalition, including those which did not deploy troops to Iraq. For those that deployed troops to Iraq in support of the US war, the appropriate punishment is to be arraigned before international legal bodies for prosecution for complicity in the breach of international law and internationally recognized human rights. Officials of the British government, in particular Prime Minister Anthony Blair, must be given top priority for prosecution, alongside President George W. Bush and other civilian and military leaders of the US government in the appropriate legal institutions, in particular the International Criminal Court.

The war criminals, ladies and gentlemen of the Jury, must be brought to trial, and soon.

Third Session

The Accountability of the Media

Economic-Political Connections of Media
Saul Landau

Overwhelmingly, corporate management of media remains attentive to the interests of its major stockholders: profit and reproduction. In order to do so, it must both validate the ruling authority (government in power) and simultaneously present a facade of fierce independence from that authority. To separate these postures requires some nuance.

In addition, the major networks, newspapers, and radio stations—Fox, owned by the outspoken right-winger Rupert Murdoch; CNN/Time Warner; CBS/Viacom; Disney et al.—shape opinion and mass aesthetics. Their main product is advertising, convincing people to want what they don't need. This means they must learn to need what they don't want. The aesthetic of the commercials and the commercial programs work together in shaping taste: thin (emaciated) is beautiful; rich (having all material desires in reach) is the object of life. The commercial and programming world identifies young, tall, and well-dressed (expensive clothes) with virtue. None of this relates to the traditional function of information and citizenship. What it does is distract the public from its citizen role and direct it toward consumption.

When the Founding Fathers guaranteed freedom of the press in the Bill of Rights attached to the Constitution, they did not guarantee that the media would provide quality information and analysis to the citizens, a role—the fourth estate[1]—that a functioning democracy requires.

Indeed, the major media has evolved as an instrument through which the dominant commercial culture—trivia to the nth degree—reproduces itself. "News" has become part of the reproductive process. Indeed, journalists learn axioms of "news reporting" as part of their apprenticeship. For example, newspaper readers and TV and radio audiences expect the "free press" to inform them of relevant facts so that the electorate can understand policy and approve or disapprove. But the media automatically validates the presidency—the result of the will of the majority, after all—by accepting its deceitful utterances as truthful, even when it knows better.

To illustrate the point, the major media "discovered" in 1982 that President Reagan had authorized a covert war against Nicaragua. The *New*

York Times and *Washington Post* both reported the CIA "scoop" in the first paragraph, providing details from inside sources of a $19 million presidential authorization to "interdict" arms supplies from Nicaragua to the Marxist rebels in El Salvador.

The second paragraph dutifully reported that the White House denied the allegations. Reporters ought to have begun their second paragraphs with the following line: "The White House predictably lied." Since the reporters and editors knew they had a solid story, based on reliable inside sources, they placed it on the front page. Why not label White House dissembling for what it was?

In addition, the major media omitted from their coverage that covert actions such as the one Reagan had "signed off on" against Nicaragua were illegal. Indeed, that's why they remained "covert." The people and government of Nicaragua certainly knew about the CIA's involvement in violence in Nicaragua. The media revealed the story but simultaneously collaborated with the administration by keeping from the public the key fact that such aggression by one state against another was barred by US law (Neutrality Acts) and a myriad of treaties, including the UN Charter, OAS Charter, and Rio Treaty.

Similarly, before, during, and after the March 2003 invasion of Iraq, the US media also cleaned its news stories of key points about Bush policy and international law. As Richard Falk and Howard Friel dramatize in their 2004 book *The Paper of Record*, the *New York Times* consistently excluded this theme from its coverage.

Preceding Bush's order to invade Iraq and during the UN debates, not one major media outlet pointed to the similarities between the argument Supreme Court Justice Robert Jackson made at Nuremberg on 12 August 1945, in explaining to the German people why the Allies had decided to try the Nazi leaders—for starting an aggressive war—and Bush's unjustified bellicosity towards Iraq:

> We must make clear to the Germans that the wrong for which their fallen leaders are on trial is not that they lost the war, but that they started it. And we must not allow ourselves to be drawn into a trial of the causes of the war, for our position is that no grievances or policies will justify resort to aggressive war. It is utterly renounced and condemned as an instrument of policy.

Under Jackson's guidelines, Saddam Hussein in the dock might well ask the court how his invasion of Kuwait differed from Bush's "aggressive war" against Iraq. "Preemptive war," as defined by Bush himself in the 2002 National Security Strategy of the United States paper, was outlawed at Nuremberg: inventing reasons that don't exist to attack neighbors cannot be twisted into any concept of a just war.

Lest people forget, in August 2002, Vice President Cheney said: "Simply stated, there is no doubt that Saddam Hussein now has weapons of mass destruction. There is no doubt he is amassing them to use against our friends, against our allies, and against us."

When reporters failed to challenge such statements and demand hard evidence, they wittingly or unwittingly allowed the administration to repeat such nonsense without investigating or questioning it. Indeed, TV, radio, and newspaper journalists gave greater authority to the lies and helped Bush justify his war goals. *New York Times* reporter Judith Miller illustrates how "the paper of record" validated Bush's charges on its front page by assuring readers that the administration possessed overwhelming evidence pointing to Saddam's possession of weapons of mass destruction. Her sources amounted to Ahmad Chalabi and his exiled Iraqi National Congress. Chalabi had received funding from the Bush administration for providing it with the "intelligence" they liked. One such source, nicknamed "Curveball," turned out to be not only a bald-faced liar but a brother of Chalabi's top aide. West German intelligence held this scoundrel and told the CIA of their doubts about his credibility. He presented himself as a defecting top Iraqi scientist who had been hired to build bio weapons stations in trucks. Bush used this man's information to warn repeatedly "of the shadowy germ trucks."

Newspaper reporters and editors loved this stuff. They referred to "Winnebagos of Death" in their accounts. Indeed, Secretary of State Colin Powell used Curveball's "data" in his February report to the UN Security Council (*Los Angeles Times*, 28 March 2004).

Curveball, in reality a low-level clerk in an Iraqi company, dismissed for stealing, claimed he personally knew that "Saddam Hussein had built a fleet of trucks and railroad cars to produce anthrax and other deadly germs."

Ironically, "U.S. officials never had direct access to the defector and didn't even know his real name until after the war." Despite this obvious lapse of tradecraft, "American officials thought it confirmed longstanding suspicions that the Iraqis had developed mobile germ factories to evade arms inspections." Ms. Miller fed the pap to her readers on page one of the *New York Times*. She also apparently confirmed the information with Chalabi, without inquiring into his close relationship to Curveball.

Only later, US officials said, did the CIA learn that the defector was the brother of one of Chalabi's top aides, and begin to suspect that he might have been coached to provide false information. Partly because of that, some US intelligence officials and congressional investigators fear that the CIA may have inadvertently conjured up and then chased a phantom weapons system.

Not only did journalists fail to ask tough questions of administration officials, but they also consistently ignored elementary logic. For example, when in September 2002 Saddam Hussein agreed to readmit the UN weapons inspectors, neither editorial writers nor pundits sucked the obvious logic from the story. If Saddam submitted and let into Iraq with full access the world's best forensic experts with the most sophisticated detecting equipment, he was sending a clear message: he had no weapons of mass destruction. The inspectors would be able to explore every nook and cranny and interview all Iraqis while going through official papers. How could even a wily dictator hide weapons or weapons programs from such a search?

By failing to explore this logic, the fourth estate failed in its obligation to serve the citizenry with information and analysis needed for a crucial decision: war or peace. Instead, the media beat the war drums in the months before the invasion. Reporters and editors aided and abetted Bush in committing war crimes by giving validity to his false claims. Instead of asking skeptical questions about Saddam Hussein's supposed deadly weapons and how they constituted a threat to the US and its allies because he planned to share these chemical, biological, and nuclear arms with the terrorists who did the 9/11 deeds, they accepted the unsupported word of the White House.

After the invasion and the absence of weapons of mass destruction and links to Al Qaeda, the reporters should have jumped all over Bush. Instead, they helped him dissemble further by participating in Pentagon-direct scripts to distract instead of inform the public. The most sensational war reporting came when the networks replayed the images of Saddam's statue falling. Later, we learned that US officials had staged this show for the cameras. Reporters also took their feed directly from Pentagon propaganda officers when they reported the "saga of Jessica Lynch."

The military's spinning of the press related to the fact that from the outset the Bush administration feared that its invasion of Iraq would not generate sufficient public support. The Jessica Lynch story emphasized the courage of a US woman soldier against the brutality of her Iraqi captors. The real story, as Lynch herself later told it, showed that the media would simply accept Pentagon lies and print them without checking. Lynch joined the military not to avenge 9/11 or serve her country against the terrorists, but because she "couldn't get a job at Wal-Mart."

A similar story occurred related to the death of former professional football star Pat Tillman, who reportedly died in Afghanistan fighting Taliban black hats. Tillman had given up his lucrative career as an athlete to fight terror. The real story surfaced more than a year after the Pentagon's phony one drenched the public in patriotic sentiment. "Friendly fire" had caused Tillman's death and the military had covered it up.

So tame had the media become that it accepted the military's dictate of "embedding" journalists with military units. As Israeli journalist Uri Avnery astutely observed, such behavior leads quickly to "presstitution." Reporters accept limits that the Pentagon imposes in order to see the war "from the inside." Unfortunately, what inside-the-military reporters see does not reflect what the public needs to know. To understand Iraq, serious readers must go to the foreign press, or the internet, for their information and analysis.

Indeed, the major newspapers and networks cannot be trusted even to check on statements that they could easily show to be false. For example, in 2002 every major news agency falsely reported that in 1998 Saddam had kicked the weapons inspection team out of Iraq despite the fact that their own news organs had reported differently.

The *New York Times* on 18 December 1998 wrote of "Mr. Butler's quick withdrawal from Iraq on Wednesday of all his inspectors and those of the International Atomic Energy Agency, which monitors Iraqi nuclear programs, without Security Council permission."

Yet, on 3 August 2002 a *Times* editorial declared that "America's goal should be to ensure that Iraq is disarmed of all unconventional weapons.... To thwart this goal, Baghdad expelled United Nations arms inspectors four years ago."

The *Washington Post* reported on 18 December 1998 that "Butler ordered his inspectors to evacuate Baghdad, in anticipation of a military attack, on Tuesday night—at a time when most members of the Security Council had yet to receive his report."

But on 4 August 2002, a *Post* editorial had the following sentence. "Since 1998, when U.N. inspectors were expelled, Iraq has almost certainly been working to build more chemical and biological weapons."

Even the venerable Daniel Schorr of NPR declared on 3 August 2002 that if Saddam "has secret weapons, he's had four years since he kicked out the inspectors to hide all of them." Schorr could have googled "UN Weapons inspector Iraq 1998" and within seconds read that fellow NPR reporter Bob Edwards had reported on 16 December 1998 that "The United Nations once again has ordered its weapons inspectors out of Iraq. Today's evacuation follows a new warning from chief weapons inspector Richard Butler accusing Iraq of once again failing to cooperate with the inspectors. The United States and Britain repeatedly have warned that Iraq's failure to cooperate with the inspectors could lead to air strikes."[2]

In 2002, whether reporters acted out of duplicity or laziness, they nevertheless added anti-Saddam fuel to Bush's invade-Iraq fire by making it appear as if Saddam had removed the weapons inspectors precisely in order to develop WMDs. Citizens without access to independent sources of information would have had no reason to doubt the accuracy of such information and thus would have been more inclined to believe Bush's argument for preemptive war.

Politics and Shopping—The Media's Role

As fewer multinational giants have grabbed control of the media over the last decades, the media's priorities have shifted accordingly, turning readers and viewers away from concerns of politics and toward shopping. Mass media distracts the citizens by distorting their priorities—sending them an average of 3,600 messages a day urging them to deal with their personal inadequacies through shopping. The gist of this message barrage: "you, the consumer—not the citizen—are inadequate in looks, dress, type of car driven, underarm deodorant used, and every other way. But you can improve your too fat, too thin, too young, too old problems by buying products for every space in your body, mind, and external life."

If news of the larger world still holds any attraction, then it lies with diverting the public's interest from war in Iraq, a frozen domestic budget, and no taxes for the rich to the pathetic figure of Michael Jackson, whose child molestation trial made more TV, radio, and newspaper "top stories" than the Iraq war.

Look at TV, listen to radio, read the major newspapers—one easily concludes that Viacom, Disney, Sony, Time Warner, and the few other transnational media goliaths have no interest in a world of citizens. They focus on a world of consumers who ideally would have no interest in politics.

Corporate media owners have good reasons to validate the state's authority. The US government works actively for them in national and international fora, like the WTO, to "deregulate" media, cut corporate taxes, make media mergers easier, and open media markets elsewhere. These mammoth business entities would be biting the hand that feeds them if they called into question the policies of a government whose help and facilities they depend on for their own profitable reproduction. It is unthinkable that such a media could act as a protector of the citizenry.

Instead, it validates illegal state policies—like invading and occupying Iraq—and distracts readers, listeners, and viewers by prodding them to focus on their personal acquisitive proclivities and not affairs of the society.

Media Wrongs against Humanity

David Miller

The preeminent wrongs against the citizens of the coalition are
  —misreporting the "threat" from Iraq (links with al-Qaeda, existence of WMD, the motives for the war);
  —misreporting the occupation;
  —marginalizing, ignoring, and undermining dissent;
  —contributing to the creation of a climate of fear.

The conduct and role of the media in the case of Iraq must be understood in terms of the underlying interests and policies of both the media institutions themselves and of the US and UK governments in relation to information. It is important to understand the philosophy, administration, and practice of the propaganda apparatus in order to understand how the media have performed. My evidence therefore focuses first on the philosophy of information control, then on the apparatus and administration of propaganda, before examining its effects on media performance.

The Philosophy of Information Control

The philosophy of information control is based on a concept called "information dominance." This basically means that information is a weapon of war and that it must be used as such. Information is not, in this model, something which can be used to evaluate how the world works in order to make decisions. Rather it is simply an aid or obstacle to information dominance. Information therefore comes in two types, friendly and unfriendly. The former is to be promoted and the latter destroyed or contained. Thus the media are not there to be manipulated or influenced but to be used or neutralized.

This is a new concept in official thinking, which collapses distinctions between the military and nonmilitary and between information and weaponry. The consequences of this for the use of media in war are profound and relate strongly to the question before the tribunal.[1]

The Apparatus of Propaganda

In keeping with information dominance, the propaganda apparatus used by the US and UK has undergone comprehensive overhaul since 9/11. The apparatus is now globally coordinated and integrated across departments internally in the US and UK. This has three consequences of note. First, that the campaign to convince the world that Iraq was a threat was coordinated and planned. Second, that the propaganda operation in Iraq was coordinated and planned (during the invasion and then during the occupation), and third and most importantly, that the internal propaganda apparatus in the US and UK which deals with the domestic "terrorist threat" is also coordinated and integrated. In other words we can talk about the creation and moderation of a climate of fear, rather than discussing a governmental apparatus reacting, perhaps clumsily, to genuine threats.[2]

The Incorporation of the Media into the Propaganda Apparatus
The process of incorporation is the effect of the philosophy outlined above, which have two basic techniques of control. These are the carrot for "friendly" media and the stick for "unfriendly" media. The stick involves threats, the use of violence and intimidation, and a refusal to treat journalists as a separate category of noncombatants. This meant that in certain circumstances journalists were regarded either as "legitimate" targets or were regarded as putting themselves in harm's way. This was the case with both the US and UK governments. The stick has identifiable outcomes in intimidated, beaten, and dead journalists. But the more important outcome is the message that it sends to other journalists to keep away from independent or "unfriendly" reporting. This is where the carrot comes into play. This tries to build up "friendly" information by allowing access in exchange for control and in socializing journalists to identify with the military. This was known as "embedding" and was spectacularly successful in securing positive (distorted) coverage. The philosophy of information control run by the US and UK reduces all information to an instrument of war and sees no effective difference between "enemy" information systems and neutral information systems (independent media).

The Lies
The lies and disinformation on Iraq were extensive and continue today. There are so many lies that it is not possible to give more than a modest set of key examples of the deceptions.

The big lies were that Iraq posed a threat to the West; that Iraq had chemical or biological weapons or active weapons programs; that it had a nuclear program; that there was some sort of link between al-Qaeda or other Islamist groups and the Iraqi regime; that the attack on Iraq would be simple and over quickly; and that the rationale for the attack was to restore democracy.

To cultivate these lies a large number of other specific lies were told. These included presentation and documentation produced by both the US and UK governments which were riddled with falsehoods and deceptions. There is a great deal of evidence now in the public domain about these lies and the way in which they were taken up and amplified by the mainstream media.[3]

The Results in Media Performance

The mainstream news media in the US and UK were overwhelmingly complicit in promoting the credibility of official sources and intelligence "information" on the alleged threat posed by Iraq. The deception perpetrated by the US and UK governments (and to a significant extent also the Spanish, Australian, and other governments) was only sporadically exposed and properly reported on. In the US, alternative views almost never made the mainstream. In the UK, while there is some more room for dissent, even skeptical journalists on antiwar papers were unable to openly express their skepticism. All the studies conducted on the mainstream media show similar patterns. To highlight just two: The Cardiff University study showed that "wartime coverage was generally sympathetic to the government's case."[4] It also found that the minority viewing channels such as Channel Four were able to show more skeptical reports than were the mainstream mass channels such as the main BBC reports.[5] The study in the US by FAIR showed that "Nearly two thirds of all sources, 64 percent, were pro-war, while 71 percent of US guests favored the war. Anti-war voices were 10 percent of all sources, but just 6 percent of non-Iraqi sources and 3 percent of US sources. Thus viewers were more than six times as likely to see a pro-war source as one who was anti-war; with US guests alone, the ratio increases to 25 to 1."[6]

Complicity in Presenting the Claims to Legality of the Invasion, and Denouncing Counter-claims

The evidence presented above in relation to the dominance of official sources is by itself evidence that official lines dominate news.

Complicity in Promoting (and the Failure to Expose) the False Credibility of the Sources and Veracity of "Intelligence" on the Claimed Threat Posed by Iraq

The overwhelming bulk of the mainstream media (including the "liberal" and "left" mainstream press) gave a false credibility to the notion that Iraq posed a threat to the West. Intelligence information was accepted as legitimate and truthful, often without attribution.

It is worth concentrating on the television news as this is the main source for most people on world events.

UK Television

Weapons of Mass Destruction (WMD): During the period of the invasion (20 March–9 April 2003), 91 percent of the reports examined contained references to WMD that suggested that Iraq had or could have had such weapons, while only 15 percent contained references which raised doubts about their existence or possible use. We might remember that this was in a period where it was known that Iraq could not have had any serious WMD.

In the run-up to the invasion, the "legitimation phase," there was some dissent in television coverage. This was, as John Theobald puts it, a "reflection" of the "deep cracks in elite solidarity" which were a result in part of the "crudity of US government positions but also in part a result of the mounting popular opposition to the attack on Iraq." These factors both fed through and were reflected in mainstream media output. "On these quite rare occasions, normally hidden information seeps out through the fissures."[7] But once the invasion was underway, the elite fissures closed up at least temporarily. This was most obviously notable in the unity of the propaganda message that we must back the troops now that they are in battle. This new phase in the propaganda was extremely successful in swinging both the mainstream media behind the war and minimizing dissent. This was candidly recognized by the head of BBC news, Richard Sambrook. There was little journalistic cross-examination during Blair's press conferences after the invasion started "partly because there is a degree of political consensus within Westminster, with the Conservatives supporting the Government policy on the war and the Liberal Democrats, whilst opposed to the war, supporting the UK forces." Press conferences are covered not to challenge ministers, but to "find out the latest information." Of course, as everyone else recognizes, press conferences are set piece spin sessions. This indicates the poverty of the BBC approach to division in the country: If it is not happening at Westminster, it is not happening. On ITV, the main alternative channel to the BBC, the political editor Nick Robinson acknowledges "it was my job to report what those in power were doing or thinking... That is all someone in my sort of job can do."

The almost complete failure to properly question the fabrications in late 2002 to March 2003 is well documented.

This highlights the twin problems of TV news. First, the tendency to take the official line at face value even in the face of overwhelming evidence to the contrary. Second, the seeming inability even to attribute official statements, so that they are reported not as the view of a particular official or government, but simply as facts. Such mistakes on attribution are very rarely made in relation to the "other side."

The structural over-accessing of official voices is acknowledged in all the academic research produced on Iraq; both studies showed that official sources dominated television.[8]

	Four UK channels %	BBC	ITN
UK/US gov't & military	46	58	66
Official Iraqi sources	30	10	9
Other media	5	-	-
Iraqi citizens	7	17	12
Others, e.g., Red Cross	12	24	22

This table shows overwhelming bias toward official sources. Note also the fact that antiwar voices do not even merit a separate category in either of these studies. But the bias is understated by these figures. As one study suggests: "many claims that came from military sources were unattributed. So, for example, when we analysed the television coverage of four stories that came from military sources—all of which turned out to be unfounded—we found that nearly half the claims made were unattributed."[9]

US Television

All the evidence of studies of the US mainstream media show that the television and elite press very largely repeated and amplified the notion of a threat from Iraq, in particular the notion that Iraq posed a threat—that it possessed WMD; that it was implicated in 9/11; and that the only way to counter this threat was military invasion.

The Coverage of Colin Powell's Presentation to the UN[10]

The lack of skepticism is echoed by the very narrow range of views allowed onto television in the US.

> "If News From Iraq Is Bad, It's Coming From US Officials: Stories Bush Missed"
>
> —*Extra!* January/February 2004, by Jon Whiten

> Despite criticism of the media by the Bush administration and its allies, US TV news coverage of the Iraq situation continues to be dominated by government and military officials, according to a new study by FAIR. The few critics of military operations that find themselves on the nightly news broadcasts rarely question the war as a whole. Nightly network news reports largely focus on tactics and individual battles, with more substantial and often troubling issues surrounding the war, such as civilian casualties, rarely being reported.
>
> The study looked at 319 on-camera sources appearing in stories about Iraq on the nightly network newscasts—ABC World News Tonight, CBS Evening News and NBC Nightly News—in the month of October 2003. Sources were coded by name, occupation, nationality, topic and network.
>
> Out of 319 sources, 244 (76 percent) were current or former government or military officials. Of these, 225 were from the United States, and a further nine were from the U.S.-appointed Iraqi Governing Council.[11]

Complicity in Promoting, and the Failure to Expose, the Myth of Progress on, and the Necessity of, the Ongoing Occupation

The vast gap between what is reported from the ground in Iraq and what appears in the mainstream media in the US and UK on the occupation and its effects is apparent from evidence cited above on the lack of reporting of credible scientific or UN reports. The coverage of the election as "free and democratic" is merely the latest example.

Can it be said that the media (by reference to identified media action) is culpable of actively silencing and discrediting dissenting voices and for failing to adequately report on the full national costs and consequences of the invasion and occupation of Iraq i.e., censorship in and by the media?

It is clear that dissent was actively silenced by both US and UK media. The over-concentration on official sources on both sides of the Atlantic ensured the effective marginalizing of antiwar voices. This was especially the case after the invasion began (as noted above). The lack of attention to dissenting voices was apparent across the mainstream and corporate media.

Covering Dissent in the UN

Scott Ritter, former chief UNSCOM weapons inspector, who was an inspector in Iraq between 1991 and 1998, claims that Iraq was "fundamentally disarmed" of 90–95 percent of its WMDs by December 1998. He also claims that inspections were deliberately sabotaged by US officials in 1998 precisely *because* the Iraqis were rapidly approaching 100 percent compliance—so removing justification for continued sanctions and control of Iraq. In December 1998, Ritter said: "What [head of UNSCOM] Richard Butler did last week with the inspections was a set-up. This was designed to generate a conflict that would justify a bombing."[12]

Last year, Richard Sambrook, then BBC's director of news, told us that Ritter had been interviewed just twice: on 29 September 2002, for *Breakfast with Frost*, and on 1 March 2003, for BBC News 24. *Newsnight* editor Peter Barron told us that *Newsnight* had interviewed Scott Ritter twice on the WMD issue before the war: on 3 August 2000 and 21 August 2002.

A BBC news online search for 1 January 2002—31 December 2002 recorded the following mentions:

George Bush Iraq, 1,022
Tony Blair Iraq, 651
Donald Rumsfeld Iraq, 164
Dick Cheney Iraq, 102

Richard Perle Iraq, 6
George Galloway Iraq, 42
Tony Benn Iraq, 14
Noam Chomsky Iraq, 1
Denis Halliday Iraq, 0
(Source: Media Lens)
Coverage of the World Tribunal on Iraq and its independent websites in *Guardian* 2003 to 10 February 2005: Zero. Not a single mention.

Coverage of Civilian Casualties

According to a two-month survey carried out by an Iraqi nongovernmental organization, the People's Kifah, comprising hundreds of activists and academics, more than 37,000 Iraqi civilians were killed between the start of the US-led invasion in March 2003 and October 2003.[13] We searched in vain for coverage of this important survey in news reports by ITN, the BBC, the *Guardian*, the *Independent, Financial Times,* and others. On 30 August 2004, we conducted an online news search, using the extensive Lexis–Nexis database, and were able to find only two mentions in the UK press: one, a brief account in the *Western Mail,* a Cardiff-based newspaper, on 26 August. The only other mention was a passing reference in a *Guardian* comment piece by activist Tariq Ali.[14]

—The *Lancet* study (100,000 deaths)[15]

—UNICEF report on Iraq October 2004[16]

—Depleted uranium[17]

—Silencing dissent in the US[18]

—The "D" notice committee: The final example considered here is the issuing of a "D" or "defense" notice in autumn 2004 by the defense, press and broadcasting committee.[19]

The example of the "D" notice indicates the fundamental orientation of British television journalism toward the powerful. This echoes the famous statement that the first director general of the BBC confided to his diary in the midst of the 1926 general strike. The cabinet had decided not to take over the BBC. Reith noted that the decision was really a "negative one": because "they know they can trust us not to be really impartial." Since that time UK news has very rarely departed from the assumptions implicit in that judgment.

The Media "Managing" News, Truth, through the Structures and Workings of Embedded Reporting

The structures of embedding are based on the principles of "information dominance," in which "friendly" information is integrated into the command and control structures of the military. (See Appendix 1 to this chapter, "Embed with the Military.")

The embedding process was regarded as a great success by the US and UK governments and has already been copied elsewhere. Some critics have alleged that the embeds were no more enculturated than other journalists.[20] This view is based on a mis-comparison of the embeds' reporting with that of news anchors.

Media Silence on Intimidation/Violence against Journalists as Systematic Practice

The silence on intimidation was not total. The deaths of journalists were reported. The notion that the attacks on journalists were either a systematic practice or the result of the information dominance approach to "unfriendly" information was almost entirely absent from the mainstream media. It was certainly not reported on the television news.

Media Failure to Inform the Citizenry of the Full Implications of the Domestic Political Consequences of the "War on Terror"

On the home front meanwhile, the propaganda campaign to talk up the "terrorist threat" has continued apace. The alleged threat from "Islamic terrorists" or al-Qaeda is constantly discussed by the US and UK governments. Indeed both governments have created new government departments and new propaganda agencies to deal with this threat. In many ways the threat has replaced the "Soviet threat" as the key organizing ideology of the powers that be. This has meant new laws which curtail civil liberties and a large number of high-profile arrests amid media stories of bomb plots, chemical attacks, and al-Qaeda cells. In neither the US nor the UK have any more than a handful of convictions been secured. Those that have been have not been for "terrorism." In other words, the creation of a climate of fear has been a deliberate tactic based on unreliable information and straightforward disinformation. The UK government created a new apparatus to coordinate this effort.[21]

In the US, the same sorts of processes applied. Adam Curtis has shown that the neoconservatives in the White House have a long record of using the media in their propaganda campaigns to close the gap between the reality of threats and the threats predicted by their ideology and interests.[22]

Influencing Public Opinion

The evidence on media performance is supplemented by evidence on public opinion. This shows important differences between the US and UK opinion which in part reflect differences in reporting. But they also reflect differences in the strength of the antiwar movement. For example, while US and UK opinion routinely prefers spending on health and education over the military, and while more people favor cutting military expenditure than raising it, there was also a clear pattern of majority support for the invasion of Iraq in the US. This was clearly built on the successful use of propaganda by the US administration. The study by PIPA showed not only that many US citizens had believed the disinformation about WMD and the link to al-Qaeda, but that the extent of misperceptions were related to support for the invasion. Furthermore, the PIPA study showed that viewers of cheerleading stations like Fox were more likely to be misled than viewers of less biased stations such as NPR/PBS.[23] In the UK, public opinion was hostile to war in the run-up to the invasion. This appeared to change after the invasion was launched. The research evidence suggests that this change was not an acceptance of the need for war, but rather a pragmatic support for the UK forces while engaged in action.[24]

But, as this study concludes, "it seems likely that, in Britain at least, the coverage of the war itself played a part in persuading a majority to support it."[25] Furthermore, the fact that some sections of the population apparently signed up to the notion of supporting the troops is itself not an ideologically neutral formulation. In fact, it mirrors the rapid ideological closure around the attack once it had started. This encompassed the UK government, the official opposition, the more critical Liberal Democrats, and notably (as indicated above) the mainstream media, particularly television news (the main source of information on international affairs for most people in the UK).

Enabling Elite Action and Coherence of Coalition

But perhaps the most significant effect of the disinformation and the way it was amplified by the media and convinced some sections of the public is the way it legitimized elite actions and buttressed the coherence of the coalition for war. This does indicate the most significant problem of the role of the media: its function as an elite sounding board and legitimator.[26]

To conclude, overall, the media are culpable for subverting the democratic rights to information and truth and for misinforming the public, convincing some of the people, some of the time of the need for war.

Appendix 1: Embed with the Military

Embedded journalists are the greatest PR coup of this war. Dreamt up by the Pentagon and Donald Rumsfeld, the "embeds," as they are now routinely described, are almost completely controlled by the military. Embeds, as is now well known, agree to give up most of their autonomy in exchange for access to the fighting on military terms. They also gain the advantage of the use of facilities such as transport and accommodation. Reporters who are not embedded are pointedly denied such facilities. Most importantly, embeds are afforded protection from physical harm by the military. So far in this war the main danger for journalists has come from the Western military. So the protection on offer is more of a threat than a reassurance for independent reporters.

Each embedded reporter has to sign a contract with the military and is governed by a 50-point plan issued by the Pentagon detailing what they can and cannot report. The list of what they can report is significantly shorter than the list of what they cannot.

According to reports, there are 903 embedded reporters, including 136 with UK forces. There are none embedded with the small contingents of other nations, such as the Australian military. Only 20 percent of reporters embedded with the US are from outside the US, and 128 of those embedded with UK forces are from the UK. Even countries with military involvement such as Australia have very little access to the embedding system, with only two reporters embedded with US forces. French journalists in particular have complained about being excluded. The Anglo-American dominance of the reporters is no accident, but a key part of the strategy.

The PR genius of the embed system is that it does allow unprecedented access to the fighting and, also, unprecedented identification by the reporters with the military. British Minister of Defense Geoff Hoon has claimed: "I think the coverage… is more graphic, more real, than any other coverage we have ever seen of a conflict in our history. For the first time it is possible with technology for journalists to report in real time on events in the battlefield." It is certainly true to say that it is new to see footage of war so up-close, but it is a key part of the propaganda war to claim that this makes it "real." In fact, the aim of the embedding system is to control what is reported by encouraging journalists to identify with their units. To eat and drink together, to risk danger, and to share the same values. Ted Koppel of US network ABC told the *Washington Post* that his feelings toward the soldiers were "very, very warm."

This identification with the soldiers works to ensure self-censorship [and] is generally effective. Phillip Rochot is a respected reporter for France 2, currently working independently in Iraq, says, "Embedded journalists do a fair amount of voluntary self-censorship, controlling what they say. In any case their views are closely aligned with the Anglo-American position. They are soldiers of information, marching with the troops and the political direction of their country. They won't say anything wrong, they feel duty-bound to defend the Anglo-American cause in this war." Christina Lamb of the London *Times* agrees that embedded journalists are "giving a more positive side, because they're with the troops… and they're not out in the streets or out in the countryside seeing what's actually happening there." Hoon has himself acknowledged the effect of this reporting in appearing to reduce opposition to the war in the first days: "The imagery they broadcast is at least partially responsible for the public's change of mood."

But toward the end of the first week of the war, US and UK officials started to mutter about too much access and claimed that it was the pressure of 24-hour coverage which was circulating misinformation. This is a straightforward propaganda maneuver designed to distract attention from the fact that the false stories have all been authorized by military command structures and also to warn journalists not to get out of line. The proof that this is propaganda is that they are not proposing to change the embed system, which has served them very well.

Some embedded reporters fell over themselves to explain that they only reported what the military allow them to. Late at night with very few people watching, Richard Gaisford, an embedded BBC reporter, said, "If we ran everything that we heard in the camp then certainly there would be a lot of misinformation going around. We have to check each story we have with them. And if they're not sure at the immediate level above us— that's the captain who's our media liaison officer—he will check with the colonel who is obviously above him and then they will check with brigade headquarters as well."

This open acknowledgement of the system of control is rare and was provoked by official criticism. It illustrates the tight censorship imposed by the military but not acknowledged in US or UK reporting. News bulletins in the UK are full of warnings about Iraqi "monitoring" and "restrictions" on movement in reports from Baghdad. The closest that they get to this on the UK/US side is to note that journalists cannot report on where they are and other security details. In fact, the embed controls are, if anything, stricter than the system imposed by the Iraqi regime.

Gaisford's comment is also interesting for the acknowledgment it makes that reporters are actually fully integrated into military command structures. This complements the identification revealed by phrases such as "we" and "our" in reports of military action. Reference to the "level above" as the press officer does indicate a fundamental subordination to military propaganda needs. But this is hardly surprising since the contract that reporters sign explicitly requires reporters to "follow the direction and orders of the Government" and prohibits them from suing for injury or death even where this "is caused or contributed to" by the military.

The unprecedented access is the carrot, but the stick is always on hand. Two embedded journalists who have allegedly strayed over the line have been expelled, and during the second weekend of the war "many embedded reporters found their satellite phones blocked for unexplained reasons." Moreover—and much less discussed in the global media, with the military a rung above the journalists' in the command hierarchy— some embeds are, according to Christian Lowe of US military magazine *Army Times*, being "hounded by military public affairs officers who follow their every move and look over their shoulders as they interview aviators, sailors, and maintainers for their stories."

Each military division in the Gulf has 40 to 60 embedded journalists, and between five and six public affairs officers "behind the scenes." They report up to the Coalition Press Information Center (CPIC) in Kuwait and the $1 million press center at CentCom in Doha.

From there the message is coordinated by the Office of Global Communications in the White House in consort with Alastair Campbell, Blair's top spin doctor in Downing Street. The fanciful notion that the misinformation of the first weeks of the campaign were due to journalists having conversations with "a squaddie who's shining his boots," as a British Minister of Defense official spun it, is itself a key part of the propaganda war. All of the myriad misinformation coming out of Iraq in the first two weeks has been fed out by the US/UK global media operation. As one reporter in Doha noted, "At General Tommy Franks's headquarters, it is easy to work out whether the day's news is good or bad. When there are positive developments, press officers prowl the corridors of the press center dispensing upbeat reports from pre-prepared scripts, declaring Iraqi towns have been liberated and that humanitarian aid is about to be delivered. Yet if American and British troops have suffered any sort of battlefield reverse, the spin doctors retreat into their officers at press centre and await instructions from London and Washington."

The Threat to Independent Reporting
If the embeds have been an opportunity, the Pentagon and British military have seen independent journalists as a threat. There have been a stream of reports of hostility, threats, and violence against independent reporters. UNESCO, the International Federation of Journalists, Reporters sans Frontières, and the British National Union of Journalists have all condemned these threats.

Some have been subtle and others less so. On the ground and away from the cameras, the threats are pointed and can include violence, as several journalists have already found out. For example, two Israeli and two Portuguese journalists were detained and deported by US troops. According to one of the Israeli journalists, Dan Scemama, the "four were denied food and water for extended periods, forced to stand in a cold tent in silence for an entire night, and said one of the Portuguese journalists was beaten by five US soldiers."

Iraqi TV facilities have been targeted in Baghdad as part of what British Defense Secretary Geoff Hoon justified as Iraqi "command and control structures."

Also, independent broadcasters such as Aljazeera have seen their hotel in Basra attacked at dawn on 1 April 2003. The Basra Sheraton was hit by two bombs which did not explode.

The subtle threats include those made by British Ministers, such as Defense Secretary Geoff Hoon: "one of the reasons for having journalists [embedded] is to prevent precisely the kind of tragedy that occurred to an ITN crew very recently when a well-known, hard working, courageous journalist was killed essentially because he was not part of a military organization. Because he was trying to get a story. And in those circumstances we can't look after all those journalists on this kind of fast moving battlefield. So having journalists have the protection, in fact, of our armed forces is both good for journalism, [and] it's also very good for people watching."

Here, Hoon takes on all the charm and authority of a Mafia boss explaining the benefits of a protection racket. The message is clear: stay embedded and report what you are told or face the consequences.

The Moral Responsibility of War Journalism

Mete Çubukçu

During the last couple of years, there has been an argument among journalists that reporters and journalists should not serve as witnesses in any sort of tribunal. When a journalist becomes a witness he might lose his job for being one-sided and non-objective.

This discussion started when journalists were invited to testify in the Hague after the Bosnian war, and has continued concerning the journalists who testified after the genocide in Rwanda.

What is the mission of the journalist?

Should he pass on the things he has witnessed to readers and viewers? Should he expose to viewers the human-rights violations he has personally seen? Perhaps the journalist should be called a messenger, if we think that the duty of the journalist is no more than that. However, at this point the journalist's duty is not only to deliver the news as responsibly as he can, but also to recognize that he has a responsibility to humanity and to the rest of the world.

I don't think journalists are any different from regular human beings.

For me it is very important to do my job as a journalist and to reflect upon what I see and what I witness, and eventually to document it for humanity. For that reason I am here in front of you.

Am I objective? *Yes.*

Am I impartial? *No.*

I am against any war exactly because I have worked as a war journalist and have witnessed what happens in wars and conflicts.

The journalist cannot be on the side of crimes or promote war. Journalists should keep the peace and promote justice between the people of world; they should not make any effort to engage in crimes or promote hatred between people.

From that point of view, the attack and occupation of Iraq are very important dates for me, since I had lived and reported from Iraq before the occupation and later during the war. After what I have seen, I know that the invasion and occupation should not be forgotten from or ignored by history.

I remember we were riding into Baghdad on 17 March 2003, three-and-a-half days after the American bombardment started. I saw that hundreds of journalists were fleeing from Baghdad along with the Iraqi people. Hundreds of these same journalists had been waiting for the war to start. However, they left Iraq for reasons of personal security or because their establishments told them to leave because, hours before the huge bombardment started, the American government had warned all the aid organizations and establishments to leave Iraq.

What their flight from Iraq meant is this: they, the journalists, are not in any way responsible for what could happen!

It could, of course, be understandable to evacuate the aid organizations and foreigners, but it is not understandable to evacuate journalists.

This exodus of the journalists had a single meaning: the US did not want it to be known what was going on in Baghdad, which very soon would be made into hell. The presence of many journalists meant a lot of news. This news could easily stain the "clean" war promised by the US. Naturally, lots of journalists yielded to this threat. But it was not the journalists who were originally responsible, but the directives which enforced them to go. However, according to the Geneva Conventions, journalists, as well as civilians and soldiers captured in war, are exempt from battle and are considered to be out of the war as much as possible. But it is naive to expect the US to abide by the Geneva Conventions when it ignored even UN resolutions. And the American bombardment turned out to be one of the most destructive and deadliest attacks the world has seen in recent years.

In the first days of the war, a few journalists, no more than a hundred, were able to report the early attacks. The US government did not want anyone anywhere to understand the destruction of the war by seeing the death and the corpses torn into pieces.

The occupying government, which opted to report the war only through their "own" journalists, started to use "embedded" journalists, a strategy which marks a turning point in the history of journalism. This institution is still at work today. For this reason, we were not able to know what was going on during the first days of the war, when the forces of the occupation were proceeding; the massacre in Falluja, the suffering of the Iraqi people, the collapse of a country and a civilization were not accessible in the news.

As a journalist who has been in Iraq, I can say that Iraq has been totally destroyed. Saddam Hussein's dictatorship has been replaced by a destroyed country abandoned to chaos. As a result of the occupation, the Iraqi people have found themselves in a situation where they cannot even satisfy their most fundamental needs. The people have to start every single day with fear of death as a result of the chaos triggered by the occupation. And we, the journalists, have turned into machines, whose single purpose is to count the number of people dying in Iraq. Hence, the occupation of Iraq has entered into the checklist of ordinary news. Just as in Palestine, the destruction in Iraq has been "normalized."

The most horrible nightmare for an occupying force is not to be able to wander about freely on the streets of the occupied country, to feel the fear of death every single moment. This brutalizes the occupying force even more.

I recall that in the first days of the occupation we would put up our hands and put down our cameras because behaving otherwise could mean death. This also demonstrated their fear of us. When I talked with the American soldiers, who had different ethnicities and many of whom were waiting for citizenship, their bemusement and their fear were obvious from their faces. They would say they came to liberate Iraq. But a soldier with whom I talked in Baghdad last year swore against Bush and said that he wanted to be swimming in Florida.

This fear of theirs brutalized them even more. In the August of 2003, the place I was told was the custody section in the American headquarters was as big as a hencoop and the temperature was 50 degrees Celsius (122 degrees Fahrenheit).

The pretext of the American soldiers who opened fire on the Palestine Hotel, or of those who killed a cameraman in front of Abu Ghraib prison, was that they thought the cameras were bazookas. The meaning of these attacks, which did not have any legal justification, was obvious: They—the US—did not want any journalists in Iraq. To be more precise, they did not want any images coming out of Iraq because the occupation required the humiliation of Iraqis on the streets and at the checkpoints. It means that houses are raided at night and men are dishonored in front of children and women. A shopkeeper in Falluja told us that "their house is raided almost every day and their doors are smashed."

The soldiers were in fear even in the open fields and on the streets. For instance, in front of Abu Ghraib a sign says, "It is permitted to open fire on those who take pictures here." We would later understand what such a mentality, which did not even allow taking pictures in front of the prison, would do inside the prison. In July 2004, I thought of how the American soldier who had put his gun against the forehead of a cameraman sitting beside me was himself full of fear, even though he could simply kill us as we sat there.

It goes without saying how the life of the Iraqi people has turned into hell while we were experiencing all this. The occupation cannot even enable the most simple, normal course of daily life. The Iraqi people have had to drink the filthy waters of the Tigris River, which has turned into garbage because of the absence of the water-refinery plants the occupation has demolished. The Iraqi people have been sentenced to live without electricity.

It is known that hundreds of women are abducted and raped in the chaotic country under occupation. The women demonstrating and blaming the occupation at Firdeus square in Baghdad were also blaming us. They were saying "Report these events, let them hear our voices!"

This does not only hold true for the occupation of Iraq but also for the things which preceded and which will follow it. Some of the American TV companies claimed that "they did not telecast the bloody scenes because the spectators would be disturbed" during the Iraqi war. But isn't war something disturbing? Was there ever a clean war?

The task of a correspondent is to reflect the true face, the disturbing side of the war. The people should face those bloody scenes so that they can be offended.

And on the roads there was always the fear of being killed, of being fired on at any moment. Because they did fire. The mercenaries with black sunglasses and automatic guns were the nightmare of the people in Baghdad. No one, including us, dared to get close to them. They would shoot people simply because of one small movement. They were not responsible for what they were doing either.

Some might say that journalism is risky in war or other dangerous regions and you have to put up with this.

Yes, it is true. But it was the occupation's deliberate attitude which did not respect the right to life of the journalists in Iraq, and which did not want the things which were happening to be known.

This was especially true in the final period after the bomb attacks, when journalists were not let close to the scene of the attack. Not far back in the past, in July last year, there were hundreds of bazooka and mortar attacks right up to the Green Line, which the Americans used to border themselves almost everyday at night. It was these attacks which broke the silence of Baghdad at night, but there was no news coming out. Journalists were not allowed to report on such events.

Some of the journalists in Iraq today are voluntary "embedded," if not official ones, which means that their understanding of journalism is "embedded." Such journalism should be allowed, but is only of value when free journalism is also made possible.

War or crisis journalism is not only writing down the death and casualty toll. Nor is it an apparatus for reflecting official statements. The forces of the occupation opt to reflect the occupation differently by establishing the institution of embedded journalism. In October 2003 in the News Xchange convention in Budapest, the American and English soldiers stated that the "application of embedded journalism has been very positive" and that they will further establish this institution. If the soldiers are content with this institution, it is obvious that the journalists are doing something wrong.

Where can you get the news, except from the journalists working behind the American soldiers today in Falluja? What are the dimensions of the massacre?

The subject of many of the Pulitzer Prize–winning photographs this year was the American soldier. These may be good pictures, but few show the true face of the occupation. This is because there is no longer free journalism in Iraq.

Iraq has become one of the most dangerous territories for journalists because the occupation has softened journalists through threats, has caused chaos, and also because Iraqi groups have targeted journalists. However, responsibility for all this lies with the occupying forces who created these conditions.

War journalism is journalism only insofar as it shows the truth of war. Journalists cannot talk of being objective in the Iraqi war because the Iraqi war is not an objective, fair war. The Iraqi people who suffered under the dictatorship of Saddam Hussein live a similar life in the hell of the occupation. Our, the journalists', real task is to convey what the Iraqi people are going through, not the fake success of the occupying forces.

In the media, it is those journalists who speak on behalf of the occupation, the officials who interfere with the news of journalists in the field, and the occupying forces who prevent the journalists from doing their work, who should be held responsible.

Military occupation is a filthy job. It is our task to show the filth in Iraq. Even if in small numbers, there are people who do this well. The journalist is a human being who does not only act with his/her pen and camera, but also with his/her conscience.

Media Wrongs against Truth and Humanity[1]

Jayan Nayar

I feel real regret that I am unable to be with you in person, unable to have the privilege of being inspired by our gathering as we rise and speak against the violent desires of power. I hope my words may at least be of some useful contribution to this imagination and spirit of a peoples' claim to judgment and action.

I am conscious that we have assumed for ourselves the responsibility of voicing a peoples' demand for justice. We gather and speak here because of failure—the failure of individuals and institutions to uphold the very basic collective promises that have been made by humanity, for humanity. We gather and speak here because we jointly reject the inevitability of such failure. But what must we say? What do we intend to do in order to carry out our responsibilities as a peoples' tribunal in ways which go beyond mere lamentations of power's wrongdoing?

We could repeat what each and every one of us here already believes, and find comfort in such repetitions. We could utter strong words against power, and applaud each other for uttering them. We could make believe that this, our moment as the WTI, by its very happening, represents a dent in power's armor of shamelessness. We could, in our excitement and rejoicing in simply being together, do all these things—necessary as they may be at times simply for the preservation of energy and hope, yet essentially self-deluding; we could do all these things and forget that we in reality stand and speak under contexts of failure, not just of institutions of power, but also of our efforts to imagine and act for a humane humanity. Despite the many ideas for a better world, despite the persistent insistence on a political and economic order governed by truly democratic law, despite the everyday demands that take place throughout the world to eliminate the impunity of power in fulfilling its desires against the social majorities of the world, we are here, again, today. How do we imagine resistance and directions for humane futures now?

I begin with this reflection more as a marker for the importance of the WTI and the challenge I believe we face. I will return to some possible implications later.

First, I address the primary theme assigned to me: the issue of "media accountability."

I am not a media analyst or commentator. Neither am I part of the "alternative media" community. I was simply part of the Rome session of the WTI, a session conceived of and carried out based on an assessment that there was a gap in the series of tribunal sessions planned for the WTI. It was felt that fundamental to any peoples' indictment of the US/UK-led invasion and occupation of Iraq and its consequences for humanity must be an examination of the role played by the institutions of the media. This in itself is nothing new; scathing criticisms of the mainstream, corporate media abound. The question we wished to confront in holding the session was how might we speak about the media with a language that recognized and placed as a matter of priority the human contexts of media voice and silence, to seek a language capable of expressing violation from the perspectives of the violated. We saw this task as essentially invoking a language of a peoples' law. It is from this position that I speak to you now.

What We Know: On the War, Media, and Disinformation

We know that the case for war against Iraq was made by the governments of the so-called coalition under various guises. Against the overwhelming opposition of the membership of the United Nations, and the unprecedented uprising of peoples' antiwar movements globally, it was asserted that what was being undertaken was a noble violence for the common good, and more particularly for the good of the Iraqi people. The same message of good against evil was repeated throughout the subsequent occupation of Iraq, and is still ongoing as the process of purported political transition reveals itself daily as a violent and impoverishing hoax. The message, however, hoax or otherwise, is crucial. At stake are the "authority" and the "legitimacy" of military-political action—of war, occupation, so-called assistance.

It is obvious that governments alone cannot create the ideological universes which we inhabit. The authority and legitimacy prized by those who rule in the name of democracy comes from a perceived congruence of power-populace worldviews, a congruence tied to perceptions of "reality" that invest in power the meanings of language and action that are understood and accepted, if not shared by the populace. It is here that the media has the most critical impact upon the political space.

That the media plays a significant role in constructing the public debate is well known. As such, the media, regarded to be bearers of truth-information, the so-called fourth estate, is taken to represent a crucial component within the democratic process, providing the ideas and knowledge link between the worlds of power and the worlds of citizenry. "Truth-telling," therefore, is intrinsically a social function, for it enables informed understandings of the realities of the world and deliberations on the political choices we may collectively make as we engage in the world. The power to construct social realities is indeed a formidable one. It bears great significance how it is wielded. It entails responsibility and accountability.

How then do we understand media responsibility in times of war?

Standards of responsibility articulated in locations of official authority are not absent in this regard. Some examples will suffice:

Charter of the Nuremberg Tribunal
Article 6.
[…] Leaders, organizers, instigators and accomplices participating in the formulation or execution of a common plan or conspiracy to commit any of the foregoing crimes [crimes against peace, war crimes and crimes against humanity] are responsible for all acts performed by any persons in execution of such plan.

UNESCO International Principles of Professional Ethics in Journalism. Principle III: The Journalist's Social Responsibility
Information in journalism is understood as a social good and not a commodity, which means that that the journalist shares responsibility for the information transmitted and is thus accountable… ultimately to the public at large…

Principle IX: Elimination of War and Other Great Evils Confronting Humanity The ethical commitment to the universal values of humanism calls for the journalist to abstain from any justification for, or incitement to, wars of aggression…

International Federation of Journalists Declaration of Principles on the Conduct of Journalists.

1. Respect for truth and for the right of the public to truth is the first duty of the journalist.…

Yet, the revelations about the lies, falsifications, disinformation, misrepresentations, and silences upon which the call to war against Iraq was based, which accompanied the brutality of occupation, and which directed the politics of "transition" remain ceaseless. You have already been presented with substantive evidence on this. Much of the "mainstream," corporate-controlled media stands implicated. This has been followed by periodic expressions of horror and outrage at the "mistakes," "omissions," inaccuracies, etc. "Apologies" to readers for inadequacies of investigation and failure to reveal competing claims to truth in the run-up to war in Iraq have even been issued. The media appears willing to confront some of the implications of disinformation that served the cause of aggression, and even their own ineptitudes in relation to truth-telling. But without consequence, it would seem, long after the event, and with a voice of professional detachment. It was not sufficient then; it is still not sufficient.

It is worth emphasizing that the recognition thus far of "media failures" has not entailed any acceptance of substantive consequence. Repeating its "failures" with respect to the duty toward the public's right to truth, it assumes that all there is by way of consequence to peddling disinformation is an inconsequential "acknowledgment" of ineptitude. Death, the consequence of the message inciting war, however, deserves greater dignity. "Failure" needs a more clearly articulated denunciation, and "apologies" a more profound content. Above all, there must be recognition that the rights to "expression" notwithstanding, the wrongs against truth which lead to patently avoidable death and the destruction of livelihoods cannot enjoy impunity. When war is the message, the "messenger" must stand accountable. As of now, as we are only too aware, they don't.

The culpability of much of the media, in conjunction with the governments that we accuse, arises from their parroting of government claims and their silence and silencing on the following substantive issues:

—The real reasons for the war, and the implications of the claim to the unilateral right to so-called preventive and preemptive violence without question or challenge.

—The celebration of the coalition's goodness in contrast to the silence on the real human and socioeconomic costs of the war.

—The silence on the prevalent spirit of resistance within Iraq.

—The impact of so-called anti-terror and other security-based laws which create structures and processes of state terror across the global political landscape.

—The human, social, and economic consequences of the spiraling militarization of polities in the name of security.

—The realities of human insecurity, the role of institutions of power in inflicting such conditions of impoverishment and insecurity, and the vitality of peoples' other visions against war and for peace.

In following and pandering to power, rather than serving to scrutinize and call power to account on these issues, those sectors of the media may be seen, perhaps, to have succeeded in serving as the ideological frontline for imperial violence. For this, we must name them complicit, and therefore guilty, in every crime committed as a consequence of the war on Iraq.

But all this said, such denunciation alone is insufficient. We have made these accusations often enough. We perhaps need to better communicate our judgments on these matters to global audiences. But in itself, this is not enough.

On the matter of general media complicity in power's designs, there is nothing stated earlier which we do not already know and have not already been powerfully claiming and demonstrating for decades. Our many alternative media activists have been bombarding the information-truth environment, through every conceivable media mechanism, with the truths not present in much of the dominant corporate media. Yet war, invasion, killing, socio-structural destruction, impunity, all of these proceeded unimpeded and still persist. We have either been insufficient in the volume of our desperate screaming for humanity and sanity, or we have not been screaming in the right way, with the right audiences in mind. I don't know. But I do know that this requires us to stop and think. The Rome session, thought of as a component of a broader WTI movement for ideological resistance and counter-creation, was an attempt to ask these questions, of how we should speak and in what languages, and how we might move for effective peoples' actions to identify and intervene at the locations of power's weaknesses.

My intention here is not to describe the Rome session on media wrongs. Rather it is to elaborate on the thinking upon which it was based, thinking not solely on the issues of the media, but importantly, on the role and potential of the WTI process as a peoples' law doing. I would like to speak now about the idea and potential praxes of peoples' law, on the visualizing of the WTI process along these lines, and its application to our judgments and deliberations on the issue of media wrongs.

The idea of peoples' law, as an opposition to what may be regarded as empire's law, is something more than an articulation of protest. It is not preoccupied with urging power to reform. It is not intended to seek an invitation to speak with the powers who seek to implement empire's projects. Rather, it is about creating a different authority for judgment and action altogether, based on other "word-worlds" of law that are authored by peoples in action. It begins, therefore, with the following repudiations of power's asserted normalities:

—Despite attempts to claim the opposite, there exists no inviolable right on the part of the powerful to govern, rule, order the weak.

—Regardless of the ideological claims being advanced, there exists no unifying or unified civilizational consensus on the naturalness of a corporate-dominated, militaristic imperialism as comprising the common values, truths, visions of human futures that prescribe a universal course for humanity's social evolution.

—Notwithstanding attempts to convince otherwise, there exists no preordained rationale for, eternal truth of, or inevitability regarding forms of socially constructed orders that form the institutions of governance, including the form of "law."

Peoples' law may therefore be understood and viewed as follows:

—As a process of reclaiming histories and futures. An underlying thrust of the conceptual and practical implication of peoples' law is the reclaiming of violated peoples' rights to "truth." An elaboration of peoples' law, therefore, impinges on the very basis upon which ideological constructions of the "world" are maintained and promoted. Much of what can be seen as people's action in this regard has been to re-tell history as a means of reclaiming the power of memory and judgment of violation.

—As a manifestation of reclaiming political action. Running through the entire range of violated peoples' political initiatives in opposition to "power" is a fundamental reclaiming of the "right to act." Peoples' law therefore brings to the fore ideas of political action which counterpose the mainstream conceptualization of democratic politics with the radical reappropriation by peoples' groups to initiate what might be termed "grassroots democratic action" of and for law.

Briefly, the following principles may be stated as describing the foundations of a people-oriented perspective of law-action:

—Judgment: the right/power of peoples to judge the "realities" that are inflicted upon them and to name as violation that which is otherwise proclaimed as normality by the dominant powers.

—Authorship: the right/power of peoples to author/create "law" and to define the structures and nature of social relationships conducive to a life of security and welfare.

—Control: the right/power of peoples to control (and not merely "participate" in) the processes of decision-making and judgment in relation to the matters which affect the daily life conditions of their communities.

—Action: the right/power of peoples to effect the "implementation" of their alternative visions of social relationships in ways that reinforce and celebrate the diversity of humanity, for humanity.

How might this then be translated into a perspective on media wrongs?

We begin with a fundamental claiming of peoples' power to judge the bearers of information for the message that they bear. We claim seriously the duties of truth telling imposed by society upon our agencies of information and journalistic messengers, even more so in times and conditions of grave consequence. Contrary to the perverted demand for media "patriotism," we proclaim that it is indeed a greater burden to truth that is borne by the profession of journalism during times of war.

A peoples' law perspective on media wrongs therefore aims to go beyond simple recognitions and denunciations of media "failure," as if such failures were merely of professional inadequacies. Instead, it seeks to transform the discourse on media responsibility from one of professional ineptitude to one of violations.

The question that follows is: how then do we name violations? First we must seek to bring into focus the different truth contexts and the human constituencies within which the questions of responsibility and culpability arise. What is significant here is that the "responsibility" or "accountability" of media institutions is not spoken of in abstract terms; the specificities of media actions and silences correspond with the specificities of human beings wronged, violated in their specific contexts. The language of violations, as spoken by the violated, is critical. In Rome, we argued for the recognition of three communities of the violated and the naming of wrongs so inflicted.

1. Against the Peoples of Iraq:
—A wrong of aggression: complicity in the waging of an aggressive war and perpetuating a regime of occupation that is widely regarded as guilty of war crimes and crimes against humanity.
—A wrong of silence: neglect of the duty to give privilege and dignity to voices of suffering.

2. Against the Peoples of the "Coalition" (in addition to the above):
—A wrong of deception: complicity, through the validation and dissemination of disinformation, in enabling the fraudulent misappropriation of human and financial resources for war, from social development.
—A wrong of incitement: culpability for inciting an ideological climate of fear, racism, xenophobia, and violence.

3. Against Humanity (in addition to the above):
—A wrong of exclusion: complicity in the marginalization, if not exclusion and non-hearing, of global voices for peace and justice.
—A wrong of usurpation: Complicity in the promotion of corporate-military perspectives on "security" against human-centered analyses and visions of peoples' security, and against the fundamental concerns and priorities of the global population.

The language of violation adopted here does not derive its validity from any formal source of law, nor from any validation by institutions of power. The object is not to plead with power for the recognition of wrongs so named, but to name them regardless, voiced by peoples claiming the power of judgment against the claimed violations. With this language of violation, it is not the case that we set out to claim that "the media" in some abstracted sense is guilty of all of the above. The assignation of guilt is not so much the priority here. Rather it is that such wrongs be named; whether or not a particular media organization, or individual, can be found to be culpable for any of the above is to be determined by examination. But the wrongs, the violations, from a peoples' perspective is to have been given a name. It is in this respect, ideally, an act of self-becoming; our naming of these wrongs enables us to become authors in the creation of norms, rather than recipients of handed-down privileges from power. I say, ideally. Whether we do so, whether such a self-becoming is realized, whether this self-becoming leads to a political consciousness and political action that is sufficiently strong to confront power, all of this is up to us. It is yet to be seen.

It is in this connection that the WTI imagination becomes central. The real significance of a peoples' law doing lies in its ability to generate imaginations for new political action, deriving from the assertion of the power of peoples' voices and judgment. Let me speak a little here about the WTI imagination as I see it and the challenges we face.

I believe that the WTI must adopt for itself three significant functions, corresponding to the original repudiations from which a peoples' law imagination is born:

—The declaratory function: rejecting the claim to "inviolability" by empire's rule/law;

—The deliberative function: reflecting on the realities of empire's rule and their implications for thought/action, thereby challenging the claim to "naturalness" by the empire's prescribed orders; and

—The mandating function: imagining strategic action for continuing peoples' law initiatives to follow from the WTI, thereby challenging the claim to the "inevitability" of empire's rule.

Applied to the issues of media wrongs, the following becomes necessary as required WTI action. The burden here is on you, the panel of the Jury of Conscience, to take up this challenge.

On the Declaratory Function:

The declaratory function requires that violations be named; that the normalcy of power's violence be repudiated and the statement of a peoples' judgment be registered in the public conscience. Naming violations, adopting the peoples' language of inflicted wrongs as discussed earlier, and declaring these wrongs as being legitimately articulated as grounded and substantiated with evidence: these would be the essential tasks for the panel. The critical function here is the validation, by a peoples' tribunal, of a peoples' law articulation of demands for justice. As such, the declaratory function announces to the world the languages of peoples' law and the determinations of violations found by our tribunal. This then forms the public record of a peoples' judgment.

On the Deliberative Function:
The declaration of a peoples' judgment through this tribunal, however, must be seen as only a first step. It is in many ways the easiest of the tasks before the tribunal. I spoke earlier about us having to confront the contexts of the failures which necessitate our gathering. Declarations of rejection, important as they are in making present and heard peoples' voices of judgment against power, need to be followed by a serious consideration of the challenges that confront us as we declare these wrongs. A declaration alone, leaving unchallenged our own assumptions and practices of "action" leaves little changed in the workings of the worlds controlled by power. It is for this reason we face the deliberative challenge.

What do we do with this language of media wrongs as presented? I do not assume that the articulation of wrongs put forward should stand unchallenged by you, the panel. Perhaps such a voicing of wrongs is not so useful; perhaps it is clumsy and requires refinement; perhaps it provides little by way of provoking new thinking on the possibilities of action against the corporate-dominated media. As a preliminary to any subsequent deliberation, all of this requires your critical assessment.

Even if this suggested language for a peoples' naming of wrongs were to be accepted, you must consider what implications may flow from such an articulation. How do we translate a peoples' law language into peoples' law actions in furtherance of justice?

Often we see the world of the media, and speak of media wrongs, simply in terms of the duality of the dominant media and the alternative media. Against the dominant media's constructions of worlds conducive to power's designs, the alternative media stands, providing powerful counter narratives. And there is no dearth in the sources of these counter narratives against power. There is no silence on truth. But why then do we still confront the unimaginable ignorance of truth among the citizenry in the centers of power, audiences that crucially matter, as it is this ignorance which enables power to pursue the hoax of democratic action for human good.

Some questions come to mind in terms of issues that require deliberation:

1. How do we translate our narratives of wrongs committed by the media into action which brings consequence to those who commit such wrongs? Perhaps we need here to think about the adequacy of confron-

tation at the level of truth-telling alone, i.e., in simply pursuing the practice of presenting to the public domain our competing truths. Silence there may not be, but ignorance, or, worse still, indifference most certainly persists. How might we impact upon this? Perhaps we need to think more specifically about naming and shaming strategies, pursued tenaciously, to bring specific instances of violations by specific institutions and individuals as the means by which the consequences of media violations may be brought into focus. Perhaps we might consider the feasibility of bringing public campaigns for test cases, using the official courts of law as theaters for a peoples' action against such institutions and individuals by adopting the languages of international criminal law. Perhaps… You the Panel of the Jury carry this burden of deliberation.

2. Do we need to rethink the directions for alternative, people-centered media action? We need to be frank. An issue which I raised in the Rome session, which did not, I believe, receive sufficient attention by way of considered response, relates to the nature of the alternative-media environment. Alternative-media activity is in proliferation. To what extent does this mean that the alternative-media environment is also dominated by a logic of competition, and what are the implications that follow from this? Money matters! We cannot pretend otherwise, and money matters also to the alternative-media sector. How might we ensure a greater coordination of people-oriented media so that the logic of competition may be overcome by a logic of cooperation? This is particularly important in connection with establishing real and meaningful spaces for voices from the global south. Can we simply continue with business as usual within the alternative-media sector? For all our brave talk, can we become of sufficient collective force to impinge seriously upon power's ability to control truth?

I have no answers to these questions. I can only ask them. I believe that this responsibility of deliberation, over and above the declarations of outrage, is a necessary burden we must bear as a peoples' tribunal. Out of such deliberation may be developed a "mandate" for future peoples' actions.

On the "Mandating Function":
The WTI exists, I believe, in a political climate where a peoples' law orientation is nascent. Consistent with the stated aims of the WTI to be a component of a creative and vital movement for peace and justice, the

"mandating function" would use the opportunity of solidarities fostered by the WTI process to give credence, and provide inspiration, to new directions for peoples' law actions. Through the voice of the WTI, therefore, may be mandated specific future initiatives which build movements across time and space, challenging the inevitability of the ways of the world as it is presently ordered. In connection with people-oriented media action, the mandating function would provide an authoritative call for relevant actors to pursue strategies identified as critical to challenge the ability of the corporate-dominated media to falsify and misrepresent our worlds as well as their impunity for these actions. WTI mandates for peoples' campaigns for truth and truth-telling responsibilities would therefore also have a symbolic potency which emphasizes the collective coming-into-being of peoples' law movements for media accountability. The specific mandates that might be deemed necessary would depend obviously on the nature and outcome of the Jury's deliberation of the issues raised earlier.

Friends, to conclude, I believe that the WTI possesses a unique potential. My wish is that it will seize what I believe to be a significant potency of voice, not merely of protest, but of reclamation. If we can believe that there is nothing inviolable, natural, or inevitable about empire's rule, notwithstanding such indoctrinations, if we can recognize within ourselves the internalizations of empire's prescriptions as we find ourselves "existing" within empire, then we might begin to accord a rightful dignity to those for whom the struggles against empire are more than theoretical postulations, more than professional activism.

I urge that you, the Panel, give significant attention to the potential of the WTI as a new beginning toward peoples' law imaginations. I hope that the outcome of your work here will provide real and new directions by which we may begin reclaiming truth for humanity. I wish you well in this important task.

The Quest for an Alternative Media

Ömer Madra

When you look at the coverage of world news for the past four years or so, the first "accurate" reporting on the plans to invade Iraq, long before the beginning of the war in Iraq, to the best of my knowledge, was in the Turkish media, about 17 months before the invasion. And this was reported in the largest daily newspaper in Turkey, or, at least, that's how it likes to describe itself, anyhow.

Now, on 7 November 2001, there is a very detailed piece of news. And the headline says, "Let's overthrow Saddam together and let's give you a share of Kirkuk [oil]." And, this is directly from Washington's mouth! The reporter states that the news originates from important sources from Washington and the Pentagon. If the names of these significant sources are withheld, the name of the reporter, Kasım Cindemir, is given nevertheless.

You see, while we are still desperately trying to make out what is going on in Afghanistan, with the bombings and all, we suddenly learn, to our amazement, about invasion plans for the bombing and invasion of another country—Iraq! Now this is an elaborate plan—and a very reliable one at that, since the newspaper reports that it is from very reliable sources in the Pentagon and Washington—consisting of eight points. Well, according to the report, it is called the "Rumsfeld Plan." Donald Rumsfeld was, and still is, the defense secretary of US, i.e., one of the highest-level planners. We also read that during Rumsfeld's first official visit to Ankara, this plan was related to the top-level authorities in Turkey, and it is reported that during the said visit he made a very detailed exposé on the "Saddam question"—whatever that means.

If we were to sum up the plan, it would consist of eight concise points: One, the war in Afghanistan will shift to Iraq.

Two, the United States, Turkey, and the UK will coordinate their efforts to bomb Iraq from the air. Very damaging strikes will be carried out, during which it is expected that there will be breakaways from the Iraqi army. Thus, Saddam Hussein will be overthrown.

Three, after the war the territorial integrity of Iraq will be preserved.

Four, in the newly set-up government, in which all the sections of the

Iraqi population, i.e., the Kurds, the Turkomans, the Shiites, and the Arabs, will be represented.

Five, Turkey will deploy its own soldiers into northern Iraq.

The remaining three articles of the "Rumsfeld Plan" are concerned with the economy—all are about "bargaining" power.

So, let me go on with the so-called Rumsfeld Plan.

Article six: After the end of the war—and, I want to draw your attention kindly to the fact that this is 7 November 2001; only a bit more than a month has passed since the atrocities of September 11 have taken place—Turkey will have a share of Kirkuk oil! The amount of the share is to be determined after the end of the proposed war.

Article seven: It is estimated that a sum of around $50 billion in new business deals and commercial opportunities will arise and a substantial part of this amount will be presented to Turkey as a special privilege or gift!

Lastly, according to article eight of the so-called Rumsfeld Plan, natural-gas pipelines and other energy resources transported will be offered to Turkey as a priority in these business deals.

And at the end of this news report in the "biggest daily" of Turkey it is stated that the "overwhelming tendency" of the Turkish authorities is to think positively toward the future—like good businessmen should, I suppose—and give "full support" to the US. And that this "full support" would include the "Saddam issue" as well, whatever that means. And finally, the news article ends with a short paragraph which asserts that Turkey had always had "legitimate" (sic!) rights to the Kirkuk oil, i.e., rights arising from "historical pacts"... These rights were nonetheless "not exercised" by successive Turkish governments. The news piece does not give any reasons for the Turkish governments' choosing not to exercise their "legitimate rights." Nor does the report makes any reference to these "historic pacts" (or agreements) which are mentioned as the basis of the said claims.

And this is the largest newspaper of Turkey, publishing this "news"!

I must nevertheless admit that this piece has been a great "eye-opener" for our radio station. We reported this on our radio broadcasts saying that Iraq was next on the agenda, and from that date on we kept on reporting the coming war in Iraq and commenting upon it. So it was very clear that the Turkish media had a very good "scoop" there at that time. Now, in the same newspaper, one of the important managers, who is also the editor in chief, is also known to pursue business interests at the government level in the capital, Ankara, for the company he belongs to. There were complaints about that conflict of interest and I remember him defending himself in the following manner. To paraphrase his words: "I am a journalist," he said, "but at the same time I am one of the administrators of a big corporate company. Since I am on the board of this company, it is natural that I assume the role of defending the interests of my corporate entity."

When I look at these extremely animated sessions of the World Tribunal on Iraq it gives me the same kind of excitement that we experienced on 1 March 2003, when we attended the great mass rally held in Ankara. On the same day and actually at the very same moment when, just a kilometer away, the Turkish Parliament was holding a historic session whereby it refused to participate in the war. And now, when I look at the first page of this same newspaper to see whether this Tribunal on Iraq is mentioned in any way, what do I see? Nothing. Nothing at all. And this is so *normal*.

Now I would like to talk to you about something which seems very interesting to me, and this is a speech reported in the US mainstream media. I began my speech today with Donald Rumsfeld, so let me finish off with Donald Rumsfeld, then. According to AP, BBC, et al., he spoke thus: "We're not losing this war, and we're not bogged down in a quagmire..." I seem to remember these words almost *mot à mot* from another war which ended thirty years ago... Yes, that was Vietnam. So, speaking after all these eminent speakers, and after listening to all the things they have said about the control of the corporate media, all the outrageous reporting and witnessing by real journalists, I have to say that, in spite of all the terrible news, I believe that things are not going so badly, in the final analysis. We are aware that a postmodern coups d'etat has been carried out in the US, and the mainstream media remained silent on this horrible situation. Yet, we also know that Rumsfeld has been forced to utter a sentence like "We haven't lost this war." And, in the United States of America, a new direction is being taken. 560,000 people have just signed a petition against the so-called Downing Street memo, which is a real scandal, and sent the petition to the White House asking for a real investigation into the matter. This doesn't seem to be bad news at all. Actually, it is very heartening news.

So, as the moderator of this session on the search for alternative media, let me say that I don't think it is significant to make a distinction between alternative media and mainstream media. I think the important thing is to be able to do journalism—real journalism. And this was very well expressed in this panel by our eminent speakers. I believe that if you have the necessary moral courage, journalism is still a profession that can be truly exercised. Let me finish by a very fresh anecdote: Some time around noon today I was asked by the Turkish service of BBC World to give them an interview on WTI Istanbul. And they asked some interesting questions, but the most interesting one was the third one. They asked "Who is going to pay attention to you?" And I said "You are. You've just done that."

Fourth Session

The Invasion and Occupation
of Iraq

Testimony on War Crimes and the Recent Situation in Iraq

Dahr Jamail

In May of 2004 I was interviewing a man who had just been released from Abu Ghraib. Like so many I interviewed from various US military detention facilities who'd been tortured horrifically, he still managed to maintain his sense of humor.

He began laughing when telling of how US soldiers made him beat other prisoners. He laughed because he told me he had been beaten himself prior to this, and was so tired that all he could do to beat other detained Iraqis was to lift his arm and let it drop on the other men. Later in the same interview when telling another story he laughed again and said, "The Americans brought electricity to my ass before they brought it to my house."

But this testimony is not about the indomitable spirit of the Iraqi people. About the dignity and strength of Iraqis, we need no testimony. This testimony is about ongoing violations of international law being committed by the occupiers of Iraq on a daily basis in regard to rampant torture, the neglect and impeding of the health-care sector, and the ongoing failure to allow Iraqis to reconstruct their infrastructure.

To discuss torture, there are so many stories I could use here, but I'll use two examples which are indicative of scores of others I documented while in Iraq.

Ali Shalal Abbas lives in the al-Amiriyah district of Baghdad. So many of his neighbors were detained that friends urged him to go to the nearby US base to try to get answers. Since he worked for civil admini-stration, he went three times to get answers as to why so many innocent people were being detained during US home raids.

On the fourth time he was detained himself, despite not being charged with any crime. This was 13 September 2003. Within two days he was transferred from a military base to Abu Ghraib, where he was held for over three months.

"The minute I got there, the suffering began," said Abbas, "I asked him for water, and he said after the investigation I would get some. He accused me of so many things and asked me so many questions. Among them he said I hated Christians."

He was forced to strip naked shortly after arriving, and remained that way for most of his stay in the prison. "My hands were enlarged because there was no blood because they cuffed them so tight. My head was covered with the sack, and they fastened my right hand to a pole with handcuffs. They made me stand on my toes to clip me to it."

Abbas said soldiers doused him in cold water while holding him under a fan, and oftentimes, "They put on a loudspeaker, put the speakers on my ears, and said, 'Shut up, fuck fuck fuck!'"

Treatment included holding a loaded gun to his head to make him not cry out in pain as his hand-ties were tightened.

He was not provided water and food for extended periods of time. Sleep deprivation via the aforementioned method was the norm.

Abbas said that at one point, "Two men came, one a foreigner and one a translator. He asked me who I was. I said I'm a human being. They told me, 'We are going to cut your head off and send you to hell, we will take you to Guantánamo.'"

A female soldier told him, "Our aim is to put you in hell so you would tell the truth. These are the orders we have from our superiors, to turn your lives into hell."

Another time one of the guards said it was time for "celebrations."

"They made some of the detainees strip naked and threw cold water on them," said Abbas, "And made them run and smash their faces against the walls while the guard was whistling."

Other treatment included, as Abbas added, "They put us on top of each other while we were naked. They made us lay on top of each other naked as if it was sex, and beat us with a broom."

A female guard told the male detainees that the penis of a dog was longer than theirs, and she made Abbas and several other detainees strip naked, then tied their hands tightly behind their backs, threw them on the ground, and made them say, "I am a donkey" over and over while they were forced to lick the ground.

Other treatment included having their food thrown in the trash in front of them and beating them on their genitals. Abbas added, "They shit on us, used dogs against us, used electricity, and starved us."

He also said, "They cut my hair into strips like an Indian. They cut my mustache, put a plate in my hand, and made me go beg from the prisoners, as if I was a beggar."

Desecration of his religion was, of course, included as part of their humiliation.

Abbas was made to fast during the first day of Eid, the breaking of the fast of Ramadan, which is *haram* (forbidden).

He told me that one day a female soldier stripped naked and other soldiers held his eyes open to make him look at her. Sometimes at night when he would read his Qur'an, he had to hold it in the hallway for light. "Soldiers would walk by and kick the Holy Qur'an, and sometimes they would try to piss on it or wipe shit on it."

Abbas did not feel this was the work of a few individual soldiers. "This was organized, it wasn't just individuals, and every one of the troops in Abu Ghraib was responsible for it."

He added, "Saddam Hussein used to have people like those who tortured us. Why do they put Saddam into trial, but they do not put the Americans to trial? I have full confidence that Saddam used to do these things, because he is a stupid student. But the Americans are the teachers."

Toward the end of his interview, Abbas stated, "America does not have a future in the world, the Statue of Liberty has been smashed by the boots of the American troops. And this is all because of Abu Ghraib. Saddam Hussein was a cruel enemy to us. I hoped that I was killed by him, though, rather than being alive with the Americans. After this journey of torture and suffering, what else can I think?"

Other Iraqis, such as Sadiq Zoman, didn't have it as good as Abbas. Fifty-five-year-old Zoman, detained from his home in Kirkuk in a raid by US soldiers that produced no weapons, was taken to a police office in Kirkuk, the Kirkuk Airport Detention Center, the Tikrit Airport Detention Center, and then the 28th Combat Support Hospital, where he was treated by Dr. Michael Hodges, a US army medic. Dr. Hodges's medical report listed the primary diagnoses of Zoman's condition as hypoxic brain injury (brain damage caused by lack of oxygen) "with persistent vegetative state," myocardial infarction (heart attack), and heat stroke.

Thus, Zoman was dropped off at the General Hospital in Tikrit by US soldiers after being held for one month. He was in a coma when he was dropped off with a copy of the medical report written by Lt. Col. Michael Hodges. His last name was listed as his first name on the report, despite the fact that all of Zoman's identification papers were taken during the raid on his home. Thus, it took his family weeks to locate him in the hospital.

The same medical report did not mention the fact that the back of Zoman's head was bashed in, or that he had electrical burn marks on the bottoms of his feet and genitals, or why he had lash marks across his back and chest.

Today Zoman lies in bed in a small home rented by his family in Baghdad. Of course there has been no compensation provided to them for what was done to Sadiq Zoman.

Such evidence that doctors, nurses, and medics have been complicit in torture and other illegal procedures in post-Saddam Iraq is already ample.

According to a Human Rights Watch report released on 27 April of this year, "Abu Ghraib was only the tip of the iceberg, it's now clear that abuse of detainees has happened all over—from Afghanistan to Guantánamo Bay to a lot of third-country dungeons where the United States has sent prisoners. And probably quite a few other places we don't even know about."

The report adds, "Harsh and coercive interrogation techniques such as subjecting detainees to painful stress positions and extended sleep deprivation have been routinely used in detention centers throughout Iraq. The earlier report of Maj. Gen. Antonio Taguba found 'numerous incidents of sadistic, blatant, and wanton criminal abuses' constituting 'systematic and illegal abuse of detainees' at Abu Ghraib. Another Pentagon report documented 44 allegations of such war crimes at Abu Ghraib. An ICRC report concluded that in military intelligence sections of Abu Ghraib, 'methods of physical and psychological coercion used by the interrogators appeared to be part of the standard operating procedures by military intelligence personnel to obtain confessions and extract information.'"

Amnesty International has also released similar findings recently.

Another aspect I shall discuss here is the catastrophic situation of the health system in Iraq. I've recently released a report on the condition of Iraq's hospitals under occupation.

Although the Iraq Ministry of Health is claimed to have gained its sovereignty and has received promises of over $1 billion of US funding, hospitals in Iraq continue to face ongoing medicine, equipment, and staffing shortages under the US-led occupation.

During the 1990s, medical supplies and equipment were constantly in short supply because of the sanctions against Iraq. And while war and occupation have brought promises of relief, hospitals have had little chance to recover and re-supply: the occupation, since its inception, has closely resembled a low-grade war, and the allocation of resources by occupation authorities has reflected this reality. Thus, throughout Baghdad there are ongoing shortages of medicines of even the most basic items, such as analgesics, antibiotics, anesthetics, and insulin. Surgical items are running out, as well as basic supplies like rubber gloves, gauze, and medical tape.

In April 2004, an International Committee for the Red Cross (ICRC) report stated that hospitals in Iraq are overwhelmed with new patients, short of medicine and supplies, and lack both adequate electricity and water, with ongoing bloodshed stretching the hospitals' already meager resources to the limit.

Ample testimony from medical practitioners in the interim in fact confirms this crisis. A general practitioner at the prosthetics workshop at al-Kena Hospital in Baghdad, Dr. Thamiz Aziz Abul Rahman, said, "Eleven months ago we submitted an emergency order for prosthetic materials to the Ministry of Health, and still we have nothing," said Dr. Rahman. After a pause he added, "This is worse than even during the sanctions."

Dr. Qasim al-Nuwesri, the chief manager at Chuwader General Hospital, one of the two hospitals in the sprawling slum area of Sadr City, Baghdad, an area of nearly two million people, added that there, too, was a shortage of most supplies and, most critically, of ambulances. But for his hospital, the lack of potable water was the major problem. "Of course we have typhoid, cholera, kidney stones… but we now even have the very rare Hepatitis Type-E… and it has become common in our area," said al-Nuwesri, while adding that they never faced these problems prior to the invasion of 2003.

Chuwader hospital needs at least 2,000 liters of water per day to function with basic sterilization practices. According to Dr. al-Nuwesri, they received 15 percent of this amount. "The rest of the water is contaminated and causing problems, as are the electricity cuts," added al-Nuwesri, "Without electricity our instruments in the operating room cannot work and we have no pumps to bring us water."

At Falluja General Hospital, Dr. Ahmed, who asked that only his first name be used because he feared US military reprisals, said of the April 2004 siege that "the Americans shot out the lights in the front of our hospital. They prevented doctors from reaching the emergency unit at the hospital, and we quickly began to run out of supplies and much-needed medications." He also said that several times Marines kept the physicians in the residence building, intentionally prohibiting them from entering the hospital in order to treat patients.

In November, shortly after razing Nazzal Emergency Hospital to the ground, US forces entered Falluja General Hospital, the city's only healthcare facility for trauma victims, detaining employees and patients alike. According to medics on the scene, water and electricity were "cut off," ambulances confiscated, and surgeons, without exception, kept out of the besieged city.

Many doctors in Iraq believe that, more widely, the lack of assistance, if not outright hostility, by the US military, coupled with the lack of rebuilding and reconstruction by foreign contractors, has compounded the problems they are facing.

According to Agence France-Presse, the former US ambassador to Iraq, Paul Bremer, admitted that the US-led coalition's spending on the Iraqi health system was inadequate. "It's not nearly enough to cover the needs in the healthcare field," said Bremer when referring to the amount of money the coalition was spending for the healthcare system in occupied Iraq.

When asked if his hospital had received assistance from the US military or reconstruction contractors, Dr. Sarmad Raheem, the administrator of chief doctors at al-Kerkh Hospital in Baghdad said, "Never ever. Some soldiers came here five months ago and asked what we needed. We told them and they never brought us one single needle... We heard that some people from the CPA came here, but they never did anything for us."

At Falluja General Hospital, Dr. Mohammed said there has been virtually no assistance from foreign contractors, and of the US military he commented, "They send only bombs, not medicine."

International aid has been in short supply due primarily to the horrendous security situation in Iraq. After the UN headquarters was bombed in Baghdad in August 2003, killing 20 people, aid agencies and non-governmental organizations either reduced their staffing or pulled out entirely.

Dr. Amer al-Khuzaie, Iraq's deputy minister of health, blamed the medicine and equipment shortages on the US-led coalition's failure to provide funds requested by the Ministry of Health.

"We have requested over $500 million for equipment and only have $300 million of this amount promised," he said, "Yet we still only have promises."

According to the *New York Times*, "of the $18.4 billion Congress approved last fall, only about $600 million has actually been paid out. Billions more have been designated for giant projects still in the planning stage. Part of the blame rests with the Pentagon's planning failures and the occupation authority's reluctance to consult qualified Iraqis. Instead, the administration brought in American defense contractors who had little clue about what was most urgently needed or how to handle the unfamiliar and highly insecure climate."

The World Health Organization (WHO) last year warned of a health emergency in Baghdad, as well as throughout Iraq, if current conditions persist. But despite claims from the Ministry of Health of more drugs, better equipment, and generalized improvement, doctors on the ground still see "no such improvement."

In conclusion, a quick summary of the overall situation on the ground in Iraq now is in order. Over two years into the illegal occupation, while Iraq sits upon a sea of oil, ongoing gasoline shortages plague Iraqis, who sometimes must wait two days to fill their cars.

Electricity remains in short supply. Most of Iraq, including the northern region, receives on average three hours of electricity per day. Even the better areas of Baghdad receive only six to eight hours per day, forcing those who can afford them to use small generators to run fans and refrigerators in their homes. Of course, this is only for those who've been able to obtain the now rarefied gasoline.

The security situation is, needless to say, horrendous. With over 100,000 Iraqis killed thus far and the number of US soldiers killed approaching 2,000, the violence only continues to escalate.

Just since the new Iraqi government was sworn in at the end of April, over 1,000 Iraqis have died in their country, and this number is increasing as I speak to you right now. This number will continue to escalate as the failed occupation grinds on, along with the number of dead occupation soldiers. As the heavy-handed tactics of the US military persist, the Iraqi resistance continues to grow in its numbers and lethality.

As I mentioned before, potable water remains in short supply. Cholera, typhoid, and other water-borne disease are rampant even in parts of the capital city, as lack of reconstruction continues to plague Iraq's infrastructure. Raw sewage is common throughout not just Baghdad, but other cities throughout Iraq.

With over 50 percent unemployment, a growing resistance, and an infrastructure in shambles, the future for Iraq remains bleak as long as the failed occupation persists. While the Bush administration continues to disregard calls for a timetable for withdrawal, Iraqis continue to suffer and die with little hope for their future. With each passing day, the catastrophe in Iraq resembles the US debacle in Vietnam more and more. It has become clear that the only way the Bush administration will withdraw the US military from Iraq and provide Iraq with true sovereignty is if they are forced to do so.

The Use of Depleted Uranium (DU) Weapons
Akira Maeda, Sayo Saruta, and Koichi Inamori

1. The Truth About the Use of Depleted Uranium (DU) Weapons by US and UK Troops

The US and UK troops in the attacks on Iraq that started on 21 March 2001 used DU weapons during the battles at various places in Iraq. The truth of the use of DU weapons by US troops was verified and admitted by Brigadier General Brooks in a press briefing on 26 March of the same year when he said, "DU bombs had been used."

Michael Kilpatrick, deputy director of deployment health support in the office of the assistant secretary of defense for health affairs, at a forum at the Massachusetts Institute of Technology on 6 March 2004, said, "The Army fired and used from tanks and armored vehicle 24 tons or less of DU bombs, and the Air Force, 10 tons or less of DU bombs from A-10 planes." These, when combined, would be equivalent to 115 tons of metallic uranium.

Also, before the outbreak of the war, on 15 March 2003, in a press briefing at the Department of Defense, Colonel Naughton stated that "Abrams tanks had been loaded with DU bombshells," and "so were A-10 planes" because "there was no other choice." Witnesses had repeatedly seen civilian facilities being targeted by A-10 planes, starting with Iraq's Planning Ministry during the aerial bombing of Baghdad. A report on the investigation conducted by Scott Peterson corroborated the statement given by Colonel Naughton at the aforementioned press briefing. Abrams tanks were the main battle tanks used in the ground assault of Iraq. It is, therefore, highly probable that aside from the facts already verified, the US armed forces have used DU weapons in large quantities, even exceeding the reported volume, in all areas of offensive operations in Iraq, even in densely populated areas, particularly Baghdad, Basra, etc.

2. Special Properties of Depleted Uranium (DU) Weapons

Storing depleted uranium is enormously expensive, and the US Department of Energy has wanted to dispose of it by any means possible. It is in military weapons that depleted uranium is used on an extremely large scale, and it is used mainly on bombshells to increase their penetration capacity, and also as armor for tanks in order to increase their defense capacity. Mainly, uranium weapons have the following advantages:

1. Depleted uranium, because of its very high density (1.7 times that of lead, 2.5 times that of iron) and hardness, when used to tip bullets, increases the penetration power of the bullets, and displays such tremendous power that it can open holes in thick iron plates and concrete.

2. Even when there are no explosives inside the bombshell, DU explodes upon impact, and its capacity to kill and injure the enemy is high because of the high temperature it causes when it burns.

3. It is very cheap because its raw materials are radioactive wastes.

However, when the depleted uranium packed in the tanks is discharged, it explodes heavily upon impact and burns at a high temperature, becoming microparticles of oxidized uranium (ceramic form aerosol of diametrical-micron; a micron is equivalent to 1/1000mm). The particles, when diffused in the atmosphere and whirled up into the sky, pollute vast ranges of the atmosphere, and those that fall on the ground pollute the environment, such as the soil and water, etc.

3. Dreadful Negative Effects of Depleted Uranium Weapons on the Human Body

Once the uranium particles are inhaled into the body, the particles attach first to the trachea and the respiratory system. Because the particles are practically insoluble, they do not dissolve easily in the blood, and stay there for a long period of time. These clinging particles continue to expose the neighboring organs to radiation. In this way, they cause the cell and the gene to mutate, and cause cancers, including leukemia and lymphoma, as well as congenital disorders and defects. Then, gradually, they are absorbed into the blood and lymph, and cause various illnesses and damages to the whole body. Also, aside from inhalation, they get into the body and enter the bloodstream by oral ingestion and through wounds. This very dangerous weapon is being diffused in large quantities all over Iraq by the US and British troops. Not only during the war, but also after the war, and an unimaginable length of time of 4.5 billion years hereafter, the people of Iraq will have to bear the burden of living in this vastly polluted land and learning how to survive with this grim reality. When they drop DU weapons, the British and US troops do not just snatch away precious lives but cause the Iraqis further and eternal miseries.

1. Physical Damages in Iraq after the Gulf War
During the Gulf war in January 1991, the US armed forces dropped 320 tons of depleted uranium weapons on Iraq. Since the Gulf war, there has been a high incidence of strange phenomenon not previously seen in Iraq. There have been a number of incidences of such phenomenon as several members of one family developing cancer, or one patient having several types of cancer, etc., cancer that spreads fast, the outbreak of infectious diseases due to fast-spreading cancer, leukemia, aplastic anemia, and malignant tumor, and immunodeficiency, massive herpes, and herpes zoster pain, symptoms resembling AIDS, syndromes due to liver and kidney dysfunction, hereditary dysphasia (hereditary damage) due to gene defects. Children, especially infants, who cannot fight back and are blameless, have become the number-one victims of this war. The southern city of Basra, which is near the battleground of the Gulf war, has been very seriously damaged, and according to a doctor at the Basra Educational Hospital, the number of people who have succumbed to cancer rose from 34 in 1988, prior to the Gulf war, to the astonishing figure of 603 in 2001, seventeen times greater.

i.) Basra Maternity and Pediatrics Hospital. Mohammed Hoji (5) was diagnosed with leukemia just a year after his own mother, who was also confined in the same hospital, died of leukemia. The physician in charge of this case, Dr. Surin Shirub, related, "What makes this case stand out is that the whole family and the brothers one by one have succumbed to cancer and leukemia. This kind of phenomenon never existed before the Gulf war." The aunt, Abed (32), who was caring for the boy, lamented, "Why do we have to suffer like this even when the war is over?"

ii.) Zein (5), who was confined in the Basra Maternity and Pediatrics Hospital five months before, suddenly developed a swollen abdomen, and was diagnosed with leukemia. Since then, he has become weak and lost his gaiety. His mother, Semal (25), sighed, "I would like America to know how the war has caused us so much miseries for many generations to come."

iii.) Abbas (5), who was diagnosed with leukemia three years ago, was sleeping soundly beside his mother, Hamdi (30). The hair on his head had become extremely thin as an effect of drugs administered to him. Hamdi said, "It's hard when you are helpless to do anything to save your child from his sufferings." Dr. Jasem (32) of this hospital related, "The damages of the war are not a temporary matter. Even after that, its innocent victims will suffer for generations to come."

These innocent children of Iraq, in fact, have been deprived of their rights to be born with good health and grow normally because of the effects of these DU weapons. Furthermore, the economic sanctions imposed on Iraq by the UN beginning in August 1990 contributed more to this pathetic situation. The UN Resolution 661 had exempted from the embargo materials to be used for medical purposes. However, the committee that was charged with the implementation of the embargo in accordance with the provision of Resolution 661 could not make this exemption operative due to opposition by commissioners from the US and UK, and thus there arose a shortage of medical supplies, vaccines, syringes, anesthetics, and medical apparatuses necessary for medical treatments. According to a UNICEF report, by February 1991, medical supplies had reached one-sixth of the normal level of stockpile. In a 1993 report, UNICEF also announced that

> at the beginning of the Gulf War, the number of children dying was more or less 100,000, but after the war, the rate of death has increased 3 times of the number before the war. Medical care, and insurance service were rendered useless due to the shortage of supplies and apparatuses for medical care and treatment. And also, due to depleted uranium bombs that were used during the Gulf War, the number of cancer patients suddenly increased after the war. If proper treatment had been provided at the early stage of the disease, death could have been avoided, but due to the shortage of medical supplies and appliances because of the economic sanctions, patients could not be treated properly resulting in the great increase in the number of afflicted victims.

Likewise, the postwar deprivation had driven the best of doctors in Iraq out of country. Many of the doctors and scholars who stayed behind were actually classified with world-class academics and had participated and presented the results of their research in international scientific and academic conferences. However, due to the economic sanctions, they were unable to obtain visas so that they could participate in international conferences and have the opportunity to continue to establish scholarly exchanges necessary for the advancement and improvement of the level of medical practice and treatment in Iraq. Even if they wanted to go overseas to receive training on radiation exposure, for example, or perhaps just to procure the necessary medical supplies, they could not do so because they could not get visas. Data on Iraqi victims was indispensable in coping with the inexperience with regard to the effects of radiation from DU weapons, and while Iraqi doctors could be in a position to provide those data and materials, the economic sanctions hampered their progress and development.

Dr. Junan, a cancer expert at the Ibn Gaswan Hospital, a Maternity and Pediatrics Hospital in the city of Basra, related, "Children's leukemia, if treated thoroughly at the early stage, has a 70 percent chance of being cured, but the kind of medicine for this ailment is not available, and so, the patients cannot be treated well, and, lamentably, just end up dying. But under the present economic sanctions, we are allowed only to procure food supplies in exchange for oil, and we are forced to make do with only 20 percent of needed medical supplies. How then can we cure the sick?" In 2001 alone, 256 cases had been confirmed as being born with congenital defects in this hospital.

2. Clinical Cases of US Veterans in this Iraqi War

Samawa, where the self-defense force is stationed, is strategically located between Basra and Baghdad. The US Army, when marching to Baghdad along this route, met with stiff resistance from Iraqi troops, and it took them a week to quell the insurgencies in towns and roads they passed by. Depleted uranium weapons were used during the fighting.

Dr. Asaf Durakovic, a specialist in nuclear medicine, advisor to the National Science Foundation, and director of the nuclear medicine clinic created by the US Veterans Department after the end of the Gulf war, established the Uranium Medical Research Center, which is an independent research agency based in Canada, and for several years has continued to examine evidence of depleted uranium contamination of American, British, and Canadian soldiers. According to a survey conducted by Dr. Durakovic, published in the *New York Daily News* on 3 April 2004, after the Iraq war, he detected depleted uranium in the urine of four out of nine US soldiers who were stationed to keep peace and order in Samawa after the Iraq war, and returned home due to bad physical condition after complaining of chronic migraine, nausea, bloody urine, partial hearing, and vision impairment, etc. The 442nd MP

Company, to which the surveyed soldiers belonged, was in charge of convoy and training of Iraqi policemen, and was not involved in direct combat. Depleted uranium was detected in these soldiers, who were doing such mission, and it was probable that they had been exposed to uranium by inhaling depleted uranium particles in the atmosphere. Sgt. Juan Vega, chief medical orderly of this company, related, "One night, 10 to 15 people just suddenly fell ill and developed symptoms such as fever of as high as 39.4°C, chill and other symptoms of unexplained nature. More than a dozen people out of 160 soldiers suddenly had been having kidney stones." He said, "Samawa is like hell."

The Dutch company stationed at Samawa after that decided to set up camp in the middle of the desert because the radiation level in the environs where the US military set up camps was just too high.

4. Medical Verification

For the sake of argument that the above-mentioned damages have been due to DU, we shall have to prove that there is a correlation between DU and its effects on the human body based on medical findings on the existence of this crisis pertaining to DU. Now, regarding Iraq after the Gulf war, which has reported the most number of DU-related casualties, we shall use as reference the data gathered by Fasy TM that were presented at the International DU Symposium held in New York in June 2003 as an unpublished medical paper.

i.) The Teratogenicity of Depleted Uranium

a.) *The Children of Iraq*: According to the data gathered by Fasy TM, the frequency rate of congenital dysphasia is 3.04 per 1,000 monitored in Basra, but in 2000, it rose to 17.6, 5–6 times higher than previously reported. This is particularly true in many reported cases where the parents were soldiers who participated in the Gulf war.

b.) *Children of Veterans of the Gulf War:* The result of a survey conducted to determine the frequency rate of congenital dysphasia on veterans of the Gulf war by the US Military Research Institute was published in the *New England Journal of Medicine*, according to Cowan in 1997. The conclusion was that there was no difference in the frequency of congenital dysphasia in children of veterans of the Gulf war and those of veterans who did not participate in the Gulf war.

But five months later, the result of research conducted by three British researchers, Pat Doyle, Eve Roman, and Noreen Maconochie was published in the same journal. Their research refuted the inaccuracy of the earlier investigations, which had been made only on children who were born and lived, disregarding aborted births and stillbirths due to massive congenital deformities and excluding one-third of the overall number of discharged soldiers.

In 2001, Kang of the Veterans Affairs Administration announced a research that would not exclude aborted births/stillbirths, and veterans in their research. The result was that compared to veterans who did not go to the Gulf war, congenital dysphasia on children of veterans who served in the Gulf war was 2.3 times for male, and 2.4 times for female. The truth about this increase in number even just on those who participated in the Gulf war is indeed astonishing.

c.) *Animal Experiments:* Based on the 2001 research conducted by Domingo JL of Spain, et al., when male rats for a period of 16 weeks ingested natural uranium, rate of pregnancy decreased, a degeneration of the testicles (male gonads) occurred, and there was a decrease in the production of sperm. Also, it was confirmed that ten days before and after giving doses to pregnant mice, ossification in litters was three to five times lower compared to the control group, and there were numerous instances of birth defects of the extremities.

In 2002, McClain DE, et al., of the US armed forces embedded depleted uranium in rats, and investigated to determine the effects of DU on the embryo. It was confirmed that the sizes of the embryos of rats were smaller after more than six months of being embedded with DU passing the placenta.

The congenital dysphasia and various diseases in children of soldiers who participated in the Gulf war resemble the conditions of Iraqi children, and this can be traced to the teratogenicity of DU.

ii.) Carcinogenicity of Depleted Uranium

a.) *Iraqi Children:* Based on the data gathered by Fasy TM, in 1990 in Basra, out of 100,000 children, there were 3.98 cancer cases, but in 2000, the number increased to 13.1 cases.

b.) *Veterans of the Gulf War:* There is no medical report showing a statistical increase of cancer in veterans of the Gulf war, but a detailed investigation on the rate of incidence of cancer in children of veterans is needed.

c.) *Experiments on Animals:* To sum up the series of animal experiments done by Miller, et al. of the Armed Forces Radiobiology Research Institute: DU increases the oncogene expression per human cell and cell disorder growth, etc., and causes cancerous growth. Also, they explain that DU—more than even nickel, which is known to cause tumors—causes a significant increase in chromosomal abnormalities usually associated with carcinogens.

Hahn, et al., reported that thorotrast and DU produce much more sarcoma (malignant tumor) when they conducted experiments by embedding tungsten, which is a heavy but nonradioactive metal, and the radioactive material thorotrast in rats. This indicates that DU is not only cancer causing as a heavy metal but is also cancer causing as a radioactive material.

d.) *Effects on the Human Cell:* In 2003, Schroeder, et al., of Germany analyzed the chromosomal abnormality of the lymphocytes of sixteen soldiers who had served in the Gulf war and Balkan war, and these soldiers were proven to have been exposed to radiation. They confirmed that the rate of specific chromosomal abnormality among these soldiers was 4.2 higher when they compared the chromosomal abnormality (dicentric and centric ring chromosomes) that was said to be specific in ionizing radiation with non-specific chromosomal abnormality. They hinted and concluded that despite the fact that the specific chromosomal abnormality cell could not survive for long (half-life being only up to 3.5 years), they observed that even after a lapse of more than ten years since the Gulf war, the body continued to be exposed to radiation due to the DU that had accumulated inside the body for over years. On top of this, they noted, based on available data from Hiroshima and Nagasaki, that this exposure to radiation could cause chromosomal abnormality in lymphocytes. Thus there is no doubt that the cause of cancer such as the increase in the number of cases of leukemia in Iraq today is connected with DU.

iii.) Verification of Gulf War Syndrome

Gulf War Syndrome includes chronic symptoms such as fatigue, headache, muscle and osteoarticular pains, insomnia, neuropsychiatric symptoms, impaired memory, impaired vision, etc.

a.) *Physical Condition of Gulf War Veterans:* It is evident that based on the data of Fukuda in 1998, which compare the physical condition of soldiers who participated in the Gulf war (hereinafter referred to as GWV) with soldiers who did not participate in the Gulf war (hereinafter referred to as non-GWV), the frequency of various symptoms of chronicity is 39 percent in GWV against 14 percent in non-GWV of light and medium, etc., symptoms, and 6 percent in GWV against 0.7 percent in non-GWV of serious illness. It is evident that frequency of such symptoms is higher in soldiers who participated in the Gulf war. It cannot be far from the truth that based on the data of Kang in 1996, the rate of death in GWV is 10.4 against 9.6 percent in non-GWV, showing statistically a difference. However, the 2002 data of Kang show that the number of accidental deaths is more numerous among GWV than among the non-GWV. Also, in 1997, Gray reported that the hospitalization rate was 10 percent higher among soldiers who participated in the Gulf war. It is true that going to war is accompanied by a great risk, and the appearance of various symptoms after returning from the war is designated as "war syndrome." However, based on the report of Harvey RW, et al., of 2002, among the soldiers returning from war, the number of the disabled persons who received services afterward was 8.6 percent of those who served in World War II, 5 percent in the Korean War, 9.6 percent in the Vietnam War, and in the case of the Gulf War, it has reached 16 percent (estimated at 110,000 persons). It is evident that the Gulf war, compared with other wars, has caused many damages, and they cannot be categorized simply as a risk of going to war. Countless research is being conducted on the causes of these symptoms, but no massive investigation placing primary focus on DU has been done. There exist, however, an extensive literature relating to depleted uranium.

b.) *Experiments on Animals:* Pellmar TC, et al., in 1999, revealed evidence that DU caused brain damage after they embedded it in rats, and they arrived at the conclusion that DU produces neurological disorder. Also, concerning the effects of depleted uranium on peripheral nerves, they observed the occurrence of cramps, pain in the extremities, gait disorder, shiver, etc., and that there is damage of calcium metabolism of the neuromuscular junction.

c.) *Psycho-neuron Abnormalities:* McDiarmid, et al., of the Department of Veterans Affairs Medical Center, in a research paper published in 2000, tested 29 people in 1997 out of the 33 veterans with fragments of DU in their body they had put under observation since 1993. They observed the neurocognizance test becoming bad in proportion to the high concentration of DU in their urines, and abnormality in the hormone function of the reproductive system. Also, they reported the genetic damage and the sperm count abnormality. Yet, while they recognize these sorts of health problems, they made it look that there were not many complaints about the symptoms when comparing them with the 21 Gulf War veterans who had not been exposed to DU. However, 11 out of the 21 were in fact suffering from some neuron abnormality and were in extremely bad condition, and a terrible deception was evidently carried out. Similarly, tests were conducted in 1999, and in the report published in 2001, 29 people with incomparably low concentration of DU in their urines to the 21 out of the previous 33 people tested were added, and this was to intentionally dilute the results in an attempt to eliminate the difference in abnormal neuron and reproductive hormone levels.

d.) *Chromosomal Abnormality:* As previously stated, the chromosomes of sixteen people who have been suffering from Gulf War syndrome are 5.2 times higher in dicentric and ring centric chromosomes. Others also, according to Uranobitz, et al., have verified seeing the chromosomal abnormality in veterans of the Gulf war who have shown such symptoms.

e.) *Increase of Depleted Uranium Density in Urine:* P. Horan, et al., of Canada examined the urine of 27 American, British, and Canadian patients, and detected a high density of DU in 14 people. This data proves that even after 8 or 9 years after exposure to DU, a high density of DU is being discharged in the urine. In addition, Durakovic, et al., have examined the uranium in the urine of eight residents of eight regions in Afghanistan who have symptoms similar to Gulf War Syndrome, and in 2003 published data on the detection of a high density of uranium in all their urine. Furthermore, in 2004, they published data on the detection of DU in the urine of four out of nine American soldiers, who were in charge of maintaining public order during the Iraq war, and returned home due to poor physical condition.

It is clear from the investigations conducted by Horan and Durakovic that DU remains in the body for several years. There is no doubt about DU's toxicity and that it is a contributing factor to Gulf War Syndrome.

iv.) There are Researchers who Recognize the Toxicity of DU.

Even within the US Military, Arfsten DP, of the Naval Health Research Center and Ritchie GD, et al., of the Wright-Patterson Air Force Base have studied in detail all US military research, etc. up until 2001, and published their dissertation under their joint names.

a.) A high density of DU was detected in the soldiers' urine after a lapse of ten years; the soldiers had inhaled particles or been pierced with fragments of DU during the Gulf war and/or the conflict in Kosovo.

b.) In mice, the DU accumulated in the testicles, bone, kidneys, and brain.

c.) In test-tube experiments, there were characteristics of genetic disorder and teratogenicity, and rats when embedded with DU developed brain tumors.

d.) It is possible to say that both heavy metals and radioactivity have a strong effect on rats' reproduction.

In this treatise is the remark that "the opinion expressed here does not reflect the opinion of the military but is based on the point of views of the authors." However, even as military researchers, they have sufficiently recognized the damage caused by DU. Recognition of the risks is not limited to their research. As previously stated, numerous medical research projects relating to DU are being conducted even with grants from the military. Even when they are being conducted under the direct supervision of the military, these projects are being given attention even when they may verify the danger of DU.

Suffice it to say, it is clear from existing medical dissertations that DU is an extremely dangerous substance that does not only cause temporary disorders, but chronic health breakdown, congenital defects, carcinogens, and other disorders.

5. Awareness of the Toxicity of DU Weapons on the US Armed Forces
The following are explanations of the fact that the US military is fully aware that DU weapons are harmful to the body from the development process of these weapons:

i.) *Letters to General Groves:* In October 1943, three physicists, A. H. Compton, et al., sent a letter proposing "research on development and protection of radioactive weapons" to General Groves, who took part in the Manhattan Project. In this letter, the three doctors proposed the organization of a team to research the handling and preparation of radioactive materials as weapons and protection from these weapons—preparation in case Nazi Germany was ahead in developing similar weapons. They hypothesized that these weapons would behave just like toxic gas weapons. In the letter, they proposed,

> as a gas warfare instrument the material would be grounded into particles of microscopic size to form dust and smoke and distributed by a ground-fired projectile, land vehicles, or aerial bombs. In this form personnel would inhale it into the lungs. The amount necessary to cause death to a person inhaling the material is extremely small. It has been estimated that one millionth of a gram accumulating in a person's body would be fatal.

Also, it mentioned:

> Two factors appear to increase the effectiveness of radioactive dust or smoke as a weapon. These are: 1. It cannot be detected by the senses; 2. It can be distributed in a dust or smoke form so finely powdered that it will permeate a standard gas mask filter in quantities large enough to be extremely damaging. An off-setting factor in its effectiveness as a weapon is that in a dust or smoke form the material is so finely pulverized that it takes on the characteristic of a quickly dissipating gas and is therefore subject to all the factors (such as wind) working against maintenance of high concentrations for more than a few minutes over a given area.

ii.) *Some of the US Government's Documentation of Harmful Effects of DU Weapons:* Documents provided by the Campaign Against Depleted Uranium (CADU) of UK are cited below to prove the harmful effects of DU:

A Federal Aviation Administration (FAA) advisory circular by M.C., dated 20 December 1984, warned FAA crash-site investigators about encounters with planes laden with depleted uranium when investigating plane crashes that "if particles are inhaled or ingested, they can be chemically toxic and cause a significant and long-lasting irradiation of internal tissue." On 7 March 1979, the US Army Mobility Equipment, Research and Development Command stated, "Not only the people in the immediate vicinity, emergency and fire fighting personnel, but also people at distances downwind from the fire are faced with potential over exposure to airborne uranium dust." (This was disclosed in accordance with a request based on the Freedom of Information Act to the National Gulf War Resources Center by Chris Kornkven, et al.) The US Army Environmental Policy Institute, in a June 1995 report to Congress, says depleted uranium has the potential to generate "significant medical consequences" if it enters the body. "The radiation dose to critical organs depends upon the amount of time that depleted uranium resides in the organs. When this value is known or estimated, cancer and hereditary risk estimates can be determined." On 26 May 1997, the *Nation* published an article about the US Army Armaments, Munitions and Chemical Command (AMCCOM) report in July 1990 that depleted uranium is a "low level alpha radiation emitter, which is linked to cancer when exposures are internal, and that chemical toxicity causes kidney damage." Also, AMCCOM's radiological task group has stated, "Long term effects of low doses [of DU] have been implicated in cancer and there is no dose so low that the probability of effect is zero." On 16 August 1993, Col. Robert G. Claypool of the US Army Surgeon General's Office, said in a letter, "When soldiers inhale or ingest DU dust, they incur a potential increase in cancer risk. The magnitude of that increase can be quantified if the DU intake can be estimated. Expected physiological effects from exposure to DU dust include possible increase in the outbreak of cancer and kidney damage." Health hazards data from the US Department of Labor says that the "[DU] increases the risk of lung carcinoma and chemical toxicity to kidney. Decay products of U-238, U-235, and U-234 are just as hazardous" (the Materials Safety Data Sheet: MSDS).

These documents indicate that before the Gulf war, and even after, the US Armed Forces and the US government had been doing investigations repeatedly on the danger of depleted uranium and the hazards of internal irradiation, and knew full well about its carcinogenicity and teratogenicity.

iii.) *Testimony of Doug Rokke*: Doug Rokke was a professor of physics and environmental science at the Jacksonville University, an army major (reserve), and in 1994–1995 was in charge of the DU Project of the Pentagon. He took the stand and answered questions from the prosecutors of the International Criminal Tribunal for Afghanistan regarding the said project. As to the background of the formation of this DU Project team of the Pentagon, he said:

Commissioned officers from the UK, Australia, Canada and Germany participated in the project to study the risk of DU weapons and I was tasked by the Army to direct the team. The objective of the project was to ensure that adequate information and training to soldiers being deployed to the battlefield are provided by making it clear to them the risks and hazards when DU bomb weapons are used, and to know what kind of countermeasures and precautionary measures should be adopted, and to make proposals as to how to clean up the DU bullets. Also, we submitted recommendations, which were completely ignored. Up to this day, the US Armed Forces has not taken any measures to protect the soldiers.

He also mentioned, "We made a proposal that clean-up was essential, but in reality, complete clean-up was impossible. Therefore, we proposed not to use DU weapons any longer. However our proposal was ignored by the upper level of the government and completely ignored by NATO, UK, Australia, and others."

Furthermore, Doug Rokke said that as part of the DU project, they made several videotapes that were supposed to be produced as videotapes on DU bombs of the Pentagon.

The first one was an advisory on what kind of danger was there when a DU bomb would explode, the second about a manual on when a clean up was being done, and the third one was on how to measure the radiation, and we made clear that a Geiger counter would not be effective in measuring DU bombs. The fourth one was about what kind of equipment should be used in destroying the residue of the DU bomb, and the fifth one was on how to handle dud [unexploded] bombs. These were produced especially for the sake of soldiers who would go on dangerous missions, but in the end, they were never used.

The US started the DU weapon project, but because of the report that was released about the extremely high risk of DU weapons, and recommendation that they should not be used, the results of the research project were classified. Through the proliferation of these information and videos, the hazardous nature of DU weapons had become clear, and the US feared being showered with criticism by the international community, and that DU weapons would no longer be used. This is how, according to Doug Rokke, et al., their recommendations were ignored, their project dissolved, and why nothing has ever been done to protect soldiers from DU weapons nor to provide them with medical care.

iv.) *Awareness of the Violations of International Law in the US Armed Forces:* Within the US armed forces, people are aware of possible violations of international law regarding the use of this type of weapon, in addition to being aware of matters relating to the danger of depleted uranium, as stated above.

The US Air Force's 1976 manual titled "International Law: The Conduct of Armed Conflict and Air Operations" names treaties, including the Hague Conventions of 1907, the Geneva Gas Protocol of 1925, and the Geneva Convention Relative to the Protection of Civilians in Time of War (1949), specifically recognized as binding by the US armed forces. The Geneva Gas Protocol outlaws asphyxiating, poisonous, or other gases, and all analogous liquids, materials, or devices, and the Hague Conventions explicitly forbid the use especially of poison or poisoned weapons. The Air Force manual defines poison as "biological or chemical substances causing death or disability with permanent effects when, in even small quantities, they are ingested, enter the lungs or bloodstream, or touch the skin." The manual says, "Any weapons may be put to an unlawful use," and unequivocally, "A weapon may be illegal per se if either international custom or treaty has forbidden its use under all circumstances. An example is poison to kill or injure a person."

It was in the 1970s that the US military began full-scale development and production of DU bombshells.

6. Environmental Pollution by Depleted Uranium (DU)

i.) *Widespread Radioactive Contamination in Iraq:* In this war on Iraq, DU weapons have been used in large cities and towns, starting with Baghdad. Many countries have a limit of public exposure to radiation prescribed by laws based on the recommendation of ICRP set at 1 millisievert per annum; the quantity of depleted uranium equivalent to this is 11.4 milligrams. The quantity of depleted uranium contained in a 30-milligram DU bomb is 280 grams. One shot of this can emit radiation surpassing the radiation limit for 25,000 persons per annum by ignition and micronization. On-the-spot investigations conducted by privately run facilities and scientists have reported that high levels of radiation have been detected from soils surrounding road ditches and inside building sites where warheads and hulls of DU bombs have been rolled, and war tanks. The exact amount used has not been publicly announced, but in a forum Michael Kilpatrick stated that even with just 115 tons, it would be enough to distribute a dosage per annum for about 100 million people. The depleted uranium has deeply penetrated people's life sphere.

On 6 April 2004, UNEP Executive Director Klaus Toefger said, "UNEP stands ready to conduct early environmental field studies in Iraq. Given the overall environmental concerns during the conflict, and the fact that the environment of Iraq was already a cause for serious concern prior to the current war, UNEP believes early field studies should be carried out. This is especially important to protect human health in a post-conflict situation where it seems apparent that DU weapons were used." Immediately afterward, UNEP published a "desk study on the Iraq environment" that contained information on the risks to groundwater, surface water, drinking water sources, and on the scattering of radioactive particles. The report of the British Royal Society in 2002 also predicts that due to depleted uranium, the radioactive contamination after the conflict will gradually permeate the soil and water sources in the years ahead.

ii.) *The Development of the Idea of Environmental Protection:* The present global environment was formed even before the human race appeared on earth, and the human race has evolved by conforming and adapting to it. However, the rapid development of scientific technology through the pursuit of comfort and convenience has brought about the destruction of ecosystems and global environmental pollution, and has caused a situation in which the very existence of mankind is now in imminent danger. Amid this situation, in 1971 the United Nations convened its first international conference with the environment as its theme, the United Nations Conference on the Human Environment, and adopted the "Declaration of the United Nations Conference of the Human Environment."

This declaration expresses the ideals that "both aspects of man's environment, the natural and the man-made, are essential to his well-being and to the enjoyment of basic human rights, the right to life itself"; "All countries, organizations and individuals at every level, all sharing equitably in common efforts, to achieve this environmental goal will demand the acceptance of responsibility and by their values and the sum of their actions, will shape the world environment of the future"; and "all countries shall bear the responsibility that their respective countries will not cause damage to the regional environment of another country."

The deepening and development of this environmental ideology was derived from movements attempting to regulate the environmental destruction brought about by war. In 1976, the treaty on the prohibition of military and other hostile use of environmental modification techniques was approved. It prohibited any technique for changing, through the deliberate manipulation of natural processes, the dynamics, composition, or structure of the earth, including its biota, lithosphere, hydrosphere, or of outer space, likely to have widespread, long-lasting, and also severe effects as a means to cause destruction, damage, and also injury. Simultaneously, the Supplementary Protocol of the Geneva Conventions also came into effect, and stipulated that "it is prohibited to use as means or method of combat intending or predicting to inflict widespread, long-lasting, and severe injury."

iii.) *Precautionary Principle:* However, without limiting it to the conduct of war, the technique and knowledge to be able to predict exactly how much effect modern human activities associated with technological progress have on the environment cannot be established at present. Consequently, the idea about the "precautionary principle" emerged in the middle of international conferences and treaties regarding the environment. At the United Nations Conference on Environment in 1992, the "Rio Declaration," specified with regard to the precautionary principle, "In order to protect the environment, the precautionary approach shall be widely applied by States according to their capabilities. Where there are threats of serious or irreversible damage, lack of full scientific certainty shall not be used as a reason for postponing cost-effective measures to prevent environmental degradation." But if this principle is prioritized, it is not difficult to imagine that profit-seeking companies, whose research will be stopped, will oppose it, and that there will be a division of opinion among nations. However, irrevocable environmental problems on the global scale, such as ecosystem abnormalities, etc., causing global warming and endocrine-disrupting substances have been observed extensively, and in 2000, an EU Commission set forth the policy "to standardize the Precautionary Principle regarding environmental problems." We human beings, who have repeatedly polluted and destroyed the environment for the sake of profit and greed and because of lack of foresight, have come to this stage; while at the same time the issues of protecting our fundamental human rights and preserving the ecosystem may motivate us to start taking notice at last of our important responsibility to the future.

In response to this problem, scientists and specialists in capitalist countries have been playing a great role, and concentrating their efforts in promoting the precautionary principle by publishing their statements in the Wingspread Conference of 1998 or the international conference on science and the precautionary principle in 2001. While they are still a minority, they have had influence in policy making. An ordinance adopted by the city of San Francisco in California is an example. Hereafter there will be a need for citizens to join hands, and to uphold the precautionary principle. At last mankind has recognized the need for voluntary restraints as a common duty and responsibility in order to prevent the complete destruction of the environment caused by people's becoming heedless of the environment, concerned only with making profits, and selfish in their attitude and mentality. This concept is the "precautionary principle," and we should bear in mind to take upon ourselves the responsibility to continue to affirm that this will become a basic ideology of mankind regarding the protection of the environment, and also to exert effort to observe it.

We believe that we should perceive the precautionary principle as something to deepen and develop an international humanitarian law and naturally apply it even to the conduct of war. The stipulation in the treaties and supplemental protocols stated previously to ban "the ways and means of military combat forecasted to cause widespread, long-lasting and severe effect and injury to the environment" should be applied at a time when some conduct is foreseen to have possible grave impact on the environment for the sake of actually demonstrating its valid restraining force. To put it plainly, if international humanitarian law—in the context of the historical development of environmental protection as achieved through the precautionary principle—is interpreted correctly, the use of DU weapons, which has been dispersing radioactivity that has a possibly grave impact on the ecosystem, is obviously an illegal act.

iv.) *The Crime of Omnicide:* On the other hand, at the International Criminal Tribunal for Afghanistan, a judgment was passed stating that the use of DU weapons threatens the existence even of neighboring countries in the region, as well as the extinction of all life forms, pollution of the air, water, and food resources, and the irreversible genetic mutation of all life forms including vegetation—in other words, it constitutes an omnicidal crime. This fact focuses attention on the danger of depleted uranium, the affects it is said to have on the ecosystem, and that its use is perceived to be an act of large-scale massacre of all life forms on earth. The failure to perceive the use of DU as criminal on the grounds that its effect on the environment has not been sufficiently established has unavoidably fostered the use and production of this environmentally destructive weapon. This is going against the tide of history in the formation of the precautionary principle, stated previously, and even in times of war, in order to make the precautionary principle effectively functional, some regulation and criminal punishment in the case of violations of that principle are necessary. Omnicide may become the basis by which to prosecute a violation, and the urgent establishment of this concept is much desired. Even to make international law function effectively hereafter, it is necessary to assimilate the concept called "omnicide" with the precautionary principle in the environmental sphere. For this reason as well, in this place, we denounce the use of DU weapons as a violation of international law, and thereby strongly appeal for banning their use.

7. The Use of DU Weapons as an Evident "War Crime" and "A Crime Against Humanity"

That the use of DU weapons is an illegal act in violation of international humanitarian law is evidently clear. International humanitarian law will not directly legalize the use of DU weapons, even when there is no explicit regulation immediately overseeing the use of individual weapons, but it has manifested the necessity of complying with 1.) the principle of prohibiting the means of causing unnecessary agony and uselessly aggravating the sufferings of disabled combatants; 2.) the principle of prohibiting the destruction of civilian targets; 3.) the principle of prohibiting weapons of mass destruction. However, as previously mentioned, the uranium pollution due to DU weapons is highly lethal, and the unnecessary suffering inflicted indiscriminately on people regardless of whether they are enemies or allies, the continuous toxicity even after the war, and the threat they pose to future posterity are clear indications of their potential to be indiscriminate, and the fact that this kind of weapons has been used in densely populated areas, including Baghdad, on both military and civilian targets, shows that the American and British Armed Forces have evidently violated all of the three abovementioned principles.

i.) *Crime against Humanity:* The use of DU weapons by the American and British armed forces is an attack aiming to murder people, plunge them into a state of deep suffering, noticeably obstruct, wreck, and steal their health through DU's genetic effects, its long-lasting destruction of the environment, and the widespread uranium pollution throughout the nation of Iraq, is an "inhumane act" committed as part of a "widespread attack or a systematic attack on civilians in an armed conflict" (Article 4 of the Official Regulations and Article 7 of ICC), and both President Bush and Prime Minister Blair, as commanders in chief, are criminally accountable for these crimes against humanity (Article 7 of the Official Regulations Article, and Article 7(a) of the ICC).

ii.) *War Crimes:* Also, this is clearly an unforgivable war, stipulated (in Articles 2(a), (d), (m) and (p) and Article 2(a), (b) of ICC) as "an attack intentionally carried out while those involved are fully aware of the collaterally long-lasting serious damages to the natural environment," "poison and toxic weapons are used" "weapons that have the quality to inflict serious injury and unnecessary suffering or have the quality to be indiscriminate are used," and both President Bush and Prime Minister Blair, as commanders in chief, are criminally accountable for war crimes (Article 4 of the Official Regulation and Article 2(a) of ICC). Long before this, in August 1996, the UN Human Rights Subcommittee adopted a resolution that the use of DU weapons constituted a violation as a weapon of mass destruction, and should be banned. Also, in July 2003, a report by Yeung Sik Yuen submitted to the UN Human Rights Subcommittee showed strong concern about the adverse effect on health, and the environment pollution caused by DU weapons, aside from the fact that "the use of DU weapons is a violation of international laws, can inflict unnecessary suffering and serious injuries, and can be a real menace to the environment, and by all means must be banned," and concluded that "these weapons... regardless of whether they are explicitly banned or not, should be prohibited." Also, in this argument, it was emphasized that states that have used these weapons in violation of international law are accountable for compensation for and decontamination of such deadly weapons.

Not only the UN Human Rights Subcommittee, but also other organizations, such as the European Union Parliament, have adopted resolutions to address this issue. In February 2003, the European Union Parliament adopted the "Resolution on the Harmful Effects of DU Bombs and Unexploded Bombs," and demanded that the European Commission monitor developments in relation to the possible serious, widespread contamination of the environment believed to be due to DU weapons, and support independent and thorough investigations into the possible harmful effects of the use of depleted uranium ammunition. In this manner, the international sentiment on banning the use of DU weapons has gained momentum, and in the midst of an awareness to observe international law, the use of DU weapons by the British and American armed forces is nothing but an insult to the international law that the international community and hitherto the human race has fostered. The whole nation of Iraq has become a testing ground for these weapons; sophisticated technology, including DU weapons, are freely used there, and by such use, the people of Iraq once again have been made to bear the pain and suffering of the fate of semi-permanent DU pollution. In the arguments expressed during the public trial of the International Criminal Tribunal for Afghanistan, the use of DU weapons was declared a crime of omnicide (the destruction of all life forms) for its threat to the survival of not only the country damaged by this use, but also neighboring countries, the extinction of life, the contamination of the air, water, and food resources, including vegetation, and also, the irreversible alteration of the genetic information of all life forms. In this regard, the use of DU weapons deprives all life forms born into this world the right to exist to the fullest, and it is an unforgivable crime against all living things.

Thus, with conviction, we prosecute the accused, President Bush and Prime Minister Blair, for the abovementioned crimes, and immediately seek compensation for all the victims, as well as the removal of radiation pollution.

Also, we hereby affirm that all nations should be legally obligated to ban the use, storage, production, and transfer of DU ammunition; that we as human beings have a mission to conclude and ratify treaties for the execution of those duties; and we affirm that through our collective efforts, we should be able to create an earth where there will no longer be any victims of depleted uranium.

The Health Effects of DU Weapons in Iraq
Thomas Fasy

It is a high honor for me to speak before the World Tribunal on Iraq. I thank the organizing committee for their invitation.

Uranium is radioactive and it is a toxic heavy metal. Inside the body, uranium exists as uranyl ions. Much of the toxicity of uranium is chemically mediated, in addition to the effects mediated by radiation. In 1986, while conducting experiments with crystal of potassium uranyl sulfate, Henri Becquerel discovered the phenomenon of radioactivity. Uranium, however, has been known to be toxic since the 1820s. In June 1942, when a commission of scientists reported to President Franklin Roosevelt that a uranium fission bomb could be built "in time to influence the outcome of the war," they explicitly warned about the toxicity of uranium, and consequently, a large-scale research program on uranium toxicology was begun in May 1943. It is now clear that uranium has multiple toxicities.

By the early 1900s, uranium was well recognized to be a kidney toxin. By the mid-1940s, uranium was known to be a neurotoxin. By the early 1970s, uranium was recognized to be a carcinogen, based on mortality studies of uranium workers and on experiments with dogs and monkeys. The first evidence that uranyl ions bind to DNA was reported in 1949 and by the early 1990s, uranium was shown to be a mutagen. Also, in the early 1990s, uranium was shown to be a *teratogen*, that is, an inducer of birth defects. The toxic effects of uranium on the kidney and on the nervous system typically occur within days of exposure and radiation probably plays little or no role in mediating these effects. In contrast, the carcinogenic effects of uranium have a delayed onset. The teratogenic effects of uranium might be due to exposure of one parent prior to conception as well as to exposure of the mother to uranium early in pregnancy.

Now let us briefly consider the routes of exposure to uranium. In the context of the dust particles derived from depleted uranium weapons, this means exposure to uranium oxides. By far the most dangerous route of exposure to uranium oxides is the inhalational or respiratory route. Absorption of uranium oxides through the gastrointestinal tract, the skin, and the conjunctivae is possible but quite limited. Following impact with hard targets, uranium metal undergoes combustion, releasing large quantities of very small uranium oxide dust particles into the environment. These dust particles derived from depleted uranium weapons are drastically different from the natural uranium that is normally present in rocks and soil. Soil particles contain uranium at very low concentrations, typically less than five parts per million; the vast majority of these soil particles, however, are too large to be inhaled deep into the lungs. In contrast, the dust particles derived from depleted uranium weapons contain very high concentrations of uranium, typically more than 500,000 parts per million; moreover, most of the DU dust particles are sufficiently small to be inhaled deep into the lungs.

Thus, compared to the uranium naturally present in the environment, DU dust contains uranium in a form that is vastly more bio-available and more readily internalized. Uranyl ions bind to DNA; they bind in the minor groove of DNA. While bound to DNA, uranyl ions are chemically reactive and can give rise to free radicals which may damage DNA. Chemically mediated DNA damage of this type may contribute to the ability of uranium to induce cancers.

I would now like to present some epidemiologic data from the Basra governate in the south of Iraq. In February 1991, more than 300 tons (possibly much more than 300 tons) of DU weapons were used in southern Iraq. After five- to six-year latent periods, increases in childhood cancers and birth defects were documented in the Basra governate. The most recent data indicate a fourfold increase in pediatric malignancies and a sevenfold increase in congenital malformations compared to 1990, the year preceding the war. The areas contaminated with DU weapons in the 1991 war and in the 2003 war are Mosul, Baghdad, Karbala, Basra, and Kuwait. The epidemiologic data that I will present were reported by Drs. Alim Yacoub and Jenan Hassan. Before the first war, the incidence rate was approximately three cases of congenital malformations per 1,000 births. This rate fluctuated considerably until 1998, when it began to rise sharply. By 2001, the rate was more than 22 cases per 1,000 births, more than a sevenfold increase compared to 1990. There has been a significant increase in the incidence rates of all childhood cancers and of leukemia (the most common childhood cancer) in the Basra governate. The incidence rates for total childhood cancers and for leukemias rose significantly between 1995 and 1998 and then began to increase sharply in 1999. There has been a striking increase in the number of leukemia cases in children younger than five. In 1990, two children under five were diagnosed with leukemia; in 2002, 53 children under five were diagnosed with leukemia.

When we look at charts and graphs of leukemia cases, we can easily loose sight of the anguish that leukemia represents for each child and his or her family. So I will close by presenting the story of Atarid, a five-year-old boy in Baghdad. This poignant photo was taken by Cathy Breen, a nurse from New York with Voices in the Wilderness. The photo was taken in mid-March 2003, a few days before the bombing of Baghdad began. Atarid was in hospital for treatment of his leukemia; his mother, Adra, has just been notified that all cancer patients in the hospital would be sent home to make room for the expected casualties from the imminent bombing. At the end of March 2003, Atarid died at home of septicemia, a blood infection.

It is not possible to establish a direct cause and effect relationship between the contamination of many populated areas of Iraq with uranium oxide dust from depleted uranium weapons and the increased incidence of cancers, leukemia, and birth defects in Iraq. Nonetheless, uranium is a known carcinogen and a known inducer of birth defects. Consequently, its dispersal into the environment in a form that is so readily internalized is, at the very least, profoundly reckless.

The UN and Its Conduct during the Invasion and Occupation of Iraq

Denis Halliday

Introduction and Background

Since 1990, the people of Iraq have been the victims of continuous US/UK-driven United Nations Security Council aggression. Triggered by the Iraq takeover of Kuwait, this aggression on the Iraqi people cannot be justified. I say that in no way defending the Iraqi invasion of Kuwait, for there can be no justification for such aggression. Instead this view reflects US rejection of peaceful withdrawal offers by Iraq. This was due to the determination of Washington to destroy Iraq's potential and violently overthrow a no longer useful former friend and ally in Baghdad.

The resulting 1991 UN-endorsed Gulf War, the war crimes committed in the name of the UN by US armed forces during that war, set a pattern of militaristic aggression toward the people of Iraq that continues today. The result has been massive loss of civilian life—some through both political and military negligence, and some intentional— as meets one essential element in the definition of genocide. This primitive response by the UN to this founding member state—via deadly UN sanctions through 2002—is now sadly sustained following the illegal invasion in 2003 and military and ideological occupation by troops of Bush II and Blair.

Since 1945, manipulated and corrupted by the five permanent members, the UN Security Council has often been brutally employed to serve the narrow interests of the powerful. This is as intended by the "victors" of World War II—if you read between the lines—in the Council's terms of reference as set out in the UN Charter.

As a result, the UN was structured to fail the people of Iraq and continues to do so in all respects. I refer to the so-called UN coalition— US led—of the 1991 Gulf War that destroyed civilian lives and infrastructure in breech of the Geneva Conventions and Protocols, massacred thousands, and buried alive in mass graves hundreds more Iraqi troops. The US leadership deployed that new nuclear weapon of choice, namely hundreds of tons of depleted uranium missiles and shells with horrific cancerous consequences still being revealed today.

In addition, the UN silently accepted the totally illegal no-fly zone bombing by the US/UK of Iraq culminating in "softening up attacks" preliminary to the unlawful invasion of 2003. More than twelve years of genocidal UN sanctions constitute a massive breach of the UN Charter itself—I refer to Articles 1 and 2 in particular—and underline the incompatibilities therein.

By these various means, the UN has itself destroyed the basic human rights of the Iraqi people through the willful neglect of Articles 22 to 28 of the Universal Declaration of Human Rights. The UN failed to protect and safeguard the children and people before and after the 2003 invasion. And as rare but honest news coverage demonstrates, the UN continues to fail Iraq—and its people—now in mid-2005, as this tribunal sits in Istanbul.

US/UK Invasion March 2003

With US invasion intentions announced, where were the UN voices of moral law and integrity? Where was the outrage? Where was the intervention of the secretary-general as per his obligations of UN Charter Article 99? Where were the many member states committed to protecting the UN Charter and tenets of international law? Given the forum of the General Assembly and the power of the majority, where were the states prepared to stop the oil/military strategic aggression blatantly being pursued by Bush and Blair? The answer is: They were nowhere to be found... or to be heard.

Respect for human rights and international law, including for the UN Charter itself, was hidden by the polluted and murky world of self-interest among UN member states that favors sweaty embraces of the Bush regime. The world watched Bush threaten the heads of state present in the General Assembly of September 2002 and then saw Bush and Blair deceive all who seemed willing to be misled, a deception culminating in General Powell lying to the Security Council in early 2003 about weapons of mass destruction and the "danger" Iraq presented!

We were asked to believe that the spirit of Article 51 of the UN Charter dealing with national self-defense somehow justified the US invasion of Iraq, as in the case of the invasion of Afghanistan. Blair informed us that Baghdad could surprise-attack London in 45 minutes with terrible and illegal weapons. He referred to chemical and biological weapons that were sold to Iraq by the UK itself, or by European and American friends, when earlier Baghdad took on Iran largely due to the urging and active support of Washington and London.

To argue that the Security Council in early 2003 was courageous in refusing to endorse the intended US/UK invasion is a nice thought, but nothing more. The UN was not, repeat not, enhanced by its action, or lack thereof, to protect the sovereign state of Iraq from raw US/UK military aggression. This was perhaps the lowest point reached yet by the UN in its short history. Even the tyranny of the "veto" did not save UN credibility, which might have been the case had the three remaining veto powers used that dictatorial device. They did not. And the failure of the remaining member states to walk out, resign, stand up, and be counted was and remains simply disgusting. When 20 months later the secretary-general remembered his responsibility to speak up as per Article 99, he mumbled off-the-record, but was sadly much too late.

Without the authority that resides in Article 42 of the Charter, and a Security Council resolution authorizing the specific use of force, the Bush/Blair invasion of Iraq is in complete breach of international law. The war crimes committed in that blatant military aggression—the most serious of international crimes—must be charged to Bush as the commander in chief, and to Blair as the prime minister who abused war powers. Bush should be charged with use of state terrorism for the opening salvo of "shock and awe" bombing strikes on Baghdad—designed to terrorize by physically and mentally attacking a civilian population. This is the kind of state terrorism that provides a tragic reminder of the US nuclear crime of bombing Hiroshima and Nagasaki. It is the kind of state terrorism beside which small-scale "terrorist" resistance pales in comparison. However, both forms of terrorism are internationally unlawful and unacceptable.

The UN member states listened mutely and swallowed—some painfully—the false arguments of Iraq's capacity to threaten not only its neighbors—none of whom appeared to share this fear—and the physical threats to the UK and US! The world tried desperately to believe the nonsense of massive stockpiles of weapons of mass destruction residing in Iraq. And to top off the US/UK lies and rubbish was the charge of a close Iraqi linkage to "al-Qaeda" and the attack on those Twin Towers of capitalistic greed in New York City on 11 September 2001. To those who understood the secular nature of the Baghdad government and Ba'athist philosophy, this supposed lineage broke the last straw of credibility. And the UN stood mutely by. Even to this day, the Security Council is unwilling to define terrorism for fear that state terrorism employed by its permanent five member states would thereby be constrained.

Thus, the March 2003 invasion took place in breach of all known international laws, executed with the application of terrorism and commission of war crimes, including further and massive use of depleted uranium. The UN, its member states, and its secretary-general failed to employ all possible means to protect the people of Iraq; worse, the UN was generally seen around the world to be acquiescent and collaborative. Ironically, at the same time, Americans were outraged that the UN had failed to support US foreign policy and their self-serving military aggression on Iraq—but that is material for another session!

UN Collaboration with US/UK Occupation

Whereas the invasion was in breach of international law, although eased by the acquiescence of the UN, and was globally condemned, the occupation was on the other hand more readily accepted as a new, if unlawful, reality. The occupation was supported by member states and donor agencies, and then actively supported by the UN. That support and active involvement constitutes collaboration. And UN collaboration with the occupying enemy was, and is, a tragic mistake. Collaboration of this kind is an unacceptable role for the UN.

We are all familiar with the rights of Iraqi self-defense and resistance to foreign military occupation, as set out in UN Charter Article 51. We are equally familiar with the often murderous consequences of collaboration, which the French Resistance made famous, and even bizarrely glorious, under occupation in the 1940s. There is nothing glorious about killing—be it of the enemy, or of one's own countrymen and women who decide, for whatever reason, to collaborate.

There was and is nothing glorious about UN collaboration in Iraq, and nothing glorious about the consequence—the deadly truck-bombing of the UN office building in Baghdad on 19 August 2003, in which some 20 UN staff died. The Security Council and particularly the secretary-general, responsible for the welfare of staff members, appear to have failed to understand that the UN was, even before collaboration, the most hated organization in Iraq. Why? Why not? After twelve years of deadly UN sanctions that cost Iraq over one million lives, mostly children, followed by conspicuous collaboration with the common Iraqi enemy, that is, the American and British occupying enemy. After twelve years of humiliation and loss of dignity under UNSCOM's intrusive search for weapons of mass destruction—why was anyone surprised?

The UN secretary-general and his staff were obligated to remain apart from the illegal occupation, at best on standby. Unless invited by a legitimate Iraqi government to assist, and there was none remaining in Iraq after the unlawful overthrow of the Baghdad government, the UN had no place in the country. The UN had no mandate to be in Iraq. A demand from Washington and/or London does not constitute a legitimate invitation. And puppet regimes cannot be recognized by the UN, even if set up by two permanent member states of the Security Council. Airlifting long expatriated Iraqis together with their own armed thugs and mercenaries and setting them up as an interim regime, does not create a representative or legal government with which the UN can legitimately serve.

However, it is considered that occupation, even unlawful occupation, comes with obligations under international law. Such obligations included the rule of domestic law, the protection of state and private property, and perhaps most importantly, the protection and well-being of the civilian population as per international law. The occupying US and UK forces blatantly failed to meet these obligations.

They allowed, even facilitated, a complete breakdown in law and order. They stood back as looting and destruction in the cities and towns of Iraq took place. As days became weeks and months, they neglected to meet the basic needs of the people, including food, housing, water, power, healthcare, education, and employment. And, tragically, the gutless UN stood back silently as the Americans and British created anarchy. The UN remained silent as the occupiers disbanded Iraqi defense forces, including border guards, thereby opening the country up to intrusion and looting by thousands intent on chaos. In addition to the cost in Iraqi civilian well-being and lives, the intruders also came to attack the occupying common enemy of the region, i.e., the intrusive and hated American armed forces— the fearsome crusaders of Bush fundamentalism. Again the UN failed to protect the sovereign rights of Iraq—the Security Council and the secretary-general were gagged.

Before the Iraqi economy could even begin the process of recovery from UN sanctions and military invasion, the American occupiers abolished the oil-for-food program. Even after the invasion, this program remained the primary source of food and other essentials for over 85 percent of the population of some 24 million. With unemployment over 70 percent, plus thousands of newly disbanded defense personnel, invasion war damage, and increased homelessness, the social and economic plight of the Iraqi people had deteriorated further.

Ignorant and grossly irresponsible, Washington looked to the modest private sector of Iraq to suddenly sell food, medicine, and other essentials to a population largely unemployed and impoverished, in the face of growing inflation. In a matter of weeks, an economy that had been centralized and public-sector driven under UN sanctions was disbanded, with very painful results. Under the US/UK occupation, for example, rates of child mortality have increased and malnutrition has risen. Where was the UN voice to protect basic civilian interests and demand that occupation obligations be fully met by the US and the UK?

The breakdown of personal security, social services, healthcare, education, and basic needs has been almost total. In other words, the occupying military forces have failed in all aspects of meeting their responsibilities under international law. And the UN has been silent. The UN has also been silent as the US set about building some fourteen military bases for their own long-term strategic military requirements in the region. These are strategies relating to regional military presence, natural gas and oil reserves, and control thereof. However, in regard to reconstruction and new investment in infrastructure destroyed by the Gulf war of 1991, constrained by UN sanctions, and weakened further by the Bush/Blair invasion, little has been done. Instead the presence of US/UK forces has created chaos and armed resistance to their military occupation. They have alienated most of the population—not unexpectedly—but in addition, they have split the secular country of Iraq into religious and ethnic divides that had been long submerged under an Iraqi national identity. Has the UN spoken up?

For the first time in many years, the dreadful possibility of civil war has been created by foreign occupation that—like an old colonial regime—has discovered the benefits of divide and rule, with disastrous results. Where is the UN demand to an end to military occupation and the belated return of Iraq to the people of Iraq?

At the time of the initial occupation of Iraq, the UN transferred some US$8 billion to a Provisional Authority headed by an American. And this was not UN money. This was Iraq government oil revenue obtained under oil-for-food program oil sales! Worse, it is now revealed that the UN did not monitor or audit the expenditure of this $8 billion and it appears much was mishandled and is unaccounted for by the US authorities. Some $4 billion was handed without the benefit of competitive bidding to the American corporation Halliburton, which is connected to the White House through Cheney, the vice president. Hundreds of millions was disbursed in cash to the "new" ministries set up with and by the Americans, staffed and managed by the Americans, without accounting. These billions improperly handed over by the UN were the property of the Iraqi people. Again the UN has failed in its responsibility.

As a diversion from its own disastrous occupation, costs, and loss of life, Washington has attacked the oil-for-food program, within which it appears there has been some UN mismanagement, poor contracting, weak accounting of Iraqi monies, and maybe even some theft—amounting to perhaps as much as $150,000. Nevertheless, this unique and largely successful US$65 billion program fed and provided basic human needs from 1997 to 2002 for some 24 million Iraqi people. The scandal is not UN mismanagement—it is Washington-approved billion-dollar oil sales by Baghdad outside the constraints of oil-for-food; it is the granting of 30 percent of Iraqi oil revenue under UN oil-for-food arrangements to Kuwait while Iraqi children died for lack of financial investment in electric power and potable water supplies. It is the genocide that the UN perpetrated on the Iraqi people over some twelve years of strangulation under uniquely comprehensive sanctions.

Conclusion

We find in Iraq today almost total political and social chaos. Foreign military occupation has influenced interim arrangements that are not representative and do not have the confidence of many Iraqis. We find chaos and misery for the Iraqi people, made homeless by brutal US/UK military action in civilian areas and towns, such as has been seen in the neighborhoods of Baghdad and Falluja, with horrific civilian casualties. For the survivors, homelessness, unemployment, and little means to survive have resulted. Healthcare and education are in disarray because families are afraid to send their children to clinics and schools for fear of bombing and kidnapping. Child mortality and malnutrition are on the increase. Personal security does not exist. University students stay away out of fear. The breakdown in policing since the occupation has led to a level of murder and killing unknown in a free Iraq before occupation. Many essentially experienced civil servants, intellectuals, doctors, and educators have been murdered. The UN is largely silent.

Despite the courage of many Iraqis to vote under these near-impossible conditions and work toward a replacement system of government, the national institutions remain in very bad shape. Financial and human capital are both in short supply. The much-needed constitution being drafted under American supervision and interference is likely to have a long and hard road to acceptance. It will undoubtedly need much rewriting once the country has an elected and representative government when free of foreign occupation. It is expected that Iraq will reject many American pressures, including privatization to foreign corporations of public-sector essentials such as water, oil resources, and power. It is feared that privatization interference will lead to structural adjustment devices that will destroy the remaining strengths of the welfare system so many Iraqis have learned to depend upon over many years.

Due to the corruption of the Security Council, and abuse of the UN Charter by the five permanent members in particular, the unlawful invasion and occupation of Iraq and the many tragic consequences thereof have not led to condemnation by the UN Security Council. Outrageously, the US and UK continue to enjoy the benefits of member states in good standing, and retain their veto powers and permanent seats on the Council. They have not been obliged to terminate illegal military action within the sovereign state of Iraq. They have not been forced to withdraw occupying military forces. They have failed to meet their occupation obligations under international law. They have stolen and abused limited Iraqi financial resources and have underspent their own funds, which they obligated very publicly for reconstruction and development.

The UN has watched the loss of life in Iraq. The UN has watched the war crimes of US/UK forces, including the negligent bombing of civilians and use of depleted uranium devices, yet again, without comment. The UN has witnessed massive loss of innocent civilian life—over 100,000 has been estimated so far. As you know, US occupation forces do not bother to count the civilians they kill and/or maim. The UN has watched the employment of some 80,000 hired guns who serve the US authorities under no known law. The UN has watched in silence American human-rights abuses, the torture and killing of Iraq prisoners, arrested and jailed without respect for their human rights or explanation to their families.

Having tragically weakened Iraq and its people under twelve years of sanctions, the UN has taken no action to stop, condemn, or punish the blatant US/UK transgressions of the UN Charter, human rights, and other provisions of international law. The world has witnessed in Iraq the most serious of international crimes—the crime of military aggression on a sovereign member state—by US and UK forces. The world waits for the people of Iraq to be given an opportunity to make their own decisions and resolve their own differences as only they can hope to do, without foreign occupation and interference. The world waits for the UN to act in keeping with the provisions of international law, including the application of International Criminal Court provisions to Bush, Blair, and their henchmen and women who have violated the core tenets of the UN Charter, the Declaration of Human Rights, and the Geneva Conventions and Protocols.

In the meantime, this World Tribunal in Istanbul has this opportunity— this obligation—to demand full international prosecution of US/UK war leaders and war criminals involved in the destruction of Iraq, the lives of its people, and their human rights and well-being, through unlawful and unjustifiable armed invasion and military occupation.

Gender-Based Violence

Hana Ibrahim

I salute you for rallying for justice as a sacred and natural right for all the people of the world. I will put in front of you a collection of facts and let us together analyze them.

I am a witness of the new era of occupation that has unleashed death that creeps around my country like a hungry monster. First of all, I would like to point out:

1) The US has not ratified the Convention on the Elimination of all Forms of Discrimination against Women. One wonders why?

2) Gender as a concept can be abused as an issue of division and strife, as sociologist experts would agree.

3) The neoliberals have used the issue of gender as a mean of strengthening discrimination against women. A quick example: Order 137 of December 2003 was issued on the watch of the occupation, by the IGC. Paul Bremer decided to cancel it and in a Saddam-like gesture gave women a guaranteed 25 percent representation in parliament. Why was the percentage set at 25? How was this decision reached? This is yet another "sectarian-like allocation."

4) The occupation came armed with its own philosophy and jargons. This phenomenon started with the Americans classifying Iraqis as Kurds, Shiites, and Sunnis, at the time the unauthorized no-fly zones were imposed, on the pretext of protecting the Kurds and the Shiites. However, they were not concerned about those who live between the two zones.

These classifications and jargons are used as instruments to break down and restructure Iraq and to arouse primitive prejudices in order to facilitate the US's plans.

The concept of gender is also being used as a means of isolating the Iraqi woman from the rest of her society and using the divisions created to facilitate the occupiers' plans.

Bush claimed to have launched his devastating war on Afghanistan in order to liberate the Afghani woman from the burka. Bush buried the Afghani woman with her burka under the rubble of war machine. Bush also stood at the UN in 2002, declaring his aim to liberate Iraqi women. What a heavy price our women have paid and are paying for this war of "liberation"—the women of Falluja, Karbala, Najaf, Kuffa, al-Qaim, and Mosul.

During the siege of Falluja, 72 women were killed in 6 days by the bullets of the snipers. All these women did was open the front door of their houses.

Bush talks about domestic-violence crimes against pregnant women being a double crime, against her and against her baby.

What of the Iraqi women living under the horrors of the continuous US wars, using their deadliest weapons? What of the Iraqi children terrorized, injured, and killed by the American bombs? What about the babies born in the American prisons; we had the testimony of ex-inmates of Abu Ghraib on this subject.

What of the grave violations of women in American custody in Abu Ghraib prison and other detention centers? There has been a complete blackout on the numerous violations of women's rights in US custody.

Our organization has documented several cases in which women prisoners were stripped naked and paraded in front of the men prisoners in Abu Ghraib prison. This is done deliberately to humiliate the women as well as the men. The occupiers want to destroy all that is sacred in Iraqi society. It is part of their strategy of subjugation of the Iraqis.

The violations of Iraqi women's rights started with the advances made by the occupiers' troops and the breakdown of law and order that they engineered. Iraqi women lost their safety, security, and their livelihood.

We have well-sourced information about the kidnapping and rape mafias by which women, teenagers, and young girls are sold into prostitution inside and outside Iraq. I have personally met someone who is in the know, but has refused to let me document his testimony.

There is a price for a raped woman (US$2,000–3,000) and another for a virgin (US$10,000).

These mafias also kidnap children for body parts abroad; a child can also fetch US$10,000.

This complete breakdown of law and order and the occupiers' failure to live up to their obligations have meant that women are resorting to seeking safety from traditional Iraqi society, whether Christian or Muslim.

This is why the number of veiled women has increased, out of fear, not out of religious belief. We conducted an impromptu survey on this issue among women university students.

Before the war, women had freedom of movement, were free to drive their own cars, and were free to be safe on the streets even after dark.

There is a dramatic drop in the number of women on the Iraqi streets nowadays. University students and schoolchildren are being chaperoned by their parents. There has been a drop in the number of girls and women in schools and colleges.

Internally displaced women are suffering from lack of shelter and the humiliation of living on handouts. Many of them have lost their husbands and breadwinners as well as their houses.

Only women and children were allowed to leave Falluja (we had the same scenario in Tal Afar and Mosul); women found themselves in charge of their families but without a safe shelter. Living in fear and sheer panic is one of the worst violations against women.

As a result of the American raids in the middle of the night and the aerial bombardment, people are resorting to sleeping in one room. Women have started to wear a trousers-like undergarment; in case their house is raided in the middle of the night, or worse bombed, they fear being exposed even when they die.

The percentage of unemployment in Iraq is put at 72 percent; for Iraqi women unemployment is 90 percent, because most women worked in the public sector.

There has been a noticeable increase in women taking casual, low-paid jobs, and serving in private houses with little or no protection. Prostitution is on the increase, with all its ramifications. Also, the number of women and children begging on the streets has increased considerably.

There is no protection or support for the widows, wives, and families of the detainees, and in those cases where a widow or wife has a right to support most of the time her rights go unclaimed, because she may be frightened to disclose that her husband was killed or is detained by the Americans.

So what will we do? We will not give in to the occupiers; we will resist them for our sake and yours. The US administration does not make the destinies of the people of the world. Another, better world is possible. I ask you to think with your hearts. Women's hearts unite humanity at times of pain and calamity.

The Ruin of Daily Life

Eman Khammas

I concur with what our friend Haifa[1] said: we need to talk about the daily struggle to survive in Iraq. But I find there are more important things to talk about than the scant supply of electricity with temperatures exceeding 50° Centigrade (122° Fahrenheit). Let us talk about the spread of crime; let us talk about the crimes of the occupiers and the Iraqi National Guards; let us talk about the total absence of security; let us talk about mass arrests.

I will be talking about the daily life in the encircled and bombed cities, about Rawa, Haditha, al-Qaim, and maybe Falluja, which is currently witnessing a much more serious assault than that of November 2003.

There are Iraq cities and towns that are labeled "insurgency strongholds" and other labels, such as the Sunni Triangle. These cities are suffering terrible human-rights abuses, with "tackling" terrorism being used as a pretext.

Just before I came here, Dr. Hamdi al-Alusi, the manager of al-Qaim hospital, was on TV imploring international aid organizations to put pressure on the British and American military to allow the injured civilians of al-Qaim access to health care, lest they die of their wounds. He called on the British and Americans to stop the bloodbath unfolding in al-Qaim.

When the American forces attack a city in Iraq, you will hear a short news item stating that the American forces have mounted a raid on such and such town. Two or three days later you will hear that they have arrested ten or fifteen terrorists and that will be the end of the matter.

In reality, what happens is: the town is completely surrounded, and all roads leading to it are cut off. Any car that attempts to approach the city will be fired on without warning.

I was in Haditha hospital myself and saw with my own eyes some of the victims.

Here is a picture of Fouad and Yousif. They were on the way to Haditha from the plaster construction factory where they worked, in a car. They were killed by American fire. One had severe head wounds and the other had severe stomach wounds. I saw the insides of their heads and stomachs sitting outside their bodies. Each one was married, with five children. This is but one example; I have hundreds of such examples.

The American raids on cities usually start with aerial and missile attacks that will last from one hour to several days. Such bombardment is more often than not indiscriminate. It does not distinguish between schools, hospitals, houses, or government buildings. The resistance is based in the city and has no headquarters, so the Americans punish all the citizens of the city. Therefore there have been many cases of innocent civilians dying under the rubble of their own houses, bleeding to death, in Haditha, Rawa, al-Qaim, and Mosul.

The doctor I mentioned earlier in al-Qaim did dispatch ambulances to reach the wounded civilians, but the ambulances were fired upon.

During the raid on the town or after it, the American forces will decide which house to take over; they force the owners to stay in one room, with a soldier guarding the door. The soldiers then proceed to act as snipers from the inside or the roof of this house. They will fire at any movement. I can understand this perhaps when they shoot at a man, because they might have thought he was a fighter, but I cannot comprehend: why do they fire on a sixty-year-old woman? Why do they fire on children? Why do they fire on the hospitals?

I asked a friend of mine, Tim, who used to be soldier, what could possibly be the reason for firing on a three-year-old girl from a distance of 500 meters and in broad daylight?

Another example is that of Dhuha— I do not know whether you can see her photo—she was in her sixties. She had just gotten out of a clinic and was trying to get into a car when the Americans started to shoot. Her son threw himself on top of her. She was injured. People inside the clinic asked her to crawl back into the clinic while the bullets were raining down. She did not make it. Dhuha died on the road. I have her death certificate, "due to gunshot wounds to the chest and abdomen," her son, his wife, and their child all badly injured; her son might not be able to walk again.

Al-Qaim has one main street with the commercial shops, the clinic, the market all situated on that main road. At the top of the road is the customs and excise office, a building that rises above the town and overlooks this street. The American forces occupied this building and they would shoot at the people of the town as the people went about their daily business. One example from al-Qaim is twelve-year-old Mustapha. I call him lucky Mustapha because the bullet that hit him just missed his spinal cord; otherwise he would have become a cripple. Many people have been crippled by the snipers' fire.

The doctors at Haditha told me that snipers' victims brought to the hospital all had serious head, stomach, or chest wounds, as you have seen earlier in the pictures of Fouad and Yousif. If the aim is to frighten people or warn them, why not aim at their limbs?

There is an army of disabled men, women, and children, thanks to the work of the American snipers.

There is also the case of a wedding motorcade (no location mentioned), which was obvious as such because the bride was dressed in her wedding dress, but whose car was fired on by the Americans. The bride was hit in the head; her father-in-law lost an eye.

There is complete lack of law and order when the Americans raid a city, no protection for the population whatsoever. No courts, no police stations. The hospitals are often occupied or bombed or burned down. I do not know whether you have heard about what happened to Falluja hospital; it was burned down deliberately by the American forces. The same was done to al-Qaim and Haditha hospitals.

I also want to talk about house demolitions. The Americans would raid a house, arrest all the men, cart out the women and children, and then dynamite the house. There are many such examples. One man, a truck driver, they even burned down his truck. They came the following day, and said, sorry, it was the wrong house! He said to them, "What do you mean you are sorry, you have destroyed my house! What can I possibly do with your apology?"

All that you hear about compensation is nonsense and a stupid lie. Some people believe it; they make a dossier documenting the damage done to their property and submit it to the American military authorities, who just discard them.

An Iraqi lawyer showed me the reply he got from the Americans on 35 such cases. The reply in all cases was a standard form, with the name changed: "The request is denied."

Before finishing, I would also like to mention the problem of the missing people. We have 10,000–15,000 men that are completely missing; no one knows their fate. This problem is not even mentioned in the press. Their families have been looking for them; they go to the offices of the human-rights ministry, to the American detention centers, the police, etc.

The officials in all these places deny the men's presence in their custody. No one seems to take responsibility for searching for these people. Their families are left in limbo, do not know where they are, what happened to them, or who to turn to.

I call on all human-rights organizations and I call on the UN to take up the cases of the missing in Iraq. Their families deserve to know the truth.

These are the main areas of the violations of human rights being committed in Iraq.

The Conduct of the US Army

Tim Goodrich

Before I start, I would like to take a moment to recognize a couple of people. In order to more accurately report on US military conduct in Iraq, I have included information collected from members of the military who served in branches other than the Air Force, which was my branch of service. Their names are Camilo Mejia, Aiden Delgado, and Dave Bischel of the US Army, and Jimmy Massey of the US Marine Corps. These people have become good friends of mine and together we have spoken out and demonstrated against the war.

Also, please do not let my youthful appearance fool you. I feel as though my time in the military has aged me prematurely.

Since the beginning of humankind's history, there has been war. Along with armed conflict, misconduct by military forces is inevitable. For anyone who has been in war, only one thing is certain: there are no rules in war, you do what you can in order to survive. The current war and occupation of Iraq is no different.

From the start, there have been allegations of misconduct. Perhaps the most infamous of these is the prisoner abuse at Abu Ghraib. Although Abu Ghraib has been widely reported across the world, perhaps what is lesser known are the everyday instances of abuse and heavy-handed tactics in Iraq. While it is imperative that the soldiers who commit these acts are punished, it is not enough to see this as just a few bad individuals who have gone astray and broken the rules. To explore the root causes of military misconduct in Iraq, we must first delve into the history and training of the military. And to do this, we must start with how people are recruited into the military, who joins the military, and the reasons why.

American society is fairly militarized. This is evidenced through the video games, cartoons, movies, television shows that our children see. And are subjected to this daily violence.

Military life is glorified; soldiers are seen as role models. In my case, I wanted to join the military since I was five years old because I had seen that my grandfathers had served.

Young adults in the US can enlist at the young age of seventeen.

Throughout high school, recruiters prey upon our youth, setting up shop outside the cafeteria and luring them with free items. Students also take field trips to military bases to learn about military life and are forced to take the armed services vocational aptitude battery, which is a test testing all the skills the student has. The results are then reported to the recruiters so that they can more accurately target their recruits.

The targeting of lower-income and minority areas is a particular problem in the US. This is what we call the "socioeconomic draft."

Lower-income kids are especially prone to joining the military, because many times their families can't afford a college education for them. Also, kids want to join the military because their families may not be able to pay the bills and the kids want to help out in whatever way they can.

Other reasons youth want to join the military are to escape poverty, a lack of job opportunities, family problems, or as a simple act of rebellion against their parents.

Minorities are often targeted as well. Recently in Los Angeles, retired General Tommy Franks, you may know him as one of the masterminds of the Iraq war, came to speak to a group of fifth graders at an intercity school. Logan Elementary School has a 90 percent Latino population. His speech was sponsored by a multibillion dollar wealth management company. And I ask you, what were the real intentions behind this speech to young children?

The misleading by recruiters continues. Many times they have been caught in the act of telling their potential recruits to lie about their past drug use, their past medical conditions, and often over-promised benefits that they will receive in the military.

Despite having different reasons for joining the military, most exit their military training having a profound sense of patriotism and become part of a unique military culture. This training indoctrinates a soldier into the military culture and this happens in a number of different ways.

Training

Military training is designed from day one to remove individuality and to dehumanize.

The goal is to break each person down and then build them up as a person who is conformed to a military lifestyle of taking orders without questioning.

The ways we do this are many. First, a recruit must ask permission to ask a question. They often are required to perform the most ridiculous tasks without questioning, such as folding t-shirts into tiny squares having all the edges aligned. Just to prove that they can follow orders without asking any questions.

At rifle practice, recruits shoot at targets depicting human bodies. This makes it easier when they have to put this into real-life practice, to shoot a human being.

During military training, recruits also learn about Geneva Conventions and the rules of warfare; however, this training is extremely limited and pales in comparison to the rest of what you learn.

We are never taught peacekeeping skills. This makes us unprepared for the situation we face in Iraq.

Regardless of a person's job in military, the first and foremost job is to kill.

Permanent Duty Station

After training, recruits are sent to the permanent duty station. There, they arrive and continue their state of perpetual training.

They also develop peer relationships.

Normal workplace rules dictate that you don't talk about race, religion, sex, politics, and other subjects of a sensitive nature. However, due to times of extreme boredom in the military, it was common to talk about these things. And it became evident to me during my time in the military that racism and ignorance are prevalent throughout the military.

If I had a dollar for every time I heard the phrase, "We should nuke the entire Middle East, it would solve all our problems," I would be a rich man.

Another example is that of the Turkish compound. I have friends who were deployed to Incirlik here in Turkey. They came back and told me of this Turkish compound where women were taken from their families and forced into prostitution to repay the debts their husbands had incurred. Obviously, this is false.

Finally, there is a great lack of knowledge about the religion of Islam. It is a prevalent idea that in Islam all non-believers are infidels and should be killed.

As time went on, it became more common to hear the words "raghead," "haji," and "sand nigger" being used on a daily basis.

Anytime someone is in disagreement with this party line of thought, they are labeled a communist. Which is funny because I am not a communist, though I have been accused of this. One time I turned around and said, "What exactly is a communist?" And of course the other person had no idea what a communist actually was. It was simply a label meant to separate you from the common train of thought. (What is a communist?)

Pre-Deployment

Before being assigned on deployment there is a lot of paperwork, processing, packing, and refresher training to be accomplished. During this time there is little emphasis on the Geneva Conventions and the rules of warfare.

My friend Jimmy Massey in the Marine Corps, before deploying to Iraq, received cultural training about the customs and courtesies of Iraq. However, it was only a 30-minute class with 150 other Marines, hardly enough to prepare him for the situation that lay ahead.

Waiting at the border of Kuwait, soldiers were trained on how to secure oil fields, but not banks, museums, and other important infrastructure within Iraq.

Let us now pass forward to the actual operations in Iraq.

Deployment

As we now know, the bombing of Iraq happened much before the official date of 19 March 2003. I was a witness to this escalation of bombing as I was deployed to Saudi Arabia from August through October 2002. Recently an article appeared in the *Sunday Times* of London, entitled "US and UK Bombing Raids Try to Goad Saddam into War." This in itself is military misconduct.

Since the ground invasion began, it was plagued with many problems as well. Among these are lack of cultural training, lack of communication, and house raids.

Lack of cultural training in the local customs and courtesies has been a problem because it has led to many innocent deaths, especially at checkpoints, when soldiers didn't know the simple hand signal in Arabic for stop. Many Iraqis mistook the hand signal as a motion to go and their vehicles were fired upon, often times killing them because of this.

Lack of communication is also a problem. This lack of communication between intelligence officials and ground troops led recently to the killing of an Italian bodyguard after an Italian journalist was freed. The Italians had provided word to the Americans that they would be traveling on the road to the airport but this was never communicated to the ground troops. There is much bureaucracy within the American military.

House raids are a particular problem. There has been much faulty intelligence leading to the arrest of innocent people. And in fact, the Red Cross has said that 70 to 90 percent of these detainees at the prisons throughout Iraq are in fact innocent.

Prison Abuse

Abu Ghraib is a symbol of the Saddam era and should not have been used. It is a sprawling complex on the western outskirts of Baghdad, housing thousands. The detainees are kept outside while soldiers stay inside the cells. This makes the detainees vulnerable to attack. The detainees are housed in tents, where they are exposed to the elements. As a common way to punish detainees, US soldiers remove their blankets and heavy clothing. One time, in uprising to protest these conditions, the prisoners started to throw rocks at the guards. The soldiers then retaliated, killing four detainees. Afterward a picture was taken of an American soldier standing above one of the dead Iraqis loaded onto a truck. The soldier was holding a spoon above the Iraqi's head as though to mock scooping out his brains.

Teenagers, adults, the handicapped, and the elderly are all kept together, handcuffed (this happened in al-Assad prison in May 2003, but the Abu Ghraib story did not break until November 2003). Camilo spooks were in charge at these detention camps—no accountability due to no rank, no name, no organization, etc...

The prisoners were subjected to sleep deprivation of 48 to 72 hours. They were kept hooded and tied. The soldiers would hit walls with sledgehammers to make loud echoing noises. They also carried out mock executions with 9mm guns; they would charge the gun next to the prisoner's head. This was not the doing of a few bad apples—abuse was systematic, and soldier misconduct prevalent throughout Iraq.

Many cases start with good intentions. However, over time the stress adds up; being away from family, working extended hours, little sleep, and fear all contribute to this. Family hardships contribute as well, such as spousal problems, child illnesses, and the like. This is particularly the case with the high level of reservists and National Guard who are activated. These citizen soldiers of the US are not used to long deployments away from home.

Sometimes Prozac or other antidepressants or anti-anxiety drugs are prescribed. But these medicines are never enough. Eventually, soldiers begin to change and take out their frustration on the Iraqis. In some cases, Iraqis have been beaten after being taken from their houses at the house raids. When dropped off at the prison, soldiers have said simply, jokingly, that they fell off the truck.

As you have just heard, there are countless numbers of atrocities happening in Iraq. In many cases these are ordered from higher in the chain of command, but ultimately the individual acts of the soldiers are a personal moral choice. What is missing is the accountability of those writing the orders and making the policies. Regardless, what has happened in Iraq is not only a betrayal of the Iraqis and the people of the world, but also a betrayal of the American troops serving there.

When a soldier signs on the line, it is with the understanding that they will risk their life for the defense of their country. They sign with the understanding that if they are sent into a war, it better be for a good (and legal) reason.

Despite all the bad news that I have just outlined, there is hope and good news.

Elements of resistance within the military itself have been increasing. This is through countless numbers of individual acts, but also growing number of large acts of resistance at home. Such as the case of Pablo Paredes, who despite being only sent overseas in a support role refused to go. He was sentenced to months of hard labor. Also Camilo Mejia, who after serving a tour of duty in Iraq refused to go back a second time. He was sentenced to a year in jail. Cases like these are becoming more common.

There are growing numbers of conscientious objector applications and growing numbers of soldiers speaking out and joining an organization I helped to co-found, Iraq Veterans Against the War.

Findings

To summarize, despite the war being illegal under international law and being based on lies, there are many other factors which contribute to military misconduct in Iraq. Among these are poor intelligence, lack of training, the stress of fighting in a guerilla war, and finally, the lack of a mission and clearly defined goals after the fall of Baghdad. Coupled with the fact that military culture already has many problems with racism, ignorance, stereotypes, and dehumanization, this clearly shows that the best solution is an immediate withdrawal of American troops from Iraqi soil.

Detentions and Prison Conditions

Amal Sawadi

L adies and gentlemen, I would like to give my special thanks to the men and women who set up the World Tribunal on Iraq. I have a great respect and appreciation for their contributions, which represent their humanity and solidarity with the people of my country who have been imprisoned by the brutal American occupying forces and their allies.

People of conscience may be able to provide answers as to why the Iraqi people have been humiliated and tortured: Why have the Muslim religious scholars been insulted? Why are the Iraqi academics and scientists being forced to leave the country or have been openly murdered? Why are children being killed? Why are women being tortured in Iraq? When will the American forces stop raping our people, stealing our homes, destroying our crops, distributing drugs, and encouraging prostitution? What do these invaders want?

Despite these questions, I have come to you with the belief that the American occupation forces and its allies, who have intentionally used violence against our people, will have to pay for their crimes.

It has now become apparent to the whole world that the Iraqi invasion is the result of a big international conspiracy. The US, UK, and their allies have insisted on a strategy of deception and distortion of the truth to convince the world that Iraq threatens world peace because it allegedly possessed weapons of mass destruction. Despite the media's support of this strategy, public opinion in many parts of the world did not support this invasion and unprecedented mass protest took place all around the world with the participation of millions of people.

The invasion was carried out and not a shred of evidence was found with regard to the alleged weapons of mass destruction. This was the first stage of the Anglo-American strategy to be completed; the next stage is still unfolding, namely, the imprisonment and torture of the Iraqi people.

There is ongoing torture in Iraqi prisons by the US and UK forces. The methods used are sophisticated and are tested previously in their laboratories of death and on other occupied nations. They employ especially trained killers who use methods of maiming and eliminating people. This is what we have come to expose.

We can divide the next sections into three stages: arrests, interrogation, and torture.

First of all, an Apache helicopter will circle above the home of the person to be arrested. This will be followed by a couple of tanks or personnel carriers. Sometimes a few Iraqi police cars are also seen participating in the raid. This usually takes place in the middle of the night, at 2 or 3 AM, when everybody is asleep. They use explosives to break down the doors, then the soldiers enter the house and they point their guns at everybody in the house.

They enter bedrooms without asking permission. They don't even let women put on their veils. The Americans tie people up and then they separate the women from the men and children. They search women in front of the men. Sometimes, Americans arrest all the family and other times they leave the women and children outside and only arrest the men.

Sacks are placed on the heads of the people who are to be taken away, while their hands remain tied. If the person to be arrested is a woman, they will tie up her hands and feet and she will be placed on the back of a lorry fit for carrying animals. The house is searched and windows, electronic goods, and ornaments are smashed and destroyed. Then they put everybody in a vehicle, piling people up without any respect. When they leave the house, the doors are left open for the thieves to rob the place. I would like to add that the American soldiers have also been known to steal money, jewelry, and official documents such as house deeds, ID cards, and car registration documents.

Before we move on to the next stage of the interrogation, we must ask: What they are they actually investigating? What are the detainees accused of? What is the evidence against them? Lawyers are not allowed to represent the detainees and no information is given about the reason or the evidence surrounding the detentions.

Iraqi women detainees are forced to undress completely; some old women beg the soldiers to spare them the humiliation. Instead the soldiers threaten to rape their daughters if they don't cooperate. What are these women accused of? Where did this accusation come from?

Some of these accusations have come from a small minority of collaborators whom the American consider "experts." Their identities are revealed to the prisoners during the interrogation to create divisions in our society, provoking groups to act against each other.

Many Iraqi women are being raped. One woman was unable to speak for three months as a result of the continued rape. Her father and son were killed in front of her, then she was "hospitalized" in the prison's hospital. The media does not mention these facts or the fact that all of Iraq has become a prison.

Even ten-year-old children get arrested. They are being accused of supporting their fathers, who are resisting the occupation. They are arrested on the basis of some unfounded evidence.

Of course, these problems existed during Saddam's time but, unfortunately, now things are much worse. Presently, all the detainees are being held together. There is no separation between men and women and children. People guilty of petty crimes are being freed, but innocent prisoners remain behind bars. The clergy is being arrested in Iraq, and we Iraqis have a great respect for our imams. Our religious people are resisting, but in return they are receiving harsh treatment. They are being humiliated and tortured. The occupation forces are showing a great disrespect toward Islam.

A conveyer belt is used, similar to the ones seen in airports that are used for transporting luggage. The detainees, especially the religious scholars and imams, are placed on them and then their backs are hit severely to break a specific vertebrate; as a result the detainees pass out. Occupation doctors then "treat" them.

The clergy are urinated on and buried in holes in the ground with only their heads above ground. Then their heads are spat on and kicked. Women soldiers sexually abuse the detainees, too.

No journalists are allowed to enter the prisons. Nobody is allowed to visit. I called the Red Cross, who did manage to enter, but I don't know what happened after that. One woman was liberated and then imprisoned once again. Her name is Houda Hafiz Ahmed and I have no idea what has happened to her now. She needs medical attention, as she has undergone an operation to extract a lump under her arm and her stitches have not even been taken out.

This is the situation of Iraq today. Thank you very much for listening to what I have to say.

Collective Punishment

Fadhil al-Bedrani

Different crimes were and are being committing against Iraq and Iraqis by the occupying American forces, but I will concentrate on Falluja. I am speaking as a journalist and as a person from Falluja. I was an eyewitness to the two strikes against Falluja in April and November 2004. In the first massacre, 518 civilians were killed, among them, according to Dr. Ahmed Hardan of the Falluja general hospital, were 216 children who were killed either by the Americans or because of the lack of food and drinking water while the town was under siege. The first massacre began on 4 April 2004, lasting till 1 May. I could never forget the killing of 25 members of two families gathered in one house in the Goulan area; this crime happened on 11 April 2004.

The second massacre began on 1 November, not on 8 November as the Americans said. Their pretext was that the Allawi cabinet asked their help. Days before the strike, flyers were distributed asking the people to stay at home because otherwise they would face danger. 150,000 of the 600,000 residents stayed in the town. Those who stayed were surprised when the bombing targeted the houses first. I saw that the women, children, and elderly people were running here and there out of fear of bombing.

On 15 November, in the Goulan area, 20 to 25 people were running barefooted when an American warplane bombed, killing and wounding them; only one elderly woman and two children stayed safe, when they hid themselves under the rubble of a bombed house. The dead bodies were left in the street for twenty days; because of the lack of the first aids, most of the wounded died.

Let me speak about Sua'ad Salam, who stayed in a bombed house with the dead bodies of her whole family in the Hasawa area of central Falluja.

The American forces considered the whole of Falluja as a military target, without taking into consideration the humanitarian issues; they destroyed the town 100 percent; they destroyed the houses and infrastructure.

I think that everyone remembers the TV images of the killing of an unarmed wounded young man; that was on 14 November in Hussein

Shalash mosque in al-Shuhada area, south Falluja. Maybe nobody knows that the same American soldier, with the same gun, killed three others.

On 25 November, fifteen American soldiers entered a house at Bathara area, central Falluja. Three civilian men were there: one was handicapped, the second was 61 years old, and the third was 52 years old. The only one who survived said, "When the Americans entered the house they saw that we were sitting unarmed; fourteen left and the last one threw us a grenade saying 'Bye.' Two were seriously wounded. I with my slight wounds tried to help them but after a while the soldiers were back; I pretended to be dead while the other two were suffering. They put a bullet in every head and left."

It would take volumes to tell all these stories, but what I want to add is that the doctors and the staff of the Falluja hospital were detained on 15 November; the warplanes bombed the alternative hospital downtown and bombed the medicine warehouses in the Nazzal area, killing four doctors and eight medical workers.

According to the numbers of the Association of the Moslem Scholars, 3,500 civilians were killed, 7,000 were wounded, and 1,200 were arrested in the November siege of Falluja. Forty-five days after the massacre, the people began returning; civil-society organizations arranged an accurate body count, according to the sources of the hospital, mosques, and official offices. The killed numbered 4,000, the wounded 7,000.

Before ending my testimony, I should speak about an old woman, 71 years old, who died because of lack of medicine; before her martyrdom, she asked me to take her condition to the Iraqi Ministry of Health and international organizations because she could not find her medicine when Falluja was under siege. Also allow me to mention Awwad Mohammed al-Dulaimi who lost his whole family: first wife, five sons, two daughters, a daughter-in-law, and two grandchildren, six months and five years old. His second wife survived but is blind, and he had a heart attack. This happened on 2 October 2004.

"Shock and Awe" Therapy: How the US Is Attempting to Control Iraq's Oil and Pry Open Its Economy

Herbert Docena

> *One of the most audacious hostile takeovers ever.*
> —Wall Street Journal[1]

> *The best time to invest is when there's still blood on the ground.*
> —a delegate to Rebuilding Iraq 2 convention[2]

> *We must find new lands from which we can easily obtain raw materials and at the same time exploit the cheap slave labor that is available from the natives of the colonies.*
> —Cecil Rhodes[3]

> *Iraq will be sold to others and will be begging the foreigners as we begged Saddam before.*
> —an Iraqi businessman[4]

> *The United States has the biggest slice, but we're confident there's enough of the pie to go around for everyone.*
> —participant in an Iraq investors' conference[5]

1) Invade

This was to be the first step in what has since become the most ambitious, most radical, and most violent project to reconstruct an economy along neoliberal lines in recent history. Since the invasion of Iraq in 2003, the United States has attempted to open up almost all sectors of Iraq's economy to foreign investors; pry it open to international trade; launch a massive privatization program to sell off over 150 state-owned enterprises; liberalize its financial market and re-orient the role of its Central Bank; impose a flat tax and remove food and oil subsidies; adopt a patents and intellectual property rights regime beneficial to corporations; and lay the ground for the eventual privatization of Iraq's oil.

While similar efforts to comprehensively restructure economies have often begun from inside the finance or planning ministries, legislative halls, universities, or five-star hotels in other countries; in Iraq, the first phase in a multi-stage and all-encompassing project began in March 2003 from the skies, with the dropping of bombs, and in the field, with the rolling in of tanks. "Shock therapy" had to be presaged by "shock and awe."

Even before the bombs fell down like rain on Baghdad, however, the blueprint for Iraq's economy was ready and waiting to be implemented—an indication that while the invasion may have been part of a larger geostrategic game plan to dominate a vital region, the goal was to implement neoliberal economic policies in Iraq, including securing access to its oil. By February 2003, the US had finished drafting what the *Wall Street Journal* called "sweeping plans to remake Iraq's economy in the US's image."[6] Entitled "Moving the Iraqi Economy from Recovery to Growth," the document laid down what was to be done with various aspects of Iraq's economy once the occupation forces had ensconced themselves in Baghdad. Michael Bleyzer, former executive of Enron, summed up the goal when he briefed Defense Secretary Donald Rumsfeld and other officials of the Bush administration: "We want to set up a business environment where global companies like Coca-Cola and McDonalds could come in and create a diversified economy not dependent on oil…"[7]

The plan called for nothing less than Iraq's comprehensive transformation from a centralized command economy with very strong state intervention into a market economy in which the state plays virtually no other role than to create, maintain, and defend the openness of this market.[8] Just as the US bombed out and physically obliterated almost all of Iraq's ministries, the plan entails the repeal of almost all of its current laws and the dismantling of its existing institutions, except those that already fit in with the US's design.[9] From their rubble is to be erected a new state from the ground up—one empowered to usher in foreign investments and facilitate the unfettered operations of multinational corporations, but disempowered to provide services to its citizens or promote development and social justice.

2) Take Advantage of the Chaos

Awarded the task to remake Iraq's economy and prepare the ground for the likes of Coca-Cola and McDonald's was Bearing Point, a private business consultancy group. Its contract with USAID, a meticulously methodical document complete with timetables, delegation of responsibilities, and assignment of tasks for specific Iraqi government posts, is essentially the master plan for the US economic design on Iraq—the "smoking gun" proving the US's intent to reconstruct Iraq's economy along neoliberal lines. The language of the contract is revealing: At one point, it says, "The new government *will* seek to open up its trade and investment linkages and to put into place the institutions promoting democracy, free enterprise and reliance on a market-driven private sector as the engine of economic recovery and growth" [italics mine]—as though this government will have no other choice.

The painstakingly systematic plan contrasts with the apparent lack of any planning for post-war humanitarian, rehabilitation, and relief operations.[10] This hinted at what the so-called reconstruction process was not going to be about. As Defense Secretary Donald Rumsfeld said, "I don't believe it's our job to reconstruct that country after 30 years of centralized Stalinist-like economic controls in that country."[11]

Having settled at Saddam's Republican Palace complex, occupation authorities quickly moved to implement the Bearing Point work plan. Little more than one month after the invasion was declared "mission accomplished" by Bush in May 2003, then Coalition Provisional Authority (CPA) chief L. Paul Bremer III unveiled the US's economic agenda on Iraq at a World Economic Forum meeting in Jordan. "Our strategic goal in the months ahead is to set in motion policies which will have the effect of reallocating people and resources from state enterprises to the more productive private firms," he said.[12] That same month, the American advisor to the ministry of industry and minerals announced the "fast-track" privatization of 48 state-owned enterprises (SOEs).[13] By the time the US handed over "sovereignty" in a secret ceremony in June 2004, key elements of its economic designs on Iraq had been put in place. The CPA had passed an array of laws that were to be the foundations and pillars of Iraq's neoliberal regime.[14]

Among the most groundbreaking was "Order 39," which was described as fulfilling the "wish list of international investors" by the *Economist* and as a "free market manifesto" by Reuters.[15] The order allows foreign investors to buy and take over Iraq's SOEs, to enter and leave Iraq as they please, to have the same rights as any Iraqi in selling to the domestic market, and to repatriate 100 percent of their profits and other assets anytime. Seen another way, the order effectively deprives the Iraqis of sovereignty over their economy.[16] By moving toward the privatization of Iraq's SOEs, the order effectively allows the transfer of the Iraqi people's assets to foreign and/or private owners whose priority is to maximize profits rather than to provide services or products to Iraqis. By removing restrictions on investments, the order denies the Iraqi state any power to regulate and control investments entering its territory. By giving foreign investors "national treatment," it deprives Iraqis of the option of supporting local businesses or pursuing industrialization policies in the hope of attaining a degree of self-sufficiency and economic sovereignty. The clause allowing full and unimpeded repatriation takes away the Iraqi state's prerogative to compel foreign investors to reinvest their profits in the domestic economy.

While oil was exempted from this order, the Bearing Point contract specifically states that it "will implement USAID-approved recommendations to begin supporting the privatization, especially those in the oil and supporting industries."[17] It was told to go ahead with preparing legislation and implementing regulations to establish an "improved fiscal regime for petroleum and mining sectors and for transit pipelines."[18] Earlier, Bush had signed an executive order giving blanket and indefinite immunity to US oil corporations involved in any oil-related activity in Iraq.[19]

"Order 12," or the "Trade Liberalization Policy," suspended tariffs, duties, and other taxes on goods entering Iraq's market, thereby depriving the Iraqis of revenue control over trade flows and an independent trade policy. "Order 40" allowed a few foreign banks to enter the Iraqi market and take over up to 50 percent of domestic banks. Combined with the other orders, this gives foreign bankers power over Iraqis' access to credit and loans and gives the government less control over monetary policy.

"Order 49" reduced the tax rate on corporations and individuals from 40 percent to a flat rate of 15 percent. Doing away with the principle of progressive taxation, the idea that those who have more should contribute more, it also means that an Iraqi who earns $100 a month will have to pay the same percentage of tax as a corporation that earns $1 billion a month.

"Order 81," which lays the ground for Iraq's intellectual property rights regime, introduces a system of monopoly rights over seeds.[20] This facilitates the entry of multinational agricultural corporations and undermines Iraqis' "food sovereignty," or their right to define their own food and agriculture policies instead of having them subordinated to international market forces.

Observers were quick to point out the similarities between elements of the plan and the structural adjustment policies imposed by the World Bank in scores of developing countries around the world since the 1980s or the "shock therapy" administered to Russia in the 1990s. Only this time, it goes further. The *New York Times* economic columnist Jeff Madrick noted that, "By almost any mainstream economist's standard, the plan... is extreme—in fact, stunning."[21] Former World Bank chief economist and Nobel prize winner Joseph Stiglitz observed that Iraq's own was "an even more radical form of shock therapy than pursued in the former Soviet world."[22] Naomi Klein was more descriptive, saying, "Iraq's 'reconstruction' makes those wrenching economic reforms look like spa treatments."[23] If all goes well, the *Economist* says, Iraq will be a "capitalist's dream."[24]

The extremism of the plan—and US officials determination to pursue it—was not just ideological; it was driven by all that was at stake. With the US expected to depend on other countries for 70 percent of its oil needs by 2025—and with both ally countries and rivals as dependent, if not more so, on oil imports,[25] securing access to oil was both a matter of survival and a source of great power. Old surveys indicate that Iraq holds around 100 to 130 billion barrels of oil, or about 11 percent of the world's total, making it second only to the world's largest reserve, Saudi Arabia.[26] But there could be more. With only 17 out of 80 oil fields tapped,[27] there's widespread belief among industry insiders that the wells run deeper and that reserves might even exceed 300 billion barrels, or about a quarter of global reserves.[28] In a speech at the London Institute of Petroleum in 1999, US Vice President Dick Cheney said, "While many regions of the world offer great oil opportunities, the Middle East, with two-thirds of the world's oil and the lowest cost, is still where the prize ultimately lies."[29]

A clear appreciation of this fact was evident during the invasion. British Petroleum engineers were embedded with the troops during the invasion and traveled with them in order to locate and secure the oil wells.[30] While virtually all other ministries were bombed, the oil ministry complex was spared. Subsequently, as much as 20 percent of the US's $18 billion reconstruction budget for Iraq was to go to oil infrastructure, including exploration and development of new oil and gas fields.[31] A Pentagon policy document had, as early as 1999, argued that a war for Iraq's oil should be considered a legitimate military option.[32] Two months before the invasion, the Pentagon officials said they "have crafted strategies that will allow us to secure and protect those fields as rapidly as possible in order to preserve those prior to destruction."[33] This mental exercise in taking over Iraq's petrol reserves had a precedent: As early as the 1970s, former Secretary of State Henry Kissinger had put forward plans for invading Middle Eastern oil fields in an essay entitled "Seizing Arab Oil."[34]

Dubbed "today's California gold rush" by the US official tasked to privatize its SOEs,[35] Iraq was giving investors a rush not just because of oil per se but also because of oil's potential to create domestic purchasing power. In theory, as the proceeds from oil trickle down to the Iraqis, demand can be expected to grow and Iraq's domestic market can be a much-needed outlet for products. For an investor, while the windfall to be reaped in the post-conflict reconstruction spending bonanza is huge, the long-term prospects in a privatized, liberalized, and deregulated Iraq looks even more promising. As US Commerce Secretary Don Evans saw it, "Their [Iraqis] collective hopes and aspirations form a valuable market for goods and services of all types."[36]

3) Disregard International Law, Placate the Resistance

For all that was at stake, two obstacles stood in the way.

All of the laws the occupation authorities passed were in clear violation of international law.[37] Article 43 of the Hague Regulations of 1907 states that an occupying power "must re-establish and insure as far as possible, public order and safety, while respecting, unless absolutely prevented, the laws in force in the country." In other words, the US could not overturn existing laws and pass new ones; only a sovereign government could. Article 55 of 1907 Hague Regulations says: "the occupying State shall be regarded only as administrator and usufructuary of public buildings, real estate, forests, and agricultural estates belonging to the hostile State, and situated in the occupied country. It must safeguard the capital of these properties, and administer them in accordance with the rules of usufruct." In other words, the US could not sell off Iraq's state-owned companies; only a sovereign government could.

But there was a bigger problem: resistance to the occupation in general and opposition to the laws themselves in particular. According to a survey conducted by the Coalition Provisional Authority itself in May 2004, up to 86 percent of Iraqis wanted the coalition forces to leave either immediately or once an elected government assumed power, as opposed to only 6 percent who wanted them to stay.[38] The Iraqi Governing Council, the 25-member proto-governing entity formed by the US in July 2003 and which it sought to project as Iraq's temporary government, was widely seen as US stooges, with a Gallup poll survey revealing that up to three in every four Iraqis believed that its actions were "mostly determined by the CPA" and only 16 percent thought it was independent.[39] In addition, according to a survey conducted by the Iraq Center for Research and Studies, 68 percent of respondents either strongly supported or somewhat supported Moqtada al-Sadr, the leader of the Sadrist movement, who has consistently called for the withdrawal of the US forces.[40]

Even if the policies had violated international law but had the support of the Iraqis, the US would have been able to rest easy. The problem was that the changes the US was introducing to Iraq did not have the consent of the Iraqis and were widely unpopular, even among those who supported the invasion. While the US Treasury Department conferred with Citigroup, JP Morgan Chase, and Bank of America over some details of the privatization process, at least one IGC ministry claimed he was not even informed of the proposal.[41] As Isam al-Khafaji, who worked with the US in the early stages of the occupation but later left, attests, "Many radically new sweeping changes, for example the law on foreign investment, Iraqis were not allowed to review it. They were not even given the chance to look at it before it was passed."[42] What was troubling the occupation officials was that the Iraqis were not just waiting for the courts to decide on the policies' legality; they were throwing bombs at them.[43]

All these threatened to turn the "capitalist's dream" into billion-dollar nightmares for those whose investments could be seized and expropriated by a future Iraqi government sensitive to popular opinion. With few buyers willing to take the risk, the illegality of the US-imposed economic restructuring and the resistance it spawned threatened the viability of the privatization program in the short term and the larger economic agenda in the long term. What the US needed to do was summed up by Sir Philip Watts, chair of Royal Dutch Shell, when asked what conditions needed to be met before oil companies could move in. "There has to be proper security, legitimate authority, and a legitimate process… by which we will be able to negotiate agreements that would be longstanding for decades," he said. "When the legitimate authority is there on behalf of Iraq, we will know and recognize it."[44]

4) Undergo a "Political Transition" Process

The US's solution was straightforward: If only a sovereign government could legally do the things it was trying to do in Iraq, then the US would have to create this "sovereign" government itself—not just any kind of government but one structurally conducive to the US's preferred economic policies, run by Iraqis willing to implement and defend these policies, and insulated from popular pressures. This seems to have been the strategy from the beginning. Bearing Point's contract, for example, takes it for granted that a cooperative government would be put in place. In May 2003, Defense Secretary Rumsfeld announced that the Bush administration would be installing a regime headed by personnel who "favor market systems" and "encourage moves to privatize state-owned enterprises."[45]

If the decisions had been entirely up to the occupation authorities, they would have preferred to go slow and make sure the conditions for managing the political process were firmly in place before letting go. While the Bush administration had conceded that at some point it would have to hold elections, it sought to postpone holding them until the time was right and the risks could be minimized. At one point, US military commanders even broke up local elections initiated and organized by Iraqis across Iraq right after Saddam's government fell.[46] The US also adamantly resisted proposals to have one-person-one-vote general elections as soon as possible, saying it was not logistically possible, despite claims to the contrary by the Planning Ministry's Census Bureau and even by some British officials.[47]

Instead of elections, the occupation authorities insisted on forming a transitional Iraqi government through a complex system of caucuses that would have given them more say in the outcome. Participants of the caucuses would be chosen and vetted by the military, as assisted by Research Triangle Institute (RTI), a USAID contractor hired to "identify the most appropriate 'legitimate' and functional leaders" [quotes around "legitimate" appear in original text].[48] As Bremer said, "I'm not opposed to it [elections] but I want to do it in a way that takes care of our concerns... Elections that are held too early can be too destructive... In a situation like this, if you start holding elections, the people who are rejectionists tend to win."[49] By "rejectionists," Bremer was obviously referring to Iraqis who opposed the presence of US military forces in the country, objected to its political and economic agenda, and refused to be part of US-installed political institutions. A senior official of the CPA was more direct when asked why elections couldn't be held soonest: "There's not enough time for the moderates to organize."[50]

When tens of thousands of people marched on the streets in early 2004 to demand direct elections or else face more violent resistance, the US was forced to relent. US officials reluctantly agreed to accelerate the political transition only because of the growing resistance to the occupation, the widening clamor for direct elections, and the consequent stalling of the neoliberal economic agenda. The US hoped that this decision would pacify the resistance and entice investors. As a Pentagon official said, "The transfer of sovereignty clearly will have an impact on security because you rid yourself of the 'occupation' label. That is one of the claims that these so-called insurgents make; that they are under American occupation. So you remove that political claim from the ideological battle."[51] Diplomatically, it would be crucial in order to give allies political cover for contributing troops and money for the reconstruction. Legally, it would provide cover for investments made under occupation and protect against possible expropriation.

But it was going to be very risky. As former National Security Advisor Brent Scowcroft said when US President George H. W. Bush was faced with a similar dilemma in Iraq after the first Gulf war: "What's going to happen the first time we hold an election in Iraq and it turns out the radicals win? What do you do? We're surely not going to let them take over."[52]

5) Bring in the Experts, Embed the Advisors

Even as they tried to defer the inevitable, occupation authorities moved quickly to entrench the foundations of a radical neoliberal free-market regime—before any future sovereign and elected government could come up with other ideas. In other words, the strategy was to preempt the Iraqi government on some of the most fundamental decisions any government has to make regarding its economy. The adopted tactic was best described by USAID's instruction to Bearing Point as it endeavored "to establish the basic legal framework for a functioning market economy." In accomplishing its tasks—from writing up laws and regulations to setting up the stock market and the Central Bank—Bearing Point was explicitly ordered to take "appropriate advantage of the unique opportunity for rapid progress in this area presented by the current configuration of political circumstances."[53]

To plant the laws and policies Bearing Point was drafting, the US placed hundreds of "advisors" with extensive corporate backgrounds, as well as dozens of organizations and agencies specializing in designing neoliberal policies, in key ministries and in the bureaucracy. Brought in to supervise Iraq's privatization spree, for example, was Thomas Foley, a former head of Citicorp who specialized in mergers and acquisitions. Charged to oversee Iraq's agricultural policies was Dan Amstutz, who, as former vice president of Cargill, the world's biggest grain exporter, drafted the controversial agreement on agriculture at the World Trade Organization.[54] A US law firm connected to Bush, called Squire, Sanders and Dempsey, was retained to provide advice on privatizing government industries, establishing regulatory agencies, and developing Iraq's tax structure.[55] Assigned to head the "advisory board" to the oil ministry was the former chief executive officer of Shell, Phillip Carroll, who was subsequently replaced by Robert McKee, a former vice president of oil giant ConocoPhillips. Bremer himself was a former aide of Kissinger, who had once said, "what is called 'globalization' is really another name for the dominant role of the US."[56] Most interestingly, the US hired the services of Yegov Gaidar, the former Russian prime minister who administered his country's own "shock therapy."[57]

Also deployed was the vast apparatus of the US government that has been promoting neoliberal free-market policies around the world for the past three decades. This included the US State Department, USAID, the quasi-governmental National Endowment for Democracy (NED), and their affiliates. Practicing what it preached, the US privatized the project to privatize Iraq by subcontracting various tasks to an army of private contractors: Creative Associates was to work toward "enhanced public-private partnerships for education service delivery"; Abt Associates was assigned to "reform" Iraq's health sector; while Development Alternatives, Inc., was to "help the rural poor move to a market-led economic transformation."

The instructions given to Bearing Point and the way it was directed to operate are illustrative of the powers given these contractors. In the name of "technical assistance," the contractor was authorized to "begin to reform, revise, extract or otherwise advise on changes to policies, laws, and regulations that impact the economy."[58] Lamenting that the existing commercial law framework is "woefully deficient in terms of establishing a market-friendly legal and regulatory environment for business formation and operation," the US ordered the contractor "to create a World Trade Organization–consistent trade and investment legal framework which will both promote competitive development of domestic business… and lay the groundwork for greater integration into international financial and trading networks."[59] On the plan to privatize the SOEs, not only was Bearing Point tasked with appraising the market price at which the SOEs are to be sold: "If changes to legislation are required," says the contract, "contractor will assist legislative reform specifically to allow for the privatization of State-owned industries and firms and/or establishing a privatization entity."[60]

While in other countries, USAID and its contractors have to negotiate with the existing government to push for their desired laws, in Iraq, as a top US military official said on another matter, "[W]e'd be negotiating with ourselves because we are the government."[61] While in other settings, they have to contend with existing bureaucracies, in Iraq, they were themselves building that bureaucracy—in this case, literally from the inside out: To establish their presence firmly within the ministries, Bearing Point was tasked with setting up "Macroeconomic Analysis Units" or "Tax Policy Units" to be staffed by Bearing Point employees within the Ministry of Finance and the Central Bank.[62]

The goal was to be visible and invisible at the same time. The US needed to lock in the laws and policies, but it also wanted to be able to show that it was the Iraqis who pushed for them. To this end, "the Contractor will employ extensive efforts to interact with government officials and leading authorities."[63] Called "instilling ownership" in USAID jargon, this entails ensuring that the adoption of "reforms" are not perceived as externally imposed. "The ultimate goal," notes the contract, "is to have Iraq's government and private sector capable to assume responsibility for appropriately structured and managed market and non-market institutions…"[64] In other words, the measure of Bearing Point's success relies on the capacity of Iraqis to continue to defend and sustain the neoliberal economic regime even without US stewardship as formal occupation is ended.

6) Put Iraqis Out Front

But the laws, structures, and institutions that the US was constructing in Iraq were not going to survive on their own. The paradox of any free-market system is that it requires strong intervention to keep it "free." In order to perpetuate its preferred economic order in Iraq, the US, from the earliest days of the occupation, had searched for Iraqis who would be willing to do its bidding—not because they were just unthinking "puppets"—but because their interests converged with that of the US. This confluence of interests has been found to be a firmer foundation for collaboration: While the US needs Iraqi faces to project "ownership" and to show that they're not colonizers imposing their will on the Iraqi people, these Iraqis need the US because, lacking constituency and legitimacy, they have no chance surviving in power without US patronage and protection.[65] Advising the US administration on how to quell mounting attacks against US forces, Thomas Friedman described this strategy as putting "more Americans out back and more Iraqis out front."[66]

In examining the US's relationship with these Iraqis, the USAID's highly developed step-by-step checklist of techniques for improving the likelihood of "reforms" being successfully embraced is illuminating. To achieve "legitimation" or the means for getting "buy-in" from the people who should be seen as owning the policies, USAID should single out "policy champions" or people who could be relied on to act as its main proponents. Drawing from its "Policy Implementation Toolkit," USAID contractors should perform "stakeholder analysis" to help them "identify individuals and groups that have an interest, or stake, in the outcome of a policy decision."[67] To do this, a catalog of stakeholders classifying them either as "supporters," "opponents," or "neutral parties" should be created and maintained.[68]

It is worth mentioning that the US's "policy champions" are not just to be put inside the formal apparatuses of the state; they are also to be lodged within "civil society." Along with the troops who entered Iraq was a silent battalion of agencies and contractors whose mission was to build up a pro-US, pro-neoliberal "civil society" by creating, funding, and supporting NGOs, trade unions, business councils, research institutions, professional associations, and other civil-society organizations. Since the beginning of the occupation, this battalion has fanned out across the country, effectively building up a national political machinery of supporters and campaigners of groups fundamentally at peace with the US role in the country.[69] On the one hand, they were being built up as a mass base to support the Iraqis that the US wanted to run Iraq's government; at the same time, they could also be used to pressure them into backing the US agenda. As the USAID put it, "Where political will for systemic reform is lacking, the main thing that foreign assistance can do is to strengthen the constituencies for reform in civil society."[70]

While the Iraqis out front may occasionally disagree with the Americans out back, on the fundamental questions they either concur or have no other choice but to submit. After all, their powers are meant to be confined to day-to-day administrative affairs; the US ultimately calls the shots on the questions that matter most. As Dilip Hiro, a Middle East historian, put it, "What Washington wanted was Iraqis who—while willing to dabble in occasional criticism of the administration—were in the final analysis beholden to it."[71] So while the relationship can at times be turbulent, the Americans know that they need the Iraqis out front as much as the Iraqis need the Americans out back.

And so, as both parties were forced to show that something was being handed from one to the other as part of a political transition, both worked in tandem to hold on to power. The story of the political transition is the story of how the US attempted to manage the process and determine the outcome every step of the way, as evidenced by its efforts to retain the power of its preferred Iraqis and preserve ultimate political, military, and economic control while appearing to be relinquishing them.

7) Hand Over "Sovereignty," But Keep All the Power
On 28 June 2004, the US reportedly handed over "sovereignty" to Iraq and began a gradual process toward installing an elected government. As

to what exactly that word meant, even US officials had varying interpretations. According to Bush, they were transferring "full sovereignty"[72]; a State Undersecretary called it "limited sovereignty."[73] For then State Secretary Colin Powell, "It's sovereignty but [some] of that sovereignty they are going to allow us to exercise on their behalf and with their permission."[74] But with the US ultimately deciding which part of that sovereignty they're going to exercise on the Iraqis' behalf and which part they're going to concede to the Iraqis, US Congresswoman Nancy Pelosi's description of the event was perhaps most accurate: It was "essentially a handover of authority from the US-led occupation to the new embassy there."[75]

Despite media coverage to the contrary, then Defense Undersecretary Paul Wolfowitz was first to caution against depicting the 28 June handover as a "magical date."[76] The Transitional Administrative Law, or the so-called interim constitution, which was drafted by American lawyers and which Bush vowed would embody "American values," was to remain in force.[77] This meant that the orders enacted by Bremer would also remain in effect. Repealing it would be extremely difficult, if not nearly impossible, because to do so would require the approval of two-thirds to three-fourths of a future assembly. As if to underscore the continuity before and after the handover, a State Department official explained, "The law doesn't expire with a new government coming in, any more than the laws passed under the Clinton administration expired when the Bush administration came into office."[78]

All US and coalition troops were to stay behind indefinitely and the Iraqi government had no power over them, no authority to order them to leave, and no control over their operations.[79] They even had no power to prosecute them if they committed crimes, because they were granted legal immunity by the US.[80] The CIA retained control of Iraq's intelligence apparatus.[81] Asked when the troops might leave, General Richard B. Myers, chairman of Joint Chiefs of Staff, said, "I really do believe it's unknowable."[82] While the occupation forces struggled to cast the Iraqi troops as Iraq's own army, they were in fact being built to function as proxies of the US military. The TAL puts them under US command, at the frontlines.[83] As a Pentagon official explained, "They will take over the fight as we move back into the shadow, out of the cities, and provide logistics, quick-reaction forces, communications, food, bullets, advice, and training."[84] One of Iraq's most important defense officials, its national security advisor, was to be appointed by Bremer and was to remain in office even after a government is elected.[85]

Apart from leaving behind the US troops to watch over the new government, the US also created new commissions and institutions that, according to the *Wall Street Journal*, "effectively take away virtually all of the powers once held by several ministries."[86] This included Iraq's inspector general; the Commission on Public Integrity; the Communication and Media Commission, which has the power to shut down media outlets; and the Board of Supreme Audit, which has authority to review government contracts.[87] Bremer appointed the chiefs of these powerful commissions to five-year terms, effectively ensuring that they could not be replaced by the incoming government, in order to "promote his concepts of governance long after the planned hand-over," according to the *Washington Post*.[88] Iraq's oil minister had hoped that "When sovereignty is regained, it means that there will be no more US advisors not only in the ministry of oil, but in every ministry in Iraq."[89] In fact, the 110 to 160 advisors in the various ministries were not told to vacate their desks and they continue to report for work in the ministries until now.[90]

Aside from having no power over the troops and having little sway over the ministries, the new interim government would also have little power over the coffers. While authority over Iraq's oil revenues was to be transferred to the interim government, the US had tied its proceeds down to projects decided by the US and to contractors chosen by the US, thereby depleting the amount of revenue to be controlled by the interim government. As the date of the handover approached, the US engaged in a massive spending spree. Issuing more than 1,000 contracts on a single day, it was, as the *Los Angeles Times* described it, "like a Barneys warehouse sale in the Wild West, with the US playing the role of frenzied shopper and leaving Iraqis to pay the bill."[91] At some point, US soldiers used the cash that they had been given from out of Iraq's oil revenues to attempt to make the Iraqis "like" them.[92] Between $4 to $20 billion of Iraq's oil revenues disbursed under the occupation authorities were unaccounted for, prompting Transparency International to warn that Iraq could be the "biggest corruption scandal in history."[93]

The US had the option to retain management control over all contracts entered before the CPA was dissolved; the interim government had no power to renege on them, reallocate previously committed funds, and enter into longer-term commitments.[94] Along with the International Monetary Fund, the US would still have a seat in the body monitoring disbursements after the handover and would still have power over the other big source of money flowing into Iraq, the $18 billion reconstruction fund from the US, and to an extent, over the amounts donated to Iraq by foreign donors.[95] In fact, Iraq's budget for 2004–2006 had to be approved by the CPA and had to meet the guidelines of the IMF.[96]

All these facts indicate that the occupation did not end; the 28 June handover merely inaugurated a new relationship between the Americans and the Iraqis. "We're still here. We'll be paying a lot of attention and we'll have a lot of influence," a ranking US official said.[97] It was an exit strategy without having to exit and the goal was to put in place handles with which to pull strings. As one senior White House official told the *New York Times* then, "We'll have more levers than you think, and maybe more than the Iraqis think."[98]

8) Choose to Whom You're Going to Hand Over "Sovereignty"

Aside from setting the terms by which "sovereignty" was going to be transferred, the US also decided to whom it was going to be transferred.

In an attempt to bestow legitimacy on the process and show that the international community had a role in the transition, the US deployed UN special envoy Lakhdar Brahimi to Iraq to hold consultations with various groups in search of the particular Iraqis to head Iraq's transitional government. Brahimi came out of the negotiations and horse-trading at first furious, then exasperated, then resigned to the outcome, saying, "I sometimes say—I'm sure he doesn't mind me saying that—that Bremer is the dictator of Iraq. He has the money. He has the signature. Nothing happens without his agreement in this country."[99]

In the end, it was the US, through Bremer and a certain Robert Blackwill, who chose Iraq's new prime minister, Iyad Allawi. The National Security Council's coordinator for strategic planning and Bush's unofficial emissary to Iraq, Blackwill was said to be the "single most influential person when it comes to decision-making in Baghdad today," according to an expert on the Middle East with the US Institute of Peace.[100] He allegedly gave Brahimi the names of the Iraqis that the US favored and reportedly "railroaded" the IGC into supporting Allawi, as confirmed by people involved in the process, because he was most willing to give in to the US demands.[101] One IGC member, Mahmoud Othman, complained, "The Americans are trying to impose their decisions on us, and we are trying to reject them."[102] The *New York Times* observed how the turn of events seemed to confirm that Brahimi "was merely bowing to the wishes of others."[103] Brahimi himself admitted that he faced "terrible pressure" that prevented him from asserting his preferences[104]; others reported that he only gave in to the Americans' choice because of their "aggressive recommendation."[105] He said: "You know, sometimes people think I am a free agent out here, that I have a free hand to do whatever I want."[106]

Blackwill's choice, Allawi, was a long-time CIA agent who provided some of the misleading intelligence reports that the US and the UK needed to justify the war.[107] He also subsequently gave the US what it badly wanted at that particular juncture: an invitation for the US-led troops to stay. With Allawi as "prime minister," agreeing not to call for the withdrawal of US occupation forces, the US secured the legal veneer it needed in the form of a United Nations resolution proclaiming that the Iraqis had regained sovereignty. Ghazi al-Yawar, the IGC member who emerged as "president," said that it would be "complete nonsense" to call for the troops to leave.[108]

For the second step of the political process, the formation of the Iraqi Interim National Council in August 2004, the US and the IGC agreed to reserve 19 out of the 100 seats for the parties that were in IGC. The method of balloting for choosing the rest of the 81 was designed such that these same parties would eventually dominate the council. The participants of the conference were self-selected; groups calling for the withdrawal of troops simply boycotted the event.[109] Those who did attend were supposed to come up with lists of candidates but since only the parties that were already in the IGC were able to consolidate their rosters in time, no voting eventually took place and a four-member panel ended up handpicking the members.[110] As one participant explained it, "They've already divided the cake among themselves. They've been negotiating in secret for weeks. We don't know who is on this list and they tell us, 'take it or leave it'!"[111]

9) Put Your Friends in Power

The third step in the process was the elections held in January 2005. Here, the US did everything its power to make sure Scowcroft's scenario did not come true.

After deciding to accelerate the transition process, the US reallocated its budget for "democracy-building" from $100 million to $458 million out of its $18-billion reconstruction chest. So important was this goal seen that its allotment was just about as big as the budget for transportation and telecommunications projects.[112] For the elections, the US allotted more than $30 million to provide "strategic advice, training, and polling data" to "moderate and democratic" Iraqi political parties in order to make them "compete effectively" and to "increase their support among the Iraqi people."[113] The Department of State was reported to be spending $1 million on monthly opinion surveys to find out "which candidates are attracting the most support from the Iraqi people."[114]

Brought in to carry out these electoral operations were the usual "democracy promotion" organs of the US such as the USAID and its contractors, the National Endowment for Democracy (NED), the National Democratic Institute (NDI), the International Republican Institute (IRI), International Foundation of Elections Systems, etc., which are documented to have supported and funded pro-US parties and candidates in Venezuela, Nicaragua, Haiti, Ukraine, El Salvador, etc.[115] The Central Intelligence Agency, whose station in Baghdad had grown to be its largest in the world, was also reported to be planning covert operations to influence election outcomes.[116] The NDI and the IRI, the foreign arms of the US's Democratic and Republican parties respectively, were given $80 million by the USAID to help their preferred parties. The NED had been holding sessions teaching Iraqis how to build up their parties' local and regional structures, how to recruit members, how to fundraise, and how to cultivate relations with media.[117] The IRI produced a database of parties, with information on each group's characteristics, their regions of operations, and estimates of their memberships.[118]

In these activities, "democracy promotion" translated to promoting the US's goals in the country in general, and to promoting Allawi's party and most of the other parties that were inside the IGC, in particular.[119] This was a tough task because the interim government, as dominated by these parties, were seen by up to 55 percent of Iraqis in an IRI survey as no longer representing their interests.[120] As it did in Nicaragua or in Haiti, the White House explicitly urged leaders of the parties it was supporting to coalesce and get their act together. Blackwill continued to perform his role mediating between the Bush administration and the Iraqis, at one point suggesting that they form a single slate for the elections supposedly to counter the power of Grand Ayatollah Ali Sistani, Iraq's most influential religious and political leader.[121]

Even as the US gave its Iraqi allies advantage, it also sought to isolate and weaken their rivals. This was not limited to giving one side an advantage in resources and organization; it also meant writing the rules to their favor. The election law enacted by the CPA gave the seven-member electoral commission appointed by Bremer the power to disqualify candidates and required it to implement a code banning candidates from using "hate speech, intimidation, and support for the practice of and the use of terrorism."[122] In practice, given how "terrorism" has been defined in Iraq's context as actions directed against US forces, this code was meant to eliminate those whom Bremer called the "rejectionists" from the electoral race. One anti-occupation force, that headed by Moqtada al-Sadr, was not only banned from joining the elections but also became the target of an all-out military offensive and assassination.[123] Other important political forces, who were not necessarily engaged in armed resistance, boycotted the elections as a matter of principle or out of a strategic calculation that even if they engaged, they would have had no chance and they would only have ended up legitimizing the winners. Needless to say, in the dispensation of cash, none was to be given to the "rejectionists." As the IRI's President Lorne Craner put it, "If you're a violent party outside the process, this is not the right place for you."[124]

Further limiting the choices for Iraqis—and in effect favoring the non-rejectionists—was the manner by which the elections were actually conducted. For example, the composition of the ballots could only have been bewildering. It contained 98 mostly indistinguishable political formations to choose from, almost none of which—except the incumbents—had any chance to campaign and present themselves to the public. The full list of the 7,000-plus candidates was announced only five days before election. Moreover, all Iraqi expatriates living outside the country, the constituency of the exile parties supportive of the US, were automatically given the right to vote.[125]

The final outcome of the tally was clouded with confusion and suspicion. At first the election commissioner announced, even before polling closed, that the turnout was 72 percent, only to be scaled down later to just 58 percent.[126] Reuters reported that the winning United Iraqi Alliance was initially informed by the electoral commission that they had won 60 percent of the vote, giving them a clear majority in the new interim government, only to be told later that they actually got 48 percent and therefore had to form a coalition government with the pro-US Kurdish parties.[127] There was no way of verifying whether fraud took place because there were no independent international monitors to scrutinize the elections. The world just had to take the US-installed Iraqi government's word for it.[128]

10) Keep Your Friends in Line

Through the first three steps of the stage-managed political process, the US has so far succeeded in installing a government supportive of the US goals in Iraq. Currently at the helm of Iraq's interim government are virtually the same political forces who came side-by-side with the Americans during the invasion and who were subsequently appointed to the IGC.

While there have been tensions and disagreements, most of them have consistently echoed the US's plans for Iraq's economy. The first appointed oil minister of the Iraq Governing Council, Mohammad Bahr al-Ulum, said he favored the privatization of downstream oil installations and production-sharing contracts upstream, saying priority would be given to US oil companies and "European companies, probably."[129] He also vigorously enticed foreign oil companies to invest in Iraq and removed senior technocrats in the oil ministry who opposed his plans. Just before bowing out of power as Iraq's prime minister, between June 2004 and January 2005, Allawi signed guidelines permitting the multinational oil corporations to develop Iraq's reserves, and keeping oil policy out of the hands of any future parliament.[130] While he reportedly had a few skirmishes with sections of the Bush administration, Ahmed Chalabi—who is even more aggressive in pushing for the privatization of Iraq's oil—went on to become Iraq's acting oil minister, after the January 2005 elections.[131] "American oil companies will have a big shot at Iraqi oil," Chalabi had promised before the invasion.[132] With Iraqis like these in front, Pentagon officials had already assured investors who signed contracts with the former occupation authority that their investments would be honored by the new government because those who were involved in the reconstruction planning will still be part of that government.[133]

While some commentators have played up the supposed contradictory relationship between the US and the winning UIA, which includes parties with Shia constituencies such as the Supreme Council for Islamic Revolution (SCIRI) and the Da'wa Party, it bears pointing out that a week before the elections, the UIA changed its platform from "setting a timetable for the withdrawal of multinational forces in Iraq" to "the Iraq we want is capable of protecting its borders and security without depending on foreign forces."[134] It was Da'wa leader Ibrahim al-Jafaari, Iraq's new prime minister, who allowed the US forces to stay on beyond the elections.[135] It was Adil Abdel Mahdi, a senior leader of SCIRI and now Iraq's vice president, who, just before the elections, said the government intends to privatize the Iraqi National Oil Company and open up Iraq's oil reserves to multinational oil companies, saying, "[T]his is very promising to the American investors and to American enterprises, certainly to oil companies."[136] As important as the new interim government's decision to allow the troops to stay and to open up the oil reserves is its decision to respect the Transitional Administrative Law, and therefore, to keep the neoliberal economic laws in place.[137]

11) Bring in the Bretton Woods Twins

Having succeeded in installing the "non-rejectionists" at the reins of Iraq's interim government and in preserving the structures it had constructed to secure its neoliberal laws, the US is confident that its "reforms" for Iraq will survive the last two steps of the political transition: the scheduled referendum on the new constitution in October 2005 and then the elections for a constitutionally elected government in December 2005. As the Iraqis' write their country's most important law, there are already indications that the US embassy in Baghdad, its largest in the world, will not sit idly by. Deputy Prime Minister Roz Noori Shawes has signified that "we might make use of foreign experts."[138] USAID "advisors" are ready with their "technical assistance." Former Secretary of State Colin Powell has clearly stated what the priorities of the largest US embassy in the world will be. "The real challenge for the new embassy, so to speak, or the new presence will be helping the Iraqi people get ready for their full elections and the full constitution…" he said.[139]

Meantime, the neoliberal agenda is moving forward. Iraq's Industry Ministry announced in May 2005 that the plans to privatize the SOEs are pushing through.[140] The plans for Iraq's oil industry have become much clearer. As proposed by US advisors, Iraq will form a state oil company that will walk and talk like a state oil company but will not be a state oil company. It will be nominally state-owned but "open to foreign investors"; "politically independent" but "run by a professional management team insulated from political interference in day-to-day affairs."[141]

Despite the relative success with which the US has managed the political transition so far, however, the US is still not assured of making the "capitalist's dream" come true. As of June 2005, the resistance to the occupation is growing, not abating. The latest survey shows that 45 percent of Iraqi respondents support those fighting the US troops, while only 15 percent back the US-led coalition.[142] Moreover, in spite of its accomplishment in putting Iraqis friendly to its interests in power, there's still opposition—even among the non-rejectionists—to the US's neoliberal economic plans, as evidenced most dramatically by the IGC's earlier unanimous decision not to participate in the proposed privatization program.[143]

To confront this defiance and to further circumscribe the power of any Iraqi government in power—whether it be run by rejectionists or non-rejectionists—the US has tapped the services of the multilateral financial institutions known for disciplining recalcitrant governments resisting economic restructuring. In November 2004, the Paris Club decided to forgive a portion of Iraq's $40 billion debt but only if it follows IMF conditions.[144] As evidenced by its reports and policy papers, the IMF's stance toward Iraq clearly hews closely to that of the US, i.e., that the country is in desperate shape because of Saddam's centralized economy, that the US has come to liberate it, that the IMF is only there to help, and that the ones resisting the occupation are "opponents."[145]

Its economic design on Iraq also fits in very neatly with the US's plans. According to Takatoshi Kato, IMF deputy managing director, "Iraq will need to embark in the near future on a program of ambitious structural reforms to achieve sustained private sector-led growth, including, among other things, the establishment of the legal, institutional, and regulatory frameworks for markets to work effectively and the design of appropriate safety nets that would support social stability."[146] IMF loans, Kato said, should "help the authorities to undertake difficult but necessary reforms, including restructuring of the public sector."[147]

Tasked with coordinating closely with the IMF is the World Bank, which is now headed by one of the US's top war architects, then Defense Undersecretary Paul Wolfowitz, who, when asked why the US invaded Iraq and not North Korea, said: "[E]conomically, we just had no choice in Iraq. The country swims on a sea of oil."[148] The World Bank has already worked on Iraq's National Development Strategy, or the overall framework for Iraq's economy and, like Bearing Point, is providing technical assistance on virtually all aspects of Iraq's economy. Like Bearing Point, the World Bank staff calls for fast action. Citing the lessons of an earlier war, a working paper states that "One of the main lessons of Bosnia and Herzegovina's experience is the need to press for investment-related policy reforms as early as feasible... [T]here is no doubt that earlier reform would have been desirable, and this is one of the most important lessons for other post-conflict environments."[149]

As it has done in scores of countries around the world, the IMF and the World Bank use debt as leverage to impose conditions that severely inhibit the policy scope of any future Iraqi government. Though the Iraqi National Assembly has rejected the Paris Club deal on the debt,[150] the interim government has promised the IMF that it will push through with "reforms aimed at reducing the role of the government in the economy," including cutbacks in government employees' wages and pensions and in subsidies on food and oil products.[151] While there are serious shortcomings in the way the assembly was constituted, it is the most representative institution in Iraq—certainly more representative than the hand-picked finance minister—and its position on the debt and the IMF's conditions illustrate the threats that the US economic agenda faces once more Iraqis are given a say.

12) Keep the Troops Ready to March Out Anytime

But there's no option of backing down. While there have been divergences among US officials on the scale and speed of Iraq's economic restructuring, there have been few cracks on the ultimate goal of transforming Iraq into an open free-market economy.[152] As long as the Iraqis out front are protected by those out back, the plans will push through. As General David Petraeus, who was tasked with overseeing training of Iraqi forces, said, "The key there is of course Iraqi leadership backed up and very firmly embraced by coalition forces."[153]

Just in case anything happens, i.e., the rejectionists take power despite all of the US's precautions or the non-rejectionists begin disobeying orders, the US can always call in the troops—or order them to march out of their bases—anytime. The indefinite presence of the US troops and the planned establishment of permanent military bases in Iraq represent the ultimate safeguard for the US's economic agenda in Iraq. US military engineers are now constructing a network of up to fourteen "enduring" military bases all over Iraq.[154] Noting how US naval bases in the Philippines gave the US "great presence in the Pacific," former Iraq administrator Lt. Gen. Jay Garner, said "To me that's what Iraq is for the next few decades. We ought to have something there... that gives us great presence in the Middle East."[155] The US has also drafted a Status of Forces Agreement, the same sort the US has with dozens of countries around the world, in order to present the US troops' continuing stay in Iraq as a deal between two sovereign countries.[156] As was the case in the Philippines, it is expected that concurrence with this agreement will be a condition for any local Iraqis wanting US support for their political ambitions.

Like missiles directly aimed at any Iraqi government, the presence of the US-led coalition will serve to threaten and restrain any Iraqi government's ambitions. Asked what the Bush administration would do if the transition government started doing things inimical to US interests, a State Department official cryptically said, "We have to make our views known in the way that we do around the world."[157] Such will be the enduring relationship between the US and the Iraqi government. One US official summed it up, saying that although Iraqis were "the ultimate determinants of their own destiny... we have 140,000 troops here, and they're getting shot at. We're also spending a lot of money. We don't dictate action plans. But we constantly remind them that we're working toward the same goal, and we have our 'red lines.'"[158] The US will ensure that, in case the laws and institutions falter or the Iraqis cross the lines, Iraq's neoliberal regime will endure as it was created: by force.

The Iraqi Legal System under the Occupation
Mohammed al-Rahoo

From Iraq, the country of civilization and law, from my country that is still bleeding, I greet you and complain to God, to you, and to everyone with good intentions who can feel human suffering and work hard to rescue people effected by tyranny and occupation. I complain to you all on behalf of a country occupied by an invading force that destroyed its sovereignty, attacked its land, humiliated its people, and killed many of them.

Before the occupation, the Iraqi legal system used to be strong. The legislative, executive, and judicial systems used to be integrated and strong, despite some chaos and flaws resulting from the internal clashes and conflicts of power between the former regime's stakeholders.

The legal system in any country is based upon four main foundations: the constitutional principles, the democratic system, the judicial system, and the international conventions and treaties. The Iraqi legal system, with its four foundations, was affected very strongly by the occupation of the country and the consequences of this occupation.

All of us realize the fact that Mr. Bremer had appointed himself as a ruler of Iraq and monopolized all the legislative, judicial, and executive power, making himself the supreme leader and the new dictator. This was announced as an order published in the Iraqi official newspaper *Al-Waqa'e*, and this was a clear violation of the legal principles.

This was followed by a number of laws and resolutions, most of which violated the legal principles regulating the legislative process. Bremer also cancelled a number of pre-occupation laws and put other laws on hold without any legal justification, and violated numerous laws as well.

Such acts are obvious violations of international law, treaties, and agreements that ask the occupying country to respect the local legal system of the occupied country (e.g., Item 45 in the Geneva Convention, 8 December 1949).

Dear audience, because of the time limitation I'll stick to a discussion of the main cases of violations of the Iraqi legal system.

A. The Constitutional Principles:

1. Issuing the Temporary Law of Administration and considering it the local constitution of Iraq was the biggest violation against the constitutional system. This TLA was prepared in a few days, not taking in consideration the legal bases and formalities for issuing such a critical document. It was prepared by mostly non-Iraqi individuals, and it included a large number of dangerous laws harming Iraq's future, sovereignty, legal system, identity, and the unity of its land and people.

2. Violating the constitutional principle of the presumption of innocence before being proved guilty. The occupation authorities detained thousands of people without any charges other than suspicion without evidence, kept them in detention camps for very long periods of time, and scanned their pupils and fingerprints, without a judge's decision or any legal basis. Thus, the occupation authorities reversed the aforementioned principle into "the presumption of guilt before being proved innocent."

3. Violating the privacy of homes, religious spaces, hospitals, and governmental buildings all of which are in breach of the constitutional principles that guarantees the privacy of such places unless a judicial order states otherwise, and according to certain procedures and legal steps. The occupation authorities raid Iraqi homes all the time without any previous notification or legal orders, and in a violent and chaotic fashion.

B. The Legislative System

The occupation authorities have violated the Iraqi legislative system in many cases, such as:

1. Paralyzing the basics of the Iraqi penal codes. The occupation authorities sabotaged the principle of local criminal laws when they granted legal immunity to their military forces and any individuals working with them. The occupation troops are immune from the Iraqi legal system for any of their military and nonmilitary actions, such as robbery, rape, assault, murder, and humiliating civilians, according to Order 17, issued 27 June 2003.

2. The occupation authorities stopped a number of other Iraqi laws, including the penal codes, the laws of criminal courts, businesses and corporation laws, citizenship laws, and estate laws.

3. The occupation authorities passed a number of unnecessary laws serving the occupation's political and economic interests, laws which many

Iraqis have criticized and ridiculed. These laws include the estate dispute laws, the de-Ba'athification law, the elections law, the army dissolution law, the ministry of information dissolution law, and the Baghdad stock market laws.

C. The Judicial System

The occupation authorities have violated the Iraqi judicial system on both the personal and legal levels.

1. On the personal level, the occupation authorities have humiliated numerous judges and dismissed them from their positions based on random and illegal claims. The occupation authorities didn't give the mentioned judges any chance to defend themselves, and the authorities didn't follow the legal procedure stated by the Iraqi judicial organizing laws. This violates Rule 54 of the Geneva Conventions, and the treaty calling for respect of the judicial system's sovereignty, passed 29 November 1985 and 13 December 1985. The occupation authorities insulted and demeaned the Iraqi judges by sending armed troops into courts and arresting some of the Iraqi judges.

2. On the legal level, the occupation authorities interfered in the Iraqi courts' work by imposing a number of restraints and procedures that contradict with the Iraqi law. The occupation authorities refused to free Iraqi prisoners who were acquitted by Iraqi courts. Furthermore, the occupation authorities interfered in the legal proceedings by attending the trials, interrupting judges, and prying in trial and investigative procedures. In addition, the occupation authorities neglected to protect the lives of judges, which resulted in the murder of a number of judges by unknown assassins. Also, the occupation authorities turned a blind eye toward a number of violations happening in the Iraqi judicial system, like the newly established sectarian courts and other illegitimate court entities, and a number of secret jails run by different parties and militias around the country. Finally, the occupation authorities gave the green light to the Iraqi police and army to go around the country and violate the rights and privacy of civilians, and detain people without taking them to court or charging the detainees, which resulted in disability or death for many Iraqis.

D. International Treaties and Agreements

1. The United Nations' principles and conventions: All of these conventions and principles were violated when Iraq was attacked without the sanction of international law. These conventions prohibit any attacks or assaults against civilians during war, including collective punishment and group imprisonment. The principle that punishment should be limited to the person responsible has also been violated; the siblings, parents, sons, and partners of wanted people have been detained and tortured and used as a hostages to put pressure on the wanted person. The conventions that prohibit torture, attacking civilians, and attacking historical sites were also violated.

2. **International Conventions and Treaties**

2.1. The occupation authorities violated many of the Fourth Geneva Convention's (12 August 1949) articles when they attacked civilians and didn't follow the rules for dealing with POWs and wounded fighters, and didn't follow the rules for defending the rights of detainees, such calling their relatives and keeping them in good conditions.

2.2. The Hague Conventions of 1907 were violated as well when the occupation authorities did not protect public property, religious sites, historical sites, art, and hospitals, and didn't respect the local laws of Iraq.

2.3. The convention against torture (Resolution 39/46, passed 10 December 1984) and the Copenhagen speech given by the UN secretary-general on 28 June 1994 was violated as well when the occupation authorities committed crimes like the ones seen in Abu Ghraib.

2.4. The treaty for respecting the independence of the judicial system passed by the general assembly in Resolutions 40/32 on 29 November 1985 and 40/146 on 23 December 1985 was violated as well.

2.5. The Roma system of 1998 was violated, too, by the aforementioned crimes.

The Transfer of Power in Iraq

Abdul Ilah al-Bayaty

No one can believe that the purpose of what is called the "political process" in Iraq is a sincere process to build a state with a permanent constitution. Neither the strategies of the parties involved in this process nor the security, economic, social, or political circumstances allow us to believe that the participants desire to or are capable of writing a constitution that all—or at least the majority of—Iraqis would approve of and respect. The real objectives behind the American presence have been announced from the first days of the occupation.

Iraq's Experiences with Temporary Constitutions

No one can disagree with the fact that the July 1958 revolution, which canceled the royal parliamentary feudal system based on the 1925 basic law, provided an opportunity to create a democratic state. The Iraqis missed this opportunity to write a permanent constitution and build a constitutional democratic state. The National Union Front had not been disbanded yet. Rather than embark on the public elections called for by Kamel al-Chaderchi, chairman of the National Democratic Party, the culture of the two main peoples' parties as well as the Kurdish movement only got involved to achieve their objectives in what was called at the time "revolutionary violence." The Communist Party focused its attention on supporting Abdul Karim Qassem against its nationalist opponents by mobilizing people in the streets and reducing the state institutions to mere committees, aiming to preserve the party leadership rather than hold elections. The Ba'ath Party was hoping that Qassem would agree to let them share some power, as seen in the political model of peoples' democracies. When it saw all other means of struggle closed off by the Communist Party, it decided a military coup was the only way to achieve its objectives. By 1962, the Ba'ath Party had adopted the theory of the vanguard one-party leadership system, derived from the Communist Party model, thus canceling the parliamentary approach which Akram al-Hourani had represented for some time in Syria.

Since then, despite the successive governments and regimes, Iraq has been living with temporary constitutions that put the executive and legislative powers in the hands of the revolution's leaders. These constitutions have not acknowledged any legitimacy other than that of the revolution's leaders. None of these governments was able to draft a permanent constitution that enjoyed the approval and respect of all Iraqis. What do all these regimes have in common? What is the political flaw from which Iraqi political thinking suffers and which has prevented Iraqis from drafting a permanent constitution?

The successive governments have justified their failure to draft a permanent constitution by the lack of stability. Undoubtedly, the ongoing armed disputes, wars, and external conspiracies don't provide the stable environment required for voting on a permanent constitution. Such a constitution should help achieve social peace and lay down the mechanisms for citizens and political forces to participate in settling disputes and achieving their interests. However, the absence of such mechanisms have surely been the reasons behind many of these conflicts.

It is obvious that any state needs to be united and to stand as one when facing dangers and challenges. It is also certain that the more citizens who participate in diagnosing and identifying the challenges and dangers, and the means to face them, the more the state is able to act as one.

We are not casting doubts on the patriotism of the governments that successively ruled Iraq or their important achievements, particularly in areas such as oil, agricultural reform, and the spread of education. However, all these governments solely controlled legislation, the management of public funds, and the nature and structure of state institutions and policies, without being subject to questioning or accountability. They all persisted in using the concept of revolutionary violence against their enemies. This led to many conflicts and tragedies that could have been avoided and dealt with in a democratic manner.

What Iraq needs is a state that uses wisdom and science to solve the various challenges society is facing. This state can only be a democratic one. There is no other democracy than that based on equality between citizens and the possession of political rights without discrimination. A democracy which derives its legitimacy from its citizens' freedom to vote and nominate in periodic and fair elections all the states' representatives and legislative institutions. A democracy that is based on the state's refraining from interfering with religious affairs or institutions, or anything related to thought, conscience, or private life. Any other form of government is merely a beautified or decorated dictatorship. Democracy is a political and functional organization of the state, the states' institutions, and mechanisms of operation, with known bases and features.

The first function of democracy is to secure social peace and coherence: respect for human rights and granting of public and private freedoms, including freedoms of the press, of political and union organizations, of demonstration, of workers' strikes, along with the organization of free fair and periodic elections of the legislative and executive powers. This guarantees that citizens and social powers can participate in drafting laws and in deciding on policies that reflect their free will. It also guarantees citizens and social powers the ability to work to change the abovementioned laws, legislations, and policies through dialogue, persuasion, and voting in future elections—thus eliminating the reasons for instability, explosions, conspiracies, and violence. This allows the state to contain social changes and to provide a space for all powers to express their interests and visions and settle their disputes in a peaceful and civilized manner.

The second function of democracy is to efficiently and effectively employ public funds. The related stages of study, approval, and implementation should fall under the supervision and control of the state's specialized institutions, such as the Financial Control Authority. These stages should also be subject to oversight by an independent judiciary that is dedicated to enforcing the constitution and the laws passed by parliament. It should also be transparent to the criticism of a free press and relevant experts in order to minimize the chances that public funds be channeled toward anything other than public interest.

The third function of democracy is to manage public affairs wisely and justly. Laws and policies should reflect the will and the awareness of the citizens. They are drafted by elected legislative institutions that should reflect the concepts of justice prevailing in society. This system prevents extremist groups from imposing their opinions on society and on the citizens. There is no group that enjoys permanent political advantages in a democracy. There are voters' representatives, temporarily elected to implement a particular policy that does not violate the constitution or the rules governing coexistence.

The fourth function of democracy is the rule of law and equality. The executive only represents one of the state's powers, as a result of their separation. The executive cannot overpower state institutions or funds according to its own interests. The legitimacy, success, and existence of the executive power depends on how much it works for public interest, honestly and fairly implements the laws, and achieves equality between the citizens.

The fifth function of democracy is to lead to an open society. The freedoms of thought, expression, organization, and the availability of dialogue and criticism, along with the rule of human rights, are factors which contribute to the development of interaction and the progress of civilization and culture. They also develop the spirit of initiative and responsibility and create open-minded generations that will participate in making the future of Iraq.

Despite all the talk about democracy and its benefits, it will remain a mere idea if we cannot build the state's military and civil institutions, which protect public interest and the constitution and are subject to the executive power only insofar as it itself is subject to the constitution and public interest. The first point to be made in the state's constitution is that employment, promotion, transfer, and retirement in state jobs should be based on efficiency and honesty and serving public interest, without discrimination. State employees should enjoy all legal and organizational guarantees that protect them from being exploited by the executive authority and enable them to prevent the executive authority from abusing its powers.

A network of specialized institutions that implement government policies and that themselves represent the will of the people should at the same time serve as a source of advice and suggestions for the government, in its capacity as representing the state's continuity. The most important such institutions are the elected local administrations, the Constitutional Court, the State Council, the Defense Council, the National Security Council, the Judiciary Council, the Financial Control Council, the Media Council, the Environment Council, the Public Service Council, etc.

The Difficulty of Drafting a Permanent Constitution under Occupation

Although occupation is an illegitimate aggression and international laws do not acknowledge laws passed and approved under occupation as permanent, by calling itself a liberation rather than an occupation force, this occupation has tried to render what is happening on the ground a basis for international and Iraqi laws. However, objections to the American presence and its laws by the international community, on the one hand, and by the majority of the Iraqi people, on the other, have created a situation in which it is impossible for the United States to achieve its objectives.

The occupation of Iraq is a war of aggression against an independent sovereign state, a member of the United Nations and the League of Arab States. Iraq did not represent any threat to the United States. The UN Security Council, the body responsible for keeping peace, did not approve the war. As such, Iraq is under the protection of the 1907 Hague Treaty, the United Nations Charter, and the Geneva Conventions. The United States' project is a blatant threat to the United Nations and the prevalent world order. In the face of protests from other countries and oppositional powers inside and outside Iraq, the United States asked the UN Security Council to issue Resolution 1533, which organizes its work as an occupying power and establishes an Iraqi civil authority alongside its military power. This was an attempt to pass its decisions and laws as Iraqi laws.

But by approving Resolution 1533, which acknowledges the US as an occupying power that will run Iraq as such, the US committed itself to the international treaties that prevent occupying powers from changing the social, economic, or political makeup of the occupied country. These international treaties also prevent the occupying power from linking the country to any agreements or treaties that exceed the reason for the occupation. Those knowledgeable about international law know that any law passed under an occupation—including the permanent constitution that United States wanted to draft for Iraq—belongs only to the occupation's administration and is binding only for the occupiers.

Confronted with an escalating military, economic, political, and legal dilemma as an occupying power, and by the majority of Iraqis asking for an end to the occupation, as well as the escalating opposition and resistance, American strategists and their Iraqi supporters came up with the temporary law called the "Bremer Law." Wolfowitz called it the "Iraqi Road Map." This law was made not only to attempt to overcome the legal obstacles facing the occupation and American projects, but to be used as a weapon against the increasing resistance.

Most of the political, religious, and social powers, for different reasons, were opposed to this law. The UN Security Council did not even mention it when issuing Resolution 1546 because it knew that the Security Council had no right to change the constitutions of a member state and because it violated the authorities an occupying power should adhere to.

According to this law, Iraq was to pass a number of steps. The first was what was called transfer of sovereignty to a government appointed by the Governing Council, itself appointed by the occupation. In reality, there was no transfer of sovereignty. According to the Bremer Law, the main state functions, such as security, defense, the economy, justice, etc., remain in the hands of the occupying power. The transfer of power process was nothing more than passing the Bremer laws and the occupation measures as Iraqi laws—taking into consideration that the transitional ministries, having acknowledged the state administration law according to which it was formed, cannot practically change any laws or cancel any institution. It was created by the occupation for itself and those conspiring with it. This means that the transitional ministries can only implement the laws of the occupation.

The second step was to elect a national assembly. The election campaign period was used to marginalize and prevent popular movements and streams from participating in the elections through military campaigns against them under different pretexts. Sometimes under the pretext that they were Ba'athists; other times that they were armed militias; other times that they were terrorist Islamist organizations; and yet other times under the pretext that they wanted to hinder the elections. This was the case with the attacks against the holy city of Najaf, the martyr Falluja, Sadr City, and Samarra. This terrorism and bloodshed added another reason, in addition to the content of the Transitional Administration Law itself, that the election commissioned lacked legitimacy. The election law and the fact that half the population boycotted the elections increased the lack of legitimacy the National Assembly enjoys. Can this assembly draft and approve a permanent constitution for Iraq?

What is a constitution and what conditions should it fulfill to become potentially a permanent constitution? A permanent constitution lays down the principles and mechanisms agreed upon by the citizens of a country to build a state to live in, depend upon, run their public affairs, and through which the citizens express their sovereignty over their land and wealth. The mere presence of the occupation renders the laws issued under the occupation temporary, because they are issued by the occupation to serve it. The verbal manipulation of calling the occupation forces "multinational forces" will not change the reality. Occupation is the highest form of dictatorship because it wishes to determine the future of the occupied country by military force, with the help of the party militias that support it. However, power does not create a right.

In addition, the occupation has created a situation in which it would be impossible to approve a permanent constitution. Currently, no one knows exactly who the citizens of Iraq who should approve the constitution are, what they number, or where they live. Due to the occupation and the measures taken by it, chaos and destruction have prevailed in such a way that no one can prove his or her citizenship. In the absence of a trusted population census, the legitimacy of any referendum over a draft will be in question.

The concept of citizenship, the basis of any modern state, has even been replaced by ethnic, sectarian, and tribal affiliations in an attempt to divide the country and cancel its Arab and Islamic civilizational and geopolitical affiliation. Those participating in the American political process no longer accept that there is one people in Iraq constituting the total of the state's citizens. The Kurds, for example, voted for independence on the same day they elected those who would represent them in drafting the constitution.

The result of destroying the infrastructure and the basic services, in addition to continued military operations, means that the referendum on the constitution will take place behind the Iraqi people's backs, as was the case with the election process.

As for freedom to participate in the American political process, there is clear evidence that the occupation wishes to determine Iraq's future through military means only. Its forces are carrying out violent attacks, which have already claimed the lives of tens of thousands. They have taken tens of thousands of political prisoners in custody; they have dismissed tens of thousands of state employees, and thus the number of those unemployed has reached millions. The occupation forces continue to wage military operations against cities and villages, along with assassinations of scientists, religious scholars, and clerics, as well as former military personnel. Will the referendum be a free one? Will the constitution be legitimate?

In reality, by occupying Iraq, the United States has canceled its sovereignty, destroyed its heritage and memory, and taken over its wealth, in an attempt to replace it with a subordinate state based on ethnic and sectarian affiliations, a state of parties, ethnicities, and religious factions, rather than a state of equal and free citizens. In doing so, the United States claims that it will establish a constitutional, democratic state that will serve as an example for the whole Middle East. However, the chaos, destruction, and ruptures it has created will not allow it to establish a state that enjoys the respect of the Iraqi people, let alone to establish a constitutional, democratic state.

The political process is only a weapon to fight the anti-occupation Iraqi people. Iraqi society, which has formed a civilizational, economic, and social unit for thousands of years, will not be able to bandage its wounds, strengthen its unity, and draft a permanent constitution until the withdrawal of the occupation and the elimination of its impact. Only then can Iraq begin in a peaceful and civilized way to build a democratic state. Only then can centralization, decentralization, or a federal system be chosen. Democracy is the road to this, and not the other way around. No democracy can exist without the sovereignty of the people.

Problems with the Current Iraqi Political Ideology

Through its projects and behavior, the occupation is giving us a caricature of democracy. It wants to pass a constitution stained with the blood of our people. For our part, we should admit that both the concepts of a constitutional state and of political activity, as well as the concept of democracy, remain foggy within prevalent Iraqi political thinking. This thinking suffers from many flaws. Among the flaws is the amazing ability of Iraqi and Arab political thinking to transform any real issue into an abstract one, into faith, and then to sanctify it. This way of thinking searches for justification not in real history but in the history of ideas and text. Its method of analysis and presenting ideas renders all ideas sacred and abstract.

Undoubtedly, the reason behind this is the age of darkness and superstitions which isolated us from Arab and Islamic civilian (secular) thinking. It is undoubtedly due to our lack of live interaction with contemporary international ideas. We merely adopt their results. Thus it is no wonder that our thinking addresses all the theories as superstitions, talismans, as a set of sacred texts. It is no wonder that occupation, a matter related to real human beings, can be portrayed as the magic recipe to spread democracy. It is no wonder that religious political ideology practices politics as a set of fatwas. Even democracy has become a set of individual ethics rather than a working project and a political act.

We should refrain from sanctifying any political thinking, or we will never be able to build a democratic state. A democratic state is a state based on equality between citizens—men and women—without discrimination. A democratic state is based on citizens managing for themselves the affairs of their country, society, and their own lives, freely, through voting, nomination, and elections. It is not the dream of enlightened intellectuals or faultless heroes. It is a functional organization of the political aspect of society. In order to avoid the way of thinking that is based on mysteries and talismans, we should discuss issues of democracy as institutions and the drafting of laws meant to organize the state and life in society in order to serve the public interest, rather than discussing these issues in terms of morality and personal behavior.

This misleading confusion in defining politics is the source of some of the flaws. The issue of politics is public. Thus its main focus is the state, and its main tasks, which involve managing public funds and drafting and enforcing legislation, are to serve the public interest. Politics does not focus on personal or subjective issues. Politics is not directly linked to human conscience, individual morals, or private lives. Politics leaves these issues to religious clerics, artists, writers, philosophers, and those concerned with human values and conscience. Political issues announce themselves and are achieved through drafting laws, programs, and measures that build state institutions, laws, and policies. The state is the vessel through which human beings exercise their common political public life. It is not the dominance of an individual, group, or class. Power is not a personal authorization. It is a set-time assignment to implement a certain policy. If Arab political thinking were able to address the issue of politics clearly, it would get rid of all the vagueness, flaws, personal tendencies, short-sightedness, and generalizations that render political thinking as undisputable theses that are not subject to reasonable research. Political thinking would no longer be an issue of individual ethics, beliefs, and sacred references incapable of coexisting with the other, let alone the opposite.

For constitutional democratic thinking to develop, the idea of the vanguard, which has brought to our countries the deepest tragedies, must be criticized. Everything is the vanguard to something else. This circle is the vanguard of the nation, and that is the vanguard of the class, this other circle claims to be the vanguard of Islam. There is even a vanguard of American democracy that wishes to crush the nationalists, Islamists, and leftists by military power. We do not deny that it is the right of any group to describe itself as a "vanguard." I even believe that political action always requires people who crystallize public opinion, be they individuals or groups. The danger of the idea of the vanguard is that it only derives its legitimacy from itself. In a democratic country, which guarantees that the generations and regions of the same country will act in solidarity and support one another, with tolerance between different religions and sects, and with the majority respecting the rights of the minorities to freedom of expression, organization, and representation in state institutions, the only source of legitimacy is the will of the citizens, men and women, expressed through voting, nomination, and periodic elections. In this case, a vanguard that enjoys permanent political privileges cannot exist, because this contradicts equality between citizens, and democratic legitimacy.

The idea of the vanguard prevalent in our countries protects those who believe in it from feeling they have to understand the will of the citizens. Vanguards believe they know what's good for the people better than the people themselves. They claim they represent the will of the people without exerting any effort to find out how to ask citizens about their will, how to prevent themselves from oppressing the people's will, or how to change the government or its procedures if the people reject them. They reduce the will of the citizens to that of the vanguard group, which in turn is concentrated in some leaders. Some vanguards claim they possess a sacred authorization of which we don't have evidence. Others depend on means of oppression and militias that we cannot face. They all believe that legitimacy is derived from reaching power, regardless of the means. Once they reach power they announce—to hinder others—that they will only be subject to their own will, that they will stay indefinitely in power, and that the legitimacy of their decisions, measures, and laws stems from their presence in power. It is no wonder that the state and society suffer a divorce and that power becomes a personal pleasure rather than a political heritage for society.

The most important point these vanguards miss is that society is a living body in which cultural, economic, and political powers grow and change. Any attempt to block the path of development of these powers within a state is equivalent to blocking Authority itself. Indeed, the nondemocratic vanguard rule always turns into the rule of a group of people, whose departure everyone awaits because its political action was restricted to violence, oppression, and, in some cases, plundering.

There is nothing sacred about the state. It is the sum of the institutions, measures, laws, and activities that organize real people's lives together. The institutions, measures, laws, and activities are made by real people. They are worldly issues even if people deal with them on the basis of their religious and spiritual values. Issues related to the state or politics should not be given a sacred character, because sacred issues can not be criticized, objected to, or asked to change. The state should not interfere in sacred issues or affairs or religious institutions, because the state's scope of activity is related to the public life of the people, rather than issues related to conscience, beliefs, thoughts, and private life.

There is nothing sacred about the state, but the state constitution should prescribe fixed principles that stem from or agree with our Arab and Islamic civilizational and geopolitical affiliation—the most important among which is that the population of Iraq is the sum of the citizens of the state of Iraq. This population is the source of sovereignty and constitutional and political legitimacy for the people's representation. The people can give confidence to or withdraw it from the government. The people should approve or reject all the state actions and laws according to the constitution, as well as the periodic free and fair elections of the legislative authority, without interference or discrimination from state institutions. Each Iraqi has the right—without discrimination—to vote and be nominated. Iraq's natural, cultural, and civilizational wealth belong to all the successive generations of the Iraqi people. The ownership of this wealth—or any part of it—is not transferable to any public or private entities. Public service and public interest are the basis of the Iraqi state's work. State bodies and institutions may not be used to serve personal or sectarian interests. The freely elected parliament, the government, and the judiciary bodies should do their best to guarantee solidarity between the citizens of the state, the generations, the regions of the country, with the sick, the elderly, the orphans, those in need, and any person that is vulnerable. This should be the basis of the social policy of the Iraqi state. Sovereignty, security, national defense, justice, health, education, water, power, transportation, basic services, managing public funds, and managing natural, cultural, and civilizational wealth constitute the main duties of the state. Every citizen, without discrimination, has the right to enjoy the benefits of state services. The freely elected parliament, the government, and the judiciary should do their best to guarantee this. The national army is the means to defend the state, in order to defend the land. The army's organization, training, weaponry, and activities are subject to the freely elected parliament. The army only receives orders from a government appointed by an elected parliament. Iraq should prohibit the building of foreign military bases on its territory, as well as prohibit armed political parties and associations.

Iraq is part of the Arab and Muslim world. Its relations with the countries of these two worlds should be based on brotherhood, peace, and cooperation, in order to exchange benefits and achieve common interests and objectives. The freely elected Iraqi parliament should make sure that Iraq does not represent a source of aggression or threat, or the passageway of any aggression, against any Arab or Muslim country.

Iraq should commit to the covenants of the UN, the Arab League, and the Islamic Conference Organization. It should also commit to the agreements and treaties within the range of these organizations; their principles should be part of Iraq's constitution.

Democracy has become a social and political necessity, a feasible program. It is no longer a dream, hard to fulfill, as was the case in the 1950s. The youth of the nation, today engaged in fighting the occupation, will build this democratic state after forcing the occupier to leave their country. With the youth struggling against the occupation and hungry for freedom, there is a democratic renaissance that will not stop, because the youth has broken the restrictions of the regimes, ideologies, and organizations, to practice action in person. They are the sons of what we call the middle and poor classes. The educated middle class in our countries have gained enough social weight to render country affairs unmanageable without them. The middle class can no longer accept being excluded by the wealthy and powerful from state affairs. This middle class can no longer accept all the cultural, political, and social restrictions that ruled their lives, because they no longer accept or believe the empty decisions, speeches, and policies. They possess the heritage, technical skills, and modernism to defend the ideas of separation of religion from the state, equality between men and women, and sovereignty over their natural resources. Thus this youth will not accept selling short the rights of the country and the nation.

The Privatization of War

Niloufer Bhagwat

Honorable members of the Jury, concerned citizens of Turkey and other nations present at this trial, which is the culmination of a global movement of people for justice against the war, defying the acquiescence of many governments and the Security Council of the United Nations in the continuing war of aggression and military occupation of Iraq that millions the world over continue to oppose; I present before you on behalf of the prosecution this indictment of the criminalized and privatized nature of this brutal war: the corporate invasion and occupation of Iraq.

I. The decision to wage a war of aggression privatized by the Bush administration that is representative of and identified with dominant US corporations, a conspiracy of an oligarchy of US and UK corporations, including the major oil and armament corporations— major contributors to the Republican and Democratic Parties in the United States and to the Labor and Conservative Parties in England. The Congress and British parliament were presented with a fait accompli and did not scrutinize the facts.

Since "War is never an isolated act," as the nineteenth-century German military theorist Carl von Clausewitz correctly articulated, but "a mere continuation of policy" by other means, the juridical task before this tribunal will not be complete by declaring that the war against Iraq is a war of aggression, or even by a detailed description of the brutal and horrific nature of the war crimes and crimes against humanity, recalling the worst atrocities of World War II. Nor will it suffice to draw attention to the widespread use of the omnicidal depleted uranium weapons, napalm, and chemical weapons manufactured and used by the military-industrial complex of the United States in Iraq for war profits and for the economic benefits to be derived from the military occupation of Iraq and by the depopulation of Iraq. This trial can only be an effective instrument if the nature of the economic and political system and the policy behind the invasion and occupation, the precise nature of the war, the participants in the conspiracy, and the ideology they represent are wholly unmasked before the bar of public opinion.

What is evident in the military aggression against the people of Iraq is the devastating and abject failure of the constitutional and political systems of the United States, UK, and other countries. The checks and balances of these democracies were unmasked for the first time, despite the control exercised by the corporate global media, which was unable to conceal the catastrophic economic crisis faced by collapsing US corporations with shares being reduced to junk bonds. The fig leaf of "rule of law" was taken over by the fraudulent "war on terrorism," which is a war on people within these countries and an even more brutal war on the people of other societies and nations, in countries like Iraq, Afghanistan, and former Yugoslavia. Invocations such as "freedom and liberty" lie buried finally in full view of international opinion in Falluja, in Ramadi, in the province of al-Anbar and in the prisons of Abu Ghraib, Guantánamo Bay, and Bagram in Afghanistan. Even as evidence emerged from the weapons inspectors of the United Nations and the heart of the intelligence agencies of these empires, new and old, that this war was neither declared nor waged in keeping with the constitution of a republic where the power to declare war is vested only in the Congress, in response to an invasion or insurrection, or after consultation with parliament, as in a parliamentary democracy. The war in Iraq was a private war of aggression declared by an oligarchy of financial and corporate conglomerates of the US and its coalition partners using their soldiers to gather the economic surpluses and raw materials of other countries. Several have borne witness to the absence of weapons of mass destruction and the inability of the erstwhile government of Iraq to launch any attack in full view of legislative committees; some may have paid for the discloser with their lives, in all probability for having revealed too much.

The global media has concentrated on one Downing Street memorandum, the "Downing Street July minutes," dated 23 July 2002, drafted by no less an authority than the head of MI6, Richard Dearlove. The year before the invasion, the memorandum reported to Prime Minister Blair that "facts were fixed around policy" in Washington. However, the press in England has referred to seven documents, all of which reveal the nature of the briefing and the fraudulent nature of the decision making of the Bush and Blair governments, among others. These documents, all Downing Street memorandums prepared for the briefing of Prime Minister Blair, are:

Downing Street memorandum I: The minutes of the meeting dated 23 July 2002, by Richard Dearlove, head of MI6, reporting to Mr. Blair that "facts were being fixed" by the British administration.

Downing Street memorandum II: Dated 21 July 2002. Memorandum to the prime minister's cabinet discussing how the war on Iraq could be justified by creating conditions to justify military action, which might include a request for the return of UN weapons inspectors.

Downing Street memorandum III: Dated 25 March 2002. The communication of British Secretary Jack Straw reporting to the British prime minister that "a legal justification is a necessary but far from sufficient precondition for legal action…"

Downing Street memorandum IV: Written by Blair's Political Director Peter Rickets, dated 22 March 2002, suggesting that "… the best survey of Iraq's WMD program will not show much advance in recent years…"

Downing Street memorandum V: By the British Ambassador to the US, Christopher Meyer, dated 18 March 2002, recording his discussions with Paul Wolfowitz, informing him that "a war in Iraq would be difficult to sell in Britain and more difficult in Europe."

Downing Street memorandum VI: Dated 12 March 2002, from British policy advisor David Manning to Prime Minister Blair, stating that President Bush had not found answers to several issues among them "how to persuade international opinion that the military action is necessary and justified."

Downing Street memorandum VII: Eight pages long, and considers the alternative legal justifications for war, including WMD and al-Qaeda, and finds all of them lacking, including the Security Resolution, which does not authorize war.[1]

These documents conclusively establish that the decision to wage war was taken conspiratorially prior to formal commencement of hostilities, without a legitimate reason for the war, before independent authorization by the Congress, which post facto rubber-stamped a private backdoor decision. However, the evidence that has been overlooked even by perceptive observers is that not only was the decision made much earlier, the attack itself commenced in 2002 before any authorization by Congress. In September 2002, a month before the congressional vote and two months before the UN Resolution on weapons inspections, approximately 100 US and British planes flew from Kuwait into Iraqi airspace, and at least seven aircrafts were part of the massive operation which dropped precision-guided missiles on Iraq's major western air-defense facility. Earlier and thereafter, bombing raids were similarly carried out on various installations.[2]

The war itself has been dictated by a conspiracy of the predatory financial and corporate oligarchy of the United States, which controls both the Republican and Democratic Parties. The flawed 2000 elections in the United States catapulted into office an administration closely allied with and openly representing the oil and energy corporations, Wall Street, and the military-industrial complex of the United States. This was against the backdrop of collapsing US corporations recording some of the largest bankruptcies in the economic history of the United States (despite creative accounting methods), which resulted in the decision to devour the national budgets and savings by the military occupation of countries or by coercion applied to diverse governments. This was in order to capture resources and markets, to revive major US corporations facing systemic decline and bankruptcy; simultaneously, to use oil as a strategic resource to dominate and/or strangulate other rival economies in order to ensure the continuing inflow of capital from China, Japan, the Arab world, and the European community, among others, into the US—not through free market operations, but by the military occupation and political control of regions rich in hydrocarbon resources. That is, several economic power centers, despite the economic distress of their own people, have indirectly fueled the war economy of the United States.

This war of economic aggression in 2003 was a continuation of the policy dictated by oil and energy companies, finance capital on Wall Street, and the military industries and defense contractors prior to, during, and after the Gulf war of 1991. To attack Iraq despite the withdrawal of Iraqi forces; to impose war and sanctions on Iraq, manipulating the Security Council and leading to the genocide of half a million Iraqi children, more than the number who died at Hiroshima, denied nutrition and medical care as a consequence of sanctions imposed on Iraq, with a view to preventing the Iraqi government and people from extracting and using petroleum resources for their own development and welfare; to bring the people of Iraq to their knees; to preserve the oil resources of Iraq for future use for the oil majors to subsidize the survival of US, UK, and other corporations of the coalition of the willing; and to control hydrocarbon regions of the world to ensure capital inflow into the United States and the primacy of the dollar.

Commenting on the first Gulf war, Sukumaran Muralidharan, an Indian journalist and political commentator, had correctly analyzed: "The far more fundamental concern is the need to protect the West's preemptive claim on the financial surplus of the Arab world. These are vital for underwriting the political stability of the US and UK which today is irretrievable, in distinct decline and need rentier economies arising from the recycling of these surpluses."[3]

Denis Halliday, former assistant secretary-general of the United Nations and UN humanitarian coordinator for Iraq, who is present before this tribunal, in clear terms denounced the amount of $4 to 5 billion received by Iraq through the Security Council from sales of the quota of permitted production for the oil-for-food program "as wholly inadequate to meet the requirement of 25 million people" and accused the United States and the Security Council of carrying out "the equivalent of a genocide against the people of Iraq." He defined "sanctions as another war" and resigned in protest. The present war is a continuity of the genocidal strategy of war and occupation of countries with hydrocarbon and other resources or those that are strategically situated.

Under the Bush administration, the US oil giants have gained direct access to the planning of military and intelligence operations on their behalf. This has been achieved through the powerful Texas oil lobby, resulting in the appointment of (former) oil company executives to key defense and foreign-policy positions, including the president, vice president, Condoleezza Rice, and the then Commerce Secretary Tom Evans, among several others. The alliance of the Anglo-American oil companies and the firm alliance between British Aerospace and America's largest defense contractors, Lockheed Martin and Boeing, is reflected in the close military cooperation between the Bush and Blair administrations in the killing fields of Iraq.

Professor Michel Chossudovsky, eminent professor of economics at Ottawa University and director of the Centre for Research On Globalization, had highlighted in his *War and Globalization: The Truth Behind September 11*, published in 2002, that the Big Five defense contractors, Lockheed Martin, Northrop Gruman, General Dynamics, Boeing, and Raytheon were shifting staff and resources from their troubled commercial/civil aviation sector into the lucrative production of advanced weapons systems, with war orders unleashing "a massive shift out of civilian economic activity into the military-industrial complex at the expense of citizens of the United States" and their social security, i.e., a massive redirection of the resources of the people of the United States toward the profits of the military-industrial complex, subsidized by military orders from the US administration initiating a policy for war.

To facilitate the conspiratorial nature of the decisions being taken, the National Security Strategy (published on 20 September 2002) of the US administration was never placed for discussion before the people during the 2000 presidential elections by either the presidential candidate or his vice presidential running mate; a wholly different posture and position was taken before the US electorate, as per recorded televised speeches and debates. This National Security Strategy announced in 2002 is an extension of the 1992 Pentagon Defense Guidelines and the Project for the New American Century's 2000 paper, "Rebuilding America's Defenses" which *inter alia* advocated for US business an accelerated globalization in the interest of US finance capital and companies. In military policy terms, this translates as the military opening up markets and the forcible seizure of resources, with direct and implied statements to the effect that the US administration in the pursuit of these policies was not bound by international law or conventional morality.

Thomas Friedman, a vocal propagandist of this phase of privatized military globalization, articulated the use of the armed forces of the United States republic in corporate private interest as follows: "The hidden hand of the market will never work without the hidden fist. McDonalds cannot flourish without McDonald Douglas [the armament corporation] and the hidden fist that keeps the world safe for the Silicon valleys technologies to flourish is called the US army, Air Force, Navy, and Marine Corps."[4] This was the militarization which was to accompany globalization.

II. The role of the Energy Task Force appointed by the US administration in 2001.

The articulation by Thomas Friedman of the use of US armed forces in achieving the objectives of corporate America is supported by the evidence of the secret role played by the Energy Task Force created by President George W. Bush and Vice President Dick Cheney in 2001 in the decision that led to the corporate invasion of Iraq. The task force's members included representatives of the major oil and energy corporations, with their names and recommendations concealed from Congress. This is not the first time in the history of the United States that the decision to launch a military invasion or carry out a coup has been taken by and dictated by oligarchies and corporate interests. The difference between the earlier decision making and the Iraq war of 2003 is that the nature of the incestuous relationship between the administration of the United States and its dominant corporations can no longer be camouflaged or concealed from the world; the identification is absolute and complete. It is "corporate rule," using as its political base the born-again Christian evangelical religious fascist movement as a diversion from policy, with homeland security and the PATRIOT Act required to secure the political system against internal revolt.

On 17 July 2003, after the military aggression and occupation of Iraq was an accomplished fact, the Commerce Department of the United States turned documents over to the public interest group Judicial Watch under a court order, as a result of a lawsuit filed by Judicial Watch (Judicial Watch Inc. v. Department of Energy, et al., Civil Action No. 01 -0981) under the Freedom of Information Act. This was in relation to some documents dated March 2001, relating to the activities of the Cheney Energy Task Force, containing a map of Iraqi oilfields, pipelines, refineries, and terminals, as well as two charts detailing Iraqi oil and gas projects and a list of "Foreign Suitors for Iraqi Oil Field Contracts," including documents relating to the oil fields of Saudi Arabia and the UAE.[5]

The concealment of the members, recommendations, and documents of this Energy Task Force by the Bush administration and its vice president from Congress, which upheld by the US Supreme Court, establishes the undisputed control of the dominant corporations over the political and economic system of the United States.

III. Two distinct features of this privatized war: the fact that it is not waged against a standing army or combatants, and the deliberate targeting of civilian, nonmilitary infrastructure for widespread destruction in order to award "reconstruction" contracts to US companies in the immediate aftermath of the bombing.

The distinct and barbaric feature of this war is that this privatized war in Iraq has not been waged against a standing army or combatants. The "shock and awe" campaign, against all established rules of warfare and with the knowledge of President Bush and Prime Minister Blair and the heads of the coalition of willing governments and senior US and UK military leaders, targeted the civilian population of Iraq as the "enemy" under the continuing military occupation. It is not an aberration that 90 percent of the victims of the US and UK military forces are noncombatants and those sympathizing with the Iraqi resistance. The occupation has committed deliberate and premeditated violations of the Geneva and Hague Conventions, the logical outcome of measures taken to depopulate Iraq, in the economic interest of US corporations, and on the lines of the fate of people in the countries of Eastern Europe militarily occupied by Nazi Germany, in pursuance of the policy of German Fortune 500 companies and banking institutions for what was termed *Lebensraum*. Permanent genetic damage has been caused in areas by the use of depleted uranium weapons that have scientifically and medically investigated carcinogenic effects, leading to silent deaths of cancer among children in particular. Consider also the fatalities inflicted by the deliberate targeting of the water supply, sewage system, and hospitals, deliberately creating a health catastrophe as a measure of depopulation. The economic objective of the war and occupation is *Lebensraum* for US and UK among other corporations in Iraq.

IV. Lockheed Martin, Bechtel, Halliburton, BKSH Associates, Custer Battles, Aegis, Loral Satellite, Qualcom, CACI, and Titan are the top ten direct beneficiaries of the Iraq war.

There is a direct historical continuity from the support extended by prominent US corporations and corporate players to the corporate rule of the Nazi Party and its pillage of the occupied countries of Europe, and the role of the dominant US corporations in the decision to launch wars of aggression. It is necessary to recall that from 1939 to 1942 Ford Motor Company produced a thousand combat vehicles for the Nazis, central to the military strategy of Blitzkrieg, and special fuels were supplied by US oil majors to the Nazi army. Of the 35,000 trucks used by the motorized German army as of 1942, one-third were Ford products. IBM received lucrative contracts from the Nazis that would be used to determine population demographs to track down Jews and other threats to the Nazi party. General Motors, Ford, Standard Oil, Dupont, Union Carbide, Westinghouse, General Electric, Gillette, and Eastern Kodak, among others, had close business and political relations with the Third Reich of the Nazi Party, which was the corporate rule of the German corporations and banking and financial institutions, the real economic and political force behind Hitler and the Nazi Party. Prescott Bush was only one of the several representatives of the banking institutions and US corporations associated with Union Bank of New York with close financial and business dealings with Thyssen, the German steel magnate, who along with prominent German banks and companies, bankrolled the Nazi Party for and on behalf of the corporations.

Lockheed Martin, whose vice president Bruce Jackson is a key player in the Project for the New American Century and had helped draft the Republican Party foreign policy platform in 2000, obtained substantial war contracts as a direct result of the war in Iraq amounting to billions, benefiting, along with other defense companies and contractors, from just about every phase of the war, with its stock tripling directly due to war. The company benefited to the extent of $21.9 billion in 2003 alone in contracts and war profits. The distinctive feature of this war is the satanic, premeditated, and systematic destruction of most of the civilian infrastructure of Iraq: of power generation units, electrification, water systems and reservoirs, roads, sewage systems, hospitals, schools, government buildings (except the oil ministry), irrigation and transportation systems, with a view to justifying the grant of construction contracts to US companies. The top ten US and UK companies deriving war profits from Iraq are Lockheed Martin, Bechtel, Halliburton, BKSH Associates, Custer Battles, Aegis, Loral Satellite, Qualcom, CACI, and Titan.

Halliburton, Vice President Dick Cheney's old company, from which he received deferred wages even as vice president of the United States, is now one of the largest oil services company in the United States, and its subsidiary Kellogg, Brown and Root provides extensive security and military support in Iraq. Halliburton has been the focus of considerable media attention in the United States and internationally for the extensive contracts granted by the Department of Defense and the US Army for the reconstruction of oil terminals and pipelines, in a secret no-bid process, worth approximately $7 billion, excluding the payments made to Kellogg, Brown and Root for services as private military contractors. The contracts were granted even before the commencement of the war.

In 2002 Halliburton was saddled with multibillion asbestos liability and the company was affected by a slowdown in domestic oil production. As a consequence Halliburton's stock prices rapidly plummeted to $12.62 from a high of $22 the year before, with rumors that the company would be filing for bankruptcy. With the no-bid contract awarded a few months before the invasion and occupation of Iraq, the fortunes of Halliburton have undergone a dramatic change. In fact Kellogg, Brown and Root, the subsidiary of Halliburton, has been a beneficiary of most of the wars waged since 1991, with contracts in countries ranging from former Yugoslavia to Afghanistan to Iraq, including the construction of new prison facilities at Guantánamo Bay, which require inmates irrespective of the justification for their incarceration.[6]

In addition to Halliburton, the Bechtel corporation was immediately singled out by USAID for a no-bid contract, for the repair and rebuilding of destroyed power generation facilities, electrical grids, municipal water systems, sewage systems, airport facilities, dredging, and the repair of Umm Qasr seaport before the seaport was occupied, as well as for reconstruction of schools, ministries, irrigation structures, and transport links, after the deliberate destruction of a substantial part of the civilian infrastructure by targeted precision bombing only with a view to justify these reconstruction contracts. Never before in history has one company been granted a contract for the reconstruction of an entire country, a contract which will eventually be worth up to $100 billion. Since 2003, more than one-third of the annual revenues of Halliburton and Bechtel have been derived from the no-bid contracts in Iraq, conclusively establishing the real objective of the war.

Several other companies figure in the list of those who have directly benefited from the war, such as Research Triangle Institute (RTI) of North Carolina for the "strengthening of management skills and capacity of local administration and civic institutions to improve delivery of essential municipal services." The president and CEO of this corporation see RTI as a vehicle for advancing corporate interests. RTI also received a contract from USAID via Creative Associates International Washington for "education system reform." The contracts to RTI signify the taking over of Iraq's education system, infiltrating its local administration and civic institutions. The former director of the Voice of America, Robert Reilly, has been appointed to "overhaul" Iraq's radio services, newspapers, and

TV, and to manage Iraq's media to "sell" US policies in Iraq and to the world media. The newly created Iraqi Media Network (IMN) established in April 2003 is being administered by Paul Reilly and the press edicts and their implementation is similar to that of Saddam Hussein's regime.

V. Extraordinary Presidential Executive Order No. 13303 signed by President Bush eliminating the judicial process with respect to the Development Fund for Iraq to which the revenues from the oil-for-food program had been credited and with respect to all commercial operations relating to Iraqi oil.

An extraordinary Presidential Executive Order was signed by the president of the United States of America on 22 May 2003. The Executive Order No. 13303 is titled "Protecting the Development Fund for Iraq and Certain Other Property in Which Iraq has an Interest." It begins with the declaration that the possibility of future legal claims on Iraq's oil wealth constitutes "an unusual and extraordinary threat to national security and foreign policy of the United States," that "any... judicial process is prohibited and shall be deemed to be null and void" with respect to the Development Fund for Iraq, as well as to any commercial operation conducted by US corporations involved in the Iraqi oil industry.

Section 1(b) of the Executive Order eliminates all judicial process for "all Iraqi petroleum and petroleum products and interests therein and proceeds." Tom Devine, legal director for the Government Accountability Project (GAP), a nonprofit legal firm, has stated: "In terms of legal liability... the Executive Order cancels the concept of Corporate accountability and abandons the rule of law." The EO exempts US oil companies operating in Iraq not only from international law, but from American civil law and criminal liability. Consequently, the production of US oil by US and other corporations is not even being metered.

In the context of Executive Order No. 13303, would anyone in the world accept that the war was waged because of nonexistent weapons of mass destruction or to restore democracy in Iraq? In this context it must be emphasized that the true content of democracy is not a "managed election." A democratic society is one in which citizens are a part of the process of decision making in all spheres, and includes sovereignty over natural resources and over the production and distribution of resources of the nation's economy in the interest of the entire people. Governments who are managing their economies in the interest of foreign or national corporate entities cannot be deemed democratic merely because elections are held, while the most basic right of livelihood, the first right of any human being, without which there can be no freedom, is denied to people. Bread and freedom are not incompatible as propaganda would have us believe.

VI. Pillage of the Development Fund of Iraq, constituted from the revenues of the oil-for-food program, and its use by the CPA to pay Halliburton, among others.
It has been reported by Christian Aid, a charity organization in the UK, that the occupying powers have failed to account for $20 billion of Iraqi oil revenues. These were oil revenues from Iraqi oil and gas exports permitted to be deposited by the Security Council into the "Development Fund for Iraq." According to an independent audit by the Multilateral International Advisory and Monitoring Board for Development in Iraq, created by United Nations Security Council Resolution No. 1483 to audit the said fund, billions have disappeared from the fund, which is not subject to judicial scrutiny as a consequence of Executive Order No. 13303, as referred to above, whereas the amounts voted on by Congress for the war remain largely unspent. The audit of the Development Fund has recorded that "… of particular concern… were contracts with sometimes billions of dollars that were awarded to Halliburton for Iraqi oil fields without calling for tenders…"

VII. The military objective of the war to privatize the entire economy of Iraq evidenced by Paul Bremer's 100 orders issued in June 2003 and renewed in 2004 to maintain varying degrees of economic and political control by the occupying power; and the transformation of the constitution and laws of Iraq and control over the entire economy, including the state-owned oil companies, for the benefit of US, UK, Australian and other companies of the coalition partners, all guilty of participating in the pillage and spoilation of Iraq.
A leaked memorandum by British Attorney General Lord Goldsmith acknowledges that Paul Bremer and the Coalition Provisional Authority in issuing the 100 executive orders may have overstepped their limits, warning British Prime Minister Tony Blair that "major structural economic reforms could not be authorized by International Law." The real policy

executed by Paul Bremer, among others in the Bush and Blair administrations, was to transform Iraq's economy into one acceptable to US and UK corporations, while eliminating local industries and local businesses, public and private, and to that purpose Iraq's legal system was to be transformed.

For every Iraqi industry, "advisors" representative of US corporate interest were appointed. To give only two examples of direct US and UK corporate control over vital sectors of Iraq's economy: for the Iraqi oil industry, the US-appointed chairman of the advisory committee is Philip J. Carroll, a major corporate player in Texas, former head of Shell Oil and of Fluor (a firm invited to bid on Iraqi construction projects). The role of Shell in Nigeria has been associated not with democracy but with violating the human rights of the Nigerian people, severe damage to the ecology of the region, and several dictatorships. UN Resolution 1472, dated 28 March 2003, transferred legal control over Iraq's oil industry from the United Nations (whose oil-for-food program, from the years under sanctions, was lifted immediately after the attack to permit the bonanza for the US and UK oil majors) to the US and its allies. As explained earlier in this indictment, the only purpose of sanctions was to prevent the development and use of Iraqi oil by the government and people of Iraq from 1991 to 2003 until total control was handed over to US and UK oil majors.

The second example which I cite as evidence of the privatized economic objectives of this war is the appointment of Dan Amstutz, former senior executive of the Cargill Corporation, the biggest grain exporter in the world, and president of the North American Grain Export Association, as advisor to the Iraqi ministry of agriculture. Amstutz drafted the original text of the main international agreements governing the trade of agricultural goods, which permits wealthy countries to devastate farmers in developing countries by dumping their subsidy-backed agricultural surpluses on world markets, pushing down prices to levels with which farmers in poorer countries cannot compete.

The vital instrument for the domination by US and UK corporations in Iraq and their complete immunity under Iraqi law are what are known as the "100 orders," issued by L. Paul Bremer III of the CPA, pursuant to the so-called Iraqi Interim Constitution, the Transitional Administrative Law—never accepted by the people of Iraq. These are clear violations of international law, the Hague and Geneva Conventions on the laws of war, and the Nuremberg Principles, which prohibit pillage of an occupied country and the altering of the laws of an occupied country. Bremer's orders divest the ownership of the Iraqi people and state-owned enterprises by providing 100 percent foreign ownership for Iraq's businesses and companies, in effect re-colonizing Iraq and directly violating Articles 46, 47, 48, 49, 52, 53, 55, and 56 of the Hague Convention IV of 1907 (to which the US and UK governments are both signatories) and the US Army's Rules of Land Warfare. Article 46 of the Hague Convention IV of 1907 specifically prohibits the pillage of an occupied country.

To ensure the implementation of the 100 orders, an estimated 200 mostly US and other international advisors are embedded in each ministry. A review of a few of these orders expose the real objectives of the war :

Order 39 provides for the alteration of existing Iraqi laws in the following respects: privatization of Iraq's 200 state-owned enterprises; 100 percent foreign ownership of Iraqi businesses; "national treatment" of foreign firms; unrestricted, tax-free remittances of all profits and funds; 40-year ownership licenses. The implication of this order is that all businesses are to be operated by US, UK, or coalition partners' companies, with repatriation of total profits to the home country without restriction or any requirement for reinvestment of any amount to service the Iraqi economy, with no guarantee of employment or public services to citizens of Iraq or the protection of workers' rights; and with corporations free to pull out without any obligations or restrictions.

Order 81 on "Patent, Industrial Design, Undisclosed Information, Integrated Circuits and Plant Variety" by executive fiat of the US proconsul Paul Bremer, amends Iraq's original patent law of 1970. Historically, Iraq's constitution and laws prohibit private ownership of biological resources, whereas Order 81 makes it illegal for Iraqi farmers to reuse their own seeds, permitting the penetration of Iraq agriculture by Monsanto, Sygenta, Bayer, Dow Chemicals—the corporate giants who control seeds across the globe—and allowing the introduction of genetically modified seeds hitherto resisted by the Iraqi government and people. The US Agency for International Development is pushing for agricultural reforms, with a contract given to the US consulting firm Development Alternatives, Inc., with Texas A&M University as an implementation partner. Part of the work has been subcontracted to Segrum International of Australia.

Order 17 grants foreign companies and contractors, including foreign private security firms, full immunity from Iraq's laws, even for killing or injuring Iraqis, or causing damage to the environment or to groups of citizens.

Order 40 turns the banking sector from a state-run system to a market-driven system overnight by allowing foreign banks to enter the Iraqi market and to purchase up to 50 percent of Iraqi banks.

Order 12 suspends "all tariffs, customs duties, import taxes, licensing fees and similar surcharges for goods entering or leaving Iraq and all other trade restrictions that may apply to such goods." As a consequence of this order, there has been an inflow of cheap consumer products, wiping out local businesses for these products. This has long-term implications for domestic production.

Order 49 reduces the tax rate for corporations from 40 percent to a flat rate of 15 percent. The income tax rate is also capped at 15 percent.

Order 77 establishes a board of Supreme Audit with a president and two deputies with powers to oversee inspectors in every ministry and authority to review government contracts, audit classified programs, and prescribe regulations.

Order 58 creates and appoints an inspector within every ministry with five-year terms who can perform audits, write policies, and have full access to all offices, materials, and employees in the ministry.

These are only some of the 100 orders which provide for a complete takeover of the economy of the people of Iraq by dominant US, UK, and other corporations with a view to establishing not a democracy but corporate fascist rule—recalling the words of Benito Mussolini, an authority on fascism, who emphasized that "fascism was corporate rule."

VIII. Privatized violence perpetrated on the people of Iraq by mercenaries and private military companies to whom the military functions of the US and UK armed forces have been outsourced, with no accountability to any authority in occupied Iraq except the private companies, who are not liable to any military chain of command.

The hiring of private military companies and outsourcing of several functions including training, logistics, and supply operations traditionally performed by the armed forces is not unique to the Iraq war. What was once a function of mercenaries is now being performed by private military companies that hire mercenaries on the direction of the Defense Department of the US, UK, Australia, and other countries occupying Iraq. The outsourcing of several functions of the US armed forces is part of a continuing policy of privatizing the armed forces, for which the initiative has been taken by members of the Bush administration. Vice President Dick Cheney, as secretary of defense in the administration of President Bush Sr., encouraged outsourcing, and Donald Rumsfeld, presently defense secretary, desires that most military functions be outsourced. It is not a coincidence that Kellogg, Brown and Root, the subsidiary of Halliburton, is one of the private military companies with the largest contracts, from former Yugoslavia to Iraq, spanning several countries and military theaters, as referred to earlier in the indictment. More than one in every five soldiers in Iraq today is a mercenary. It is estimated that apart from private military companies there are 20,000 private security contractors in Iraq.

The irony of the situation is that according to a recent report by the United Nations, South Africa is among the top three suppliers of personnel for private military companies operating in Iraq, next to the US and UK. At least ten South African companies have been sending people to Iraq, and several South African mercenaries, it is reported, have fought alongside the Americans and British in Falluja. The South African company Erinys International has been performing a vital role for the US- and UK-led coalition in the recruitment of mercenaries to serve as bodyguards to US and UK top military officials and even to protect the "Green Zone." The most heavily recruited are the apartheid-era security groups, many of whom received amnesty from the Truth and Reconciliation Commission, to be once again used against humanity in Iraq in what is a brutally racist war.

The policy of the Bush administration and earlier US administrations is to outsource vital military functions in order to allow corporations to profit from government contracts. Similarly, the Blair government, on the basis of advice received from corporate advisors, has decided to outsource functions of the military, at the cost of the exchequer and the serving soldier, who comes cheap. A soldier in the lowest rank in the US army earns $15,489 a year ($1,000 more than the average pay for a movie usher in the United States) and a corporal with three years experience earns $19,980 a year, whereas the US and UK governments pay private firms between $500 to $1,500 a day for each mercenary they supply.

The hiring of mercenaries and the use of private military companies of the US, UK, Australia, and South Africa, among others, in Iraq is a logical extension of the privatized, brutal, and illegal nature of the war and the secret agenda for Iraq and its people drawn up by the dominant US and UK corporations, in order to rake in war profits by establishing private military companies who can be hired from one war to another, from one covert operation to another. Moreover—although the deployment of mercenaries is forbidden in accordance with the laws and customs regulating war, and by Article 47 of the Additional Protocol to the four Geneva Conventions in 1949—the US and UK are reluctant to deploy skeptical and disillusioned soldiers and reserves, who are suspicious of the real reasons for their deployment and operating increasingly more reluctantly, and prefer to deploy the mercenaries of private military companies as "death squads" against the civilian population.

A confidential army report addressing the shocking revelations of American abuse of Iraqi inmates at Abu Ghraib and other prison centers has reported that employees of private military companies CACI and Titan, which were among the top ten companies given contracts for interrogation and translation, along with other functions, were involved in the abuse of prisoners. Even though termination of employment was recommended, neither corporation removed them because there is no legal liability whatsoever for the extreme brutality of the employees of private military companies operating in war zones.

Mercenaries are the second largest group of soldiers in Iraq today, which is one reason for the extreme brutality with which the war is being conducted, as witnessed in the destruction of Falluja in several operations, with the use of DU, napalm, and prohibited chemical weapons. The reprisals in the ratio of 100:1 for the killing of four mercenaries of the private military company Blackwater Security Consulting, which supplies mercenary military personnel on a contract basis, indicates the brutal military strategy and tactics of the private military companies that have reaped the bonanza of military aggression and occupation determined to root out the resistance of the Iraqi people.

The real character of this war is revealed in the nature of security provided to L. Paul Bremer III and other highly placed officials, which was entrusted to private military companies rather than US soldiers, indicating who is running the war, in whose interest. Though the hiring of private military companies is "military expenditure," it is estimated that as much as one-quarter of the reconstruction budget of $18 billion voted on by the US legislature (the money of the American people) was not spent on reconstruction, but is being paid out to these private military companies. The Iraqi Development Fund of the people of Iraq has been used for similar purposes, including the military outsourcing to Halliburton, as mentioned in the official audit, which, according to the Executive Order No. 13303 referred to earlier, is not subject to judicial scrutiny.

IX. The "El Salvador" and "Colombian" options; namely, the use of private militias of thugs and mercenaries being funded, trained, and utilized as private armies and death squads by the US against the people of Iraq and the resistance, in order to fan fratricidal civil war between Shias, Sunnis, Turkmen, and Kurds, which would criminally Balkanize Iraq, recalling the partition of countries under colonial rule by covert operations, which created ethnic/religious conflict in keeping with the geostrategic and economic objectives of the colonial powers. The Balkanization of Iraq would have a serious impact on countries such as Turkey and Iran.

The Bush and Blair administrations having failed to subdue the national resistance of the people of Iraq and have been resorting to criminal tactics and the use of what is being termed as the "El Salvador" or "Colombian" option. These tactics include the use of private militias of thugs and mercenaries referred to by various names, such as the Muthana Brigade, Defenders of Khadamiya, Special Police Commandoes, and other diverse names, which use torture, kidnapping, and sectarian killings falsely attributed to one ethnic/religious group or another to ignite a fratricidal civil war among Kurds, Arabs, and Turkmen, as well as Shias and Sunnis. The aim is to break the unity of the national resistance of the people of Iraq and to resort to an El Salvador or Colombian situation, where mass executions were carried out against various sections of the population. In Iraq, all over the country, mass graves are now being found of civilians, whom the resistance does not target, with bodies floating down rivers, hooded and with hands tied behind them. This covert criminal policy, which has been used before in many countries in Latin American and during British colonial rule to partition countries, and recently in former Yugoslavia, to Balkanize and alter the political boundaries of existing states by inciting religious or ethnic warfare in the economic interest of the colonial power, poses a threat not only to the integrity and unity of Iraq, but also of neighboring countries, such as Turkey and Iran, among others.

X. The deficiencies of the Nuremberg and Tokyo trials: the camouflage of the economic and political systems of the Allied and Axis powers, which had led to the rivalry for economic domination and seizure of resources, with certain exceptions; the failure to convict the directors of Krupp, I.G. Farben, and other conglomerates and companies for the conspiracy to wage a war of aggression; and failure to regard the nuclear bombing of Hiroshima and Nagasaki and the fire bombing of undefended towns and cities like Dresden as war crimes.

The following facts were established by the International Military Tribunal at Nuremberg in the case of Goering and the political and military leaders of the Third Reic;: 1. That the Reich adopted and pursued a general policy of plunder of occupied territories in contravention of the provision of the Hague Conventions with respect to the plunder of both public and private property; 2. That territories occupied by Germany had been ruthlessly exploited, without consideration for the local economy and as a consequence of deliberate design and policy; 3. That in the occupied territories in the East and West, the exploitation had been carried out by putting local industries under German control, using forced labor, and transporting raw materials and goods to Germany.

The trial of the political and military leadership of some of the Nazi leaders was followed by the trial in 1948 of the directors and executives of a few of the German Fortune 500 Companies, mainly Krupp, the armament company, and the chemical giant I.G. Farben, as well as a few others, charged with "the participation in the planning, preparation, initiation and waging of wars of aggression and invasions of other countries" and the "plunder of public and private property... conspiracies to commit crimes against peace, war crimes and crimes against humanity" including the use of slave labor.

The tribunal in the case of the United States v. Flick (case no. 5) held that "Acts adjudged criminal when done by an officer of the government are criminal also when done by a private individual… the application of International Law to individuals is no novelty." Yet the directors and executives of these companies were acquitted of the far more serious charge of conspiring to wage a war of aggression; they were convicted and given minor sentences for the spoilation and pillage of property and the use of slave labor, in what was a major miscarriage of justice. This is for jurists the incomplete task of the Nuremberg trial and Tokyo trials. The reasons for this failure are to be found in the common economic and political system of the Allied and Axis powers (with the exception of the former USSR), and the manner in which these economic and political systems had been operating—using war as a means for the seizure of resources and markets during the two World Wars and the colonial and other wars inflicted on the developing nations. The Nuremberg and Tokyo trials failed to focus attention on certain serious war crimes committed, including the bombings of Hiroshima and Nagasaki and the fire bombing of undefended towns like Dresden by the Allied powers.

While the propaganda systems after World War II focused on the gulag in the former USSR and the restrictions on civil liberties—which undoubtedly were legally and morally inexcusable for a socialist society, which must always be firmly rooted in democracy, with the participation of the people—the serious pillage and murder of the peoples of the world was concealed by the world media, which was controlled by the corporations. As a consequence, humanity continues to be the victim of the barbaric economic and political system which has been described in the indictments at this trial. Humanity is already facing an apocalypse with the technological superiority of weapon systems conceived by the mind of men and women who have hired themselves out to an anti-human economic system that is destroying the species to which they belong, with devastating effects on the ecology of this planet, a common home for the people of all nations.

XI. Democracy not compatible with economic systems which allow dominant corporations to control the economic and political space within and across nations.

It is a contradiction to hold that corporate oligarchies with dominant control over the economic and political life of a country and with financial resources several times the size of the annual budgets of many countries are compatible with or can usher democracy and the rule of law into any part of the world. Their capacity to keep the systems they operate democratic can be compared to the democratic tendencies, if any, in absolute monarchies. Both citizens and political philosophers the world over concluded that absolute monarchies were antagonistic to the rights of the citizen and defeated these systems by revolutions in which the entire people participated. Judging from historical experience of these systems, can political systems in which dominant and monopolistic corporations control the economic and political sphere financially and industrially meet the democratic test?

No trial of the Bush and Blair administration and others who have collaborated with them would be complete without an analysis of the symbiotic relationship these governments have forged, through the existing political and economic system, with their Fortune 500 companies, in order to oppress their own citizens along with the rest of humanity.

It is necessary for me to cite Professor Samir Amin, an eminent economist in support of this indictment. In "Confronting the Empire" (*Monthly Review*, April 2005), referring to the military aggression and occupation of Iraq, Professor Amin highlights that the United States government is openly in the service of satisfying the

> demands of the dominant segment of capital made up of US multinationals... if it is the question of making additional fifteen million dollars in profit for the American multinationals at the expense of 300 million victims, then there will be no hesitation... instead it aims only at looting their resources... in the short term putting the military at the disposal of capital and delinking this capital from any system of human values... it is infinitely more brutal... and it is closer to the Nazi program... the US advantage is that of a predator whose deficit is covered by loans from others, whether obtained by consent or fraud... nothing to do with the laws of the market... There is a single party of Capital which includes Republicans and Democrats.

Honorable members of the Jury, we are before the bar of humanity; let it not be said that we lacked the courage, honesty, or the perspective to speak the truth. In conclusion I submit that the resistance of the people of Iraq to the tyranny described in the indictments before this World

Tribunal is sanctioned by a constitutional document maintained in the archives of the United States: the Declaration of the Independence of the United States from British colonial rule.

The Occupation as Prison

Nermin al-Mufti

First, I would like to tell you that I am not going to give my testimony in English because it is the language of the occupation. The second thing I would like to tell you is that I present myself as an Iraqi Turkmen in order to clarify that we in Iraq are one nation; those who are speaking about the Iraqis as "the Iraqi nations" in separating the Iraqis are assisting the American agenda of dividing Iraq. Arabs, Kurds, Turkmen, and others are the Iraqis or the Iraqi nation; so please, when speaking about us do not say "nations," say "Iraqis." Thank you.

If I were to ask the friends who are attending this tribunal to define the word "jail" or "prison," the first answer would be immediately: high walls; barbed wires; limited drinking water, electricity, and food; and neglect of the humanity and environment. If I were to ask you to define a "notorious prison," the answer would be in addition to what was said, the following descriptions: continuous violations of human rights, random killings, executions without trials, torture, and rape. Sure, there are many other descriptions, but I am referring to the basics. So according to both definitions and to the ongoing humanitarian, political, social, and economic situations in Iraq created by the occupation forces, we would find Iraq has become a great prison—it could be in the *Guinness Book of World Records* for being the largest prison in the world, with 26 million prisoners!

"A jail has high walls and barbed wires"—I will not speak about the besieged Iraqi cities and towns, but I will speak about one street in Baghdad, al-Sadoon Street. This street begins from Tahrir Square, Baghdad center, and continues about 750 meters toward Firdous Square, where there are hundreds of concrete barriers of different sizes with tons of barbed wires; we find the same situation on Abu Noaas Street, which runs parallel with Sadoon Street from the riverside, but with the addition of hundreds of huge sand bags and tens of check points. To be fair, while speaking about Iraq the jail, I should admit that the American occupation forces did achieve many "good" things in Iraq! The first achievement was in making the cities clean from pollution. I don't mean clean from the pollution of DU and other explosives, but from car pollution; because of the thousands of concrete barriers blocking many streets and bridges, the cars began going through only three or four streets. In our turn, we will enjoy another achievement: being slim without surgeries and gyms because we have to walk long distances to our schools and offices, again because the streets are blocked.

The barriers are not enough; at any time, any street could be blocked without respect to the time and leaving thousands waiting in their cars and public buses for long hours, either in hot weather (which is very hot in Baghdad, about 50°C in July and August) or in the very cold winter. Whoever dares to ask or to criticize will face harsh words or maybe even detention. At any time, any car could be stopped and checked while the occupation forces put out statements every so often about the models and plate numbers of the supposed car bombs—asking the Iraqis to help them in arresting their drivers!

In Iraq the jail, there is no respect for human rights or the international treaties and accords. I will not speak about Abu Ghraib Prison because I'm sure that everybody here knows plenty about it, but let me tell you something: the photos of Abu Ghraib were not published by a "noble American" who respects human rights, but were published according to the American administration's instructions to make the Iraqis feel how weak and humiliated they are, unable to do anything while Iraqi men are tortured and raped. Yet the Iraqis have continued and will continue, *inshallah*, their resistance against the occupation forces and their "Iraqi" puppets.

Every Iraqi is treated as a terrorist until he can prove otherwise! Thousands of Iraqis are being detained in Puka jail in Basra, southern Iraq, because they are supposedly a security risk—they have no evidence against them, but freeing them will "harm" the security in Iraq.

Soon, you will see what the American forces committed while raiding my apartment (on Haifa Street). They broke the glass of the windows and the doors, broke the dishes in the kitchen, and messed up my books and furniture, in addition to stealing many cameras and other things. I could not reclaim the stolen things for a simple reason: the unit that raided my apartment had left Iraq! I am not the only Iraqi who has had things stolen by the Americans; many have lost valuable things during the Americans raids; they have all heard the same excuse I heard.

It is very easy for Americans to kill Iraqis. The American vehicles raise banners warning the Iraqis to stay at least 100 meters away. Sometimes an American convoy comes from the wrong side and the Iraqis have no time to stop or change direction and simply will be crushed in their cars in cold blood because the Americans have the right of self-defense! Tens of Iraqis are killed every month at the checkpoints and the pretext always is: failure to stop at the checkpoint. In Kirkuk, for example, the American tanks crushed and killed engineer Muhammad Mousa and four of his friends while they were on their way to their work at the Northern Gas Company and the tanks were coming the wrong way in their lane. On Sayidiya Bridge, Baghdad, two women were in a car in the right lane when American tanks took the wrong side and crushed the car, killing both women. Six civilians were crushed by the occupation tanks in two days.

Every day, one can read in the local newspapers about Iraqis being killed at the checkpoints. And the Iraqis are not the Italian journalist Sgrena, whose bodyguard was killed at an American checkpoint on the way to the Baghdad airport, and the Americans did apologize to his government and his family was compensated.

Who would ask about an Iraqi in an occupied country? The occupiers have instated a law that prohibits Iraqis from filing any suit against those who have come from the United States and Britain, whether civilians or members of the military. The American shootings that kill Iraqis are called "friendly fire"; their families receive nothing, not even an apology, because the victims were too close to an American convoy or they are passing through a crossfire area (an area where the Americans are attacked suddenly)—according to this reasoning, every Iraqi is suicidal if he goes to his office and back while the Americans are in the streets.

The Iraqi POWs who returned from Iran said that the Iranian authorities separated them according to their sects and ethnicities in order to make them feel isolated and to incite each group against the others. I am telling you this trying to clarify what the Americans and those "Iraqis" who ride in back of the American tanks have done and are still doing in Iraq; they have deepened the sectarian and ethnic feelings in Iraq in an attempt to divide Iraq and Iraqis and to achieve the imperialist and Zionist agenda of destroying Iraq, reshaping the region, and redrawing Sykes–Picot in order to have more bases and to claim the vast natural resources of the region.

So-called governments formed after the day of the government handover (28 June 2004) and the dissolution of the bad Governing Council, have all been formed on sectarian and ethnic bases; although the majority of the Iraqis are against this tendency, it benefits the Americans and their Iraqi puppets.

Brainwashing is a daily practice in prison, any prison, yet in Iraq the jail, brainwashing is being committing every moment through different TV channels and dailies, especially after the looting of the Iraqi museums and libraries and the ongoing illegal digging and smuggling the archeological sites of Iraq. Here I will refer to two examples (are they simple?): The first is that law put out by the GC saying that modern Iraqi history began on 9 April 2003. The second is the English-language curriculum that was going to be instated in the first intermediate schools; they included a statement that the "former" Iraqi military forces were killing the Iraqis. This attempt was stopped by the Iraqis; yet there are many similar crimes that go undiscovered.

In jail, one is not allowed to tell the truth if it means giving a conflicting opinion; the situation that Iraqis are facing now after "liberation" is like this, as though their country had been converted into a jail. Paul Bremer III (this is his official name), the American governor of Iraq from May 2003 to July 2004, created a law that punishes any journalist, writer, or paper who publishes an article that incites resistance; as a result many dailies and weeklies were raided, equipment and materials were confiscated, and many journalists and editors were detained; especially the papers that refused the American funding and took the patriotic path. I'm referring to *Al-Istiqlal* ("the independent") weekly, whose owner was arrested and its computers were confiscated, and then it stopped coming out. "Free media" in the "liberated" Iraq means how to hide high-ranking officials' corruption (corruption in Iraq is about 70 percent, according to the Transparency International) and what the occupation and the different transitional governments are committing against Iraq and Iraqis.

In Iraq the jail, the high-ranking officials in charge, especially those who got their power through the Americans, are afraid of the prisoners' anger, so they have spent millions of dollars to protect themselves and the Green Zone—the only zone where ordinary life is possible.

After the dissolution of the Ministry of Information, the Iraqi military forces, police forces, and many other offices, more than one million families lost their salaries and dropped below the poverty line (about 25 percent of Iraqis are below this line). But if we examine the dismantling of the military forces, police, and intelligence agencies, we will discover that Bremer and his Iraqi cooperators were planning to open Iraq up for thieves (local and international) and terrorists to liquidate their accounts with the Americans in Iraq, no matter how many Iraqis were and are being killed. Here I refer to Bush's statement before the invasion that Americans could not overcome the terrorism only through terrorism!

I do not how we have been "liberated" while the communiqués of the occupation forces describe the Iraqis as enemies in the areas where their forces are attacking or confronting the Iraqi resistance-fighter heroes. Now I am recalling again what Bush said about Iraq early on in the occupation, that he would resist if his country were to be occupied… So the Americans can resist, and part of this resistance is destroying Iraq. We, the enemies of the US, according to the communiqués, have no right to resist and no right to live, although our country is occupied everywhere, with banners of "forces authorized to kill"!

Not only was the pretext of making the world safer for Americans used for destroying Iraq, but by prolonging the atmosphere of insecurity, the occupation could claim that Iraqis needed the occupying forces.

Because of ongoing insecurity (American-made), the rebuilding of Iraq has not started; the only facility to be reconstructed was Abu Ghraib prison, which was rebuilt and widened; almost all the former Iraqi air bases have been turned into jails. The occupation forces and their Iraqi cooperators are dealing with Iraqis as though they have come to take their revenge.

The prolonging of need, fear, and insecurity is part of the psychological war Iraqis are facing in their country, which has been converted into a jail. I won't forget to refer to the collective punishment principle in the notorious prisons, which is the main principle through which Americans are dealing with Iraqis. Falluja, Najaf, and Telafer are examples of such punishments; the whole of Falluja was destroyed, as you will see in my photos. My photos were the first showing the destroyed city; I mean they were the first photos uncensored by the Americans because I entered the city with the Iraqi Red Crescent and not embedded with the occupation forces.

Falluja will not be the last town attacked by the Americans; they have attacked and are ready to attack any city that has refused or refuses the presence of the occupation forces.

Because the number of Iraqi civilian victims is a top official secret, I tried to discover the average through the black banners. A black-clothes seller told me that he usually sells 300 meters per month; Iraqi women wear black when they lose beloved ones, and the Iraqis announce this loss by hanging a black banner displaying the name of the victim (martyr). The next shop was selling white clothes; the Muslims buried the dead by covering them by white shrouds. The banner writer next to both shops told me he usually writes ten black banners per day, among them six to eight for civilians killed by suicide explosions or by "friendly fire."

In our greatest jail, we have no right to a lawyer, so I appeal to the WTI to give Iraqis the feeling that they are not alone in their battle and their resistance is indeed the resistance of the world; condemn Bush and Blair and whoever cooperated in destroying Iraq.

Covert Practices in the US War on Terror and the Implications for International Law: The Guantánamo Example

Barbara Olshansky

I want to thank everyone that put the tribunal together and everyone here today for inviting me to participate in this gathering of what I think are some of the greatest advocates of humanity in our era. It's really truly great for me to be with so many people who are working so hard to hold the United States and its leaders accountable for the terrible war crimes they committed. I really can't start my talk today without saying something that I hope people don't misunderstand. I feel personally that I need to say that I am truly profoundly sorry for what the United States has brought upon the world. I know that this is not my obligation to do, but I feel that I must do it because I don't think any US government official will ever say it, and I know that it doesn't mean much coming from one individual, but I mean it with all my heart and I couldn't start without saying it today.

So I imagine that some people have been wondering why I am here talking about Guantánamo, especially given the fact that we at the Center for Constitutional Rights have also been working on the situation in Iraq and have sued American defense contractors on behalf of Iraqi citizens who were tortured and abused by them. So why am I speaking about Guantánamo? I am speaking about Guantamano really literally because the folks at the tribunal invited me to speak about that, and I don't think I understood why I was asked to speak about it until today, I think. I am speaking about Guantamano because that is the place where the US policies were initiated, policies that involved the deliberate violation of not only our domestic constitutional law but virtually every international humanitarian human rights law. That's where the policy started that has caused so much suffering for so many people.

The United States government's unlawful practices started very early on. I am just going to say this to give people a picture of how quickly this administration seized on the opportunity to repress people. Within one day of the attacks on the United States, the government started rounding up in excess of 1,500 people—that's a guess; we will never know how many—immigrants and foreign visitors to the United States of Middle Eastern origin and/or of the Muslim faith, and put them in jails and detention centers around the US and ordered the guards at those jails to lie to the attorneys who came to the jails and to lie to the foreign consoles about who was in prison there. This was a deliberate order by our attorney general then, John Ashcroft, to lie to everyone that came to the door about who was there. When we filed under federal law seeking information about who had been arrested because people had come to us and said, "they took my husband, my brother, my son, my nephew and I don't know where they went," we had to go literally door to door to try and find people; when we asked for information about how many people were taken, what was the justification, whether they had attorneys, whether their families knew, we got an answer from our Department of Justice that we were not entitled to know. We won in the trial court but we lost in the highest court in the land, and that means we'll never know. What we do know is that people were arrested and they were arrested for civil violations; they committed no crimes, were not accused of any relationship to any terrorist organization. They were arrested on the basis of unsupported tips that people called in all over the United States about not liking too many Middle Eastern men working in this grocery store— those were the kind of tips people were arrested upon. When they were in jail, given the opportunity by an immigration judge to go back to their home countries, the United States had kept them for two years longer without any charge, without any trial until they had decided that they had investigated them enough. The US deported them in the middle of the night, so that none of them could see where they were going; this was our first inkling of what we were going to be facing with regard to human-rights violations by the United States. That sort of is the beginning of my entrance into these issues.

Guantánamo opens up a new chapter after this. With the creation of Guantánamo came the Bush administration's revision of all existing laws, and in fact its start on a road of utter disregard of the rule of law all together. What we see early on—and this we know now from White House memorandums and letters that were released in the summer of 2004—what we know is that Guantánamo was the result of a desire, expressed at the highest offices in our country by the president and his chief council, Alberto Gonzales, who unfortunately now is our attorney general, to create a prison beyond the law. This was their expressed desire, to create a black hole into which the United States could place people in order to hold them indefinitely and to interrogate them under torture. This is expressly stated in a memo from John Yoo, a man who was a legal advisor to President Bush, who wrote a memo in the end of 2001, selecting the naval station at Guantánamo Bay, Cuba, as a place where he thought it could be safe to hold prisoners, because no US court could examine the military's actions on that base. At the same time that Guantánamo was selected as one of the government's prison sites, the Bush administration was also discussing how it would phrase its decision to deny everyone captured or arrested all of the protections of the Geneva Conventions. I know it doesn't take a legal education to understand that the Bush administration wanted to dispense with the Geneva Conventions so that it could deny Taliban soldiers the protections of the Third Geneva Conventions, which would have required the United States to treat them as prisoners of war.

The Bush administration's refusal to acknowledge the applicability of the Geneva Conventions also did three other things. Article Five of the Conventions aims to separate civilians from soldiers, innocents from war criminals. So first of all, this refusal means that that protection is lost. Second, the refusal to comply with the Geneva Conventions meant that the Bush administration did not afford the children that it took to Guantánamo Bay the special privileges that are afforded to them under the conventions. Instead of granting them these privileges, to continue to education and care, juvenile detainees were placed in adult camps. Third, dispensing with the Geneva Conventions meant that the administration escaped from the requirement of releasing war detainees upon any cessations in hostility. What this would have meant is that when the United States recognized the provisional government in Afghanistan, it would have had to release even those Taliban soldiers that it was holding, the way that all prisoners of war have to be released. Instead, according to the Bush administration, people in Guantánamo can be kept in there indefinitely without charge or without trial.

Also created contemporarily with the discussions of Guantánamo was the administration's redefinition of the word "torture." There was some reference to this today, but I don't really know, unless you are looking at the documents that were put out by the White House, what this actually meant. The definition that has been included in key human-rights treaties and cases, according to the administration, is incorrect. The lawyers at the White House decided that the term is actually much narrower than you would see in the Convention Against Torture, and applies only to the instances of physical harm that put a person at risk for major organ failure or death. Redefinition of torture apparently opened the door for the use of Guantánamo as a prison laboratory for creating effective abuse and torture strategies. We've pretty much confirmed, having seen what has happened in Guantánamo and what has happened in the prisons in Iraq, that in fact Guantánamo was the laboratory for testing all of these different procedures.

It was in Guantánamo that the United States first used dogs to instill fear in detainees, forced people to strip naked and remain that way for days and in front of others, implemented sexual humiliation techniques, engaged in religious degradation, and manipulated the conditions of confinement. What did this manipulation include? Extremes of hot and cold, earsplitting noise, use of light and darkness to deny people sleep, complete isolation for months at a time. What was the effect of these measures? For some, complete decompensation, personality breakdown; for others, complete despondency and despair. After reporting 34 suicide attempts at Guantánamo, the United States Department of Defense decided that it did not really want to report these anymore. Now suicide attempts are called "manipulative self-injurious behavior." So that meant that in late 2003, there were massive numbers of suicide attempts and that information did not make its way to us.

I want to point out two more things. With Guantánamo came the Bush administration's development of the idea of the "enemy combatant." Enemy combatants are people who are suspected of some kind of connection to a terrorist organization, and therefore may be indefinitely detained. The government's explanation of what this phrase means is constantly changing. To be called an enemy combatant is to be accused of an offense, convicted of the offense, and sentenced to life in prison. If you are an enemy combatant when the president or Secretary of Defense Rumsfeld says you are, you go away, and it is not necessarily clear that anyone will ever know where you are going. What is the other significance of enemy-combatant status? According to the Bush administration, this new phrase, which does not exist in human rights or in humanitarian law at all, permits the US government to kidnap any person from any country around the world. Without notifying your government, without notifying you, without making any charges, without giving you access to a lawyer or a court. It is happening right now. It has happened to people that are in Guantánamo—and maybe some people here know this, but in the United States no one knows this—but in Guantánamo there were people that were picked up in countries halfway around the world from the battlefield in Afghanistan. People were picked up in Belgium; there were Algerians kidnapped in Bosnia; they are all in Guantánamo. They were going about their daily lives and they ended up in Guantánamo. Did we even have enough evidence to charge these people criminally? No! In court, where we argued with the government about what this means, the judge asked the attorney for the Department of Justice, "Are you saying that you can decide at any time that anyone is an enemy combatant?" and they said yes. This was the hypothetical that the court gave: "There is a grandmother in Switzerland, who on her death bed is deciding to give money to a charity in Afghanistan, because she feels terrible about what the United States has done there, and it turns out that some of the money at some point along the line goes to a terrorist organization, is she an enemy combatant?" The United States government lawyer said, "Yes, we can take her on her death bed and put her in Guantánamo." That is what it means to be an enemy combatant: you don't have to act, all you have to do is think about something and the government will claim you are an enemy combatant.

With the creation of Guantánamo there also came an exponential growth in the CIA's extraordinary rendition program. Under this program, United States special forces charter private jets and fly around the world and pick up people. Now, these are not usually enemy combatants; for those we use our own army and Air Force planes. These are people who are seized, hooded, and brought from the country in which they are captured and sent to third countries for interrogation under torture by the United States' request. It happened to two Egyptian men who were taken from Sweden, two people who were transiting from one flight to another and ended up in Syria being tortured for a year. This has been confirmed by a CIA official and now by private citizens who have helped to set up the operations for the charter companies.

These are the things that started with Guantánamo. What they prove is that every statement made by US officials about the abuses in Abu Ghraib and other places in Iraq being the work of only a few individuals is a monstrous lie. They are official policies, certainly not the policies of a few individuals. While this has been going on, there has been a failure of leadership in the United States. Neither the judiciary nor the Congress has been able to hold back this tide of militarism and brutality committed by the military and by the Bush administration. That is why I think that it is important for me to be here today, to see that there are so many people to work with, to try and limit a country that has alienated itself and the rest of the world, from the people of the United States.

Thank you.

Testimony on Falluja

Rana M. Mustafa

First of all, I would like to thank each person participating in this beautiful mosaic meeting that brings different types of people from different countries together around one issue. And all of us have the same enemy, and we will finish off this enemy in Iraq.

First of all, I would like to start by giving people a background about the history of Falluja and how it has always been a city with a strong resistance.

We can start from the period of British occupation. Falluja was one of the strongest cities in Iraq in its resistance to the British occupation. And we have today a slogan handed down from generation to generation: Resist any occupier in Iraq.

Then look at the period of the previous regime: One of the military coups against Saddam's regime began in Falluja, which is located in al-Anbar province.

Then look at how Fallujan resistance was born under the American occupation: Resistance in Falluja began when residents there protested the US military occupation of an elementary school in April 2003. US soldiers gunned down seventeen protesters and began raiding homes and detaining people. That is how resistance was born in Falluja.

Then we have the 82nd Airborne Division that was deployed in al-Anbar province. Iraqis call this the dirty division because of the horrible way they treated the people in the whole of al-Anbar province. All of our traditions were disrespected by these occupiers and so many horrible things were done by these soldiers. For example, the nighttime home raids, the illegal detentions, innocent people being killed for no reason. Then the American military itself admitted the need to change its policy in al-Anbar province, so they started to send in the marines to replace the dirty unit, which is the 82nd Airborne Division, and to treat the Iraqis better. The marines arrived at the end of March and were sent to al-Anbar. Then ten days after they arrived, four contractors, as they called them, who were CIA guys and all of you know that, were killed inside Falluja. Iraqi resistance knew these mercenaries and killed them. Then the resistance fighters who carried out this operation left. And it wasn't the resistance fighters who cut them to pieces and hung them from the bridge and burned them, as they told and showed people. It was the people, who wanted to get their revenge on those mercenaries who work for the Americans.

On 4 April, the first siege of Falluja began. I was an eyewitness inside Falluja during that siege. I never saw a single foreign fighter, as opposed to what their propaganda says. They said Falluja kept terrorists inside the city. I saw only Fallujan people or Fallujan men holding their weapons to defend their land because they have the right to resist any occupier. They don't want any American presence inside their city. After about a month, the marines had taken many casualties and it was clear that the fighters in Falluja had won the battle. So the American and Iraqi governments agreed to negotiate and stop the siege by having a cease-fire.

10 May was victory day in Falluja. One of their demands in the cease-fire was that they wanted to patrol inside Falluja again—I mean the American marines with the Iraqi National Guards and the Iraqi police. If they did this, it would mean that there would be another mess inside Falluja. It was a hard day that day. As I arrived, I saw a US patrol in front of the City Council, surrounded by a human shield made up of Iraqi National Guards and Iraqi police. And then they withdrew from the City Council toward the main gate of Falluja, one kilometer away. And that was the amazing day of Fallujan victory. All these fighters came out on the streets and all the families were celebrating together. At that moment I had a very strange feeling, which was a mix of happiness and sadness: Happiness for my people because they won this battle, and they put these marines in a very hard situation. Sadness because I felt sad and worried about my people, because the marines that fought in that battle—and they are described as the best soldiers in the military—would go now and prepare the real attack on this small city, the city of the faithful.

And then as all of you know, the second siege in November started. And one of those guys who cooperate with the Americans, ex-Prime Minister Iyad Allawi, announced to the people: "You have to leave your city."

On the US Killing Civilians

I was an eyewitness. I entered Falluja during the second siege. These are the things that I saw the Americans do and that I heard from the eyewitnesses who didn't leave Falluja at all.

The Americans used different sorts of illegal weapons like napalm, chemical weapons, and different sorts of this stuff, all of which are against international law. It was like a massacre of civilians. I saw the dead bodies that were in the streets. One of the guys I know was with a group that went with the Americans into the city. They let them get some dead bodies from inside, but they did not let them get all the dead bodies because the dead bodies were chosen by the Americans. This means dead bodies with clear signs of chemical weapons were eaten by dogs inside Falluja. After the siege, Americans handed out papers telling people not to drink water or eat any food from inside the city. I got one of these papers, warning me: "Don't eat or drink any sort of food or water inside the city." Why, if they did not use any of these illegal weapons?

Conclusion
Falluja is 80 percent destroyed. And there is no outside assistance for reconstruction. Falluja was a massacre, and people are still being massacred in this way. Iraq has a severe wound and this severe wound will be affected because of the bacteria that have entered it. There is only one way that we will have peace in Iraq and solve this disaster. All of us, we have to hold hands and get these bacteria out; we have to force the Americans to leave Iraq. Then there will be real peace in Iraq. The peace in Iraq will be when the last soldier leaves Iraq, and the end, the defeat of this empire, which is the United States, will be at the hands of the Iraqi resistance. And I would like to get your support for the Iraqi resistance in its different types: the Iraqi resistance with weapons, with cameras, with pens, with different sorts of resistance.

I would like now to show you our documentary that we filmed, Mark Manning and I. We filmed under hard conditions. Some of our tapes were confiscated by the administration of freedom and democracy in the United States from my colleague Mark Manning. I would love to show our documentary to you. Thank you very much.

Human-Rights Violations and the Disappeared in Iraq
Abdul Wahab al-Obeidi

I have written a great deal about what is happening in Iraq, but I feel there is still a great deal to be said.

Bush has invited you to see Iraqis as he sees them, enjoying American democracy. He knows very well that it is not safe for you to see Iraq for yourself, as you would become yet another target for the occupiers' military, just like the rest of the Iraqis.

I have photos and films that document the real "democracy" Iraqis are experiencing. You will see for yourself the realities and the sufferings of the children in Iraq. I recall a warning being issued for children to stay away from this hall, to protect them from the disturbing scenes about to be shown. Iraqi children are confronted with these scenes every single day. What of the children of Iraq, do they not need care and protection?

This war has brought with it a strange philosophy that turns all the standards and values of the norm upside down. Those who defend themselves, their communities, their country, and everything that is sacred to them are called terrorists! Those who bomb from the air, destroy cities, ruin communities, and loot resources are the civilized! These are the values of the new era of globalization!

I wish first to speak about what American democracy has brought about for the Iraqi woman. The aggression toward Iraq started with the criminal economic siege that was given legitimacy through the United Nations. Then, on top of all that, we had war and invasion with all its destruction and horrors. What of the women who lost their parents, their husbands, and their children? What of the women whose homes were destroyed?

41 innocent people, including women and children, were killed when 13 American bombs fell on a wedding ceremony in al-Qaim. Bush's democracy is the democracy of killing, destruction, displacement, and forcible relocation.

I wish to salute you, and commend your work, at a time when Iraqis might be feeling desperate and despondent, as all these acts of mass killing and destruction are taking place.

To save time, I will put forward my testimony in sections:

1. The legality of the war: The war on Iraq was illegal; the secretary-

general of the UN himself said so two years after the event. All the claims of Iraq being a danger to security have all been proven to be false.

There is no proof of any connection between al-Qaeda and Saddam. No weapons of mass destruction were found and no nuclear program. Even the US administration itself has admitted that its information on Iraq was wrong. In that case, in accordance with the rules of truth and justice, the US and its allies should compensate Iraq for all the grave damage done to all the infrastructure, all government institutions, health, educational, and cultural centers—all the destruction that took place since the first bomb was dropped until the date of UN Resolution 1483 of 2003 that regulated the occupiers' presence thereafter.

On top of the acceptance of responsibility, according to international law this war was an act of blatant aggression.

2. Human-rights abuses that accompanied or were committed straight after the illegal aggression: These include mass arrest and detention without charge or trial; maltreatment; torture and abuse of detainees; excessive use of force; use of weapons of mass destruction; dropping massive bombs on civilian areas; severe damage to towns and villages; bombing of farms and orchards; displacement and forcible repatriation of civilian population by conducting lethal military operations on cities, towns, and villages; restricting freedom of worship; desecrating places of worship and insulting religious sensitivities by deliberately damaging copies of the Qur'an. This is not to mention the daily maltreatment of Iraqis at the hands of the occupation soldiers.

3. Violation of the Geneva Conventions through interference in the affairs of the occupied, by enforcing the following measures: Dissolving the army, security forces, and the information ministry that I worked at; issuing orders to override existing laws, which caused a great deal of confusion and destabilization of law and order. Then they prepared for the fomentation of civil strife by putting together the Governing Council based on sectarian and ethnic representation, introducing the temporary constitution TAL (Transitional Administration Law), and holding the illegitimate elections. Illegitimate and invalid, because the situation in Iraq under occupation did not allow the people to express their genuine wishes for their country.

Then we also had Order 17, which granted immunity from prosecution to all American forces, despite their crimes. This order claims to have been based on UN Resolution 1483, although this resolution expects the occupiers to adhere to international law, the Geneva Conventions, and the Hague rulings that prohibit all acts of revenge and violation of the rules of armed conflict. This order was issued by Bremer, the American ruler of Iraq; it also includes all those who offer logistic assistance, catering, or other services, whether Iraqi or not. The order is four pages long; if you read it, you would cry a lot and laugh a little, to see how there is no value attached to the lives and livelihoods of the Iraqis.

4. The siege: Cutting off water and electricity and dumping tons of explosives on the civilian population in villages, towns, and cities. Surrounding the town with barbed wire, restricting civilian movement, and violating humanitarian law by restricting the population's access to water, electricity, health clinics, and hospitals. Reckless disregard for the lives and welfare of civilians. Use of excessive force in disproportionate response by using lethal weapons on civilians. Most of you have heard of Falluja, Najaf, al-Qaim, Buhruz, Tel Afar, Samarra, and al-Sadr City. These towns now have their own mass graves—yes, new mass graves—of innocent people killed by Bush and his allies. Moreover, the occupiers make sure that there is a news blackout while there is an assault on an Iraqi city.

5. The atmosphere created by the existence of absolute and unaccountable power for the Americans and those appointed by them. We also have militias that seem to operate above the law, been given a free hand to commit crimes of mass killings, assassinations, kidnapping, torture, and destruction of property, and there is no recourse in the courts. Some of these operations seem to deliberately target the academics and scholars of Iraq, with the government doing absolutely nothing to protect them. A complete breakdown of law and order, the occupation and a client government failing to protect the people.

Such an atmosphere is ideal for acts of terrorism, for armed groups to operate freely in Iraq, whether criminal gangs or village-based armed groups operating against the American attacks.

We in the organization Voice of Freedom for human rights have forty lawyers and legal advisors. We have discovered that it is possible to take cases against the Americans to the American courts. We have filed 275 such cases of crimes committed against ordinary Iraqis. Please do not ask me how I managed this. I have with me the full documentation for 85 cases or crimes, which can be heard in any court of law anywhere in the world. We have a total of 450 such cases, and I will be happy to pass to you the details after my testimony.

There is also the issue of arbitrary arrests or those carried out on the basis of information received from informants with a grudge. We have documented cases of people held in US custody for months, some a year, suffering torture (physically and psychologically) and mistreatment, but not interrogated. These people have been held without a charge or trial.

All the good people around the world who believe in standing up for justice and supporting the oppressed must condemn these practices. The occupiers are not just oppressing the Iraqis, but they try to cover their crimes with a tissue of lies about democracy, freedom, and human rights, women's rights, and children's rights.

You have seen for yourselves the truth about human rights in Iraq. You have seen the children, killed, maimed, traumatized, and psychologically damaged by all the violence of warfare, raids, and subjugation.

I hope that good people like you will "clean the reputation" of freedom, democracy, human rights, and women's rights after Bush and Blair have given them a completely new meaning. I hope your conclusions will include the following points:

1. An International Criminal Court investigation into the war crimes committed in Iraq. An international team to investigate the daily sectarian and ethnically motivated crimes in Iraq.

2. Protecting Iraq's academics and intellectuals as well as the national and religious leaders.

3. Replacing the occupying forces with forces from neutral countries.

4. Ensuring access, protection, and support for the independent human-rights organizations, facilitating their access to the prisons and detention centers. Such organizations should be allowed to document and investigate human-rights abuses and report them. Such reports should be made public.

5. The release of all prisoners of war and their freedom to determine their own fate after the end of hostilities.

6. The immediate release of all prisoners detained without charge or trial, ensuring that those charged received a fair trial.

7. Discussing the possibility of holding sessions such as this inside Iraq.

Now you will see a film about a recent operation in Iraq. The Americans demolish a house while a woman and her two daughters are inside.

I wish you all success in serving the truth and humanity. Peace be upon you.

Human Rights and the US/UK Illegal Attack on Iraq
Johan Galtung

Distinguished members of the Jury of Conscience, fellow advocates, ladies and gentlemen, friends:

The testimonies have brought the reality of an Iraq tortured by the US/UK (and a coalition of willing clients') illegal attack, and illegal occupation, into our minds and hearts. With a sense of deep anger at the continued aggression and deep compassion with the victims, we have witnessed the reality of crimes against peace, war crimes, and crimes against humanity, including nuclear war through the use of depleted, radioactive uranium, on top of the genocidal economic sanctions, and the general "softening up" of Iraq for a quick, decisive war and remolding to the taste of the aggressors.

Members of the Jury, what we are witnessing is the geo-fascist state terrorism of US imperialism, following the defunct British Empire, soon to follow it into the graveyard of empires—in my research-based opinion, at the latest by 2020, but, past experience being a guide, there is more to come. By some counts, the attack on Iraq is US aggression no. 239 after Thomas Jefferson's start in the early nineteenth century, and no. 69 after World War II, with between 12 and 16 million killed in that period alone. All in flagrant contradiction of the most basic human rights, like the "right to life, liberty and security of persons" (UD:3) and the condemnation of "cruel, inhuman or degrading treatment or punishment" (UD:5). In a Pentagon planner's chilling words: "The de facto role of the United States Armed Forces will be to keep the world safe for our economy and open to our cultural assault. To those ends, we will do a fair amount of killing."[1]

And in my drier words: "Imperialism is a transborder structure for the synergy of killing, repression, exploitation, and brain-washing."

I hold up against this organized atrocity—whether its legitimization is attempted through packs of lies about weapons of mass destruction and links to al-Qaeda, or by invoking a divine mandate or a mandate to export democracy and human rights through dictatorship and world crimes—a slip of paper, Article 28 of the Universal Declaration of Human Rights: "Everyone is entitled to a social and international order in which the rights and freedoms set forth in this Declaration can be fully realized" (UD:28).

This admirable formulation provides an excellent linkage between various levels of social organization, from the individual level at which these rights are implemented or violated, to the structure of the social and world spaces. It indicates the spaces in which these conditions may be identified. The basic needs served by human rights are located inside the individual, but the conditions for their satisfaction are social and/or international, generally speaking. UD:28 is a meta-right, a right about rights, with nothing short of revolutionary implications.

US imperialism in general, and its articulation in Iraq in particular, invokes the whole International Bill of Rights, but the focus is on the UD:3 right to life, in the context of Article 29: "Everyone has duties to the community in which alone the free and full development of his personality is possible" (UD:29).

There are no rights without duties, and right-holder and duty-bearer may also be the same actor. The word "community" rather than, but not excluding, "country" is used. This is very realistic, as human beings developed personalities long before there were countries run by states and peopled by nations in our sense. But "communities" are as old as humankind itself. To a growing part of humanity, the most important are non-territorial, like the NGOs.

Problem: What are the rights that flow from the conjunction of UD:3 with UD:28, and what are the corresponding UD:29 duties?

First Exercise: The entitlement to a social and international order where everything is done to resolve conflicts nonviolently.

Obvious, but worth emphasizing: the US/UK continued warfare is not only criminal, even by intent as demonstrated by the Downing Street memorandum, but also plainly stupid, a folly. The criminal and the stupid can operate singly, but they also often combine and reinforce, due to a simple mechanism. Criminal acts have to be planned in secret, also to deceive their own peoples, by small gangs with "cojones," in Bush's words. They do not benefit from the dialogue of open agreements openly arrived at in an open society, also known as a democracy. Democracy's traitors easily become its fools.

Barbara W. Tuchman, in her fine book *The March of Folly*,[2] gives us some leads. She studies Troy in the Battle of Troy, the Renaissance Popes during the Protestant Reformation, England and the American Revolution, and the US in Vietnam, and concludes that their actions were simply foolish.[3] And she presents three criteria for a policy to be characterized as a "folly"[4]:

1. It was perceived as counterproductive in its own time;
2. A feasible alternative course of action was available; and
3. The policy was not the policy of one particular ruler only.

All criteria are met in the illegal US/UK attack on Iraq. Hardly ever has a policy been so massively critiqued for being "counterproductive," including the 15 February 2003 demonstration of 11 million in 600 places around the world, the biggest in human history. As I shall indicate, alternative courses were available. And there was more than one ruler involved, a whole coalition defying their people, headed by 2B, Bush–Blair, followed by clients like 2b, Berlusconi-Bondevik (the Norwegian fundamentalist prime minister). Only two countries were democratic in the sense that executive, legislature, and public opinion coincided: the US, for the war, and our host country, Turkey, against. EU, take note.

Two Security Council members, France and Germany, put forward an alternative course of action: continued, deeper inspection that could then be extended to a human rights inspection, gradually eliminating two of the pretexts for a war which obviously was for geo-economic, geo-political, and geo-cultural aims (Judeo-Christian and anti-Islam, that is what the content of the torture and the desecration of the Qur'an are about). This proposal could easily have been developed into something that could serve to organize a General Assembly Uniting for Peace resolution, possibly also using the highly successful Helsinki Conference for Security and Cooperation of 1973–1975 as a model (also to avoid a US/UK veto).

But this was not the road traveled. Not to do so was not a US/UK brutal act of commission, but an act of omission that always comes as a poor second in Judeo-Christian philosophy and Western jurisprudence. Many can be blamed, including France and Germany themselves, for not having followed up, lesser coalition members, the UNGA for not mustering the collective courage against the bullying by Colin Powell, who said that Uniting for Peace (in the UNSC-run UN) was seen by the US as an "unfriendly act."

We are sensing here a missing human right with corresponding duty: the right to live in a "social and international order" where everything is done to solve conflicts nonviolently. That right can only be implemented if others fulfill certain duties. It is not possible for everybody to have an impact on the "social and international order" in such concrete and partly technical issues. In other words, for the right to be implemented, somebody "high up," socially and/or internationally—indeed, including the media—will have to do a better job, being more open to nonviolent alternatives and more closed to violence, war, and the "military option" in general.

This point becomes even more clear in the next example, Saddam Hussein's peace proposal in the *New York Times* (6 November 2003), "Iraq Said to Have Tried to Reach Last Minute Deal to Avert War": In February 2003 Hassan al-Obeidi, chief of foreign operations of the Iraqi Intelligence Service, met with Imad Hage, a Lebanese-American businessman, in his Beirut office. Mr. Obeidi told Mr. Hage that Iraq would make deals to avoid war, including helping in the Mideast peace process. He said, "If this is about oil, we will talk about US oil concessions. If this is about weapons of mass destruction, let the Americans send over their people." Mr. Obeidi said Iraq would agree to hold elections within the next two years. Of all people, Richard Perle seems to have been willing to pursue this channel, but was overruled by higher officials. Said Perle: The message was, "Tell them that we will see them in Baghdad."

The blame for this act of omission falls on the US itself. But this is entirely in line with a very transparent US approach: the US reports its own proposals but not those of the other side, as in Vietnam, in the Rambouillet negotiations over whether or not to bomb Serbia, or in general over Israel–Palestine. When the other side, denied access to public space by the compliant media of the military-corporate-media complex, fails to accept US proposals, they can more easily be portrayed as being "against peace."

In a Helsinki-style conference for security and cooperation in and around Iraq, these proposals would be on the table, as "it" was about all those issues, holding Saddam Hussein to his words. "Oil issues" could be translated into quotas and put the US in a negotiating rather than dictating position. WMD: the US knew the program had been discontinued in 1995; the CIA is hardly that badly informed. And even if

Hussein is not credible as a guardian of democracy, these elections would not be under the US/corporate press/"one dollar one vote" control that gives democracy such a bad name, close to a synonym for "US client state." However that may be, to have closed this channel was both criminal and stupid.

Second Exercise: The entitlement to a social and international order where perpetrators of (major) crimes are brought to justice.

With major perpetrators having major power through major veto, the UN today is not an adequate instrument for bringing the US and UK to justice, the US even having exempted itself from ICC adjudication. Yet they should not get away with impunity. Justice has to be done.

When a government fails to live up to its duty, civil society, meaning nongovernment, has to step in. When the major international instrument of governments, the UN, fails to live up to its duty, the international civil society has to step in. This World Tribunal on Iraq is an example of a tribunal based on the international civil society. But how about the instruments of punitive justice

The answer is that the international civil society, everyone of us, has that instrument: an economic boycott of US/UK products. A boycott could include consumer goods (drinks and food of iconic nature, fuels), capital goods (like not using Boeing aircraft, a major death factory, whenever there are alternatives), and financial goods (like using currencies other than dollars for international transactions, including tourism and price denomination; divestment from US/UK stock and bonds). It could relate to all products, or only to products from the most obnoxious, empire-related companies, like US/UK oil companies. It could be combined with a "girlcott" favoring non-coalition countries and acceptable US/UK companies.

Members of the Jury, everybody could find his/her own formula, seeing some boycott not only as a human duty but as a human right not to be interfered with. For Iraq, a focus on oil is recommended.

However, channels of communication should be kept open for dialogue. The goal is less to inflict pain than to bring about an end to an illegal aggression and, by implication, atrocities and illegal occupation. When the occupation is over, so is the boycott.

Third Exercise: The entitlement to a social and international order without imperial structures perverting the order.

We are today talking about a US empire, which may or may not have successors, in which case what follows also applies to them.

The empire is a structure based on unequal exchange in the military, political, economic, and cultural fields, and has to be counteracted in all four fields. Being the negation of the social and international order in the sense of UD:28, there is not only a human duty for people at all levels to counteract an empire, but also a human right, not to be interfered with, to do so.

Unequal exchange is injustice. To counteract it will be construed as hostile action, as "terrorism," interfering with the "normal" flow of resources and products, "normal" as established by the empire (see Article 24 of the new NATO Pact of 1999).

In reality, not to interfere is complicity, and to interfere is justice, and more particularly restorative justice. It restores not only victim countries, groups, and individuals, but also the perpetrator, to normalcy and sanity, coexisting peacefully in a world of more equal, or at least less flagrantly unequal, exchange.

The country to benefit most from the dismantling of the US empire is the US, which, while enriching its upper classes, at the same time has degenerated into a paranoid, angst-ridden country tormented by the existential fear that "one day they will do to us what we have done to them" (yes, one day they did, 11 September 2001).

I join the ranks of those who say, "I love the US republic, and I hate the US empire." The question is how to engage in these colossal acts of restorative justice. And the answer is that it is happening all the time militarily and politically, that more can and should be done, and that there is a need for action in the economic and cultural fields. And who are the actors? Everybody.

How can it be done? Four examples, covering the four fields:

Militarily, this is happening all places in the world where that "most powerful country" is challenged by people shedding their uniforms, dressing and living like the people around them, with their total support and more dedicated than soldiers fed packs of lies.

Members of the Jury, all resistance against an illegal attack is legitimate, and the Iraqi resistance is fighting for us all. But I also blame us in the peace movement for having been unable to share our insights in nonviolent resistance with our Iraqi friends.

Politically, regionalization is happening all over the world, in part motivated by getting out of the US grip: the EU, the AU, and similar incipient movements in Latin America, OIC, and East Asia.

Economically, there is the economic boycott, adding to punitive justice the restorative, Gandhian aspect of taking on the challenge of developing one's own products and helping the US adjust to a reasonable and equitable niche in world trade. John Perkins's *Confessions of an Economic Hit Man* displays the depth of US insanity.

Culturally, we are confronted with US/UK legitimacy. It used to be that "the US is chosen by God; the UK by the US"—like a pale moon reflecting that divine Anglo-American light. Today the idea of God using Bush as his instrument is sheer blasphemy, and countries chosen by the US should ask, "What is wrong with me?" If you are so immature as to need a strong father, seek psychotherapy, not a mafia boss. To kill Iraqis as therapy is despicable.

Members of the Jury, my own Buddhism is sufficiently close to the gentle Christianity of a St. Francis to sense the blasphemy. I call on the Jury to call on Christian communities to protest this blasphemy, including Pope Benedict XVI, Joseph Cardinal Ratzinger, who has the task of protecting the faith. The time to act is now.

Fifth Session

Cultural Heritage, the Environment, and World Resources

The Destruction of Cultural Heritage: A Report from the Istanbul Initiative

Gül Pulhan

Ancient Mesopotamia, the land between and along the rivers Euphrates and Tigris, corresponds to modern-day Iraq. In the third millennium BC, the southern part of the country was called Sumer and the northern part Subir; later they were known as Babylonia and Assyria, respectively. The first cities in the world were established here, 5,000 years ago. Their economy was based on irrigation agriculture, animal herding, fishing, and long-distance trade. The origins of the first centralized states were also discovered here. These primary states soon grew into empires ruling the foreign lands. The first rulers of these city-states were priest-kings, and they appear on various works of art, such as stone reliefs, statues, and vases.

Ancient Sumerian cities had temples, palaces, houses, workshop areas, gardens, and were surrounded with fortification walls. Agricultural production was collected and redistributed by the central authority. This required a precise accounting and recording system which gradually led to the invention of writing. Sumerian is the oldest written language in the world. Thousands of clay tablets that carry the writings of ancient Mesopotamians, be they Sumerians, Akkadians, Babylonians, or Assyrians, are the oldest historical records of humanity. Religion, literature, mythology, law, medicine, astronomy all had their roots in this land. Gilgamesh is mythological figure that everyone knows. He became immortal because of his quest for eternal life. Gilgamesh was a king in the city of Uruk in the third millennium BC.

As we speak, the sites, i.e., ancient mounds, that bear all the evidence of our past are being looted and destroyed. The loss of knowledge and the destruction of the record of a very crucial period of human history is unmatched. In Dr. Neil Brodie's terminology, the archaeological record soon will become "extinct."[1] Some of the world-famous sites, such as Babylon and Kish, were turned into military bases and destroyed by the occupiers. Others such as Umma, Larsa, and Nineveh became prey for wanton looters. The lack of protection for sites is a cultural emergency that has existed for the past two years.

The Looting of the Iraqi National Museum in Baghdad

In fall 2002, as the American and British troops were preparing for the potential war, archaeological communities around the world were fearing for Iraq's archaeological treasures and sites, particularly for the museum in Baghdad. Following the 1991 Gulf War, during the uprisings in Iraq, nine local museums (Basra, Imara, Diwaniya, Kufa, Kut, Babylon, Kirkuk, Dohuk, and Sulaymania) were looted and damaged. An estimated total of 4,000 archaeological objects were taken from these museums. An Iraqi appeal for UNESCO experts to conduct a damage assessment mission was blocked by the UN Security Council. Three volumes, titled "Lost Heritage: Antiquities Stolen from Iraq," were prepared by international scholars in coordination with Iraqi colleagues and distributed around the world to stop the trading of these artifacts.

The UNESCO Convention of 1970, signed by 96 states including Iraq, the United States, and the United Kingdom, prohibits any import, export, and transfer of ownership in cultural property that has been taken out of a country in contravention of its laws. In implementation, the country of origin has to prove the illicit—therefore clandestine—nature of the trade, which in most cases is very difficult, if not impossible. Regarding the 1991 museum lootings, although Iraq was able to provide complete inventories and photographs of the stolen objects, approximately 12 out of 4,000 were returned.

Based on this experience, and tragic lootings in Cambodia, Lebanon, and most recently in Afghanistan, and in fear of the worst, on 24 January 2003, American archaeologists met with Joseph Collins, deputy assistant defense secretary for stability operations.[2] Collins promised to look into the subject. On a few other occasions, Pentagon officials were given the coordinates of the most important archaeological sites and reminded of the necessity of safeguarding the country's archaeological heritage.

On the other hand, some museum people and antiquities collectors were also meeting with the military and lobbying to ease the antiquities trade with Iraq after the war. The director of the Metropolitan Museum in New York, Philippe de Montebello, proposed that future American museum excavations in Iraq should be able to export their finds.[3] This group's opinion culminated in an article written by a well-known collector, Andre Emmerich, and published in the *Wall Street Journal* on 24 April, ten days after the looting of the museums in Iraq. The title of the article was

"Let the Market Preserve Art, What Were all those Antiquities Doing in Iraq Anyway?"

On 26 March, the Office of Reconstruction and Humanitarian Assistance (ORHA) prepared a list of key institutions in Baghdad that would require "immediate protection, to prevent further damage, destruction and/or pilferage."[4] On the list, number one was the Central Bank (ironically, the most valuable collections of the Baghdad Museum had been deposited there for safe keeping) and number two was the Iraqi National Museum together with the Abbasid Palace. The document stated that "the museum will be prime target for looters and it contained literally thousands of priceless objects."[5]

On 27 March, UNESCO assistant director Dr. Bouchenaki said that he has been told that US and allied forces were instructed not to hit the archaeological locations, and UNESCO sent a map of sites to Washington, along with a list of key museums.

On 5 April in Kuwait, army civil affairs officer Major Christopher Varhola expressed special concern for the risk that the National Museum was facing, but no military order was issued for US forces to be stationed to protect the museum. On 9 April, Baghdad fell to US forces. On 10 April, a senior military officer made an urgent request to protect the museum. He received a written answer stating that US forces were on their way.[6]

On 11 April, Secretary of Defense Donald Rumsfeld communicated his opinion on the ongoing lootings in Basra: "The images you are seeing on television you are seeing over, and over, and over again, and it's the same picture of some person walking out of some building with a vase, and you see it twenty times, and you think… My goodness, were there that many vases? Is it possible that there were that many vases in the whole country?"

The National Museum in Baghdad was founded in 1923 and moved to its current location in 1966. In terms of ancient Mesopotamian and Islamic artifacts, it was one of the richest museums in the world, and certainly the most representative one. Collections ranged from the Paleolithic cave finds to monumental palace reliefs from the Assyrian Empire. A small portion of this priceless collection was displayed in twenty chronologically arranged halls and the remaining objects and cuneiform tablets were kept in storage rooms.

The museum had been closed since February. The most prominent collections, such as the treasures from the Royal Burials of Ur and Nimrud, had been stored in the safes of the Central Bank since the Gulf war. Prior to the allied occupation, another group of objects were also hidden in a secret location in Baghdad. Still, the remaining objects numbered around 150,000.

Various types of looters entered the museum on Thursday, 10 April, and the pillage, theft, and destruction continued for three full days. Some of the museum personnel, journalists, and television crews managed to enter the building on Sunday, 13 April. The senior Middle East correspondent of the *Independent* newspaper, Robert Fisk, tried to send some soldiers to the museum after witnessing the horrible situation: "The looters had left only a few hours before I arrived [after witnessing the situation in the museum]... Half an hour later, I contacted the civil affairs unit of the US Marines in Saadun Street and gave them the exact location of the museum and the condition of its contents. A captain told me that 'we're probably going to get down there.'" Fisk published his account in the newspaper the next day. His article was titled "A Civilisation Torn to Pieces."[7]

The situation was getting worse and worse, but no US tanks were on the horizon. On Monday, 14 April, Secretary of State Colin Powell held a press conference in Washington, DC, and stated that, "The US understands its obligations and will participate in restoring that which was broken, and will be taking a leading role with respect to antiquities in general, but this museum in particular." He also added that, "objects taken from museums and archeological sites in Iraq are the property of the Iraqi nation, under both Iraqi and international law," and he warned, "Americans who purchase or trade in such items... face prosecution under the US National Stolen Property Act." Secretary of State Powell was trying to control the damage, but he was left alone.

The following day, on Tuesday, 15 April, at a Pentagon news conference, Secretary of Defense Donald Rumsfeld dismissed charges that the American war plan failed to protect Iraq's antiquities: "I would suspect that over time we will find that a number of things were in fact hidden prior to conflict. That is what most people who run museums do prior to a conflict which was obviously well telegraphed in advance."

On the same day at a press conference in Doha, Qatar, Brigadier General Vincent Brooks expressed his take on the events, "I don't think anyone anticipated that the riches of Iraq would be looted by the Iraqi people. And indeed it happened in some places... The richness of the Iraqi population are of interest to the world... US troops were involved in very intense combat, and a 'vacuum' was created."

Exactly a week later, on Wednesday, 16 April, the US tanks secured the looted museum. On 22 April, a military investigation team under the directorship of Colonel Matthew Bogdanos began their inquiry, and after two months of meticulous work at the crime scene, concluded that circa 15,000 objects had been looted and damaged. According to the Bogdanos report, one group of looters had inside information and access to the keys of the storerooms, but dropped them during the mayhem. Still, they took the museum's invaluable cylinder seal collection, consisting of 5,000 pieces, but could not get to the gold and silver coin collections. A general amnesty and no questions asked policy was applied, and as a result, to this day nearly 6,000 objects have been recovered both in Iraq and abroad. Among them are prize pieces like the Lady of Uruk, the bronze statue of Akkadian king Naram-Sin, and the famous Uruk Vase.

On 22 May, UN Security Council Resolution 1483 banned international trade in Iraqi cultural property and other archaeological, historical, cultural, religious, and rare scientific items illegally removed from the National Museum, the National Library, and other institutions.[8] Despite these measures, every week another cache of Mesopotamian antiquities surfaces on the internet auctions, particularly on eBay.

The museum remains closed, circa 8,000 objects still hidden in secret locations. The director at the time of the events, Dr. Nawalla al-Mutawalli, has been replaced by Dr. Donny George Yukana.

International Conventions and Legal Responsibilities

The main document concerning the protection of cultural heritage in time of war and its aftermath is the Hague Convention for the Protection of Cultural Property in the Event of Armed Conflict. It was first drafted in 1899 and 1907, but failed to prevent destruction of cultural property during World War I. The 1949 Geneva Conventions and the 1954 Hague Conventions were formulated as a reaction to the cultural losses of World War II. In the Nuremberg Trials, confiscation, destruction, and damage to cultural property was treated as a war crime subject to prosecution and punishment.[9]

The Hague Convention was signed in May 1954 and entered into force in August 1956. It has been ratified by over 100 states, Iraq among them. The United States and the United Kingdom are not signatories to the 1954 Convention. In 1996, the US State and Defense Departments recommended ratification, and in 1999 President Clinton submitted the Hague Conventions and its Protocols to the Senate, and to this day they await the US Senate's advice and consent.[10] The UK started the process of ratifying the original 1954 Hague Convention and its added Protocols. Professor Patrick Boylan, a British legal expert on cultural property indicated that *lex situs* rule under both national and international law applies to the case of Iraq because the convention applies to territory.[11] And prior to the invasion both the United States and the United Kingdom claimed that they would observe its provisions.

According to Professor James Nafziger's summary, these three sets of treaties set the framework for protecting cultural heritage against deliberate attack, incidental damage, pillage, and outright theft.

Precisely a year ago, during the international symposium organized by the Istanbul Initiative on redefining the concept of cultural heritage and its protection based on the recent events in Iraq, Murat Cano proposed that offenses concerning cultural property, including all the exceptions of "military necessity," should be characterized as crimes against humanity and the jurisdiction of the International Criminal Court be redefined accordingly.

Even if it was due to pure ignorance and negligence, political and military parties that are responsible for the looting, burning, and destruction of museums, archaeological and historical sites, libraries, archives, and universities in Iraq should be held accountable for their acts. We owe this to ancient Mesopotamians and to modern Iraqis.

Thank you.

Testimony on the Destruction of Cultural Heritage
Amal al-Khedairy

My presentation does not claim to be scholarly research, but it is an outcry by a witness of an atrocious aggression, a bearer of personal and collective suffering—the result of this aggression that has violated all human rights and the decency of mankind. It is an aggression against a country that is not even the size of California and with less population, a cradle of 5,000-year-old civilization, an active member of the United Nations, and the first independent country in the Arab world in the twentieth century. This aggression defied the United Nations and worldwide free opinion as expressed in global demonstrations, ironically, of which the one in the United States was the loudest! The slogans were hoisted all over the globe. "No Blood for Oil" exposed the lies and the fragile pretext for this colonial war that inaugurated the third millennium with a setback to the Dark Ages, killing all that the United Nations stands for and what it represents: all human yearning for a world of peace, prosperity, equal rights, and independence…

Unfortunately, the world's awareness of the coming catastrophe was a delayed reaction to a strategy which has been building up stealthily since the 1970s, when Iraq announced the nationalization of its petroleum.

From then on, Iraq's oil ignited a ferocious hunt by world powers, particularly China and Russia. Iraq (at the peak of its development, stepping up to self-fulfillment and reclaiming its role in history) was entangled in this network of world politics, which led to its present destruction, destitution, and the defacing of its identity. For two decades Iraq has been demonized, and its population of 25 million and its 5,000 years of cultural heritage reduced to a personification of one man: Saddam Hussein, who has been depicted by vindictive pens and biased media. That is how Iraq became an available prey to wolfish power and that is why the world protest came too late.

The cancerous power had already spread through Iraq's body through the Iran–Iraq War, through the invasion of Kuwait, through the unjust embargo of the oil-for-food program, through the arbitrary dissection and bisection of Iraq into zones, through pushing Iraqi people into the Dark Ages by destroying their infrastructure and cornering them into a cocoon that imprisons their spiritual, social, and intellectual life. The pyramid of 5,000 years of cultural heritage of different strata of civilizations and religions has been reduced to warring sects and ethnicities, and defining the notion of who is Iraqi has become a pastime for computer fans at the military.

Mr. Bush and the military defined the situation, in opposition to the world and despite the United Nations, as: "We are using a sledgehammer to crush the nuts." The nuts are supposed to be the Iraqis, whom Bush promised the world he would liberate, and establish his democracy. His sledgehammer turned out to be everything destructive his arsenal contained, from rockets to cluster bombs, which devastated the country—burning, looting, and destroying even what was necessary for the most primary needs of human beings. Not sparing anyone or anything except the Ministry of Oil, Rasheed Hotel, and Congregation Palace, which were spared to serve the interests of the occupiers.

Posing in a uniform on his safe aircraft carrier, Mr. Bush eloquently summed up the Iraqi people's grief, humiliation, and devastation in two words: "Mission accomplished." Yet he gave Iraqis no respite from his destructive invasion. With "shock and awe," he inaugurated his occupation of Iraq. A new page of another downgrade in all human values. Before the Iraqis woke up from the nightmare of the invasion to collect their dead, lick their wounds, and gather their shackles, they were dumbfounded by the atrocities of the occupation and its fathomless abyss. Since then, the American army (the mercenaries and militias they have been training) have wreaked and are still wreaking havoc in every aspect of life: political, economic, social, cultural, educational, religious.

As a witness to this tragedy, I, or what is left of me after living through this tragedy, have an opportunity, albeit brief, to reveal what we lived through.

The fact that the country and its people are under a brutal occupation must be addressed in the political arena. The people lack a sovereign government; the government has the vote but not the power. Its real army and police have been dismantled and replaced by mercenaries and militias (they owe their allegiance either to their ethnic leaders or religious leaders). There is an absence of judicial and international organizations. The Iraqi educated elites have lost their weight as arbiters under the occupation. The bankrupted economy (previously sapped by three wars and an embargo)—presently collapsing under the huge American machine of the monopoly by its global corporations, which are jealously barring "intruding outsiders" who did not participate in the military campaign—simply cannot support this skeleton government. Nor does this skeleton government have a say in this privatization—a major surgical operation before the country has healed from its different wound—before its national financial power and manpower have recuperated enough to face the grinding World Bank machine.

This collapse of economic and political life and the heavy burden of an occupation that harasses Iraqis in their streets, even in their private lives, has scattered society. It tears the very warp and woof of their religious, social, and moral, as well as long-living tribal, values. Witness the scandal of Abu Ghraib, of burning churches and destroying mosques, bursting into Abu-Hanif Mosque during Friday prayer, arresting men without charges. Molesting women with sound bombs. Women and children seeing their husbands and fathers trampled by American boots; the detention of wives, daughters, and mothers in order to force the resistance out into the open. Barricades and cement walls raised to protect the aggressor have wiped out the beautiful face of Baghdad and forced its life into ghettos. Landmarks of Iraqis' historical and cultural heritage have been destroyed, burned, and looted. I have very little time to cite them all.

Intellectual and educational life have disintegrated, because generations of Iraqis are losing the right to education already damaged by the embargo (Iraqi children were bereft even of pencils and papers), and then by the vicious and barbaric burning and looting of libraries and the destruction of the infrastructure of universities and academies. The Ministry of Education itself was destroyed, burned, and looted. According to a report from the Ministry of Education issued in 2004, 80 percent of the schools need to be rehabilitated, 1,334 schools to be reconstructed, 4,500 to be rebuilt. The whole educational system is paralyzed and conditioned by the absence of security, by a "shock and awe" policy imposed by the dominating occupation on one hand and an unprecedented phenomenon of fundamentalism on the other, pushing the education system and the role of women to the Dark Ages.

Needless to say, the institutional bases of intellectual and academic life in Iraq now depend upon American authorities, for funds, security, and aid are predicated first and foremost upon American ideological and strategic interests.

Consequently, Iraqis face a dilemma. We are all responsible for rectifying the damage caused by this spiritual and material destruction. This earth is home to us all. It is our common wealth and no country has the right to possess it all, even if it possesses the greatest technology in the world.

The welfare of mankind is our shared responsibility. It is for this very reason that we are gathered here now. We must all act together to stop this destruction of all human values.

Here is a list of sites that have been devastated in Iraq: the Iraqi National Museum in Baghdad; the Islamic Museum in Tikrit; the Archeological Museum in Mosul; all the libraries belonging to these museums. Hundreds of sites have been robbed. Also, Babylon; the Academy of Sciences; Beit al-Hikma ("house of wisdom," established during the Abbasid period, and where scholars from across the Islamic world met to publish books and translate books from Greek and Latin into Arabic); the Academy of Fine Arts; the Art Center (180 sculptures of Mohamed Ghani, hundreds of paintings); the National Theater; the Rashid Theater; the People's Theater; the National Library; the Awqaf Library; the Munir al-Qadi Library; art galleries: Beit al-Iraqi; Widad al-Urfali; Mustansarriyah University. 80 percent of schools have been damaged, according to a report by the Ministry of Education in 2004. Also, the Ministry of Information; the Ministry of Planning (designed by De Ponti); the Ministry of Finance (designed by Kahtan al-Madfai). The sports stadium (designed by Le Corbusier) has been occupied by the military. The Martyrs' Building has been occupied. Also devastated are the Zewra Park and Zoo; the Malwiyya Tower in Samarra; Abu Hanifa Mosque (the tower and the historic gate); Gushla and the Wali Palace.

The Ecological Implications of the War

Joel Kovel

The title of this presentation requires a brief introductory comment, since the notion of the "ecological implications" of war—or of anything else, for that matter—is not commonly brought forward. And when it is, the word "ecology" is often confused with the notion of the "environment." Of course the two terms are intimately related, as referring to the side of things having to do with nature and the external world; in many instances they can be used interchangeably. But there is a major difference as well, which has to do not with facts but relationships. When we speak of our environment, we mean that which is outside us and surrounds us. When we speak, however, of our ecology, we are talking about a pattern within which we are a vital participant. We speak also, when we use ecological language, of these relationships as they form a "whole" that cannot be reduced to the sum of its parts. From an environmental standpoint, humanity appears as essentially separated from nature, which appears externally, as resources, or assaults us with storms or tsunamis. From an ecological standpoint, however, we are part of nature and nature is part of us. Our relationships with other people as well as animals are ecological in form, and our built society is also a set of ecological relationships. Each structured instance of such relationships we call an "ecosystem." Environmental data are necessary to assess the components of an ecosystem, yet the environmental facts can never account for an ecosystem, which, because we are part of nature, can be human as well as nonhuman. This enables us to relate society to nature, and to see it as a human ecosystem in which our lives are lived out.

Or, in the case of warfare, destroyed. The goal of war is to dominate another's society. To do this, armies since the beginning of history have recognized, without of course using the word, that destruction of the ecosystems upon which life depends is as essential as defeating the opposing army, whether this entails the annihilation of cities or the interruption of basic environmental inputs like water. He who makes war enters into a systematic and deliberate attempt to tear apart existing ecosystems on an expanding scale in order to get his way—and it follows that he who makes war aggressively, attacking a nation which has not threatened him, and violating the truth to do so, has committed this offense on a larger scale. Therefore the United States/British war on Iraq is *prima facie* an ecological catastrophe because it sets into motion an expanding and chaotic breakup of ecosystemic relationships. From this standpoint the invasion/occupation and the insurgency against it are both implicated—although from a legal or moral standpoint the primary burden of responsibility must fall upon the aggressor, who sets the whole catastrophic mass into motion.

Aggression, moreover, extends beyond the realm of the military, and this lesson applies to ecological damage as well. War is always an ecological devastation, yet an ordinary, well-functioning economy can also be ecologically devastating, and a ruined economy that causes the social ecosystem to collapse can be, paradoxically, less of an ecological insult to the planet as a whole. For example, as a result, in great part, of the protracted assault upon it since 1991 by the United States and Great Britain, Iraq by the end of 2002 was consuming 47.2 million BTU of energy per capita while the United States consumed 339.1 million BTU per capita. This translated to the release each year of 3.2 metric tons of CO_2 per capita for Iraq compared to 20.0 tons for each citizen of the United States, almost a 7:1 ratio.[1] Given the absolute difference in size between the two countries, we have roughly a hundredfold greater negative impact on the global ecology by the United States as compared to Iraq. The reason is that America aggressively sucks resources and energy from the rest of the planet by a combination of economic exploitation and the projection of brute military force, and in the process inflicts a burden on the planetary ecosphere such as has never before been seen. This is what it means to be a "superpower," or in the case of the United States, a "hyperpower," and the invasion and occupation of Iraq is no small part of the process. Every war diminishes and afflicts humanity. But the war against Iraq acquires special status because of its strategic value to the hyperpower, and its ecological costs are planetary and not limited to this one country.

It is said that the Iraq war is about much more than oil. Well, that is no doubt true. But try to imagine what would have happened if the chief product of Iraq were sunflowers, and you will not get the same story. The key fact is that Iraq sits atop the second-largest—and largely unexplored—reserve of hydrocarbon fuel on a planet facing static or declining supplies. Its Oil Ministry was, along with the Ministry of the Interior—i.e., the keeper of police records—the only official institution that the invading forces took care to physically protect. In addition, exceptional care was taken to immediately seize the oil fields themselves in order to prevent a repetition of Saddam Hussein's unconscionable fire-setting of 1991 after his defeat became inevitable.

From this standpoint it will be argued by those who would buy into the Bush-Rumsfeld line, that just as America is bringing the blessings of democracy and progress to Iraq, so has the invasion been "environmentally friendly" compared to Saddam. Now there can be no doubt that the Saddam Hussein regime was an odious one from every angle, including the ecological. Nonetheless, there is no question of the greater ecodestructive impact of the American-led invasion, inasmuch as the havoc America has wrought in Iraq occurs as part of a desperate search to prolong the hydrocarbon era that has fueled capitalist industrialization and has led to global warming, massive species extinctions, and general planetary degradation of a degree that threatens the very future of civilization and the human species itself. By comparison, Saddam's regime was a retail operation, multilateral and more negotiable, compared to the brutal seizure represented by the invasion. Make no mistake, it is the *success* of the American effort to "modernize" Iraq that will increase the threat to planetary ecologies well beyond the immediate damage to this one country. Certainly nothing will be done by a fully victorious America, with another 120 billion barrels of crude petroleum under its control, to encourage nations to bring hydrocarbon emissions under control. We may have been spared the gruesome spectacle of burning oil fields this time around, but what is the overall benefit if that fuel is burned more slowly in millions of automobiles and diesel trucks, with all the associated ecological devastation, from urban sprawl to endless degrees of pollution and the degradation of everyday life, that this mode of transport has brought about? The fact that the Iraqi resistance has so far been successful in resisting America's petroleum ambitions[2] is to be registered therefore as both an ecological and an anti-imperial advance.

Another complication in defining culpability for ecosystemic destruction in Iraq arises from the unprecedented and wanton manner in which the military invasion has provided cover for a second invasive wave, of privatization. As soon as Paul Bremer (who had been on the corporate board of Bechtel) took command of the occupation, he proceeded to open the country to investment. The strategy reached fruition on 19 September 2003, when Bremer issued Executive Order 39, mandating privatization and guaranteeing 100 percent repatriation of profits for 40 years for all enterprises save natural resource—i.e., oil—extraction (though including water in the zone of privatization—see below). Never has a nation been turned over so swiftly to "free enterprise" and rampant profiteering—only compare in this respect the re-installation after World War II of the national bourgeoisies of Germany and Japan, countries that had inflicted incomparably more harm on humanity in general and the United States in particular than Saddam Hussein's Iraq. In the earlier case, it was a matter of restoring a global capitalist system that had gone haywire, whereas Saddam's Iraq had essentially stood apart from such a system except for providing some of its fuel.[3]

Be that as it may, the opening of Iraq to US capital also opened it to what capital does ecologically, which is to destabilize ecosystems by converting nature to commodities on an expanding scale.[4] This has profound and negative ecological consequences; yet though it would never have happened absent the invasion, the ecodestructive effects are not seen as such by most people, nor are they appreciated as invasion's necessary consequence. To cite one example, no sooner had big business established its beachhead in the country than it proceeded to destabilize ancient foundations of Iraqi agriculture. As a recent study put it:

> For generations, small farmers in Iraq operated in an essentially unregulated, informal seed supply system. Farm-saved seed and the free innovation with and exchange of planting materials among farming communities has long been the basis of agricultural practice. This is now history. The CPA has made it illegal for Iraqi farmers to re-use seeds harvested from new varieties registered under the law. Iraqis may continue to use and save from their traditional seed stocks or what's left of them after the years of war and drought, but that is not the agenda for reconstruction embedded in the ruling. The purpose of the law is to facilitate the establishment of a new seed market in Iraq, where transnational corporations can sell their seeds, genetically modified or not, which farmers would have to purchase afresh every single cropping season. While historically the Iraqi constitution prohibited private ownership of biological resources, the new US-imposed patent law introduces a system of monopoly rights over seeds. Inserted into Iraq's previous patent law is a whole new chapter on Plant

Variety Protection (PVP) that provides for the "protection of new varieties of plants." PVP is an intellectual property right (IPR) or a kind of patent for plant varieties which gives an exclusive monopoly right on planting material to a plant breeder who claims to have discovered or developed a new variety. So the "protection" in PVP has nothing to do with conservation, but refers to safeguarding of the commercial interests of private breeders (usually large corporations) claiming to have created the new plants.[5]

The occupation undermines an 8,000-year-old collective practice that has sustained the ecologically rational form of society known as the commons, in the process opening Iraqi society to ravaging by the global market. Thus are eight millennia wiped out by fiat of the proconsul. All is made to look normal, and celebrated by the propagandists. In other societies of the South, mechanisms of indebtedness have had the same result; and perhaps Iraq would have gone this way, too. But this ecological insult is specifically a product of the US invasion.

It is the task of this tribunal to arrive at an assessment of criminal activity as carried out by the United States and Britain in the course of their invasion of Iraq. Yet there is no Geneva Convention or equivalent covenant governing the destruction of ecosystems through warfare. There is a body of international environmental law, but it refers more or less exclusively to the regulation of pollution across national borders in the course of ordinary commerce. Some progress has been made with respect to military conflict; but, as the most comprehensive study issued from the United States military puts it: "The notion that the rules of general international environmental law continue to apply during armed conflict is now well accepted, but the principles that are usually cited remain at a very high level of abstraction." Even so, the focus is mainly on naval involvement between equally balanced states, and virtually none on the kind of aggressive intervention we are dealing with here. Moreover, as the report states, for "treaties that are in principle applicable during armed conflict. . . analysis shows that, under international law, belligerent and neutral states have the legal right to suspend those treaties, wholly or in part."[6]

Given the increasingly devastating effect of modern weaponry and the increasingly total character of modern warfare, it is unconscionable that states cannot be held accountable under international law for the ecological devastation they inflict on nature as well as humanity. As if in anticipation of the development of accountability, the Pentagon has taken preemptive measures against it. Since Bush came to office, the military has won exemptions from parts of the Migratory Bird Treaty Act, the Marine Mammal Protection Act, and the Endangered Species Act. As of this presentation, administration officials are back at the congressional trough, asking for relief from the Clean Air Act and the Resource Conservation and Recovery Act, which governs hazardous waste. These exemptions are meant to apply to domestic military bases, the 25 million acres of which in the US are home to 131 hazardous waste sites. Indeed, the Defense Department accounts for more than 10 percent of the country's top-priority Superfund cleanup sites, and generated 16.5 million pounds of toxic waste in 2002, according to government estimates.

Why make this worse? The reasoning, as given by Defense Secretary Donald Rumsfeld in a 2003 testimony to Congress, is that without waivers to environmental laws, "We're going to end up sending men and women into battle without the training they need."[7] Training for what? Seizing Iraq, no doubt, for without this war the others cannot be fought.[8] But this war, as bad as it has been, is no more than one phase in a grander scheme set into motion by the forces driving United States policy. Terror is their rallying signifier, providing all-purpose justification for an epoch of endless warfare. The totalization of warfare under the present regime extends in time as well as space; war is permanent as well as unbounded; it is the essential condition of the world as seen through the lens of the United States security apparatus, and it sweeps nature as well as civilization into its devouring mouth. The ecological effects of the war on Iraq are not confined to Iraq, then. The administration does not merely wage war—in Iraq, Afghanistan, and against "terror"—but it uses these wars to get what it craves: unbounded domination, a dominion now extending into outer space and across nature. And by leveraging the war to weaken hated environmental legislation, they also come closer to a fundamental goal of accumulation: the total commodification of nature.

Having said this, the fact remains that of all the myriad points at which the system operates, the military represents the most wanton destabilizer of ecosystems and the number-one polluter. The statistics above give some sense of this, as does the following: that an Abrams tank, the US Army's leading ground-assault weapon, consumes 8 gallons per mile of fuel while operating off-road and 3 gallons a mile on the road, i.e., about 200 times as much as an ordinary sedan when in full combat mode. No matter where one looks for indices of ecological function, war-making exceeds all other endeavors for sheer destructivity and the production of chaos—whether, as here, by consumption of resources; or through the introduction into a fragile desert ecosystem of the lumbering machinery of war; or from the virtual impossibility of any recycling or cleaning up; or, overall, the deliberate tearing apart of the filaments by which ecosystemic elements interrelate and form themselves into wholes. And when warfare turns into occupation, and occupation into resistance, we add the hatred of subjugated people, the racism of the occupiers, and the moral nihilism that inevitably accompanies sustained combat and degenerates the human connections to ecosystems, leading to every conceivable crime and turning a defeated and occupied country into a special corner of Hell.

Thus it was that on 2 June 2005, two years after an initial and somewhat hopeful report had been issued on the state of Iraq's environment, the following gloomy assessment was made by Pekka Haavisto, the Iraq task force chairman of the UN's Environmental Program: "Iraq is the worst case we have assessed and is difficult to compare. After the Balkan War we could immediately intervene for protection, such as the river Danube, but not in Iraq." Lack of spare parts and Iraq's inability to maintain pollution standards during two previous wars and more than a decade of crushing sanctions have damaged the environment, including the Tigris and Euphrates Rivers, where most of Iraq's sewage flows untreated.

The situation became worse after the 2003 US-led invasion, in which depleted uranium munitions were used against Iraq for the second time, and postwar looting and burning of the once-formidable infrastructure caused massive spills and toxic plumes. "The bombing and war carried a cost but the looting cost the environment more, such as in the Dora refinery or Tuwaitha nuclear storage," Haavisto said. "There has not been proper cleanup and only assessment work at some of these sites. Very little has changed and Iraqi teams are in the process of getting in some of these locations." The UN official was referring to the 56 square km (22 sq mile) Tuwaitha complex south of Baghdad where 3,000 barrels that stored nuclear compounds were looted.

In the Dora depot on the edge of Baghdad, 5,000 barrels of chemicals, including tetra ethylene lead, were spilled, burned, or stolen, a UN survey showed. Contaminated sites near the water supply also include a 200 square km (77 sq mile) military-industrial complex, torched or looted cement factories and fertilizer plants—Iraq was one of the world's largest producers of fertilizer—and oil spills.

> "Iraq was a modern industrial society in many ways. The chemicals are very risky to its future. The more time passes, the more consequences on health," Haavisto said. He added that "postwar assessment of the environmental damage was proceeding despite threats to the 1,000 [person] staff of an Iraqi environment ministry, set up as an independent unit after the American invasion. The field studies will eventually include depleted uranium, a toxic, heavy metal used to make bombs more lethal, of which the United States used an estimated 300 tonnes in the 1991 Gulf War and an unknown quantity during the last invasion."[9]

Predictably, this report, from Reuters, was ignored by virtually all the major news media. We may summarize some of its main implications, adding a few points here and there.

First, any report on the environmental or ecological damage to contemporary Iraq, however conscientious, can provide only a tiny portion of what we need to know. How can the full extent of damage be assessed in a country most of which is off limits due to insurgency? Note the "threats" to the 1,000 staff personnel who are supposed to be studying the problem. Thus any decent degree of assessment has to be put off to an indefinite future. Nevertheless, the fact remains that, all the propaganda notwithstanding, the ecology of Iraq has slid sharply downhill in the two years since the invasion was supposed to liberate the country.

Second, Haavisto makes an important point that needs to be underscored: an industrial society—and Iraq was the most developed instance of this in the Arab world before it began its decline—is more vulnerable to severe ecological decay as a result of war than a pre-industrial society. This is for the very cogent reason that industrialization builds a thick and complex wall separating society from nature, introducing along the way all sorts of intermediate agents that must be sequestered lest they undergo chaotic reactions with living creatures and other ecosystemic bodies.[10] War, with its overarching goal of smashing ecosystems, is the nonpareil force capable of breaking down the barriers that protect industrial societies from ecological disintegration.

Third, take note of Haavisto's informed opinion that looting has been a greater factor than direct military engagement. This is consistent with what was said above, that war induces moral nihilism (which is a kind of decay of the human ecosystem) and erases the inhibitions built up against the ruthless acquisitiveness built into our so-called advanced society. But the notion of looting is a complex one, and requires some analysis. There is, on one side, the looting set free by the collapse of Saddam's authoritarian regime—and from the side of the occupation, what might be called a climate of looting compounded from the aggressive arrogance of the hyperpower's militarism and the extraordinary greed shown by its corporate grab of Iraq's economy. It would be interesting to pursue the connections between these currents. Certainly the United States could have prevented much of the orgy of looting—especially of cultural treasures—which followed the fall of Saddam had it simply posted troops to do so. That it did not (except, as noted, for the oil and police ministries) tells us volumes about how looting and economic activity converge for it, and of the immense corruption the occupation has spawned.

Military combat, however brutal, operates according to rules. Within the human tsunami represented by the "invasion within the invasion," of "free-market" capitalism, however, the supreme rules are those that get you the most money the fastest. An indifference to such portions of humanity and nature as cannot be readily turned into cash is basic here. As a result, phenomenal corruption has been built into the United States' invasion/occupation of Iraq, far greater, one fears, than will ever be brought to light. But we can at least recognize that this has ecological as well as economic effects.

One of the most prominent of the former pertains to the question of water, where callous indifference, greed, corruption, and the raging hunger for privatization have come together to destabilize this precious resource, and with it, the entire fabric of Iraq's ecology. Mesopotamia became the cradle of civilization because of the geographical gift of being "between two rivers." But this same fact has always been associated with a fragility of the water supply and its tendency to salinization. Today, control of water in this part of the world is as strategic as control of oil. Its provision is part of a complex of infrastructural factors that include functioning electrical networks and sewage facilities, in addition to sources of potable water. Enter the Bechtel corporation—with Halliburton, one of the two biggest instruments of US capital in Iraq[11]—a major figure in infrastructural construction and one of the world's leaders in the privatization of water (for example, in Bolivia).

All of which has proven very bad news for the people and ecology of Iraq. Given over $3.8 billion since April 2003, in cozy no-bid contracts to take care of vital infrastructural needs through December 2005, Bechtel has succeeded mainly in putting forth lame excuses and glossy public-relations brochures while selling the Iraqis on the benefits of privatized water (can it be that they are deliberately allowing the system to deteriorate in hopes of creating a market demand for their services?). Meanwhile, appalling conditions persist. In the most recent press inquiries, from March and April of this year, the *Los Angeles Times* reported that at least 40 of Bechtel's water, sewage, and electrical projects do not work properly. According to an internal memo of coalition officials, throughout Iraq renovated plants "deteriorate quickly to an alarming state of disrepair and inoperability." One US official involved in reconstruction projects estimated that "hundreds of millions" had been squandered.[12] And as of June 10, Dahr Jamail relays (personal communication) that

> It's safe to say though, that the water situation is just as bad and probably worse than when I reported on it in January/Feb. 04. In Falluja now everyone has been instructed to boil their water, and even in parts of Baghdad, particularly Sadr City, there are cholera, hep[atitis]-E, and Typhoid outbreaks. [This information] comes recently from Iraqi doctors I know who are there now.

In short, nothing essential has changed, including the lack of oversight and conscientious supervision by the occupation. How can it, in a climate of built-in chaos that induces the most corrupt and nihilistic behaviors? Thus arise innumerable vivid and heart-breaking personal accounts of the misery of living under conditions of collapsed water, sewage, and electrical systems. These summate in surveys showing, for instance, that 78 percent of Iraqi households report "severe instability" in electricity, and 66 percent report the same for piped water, while over 50 percent say the same for sewage.[13] And these in turn bear witness to the greed, incompetence, and nihilism which are the prime legacies of the assault on Iraq.

Here is one entirely characteristic account, obtained by Dahr Jamail, from early in 2004:

> Sadr City, formerly Saddam City, a large slum of Baghdad, has a largely Shiite population of over one million poverty stricken inhabitants. The water situation is at a crisis level. Ahmed Abdul Rida points to his tiny, dilapidated water pump which sits quietly on the ground in his small home in Sadr City. "We have one hour of electricity, then none for 8 hours," he says. "This pump is all we have to try to pull some water to our home. So whenever we get some electricity we try to collect what water we can in this bowl." He points to an empty metal bowl that sits near the lifeless pump. When Mr. Rida and other Sadr City residents do get water, most of the time it is brown water from the Tigris. Due to all of the dams upriver from Baghdad, the volume of flow from the Tigris has dropped from 40 billion cubic meters in the 1960's to 16 billion cubic meters today. So the water Mr. Rida gets during his two and a half hours a day of electricity is a concentrated cocktail of pesticides, fertilizers, heavy metals from antiquated piping, and unknown amounts of depleted uranium, raw sewage, and other chemicals released from American and Iraqi munitions from the 1991 Gulf War, and the more recent Anglo-American invasion. He points to a bottle of the last water they collected to show a sample of what his family has to drink. It has the color of watered down iced tea and smells like a dirty sock. It is no wonder he and his family are constantly plagued by diarrhea, with many of them suffering from kidney stones. And these are just the most obvious effects for the families in Sadr City who drink the contaminated water; heavy metals in their water also damage the liver, brain, and other internal organs.

Note that in the cocktail that Mr. Rida and his family have to use for life-sustaining water is an "unknown amount" of depleted uranium left over from the two Anglo-American invasions. This echoes the observation of the UN's Haavista and calls for some additional reflection, as the use of DU introduces an entirely new dimension into the ecological disruption brought about by Anglo-American aggression.

The United States admits having used DU in the 1991 war, and the figure of 300 tons has been calculated.[14] There has been no admission to having used it in the 2003 invasion, nor will the United States admit that DU poses a health hazard—although its own training manuals warn troops of its toxicity, as does a video made by the DoD in 1995. There is, however, no question that an as yet undisclosed though undoubtedly substantial amount of DU was sown over at least Baghdad and the Basra region in 2003,[15] nor can its use since be ruled out. The hard fact remains that the use of this substance in ordnance, chiefly "bunker-busting" bombs and anti-tank shells, is much cherished for two reasons: because of its superb ability to penetrate even the hardest armor or thickest wall and then ignite; and because it is essentially free and unlimited in quantity, hundreds of thousands of tons having collected over the era of nuclear production for bombs and power plants. As DU, with its radioactivity and half-life of 4.5 billion years (the age of the solar system) is radically indisposable, the military has chosen to dispose of it against the "enemies of freedom," nor will they be budged in this decision.

This tribunal has already heard testimony regarding DU. Here it only needs to be pointed out that the term "sown," as a descriptor of how DU has been loosed on Iraq, is morbidly accurate. Because the vectors are tiny dust particles, chiefly of uranium oxide, produced by the ignition of DU munitions; and because these can spread anywhere and are virtually imperishable; and because they can be borne through the air and in the water; and because children play in the dust and in and around the many remaining hulks of destroyed targets; and because the dust has also been ingested though polluted water and air; and because the particles, once in the body, can lodge anywhere and produce a host of diseases; and because they also alter germ plasm and so are passed down through the generations; and because also in Iraq, health facilities have suffered the general ruin of the infrastructure… for all these reasons, it must be said that an immense eco-catastrophe has been set loose in Iraq, manifest in horrible disease and genetic defect that will continue through the years into an indefinite future. The same should also be said for the military personnel who have been exposed and have gotten ill—and who, although they live in countries with advanced health facilities, have to suffer the calculated neglect of a system that cannot afford to admit its crimes.[16] And, *inter alia*, the same can be said of all of us who are downwind of the particles set loose by the military machine.

It follows that among the ranks of particular crimes against nature and humanity wrought by the invasion and occupation of Iraq, the leading place should be given to the wanton usage of depleted uranium, in clear violation of international covenants against the use of nuclear weapons, and in particular, this weapon. For it is necessary to call things by their right names, and the right name for this is nuclear war, the supreme dismemberment of ecological relationships that have evolved over four billion years.

Eventually there will be a re-equilibration in Iraq, though at the cost of what suffering can scarcely be imagined. We can only do what we can to see to it that in this as yet unforeseeable future the aggressors of today will have been brought to justice.

Environmental Damage of Military Operations during the Invasion of Iraq (2003–2005)

Souad Naji al-Azzawi

I. Introduction

The Iraqi population and environment have suffered a great deal of damage due to the continuous state of war and economic sanctions from 1980 to this day. During these destructive war operations, the US administration and the Pentagon decided to make Iraq's people and environment a laboratory for DoD testing of all types of DU radioactive, thermaboric, chemical, robust earth penetrators, microwave, and other types of weapons. They also decided to distribute all the 750,000 tons of radioactive waste from their backyard to certain parts of the world—beginning with Afghanistan, Iraq, Palestine, the Balkans, and on down the list of similar countries—after converting this waste to deadly weapons that can be sold for billions of dollars. Part of the technique to bury evidence of the catastrophic crimes that are being committed every single minute against the people and environment in Iraq is the destruction and looting of research centers and the imprisonment and assassination of Iraqi scientists.

This paper is an oversimplified presentation to define some of the environmental damage resulting from the Iraq Invasion and Military Operations (hereafter abbreviated as IIMO) starting on 19 March 2003 and continuing to this very day.

Operation Iraqi Invasion: Military Operations and Weapons

Tremendous types and generations of deadly military weapons have been used during the invasion of Iraq (19 March–21 April) some of which are shown.[1]

Table 1: Types of Weapons Used in IIMO March 2003–today

Munitions	Ground Weapons
AGM-88	Up-armored Humvee
AGM-154A	M1A1 Abrams battle tank
SCUD C	M2A3 Bradley fighting vehicle
Tomahawk	M6 Bradley Linebacker
AGM-65	Humvee
AGM-84D	M109A6 Paladin Howitzer
GBU-12	Saxon Armored personnel carrier
Hellfire air-to-surface missile	Scimitar reconnaissance vehicle
TOW anti-armor missile	SA-80 rifle
Stinger anti-aircraft missile	A590 Braveheart
Massive Ordnance Air Blast Bomb (MOAB)	
	M270 multiple-launch rocket system
JDAM air-to-surface bomb	Patriot missile system
JSOW air-to-surface bomb	Avenger Humvee
GBU laser-guided bombs	Light-armored vehicle
GBU-28/27 bunker buster	M88A2 Hercules Recovery
Daisy cutter 15,000 lb bomb	US infantry weapons
MK-82 (500 lb bomb)	Challenger II battle tank
MK-84 (2,000 lb bomb)	Warrior combat vehicle
Termoborik weapon	Striker anti-armor vehicle
Tomahawk / AGM, cruise missile	Sabre reconnaissance
Maverick air-to-surface missile	Land Rover light truck
HARM anti-radar missile	
AIM-120 air-to-air missile	

Also, the following weapons have been used (References [1] to [20])
—Napalm bombs
—Cluster bombs (BLU-97 A/B, RBL 755, and CBU-105), and
cluster munitions and MLRS
—Chemical agents (as in Falluja, al-Dor, Ballad, Tikrit, etc.)
—DU weapons (including those in bunker-buster bombs and
Tomahawk missiles).

Reminder: The first generation of bunker busters (GBU-27) were also tested for the first time in Iraq on 13 February to destroy al-Amariyah shelter in Baghdad. It has been proven successful, with 2,000 lbs of explosives incinerating 408 women and children sleeping in the shelter.

II. Air Pollution

Major air pollution sources as a result of IIMO are:

1. Toxic hydrocarbon (HC) soot and fumes from the burning of thousands of barrels of oil from wells or oil pits surrounding Baghdad and other cities. Smoke and soot from oil burning contains toxins and carcinogens.[2] Substances like polycyclic aromatic hydrocarbons or PAHs, dioxins, furans, mercury, sulfur.

Figure 2 shows these HC and soot plumes and Table 2 shows pollutant loads from burning different types of fuel.

Table 2: Pollutants Loads Generated from Burning of Hydrocarbons Fuels

Fuel type	Suspended Particles	SO_2	NOx	HC	CO
Gasoline	2.0	0.54	10.3	14.5	377.0
Gas Oil	2.4	19.00	11.00	2.6	43.5
Kerosene	3.0	17.00	2.3	0.4	0.25

Kg Pollutants/Ton of Burned Fuel

2. Explosions plumes from conventional weapons (NOx, SOx, COx, etc.).

3. Thermal and heat pollution as a result of using napalm and thermaboric bunker-buster bombs.

4. Noise pollution during air raids and what was known as "shock and awe," during which noise intensity exceeded 130 dB or close to the threshold of pain to human beings.[3]

5. Increase of TSS (total suspended solids) in air due to tanks and heavy artillery traffic and bombardment deep into the earth using the bunker-buster bombs and other heavy missiles.

6. Increase in the number or frequency of sand and dust storms compared to previous years due to the destruction of the soil's molecular structure and the damage to vegetation cover. Table 3 shows the frequency and concentrations of total suspended solids (TSS) in selected years in Iraq.

Table 3: Frequency and Concentrations of TSS in Selected Years in Iraq[4]

Year   Storm Frequency   Highest & Lowest Concentration of TSS ($\mu gm/m^3$)

Year	Storm Frequency	Highest & Lowest Concentration of TSS ($\mu gm/m^3$)
1985	2	950–319
1986	1	1,211–213
1988	—	461–113
1990	—	580–167
1991	3	8,800–139
2003	5	

7. Ionized radiation as a result of using more than 1,100–2,200 tons of depleted uranium weaponry.[5]

8. Complex plumes of absorbed DU oxides on fine suspended dust (clay particles of <5 microns) with hydrocarbonic soot and smoke.

III. Water Pollution

The surface and ground water in Iraq includes the Tigris and Euphrates Rivers, their tributaries, storage lakes, marshes, and shallow and deep ground water aquifers connected to these water courses. Heavy bombardment of understorage tanks and infrastructures caused a great deal of seepage of hazardous and toxic chemicals and hydrocarbons and sewage water to nearby watercourses or to groundwater then to surface water.

Polluted surface runoff after each rainstorm adds dissolved air pollutants to soil or surface water.

There has been an increase in waterborne diseases like cholera, typhoid, infectious hepatitis, malaria, and dysentery, especially after the degradation of sanitary conditions due to the lack of disinfection chemicals after the major mechanical and electrical parts of the water purification and sewage treatment plants in Baghdad and other cities were looted.

WHO, UNEP, Oxfam, and Voices in the Wilderness have written about the deterioration of sanitation and the outbreak of some serious, dangerous diseases, such as leishmaniasis, which leads to disfigurement of the face and the hands.[6]

IV. Soil and Land Degradation

The month of continuous and heavy bombardment caused tremendous damage to the soil structure. The soil has been contaminated and degraded by:

—Spilled chemicals and oils. There have been about 217 attacks on oil pipes[7] and refineries, resulting in the spillage of thousands of oil barrels into soil and ground and surface water.

—Sewage with high TDS and biological oxygen demand (BOD).

—Heavy artillery, tank, and armored vehicle traffic.

—The bulldozing of huge areas of trees and date palms by American troops as a collective punishment for resisting the occupation,[8] or as a security measure to reduce the resistance attacks on occupying forces. Figures 3, 4, 5, and 6 are Landsat images that show how more than 50 percent of previously vegetated areas on the way to Baghdad airport, Samarra, floodplains of the Tigris River in Baghdad and other cities have been removed and bulldozed. These are green belts preventing desertification in these areas.

As a consequence, endangered Iraqi desert species, including the Asiatic jackal, wolf, fox, gazelle, and falcons have disappeared from the few areas sheltering them on the edges of urban areas.

V. Radiological Pollution Associated with the IIMO

Since 1991 Iraq has been subjected to radiological pollution as a result of the use of depleted uranium weapons by the US and its allies in the first Gulf war. This contamination has caused an increase in cancer incident rates and congenital malformations to six times more than prior to the war in southern Iraq, where more than 320 tons of DU munitions have been fired in areas west of Basra. Other areas in Iraq have been proven to be contaminated (Table 4), but to a lesser degree.

During IIMO in 2003, DU munitions were also used directly or indirectly through new generations of weapons with extraordinary penetrating capabilities, such as cruise missiles and bunker-buster bombs.[9]

To assess the impact of these radiological and toxic weapons on the population in the area, we need to know the exact amount of depleted uranium used. IIMO officials wouldn't release this information even after the international community's outrage about DU weapons' health and environmental consequences on Gulf war veterans and the Iraqi people.

Table 4: Measured DU Contamination Areas in Iraq during and after the Gulf War of 1991

Authors	Year	Measurements	Areas
Maarouf, B.A. et al.	1993	Exposure, soil sampling to define (U-238, Th-234, Ra-226) increase radioactivity	Artawee, northern and southern Rumaila oil fields, Grange (south of Iraq)
Al-Azzawi, S.N. et al.	1996	Exposure, soil, water, vegetation cover and animal tissues	Safwan, Jabal Sanam, al-Zubair, southern and northern Rumaila oil fields (south of Iraq)
Khalil, M.A. and Fethi, F.M.	1996	Exposure, soil, water, plants and animal tissues	Al-Muthana and Thee-Qar Governorates
Tawfiq, N.F. et al.	2000	(Alpha) activity in soil samples	Al-Muthana, Al-Basrah, Thee-Qar Governorates
Maarouf, B.A.	2000	Exposure, activity measurements in soil	Basra and al-Mutharan Governorates
Al-Azzawi, S.N. and Aref, A.	2000	Water and river sediments	North of Basra waterways and Shatt al-Arab
Al-Azzawi, S.N. and Shawkat, Nashwan	2000	Exposure, soil, water, sediment	Mosul City and Nineveh Governorate
Al-Azzawi, S.N. and Hassan, A.	2000	Exposure, soil	Safwan City, al-Zubair, Jabal Sanam, northern and southern Rumaila oil fields, Basra

Elias, M.M. et al. 2001	Radioisotopes in drinking water	Baghdad City municipality
Tawfiq, N.F. et al. 2000	U-238 concentration in Tigris and Euphrates Rivers	Basra, al-Suweirah and other loc.
Butrus, S.M. et al. 2001	Soil sampling	East, central & west areas of Basra
Kinani, A.T. et al. 2001	U-235/U-238 in soil samples	Basra, Safwan, northern & southern Rumaila oil fields

VI. DU in Cruise Missiles

Since the first test of AGM 154JSOW cruise missiles in the no-fly zone in 1999,[10] a comprehensive radiological detection, sampling, and testing program has been conducted by the Environmental Engineering Department in Baghdad University in the following areas.[11]

Table 5: Number and Types of Sampling Programs

Area	No. of Exposure Measurements	No. of Soil Samples	No. of Water Samples
Mosul			
city center	86	57	3
Nineveh			
Governorate	24	24	1
Total	110	81	4

Extensive studies of the following were done before the sampling program:
—Population distribution
—Climatological conditions (rainfall, temperature, prevailing winds, etc.)
—Surface geographical features
—Hydrology of the area
—Soil conditions
—Geology of the area
—Previous contamination from the Chernobyl accident

Results of Field and Laboratory Tests

Tables 6 and 7 show three major test results.

Table 6: Average Exposure Measurements

Area	Average Exposure µR/hr	Natural Background Level
Mosul city center	11.38	< 7.0
Nineveh Governorate	10.11	< 7.0

Table 7: Soil Sample Average Activity Measurements

Area	Average Activity in Soil Measurement (Bq/Kg)	Natural Background Soil Activity Measurement (Bq/Kg)
Mosul City Center	95.4	< 60
Nineveh Governorate	75.1	< 60

All higher measurements are close to or in the windward direction of the three targets destroyed by the AGM 154 AJSOW cruise missiles.

An important conclusion of this study is that the cruise missiles used to destroy these three targets contained uranium or depleted uranium. Considering this conclusion, the amount of DU (800–1,200)[12] from the Tomahawk cruise missiles and the bunker-buster bombs used from 2003 to 2005 is much higher than the figures released by the IIMO leaders or even estimated by the other concerned organizations or groups (1,100–2,100 tons).

VII. Other Radiological Contaminations
1. Al-Tuwaitha Nuclear Complex Disaster

In an attempt to eliminate the evidence of DU contamination from 1991 or from IIMO in 2003, the occupying forces allowed looters to sabotage the Tuwaitha nuclear complex south of Baghdad.[13] About 600 tons of natural uranium and Cobalt-60 in the complex, contained in sealed, isolated, and fenced areas under the inspection and monitoring of the IAEA, were all looted.

On the same site, the two Tamouz nuclear reactors' storage areas, containing highly contaminated parts, instruments, motors, pipes, tools, etc., were also looted, in addition to about 500 barrels of radioactive waste. The looters knew nothing about the health hazards of radioactive materials, spilled the uranium, the radioactive waste, and the Cobalt-60 on the ground and some in the segment of the nearby Tigris River close to the complex. They wanted to use the nice, colored, standard radioactive waste barrels to store food and water in their houses. Greenpeace found that radioactivity measurements in some of the Tuwaitha village's houses reached 1,300–10,000 times the natural background levels.[14]

2. Al-Mosul Uranium Extraction Site
Highly contaminated instruments, tools, machines, and waste ponds are located here and were monitored by the IAEA and all inspection teams during the 1990s.

The looters took the contaminated instruments and destroyed the radioactive waste ponds to take the concrete reinforcements, resulting in serious groundwater contamination in the area surrounding. The whole area needs an emergency plan to define the heavily polluted spots and act accordingly.

VIII. Concluding Remarks
The Iraq Invasion Military Operations (IIMO) from 1991 and 2003 to this day have imposed catastrophic environmental problems in plain view of the international community, the United Nations, WHO, UNEP, UNDP, and all other international organizations.

The addition of huge radioactive DU contaminants to what already exists from 1991 proves that a genocide is gradually being implemented not only against the Iraqi population, but to all natural ecosystems in the region. Chemical, biological, and radiological pollution is causing an increase in human suffering and an increased degradation of human health; hospitals are not allowed to release any information, photos, or records. An outbreak of cancer cases, miscarriages, fertility problems, and congenital malformations have already begun in Baghdad, Ramadi, Balad, Tikrit, and Mosul, in addition to what has been going on in the southern cities since 1991. Universities and research centers and scientific communities are forbidden from touching the issue of depleted uranium or even conducting any type of risk assessments related to the war and occupation military operations.

International organizations and groups should conduct an emergency comprehensive radiological survey and risk assessment to define hazardous high-radioactivity areas before it is too late. The risk model should include the combined effect of hydrocarbons, soot, dust, and DU oxide plumes during the first three weeks of the IIMO.

Acknowledgments

To all the groups, activists, countries, and people who stood firm against the war in Iraq and other parts of the world; to all the scientists who have been detained or killed by occupation forces because they revealed the truth about the dangers of DU weapons in Iraq in 1991; to Dr. Alim Yacoub and Dr. Huda Ammash; to all of you honest, brave women and men who have committed your lives and continue the struggle against all kinds of atrocities in the world; to all of you I present my appreciation, deepest respect, and love. Thank you.

Sixth Session
The Global Security Environment and Future Alternatives

Militarism and the Culture of Violence

Ay e Gül Altınay

Exactly 100 years ago, in 1905, Leo Tolstoy published his essay "Patriotism and Government," where he said the following: "Continental powers without a murmur submitted to the introduction of a universal military service, that is, to the slavery, which for the degree of degradation and loss of will cannot be compared with any of the ancient conditions of slavery."[1]

Introduced by the French Revolution and perfected by Prussia, universal military service had turned the formation of "citizen armies" into a foundational process in the emerging nation-states of Europe. A state's soldiers would no longer be limited to its paid mercenaries. With the introduction of military service as a foundation of citizenship, the states would have access to the minds and bodies of at least half of their citizen body. This enabled a cheap and effective form of military mobilization, which soon created the catastrophes of WWI and WWII.

I don't know if this was your reaction a minute ago when I read Tolstoy's quote, but when I first read the statement by Tolstoy, calling military service the worst form of slavery, I was quite surprised. These views are quite radical even *today*; they must have been like science fiction in 1905. How could he have been so clear, so unambiguous, so sharp in his critique? Soon I realized that the problem was not with Tolstoy. It was with my assumptions about history and historical change. Deep down, I was assuming that we, as the critical thinkers of late twentieth and early twenty-first century, were more radical in our views about military service and militarism than our predecessors from the previous century. The more I read about militarism, the more problematic this assumption has become.

The twentieth century has been a century of war and destruction. It has also been a century of militarized nationalisms defining the order of our lives. Nationalism and militarism have strongly reinforced each other and have together made it very difficult to remember and appreciate Tolstoy's remarks on military service. After all, serving in the military, whether as part of a compulsory system or as a "volunteer," is the most valued citizenship practice. Who can talk against those "men and women who bravely put their lives at risk for all of us"? We can only be grateful.

Yet, as critic Elaine Scarry reminds us, the most fundamental activity in war is killing.[2] In the words of Tim Goodrich, who spoke yesterday, "a soldier's foremost job is to kill." Therefore, those men and women to whom we are asked to be grateful are not dying for us, they are *killing* for us. In our name; with our direct or indirect support...

According to historian Alfred Vagts, "if the members of a whole nation are to be made soldiers, they must be filled with a military spirit in time of peace."[3] It seems as though nation-states initially had two main tools to create citizens with a military spirit: universal compulsory military service and universal compulsory education. These were the two institutions through which the state had direct contact with its citizens and, in early years of nation-state formation (and particularly during times of war), there was a close link in the way these two institutions were perceived. The military was seen as a school, in Eugen Weber's terms "the school of the fatherland,"[4] and the schools were given a nationalizing and militarizing role. During and after World War I, there were fierce debates about militarism and education in the United States and Britain (there have been numerous reports, articles, and books published on this issue). Educator and philosopher John Dewey, for instance, was vocal in his critique of military training in schools:

> Military Training in schools cannot be defended on the ground of physical training.... Its real purpose is to create a state of mind which is favorable to militarism and to war.... Now that war has been outlawed by agreement among the nations, it ought to be recognized that it is criminal to produce in the young, emotional habits that are favorable to war.[5]

In Britain, John Langdon-Davies wrote a book titled *Militarism in Education: A Contribution to Educational Reconstruction*, and argued that schools were being configured as the thresholds of conscription. He urged the public to "beware of the insidious advance of industrial and military conscription" and suggested that they "must cease to educate for war, and to inculcate the doctrine of force."[6]

So let us ask ourselves: A century into these debates, has this marriage of nationalism and militarism through such practices as military service and national education ceased to exist in the national and global order of things? If not, have we as scholars and activists paid enough attention to them? Or have the sciences and the social sciences, as well as our oppositional political struggles, been complicit in the *normalization* and *invisibilization* of the everyday forms of militarism?

If you do a search on books that have "militarism" in their titles, you would be surprised (or perhaps not) to find that quite a few of your major resources will be books from the first part of this century. Despite the critical thinking, at least in academia, on nationalism since the 1980s, there are still very few works that discuss militarism, apart from the militarism of Japan and Germany during World War II.[7] For some reason, militarism as a concept has been absent from our critical vocabulary. Does this mean that it has been absent from our lives? Or have we, as Issa Shivji's paper suggested on the first day, been *embedded* in military structures and militarized language as intellectuals as well?

In the past years, as I was studying militarism in Turkey, one of the things I looked at in the context of the militarization of education was a high-school course on national security.[8] Every single Turkish person you have met who is a high-school graduate has taken a one-year course focusing on military issues, as part of a curriculum and textbook developed by the military. The teachers of this course are military officers. As I was doing ethnographic research on this course, my interest was met with surprise by many of the people I interviewed. Almost everyone suggested that this course was "not important at all." It was an "easy" course which did not "mean anything to the students." Many remembered that the students often made *fun* of this course and its teacher. The suggestion that the course might have had an impact on us in any way was "absurd." "No one takes the course seriously, why are you?" was the response I often received. I ultimately concluded that these responses themselves were the utmost expression of the widespread nature of militarization in Turkey. The fact that all high-school students were educated in military affairs by a military officer was something to simply make fun of. The presence of the military in civilian schools was so normalized that there was nothing to take seriously.

We are here today discussing war. A horrific human tragedy has taken place—is taking place—in Iraq. Even as someone who has been following this war pretty closely, I was shocked and utterly disgusted at the testimonies provided at this tribunal. The crimes committed against the Iraqi people are crimes against all of us. We are all asking ourselves a simple yet very difficult question: "How has this been possible?"

I would like to suggest that in seeking this answer, we remember Tolstoy and many others who have taken similar positions, and pay more attention to *peacetime* war preparations and *peacetime* militarization.

I understand militarism to be an ideology that glorifies practices and norms associated with militaries.[9] Fundamental here is the *normalization* of the use of violence. Military thinking and practice rests on the use of violence and makes everything else unimaginable. It is *unrealistic*, we are often told, to imagine nonviolent solutions to serious international conflicts. Nonviolence *may* be the ideal, but we all have to be realists and "bite the bullet," so to speak. Very successful acts of nonviolent opposition to colonialism and racism, such as the Gandhian resistance, which resulted in the independence of India, or the African-American struggle for civil rights, which resulted in the desegregation of the United States, are presented as exceptions to the rule that violence is necessary to initiate social and political change.

It is this argument about the "inevitability of violence" that militarizes our notion of resistance, our notion of opposition, our politics in general, often times even in the antiwar movement.

It is very significant in this sense that one member of the Jury of Conscience in this tribunal is a conscientious objector. Mehmet Tarhan is not against the Turkish military; he is against all militaries. Most importantly, he is against the very institution of military service, which even in the absence of war—perhaps more effectively then—militarizes our minds, our bodies, our relationships with one another, and our own self-understanding.

As we hold this World Tribunal at the turn of the twenty-first century, what do we have to say about our embeddedness in the prevailing discourses of militarism, in the subtle processes of militarization, and in the normalization of violence in both hegemonic and oppositional politics? What would Mehmet Tarhan say if he were here with us today instead of being detained in a military prison for "persistent insubordination"? What does his insubordination tell us about *our* subordination? I am personally saddened by our lack of attention to the militarization of Iraqi resistance and the crimes committed by armed resistors against civilian Iraqis. Are we once again suggesting that "there is no other way"? And whose language does this mimic?

This session is about the global security environment and future alternatives. Having talked about the urgent need I perceive in taking militarism and processes of militarization seriously as a way of understanding global *insecurities,* I would now like to concentrate on the issue of alternatives and point to a very creative form of political action carried out by antimilitarists in Turkey in the past two years. I want us to join their tour of militarist sites for a few minutes and reflect on similar sites in our own neighborhoods, in our own lives.

On 15 May 2004, militourists gathered in Istanbul and started their day-long tour of selected militarist sites. In the Haydarpasa train station, where one often witnesses the farewell ceremonies of young men going to their military units, antimilitarists greeted the conscientious objectors arriving on the train, throwing one of them up in the air, shouting "our objector is the greatest objector." The next stop was the Gulhane Military Hospital. A case of apples was to be presented to the soldiers "defending" the hospital. They would be asked to separate the good apples from the "rotten" ones, as they were experts in this procedure. This did not happen, because the group was not allowed to get close to the hospital, but instead they left the apples in a park nearby, asking the soldiers to come and get them. Why was this site important? The brochure of the militourism festival announced the Gulhane Military Hospital as the only "state-sponsored institutional gay porn archive" in Turkey. This was due to a widespread procedure whereby those men who declare themselves to be gay are asked to present photographs or videos that show them in a homosexual relationship. These photographs are meant to qualify them for the "rotten" (or "unfit") report that they would be given. This was part of Mehmet Tarhan's objection. He refused to get this report, saying that this procedure was a proof of the rottenness of the militarist system itself, not of him as a gay man.

The militourism festival continued with a stop at a corporation, the Nurol Holding, that produces weapons, in addition to many other products for civilian consumption. The group read a declaration in front of this corporation and placed an order for "broken rifles." The next site was a military recruitment office in Be ikta . After a very loud concert of anti-militarized songs (that is, songs whose lyrics were turned into antimilitarist messages) in front of the recruitment office, the militourists proceeded to Taksim, where the new objectors, among them three women, read their objection declarations.

In May 2005, militourists were this time in Izmir, making visible the militarist symbols and sites of this beautiful Aegean city. Attended by a Greek conscientious objector, this tour covered a castle, a NATO base, a militarist statue, the central office of a company (TUKA) owned by the big military corporation OYAK, and a military port facility. The final stop was the cultural heart of the city: Kıbrıs ehitleri Caddesi, the Cyprus Martyrs' Street. The street was in a neighborhood called Alsancak (literally, "red military flag"), which we approached by driving on the Talat Pa a Boulevard (Talat Pa a being the main architect of the Armenian deportation law of 1915), passing the Veteran Primary School. As the brochure of the second militourism festival suggested: Militarism was in every aspect of our lives.

The tour ended with a non-militarist, nonviolent, yet very loud walk (because it was non-militarist, I will not call it a "march") along the Cyprus Martyrs' Street, where the group shouted over and over again: "We will not kill, we will not die, we will not be anyone's soldiers."

Before this walk, eleven people, four of them women, read their conscientious objection declarations. Why were women refusing? many people who witnessed this event asked. After all, military service is only obligatory for men. To answer this question, I will refer to a very revealing story that was published in the 1930s in a major Turkish monthly.

In the story, Hüsmen, a young peasant from Bergama, is spending his last day in the barracks. He is very excited that it is his last day, *not* because he is leaving the military, but because he will be able to put to use the things that he learned in the military in his civilian life. He starts daydreaming:

> After he is back in the village and has his wedding, he will tell Kezban all about the things he learned in military service... When Hüsmen says it all to Kezban, she will be dumbfounded; the fascination of his wife... will make Hüsmen proud. He will first teach Kezban how to identify herself [in the military way]. When he calls 'Kezban,' Kezban will run to him like a soldier, stand in front of Hüsmen and after giving the official greeting, she will say 'Ali's daughter Kezban... yes, sir!' and will wait for his orders.

Such was the daydream of a young peasant man as it was narrated by Celal Sıtkı, the writer of this short story, in 1933.[10] In this story, participation in the military is linked directly to masculinity, where *military knowledge is power over women*. Hüsmen may have been a private accepting orders in the military (or a slave in Tolstoy's terms), but he is guaranteed the *unconditional* position of the commander at home, with the position of the slave designated for his wife.

Like the Israeli women who have run a campaign called "Women Refuse" (and we are very fortunate to have one of the initiators of this campaign, Rela Mazali, here with us today), the women objectors in Turkey point to the crucial role that women play in normalizing and reproducing militarism in our contemporary societies. They point to the intricate links between militarism, sexism, and heterosexism, and challenge everyone to recognize those links. Mehmet Tarhan does the same.

To repeat my earlier questions: What would Mehmet Tarhan say if he were here with us instead of being detained in a military prison for "persistent insubordination"? What does his insubordination tell us about *our* subordination, *our* embeddedness in reproducing militarized politics, militarized lives, a militarized world order?

Amy Bartholomew was suggesting earlier that we need to re-theorize empire. I would like to insist that we re-theorize militarism as well, and that we do this with "feminist curiosity,"[11] to borrow Cynthia Enloe's beautiful formulation. This re-theorizing is necessary if we want to understand how Tolstoy can be more clear and more radical than most of us a century later.

I want to finish with an anonymous antimilitarist statement:
"Imagine that there is a war, and no one is going."
Can we?

Gender and War: The Plight of Iraqi Women[1]

Nadje al-Ali

Introduction

Despite the common rhetoric of democratization, women's rights, and inclusion, Iraqi women might turn out to be the biggest losers in the current and future political and social map of Iraq. Having already suffered from the steady erosion of socioeconomic rights, which had been gained in the early years of the Saddam Hussein regime, women and gender relations have been particularly hard-hit by economic sanctions (1990–2003), as well as the recent war in 2003 and its ongoing violent aftermath. UN Resolution 1325, calling for the mainstreaming of gender in all aspects of reconstruction and political state building, has taken on a tragic twist: To start out with, the question of reconstruction appears immature at a time when the increasing levels of violence and conflict prevent any serious development projects and processes. Secondly, there has been the danger of a backlash against women's rights and gender relations because the call for the mainstreaming of gender is being linked to the wider issue of foreign occupation, neocolonial configurations, and an interim government that lacks widespread credibility among the Iraqi population.

This political dilemma should not, however, prevent political debates and academic analyses that put gender on the map. Without doubt, the differentiation and relative positioning of women and men is an important ordering principle that pervades systems of power and is sometimes its very embodiment:

> Gender power is seen to shape the dynamics of every site of human interaction, from the household to the international arena. It has expression in physique—how women and men's bodies are nourished, trained and deployed, how vulnerable they are to attack, what mobility they have...[2]

Gender also has expression in prevailing ideologies and norms, in laws, in citizenship rights, in political dynamics and struggles, and, of course, in economics—how money, property, and other resources are distributed between the sexes. However, what is important to point out here is that gender does not necessarily constitute the most significant factor.

Economic class, ethnic and religious differentiation, sexual orientation, and political affiliation also shape power hierarchies and structure political regimes and societies. And these differentiating factors, in turn, are gendered and are part of the specific constructs of men/masculinities and women/femininities.

In this paper, I will first provide a brief theoretical background about the significance of gender in war and conflict, in reconstruction and nation-building processes, before exploring the role of women and changing gender relations in contemporary Iraq. A historical background aims to shed light on the changing gender ideologies and relations during the regime of Saddam Hussein. I will focus particularly on the impacts of the early developmental-modernist discourses of the state to the impacts of war (the Iran–Iraq War of 1980–1988 and Gulf War of 1991) as well as the comprehensive economic sanctions regime (1990–2003). The latter involved wider social changes affecting women and gender relations but also society at large, i.e., impoverishment of the well-educated middle-class, wide-scale unemployment, an economic crisis, and a shift toward more conservative values and morals.

It is against this backdrop that the impact of the latest war (2003), the occupation, and reconstruction attempts need to analyzed. In addition to the most immediate effects of the current situation (lack of security and mobility, humanitarian crisis, and political marginalization of women), the paper will explore more long-term issues related to the issue of mainstreaming gender.

Nationalism and National Identities: Gendered Perspectives

One of the key issues in delineating gender differences is the relationship between nationalism and gender, that is, the ways in which nationalism and the nation-state are gendered as well as the various ways in which women participate in or challenge nationalist processes. Case studies of women in a variety of geographical and political contexts substantiate the theoretical model sketched out by Yuval-Davis and Anthias[3] to describe the various ways in which women can and do participate in ethnic and national processes: 1) as biological reproducers of members of ethnic collectivities; 2) as reproducers of the boundaries of ethnic and national groups; 3) as actors in the ideological reproduction of the collectivity and as transmitters of its culture; 4) as signifiers of ethnic and national groups;

and 5) as participants in national, economic, political, and military struggles.

The most "natural" way in which women participate in national and ethnic processes is the "biological reproduction of the nation," which corresponds to the notion of *Volksnation,* a nation of common origin, common "blood and belonging."[4] The relationship between cultural reproduction and gender relations can be articulated in terms of a *Kulturnation.* Here, gender relations are at the center of cultural constructions of social identities and collectivities, where women tend to constitute their symbolic "border guards." Being constructed as carriers of the collectivity's "honor" and the intergenerational reproducers of its culture, specific codes and regulations delineate the "proper women" and "proper men."[5] Often women are perceived to be both biological and cultural reproducers of a nation. In Iraq, for example, women were asked by the regime of Saddam Hussein to "produce" future soldiers, while they were also increasingly being used as symbols for the honor and stamina of the nation. In post-Saddam Hussein Iraq, women are increasingly being used as symbols against the previous, largely secular regime as well as Western cultural and political imposition.

Cockburn argues convincingly that the more primordial the rendering of people and nation, the more are the relations between men and women essentialized: "Women are reminded that by biology and by tradition they are the keepers of hearth and home, to nurture and teach children 'our ways.' Men by physique and tradition are there to protect women and children, and the nation, often represented as the 'motherland.'"[6] This process can also be observed in Iraq, where the increased significance of primordial ethnic and religious identities goes side by side with more conservative and restrictive gender ideologies.

Gender in War and Conflict

When violence and conflict erupt, women tend to suffer in gender-specific ways in addition to the suffering endured by all of the population. Men continue to be the major decision-makers, politicians, generals, "leaders," and soldiers involved in "making war." Yet, it is estimated that close to 90 percent of current war casualties are civilians, the majority of whom are women and children. This has to be compared to a century ago, when 90 percent of those who lost their lives were military personnel,[7] or in World

War II, when civilians were half the casualties. Increasingly, wars are fought on the home front. In Iraq, just as in Bosnia-Herzegovina, for example, marketplaces and bridges are bombed, as well as houses and shelters.

Sexual humiliation and mutilation, forced prostitution, rape, and forced pregnancy are among the gender-specific violence occurring during wars. Historically, rape has certainly been the most widespread form of gender-specific violence. It can occur as a random act within the context of general lawlessness, anarchy, chaos, and aggression. This seems to have been the case in Iraq in the early months after the downfall of the previous Iraqi regime. However, in some contexts, rape has also been used systematically as a deliberate weapon of war and means of torture to inflict maximum harm. Rape is not only used to attack and humiliate the "enemy woman," but through her to attack her male supposed protectors. With women being universally used as symbols of a nation's honor and pride, raping a community's womenfolk traumatizes and violates women individually and also humiliates and attacks the whole community. Rape and sexual abuse have been rampant in the accounts of political prisoners and victims of the Saddam Hussein regime.

In the case of the wars in former Yugoslavia, women's bodies were used as "ethnic markers" in nationalist ideology.[8] Yet, when men are raped or sexually abused and humiliated, as also happens during wartime, these acts are also gendered. Aside from the individual abuse, it is the enemy's masculinity and ability to protect the nation which is under attack. These acts of aggression and humiliation are particularly devastating in societies where sexuality is perceived to be a taboo and associated with shame. However, it would be misleading to overemphasize culture or religion: it is not only Iraqi men in Abu Ghraib prison who experienced severe humiliation and a sense of emasculation—any Western man who experiences rape experiences similar trauma.

The Continuum of Violence

Instead of thinking about armed conflict and warfare as isolated instances of violence, feminist scholars and activists have alerted us to the "continuum of violence." On one level, many societies experience what has been called "structural violence" in the period prior to open conflict. According to this conceptualization, violence exists whenever the potential development of an individual or group is held back by the conditions of a relationship, and in particular by the uneven distribution of power and resources.[9]

Many war-torn countries in the post–Cold War era have experienced severe economic crises as a result of the disintegration of the Soviet Union, as well as IMF-imposed structural adjustment programs. The countries of the former Yugoslavia, for example, witnessed high unemployment, depressed wages, and a general economic crisis prior to the outbreak of war. During this time, women were urged to leave paid employment and pursue their "natural roles," with restrictions imposed on their reproductive freedom.[10] The developments in the former Yugoslavia parallel state rhetoric and policies toward women and gender during the period of economic sanctions (1990–2003) in Iraq. Here the government also retreated from its previous policies of social inclusion of women and the mobilization of the female workforce once the country was faced with a severe economic crisis. Instead, Iraqi women were told to leave their workplace to let men take over and to return to their "natural place" at home as mothers of future citizens and soldiers.

Feminist scholars have also argued that, in addition to "structural violence" based on the unequal distribution of resources, women experience the gendered phenomenon of violence within the context of patriarchal social relations.[11] According to some analysts, all such violence should be situated within a "sexual violence approach,"[12] even where no overtly sexual act is involved. In this interpretation, a whole set of violent acts is subsumed under a broad definition of male sexual violence[13]: "Violence which takes place in the home or the workplace and on the street corner; violence involving racism, homophobia, xenophobia and other prejudices; violence on international and global levels including trafficking in women and women's experiences of war violence."[14]

However, I concur with the view of some authors that this approach essentializes men and masculinities as well as glosses over the multiple causes for violence, which are not merely rooted in male sexuality. This is not to deny the relationships between forms of violence within the home, on the street, and within society at large and the violence occurring during conflict and war. But it is important to recognize the complex causes for violence, and acknowledge that men and women can be active agents in perpetrating and resisting violence. Lentin, for example, argues that "Viewing women as homogeneously powerless and as implicit victims does not allow us to theorize women as benefactors of oppression, or the perpetrators."[15] Nor does it help us to theorize and explain women's agency with respect to peace initiatives and resistance to patriarchal gender ideologies and relations.

The links between patriarchy,[16] nationalism, and militarization of society have widely been demonstrated.[17] Militarism is the culture, and national militaries supply the force, that tends to sustain national movements and help them to achieve their goals.[18] Militarism, like any ideology, entails a whole set of core beliefs that are tied to militarized gender regimes[19]—institutionally manifested gender relations. Among these core beliefs are:

> a) that armed force is the ultimate resolver of tensions; b) that human nature is prone to conflict; c) that having enemies is a natural condition; d) that hierarchical relations produce effective action; e) that a state without a military is naïve, scarcely modern and barely legitimate; f) that in times of crisis those who are feminine need armed protection; and g) that in times of crisis any man who refuses to engage in armed violent action is jeopardizing his own status as a manly man.[20]

Militarized gender regimes often exaggerate gender differences and inequality, and dictate complementary worlds for men and women, prior to, during, and after wars. Men are frequently equated with the worlds of arms and glory, and women relegated to birthing and mourning.[21] This process was very evident during the prolonged Iran–Iraq War (1980–1988), for example. The state shifted its previous modernist-developmentalist discourse on women to emphasize her reproductive roles and capacities, while glorifying Iraqi men's military involvement.

While militarized gender regimes generate a form of masculinity that tends to be oppressive to women and prone to violence, it is important to differentiate hegemonic masculinities from marginalized, subordinated, and even subversive masculinities.[22] Masculinity is not a homogeneous entity, but, like femininity, differentiated by economic class, education, religious, racial, and ethnic background, sexual orientation as well as political affiliation. In the Iraqi context, it has been well documented that Kurdish and Shia men, and those of low socioeconomic status did experience marginalization and subordination vis-à-vis Sunni Arabs of middle-class background. However, it would be simplistic to equate specific political orientations to ethnic, religious, and socioeconomic backgrounds.

At times of sociopolitical tension and economic crisis prior to conflict, as well as during conflict itself, hegemonic militaristic masculinities are celebrated and promoted more than others.[23] Yet male experiences of the military are fundamentally shaped by "race"/ethnicity, sexuality,[24] and class. The disproportionate number of Afro-American and Hispanic soldiers in the US army is telling of the racial, ethnic, and class differences within the US, where impoverished communities tend to bring forth more male soldiers than those privileged.

Gender and Post-Conflict Periods

Peace for women does not mean the cessation of armed conflict. Women's security needs are not necessarily met in "post-conflict" situations as gender-based violence still remains rampant in reconstruction periods.[25] Enloe's definition of peace is "women's achievement of control over their lives."[26] Peace, as defined by Enloe, would require not just the absence of armed and gender conflict at home, locally, and abroad, but also the absence of poverty and the conditions which create it.[27]

In reality, women often experience a backlash in post-war situations when traditional gender roles inside the home or outside are evoked. Violence against women is often endemic in post-war situations, partly due to the general state of anarchy and chaos but also as an element of heightened aggression and militarization, and prevailing constructions of masculinity promoted during conflict. An extreme example of this situation is contemporary Iraq, which despite the official ending of military conflict is extremely violent and insecure. As a matter of fact, the level of everyday experienced violence is even greater now than during the period of formal military intervention. Women have particularly suffered from the chaos, lawlessness, and lack of security and have been subject to increased harassment and abductions as well as sexual abuse and rape.

For women at home and within the diaspora, it often seems as if the challenges posed to traditional gender ideologies and roles during times of war become too great for patriarchal societies to accept in peace. Women often have less political space to challenge gender relations and to contribute to political processes in the aftermath of conflict. According to Pankhurst (2004):

The ideological rhetoric is often about 'restoring' or 'returning' to something associated with the *status quo* before the war, even if the change actually undermines women's rights and places women in a situation that is even more disadvantageous than it was in the past. This is often accompanied by imagery of the culturally specific equivalent of the woman as 'beautiful soul,' strongly associating women with cultural notions of 'tradition,' motherhood, and peace.[28]

Historically, women rarely sustain wartime gains in peacetime. Societies neither defend the spaces women create during struggle nor acknowledge the ingenious ways in which women bear new and additional responsibilities.

Absence of Women in Formal Reconstruction Processes

In many post-conflict settings, women have been sidelined or marginalized from formal peace initiatives, political transitions, and reconstruction efforts. Formal peace negotiations among warring parties and their mediators serve to define basic power relations and to identify priorities for immediate post-war political activity.[29] Traditional militarized gender regimes tend to endow men with the power in politics and locate women's importance within the family.[30] However, women within conflict-ridden societies as well as within diasporic communities do find ways to work for peace and reconciliation through grassroots activism. Women from all walks of life participate in this informal peace-building work, but their activities are often disparaged as "volunteer," "charitable," or "social," even when they have a political impact.[31]

Despite UN Resolution 1325, which was passed in October 2000 and stated the importance of the inclusion of women and mainstreaming gender into all aspects of post-conflict resolution and peace operations, the reality of post-conflict situations is often quite different. If it is heeded at all, UN Resolution 1325 is frequently translated into adding a few women into governments and ministries. However, the mainstreaming of gender would involve the appointments of women to interim governments, ministries, and committees dealing with systems of local and national governance, judiciary, policing, human rights, allocating funds, free media development, all economic processes. It also aims at encouraging independent women's groups, NGOs, and community-based organizations.

In some post-conflict settings, especially with respect to Muslim societies, UN Resolution 1325 is perceived to be part of a Western plot to destroy a society's traditional culture and values. This is particularly the case in contexts of US-led military intervention, such as in Afghanistan and Iraq. Paradoxically, people who might otherwise be sympathetic to issues pertaining to women's rights and women's equality could express strong opposition to women's inclusion in post-conflict reconstruction if this is made one of aims of the occupying powers. The political involvement, or even return, of diaspora women might evoke resentment and a backlash for local women's rights activists. This trend has been particularly evident in the Iraqi context, where the diaspora has played a disproportionate role in the new Iraqi leadership supported by the US. Diaspora women have tried to put their mark on emerging women's organizations within Iraq, but have frequently been perceived as patronizing and being part of a Western ploy.

It is important to point out that Iraqi women have been very much part of the "public sphere" until a decade or so ago. Despite the context of general political repression by the Ba'ath regime of Saddam Hussein, Iraqi women were among the most educated in the whole region. They were part of the labor force and visible and active on almost all levels of state institutions and bureaucracy. These days, however, women are prevented from leaving their houses due to fear and a great sense of insecurity. Violent burglaries, mafia-like gangs that roam the cities at night, increased sexual violence, including rape, as well as militant resistance and US snipers have pushed women into the background. The demise of women's gains during the 1970s and early 1980s was already evident prior to the war in 2003. Aside from most obvious effects related to the atrocious humanitarian situation, there have been changes in gender relations and ideologies in the context of wider social changes related to war, sanctions, and changing state policies.

Even before this last war, due to sanctions, there was a massive deterioration in basic infrastructure (water, sanitation, sewage, electricity) that severely reduced the quality of life of Iraqi families, who often have to get through the day without water and electricity. High child mortality (about 4,000–5,000 per month), rampant malnutrition, and increased rates of leukemia, other forms of cancer, epidemic diseases, and birth defects were among the most obvious "side effects" of the sanctions regime.

However, everyday lives changed not only with respect to a drastic deterioration of economic conditions and basic infrastructure: the social and cultural fabric of Iraqi society has also been affected.

Iraqi women have experienced a number of profound social and cultural changes linked to gender relations and ideologies. These changes are not easily quantifiable and visible to an outside observer. But when war and economic hardship are brought to a civilian population, women suffer in various ways. Data on war and conflict-ridden countries such as Iraq tend to conceal gender-specific forms of hardship. In this paper, I focus on a number of social and cultural changes that have had an impact on women and gender relations. It is too early to address with certainty the impact of this last war, occupation, and the ongoing conflict in Iraq, although some trends are already evident.

More long-term and quantitative research would be needed to provide statistical information and evidence, so I can only provide a broad sketch of certain trends and transformations. My findings are based on observations during my own visits to Iraq (the last two were in 1991 and 1997); interviews with Iraqi refugee women in the UK and Germany who have recently left Iraq; discussions with my parents and friends, who have been visiting Iraq more regularly; phone contact with relatives; and discussions with my PhD student, who has been doing fieldwork in Iraq.

Historical Context
An analysis of the impact of economic sanctions and war on women in Iraq must be prefaced by a brief historical background addressing the general situation of Iraqi women before the sanctions regime came into place in 1990. Despite indisputable political repression in the 1970s and early 1980s, the majority of the Iraqi population enjoyed high living standards in the context of an economic boom and rapid development, which were a result of the rise in oil prices and the government's developmental policies. These were the years of a flourishing economy and the emergence and expansion of a broad middle class. State-induced policies worked to eradicate illiteracy, educate women, and incorporate them into the labor force. The initial period after the nationalization of the Iraqi oil industry in 1972 was characterized by economic hardship and difficulties. But the oil embargo by OPEC countries of 1973, known as the "oil crisis," was followed by a period of boom and expansion. Oil prices

shot up and oil-producing countries started to become aware of their bargaining power related to Western countries' dependence on oil.

In the context of this rapid economic expansion, the Iraqi government actively sought out women to incorporate them into the labor force. In 1974, a government decree stipulated that all university graduates—men or women—would be employed automatically. In certain professions, such as those related to healthcare and teaching, education itself entailed a contract with the government, which obliged the students to take up a job in their respective professions.

Policies of encouraging women to enter waged work cannot be explained in terms of egalitarian or even feminist principles, however, even though several women I interviewed did comment positively on the early Ba'athists' policies of the social inclusion of women. The initial ideology of the Ba'ath Party, the ruling party of Iraq, was based on Arab nationalism and socialism. It is beyond the scope of this paper to explore in detail the specific motivations and ideology of the Ba'athist regime with respect to women's roles and positions. What can be said is that human power was scarce, and that, as the Gulf countries started to look for workers outside their national boundaries, the Iraqi government also tapped into the country's own human resources. Subsequently, working outside the home became for women not only acceptable, but prestigious and the norm. Another factor to be taken into account was the state's attempt to indoctrinate its citizens—whether male or female. A great number of party members were recruited through their work places. Obviously it was much easier to reach out to and recruit women when they were part of the so-called public sphere and visible outside the confines of their homes.

Whatever the government's motivations, Iraqi women became among the most educated and professional in the whole region. How far this access to education and the labor market resulted in an improved status for women is a more complex question. As in many other places, conservative and patriarchal values did not automatically change because women started working. Furthermore, there were great differences between rural and urban women as well as between women from different class backgrounds.

During the years of the Iran–Iraq War (1980–1988), women's increased participation in the public sphere to replace male soldiers coincided with the further militarization of society and a glorification of certain types of masculinity, i.e., the fighter, the defender of his nation, and the martyr. Women were simultaneously encouraged by the state to replace male workers and civil servants who were fighting at the front, and to "produce" more Iraqi citizens and future soldiers. The glorification of a militarized masculinity coincided with the glorification of the Iraqi mother.

Only two "peaceful" years were followed by the invasion of Kuwait (August 1990) and the Gulf war (January–March 1991). The latter was particularly traumatizing, as night after night of heavy bombing not only disrupted sleep and family lives, but left many in deep shock and fear. Iraqis invariably have vivid memories of the Gulf war, and even prior to the latest war, many Iraqis spoke about ongoing nightmares, a sense of anxiety, and a great sensitivity to certain noises that could only remotely be mistaken for bombs. Unlike other war-torn countries, like Bosnia-Herzegovina, for example, "post-traumatic stress syndrome" has not been recognized as a medical condition in Iraq. And even if it were acknowledged, lack of resources and expertise make systematic treatment impossible.

Impact of Wars and Economic Sanctions

Despite common generalized depictions of Iraqis as either culprits or victims, a closer look at Iraqi society reveals the obvious fact that Iraqi women as well as men are not a homogeneous group and have been affected by sanctions and war in different ways. Among the numerous differentiating factors are place of residence (urban versus rural), ethnic (Arab or Kurd) and religious (Shia, Sunni, Christian) backgrounds, and, perhaps most important, social class. However, the previously existing class system itself has been inverted, most notably through the impoverishment of a previously broad and stable educated middle class and the rise of a class of war and sanctions profiteers. The latter group tended to be closely related to the Iraqi regime and to constitute political and economic networks of privilege. Another extremely significant factor affecting the ways sanctions and war impact on daily lives is the existence of relatives or close friends in Western countries. Remittances sent by relatives from all over the world, but most notably from northern Europe and the United States, often make the difference between misery and coping.

For women of low-income classes in urban areas or poor women living in the countryside, sheer survival became the main aim of their lives. There is no doubt about the fact that it was particularly the poor mothers whose children are more likely to become yet another statistic in the incredibly high child-mortality rates or to suffer from disease and malnutrition. Yet even for educated women who were part of the broad and well-off middle classes of Iraq, feeding their children became the major worry and focus. Hana', who left Iraq in the late 1990s and now lives in London, recalls:

> I would feed my children and my husband before eating anything myself. Often I would stay hungry. I would also feed my children before visiting anyone. Before the sanctions people were very generous. You would always serve tea and biscuits if not a meal when a visitor came. Now people stopped visiting each other so that they do not embarrass each other.

During the time of sanctions, about 60 percent of the population was dependent on the monthly food rations given out by the government and paid for by the oil-for-food program. In the aftermath of the downfall of the regime, 100 percent of the Iraqi population have become dependent on food aid, which currently needs to be distributed by the occupying forces.[32] Sanctions and war have led to massive impoverishment and insecurity, which have subjected women of various social backgrounds to considerable material strain. Household management in the context of electricity cuts and water shortages has been time-consuming, exhausting, and frustrating.

Widespread unemployment, high inflation, and a virtual collapse of the economy have affected most women in their daily lives. For a population that was used to plenty and abundance—one often-quoted example is the well-stocked home freezers—scarcity has come as a shock. Many women have had to revert to or learn homemaking skills practiced by their grandmothers. For example, bread has been too expensive to buy on the market and many Iraqi women have had no choice but to bake their own bread on a daily basis, using the flour ration distributed by the government. Furthermore, for many women, especially those living in the countryside or in the south of Iraq, food storage has been largely impossible because of the frequent electricity cuts.

Aside from the more obvious effects related to basic survival strategies and difficulties, the sanctions and war have also left their mark on the social and cultural fabric of Iraqi society. Without doubt, Iraqi women have lost some of the achievements gained in the previous decades. They can no longer assert themselves through either education or waged employment, as both sectors have deteriorated rapidly.

The breakdown of the welfare state had a disproportionate effect on women, who had been its main beneficiaries. Women were pushed back into their homes and into the traditional roles of being mothers and housewives. From being the highest in the region, estimated to be above 23 percent prior to 1991, women's employment rate fell to only 10 percent in 1997, as reported by the UNDP in 2000. Monthly salaries in the public sector, which since the Iran–Iraq War had increasingly been staffed by women, dropped dramatically and did not keep pace with high inflation rates and the cost of living. Many women reported that they simply could not afford to work anymore. The state withdrew its free services, including childcare and transportation.

There has also been a sharp decrease in access to all sectors of education for girls and young women due to the fact that many families have not been able to afford to send all their children to school. Illiteracy, drastically reduced in the 1970s and 1980s, rose steadily after the Iran–Iraq War and between 1985 and 1995 grew from 8 percent to 45 percent. The dropout rate for girls in primary education reached 35 percent, according to the United Nations Development Fund for Women Report of 2004. According to UNICEF, 55 percent of women aged 15–49 years are illiterate.

The deterioration of the general education system was already evident in the early 1990s. Wadat, an educated middle-class woman in her late forties, had worked as a teacher in a high school until 1995. She told me:

> We did not feel it so much during the first years of the sanctions, but it really hit us by 1994. Social conditions had deteriorated; the currency had been devalued while salaries were fixed. Many women started to quit work. Some of my friends could not even afford transportation to the school. Before the sanctions, the school made sure that we were picked up by a bus, but all this was cut. For me, the most important reason was my children. I did not want them to come home and be alone in the house. It has become too unsafe. And then, I know from my own work that schools have become so bad, because teachers have quit and there is no money for anything. So I felt that I have to teach them at home.

Because of the bad conditions in schools due to the lack of resources and teachers, many parents have felt that they had to contribute to their children's education.

Higher education has virtually collapsed, and degrees became worthless in the context of widespread corruption and an uninterrupted exodus of university professors in the 1990s. During the period of economic sanctions, even the few academics who were still employed were often not paid their salaries. In the current post-Saddam period, salaries have risen considerable. However, unemployment rates are still very high and, due to the lack of security, women are extremely reluctant to take up work again. There have also been numerous reports of absolute chaos at universities, looting of libraries, professors being forced to step down, and many have had their lives threatened by students because they were perceived to be Ba'athist.

Working women like Wadat suffered from the collapse of their support systems. One previous support system, funded by the state, consisted of numerous nurseries and kindergartens, along with free public transportation to and from school and to the women's work places. The other major support system was based on extended family ties and neighborly relations, which helped with childcare. Ever since the sanctions regime, women have become reluctant to leave their children with neighbors or other relatives because of the general sense of insecurity.

Crime rates have been on the increase since the Gulf war in 1991. Many women reported that prior to the imposition of sanctions, they used to keep all their doors open and felt totally secure. During the sanctions regime, there were numerous accounts of burglaries—often violent ones. And in the current situation of occupation, looting, burglaries, killings, and rape are widespread. Aside from mafia-like gangs that roam the cities at night, most Iraqis do not want to hand in the weapons they have as they feel they have to protect themselves and their families. In light of the failure by US and UK soldiers to protect hospitals, museums, libraries, etc., the only people perceived to have provided security in a systematic way are the religious authorities, especially local imams at mosques.

Changing Family and Gender Relations

Although Iraqi families used to be very close-knit and supportive of each other, family relationships have been strained by envy and competition in the struggle for survival. In the past, children grew up in the midst of their extended families, often spending time and sleeping over at the houses of their grandparents, uncles, and aunts. These days, nuclear families have become much more significant in a context where people have to think about themselves and those closest to them first.

Some women reported that they had stopped visiting their relatives because they did not want them to feel embarrassed because they could not provide them with a meal. Hospitality, especially where food is concerned, is a very important aspect of Iraqi culture. During the time of sanctions, most Iraqi families could not provide their guests with full meals because of widespread unemployment and low salaries. The same holds true in the current context of chaos, lack of security, and widespread unemployment during occupation. This fact has had a damaging impact on family and social life in contemporary Iraq. Aside from sadness, depression, and sometimes anger, Iraq women and men of all ages have become remarkably fatalistic and have built up an incredible resistance to pain and suffering.

The loss of loved ones has become a common aspect of the pool of experiences of Iraqi women. Three wars, ongoing political repression, widespread disease, malnutrition, and a collapsed health system account for the great number of deaths that occur in present-day Iraq. According to UNICEF, 4,000–5,000 children have been dying each month since 1991 due to malnutrition and water-borne diseases, but also various forms of cancer, which have been related to the impact of depleted uranium.

The demographic cost of two wars, political repression, and the forced economic migration of men triggered by the imposition of international sanctions account for the high number of widows and female-headed households. In Basra, up to 60 percent of all households were female-headed in 2003, according to the October 2003 UNICEF report. The Human Relief Foundation estimates that there are approximately 250,000 widows in Iraq. A recent UNDP-commissioned study on widows in Baghdad found that, in one small district of al-Sadr City (Hai'our), almost every multi-family household had one widow. It is not only widows who find themselves without husbands, but also women whose husbands went abroad to escape the bleak conditions and find ways to support their families. Other men just abandoned their wives and children, being unable to cope with the inability to live up to the social expectations of being the provider. During the 1990s, female-headed households, rural areas, and poor households had the highest rates of infant and child mortality. While those whose husbands were killed in battle have received a small government pension, those whose husbands were killed by the former regime for political reasons have received no benefits and have been left to fend for themselves.

But even those women who still have husbands that are alive are struggling: The difficult economic and political situation seems to have taken their toll in terms of relationships between husbands and wives. There are no concrete figures, but it seems that the divorce rate has increased substantially. A caseworker working with Iraqi refugees in London reported that there is a very high divorce rate among couples who have recently come from Iraq. About 25 percent of Iraqi refugees in the UK are either separated or divorced. A few women stated that their husbands have become more violent and abusive during the past years. Widespread despair and frustration and the perceived shame of not being able to provide the family with what is needed evokes not only depression but also anger. Women are often at the receiving end of men's frustrations.

Family planning has become a big source of tension and conflict between husbands and wives. Before the Iran–Iraq War all kinds of contraception were available and legal. During the war, contraception was made illegal as the government tried to encourage Iraqi women to "produce" a great number of future citizens to make up for the loss in lives during the war. Many incentives were given, such as the extension of maternity leave to a year, of which six months were paid. Baby food and papers were imported and subsidized.

After the Gulf war in 1991, contraceptives were still not available, but women's attitudes toward children had changed because of the material circumstances and the moral climate. There has also been fear of congenital diseases and birth defects, which are incredibly high since the Gulf war in 1991. Unlike the case in previous times, Iraqi women are reluctant to have many children. Abortion is illegal, so many women risk their health and their lives to have illegal back-alley abortions. The director of an orphanage in Baghdad stated in 1997 that a new phenomenon has emerged in Iraq: women abandoning newborn babies on the street. These babies may be a "result" of so-called illicit relationships, but, according the director, they are often left by married women who just can't face not being able to feed their children.

Despite the overall strain on marital relationships, some women state that their relationships to their husbands have improved. Aliya, a housewife in her late thirties, says:

> My husband never did anything in the house before the sanctions. He used to work in a factory outside of Baghdad. Ever since he stopped working, he helps me to bake bread and to take care of the children. We get along much better than before because he started to realize that I am working very hard in the house.

While families and marriages are affected in multifarious ways, many Iraqi women can only dream of marriage and having their own families. One of the numerous consequences of the current demographic imbalance between men and women is the difficulty for young women to get married. Polygamy, which had become largely restricted to rural areas or uneducated people, has been on the increase in recent years. There is also a growing trend among young women to get married to Iraqi expatriates, who are usually much older than they are. This is largely due to economic reasons as most Iraqi men will not be able to provide for a new family. According to some women, there are numerous of cases of women who have not been able to cope with living abroad, and who feel totally alienated from their husbands and the new environment in which they find themselves. Others are being married off to older men within Iraq, often to settle a debt within the family.

A further common phenomenon is what one Iraqi woman called "marrying below one's class." Iraq has traditionally been a very class-oriented society where one's family name and background might open or close many doors. Now one can detect greater social mobility and less rigid class barriers. This is partly due to the uneven demographic situation between men and women but it also relates to the radical inversion of class structures mentioned above. The impoverishment of the previously well-off middle classes goes side by side with the emergence of a *nouveau riche* class of war and sanctions profiteers.

While the majority of the Iraqi population have been impoverished and have suffered greatly from the policies of their own government as well as war and sanctions, a small percentage of people have actually managed to profit from the situation. These people are mainly working in the black-market economy, engaging, for instance, in smuggling goods across the Jordanian, Syrian, Iranian, or Turkish border. These profiteers used to have close ties to the Iraqi regime. Living in luxury in the midst of widespread suffering and poverty asks for envy and contempt. But it also guarantees greater marriage prospects and access to social circles previously exclusive to the educated middle and upper middle classes.

Islamization and Increased Conservatism

At the same time that marriage has become a relatively difficult undertaking, young women in particular feel pressured by a new "cultural" environment that is marked simultaneously by a decline in moral values like honesty, generosity, and sociability, and an increased public religiosity and conservatism. Many women I interviewed concurred with one of my female relatives in Baghdad when they spoke sadly about the total inversion of cultural codes and moral values. I will never forget when one of my aunts told me: "You know, bridges and houses can easily be rebuilt. It will take time, but it is possible. But what they have really destroyed is our morale, or values." She, like many other Iraqi women I talked to, sadly stated that honesty was not paying off any more. People have become corrupt and greedy. Trust has become very rare word and envy even exists among closest kin.

Young Iraqi women frequently speak about changes related to socializing, family ties, and relations between neighbors and friends. Often a parent or older relative was quoted as stating how things were different from the past when socializing was a much bigger part of people's lives. Zeinab, a fifteen-year-old young woman from Baghdad, spoke about the lack of trust between people. She suggested the following as an explanation for the change in dress code for women and the social restrictions she and her peers experience constantly:

> People have changed now because of the increasing economic and various other difficulties of life in Iraq. They have become very afraid of each other. I think because so many people have lost their jobs and businesses, they are having loads of time to speak about other people's lives, and they often interfere in each other's affairs. I also think that because so many families are so poor now that they cannot afford buying more than the daily basic food, it becomes so difficult for them to buy nice clothes and nice things and therefore, it is better to wear *hijab*. Most people are somewhat pressured to change their lives in

order to protect themselves from the gossip of other people—especially talk about family honor.[33]

In addition to increased responsibilities and time restrictions related to economic circumstances, teenage girls in particular complain about the increasing social restrictions and difficulties of movement. While the parents of the predominantly middle-class young females who were interviewed used to mingle relatively freely when they were the age of their children, today's young Iraqis find it increasingly difficult to meet each other. Schools are often segregated between sexes, but even in coeducational schools interaction between boys and girls has become more limited. Girls are extremely worried about their reputations and often avoid situations in which they find themselves alone with a boy. These fears may have been aggravated by the not uncommon occurrence of so-called honor killings during the past decade. Fathers and brothers of women who are known or often only suspected of having "violated" the accepted codes of behavior, especially with respect to keeping their virginity before marriage, may kill the women in order to restore the honor of the family. Although this phenomenon is mainly restricted to rural areas and uneducated Iraqis, knowledge about its existence works as a deterrent for many female teenagers.

Others may be less worried about the most dramatic consequences of "losing one's reputation." For educated middle-class women from urban areas it is not so much death they fear as diminished marriage prospects.

The most obvious change that has taken place over the past decade or so is the dress code of young women. Aliya (sixteen years old) is clearly unhappy about the changes:

> I do think that our life was much more easy and happy in the past than it is now. My father used to be so open and believe in women's freedom. He would let my mother go out without covering her hair when they visited our relatives in Baghdad. We only had to wear the *abbayah* in Najaf because it is a holy city.[34] Some years ago, he started to change his attitude to many things. And lately he has become so conservative that he thinks covering the hair is not enough, and he demanded that my mother wear *abbayah* everywhere outside the home. He said that I also should keep the cover on my hair when I go to Baghdad. I am now not even allowed to go out with trousers outside

our home. My mother and I have to wear long skirts with a long wide shirt covering the hips when we go outside our home.[35]

As much as Aliya detests the imposed dress codes and her father's new conservatism, she understands the underlying reasons. She explains:

> I know why my father is doing this and I am not angry with him. I discussed this issue with him many times, and I really do not blame him for this change in attitude. I think it is not only my father who is doing this, but that it may be all fathers in Iraq. They are doing the same in order to protect their daughters from the risks of becoming victims of bad rumors.

These days there have been numerous reports of unveiled women being harassed on the streets by Islamists who demand that all women wear a headscarf or *abbayah.*

Increased social conservatism and the threat of gossip that would tarnish one's reputation are a common complaint among young Iraqi women. Girls especially suffer in a climate where patriarchal values have been strengthened and where the state has abandoned its previous policies of social inclusion with respect to women.

Economic hardships have pushed a number of women into prostitution—a trend that is widely known and subject to much anguish in a society where a "woman's honor" is perceived to reflect the family's honor. In the mid-1990s, the government condemned prostitution and has engaged in violent campaigns to stop it. In a widely reported incident in Iraq in 2000, a group of young men linked to Saddam Hussein's son Uday singled out about three hundred female prostitutes and "pimps" and beheaded them.

The drastic increase in female prostitution does not stop at the Iraqi border, however. Most of the female prostitutes in Jordan, for example, are Iraqi women. The imposition by the government of the "*mahram*" escort for females leaving Iraq did not succeed in stopping this trend. This law does not allow women to leave the country without being accompanied by a male first of kin, unless they are over forty-five years old. It was enforced after the Jordanian government complained to the Iraqi government about widespread prostitution by Iraqi women in Amman.

Men often feel compelled to protect their female relatives from being the subject of gossip and from losing the family's honor. The increasing social restrictions imposed on young women have to be analyzed in the context of wider social changes, particularly with respect to the increase in prostitution, significant numbers of female-headed households, rampant unemployment, and the appropriation of Islamic symbols by the Iraqi government under Saddam Hussein, the general religious revival within Iraqi society, and the rise of Islamist forces in contemporary Iraq.

Processes related to the Islamization of society and Islamist politics are not only leading to increasing conservatism in gender relations, but are also dominating Iraqi political power struggles in the post-Saddam era. One example of the increased impact of Islamist tendencies was the attempt in December 2003 to scrap secular family laws in favor of Sharia-based jurisdiction (Islamic law) by the Iraqi Governing Council under then chairman Abdel Aziz al-Hakim, head of the Supreme Council for the Islamic Revolution in Iraq. The secular code established in 1959 was once considered the most progressive in the Middle East, making polygamy difficult and guaranteeing women's custody rights in the case of divorce. Although unsuccessful, the attempt to change the law and the discussion around it reveals the current climate and the possible dangers lying ahead. This is particularly important in a context where women's rights and equality are perceived to be part of Western agendas to impose alien culture and morals. Many Iraqis, who under different circumstances might have been sympathetic or even supportive of women's rights, view women's roles and laws revolving around women and gender relations as symbolic of their attempt to gain independence and autonomy from the occupying forces.

Many women in Basra, for example, report that they have been forced to wear a headscarf or restrict their movements out of fear of harassment from men. Female students at the University of Basra say that since the war ended a year ago, groups of men began stopping them at the university gates, shouting at them if their heads were not covered. These reports are symptomatic of wider conservative trends and various ways in which women are being used in Iraq—as in many other societies—to demarcate boundaries between "us" and "them." Islamicization here fulfills two objectives: a break with the previous secular regime of Saddam Hussein, and resistance to the occupying forces.

Women's Political Participation

Although Iraqi women have a history of some political participation and activism prior to Saddam Hussein's regime, their autonomous political participation came to an end in the 1970s. Women were encouraged to join the Ba'ath Party and to run for the rubber-stamp parliament. Scores of Iraqi women contested elections in 1980 and 16 won seats in the 250-member Council. In the second Ba'athist parliamentary elections in 1985, women won 33 Council seats (13 percent). But even this sponsored participation was reduced toward the end of Saddam's regime, as evidenced by the decrease of successful women candidates to 8 percent of members elected to the parliament of 2003.

The major vehicle for women's participation was the General Federation of Iraqi Women (GFIW), founded in 1969. It had branches all over Iraq and it is estimated that about one million Iraqi women were members. Despite the fact that the federation was a branch of the ruling party and lacked political independence, the government's initial policies of social inclusion and mobilization of human power did facilitate a climate in which the federation could play an implementation role in promoting women's education, labor force participation, and women's health, as well as providing a presence in public life. The role of GFIW changed drastically in the 1990s, when the state abandoned its policies of social inclusion and began to promote women's traditional roles. The GFIW then concentrated on humanitarian aid and the provision of health care.

At the same time that Iraqi women were losing state support in terms of socioeconomic rights, semi-autonomy in Iraqi Kurdistan allowed women there to establish civil society associations and become involved in party politics. While only two of the twenty ministers in the Kurdistan Regional Government were women in 2003, women gained employment in the civil service. But it is also the case in the Kurdish areas that women's initiatives and political participation have been opposed by conservative male political actors. Women activists campaigning against widespread honor killings in the north have been subject to harassment, and a newly established women's shelter for victims of domestic violence had to close down due to political opposition.

Since April 2003, women's organizations and initiatives have been mushrooming all over Iraq. Most of these organizations, like the National Council of Women (NWC), the Iraqi Women's Higher Council (IWHC), the Iraqi Independent Women's Group, or the Society for Iraqi Women for the Future, for example, have been founded either by members of the Iraqi Governing Council (IGC) or prominent professional women with close ties to political parties. While mainly founded and represented by elite women, some of the organizations have a broad membership and have branches throughout the country. Their activities revolve around humanitarian and practical projects, such as income generation, legal advice, free health care and counseling, etc., as well as political advocacy. The two main issues that have mobilized women of mainly educated middle-class backgrounds throughout Iraq are 1) the attempt to replace the relatively progressive personal status law governing marriage, divorce, and child custody with a more conservative law (Paper 137), and 2) the issue of a women's quota for political representation. Although women were unsuccessful in obtaining a 40 percent quota in the transitional constitution, they managed to negotiate a 25 percent quota.

However, the actual long-term status of the transitional constitution and the decision of the IGC as well as CPA remain to be seen. In recent months, women's organizations have been seriously impeded by the security situation, which often stops women from leaving their houses altogether. This has also prevented many women from running for election in January 2005. As the candidates were largely unknown to the Iraqi public, it has yet to be seen whether parties did actually adhere to the 25 percent quota.

Lack of Security

The fact that only a relatively small number of women have expressed their political dissent and wishes is not only due to the lack of democratic political culture within Iraq. It is also due to the fact that the biggest problem for women in Iraq today is the lack of security. Aside from the more recent threat of militant resistance and suicide bombings, of which Iraqis have been the main victims so far, women suffer from gender-specific threats and violence. "This violence is still a daily occurrence, especially on the streets of Baghdad, without attracting the least attention of the soldiers," Yanar Mohammed, director of the Baghdad-based Organization for Women's Freedom, told the press a few months ago.

A Human Rights Watch Report published in November 2003 gives evidence to numerous reports of sexual violence and abduction of women and girls. Medical practitioners, victims, witnesses, and law enforcement authorities have documented some of these crimes. However, many cases go unreported and uninvestigated. Some women and girls fear that reporting sexual violence may provoke "honor" killings and social stigmatization. For others, the obstacles to filing and pursuing a police complaint or obtaining a forensic examination that would provide legal proof of sexual violence hamper them from receiving medical attention and pursuing justice. Whatever the reason, both documented and rumored stories of sexual violence and abduction are contributing to a palpable climate of fear: "Women and girls today in Baghdad are scared, and many are not going to schools or jobs or looking for work," said Hanny Megally, executive director of the Middle East and North Africa division of Human Rights Watch. "If Iraqi women are to participate in post-war society, their physical security needs to be an urgent priority."[36]

According to Human Rights Watch, many of the problems in addressing sexual violence and abduction against women and girls "derive from the U.S.-led coalition forces and civilian administration's failure to provide public security in Baghdad. The public security vacuum in Baghdad has heightened the vulnerability of women and girls to sexual violence and abduction" (Summary, "Climate of Fear," 2003). This resonates with the Organization for Women's Freedom in Iraq, which chided coalition forces for their failure to protect women in post-war Iraq, asserting that over 400 have been raped since the end of the war.

Due to the fact that the police force is considerably smaller and relatively poorly managed, there is limited police street presence. This has even become worse during the past months as the newly established Iraqi police has been frequently targeted by militant resistance. The insecurity plaguing Baghdad and other Iraqi cities has a distinct and debilitating impact on the daily lives of women and girls, preventing them from participating in public life, reconstruction processes, participation in the labor force and in shaping the political future of Iraq.

Conclusion

The rather bleak picture I have sketched out only touches upon some aspects of the numerous ways war, sanctions, and occupation have affected women and gender relations in contemporary Iraq. In this paper, I have tried to point to the social and cultural phenomena that have emerged during the past years and have to be viewed as mainly triggered by the sanctions regime and the government of Saddam Hussein. It is too early to be able to grasp fully the complex and multifarious ways the recent ongoing war and occupation is affecting daily lives as well as wider gender ideologies.

What can be said about the current situation, however, is that, so far, women have been pushed back even more into the background and into their homes. They are suffering both in terms of a worsening humanitarian situation and an ongoing lack of security on the streets. Aside from the fact that basic needs (including water, electricity, medical care, and food) as well as security are not addressed adequately, there is the more long-term issue related to women's future roles in society, wider gender ideologies, and the threat of an ongoing backlash. It remains to be seen whether the women's quota of 25 percent will actually be implemented or whether a push for women's political participation during the period of occupation might eventually backfire. Moreover, women will continue to be the symbols of both religious conservative and secular progressive forces, both instrumentalizing women's issues to get support for their political agendas.

Because they represent both the majority of the population as well as an increasingly vulnerable and marginalized group, it is of ultimate importance to support women's political participation. However, due to the fact that women are perceived to be symbols and markers of cultural boundaries and "authenticity," any insensitive promotion of women's rights and women's equalities as part and parcel of "liberation" will strongly backfire in the current context of occupation as well as in the aftermath. Not only in Iraq, but in most other countries in the region and the Muslim world, feminism is negatively identified with the imposition of Western values and the eradication of indigenous culture and morals. Any women's rights initiatives and organizations promoted by the occupying forces or the Iraqi Interim Government will not only be short-lived, but will also negatively impact on locally initiated women's organizations and gender roles and ideologies more generally. Similarly, Iraqi women's organizations and activists based abroad lack legitimacy and credibility among the majority of the population and should not be used to either represent or short-cut locally based initiatives.

At the same time, it is important to point out that Iraq, like other countries in the region and the Muslim world, has a history of indigenous women's rights struggles and women's movements. There are many mainly educated middle-class women who are already involved in humanitarian assistance, as well as political lobbying and advocacy related to social justice with respect to women and gender relations. It would be detrimental for Iraqi women if they were not given special support in the process of reconstruction and political transition.

One way to sensitively support women is to change the language from a feminist rights approach to a language stressing education, training, and participation in reconstruction, thereby appealing to a modernist-developmental discourse. The other main strategy is to link women with organizations, experts, and initiatives in other countries in the region or the Muslim world. Based on research I carried out among women's organizations in Egypt, for example, I found that women felt much more empowered by the exchange of experiences and training from non-Western women activists from countries of the "South."

The current situation in Iraq leaves doubt about the intentions of the US in terms of good governance, its commitment to human rights, and democracy-building. Especially where women and gender relations are concerned, I personally do not expect too much from the occupying forces, considering Bush's record of conservative policies toward women in the US. The case of Afghanistan is a sad example of the US government paying lip service to women's rights, but not actually seeing it through in the aftermath of the war. In fact, Afghanistan is an example of how not to do it, as the mere appointment of a women's minister without resources (who subsequently had to resign) was a cynical token towards a human and women's rights agenda.

Let me finish this paper on a slightly brighter note. It is very important to stress that Iraqi women are not just passive victims. And here I am not talking about those women who were implicated in the previous regime or are now made token women in the current political structures. I am talking about ordinary women of various social class backgrounds. Contrary to common media representations of oppressed Arab women, in many ways Iraqi women have been more resourceful and adaptable in response to the changing situation than Iraqi men. Small informal business schemes, such as food catering, mushroomed during the period of economic sanctions. Skills in crafts and the recycling of clothes and other materials have given evidence to an incredible creativity. In the post-

Saddam period, women activists have defied simple ethnic, religious, and political party divisions and have pulled together to lobby around several issues. Any analysis of women and gender relations in Iraq needs to pay tribute to the dignity, humanity, and courage of women despite ongoing hardship and struggle.

Further Resources

Belhachmi, Zakia, "Contextualizing Women in Iraqi Governance: Al-Nassiriyah Model," Report for Iraq Local Institutional Support and Development Program (Local Governance Program), USAID/RTI/Iraq, March 2004.

CASI—Campaign Against Sanctions on Iraq (2000): background, consequences, strategies. Proceedings of the conference hosted by the Campaign Against Sanctions on Iraq, 13–14 November 1999, Cambridge (Cambridge: CASI).

Center for Economic and Social Rights, "The Human Costs of War in Iraq," March 2003.

Cockburn, C., *The Space Between Us: Negotiating Gender and National Identities in Conflict* (London and New York, Zed Books, 1998).

Human Rights Watch, "Climate of Fear: Sexual Violence and Abduction of Women and Girls in Baghdad," 15 (8), July 2003.

"Iraq: Female Harassment from Religious Conservatives," Irinnews.org, 14 April 2004 <Irinnews.org/report.asp?ReportID=40560&SelectRegion=Iraq_Crisis&SelectCountry=IRAQ>.

UN Office for the Coordination of Humanitarian Affairs, "Iraq: Focus on Widows," Irinnews.org, 23 April 2004 <Irinnews.org/>.

UN Office for the Coordination of Humanitarian Affairs, "Iraq: Focus on Disabled People," Irinnews.org, 23 April 2004 <Irinnews.org/>.

UNDP (2000) *1999–2000 Country Report*. Iraq Country Office, June 2000.

UNICEF, "Iraq: Facts and figures," accessed 22 April 2004 <www.unicef.org/media/media_9788.html>.

UNICEF (2001) UNICEF Humanitarian Action: Iraq Donor Update.

UNIFEM (2004) Gender Profile, Iraq <www.womenwarpeace.org/iraq/iraq.htm>.

Organization For Women's Freedom in Iraq <www.equalityiniraq.com/whowe.htm>.

Creating Racism and Intolerance

Liz Fekete

I have been asked to speak about the threat posed by racism and intolerance to the global security environment. But the question on everyone's lips over the last few days has been, if, as so many of us believe, the US's war on Iraq is an imperialist venture, isn't it also a racist war? When a massive military force, which boasts its superior civilizational values, destroys the civilizational heritage of a country, isn't that racism? When the occupiers of Iraq impose their language as the common language of educational instruction, isn't that racism? When the occupiers humiliate those it detains in their culture, denigrates their religion, tramples on the Qur'an, isn't that racism?

"The Istanbul session bears the responsibility of culminating a process already initiated, and initiating a process yet to be imagined." These are the words of the International Coordination Committee of the World Tribunal on Iraq, which also advises us, the Panel of Advocates, of our duty to provide "a point of departure for further initiatives... and elaborate on issues that may not have received the attention they deserve." So what I ask the Jury to consider today is this: when they come to examine the question of whether the war in Iraq creates racism and intolerance, they also take into consideration the global situation, and in particular they look at the creation of a global architecture of repressive laws that have been instigated by the UN Security Council post-9/11 in order to create a global security regime that aligns anti-terrorist legislation in major regions of the world to the security needs of the US.

A racist power is also an arrogant power. And the arrogance and racism of the US is spreading like an oil slick around the world. The global security regime which I will describe was instrumental in facilitating the invasion of Iraq. It brought together a motley crew of authoritarian regimes and "democratic" governments around a dangerously simplistic definition of "international terrorism." As such, the global security regime provides the justification for future illegal wars. It isolates democracy movements in the South and erodes civil liberties in the North. It intensifies all forms of racism and discrimination, and generates new ones.

Naturally, it was the US which was to fashion this new global security state into a design capable of meeting its economic and security interests. In the immediate aftermath of 9/11, and under pressure from the US, the UN Security Council passed Resolution 1373. This imposed an obligation on all states to a) take broad measures to counter terrorism and b) work with the international community to strengthen the "global response" to threats to international security. A Counter-Terrorism Committee was set up to enforce global compliance with Resolution 1373. The result was an interlocking system of national, sub-regional, regional, and international anti-terrorist structures—all, seemingly, under the jurisdiction of the UNSC. Those states that complied with the UN Security Council's demands were now part of the International Coalition Against Terrorism; they were part of a privileged club which had responded to Bush's call to arms—that "those who are not with us are against us."

It was not long before authoritarian states throughout the world were pointing to the convergence between emergency rule in their own countries and the stance now being taken by the US and the UN. The (then) Malaysian prime minister, Mohammed Mahathir, offered its notorious 1960 Internal Security Act as a model for every other Asian country to follow. And the Egyptian prime minister cited the "war on terrorism" and new security laws passed in the United States and elsewhere to justify Egypt's own emergency laws.[1] Authoritarian states had long since pressed the international community to outlaw as terrorist the political, cultural, or religious oppositional movements that their human-rights abuses had engendered. Thanks to the formation of the International Coalition Against Terrorism, the criminalization of oppositional movements as terrorist could now come to pass. After all, international terrorism, now considered an amorphous and all-pervasive threat, takes in any "foreign terrorist organization" that threatens the security or economic interests of the US.[2]

In this way, then, a number of very different local insurgencies came to find themselves added to UN and US lists of proscribed organizations— seen as linked to al-Qaeda, spun into a spider's web of international terrorism. And into this web, Iraq was also woven. (Remember that the first justification for the invasion was that Saddam Hussein had been financing al-Qaeda and international terrorism.)

As the global security state took shape, small wonder that campaigners in the South, working for an end to emergency rule and for the peaceful resolution of protracted internal conflicts, spoke of their isolation and a sense of betrayal. Meanwhile, in the "democratic" North, the global security state was also laying down roots, albeit in a different form. The myth that the security of rich industrialized nations was under perpetual threat from foreign terrorists was used to justify the passage of new, more embracing anti-terror laws. These removed foreign nationals from the protection of the rule of law and corralled them into a parallel, shadow criminal-justice system based on lesser rights for "suspect communities."

The USA PATRIOT Act authorized the government to detain foreign nationals indefinitely without charge (even if they have committed no crime), deny entry to foreigners because of their views rather than their actions (see the case of the Swiss professor Tariq Ramadan who was not allowed to take up his position as chair at Notre Dame), and to deport even permanent residents who innocently supported disfavored political groups.[3] Subsequently, immigration provisions in the Iraq War Appropriations Bill make it possible to deport any foreign national who has ever joined or made a donation to any organization, of two or more people that have ever used or threatened to use a weapon. (It is no defense to prove that one's support or membership was not intended to further terrorism or violence.)[4]

Similar processes were underway across the European Union (as evidenced by broad definitions of terrorism, which could be either "active" or "passive," in the EU Common Positions and Framework Decision on combating terrorism). The UK Anti-Terrorism Crime and Security Act (2001) introduced internment without trial for foreign nationals only. And foreign nationals (including asylum seekers) suspected of posing a security risk were deported from countries such as France, Germany, Sweden, and Italy, in defiance of the principle of *non-refoulement*, whereby foreign nationals cannot be extradited to a state where they risk persecution, the death penalty, or torture.

In this way, then, was a new and more virulent anti-foreigner racism—xeno-racism—woven into the state apparatus.[5] It is "xeno" in form in that it is directed against foreigners irrespective of color; it is racism in substance in that it bears all the hallmarks of demonization and exclusion of the old racism—and the mechanisms that entrench it are legal and structural and institutional.

And foreignness, now, is not merely associated with the "enemy alien" but also with the "enemy within." The parameters of institutionalized xeno-racism have been expanded to include settled minority communities—simply because they are Muslim. Racial and religious profiling of Muslim communities by the intelligence services and law-enforcement agencies is growing. In the US, executive orders have encouraged racial profiling by law-enforcement officers, leading to the surveillance of mosques, the targeting and "special registration" of male visitors from 25 Muslim or Middle Eastern countries as well as North Korea, and the targeted monitoring of persons of Arab or Muslim origin.[6] In Europe, punitive policing—drawing force from the creation of mass databases on foreign nationals and Muslims—manifests itself in raids on Muslim meeting places and religious places of worship and in the increase in identity checks on people judged to be of Muslim appearance. And it is at this point, on the streets, that the political decision to target the Muslim community as a national security threat spills over into racial profiling, as it is most often "racial characteristics" that signify religious identity to the police. In the UK, for instance, the number of people from Asian backgrounds stopped and searched by police under anti-terrorist legislation has increased by 300 percent.

But what has really set a seal on institutionalized xeno-racism is the way in which European states are steering "race relations" policy away from multiculturalism toward monoculturalism and cultural homogenization. Assimilation is being forced through by the adoption of a number of measures. One of these is the cultural code of conduct for Muslim girls and women, who, in some areas of Europe, are forbidden to wear the *hijab* in state schools and other state institutions.

Another such measure is the recasting of citizenship laws and immigration laws according to security concerns. Immigration laws are being changed in order to deport naturalized citizens and long-term residents deemed guilty of "speech crimes." Speech crimes represent the latest infringement on individual liberty—except that what is a crime applies only "to some citizens (the naturalized) and not to others (the natives)." The Enlightenment value of freedom of speech is meant to be universal; but now freedom of speech "belongs in its pristine glory to 'natives' only."[7] For in a clear double standard, the intelligentsia can freely bait the Muslim community, mock them as the "messengers of the utmost backward darkness" or "a fifth column of goat-fuckers" (the words are those of Theo van Gogh) or "vile creatures who urinate in baptisteries" and "multiply like rats" (Oriani Fallaci). As "cultural commentators" promote the idea of superior Western (Christian) civilizational values, some Muslims are drawn to the preaching of fundamentalist Islamic clerics whose hate speech mirrors that of the Western intelligentsia, only this time Salafists claim Islam as a superior civilizational force. This message appeals to some sections of the marginalized, particularly the youth, whose sense of injustice has been compounded by their anger at witnessing what is happening in Iraq. For in the way it has been pursued, the war in Iraq has substantiated the notion of a fundamental conflict between Christianity and Islam. In such a climate, intolerance can grow, with incidents like the assassination of Theo van Gogh in the Netherlands in November 2004 acting as a conductor setting ablaze increasing anti-Muslim violence and counter-attacks.

If we are, in the words of the International Coordination Committee, to "stop the establishment of a new imperial order as a permanent 'state of exception' with constant wars as one of its main tools," then it is vitally important that we dismantle the global security state—in *all* its manifestations. In the South, the global security state has been superimposed on existing national security regimes and manifests itself in a fortified authoritarianism. In the North, the global security state mutates and forms a destabilizing underlayer of draconian and racist laws that serve to unsettle multicultural societies. The political, ethnic, and cultural diversity of the world is under threat—and the people are rebelling. Authoritarian regimes aligned so brazenly with a deeply unpopular imperial power provoke political and cultural resistance. The antiwar movement strengthens the multicultural fabric of civil society, bringing into closer dialogue people of all faiths, and none. But as, one by one, the countries aligned with the US in the International Coalition Against Terrorism bow to public pressure and withdraw their troops from Iraq, a major body blow can be dealt to the architects of the global security state.

The Militarization of Economy and the Economy of Militarization

Samir Amin

War and militarization are certainly not something new in history—neither in history in general, nor in modern history of the capitalist system. But in order to meet this challenge and design an efficient alternative strategy, one has to be very careful and first analyze, as scientifically as possible, the nature of war in the concrete circumstances of the time. That is, articulate the choice of war by state, nation, class, in the frame of the variety of economic and social interests. And in the light of that analysis, consider what problems can be solved by war. Liberation war has solved some problems, and other wars also have solved some problems which ought to be identified in accordance with the circumstances. It is said, for instance, that the current war in Iraq is the condition necessary to create democracy in that country and the region. I believe this is not true. The aims of the war are in fact different: plunder the oil, establish US military control over the planet. Yet this is not always understood and some people tolerate, if not legitimate, this war. My point is that the type of war that we are facing not only in Iraq, but since 1990 in Yugoslavia, in Afghanistan, and in other places to come for sure, is operating in a frame very different from the frame of previous periods which included also the use of war.

I submit that the pattern of war today is the result of the combination of two characteristics of the present system: on the one hand, the movement of the system from a number of conflicting imperialist powers, in plural, to what I am calling a collective imperialism of the triad, the US, Europe—Western Europe—and Japan. And on the top of that collective imperialism, the specific and particular project of the US—not hegemony, but leadership. Now, what does this mean concretely? It means a lot. It means that the dominant segments of capital, which in vulgar language could be called the transnationals, have a common interest beyond the conflicts between them, which is very usual ("Every capitalist is the enemy of all the others"). But common interest; why? Because the degree of centralization of capital which has been reached today goes far beyond what it was fifty years ago. And therefore those segments of capital need to have access to the global market; they cannot crystallize and be successful on the basis of less than the global market. And therefore they need to have common instruments and, to a certain extent, a common strategy to operate at this level. This is the very strong basis for the intimate solidarity between capitalist ruling classes, whether Democrats or Republicans in the US, right or left as they are electorally in Europe.

We ought to know this and to know that, therefore, even if there are disagreements in the way this global system should be managed (and, more particularly, if Iraq should have been invaded or not), there is a common stand on fundamentals, which is expressed in the policies of the collective instruments of that collective imperialism. I refer here first to the economic instruments: the IMF, which I'm calling a "collective colonial monetary authority"; the WTO, which is not a trade organization but a "collective ministry of colonies," since it administers the division of labor and the organization of production at all levels globally; and the World Bank, which I think is a "ministry of propaganda" of the G7. I refer also to the political instruments of that collective imperialism, the G7 and NATO, considered more important than the UN. This is why imperialism does not accept the very concept of the UN and rejects the rule of international law. On top of that, we have the US's specific project, which is not that of only the extreme right of the Bush administration, but reflects the view of the majority of the ruling class of the US, including the Democrats.

This US plan is not very new; it started in 1945. It was, and is, a plan which—I will use a very short phrase to describe it—aims at "extending the Monroe Doctrine to the whole world." That is, not only to govern the whole Western hemisphere according to the US's own specific interests and to deny the interests of the other peoples of the continent, but to do the same at the global level. This plan has always been based on the advantage of weapons. It started not in Yalta, but in Potsdam, because at Potsdam the US had the monopoly at that point on nuclear armament, which they used. Consequently, that monopoly was broken by the Soviet military achievements and the US had to postpone further steps needed to implement their project. But what we saw in 1990 with the breakdown of the Soviet Union, very brutally, was a step forward in the implementation of the project. At that point in time, the project was fully supported by the Europeans and the Japanese. This is what explains the clashes of 1990, the wars in Yugoslavia, etc., etc.

This plan is presented in an "attractive" way. The US pretends to be acting in the interest of "everybody," i.e., the collective imperialism. Additionally, they pretend that their intention is to expand the rule of democracy globally and that NATO, being an organization of "democratic nations," cannot do otherwise. This is far from the truth: Salazar was one of the founding fathers of NATO; the Greek colonels and the Turkish generals, whom I doubt as exemplary democrats, have been strong allies and supporters. In fact, the discourse on democracy is an ideological, propagandistic discourse. I do not think that the ruling classes believe in it; they are cynical enough not to do so; perhaps a number of intellectuals believe in this discourse, but not those within the system of power.

It is important to identify the weaknesses of the project in order to develop an effective counter-strategy for an effective alternative. The weakness is that the US is not in a hegemonic position, in the sense that if the rules of the game, i.e., liberalism, transparent competition, were implemented, the US would not be victorious in their competition with Europe in some segments of most modern industries; with China, India, Brazil, and others for common industries, say, the automobile industry; with Europe and the southern cone of Latin America for agricultural products, etc. Therefore, the US has no choice but to impose themselves through military control of the planet, with a view to occupying the areas which are providing strategic resources, particularly energy and oil. This is the reason for their choice of the Middle East as the target for the first blow, not the last one. Additionally, the region is in the heart of the old continent, at equal distance from London, Singapore, Beijing, Johannesburg, and Moscow. Therefore, US military control of the region makes very difficult an eventual Euro-Asian rapprochement. The axis which at some point in time seemed possible (Paris, Berlin, Moscow, Beijing, and Delhi), and which would mean that "You Americans have nothing to do here! Go back to America!", is made much more difficult. It is at this point that political contradictions (a concept distinct from the contradictions between the interests of economic dominant capital in Europe and in the US) reemerge. I refer here to the eventual effects of the distinct political cultures of Europe, on the one hand, and of the US, on the other.

I derive some conclusions from this analysis. One is that the US project is based on abrogating international law, a big step backward to before 1945. This abrogation has been achieved thanks to many complicities, including that of the secretary-general of the UN personally. This stands as an obstacle to the alternative, which ought to be based on the concept of a multipolar system, that is, a system in which globalization is negotiated on the basis of a recognition that the different interests are conflicting. A multipolar system is the condition for associating social progress (I am not saying "socialism"), immediate social progress everywhere and for everybody, with democratization (not a blueprint of the so-called democracy which is a caricature in most cases) understood as a long process. That in turn implies full respect for the autonomy of nations and sovereignty of peoples.

This is the alternative for everybody, including the Iraqis. What the Iraqi resistance may or may not achieve and how the resistance should be supported should be discussed within that perspective.

The Iraqi resistance must be supported. As long as the Iraqis, who are the direct victims of the demented and criminal plan of the US and its allies, feel that they are almost alone to face the aggression, many negative things could happen and will continue to happen.

That leads me to my conclusion, which I am addressing to the Jury, of course. My conclusion calls for a much stronger solidarity with the Iraqi people (and some others, like the Palestinians). To that effect, I suggest organizing a global campaign under the slogan "US go home!", which could be associated with a North American campaign, "US back home!" The demand is that the US should quit every place they occupy, irrespective of the possible so-called negative effects for the future of the countries involved. I am not over-optimistic—I don't think that necessarily everywhere beautiful developments will happen. But it is, for sure, not the American military occupation which will help to solve any problem, big or small. Because the exclusive target of this occupation is to plunder natural resources and oil, and through this plunder to exercise US domination over even its allies—in this case, the Europeans and the Japanese. A global campaign, "US go home!", means also dismantling US military bases, and for the Europeans to consider the dismantling of NATO necessary. And now how to start that campaign? I suggest a "Guantánamo Day," a day like 15 February, when tens of millions of people walked down in the streets everywhere in the world. The slogan for this day would be: "Wherever the US military is, they are building Guantánamos!" This is the way to reconstruct the solidarity between the peoples of the world, including the people of the United States, rebuilding that solidarity and not leaving the Iraqi and the Palestinian resistance to face, almost alone, the strongest and ugliest criminal enemy in modern history.

Thank you.

The Relationship between Iraq, Palestine, and Israel
Ahmad Mohamed al-Jaradat[1]

From the very beginning, there has been a link between what is happening in Iraq since the American invasion and what America and its allies—especially Israel—are planning for the whole area. Their aim is to secure by force complete control over the wealth and natural resources of the Middle East. In addition, strengthening the Israeli role and military-economic superiority over the region will keep it as a strike-force against any opposition or liberation movement in these countries.

Any future plan for the region is doomed to failure in the absence of a just and lasting peace and a fair solution to the Palestinian question.

Within this framework came the Madrid Middle East Peace conference in 1990, directly after the first Iraqi war, which was known at that time as "the war to liberate Kuwait" from the Iraqi occupation.

What is currently happening in the Iraqi arena mirrors the Palestinian situation, in which Israel has refused to meet the minimum agreements regarding Palestinian rights as stated in the Oslo agreements in 1993.

This American policy is clearly evident in the strategy drawn and led by the new conservatives in the White House under the Bush administration. The philosophy of this new policy originates from the vision that the world's capitalist regimes have achieved a real success by defeating the socialist regimes, thereby becoming the only option for the whole world. This policy is led by the United States of America, which considers itself the world's sole superpower. They understand that this superiority entitles them to lay down the conditions and spell out new visions for the economic, military, and political shape of the world map—their version of "globalization."

From this vision came the new Bush strategy, which includes:
1. Restructuring the world's systems to secure America's superiority;
2. Spreading democracy as defined by America;
3. Preventing any country from maintaining any sense of power;
4. Declaring war against any force or regime or party that would oppose this American policy.

Consequently, we see American slogans like "the war against terrorism," "the axis of evil," "He who is not with us is our enemy," etc.

The American-British-Israeli alliance is the best translation and example of this aggressive policy. The sequence of recent events demonstrated that world equations and contradictions are far more complicated than this naïve policy set forward by the American administration and its allies. It echoes in the worldwide crisis through which America is passing due to its short-sighted policies in Afghanistan and Iraq.

To connect what is going on in Iraq with what is currently taking place in Palestine, we need to stop and discuss some relevant issues:

1. Rearranging the whole area according to the American–Israeli vision;

2. Peace according to the Israeli vision and the American evasion of the issue;

3. The current Israeli policy and plans in the occupied Palestinian territories.

Why the New Rearrangements as Drawn by America and Israel?

Speaking about these arrangements, one would think that they are a new American solution for the problem, when in fact they reflect the Israeli interests and aims in the region. Not only that, but it seems that Israel has played a role in shaping and formulating these projects.

Some may observe: If most of the Arab regimes would eventually voluntarily implement a pro-democracy/pro-American policy, then it does not ring true for America to adopt such an aggressive policy; it is forced to defend it under the pretext of "democratizing" the Arab world or protecting human rights in these countries. Some Arab countries are implementing a fully American policy, and others went as far as to sign peace agreements with Israel, making the Palestinian issue a secondary one in their foreign policy.

America knows very well that these despotic Arab regimes are far away from any democracy, and that there is a wide gap between the governments and the people they govern. In addition to a deteriorating economic situation in these countries, the widespread exercise of dictatorship at the expense of human rights increases the hostility between these corrupt regimes and their peoples, igniting the opposition which calls for social, political, and economic reformation, as well as an improvement in human rights and the rights of women.

What has made things worse for these Arab regimes is that people in these countries came to realize—through the help of the world media—

the corruption of their leaders and governments. These regimes can no longer hide from their own people their injustice, corruption, or aggressive policies against their citizenry. The American administration and the Israelis are well aware that the winds of change are blowing strongly in these countries, and the growing opposition in these countries scares the Bush administration as well as Israel because these changes do not serve their future projects for the area.

For this reason, America started its precautionary measures and steps to contain these regimes and initiate a change in them in an attempt to beautify these regimes and make them look acceptable to their peoples.

But the main target of the United States does not change at all; namely, to succeed in controlling and exploiting the wealth of other countries and prolonging the time for these puppet regimes to continue running within the orbit of US policy.

So much for our discussion of pro-US regimes. What about Arab regimes that try to oppose US policy? Some have made steps in developing their systems and situations to be independent, especially economically. Nevertheless, the US regards them as a threat to her policy and consequently to Israel. The best solution—according to the American vision—is to eliminate these regimes by force. That is what has happened in Iraq and may happen to Syria and Iran, if one considers the warnings and threats being made to these regimes.

We have to remember what happened in Iraq in 1981, when Israel destroyed the Iraqi nuclear reactor. We must note that the continued threats to the Iraqi regime since that time by the United States and Britain fall into the same category. These imperialist regimes noticed that Iraq was developing very daring economic and military projects which were considered as a threat. So, in their view, it is necessary to put an end to such ambitions and deter these regimes from such policies, because they could prove to be a threat to Israel and the American/British interests in the region. The aim of Israel and America is to put an end to the Palestinian question by creating a new set of facts on the ground and inserting radical changes in the Arab world to the benefit of Israel and America.

What Sort of Peace do America and Israel Want with the New Rearrangements in the Area?
Israel, and especially the current right-wing government headed by

Sharon, has theoretically and practically put an end to all Oslo agreements in order to impose a political solution that serves the goals and ambitions of Israel. This policy states that Israel reoccupies the cities from which Israel has withdrawn according to the Oslo Accords. The Sharon government made it clear from the very beginning that the Oslo agreements were something of the past. Sharon even went further by claiming that it was in the interest of both Israel and the Palestinians to end the Oslo agreements and think of a new mechanism for peace as envisioned and planned by Sharon himself.

This so-called Sharon peace plan can be summarized as follows.

Since the beginning of the war against Iraq in 1990, the American–Israeli policy was to put an end to the conflict in Palestine by taking advantage of the very hard situation in the Arab world (especially after the collapse of the socialist regime in the Soviet Union).

Both Israel and America came to realize that it was almost impossible to implement any new arrangements in the area without terminating the Palestinian problem as they see it. It has been clear from the very beginning that both countries wanted to impose a solution and not seek a just and durable solution that would meet all or part of the Palestinian rights on the ground. They wanted to bring about the solution of the victorious; a solution that would meet both countries' interests in the Middle East as well as the approval of the world community (as represented by the UN Security Council and the United Nations—through the escalating pressure exerted by the United States in these world forums). By using the veto and justifying Israel's actions and behavior during the current intifada, America did its best to marginalize any role played by the United Nations in exposing the continued Israeli violations and consequently condemning such policies in the West Bank and Gaza.

It is important to track the Israeli behavior on the ground since the American campaign against Iraq in 1990 and its invasion of it two years ago. Israel has initiated a number of procedures that showed a direct connection with what was happening in Iraq, trying its best to take advantage of the circumstances.

Here is a list of some of these Israeli actions and policies during this period:

1. As regards settlements and the annexation of land, Israel doubled this policy during this period and surrounded Palestinian cities and towns

by settlements with the new wall, and enlarged the present settlements by confiscating more land.

We have to remember that the axis of the conflict between the two sides is the land. We cannot speak about any peaceful settlement without speaking about Israeli withdrawal from the Palestinian land occupied in 1967. On this land the Palestinians plan to establish their future state and start their independence.

But what we see now is a frenzied expansionist attack and the confiscation of wide areas of land, which gives the impression and belief that Israel is not interested in reaching a peaceful solution. The settlements and the winding roads have formed geographical barriers between Palestinian cities from the north to the south. There are huge settlements between one Palestinian city and the next.

2. The siege imposed on the Palestinian leadership—especially that on the late President Arafat when he refused to concede any of the Palestinian rights during the Camp David negotiations in July 2000. Then came the provocative visit by Sharon to the al-Aqsa Mosque in Jerusalem during the Labor government of Barak and the massacres that followed the protests against that visit and the escalation of the situation until it led to the present intifada.

3. The reoccupation of the Palestinian cities from which Israel had withdrawn according to the Oslo Accords—followed by clear statements from Sharon that these accords are out of date. We have also witnessed the devastation and destruction of huge quarters and parts of Palestinian cities and towns in the West Bank and Gaza. Israel also made it clear at that time that its aim is to destroy the present Palestinian authority and its organization.

4. The building of the apartheid wall through the West Bank has had a profound and harmful impact upon the Palestinian land, as seen in the uprooting of trees and the siege of cities and towns, effectively isolating their residents. Even worse is the wall's political impact, which shows that Israel is not considering the land as "occupied," but as land that effectively belongs to the State of Israel. It is worth mentioning that 85 percent of the wall is built within the 1967 borders.

This apartheid wall also means that Palestinians cannot establish their future state, since most of the land is occupied and the settlement projects are isolating the cities, making it impossible to form a state likely to survive.

The idea behind the building of this wall by Israel is to continue the occupation and minimize losses by besieging Palestinian towns and villages. The wall will annex 8 percent of the West Bank and isolate the remaining area of 631,200 dunums. So far, more than 250,000 dunums have been confiscated to build the wall, most of which is agricultural land. Because of this, the Palestinians will lose a main source of their income, agriculture.

5. The start of talking about new peace projects—especially the "road map." Although this project doesn't comply with many of the Oslo Accords, it is a security project more than a political one, since it does not deal justifiably with the central issues of the conflict. Still, the Sharon government has forwarded fourteen reservations against the project. The differences were wide between the vision of Israel and that of the Palestinian Authority regarding the terms of the Oslo Accords. The Authority states that the accords have been agreed upon by both sides and awaits implementation of their items. Israel, on the other hand, says that the items of the Accords are negotiable.

All these facts confirm beyond any doubt that Israel, supported by the American administration, is not actually interested in a lasting and durable peace—which means that there are no new projects or real intentions for peace in the near future.

The most important relationship between what is going on in Iraq and Palestine is the Israeli role in the region. This role played by Israel in restructuring the map of the new Middle East has full American support and partnership in order to rob the resources of the area to satisfy and meet their interests.

This is ample proof that Israel is not interested in a genuine peace, at least at the time being. They seem satisfied to await the outcome of potential changes among Arab regimes—especially in Iraq—since any American success there would open the door to implement a broader new Middle East project as wanted and desired by America and Israel.

Therefore, we are witnessing a clear and subjective relationship between what is going on in Iraq and in Palestine. We must not forget that the Palestinian problem is also reflected in and influenced by its Arab depth and dimensions. No matter how difficult the Arab situation is, the Palestinian problem will always be an integral component of its outcome. The resolution of the Palestinian problem will be affected negatively or positively depending upon what is going on in the Arab world—and particularly what is happening in Iraq, since it is considered one of the most strategic areas in the Arab world.

The United States, as well as Israel, is aware of this relationship, and thus they try to influence what is going on in Iraq to achieve a tailored solution to this problem that will not meet even the smallest rights of the Palestinians—their right to return, to statehood, to real independence, and Jerusalem, their future capital.

Comparison Between What is Going on in Iraq and Palestine

There are two axes for comparison.

The first axis is the common situation prevailing in the two countries, as both of them are currently occupied by force. There is a national resistance against the occupier in both countries. There are violations of human rights in both countries (collective punishments, siege, curfews, destruction of infrastructure and property, killings, kidnapping of civilians, arrests, torture, and the use of prohibited weaponry).

In both countries there are violations of the Fourth Geneva Convention and all international laws and agreements regarding civilians.

The second axis: in both cases we are confronted with occupation forces that control the resources and future of the land in a way that is designed to benefit the occupier. This is a clear usurpation of the wealth of both countries. In Iraq, America aims to establish a puppet political system that would protect its interests there by making Iraq an American base in the region from which America could direct its future projects in the region. America is investing its military presence in Iraq to draw a new map for the Middle East according to its vision.

In Palestine, Israel wants to see a Palestinian Authority working to maintain its security. This was clearly shown during Israel's negotiations with the Palestinian side over the past ten years.

Israel considers its occupation of the land as a strategic dimension, using it as a spearhead to play an influential role in future changes throughout the Middle East.

This parallel American/Israeli strategy in Iraq and Palestine emanates from their mutual economic and military interests in the region. Both countries are implementing their policies by disregarding the interests of the people of the area under the pretext of fighting terrorism.

What are the Other Options?

In the face of this dark and cruel map of the area—where America and its allies are playing with the destiny of the people, plundering their resources—there is a great need for stronger relationships and ties between the peoples in these countries to resist this American globalization. The gap between the rich and poor, the developed and the underdeveloped countries, must be breached, to become narrower and narrower. The leaders of the Middle East must build bridges between them and their peoples and work for trust-building measures for the welfare of the people of the area.

As regards Palestine, the other alternative for what may be called the Israeli-American peace projects is a genuine peace that would give the Palestinians (who have suffered most and who continue to suffer) an independent state, and give those who want to return to their occupied land the right to do so. This could be reached through the withdrawal of Israeli forces from all Arab territories occupied since 1967, and the dismantling of the settlements.

All the political projects in this respect have so far failed to achieve their goals due to their neglect of inalienable Palestinian rights. The present Palestinian intifada could be the best and last lesson to be learned in this respect. Peace between two independent sovereign states, or one democratic state for the two peoples in historic Palestine—this last option has its supporters and followers on both sides.

Polarization and the Narrowing Scope of Political Alternatives

Wamidh Nadhmi[1]

Presented by Ay e Gül Altınay:
The first speaker on this panel was going to be Wamidh Nadhmi from Iraq. Unfortunately, he is not here with us. I would still like to introduce him and to read a statement by the Iraqi National Foundation Congress, of which he is a member. Wamidh Nadhmi is a professor of political science at Baghdad University, and the official spokesman of anti-occupation front Iraqi National Foundation Congress, which is composed of academics, community leaders, religious scholars, and veteran moderate Arab nationalist politicians, the credibility of whose members is largely due to a record of independence and opposition to Saddam Hussein's policies, on the one hand, and to the history of criminal sanctions, invasion, and occupation on the other. He is also editor-in-chief of the Baghdad-based journal *Riya dul Arab*. Here is the message he has sent to the WTI:

Dear Madams and Sirs,
On the eve of the war on Iraq, Ms. Rice declared that he who will support us will be rewarded, he who will abstain will be neglected, and he who will defy us will have his bones crushed. And this was exactly what happened.

When the Governing Council was established, 17 out of its 25 members were people who were living outside Iraq, i.e., self-exiles. Only eight came from inside Iraq, and only two out of these eight members were slightly known (Mr. al-Chadirchi and Dr. Abdul Hamid). The rest were completely unknown and insignificant. If we were to look into the origin of the 25 GC members, we would find that they were chosen on a sectarian and ethnic basis only.

In most countries of the world, social harmony is essential. Some countries need it in ethnic terms, others in social and religious terms, and the rest in sectarian terms. Iraq was not an exception. But what really happened in Iraq after the occupation is that its national harmony was divided between Arabs, Kurds, Turkomans, some non-Arab entities, and

Christians. The Arabs were 75 percent, the Kurds 18 percent, and the Turkomans 2 percent. However, since the establishment of the modern Iraqi state, there have been no official statistics showing the right percentage of the Sunni and Shia Arabs. But this did not prevent the occupiers from deciding who is in the majority and who is in the minority and what percentage they have.

When the Iraqis insisted on elections as the only just remedy for the growing disintegration of the Iraqi state, the Americans refused on the basis that there is no census showing the evident and exact components of the Iraqi population. They both refused to carry out such a census or to regard the existing calculations of such ratios as the main basis for elections.

Hence, the GC was established of 30 percent Kurds, 58 percent Shia, 16 percent Sunnis, 4 percent Turkomans, and 4 percent Assyrians. They have excluded the main current (trend) in the Shia sect of Moqtada al-Sadr, Sheikh Jawad al-Khalisi, and the secular Shias. From the Sunni sect they excluded all anti-occupation forces, and from the Kurds they excluded all the Kurdish Islamic parties. This was the real implementation of the policy of divide and rule. As a result of this policy, divide and rule, all pro-occupation forces were involved, and the percentage they got was 99.9 percent through the GC and the transitional government.

One wonders if 99.9 percent were with the Americans, then, who were behind the killing of 1,800 American soldiers, the 15,000 wounded. Who is behind the large numbers of attacks on and killing of the American-established and sponsored Iraqi police and national armed brigade. And who should be held responsible for turning Iraq into a chaotic, unstable and lawless state?

Appendix
Iraqi National Foundation Congress
Second session: Baghdad, 7 May 2005
Concluding statement (as sent by Wamidh Nadhmi)
The Iraqi National Foundation Congress convened its second session on Saturday 7 May 2005 in the Iraqi Law Association hall in Baghdad. The gathering of anti-occupation political parties, movements, and personalities discussed the current changing political scene and the conduct of the congress over its first year. They addressed the events that preceded, accompanied, and followed the elections, and the consequences

of the continuing raids and attacks on Iraqi towns. They noted the grave tendency to implant division and strife among the Iraqi people through the adoption of sectarian and ethnic quotas in the formation of government bodies, and the mounting insecurity and chaos in all areas of the country.

The congress critically reviewed its activist, political, organizational, and media roles, and resolved to uphold the patriotic principles expressed in the Charter of National Mutuality and Action, with emphasis on the following points:

1. The congress rejects the foreign occupation of Iraq and will work to end it by all possible means, including annulling all its political, economic, educational, and moral consequences. The minimal demand of the current government should be a declaration of an unconditional schedule of withdrawal of foreign troops from Iraq. This is the minimal condition for us to participate in the writing of the constitution, in the coming elections, and in any other political process.

2. The congress upholds the legal right of the Iraqi resistance in all its forms as the inalienable right of a people under occupation. The resistance constitutes, in all its kinds and options, as an essential part of the national liberation movement. The Iraqi resistance, together with the Palestinian resistance, and the peace, anti-globalization, anti-hegemony movements in the world at large, are together the main barrier to the US imperialist and Zionist plans to impose their will on humanity.

3. The congress upholds the unity of Iraq as a people and territory, and its Islamic–Arabic identity in cultural non-ethnic terms, upholding all the cultural and national rights of the components of the Iraqi people. To reject all plans that aim to undermine sovereignty and lead to partition, especially in the federal form recorded in the administrative law.

4. The congress condemns the security breakdown in Iraq, and calls for combating organized crime, the assassination of scientists, and the kidnapping of citizens. It also condemns the suspect terror inflicted on innocent Iraqi lives and public utilities and property, declaring it totally alien to the history and practices of people in Iraq.

5. The congress condemns all the suspect feuds that have flared of late, which threaten to sow seeds of strife and ethnic, religious, and confessional hatreds. It places the responsibility for these on the occupation forces, the interim Governing Council, and the transitional government. It calls for efforts to uncover those behind them and for the formation of national

committees to monitor such terrible moves and to offer guidance about them.

6. The congress calls for the reconstitution of Iraqi armed forces under the command of Iraqi officers with well-attested qualifications, integrity, and loyalty, following the removal of those who have caused harm to the people and the country. One of the first steps in this respect is the re-activation of the long-established Iraqi military colleges, so as to rebuild the Iraqi army in the service of our people.

7. The congress affirms its rejection of the transitional administrative law which has been imposed by the occupation forces. This is an illegal document, internationally rejected because it is not part of any voluntary decision.

8. The congress affirms its esteem and commitment to Arab–Kurdish brotherhood, and declares its readiness for dialogue with all and any of the Kurdish fraternal groups to arrive at a peaceful brotherly solution that guarantees legitimate aims and strengthens the unity and stability of Iraq.

9. The congress strongly condemns the increase in the number of political prisoners, whose numbers are now in the tens of thousands, and the indeterminacy of their terms of arrest. The international community that upholds human rights and individual freedoms should take into consideration the torture to which many of the prisoners have been subjected, and note that the abuses include denying family visits and other basic rights. The congress appeals to all international organizations to support its own efforts to put a stop to these illegal and inhuman practices, to submit those accused of crimes to independent Iraqi courts, and to release all the innocent rest.

10. The congress calls on the Iraqi army and police forces to carry out their patriotic duties with courage, to ensure the safety and security of citizens, and to be steadfast in opposing plans to enroll them in actions against their compatriots, since their charges are the citizens not the occupiers.

11. The congress declares its hope in establishing good neighborly relations with all countries bordering Iraq and its refusal to interfere in the internal affairs of others. It warns against the use of Iraqi territory against its neighbors, especially Syria and Iran, among other Arab and Islamic countries, and places the responsibility for the grave consequences of such action on the occupying forces.

12. The congress declares it total support for the valiant struggle of the Palestinian people toward the attainment of their will and sovereignty. It rejects the establishment of any political or normalization links with the Zionist, usurper, settler entity.

13. The congress affirms its eagerness to widen its membership to include all patriotic movements, bodies, and personalities which share its principles, and its eagerness for national dialogue with all forces under the banner of Unity and Independence.

Long live free and independent Iraq, with sovereignty intact.

Long live inclusive, resolute Iraqi unity.

The Iraqi National Foundation Congress
Information Bureau

Collateral Damage: The Mexican Example

John Ross

Introductory Note

"Poor Mexico, so far from God and so close to the United States" is a popular saying among the Mexican people, one that quite accurately accounts for the collateral damage this country has suffered as a result of the illegal aggression of the United States against Iraq.

Although Mexico is not a member of George Bush's disintegrating "coalition of the willing" and, in fact, strenuously opposed the invasion of Iraq and its continuing occupation by Washington's troops, it has been affected by the war because of its geographical propinquity to the aggressor.

Since 2003, the US aggression has cost Mexico the lives of nearly 100 of its sons and daughters, the over-exploitation of precious natural resources to fuel Bush's war, and immeasurable damage to its national sovereignty.

Collateral Damage

In military terms, collateral damage is generally limited to damage inflicted on civilian infrastructure destroyed or downgraded during long-range aerial attacks on designated targets. The military damage is almost always confined to unintended material damage caused to sites adjacent to primary targets and does not include the loss of life or grievous destruction inflicted upon civilian populations when an errant weapons systems cuts a swath through a non-military neighborhood or community, such as occurred repeatedly during the first days of the illicit invasion and occupation of Iraq, when hospitals and marketplaces fell victim to US air attack. Whether intentional or not—and attacks on civilian sites are often intentionally directed to terrorize a resistant population into surrender— the military deliberately calculates such horrendous events in terms of material loss and sometimes pays a stipend to the families of the victims— if indeed it concedes that these mass killings happened at all.

But seen from the ground up, the collateral damage done is devastatingly human—not only in respect to the dead and wounded but also in the cost to the well-being of civilian populations. A hit on a military target that damages a potable water treatment plant, an electricity generating facility, or a communications center have incalculable impacts on the quality of life for the survivors, one that will potentially breed disease and death a bit further down the line.

Moreover, US aggression in Iraq has generated collateral damage far beyond the borders of that beleaguered land. The world's nations—and the planet itself—have been affected by this illegal invasion and occupation in ways often masked by the cut-and-dried military definition of collateral damage. The destruction of archeological sites in Iraq, for example, both in the 1991 Gulf War and in the second Bush's atrocities have trashed the cradle of civilization, from the graffiti-stained walls of Babylon to the looting of the Iraqi National Museum, a loss for all of man and womankind. The devastation of Iraq's environment is not confined to just one country but has poisoned the world's water and air and the species, both human and not, which depend upon these essential elements for survival. The accelerated depletion of the world's energy sources to sustain the destruction of Iraq is as much collateral damage as the maiming of women and children in Baghdad.

Because we live on an integrated, finite planet, all of the world's nations and peoples have been collaterally damaged by Bush's ongoing criminal enterprise in Iraq. It is incumbent upon each of us as citizens of a specific place or state to assess this damage upon where we live and bring charges against those responsible for these crimes before such tribunals as this one.

As a longtime resident of Mexico, I have been asked by the Mexican antiwar movement and the Not in Our Name Initiative to present such charges before the World Tribunal on Iraq meeting in Istanbul 23–27 June 2005. We encourage others who have suffered similar collateral damages in their own country to prepare parallel reports.

Petroleum

With the world's eleventh-largest reserves and currently its eighth-largest producer, Mexico accounts for about 14 percent of the US oil basket, a percentage that has become increasingly vital to US supplies, given uncertain relations with Venezuela.

In the first months of the Iraq conflict, and in an effort to improve relations with a Washington that had become estranged over Mexico's intended vote against the invasion in the United Nations Security Council,

President Vicente Fox upped Mexico's daily export platform from 1.2 million barrels to 1.6, nearly all of it being shipped up the Gulf of Mexico to US ports. The increased exports have enabled Bush to both wage a war in Iraq and keep domestic prices below US$3 at the pump, crucial to the US president's continuing mandate.

But this gratuitous concession to the White House is a heavy drain on diminishing Mexican resources. With between only 10 and 12 years of proven reserves left, Mexico is essentially betting its energy future on Bush's faltering war in Iraq.

Moreover, costly environmental damage caused by increased pumping both offshore and in the oil-producing states of Tabasco and Veracruz has compounded the problem, and pipeline explosions and massive leaks are reported on a weekly basis.

In Mexico, petroleum is a patriotic resource. Under President Lazaro Cardenas (1934–1940), Anglo-American oil interests were expropriated and nationalized and, in effect, Mexico's oil is the property of its people. Depleting these national reserves to accommodate Washington's illicit aggression in Iraq is a grave violation of Mexico's national sovereignty. Sadly, it is not the only one that the Bush government has imposed upon its immediate neighbor to the south as the bitter fruit of the illegal war on the Iraqi people.

National Sovereignty

In the months prior to the invasion of Iraq when the matter still lay before the United Nations Security Council, on which Mexico then had a seat, President Vicente Fox's reluctance to sign on to the US war plans led to pressures against the Mexican delegation. According to accounts offered by then ambassador Adolfo Aguilar Zinser, electronic eavesdropping devices were found in his offices, where meetings of Security Council members who had not yet committed their vote were often held. "We would then meet with Negroponte [John Negroponte, then the US ambassador to the UN] and he would quote back to us what we had been discussing," Zinser reported in an interview with the British weekly *Observer*.

The bugging of Mexico's United Nations office suite was corroborated by former British Intelligence operative Katherine Gunn, who told the *Observer* that Washington had requested the British plant and monitor the bugs, presumably to avoid a diplomatic showdown with Mexico prior to a crucial vote. The illegal eavesdropping by the United States and British governments constitutes a serious violation of both United Nations neutrality protocols and Mexican sovereignty.

Mexico's refusal to back the US invasion provoked swift retaliation from Washington. Any prospect of much-needed immigration reform was shelved indefinitely and even Mexico's upping of its export oil platform and the permission granted to US security agencies to station their agents on both Mexican borders and the Mexico City international airport—yet another infringement of national sovereignty—could not reheat relations between Mexico and the country with which it shares a 3,000-kilometer border.

Other violations of national sovereignty have been just as egregious. Since the Iraq carnage began in March 2003, armed US troops have deployed at least four times on Mexican soil at funerals held for Mexican nationals killed in Iraq, acting as honor guards, accompanied by US generals, and bearing arms expressly forbidden by Mexican law. Indeed, during the 4 July 2004 interment of Juan Lopez Rangel, a 20-year-old son of Guanajuato killed in Falluja in June of that year, the Mexican army was called upon to disarm US troops accompanying the bier.

Historically, the United States has invaded Mexico on at least eight occasions and the deployment of US troops anywhere south of the border is not looked upon kindly. One of the key missions of Mexico's armed forces is to repel an invasion from the north.

Mexican Lives

But it has been the loss of young lives to Bush's genocidal campaign in Iraq that has most wounded Mexico. Although a recent US Department of Defense count lists 22 Mexican nationals killed in Iraq, Pentagon criteria for who is a Mexican does not take into account native-born Mexicans naturalized in the US or the sons and daughters of Mexican-born US citizens whose citizenship is undefined.

A closer inventory of Mexican deaths in Iraq that includes these parameters is kept by Fernando Suarez del Solar, father of a marine killed in Iraq. Suarez lists 89 Mexicans as having died in Iraq between March 2003 and April 2005—no numbers for wounded are available. The first to be killed was Rodrigo Gonzalez, the son of farmers from the Coahuila desert, who died in a Kuwaiti helicopter accident 23 February on the eve of the invasion. Of the first 1,000 reported US deaths in Iraq, at least 50 were Mexicans.

Although Mexico is not a part of Bush's bloody coalition, it stands third on the list of fatal casualties per nation, behind Iraq and the US but ahead of Great Britain (87 at the end of April 2005), Bush's most loyal ally in the slaughter.

The combined United States armed forces count 134,000 troops of Latin descent, half of whom are Mexicans. Other Latin American countries represented in the mix include Puerto Rico (a US possession), the Dominican Republic, Honduras, El Salvador, and Ecuador. Similarly, of the 37,000 non-citizens serving in the US military, an estimated 20,000 are Mexicans.

A study done by the Chicano organization Aztlan Nation determined that 13,000 Mexican and Mexican-descent troops are currently serving in Iraq as part of the US occupation forces. Newspaper reports also indicate that at least 40 Mixtec Indians from the central state of Puebla are currently subcontracted as laborers by international construction corporations working in Iraq.

Mexicans have historically joined the US military to obtain United States citizenship. After the 11 September 2001 terrorist attacks on New York and Washington, President Bush promised that all non-citizens joining the military would be placed on the "fast track" to citizenship. But when the invasion of Iraq began, the only way a non-citizen soldier could actually obtain US citizenship was to be killed in action.

Jesus Suarez, a 21-year-old marine from Tijuana, Mexico, was killed near Nazariya in the first weeks of the war. But when Washington conferred automatic citizenship upon Jesus, his father Fernando Suarez del Solar, angrily rejected it. "My son was proud to be a Mexican," Fernando told the Pentagon authorities.

Like many Mexican youths, Jesus was recruited into the US Army under false pretences. Promised by Marine Corps recruiters that they would help him become a drug enforcement agent to combat narco gangs in his native Tijuana, he was instead sent with an ill-trained and poorly equipped unit to Iraq, where he was killed early in the war.

Because the percentage of Latino and Mexican soldiers in the US armed forces is lower than their percentages in the general population (Latinos, including Mexicans, are now the largest US minority, accounting for 15 percent of the population), military recruiters have intensified efforts to bring their numbers up to parity. Led by the Marine Corps, whose aggressive recruiting is well documented, the military targets Latino-Mexican populations, often bringing in Spanish-speaking recruiters and running come-on campaigns on Spanish-speaking radio and television.

US recruiters routinely cross south to border cities like Tijuana and Ciudad Juarez, head-hunting the high schools for young people with dual citizenship, often promising enhanced educational opportunities and pledging to clear up immigration problems. The recruiters' access to schools in Mexico is another glaring example of how Bush's war has impacted Mexico's national sovereignty.

North of the border, military recruiters have long had unblocked access to high schools, particularly in areas of high Mexican and Latino density such as Texas and California, where kids from these communities graduate into dead-end jobs flipping Big Macs, if they are lucky.

One reason why the Marine Corps now has the highest number of Mexican recruits (13 percent) is that the service enjoys a long-standing exemption allowing it to recruit non-citizens. The 1985 Immigration and Reform Act (IRCA) legalized many Mexicans living in the US who then brought their families over, but many of the children were never covered. A good number of the estimated 20,000 Mexican non-citizens in the US armed forces are believed to have joined up to clarify confused immigration statuses.

Much of the blame for this lamentable situation can be laid on the doorstep of a recruitment policy that fills quotas by any means necessary. Abuses by overzealous recruiters range from procuring fake diplomas for prospective recruits and falsifying drug tests to promising that the inductee will never participate in military combat.

Now in the third year of the Iraqi occupation, military recruitment numbers have diminished alarmingly from month to month and the services are forecasting shortfalls that will leave the US unable to respond to crisis situations in the near future. Given this very likely scenario, pressures by military recruiters on Mexican and Mexican-descent youth are expected to ratchet up.

At this writing, 89 Mexican families have received the sad notice from the US government that their loved ones were killed in Iraq, a desert land far from their own. One reason for the high kill rates is the concentration of Mexican recruits into front-line combat units. Mexicans and Mexican-descent youth recruited in southern California are concentrated at Camp Pendleton, adjacent to San Diego. It was marine units from Pendleton that led the initial March 2003 assault—fourteen Mexican and Mexican-descent casualties were reported in the first month of the fighting. The same units were sent into Falluja in November 2004, the vanguard of US forces who would level that Sunni Muslim stronghold.

Lance Corporal Andres Raya, nineteen, the son of Mexican farm workers from Ceres, California, was a member of a transportation unit based at Camp Pendleton. For seven harrowing months, he drove an unprotected Humvee without armor plating between Falluja and Baghdad along roads laced with deadly bombs. After being returned to Camp Pendleton, rumor circulated that the unit would soon be sent back to Iraq for a second tour. At home in Ceres over Christmas 2004, Raya committed suicide by opening fire on local police, killing one, and prompting his own death in a hail of police bullets. At subsequent public inquests, Raya's neighbors insisted that he had died "on his feet like a Mexican."

The ongoing occupation of Iraq is killing off Mexican men and women at an unacceptable rate. Andres Raya, every bit as much as Jesus Suarez, is a victim of this imperialist war.

The Iraq war is also turning Mexican and Mexican-descent US soldiers into war criminals. Sergeant Jonaton Cardenas Alban, 28, was sentenced last October to a year in jail and stripped of rank for gunning down a 16-year-old garbage man in the Sadr City area of Baghdad in August 2004. Other higher-ranking Mexican and Mexican-descent soldiers who stand accused of war crimes include Brigadier General Ricardo Sanchez. General Sanchez, a poor kid from the Rio Grande Valley whose parents crossed the river to find work, rose to become commander of US forces in Iraq. As commander, Sanchez presided over the reign of terror at Abu Ghraib prison, but thus far has not been charged for his complicity in the widespread torture of Iraqi prisoners.

Mexican immigration to the US is fueled by poverty and political repression. While this migration has a long history (the first migrants arrived in California in 1879), it has been exacerbated in recent years by free-market projects like the North American Free Trade Agreement, which has driven tens of thousands of poor farmers off their land and into the migration stream. Since that treaty was signed in 1992, over 4,000

Mexicans, many of them displaced farmers, have died trying to cross the US border to find employment—more than were immolated in the World Trade Towers on 11 September 2001.

Mexicans have fought in four US wars in the past 100 years—World War II, Korea, Vietnam, and now Iraq. Traditionally, when a young Mexican goes off to fight a US war, their families travel to the Shrine of the Holy Child of Atocha in the central state of Zacatecas to light candles and offer *plegarias* (written prayers) for the safety of their children. Today, once again, the formal portraits of young men—and now young women—in military dress line the walls of the stone chapel, further evidence that the collateral damage from another US war is pounding down upon the Mexican landscape.

(This report was prepared by John Ross for the "Initiativa No En Nuestra Nombre" in Mexico City, to be submitted as testimony to the World Tribunal on Iraq to be celebrated in Istanbul, Turkey, 23–27 June 2005.)

Human Security vs. State Security

Christine Chinkin

The concept of international peace and security in international law has classically been understood narrowly as protecting the political and physical integrity of sovereign states. In its traditional form, state security is centered on the preservation of the sovereign state from external threats and the activities of other states. It thus requires internationally recognized boundaries protected if necessary by military action, prohibition of the use of force between states, and non-intervention in the affairs of other states.

Under the UN Charter, individual state security is supported by collective security, that is, according to the Security Council primary responsibility for the maintenance of international peace and security. The Security Council can authorize the use of "all necessary means" in response to a breach of the peace, threat to the peace, or act of aggression (UN Charter, Articles 39 and 42). The "collective" is circumscribed in that it is defined simply as the Security Council, rather than as any broader community of states or other interests. The veto (UN Charter, Article 27 (3)) ensures the agreement of the five permanent members in any such collective action and is thus a safeguard against contested action. The decision to use the veto is political. The concept of an "unreasonable veto" raised by Prime Minister Blair in the period before March 2003 (when a further Security Council resolution explicitly authorizing the use of force in Iraq was being sought) has no basis in international law. In Resolution 678 the Security Council authorized "all necessary means" (i.e., the use of force) against Iraq after the invasion of Kuwait in 1990, but no such resolution was adopted in 2003. The divisions between member states on when the Security Council should authorize collective action has led the secretary-general to recommend the adoption of a resolution setting out the principles which will guide it in making such decisions ("In Larger Freedom" [March 2005]).

Since the end of the Cold War, the Security Council has to some extent moved beyond the narrow understanding of state security epitomized by the invasion of Kuwait. It has, for example, authorized collective military intervention in response to humanitarian crisis (Somalia,

Bosnia–Herzegovina), internal unrest and conflict (Haiti, Sierra Leone), and refugee flows (Haiti, Iraq). It has also recognized the particular insecurities faced by children and women and those caused by HIV/AIDS.

Collective security is a protection against unilateral use of force by one state (or group of states) against another state, with the potentially destabilizing effect on international relations that entails. Accordingly, exceptions to the prohibition against the use of force are narrowly expressed. The only Charter exception to the prohibition of unauthorized force is the inherent right of individual and collective self-defense in response to an armed attack against the state, which is preserved within the UN Charter, Article 51. The focus upon state security (rather than that of individuals within the state) was emphasized in the Advisory Opinion of the International Court of Justice on the Legality of the Threat or Use of Nuclear Weapons (1996) when it stated that

> ... in view of the current state of international law, and of the elements of fact at its disposal, the Court cannot conclude definitively whether the threat or use of nuclear weapons would be lawful or unlawful in an extreme circumstance of self-defense, in which the very survival of a State would be at stake.

The state-centered concept of security extends to the assumption that it is state action that threatens the security of other states. This means that less attention has been paid to the role of non-state actors, such as multinational corporations, in generating insecurity. However, in the context of terrorism this has now changed. For example, in the preamble to its Resolution 1368, 12 September 2001, the Security Council recognized terrorist acts as constituting a threat to international peace and security (as indeed it had done in the context of Libya some years earlier) and went further by accepting that force could be used in self-defense as a legitimate response to the armed attacks by non-state actors in New York and Washington on the previous day.

The fact that self-defense is the only Charter-based justification for unilateral use of force has meant that states have endeavored to present any military action as coming within its ambit, or as expressly or impliedly authorized by the Security Council. The lack of legal certainty this has caused in the decentralized international legal system has generated further insecurity.

Not content with the Security Council recognition of terrorist acts as a threat to international peace and security and its authorization of self-defense in response to terrorist acts, certain states, notably the US, have sought to define state security more broadly. In the context of terrorist attacks and the possession of WMD it has been argued that protection of a state's own borders (territorial integrity) is not sufficient, but that preemptive action against another state, within that state's borders, is required. While there is perhaps little disagreement that UN Charter Article 51 includes the right to anticipatory self-defense (when the need to respond to an anticipated armed attack is instant, overwhelming, and the action is proportionate), the conformity with international law of the more far-reaching claim of preemptive self-defense (that is, the use of force in advance of any immediate threat) as expounded in the United States National Security Strategy 2003 is highly controversial and largely rejected.

Despite its broader understanding of the concept of security, the Security Council has not moved beyond state security to adopt any comprehensive approach to the concept of personal security. However, other bodies have developed this notion of personal, or human, security that looks to individuals rather than to states and state boundaries. The Commission on Human Security report, May 2005, has defined the objective of human security as being "to protect the vital core of all human lives in ways that enhance human freedoms and fulfilment."

Human security denotes individual freedom from basic insecurities, whatever the root of those insecurities. Insecurity is generated by military conflict between states. Thus the uncertainties in the international legal regime for the prohibition of the use of force and its contested unilateral use as in Iraq in 2003 are a basis for human insecurity. It is also caused by internal conflict, by the collapse of state institutions and structures (especially those relating to law and order), by authoritarian regimes, by human rights violations by state agents, and by environmental degradation. It also emanates from violence and abuse by non-state actors: by experiencing or fearing terrorist acts; by being (or fearing being) caught up in violence between rival groups; by being targeted by such groups for violence, whether those groups are involved in conflict, or are more accurately seen as criminal gangs; by an environment of random violence which law and order agencies are unable to control. Human insecurity is also caused by violations of economic and social rights such as the right to food, health, and housing, as well as civil and political rights such as fearing torture and deprivation of life and liberty. However, although denial of human rights contributes to human insecurity, which in turn generates further violations of human rights, human security is a wider concept than human rights. It encompasses physical security, economic security, legal security, political security, food security, gender security, and relational security. Human security is perhaps best summarized by the inclusion of "freedom from fear" and "freedom from want," among the four freedoms proclaimed by President Roosevelt during World War II. The May 2005 report of the Commission on Human Security added that it also includes the freedom to take action on one's own behalf, that is, the enjoyment of autonomy and self-esteem.

Human security thus goes beyond and supplements state security. The May 2005 Commission on Human Security report explains that it complements state security by being people-centered and by addressing insecurities that have not been considered as state security threats. It includes the insecurity generated by the use of force by one state against another (international armed conflict). Insecurity is also caused by state violence within the state and by state failure to provide a secure legal and economic framework and to protect against violence generated by non-state actors. Human (in)security does not depend upon international law distinctions between conflict, military action, internal affairs, and police action. In so-called post-conflict situations, the forms of violence typically mutate from conflict (bombings, military attacks) into criminal violence (murder, looting, abductions, kidnappings, corruption, armed crimes, organized crime). Where the state government cannot guarantee security within the state, other actors may assume that responsibility, for example an occupying army, or international peacekeepers. However such bodies tend to perceive security within state security terms (or in terms of the security of their own forces) rather than in that of the human security of civilians within the state.

Forms of human insecurity include genocide and gross violations of human rights that constitute crimes against humanity as defined in the Rome Statute for an International Criminal Court, 1998. It has been argued that the use of military force may be justified under international law where it is used to save human lives, that is, to promote human security. So-called humanitarian intervention is the classic instance of a claim based upon the security of individuals within the targeted state and where moral and ethical considerations are used to support arguments of legitimacy. The Security Council has given limited recognition to humanitarian intervention (Somalia, East Timor), but there is a great deal of disagreement as to whether humanitarian intervention without Security Council authorization in circumstances of gross violations of human rights in the target state (such as in Kosovo in 1999) is either legitimate or justified under customary international law and, if so, the circumstances in which it is warranted. The report of the International Commission on Intervention and State Sovereignty, "The Responsibility to Protect" (2001) is an important reformulation of the underlying principles of humanitarian intervention and suggests criteria for such intervention. Scholars in the US have also promoted a so-called duty to prevent, whereby states that are subject to no internal checks on government power must be prevented from developing weapons of mass destruction, or harboring terrorists. The duty to prevent has been presented as a corollary to the Responsibility to Protect and to the nonproliferation weapons regime. There are three features of the proposed regime: the focus is on the control not just of weapons but of the people who possess them; the emphasis is on prevention; and collective action through global or regional organization is preferred. Force (when used) should be used alongside and to support diplomacy. Apart from preemptive self-defense this is the most explicit—and extreme—claim for the development of new international legal norms for the security needs of the intervening state(s).

Human security is also closely linked with development, as for example through the Millennium Development Goals. In his report, "In Larger Freedom" (March 2005), the UN secretary-general linked freedom, security, and development and human rights. He argued that an illiterate person with AIDS who lives close to starvation, but who has the right to vote, cannot be called free. Nor can a woman who lives in the shadow of daily violence be called free. One could also say that these people exemplify human insecurity. In the words of the secretary-general: "Accordingly, we will not enjoy development without security, we will not enjoy security without development, and we will not enjoy either without respect for human rights."

What is evident from the attempts to extend the instances when force may be legally used by one state against another under international law is that the right to human security of individuals within the target state is likely to be at odds with the same right of individuals within the perpetrator state. For example, in the context of the war against terror, the claim is that to protect individuals within, for example, the US from terrorist acts, the US is justified in using force against those within a state supporting or harboring terrorists (Afghanistan) or suspected of flouting UN Security Council resolutions and failing to disarm (Iraq). While it is undoubtedly true that all individuals have the right to life and that a state has the obligation to "respect and ensure" the right to life of those within its own territory and subject to its jurisdiction, this cannot be done with disregard of the right to human security of those in other states. While the war against terror is supposedly about human security, its pursuance through war rather than, for example, through the criminal justice system is deeply destabilizing for the human security of all those in the target state. In the case of Iraq, it has emerged that there was no evidence of WMD and that the Ba'athist regime presented no immediate (if indeed any) threat to human security in the US or UK—the leading partners in the coalition. Arguments for the legality of military action based either on the revived effect of Security Council resolutions adopted during and after the use of force in Iraq in 1991 or on the need for the removal of an oppressive and brutal regime are of doubtful legal force under the rules relating to state security and ignore the broader issues of the human security of Iraqi civilians. It should also be noted that militarism and military action can also generate human insecurity in the state seeking such action, for example through fear of revenge attacks, anti-terrorist legislation, and military rather than social justice priorities.

Many Iraqis suffered great insecurity throughout the previous repressive regime, with its disregard for human rights, and through the imposition of economic sanctions since 1990. However, since human rights protection is not synonymous with human security, the removal of the previous regime has not necessarily removed those insecurities, for example, the effect of continued disappearance of family and friends. Nor has it necessarily delivered human security for Iraqis. There is no doubt that security for all Iraqis against some forms of abuse has improved since March 2003, but the invasion and occupation of Iraq has also seen the human security of Iraqi civilians undermined in other ways and by a range of state and non-state actors. The lack of formal data about the deaths of

Iraqi civilians and the other forms of harm they have suffered (including the refusal by the US and UK governments to collect such data) makes it difficult to quantify the level of human insecurity in Iraq. What is indisputable, however, is that civilian deaths and destruction of civilian facilities during the active military operations (including through violations of the laws of war), denial of human rights during the conflict and after the cessation of major combat operations (May 2003), the breakdown of law and order and the failure of the authorities to restore it and to protect individuals from the daily occurrence of violence and lawlessness have all contributed to the unacceptable levels of human insecurity.

Examples of human insecurity that have occurred at different times throughout Iraq after March 2003 and have been caused by state actors include:

—The use of cluster bombs and other weaponry throughout the active hostilities

—Bombings of civilian areas (marketplaces, restaurants, media facilities)

—Military action by coalition forces against targeted areas, for example in Falluja

—Use of combat forces for policing tasks; shootings, arrests throughout military patrols in civilian areas

—House raids by armed combat forces

—Failure to carry out adequate investigations of deaths and injuries that have occurred through raids, street patrols, and other activities

—Detentions of Iraqi civilians without charge or trial; conflation of the use of force against Iraq, the war against terror and insurgency, allowing detainees to be labeled as suspected terrorists and denied the international legal protections for either prisoners of war or those accused of criminal offenses

—Use of torture, cruel, inhuman, degrading treatment in detention facilities, including sexual abuse and humiliation

—Roadblocks and shootings at roadblocks

—Failure to protect public and private property; failure to deploy sufficiently trained and equipped forces for law-enforcement responsibilities

—Failure to redress high unemployment

—Destruction of housing and essential services and failure to restore them

—Inadequate access to health facilities and ill health caused by such deprivations

Extreme human insecurity has also been caused by non-state actors, for example:

—Extreme violence and intimidation by armed groups opposed to the occupation and regime change committed against coalition forces, civilians, police facilities, places of religion, government bodies, public spaces. These include bombings, suicide bombs, and other terrorist attacks

—Looting of military weapons, proliferation and availability of many forms of weapons

—Looting, hostage taking and killing, abduction, kidnapping, raping by armed groups without effective response from the authorities

—Attacks on oil fields, transportation, and communication lines; destruction of private and public property

—Organized criminal activities, black markets, etc.

—Taken together, these various forms of insecurity have inhibited moves for development in Iraq after the end of active military operations, and such lack of development is another source of human insecurity

Some people have been especially vulnerable to violence. These include civilian police and those applying to become members of the police forces, medical personnel, academic personnel, journalists, and NGO and civil society leaders, all of whom have been targeted by terrorist/insurgent gangs. Children, the elderly, and the disabled also suffer insecurity from the failure of institutional infrastructures, as well as from the many manifestations of violence.

Human insecurity is closely bound up with unequal relations between women and men and is highly gendered. There are many particular forms of insecurity that women suffer because they are women. Such insecurity continues in the aftermath of military action, and even more so in the conditions that prevail in Iraq. Such insecurity comes both from coalition forces, armed groups within Iraq, religious extremists, and from family members and acquaintances. Forms of insecurity stemming from the latter may be associated with, or resultant from, the invasion, occupation, and its continuing aftermath. In addition to the forms of human insecurity suffered by all Iraqis, the following gender-based harms cause insecurity for women:

—Detention, including being detained in order to convince male relatives to provide information

—Torture and sexual abuse in detention

—Loss of male breadwinners and other family members through death, wounding, and detentions; uncertainty caused by not knowing the place or likely length of detention of male relatives or their physical well-being
—Rape, sexual assault, death, abductions
—Fear of leaving home because of the incidence of public violence, coupled with the need to leave home to carry out their traditional family duties, including seeking care for wounded family members, obtaining food and other daily supplies, and attending to the needs of children
—Intimidation and harassment for failure to observe forms of dress code, resulting in restriction of movement
—Invasion of private space within the home by house raids
—Domestic violence
—Honor killings, including raped women being killed by their own families, to clear the "shame" of being raped
—Intimidation and fear of violence
—Murder of women who have entered the political scene and women's rights advocates and activists
—Denial of, or discrimination in access to, economic and social rights including healthcare, education, and employment
—Poverty and vulnerability to being trafficked, forced prostitution
—Inadequate protection from law (continued discrimination and legal subordination) and legal enforcement agencies.

Military action that is deemed to be for the protection of the civilian population creates a relationship of protector/protected between the military forces and that population. Where insecurity is in fact generated directly or indirectly by such forces this dichotomy is exposed as meaningless.

Criminal acts by non-state actors (armed gangs, insurgents, terrorists) are subject to trial and punishment by the national courts and may also reach the threshold of severity that makes them in violation of international criminal law. However, inadequate and weakened state institutions reduce the likelihood of detention and legal process, and much of the response is through further action carried out by military forces rather than by police action. Violence by non-state actors and the authorities' responses cause an ongoing spiral of insecurity that appears impossible to break.

State actors are also subject to international legal obligations. During the military hostilities, the coalition forces were under an obligation to comply with the laws of war. After May 2003, the CPA as an occupying body had the obligation to "to restore, and ensure, as far as possible, public order and safety" (Hague Regulations, Article 43). This includes the obligation to ensure food and medical supplies for the population (Geneva Convention IV, Article 55); the medical and hospital establishments (Geneva Convention IV, Article 56); to maintain the orderly government of the territory (Geneva Convention IV, Article 64); and to continue the functioning of penal law and tribunals (Geneva Convention IV, Article 64). The occupying force was also bound by fundamental human-rights guarantees. These legal obligations go to the heart of human security. Since the formal end of occupation and the handover to the interim Iraqi government in June 2004, the Iraqi government is responsible for complying with the human-rights instruments to which Iraq is party and ensuring the human security of its citizens. The state has an obligation to exercise due diligence to prevent human-rights violations, and to investigate and punish them when they occur. The state's failure to take preventive or protective action "itself represents a violation of basic rights on the State's part. This is because the state controls the means to verify acts occurring within its territory" (Velasquez Rodriguez v. Honduras, American Court of Human Rights). Such control may not of course be possible and the state may seek assistance in providing such security. The inability of Iraqi security forces to do so means that coalition forces remain in the country, now as the multinational force "requested" by UN Security Council Resolution 1546, 8 June 2004.

Iraqi civilians have no recourse against abusive acts committed by the CPA or subsequently by coalition forces. Order 17 accorded immunity from the Iraqi legal process to personnel of the CPA, coalition forces, and Foreign Liaison Mission. CPA Revised Order 17 was adopted on 27 June 2004, the day before the "handover" to the Iraqi interim government. This continued the immunity into the period of the interim Iraqi government and extended its scope. This order provides that the multinational force (MNF), CPA, Foreign Liaison Missions, and all international consultants shall be immune from the Iraqi legal process. This immunity extends to foreign contractors "in matters relating to the terms and conditions of their contracts" and "with respect to acts performed by them pursuant to the terms and conditions of a Contract or any sub-contract thereto." Thus legal impunity with respect to the acts of international personnel is added to other forms of insecurity experienced by Iraqi civilians.

States respond to national security issues through defense policies, military spending, and arms development and spending. The May 2005 Commission on Human Security report recommends two responses to human insecurity: protection and empowerment. Protection requires focus on public safety (rather than military operations) and "concerted effort to develop norms, processes and institutions that systematically address insecurities," while empowerment "enables people to develop their potential and become full participants in decision-making." Law and order is key to ensuring human security. What is evident in Iraq is that coalition forces through the invasion, occupation, and since the June 2004 handover have contributed to the insecurity of Iraqi civilians both directly and indirectly and have failed to provide adequate protection against insecurity generated by other actors. Further, while elections and constitutional change seek to establish new legal, economic, and social institutions, they are insufficient mechanisms for protection or empowerment.

Next Steps for the Peace Movement

Ken Coates

Our people need to know what has been happening in Iraq: but a systematic analysis of the terrible events there is necessary for more reasons than those of public instruction. Unless we learn from these events, they will be repeated: and the signs are that the repetitions could be soon. In a word, the detailed examination of the war in Iraq is important throughout the world, and above all to peace movements because of the light it throws on military intentions, on the balance of military power, and on overall threats to the peace of the world.[1]

Like the generals who always get ready to fight the last war, peace movements do tend to be dominated by the thinking of a previous generation of strategists. They have more excuse than the generals, because they are not normally privy to what generals know about the state of the world, and the nature of power. They do also tend to be more innocent. However, to paraphrase Donald Rumsfeld, not the least consequence of the war in Iraq has been that many things that were previously unknown are now known.

For a very long time, peace activists have been left to pick the bones out of the remnants of the Cold War. We have not been very good at that. In the 1980s, campaigners for European Nuclear Disarmament called for the simultaneous dissolution of the great nuclear alliances, NATO and the Warsaw Treaty Organization. Following the rise of Gorbachev, the Warsaw Treaty quickly fell apart, but NATO, after a very momentary quiescence, simply grew and grew, until it directly embraced large numbers of territories in Eastern Europe, and indirectly entered formal "partnerships for peace" with large parts of the former Soviet Union. The peace movements, to give them their due, were uneasy about this expansion, but they were quite unable to stop it. By March 2004, Bulgaria, Romania, Slovakia, and Slovenia all became full NATO members. The Czech Republic, Hungary, and Poland had joined five years earlier, in March 1999. Three countries which are now independent, but were formerly constituent parts of the Soviet Union— Estonia, Latvia, and Lithuania—also enrolled themselves on the 29 March 2004. Other accessions are undoubtedly slated.

In the years of this transition, numerous conflicts were seeded, which even divided the peace movements, as happened in Yugoslavia and Afghanistan. It has taken some time, and a number of alarming developments in weapons systems and nuclear military technology, to give rise again to a halting renaissance of the demand for the removal of all nuclear weapons from the area of Europe.

Of course, the fundamental result of the end of the Cold War has been the ending of bipolar conflict and the emergence of a single dominant megapower.[2] The American military quickly codified the new balance by developing the new doctrine of "full-spectrum dominance." This is proclaimed to be:

> The ability of US forces, operating unilaterally or in combination with multinational and interagency partners, to defeat any adversary and control any situation across the full range of military operations... It includes theater engagement and presence activities. It includes conflict involving employment of strategic forces and weapons of mass destruction, major theater wars, regional conflicts, and smaller-scale contingencies. [It implies] freedom to operate in all domains—space, sea, land, air and information. (See US Department of Defense Website)

As with many doctrines, there is more than one slip betwixt cup and lip. It is easy to proclaim military supremacy, but can be more difficult to secure it. However, even before the new doctrine, the United States had indeed already enjoyed long years of military invulnerability. Nobody has been or is in a position to invade the country even without the best efforts of the military-industrial complex: there are no land forces able to assault the United States from Mexico, or Canada, and all Latin America is comparatively weak and poor, seriously divided, and largely introspective. At the same time, there is wider dominance. The United States has an impressive control of the seas. Britain certainly does not rule the waves any more, and has sublet its remaining outposts of naval power to the United States. Notably, Diego Garcia has been illegally expropriated by the British for the benefit of the American air force, and to the immense detriment of America's chosen enemies in the Middle East and Africa.

All this concerns only conventional domination, long since surpassed. Joint Vision 20/10 proclaims a coming bonfire of the treaties, because the medium of space is the fourth medium of warfare—along with land, sea, and air. Space power (systems capabilities and forces) will be increasingly leveraged to close the ever-widening gap between diminishing resources and increasing military commitments.

And, in case we were in any doubt, "information superiority relies heavily upon space capabilities."

With such unchallengeable ascendancy in arms, it is hardly surprising that America has effortlessly sought to rig the balance of power in Eurasia to its advantage. Hence, formerly Soviet oil courses from Azerbaijan across Georgia into Turkey and thus to the Mediterranean. American bases are scattered across former Soviet Central Asia, so that NATO cannot today criticize the repression in Uzbekistan for fear of annoying American clients in that country. There is really a vast accumulation of force and potential force, enough to daunt all conventional military rivals.

And yet, in the attacks of al-Qaeda, a handful of people employing weapons no more deadly than Stanley knives were able to mount a destructive foray against New York, destroying the Twin Towers of the World Trade Center. This was not, contrary to official propaganda, the opening of a war. There was no warring power capable of concluding such a war. Legally, the atrocity of 9/11 fell under the criminal law, and this appreciation was at least partially refracted in the subsequent decision of the American government that its "war" on terrorism did not fall within the provisions of the Geneva Conventions.

Once again, international law has been rewritten by the marshals, who routinely annul all lingering notions of right or justice. These processes have been at work on a larger stage.[3]

Of course the United Nations was the creation of the wartime alliance against Hitler's Germany and the axis powers. Its founding conference in San Francisco took place at a time when the alliance had never been stronger, and would never be closer. The Charter of the new organization was carefully sculpted to maintain the unity of the wartime alliance—and to safeguard the rights of its principal contenders. The veto, or rule of unanimity, assured that the five great powers in the alliance—the US, the USSR, Britain, France, and China—would never have their vital interests violated by any decision of the new body. This prudent precaution soon gained an altogether new meaning, as the alliance fractured into the Cold War, which more than once ran the risk of becoming hot.

Viewed in retrospect, the more than half-century of the UN's history is a remarkable achievement. Those who designed this structure had learned well from the difficult story of the League of Nations, which proved much more vulnerable to events in the interwar years than did the UN in the seismic period of the nuclear arms race. Certainly the nature of this threat did, in itself, contribute to the will to maintain a viable international organization.

Now the need for the reform of this organization has been widely accepted, and has generated an official report by the high-level Panel on Threats, Challenges and Change, set up by the secretary-general. Reform, however, is not so easy. Much argument has been lavished on the injustices of the veto. For the great powers, the objection is usually to other people's vetoes.

There is a special problem which attaches to the maintenance of a United Nations organization when one nation has unchallenged preeminence over all the others. As Jack Straw, the British foreign secretary, argued, when seeking to persuade the British Parliament that they dare not defy American wishes and refuse the war in Iraq:

> ... you are right it is the United States which has the military power to act as the world's policeman, and only the United States. We live in a unipolar world; the United States has a quarter of the world's wealth, the world's GDP, and it has stronger armed forces than the next 27 countries put together. So its predominance is huge. That is a fact. No one can gainsay it; no one can change it in the short or medium term. The choice we have to make in the international community is whether, in a unipolar world, we want the only super-power to act unilaterally and we force them to act unilaterally or whether we work in such a way that they act within the multilateral institutions. What I say to France and Germany and all other European Union colleagues is to take care, because just as America helps to define and influence our politics, so what we do in Europe helps to define and influence American politics. We will reap a whirlwind if we push the Americans into a unilateralist position in which they are the centre of this unipolar world.

But undoubtedly the foundation of the UN rested on the appreciation, derived from Immanuel Kant, that the foundations of the international order rested on nation-states. A state is a society of human beings, Kant taught, that no one other than itself can command or dispose of. The collaboration of such states depended on the appreciation that each was, in truth, inviolable. As Kant himself said in his proposal to secure perpetual peace, "No State shall forcibly interfere in the constitution and government of another State." "Limited" sovereignty, or the doctrine that "sovereignty is less absolute than in earlier times," would sap the fundamental agreement on which the United Nations rests, which is why Kofi Annan, no firebrand, nonetheless insisted that the war on Iraq was illegal, insofar as it was undertaken without either direct justification in self-defense, or the mandate of the Security Council of the UN.

Surely the modern world has moved beyond the age of Kant? The answer has to be yes, and no. If political economy is the true foundation of civil society, then globalization is assuredly eroding the powers of nations. There are also more beneficial pressures which enlarge the cooperation between the institutions of civil society across frontiers. But civil society has certainly not attained a fully integrated global presence.

The word of Amnesty International resounds around the world but the limitations of the influence of that organization are all-too evident. Kant thought that if reforming states could aspire to similar "republican" governments, they could then federate in a League of Nations which "need not be a state of Nations." But similar and parallel evolution of institutions is only the beginning of a very long march to the integration of civil society across national frontiers.

For a time, it looked as if the European Union could fulfill the dreams not only of Kant, but also of Tom Paine and William Penn, growing into "an ever closer union." We may well think that links between peace movements and wider common actions between voluntary bodies are the groundwork upon which another world becomes possible. But this does not imply that we can simply jump over the inherited institutions. These institutions have nuclear teeth, and their military rationality remains untamed, even if a new, more humane rationality is slowly evolving among the peoples.

We tried to build the Russell Tribunals on war crimes in Vietnam and on repression in Latin America on this foundation. In the words of Lelio Basso, the tribunals became necessary because "human rights are at the same time proclaimed and left unprotected, devoid of international or national safeguards."

It is clear that the problems have all been aggravated since those days: but the war in Iraq shows with fierce cruelty how little progress we have made in our institutional responses to those problems.

Today we see in the flood of embarrassing documents on the true origins of the Iraq war a fierce tension between the constitutional foundations of the UN, and the real power relationships. The United States believes that it exercises "full-spectrum dominance" in military terms, and that it does not need any permission to assert its will wherever it feels the need to do so. Why else expend all that treasure, all those efforts to create an armed power beyond compare, if it is to generate no dividends in actual behavior? But it takes two to tango, as was seen in the case of Turkey, not the strongest member of the North Atlantic Treaty Organization, who refused to fall in behind George Bush and Jack Straw in declaring war on Iraq.

The culmination of the recent revelations was perhaps the publication on 1 May in the *Sunday Times* of London of the so-called Downing Street memo, now generally described in the United States as Downing Streetgate.[4]

A spate of leaks of classified memoranda shows that British officials in Washington believed in July 2002 that "war was inevitable," and that "the intelligence and facts were being fixed around the policy." These documents have provoked sustained enquiries in the United States, and a powerful campaign by Representative John Conyers, Jr. They show us the sense in which it is true that domination is not enough. American satellites could pinpoint every movement in the Iraqi desert, but could not control the growing apprehensions of public opinion around the world.

It was presumed that those things which could not be accomplished by military gadgetry might be brought about by the expenditure of money. But, astonishingly, bribery was not a sufficient weapon to bring the Security Council of the United Nations on side with the projected war. These intransigent facts could not stop the war, and the slaughter of at least 100,000 Iraqi civilians. But they could deny that war legitimacy, and thus establish a large space in which the movement for peace and human rights can develop.

This will require a hard-headed appreciation of the scope and limitations of agreements between nations, and their institutional arrangements. In defending the United Nations, we are defending not what has been passed down to us—a long history of shabby compromises—but a continuous space for cooperation and democracy, a Commonwealth that is to come. When the British working people demanded the extension of the franchise, they were not seeking to consummate the somewhat raddled history of the mother of Parliaments: rather they were struggling to pass beyond the old corruption, into a new and better world. Another world is, truly, possible.[5]

Towards a New Political Imaginary

Corrine Kumar

1.

We have entered the night to tell our tale
to listen to those who have not spoken
we who have seen our children die in the morning deserve to be
listened to:
we have looked on blankly as they have opened their wounds
Nothing really matters except, the grief of the children
their tears must be revered
their inner silence speaks louder than the spoken word
and all being and all life shouts out in outrage
we must not be rushed to our truths

whatever we failed to say is stored secretly in our minds
and all those processions of embittered crowds
have seen us lead them a thousand times
we can hear the story over and over and over again
our minds are muted beyond the sadness
there is nothing more we can fear.[1]

Friends of the World Tribunal on Iraq, members of the Jury, friends from
Iraq, friends from Turkey,

We live in fearful times:
We live in violent times:
times in which our community and collective memories are dying;
times in which the many dreams are turning into never-ending nightmares,
and the future increasingly fragmenting;
times that are collapsing the many life visions into a *single cosmology* that
has created its own *universal truths*—equality, development, peace;
truths that are inherently discriminatory, even violent.
Times that have created the globalized world order that dispossesses the
majority, desacralizes nature, destroys cultures and civilizations, denigrates
the women; times in which the war on terrorism à la Pax Americana brings
a time of violent uncertainty, brutal wars:

wars for resources—oil, diamonds, minerals: wars of occupation, state terrorism, going global patented by the USA, times that are giving us new words; preemptive strike, collateral damage, embedded journalism, enemy combatants, new words: words soaked in blood.

Times in which the dominant political thinking, institutions and instruments of justice are hardly able to redress the *violence* that is escalating, and *intensifying*, times in which *progress* presupposes the *genocide* of the many; times in which human rights have come to mean the rights of the privileged, the rights of the powerful times in which the *political spaces* for the other is diminishing, even *closing*.

The world, it would seem, is at the end of its imagination.

2.

Only the imagination stands between us and fear: fear makes us behave like sheep when we should be dreaming like poets.

So let me gather some stars and make a fire for you, and tell you a story:

It is a story of horror and hope; a story of the missing, the disappeared; a story so real, yet magical: a story from Lawrence Thornton in *Imagining Argentina*.

It could be from Iraq.

I tell this story for Eman and Hana, Rana, Amal; and for the children in Iraq.

It is a story about Argentina under the dictators. The hero is a gentle person, Carlos Rueda, an intense man who directs a children's theater and is at home in the world of children. During the time of the dictators, Carlos discovers that he has an extraordinary gift. He realizes that he is the site, the locus, *the vessel for a dream*. He can narrate the fate of the missing. From all over Argentina, men and women come to his home and sitting in his garden, Carlos tells them stories: tales of torture, courage, death, stories about the missing, about the *disappeared*.

One day the regime arrests his wife Celia, for a courageous act of reporting. The world of Carlos collapses till he realizes that he must keep her alive in his imagination.

Only the imagination, says Carlos, stands between us and fear; fear makes us behave like sheep when we must dream like poets.

As the regime becomes more violent, it is the women who object. It is the women as wives, as mothers, as daughters who congregate in silence at the Plaza de Mayo. Silently, each carries a placard announcing or asking about the *missing*. The women walk quietly, sometimes holding hands.

It is not just an act of protest; it is *a drama of caring*; each listening to the other's story, each assuring the other through touch, weaving a sense of community.

The community grows as the men join them.

All the while, through the window, the Generals watch them.

People realize that they cannot be indifferent observers, spectators, bystanders, *even experts*. The indifference of the watchers to the regime is not enough.

One must be a witness.

A witness is not a mere spectator.

S/he *looks* but she also *listens*.

S/he remembers.

Everything must be remembered. Nothing must be forgotten.

We must retrieve history from memory.

We must explore the new imaginary not as experts but as witnesses.

The Mothers of the Plaza de Mayo in Argentina express this new imaginary.

3.

Our imaginaries must be different:

The new imaginary cannot have its moorings in the dominant discourse, but must seek to locate itself in a *discourse of dissent* that comes from a deep critique of the different forms of domination and violence in our times: any new imaginary cannot be tied to the dominant discourse and systems of violence and exclusion.

This new imaginary will move away from the eurocentric and androcentric methodologies which only observe and describe; methodologies which quantify, percentify, classify, completely indifferent to phenomena which cannot be obtained or explained through its frames. We need to deconstruct the dominant mythology, disallowing the invasion of the dominant discourse; refusing the integration of the *South* into the agenda of globalization and the war on terrorism. The new imaginary invites us to create a new spectrum of methods which depart from the linear mode of thought and perception to one that is more *holistic, holographic*. It urges us to search more qualitative methodologies in oral history, experiential analysis, using fluid categories, *listening for the nuances, searching for the shadow*, in poetry, in myth, in metaphor. It invites us to a way of knowing that refuses to control and exploit Nature, but one that finds our *connectedness to Nature*: to place together these fragments, to discern the essence, to move into another space, another time, recapturing hidden knowledges, regenerating forgotten spaces, refinding other cosmologies, reweaving the future. It is here perhaps, that the notion of the sacred survives; it is here in the cosmologies and rootedness of cultures; here with peoples on the peripheries that we must seek the beginnings of *an alternate discourse*.

It is not difficult to see that we are at the end of an era, when every old category begins to have a hollow sound, and when we are groping in the dark to discover the new. Can we find new words, search for new ways, create out of the material of the human spirit *possibilities* to transform the existing exploitative social order, to discern a greater human potential?

What we need in the world today are new universalisms; not universalisms that deny the many and affirm the one, not universalisms born of eurocentricities or patriarchies; but universalisms *that recognize the universal in the specific civilizational idioms in the world*. Universalisms that will not deny the accumulated experiences and knowledges of past generations but that will not accept the imposition of any monolithic structures under which it is presumed all other peoples must be subsumed. New universalisms that will challenge the universal mode—militarization, nuclearism, war. Universalisms that will respect the plurality of the different societies, of their philosophy, of their ideology, their traditions and cultures; one that will be rooted in the particular, in the vernacular, one which will find a resonance in the different civilizations, *birthing new cosmologies*.

We need to imagine alternative perspectives for change: to craft visions that will evolve out of conversations across cultures and other traditions; conversations between cultures that challenge and transcend the totalitarianism of the Western logos; conversations that are not mediated by the hegemony of the *universal discourse*.

Members of the Jury, the new imaginary invites us to another human-rights discourse; one that will not be trapped either in the *universalisms* of the dominant thinking tied as it is to a market economy, a monoculturalism, a materialistic ethic, and the politics and polity of the nation-state; neither must it be caught in the discourse of the *culture specific* but one that will proffer universalisms that have been born out of a *dialogue of civilizations*. And this will mean another *ethic of dialogue*. We need to find new perspectives on the universality of human rights: *in dialogue with other cultural perspectives of reality*, other notions of development, democracy, even dissent, other concepts of power (not power to control, power to hegemonize, but power to facilitate, to enhance) and governance; other notions of equality; equality makes us flat and faceless citizens of the nation-state, perhaps the notion of *dignity* which comes from depth, from *roots*, could change the discourse, the Iraqis at the tribunal speak of *dignity*: other concepts of justice—*justice without revenge*, justice with truth and reconciliation, *justice with healing* of individuals, of communities, because *human kind proffers many horizons of discourse*, and because our eyes do not as yet behold those horizons, it does not mean that those horizons do not exist.

Take the *universal* discourse on *democracy*: the new magical word to *reform* the world, the Greater Middle East: the dominant understanding on democracy is tied to the notion of individual rights, private property, the *market economy*; we are all equal we are told but the market works as the *guarantor of inequality*, of unequal distribution, of how only a few will have and how the many must not have. What shall we do with the rhetoric of political equality on which this democracy is built, while the majority are increasingly dispossessed, living below poverty lines? We must seek new understandings of democracy; that will include a concept of freedom that is different from that which is enshrined in the Enlightenment and its Market. There is an urgent need to reinvent the political; to infuse the political with the ethical.

The new political imaginary speaks to an ethic of care:

In 1996, Madeleine Albright, the then US secretary of state, was asked what she felt about the 500,000 Iraqi children who had died as a result of US economic sanctions (in the name of UN Security Council), in the context of the continuing war. Was it a high price to pay? Was it worth it? She replied: *Yes, all things considered, we think that the price is worth it.* Lives of children lost in wars are considered *collateral damage*.

But in the world of rights we all are equal; each has the fundamental right to life.

But what does the right to life mean to the genetically damaged children born all over the world because of depleted uranium? Depleted uranium that was used in wars in Bosnia, Kosovo, Afghanistan, and in Iraq for this generation, and for the generations to come.

The new political imaginary invites us to write another history: *a counter hegemonic history*, a history of the margins. It is a journey of the margins: a journey rather than an imagined destination: a journey in which the dailiness of our life proffers possibilities for our imaginary, survival and sustenance, for connectedness and community. For the idea of the imaginary is inextricably linked to the personal, political, and historical dimensions of community and identity. It is the dislocation expressed by particular social groups that makes possible the articulation of new imaginaries. These social groups, the margins, the global south, *the south in the north*, the *south in the south*, are beginning to articulate these *new imaginaries*.

The peasants in Chiapas, Mexico, describing their *new imaginary*, explain their core vision in their struggle for their livelihoods and for retaining their life worlds. And in their profound and careful organization, in their political imagining and vision, do not offer clear, rigid, universal truths; knowing that the journey is in itself precious, sum up their vision in three little words: asking, we walk.

The asking in itself *challenges master narratives*, masters' houses, houses of reason; universal truths, of power, of politics.

The Zapatistas in offering another logic, draw the contours of this new imaginary.

The new political imaginary invites us to *dismantle the master's house*; and as the poet Audre Lorde said, the *master's tools will never dismantle the master's house*. There is an urgent need to challenge the centralizing logic of the master narrative implicit in the dominant discourses of war, of security, of human rights, of democracy. This dominant logic is a logic of violence and *exclusion*, a logic of developed and underdeveloped, a logic of superior and inferior, *a logic of civilized and uncivilized*.

This centralizing logic must be decentered, must be interrupted, even disrupted.

The new political imaginary speaks to this disruption; to this trespass.

4.

The World Tribunal on Iraq speaks to this disruption: It is a disruption of the dominant discourse and the dominant politics of our times and public hearings, people's tribunals, Courts of Women are all expressions of people's resistance: expressions of the new imaginary that is finding different ways of speaking *Truth* to *Power*, recognizing that the concepts and categories enshrined in the dominant thinking and institutions in our times are unable to grasp the violence.

We must ask where can sovereign people go for redress, for reparation for the crimes committed against them? Where will the *people of Iraq seek the reparation* that is *owed* to them?

There are no mechanisms in the rights discourse/praxis where *sovereign people* can take sovereign nation-states to task, locked as it is, into the terrain of the nation-state: the state on signing the international covenants/Universal Declaration on Human Rights become the *guarantors* of human rights and freedoms for their citizens; but what often happens is that the *state become the greatest violator*. We know that the International Criminal Court has been ratified by many countries but remains state-centric: the greatest violator, the US, refusing to ratify the Rome statute, continues to make bilateral treaties with other states assuring that the US will not be prosecuted for war crimes that they will continue to commit with impunity.[2]

So, where shall we find justice?

Perhaps it is in the expressions of *resistance* seeking legitimacy not by the dominant standards, not from a dominant paradigm, not by the *rule of law*, but by claims to the truth offering *new paradigms of knowledge*, of politics: the truth commissions, the public hearings, the peoples' tribunals, the Courts of Women are movements of resistance that are *speaking to Power, challenging Power, creating other reference points*; sources of other inspiration, speaking to the *conscience* of the world, returning *ethics to politics*, decolonizing our minds and our imaginations.

The *South* has for too long accepted a world view that has hege-monized its cultures, decided its development model, defined its aesthetic categories, outlined its military face, determined its science and technology, its nuclear options, and molded its modes of governance through the modern nation-state. For the modern idiom of politics is the eurocentric world of nation-states, centralized, bureaucratized, militarized, some even nuclearized. The nation-state in its homogenization of the polity has subsumed all cultural diversity, all civilizational differences, into one uniform political entity, which now belongs to the *New World Order*. A cosmology constructed of what has come to be known as *universal values*; a cosmology whose philosophical, ideological, and political roots were embedded in the specific historical context of the culture of the West. What qualified it then to be termed *universal?* The vision of the world in which the center of the world was Europe and later North America (the West) encapsulated all civilizations into its own Western frames: it reduced their cultural diversities into a schema called *civilization*; it made universal the specific historical experiences of the West. It announced that what was relevant to the West had to be a model for the rest of the world: what was good for the center had to be meaningful for the periphery. *All that was Western simply became universal.* Every other civilization, every system of knowledge came to be defined and compared vis-à-vis this paradigm submitting to "its insights as imposition, its blindness as values, its tastes as canons, in a word to its eurocentricities."

The *Other* in this cosmology were the civilizations of Asia, the Pacific, Africa, Latin America, the Arab world. *Scarcely twenty years were enough to make two billion people define themselves as underdeveloped,* vis-à-vis the post-war growth model, the market economy, and the international economic order conceived of at Bretton Woods. It minusculed all social totalities into one single model, all systems of science to one mega-science, all indigenous medicine to one imperial medicine, all knowledge to one established regime of thought, all development to gross national product, to patterns of consumption, to industrialization, to *the Western self-image of homo economicus with all needs commodity defined,* and *homo economicus has never been gender neutral.*

This cosmos of values has determined the thought patterns of the world, as well as the world's ecological patterns: indicating its scientific signs, giving it development symbols, generating the military psyche, defining knowledge, truth: *universal truths which have been blind to cultures, race, class, gender.* Universal *patriarchal* truths, whatever the cultural ethos, whatever the civilizational idiom.

5.

What is essential is not to develop new doctrines or dogmas, or to define a new, coherent political schema; but, to suggest a *new imaginative attitude,* one that can be *radical and subversive* and which will be able to change the logic of our development. Perhaps, as the poet says, we *should now break the routine, do an extravagant action that would change the course of history.* What is essential is to go beyond the politics of violence and exclusion of our times and to find *new political imaginations.*

An imaginary where people of the margins, of the *global South* are subjects of our own history, writing our own cultural narratives, offering new universals, imagining a world in more life-enhancing terms, *constructing a new radical imaginary.*

We must seek new imaginaries from the South: the South not only as third world, as the civilizations of Asia, the Arab world, Africa, Latin America; but the South as the voices and *movements of peoples*, wherever these movements exist;

the South as the visions and wisdoms of women;

the South as the discovering of new paradigms, which challenge the existing theoretical concepts and categories, breaking the mind's constructs, seeking a new language to describe what it perceives, refusing the one, objective, rational, scientific world view as the only world view; the South as the discovery of other cosmologies, as the recovery of other knowledges that have been hidden, submerged, silenced: the South as an *"insurrection of these* subjugated knowledges";

the South as history; the *South as memory;*

the South as the finding of new political paradigms, inventing new political patterns, creating alternative political imaginations: the South as the revelation of each civilization in its own idiom: the South as *conversations* between civilizations;

the South then as *new universalisms.*

It invites us to create a new imaginary.

The South as new political imaginary.[3]

6.

The Courts of Women are an articulation of the new imaginary: The *Courts of Women* are an unfolding of a space, *an imaginary*: a horizon that invites us to think, to feel, to challenge, to connect, to dare to dream.

They are an attempt to define a new space for women, and to infuse this space with a new vision, a *new politics.* They are a gathering of voices and visions of the *global South.* The Courts of Women reclaim the subjective and objective modes of knowing, creating richer and deeper structures of knowledge in which the observer is not distanced from the observed, the researcher from the research, poverty from the poor. The *Courts of Women* seek to weave together the *objective* reality (analyses) with the *subjective* testimonies of the women; the rational with the intuitive; the personal with the political; *the logical* with the *lyrical* (through video testimonies, artistic images, and poetry); *we cannot separate the dancer from the dance*. It invites us to discern fresh insights, offering us other ways to know, urging us to seek deeper layers of knowledge towards creating new paradigms of knowledge.

The *Courts of Women*, like the World Tribunal on Iraq, are public hearings: the *Court* is used in a symbolic way. The *Courts* are *sacred* spaces where women, speaking in a language of suffering, name the crimes, seeking redress, even reparation.

They are a rejection of the silencing of the crimes of violence:

Silence subjugates; silence kills: breaking the silence signifies the point of disruption and of *counter-hegemonic truth telling*.

While the *Courts of Women* listen to the voices of the survivors, they also listen to the voices of women who resist, who rebel, who refuse to turn against their dreams. They hear challenges to the dominant human-rights discourse, whose frames have *excluded the knowledges of women*. They repeatedly hear of the need to extend the discourse to include the meanings and symbols and perspectives of women.

They speak of a new generation of women's human rights.

The *Courts of Women are a tribute to the human spirit:* in which testimonies can not only be heard but also legitimized. The courts provide witnesses, victims, survivors, and resistors not only the validation of their suffering but also the validation of the hopes and dreams that they have dared to hold. This speaks to the right of the subjugated and the silenced to articulate the crimes against them; it is a taking away of the legitimizing dominant ideologies and returning their *life worlds* into their own hands.

The Courts of Women celebrate those disruptive voices, voices that disrupt the dominant narrative of war and occupation, of security, of justice, of patriarchy...

7.

With our partner organizations, and drawing from the methodology of the Courts of Women, we have held two sessions of the World Tribunal on Iraq.

In January 2004 at the World Social Forum in India, we held the

World Court on US War Crimes with a central session on Iraq, and many voices from other sessions of the WTI were heard in the court. The focus of the WTI-Mumbai session was on the War Crimes of the US over the last fifty years. It was clear that the US was and continues to be the only country in the world that has *actually used weapons of mass destruction*: the atomic bombing of Hiroshima and Nagasaki, the hydrogen bomb testing on the Bikini Atoll in the Pacific, the use of depleted uranium in the wars in Afghanistan, Kosovo, the first 1991 Gulf War, and now again in Iraq; Agent Orange, chemical warfare in Vietnam, and now again the use of MK-77, a version of napalm, in Iraq; bacteriological warfare in Cuba; the creation of military bases all over the world, about 130, and still building...

Members of the Jury, we ask that the rationale for the aggression and war on Iraq—the search for weapons of mass destruction—be placed in the context of the *global hegemon* and its actual use of weapons of mass destruction all over the world.

It has done all this with impunity.

Somebody in this session said that Nuremberg was the justice of the winners, and I wonder if the face of the world, of *realpolitik,* would have changed had the world demanded that America apologize and that *justice and reparation* be given to the *hibakusha* of Hiroshima and Nagasaki: *We must right the many wrongs of history.*

Perhaps we must add our voices to the movements for compensation and reparation to the victims of America's wars: the greatest rogue state of our times.

Last week we held in Tunis the Arab session of the WTI which focused on US war crimes, the Project of the New American Century, and the Arab street. There were several recommendations made at the WTI-Arab session, and we proffer some recommendations to the Jury:

1. To demand the unconditional *End of the Occupation* which is illegal and immoral: for Iraq, for Palestine.

2. The WTI-Arab session asks for an independent investigation into the crimes at Abu Ghraib, placing it in the context of America's systematic and systemic *use of torture* and abuse of prisoners, now known as enemy combatants: from Bagram in Afghanistan to Guantánamo in Cuba.

3. The creation of a world commission comprised of scientists, witnesses, experts, scholar-activists, on the weapons of mass destruction of

the US; what it has used, and what it has in stockpiles, which could be used in preemptive strikes.

4. An independent investigation on the *nuclear war* unfolding in Iraq, the use of depleted uranium since 1991 and napalm (MK-77), and the effects of depleted uranium and napalm on the peoples of Iraq, especially the children.

Perhaps, we can then make a case for sanctions against the US: Embargo the US!

5. The need to hold peoples' courts all over the Arab world challenging the dominant thinking and praxis of wars and violence in our times, gathering and listening to the voices and visions from the Arab street:

Let me bring to the tribunal a little corner of the Arab street:

It speaks with another logic: the Arab street in privileged and *civilized* parlance is a *street of violence*, of extremism, peopled by killers, by terrorists, by savages, by *barbarians*. The *barbarian* of course, is the evil one, the *uncivilized*: and its *civilized* range is full-spectrum dominance, from communist to terrorist.

The word *barbarian* invites us to remember a story:
Once upon a long time ago, in another place, another time, women and men turned away from the Empire, they withdrew from the civic life of their times and gathered their strengths to withstand the coming hordes of barbarians, a story much like today's: with one very important difference.

This time we are not warned that the *barbarians* are coming, that they are waiting at the borders, knocking at the gate because they have already been there for sometime in Washington, inside the White House, inside our lives. Destroying our heritage, rewriting our history, killing our collective memory, overtaking our dreams.

Do you still wonder why there is so much anger, even hatred?

As Bush asks why, especially when *we are so good* especially when we are so democratic perhaps its is our *Wealth?* perhaps it is our *Freedom?* echo the Washington clique. Perhaps if they listened carefully to the Arab street they would hear other stories; stories of why people burn the American flag, stories that point to the US unilateral support to the Israeli occupation of Palestine.

Stories of its support of corrupt leaders, brutal regimes in the region, in order to secure its own *strategic interests* controlling oil reserves, preserving its own *economic interests*. It is a story of the last forty years of US foreign policy in the Arab region, its petro-military complex more vicious now with its *ambitions of global hegemony*, the new world order, and the new American Century:

But there are other voices: voices of conscience, voices of compassion: voices from the American street, here is the voice of a poet, that reaches across to a little corner on the Arab street, the poem written in another moment of time:

> Tremors of your network
> cause kings to disappear.
> Your open mouth in anger
> makes nations bow in fear.
>
> Your bombs can change the seasons,
> obliterate the spring.
> What more do you long for?
> Why are you suffering?
>
> [...]
>
> Seas shift at your bidding,
> your mushrooms fill the sky.
> Why are you unhappy?
> Why do your children cry?
>
> They kneel alone in terror
> with dread in every glance.
> Their nights are threatened daily
> by a grim inheritance.
>
> You dwell in whitened castles
> with deep and poisoned moats
> and cannot hear the curses
> which fill your children's throats.[4]

Listening to the poem from across the seas, understanding the story of the barbarians across time, knowing the wisdoms written in our history, in our memory.

As they gather today in Brussels for a US/EU/UN/NATO meeting to cancel the debt of Iraq, we must ask them what debt is *owed to Iraq*, what *reparations* will they pay for all the death and destruction of a people, of a civilization?

How will they calculate what is owed?

As they look into the eyes of the children, what stories will they tell them?

Will they tell them that once, not-so-long-ago, when thousands of Iraqis were being massacred, they looked away; that they preferred to look to the future created by the warmongers.

That they listened to their doublespeak, validated their political somersaults, erasure and extermination was their script: even as they made the UN irrelevant *empire building* is their finale.

And as they look into the eyes of their children, will they tell them that they had *no answers* and that all that they accepted were only *violent* ones? What will they tell the children?

They must listen to other stories: stories that come from the *corners of the Arab street*—stories from Iraqi mothers, from Abu Ghraib,
stories that come *from people of conscience* all over the world,
stories of courage and commitment; stories of harmony and hope:
stories of the dignity of a people,
stories that come from the children
tortured, terrorized, traumatized
in wars, civilized or uncivilized,
children from the tears, *children of the storm*,
children of the stars;
they offer a hope,
they speak of a justice,
a justice that will stop the curse of *greed and violence and war*;
Is not this what this war of occupation is all about?
Because only justice, only justice can stop a curse!

May I leave you with the very poignant hope of the Palestinian poet Mahmoud Darwish who reminds us to:

pay attention to the drunkenness of light

even as light as the butterfly
in the darkness of the tunnel.

I thank you for listening.

Appendix
The Courts held over the years (1992–2005) are:

Asian Court of Women on Violence Against Women
December 1993–January 1994. Lahore, Pakistan.
With the Simorgh Women's Collective.

Asian Court on War Crimes Against Women
March 1994. Tokyo, Japan.
In collaboration with 64 women's groups in Japan.

India Court of Women on Crimes Against Dalit Women
March 1994. Bangalore, India.
With the Women's Voice, India.

International Court of Women on Women on Reproductive Technologies
September 1994. Cairo, Egypt.
With UBINIG of Bangladesh

"Speaking Tree: Women Speak"
Asia Court of Women on Crimes Against Women and the Violence of Development
January 1995. With Vimochana, India.

Asian Court of Women on Trafficking and Tourism
June 1995. Kathmandu, Nepal.
With 200 Nepali NGOs working on trafficking issues.

Mahkamet El Nissa: Permanent Court of Women in the Arab World
June 1995. Beirut, Lebanon.
With women's and human-rights organizations in Tunisia and Lebanon.

World Court of Women on Violence Against Women
September 1995. Beijing, China.
With over 100 women's human-rights groups from all over the world.

Mahkamet El Nissa: Women and the Laws
March 1998. Beirut, Lebanon.

Mahakama Ya Wa Mama Wa Africa: Africa Court of Women
24–26 June 1999. Nairobi, Kenya.
With women's human-rights groups in Africa.

Nga Wahine Pasifika: The Pacific Court of Women on Uranium Mining, Nuclear Testing, and the Land
September 1999. Aotearoa, New Zealand.
With the Maori Women's Network.

Mediterranean Forum on Violence Against Women
November 1999. Casablanca, Morocco.
With Amal, Morocco and Crinali, Italy.

International Court of Women on the Economic Blockade
November 1999. Havana, Cuba.
With El Taller, Central America, Cuban Women's Federation and Institute of Philosophy.
Reheld during the World Social Forum, Puerto Allegre, January 2003.

World Court of Women Against War, for Peace
8 March 2001. Cape Town, South Africa.
With an International Coordinating Committee and
a network of local women's and human-rights organizations

World Court for Women Against Racism
30 August 2001. Durban, South Africa.

With the Institute for Black Research, University of Natal; the University of the Western Cape, Women's Support Network, Cape Town; the Durban Social Forum, Sangoco and several other national and international NGOs

Australian Court on Refugees and Indigenous Women
4 December 2001. Sydney, Australia.
University of New South Wales with ANCORW

South Asia Court of Women on the Violence of Trafficking and HIV/AIDS
11–13 August 2003. Dhaka, Bangladesh.
With United Nations Development Program and UBINIG, Bangladesh

World Court of Women on US War Crimes (WTI-Mumbai)
18 January 2004. At the World Social Forum, Mumbai, India.
With International Action Center, US; Arab and Africa Research Center, Egypt; Institute for Black Research, South Africa Center for Development Studies, India; and several other local and international NGOs.

Australian Court on Refugees and Indigenous Women
April, 2004. Sydney, Australia.
University of New South Wales with ANCORW

Africa Court of Women on the Violence Against Women
10 December 2004. At the Africa Social Forum, Lusaka, Zambia.
With the Africa Social Forum and several other local and regional NGOs

Africa Court of Women: Lives, Livelihoods, Lifeworlds
29 January 2005. At the World Social Forum, Porto Alegre, Brazil.
With the Africa Social Forum and several other regional and international NGOs

International Court of Women against Neoliberal Policies in Latin America
February 2005. Havana, Cuba.
In association with the Institute of Philosophy and Galfisa

Alternatives for an Alternative Future
Biju Matthew

I cannot speak of this war by itself, but as many of you have constantly reminded us over the last three days—this war and its waging is deeply embedded in a social and economic trajectory.

But I do want to begin with a statistic that has also been mentioned several times over the last three days—that over 100,000 Iraqi civilians and close to 2,000 US soldiers have died. However, I wish to use this statistic in a way that may seem initially irreverent and I want you to bear with me for a few seconds. In this equation of the number of dead, there is one problem... that the number of civilians are endless and the number of troops are limited, especially when we note the fact that for the third straight quarter the US army has fallen short of its recruitment targets, and given that one of the most significant recruitment communities—the impoverished African-American youth—have not come forward to join the army. In other words, it is almost certain that the US will lose this war. However, the problem behind such a statement is the process of losing, and what they will do in the process of losing:

1. They will have made irreparable changes to the Iraqi economy, which are already well underway; 2. They will have torn asunder the fabric of Iraqi social and cultural life; 3. They will have inserted into the political orbit a whole bunch of political actors who are just as bad if not worse than Saddam; 4. And as the army bottoms out, there will more madness in terms of numbers killed for no cause, and the Abu Ghraibs, systematic as they already are, will only get worse.

I develop this context of inevitable loss but unimaginable pain and suffering to put into place two broad points:

1. That this context tells us that if the objective of the antiwar movement is to end the occupation in the shortest possible time frame, then it must find ways of weakening the American state and not believe that moral suasion or simple political pressure will do the task. I say this in such a pointed way because I believe that the global antiwar movement, which achieved something that has never before been achieved in history—produced a united cry of no to the war by fifteen million people—needs to shift course. The movement's logical starting point was

indeed to appeal to the idea of democracy and freedom and self-determination within the liberal bourgeois state, and hope that a moral and legal framework would crack the American and British states. What this does not factor in is imperialism and the very specific and current context of global capitalism. The relationship between neoliberalism and imperialism is precisely in the fact that what was an emergent neoliberal regime has been captured by the neocons, who find imperialism the far more attractive option. We must understand that this last 25 years is, historically speaking, the most serious moment of consolidation of class power since the periods immediately preceding and following the bourgeois revolutions. In other words, we must cease to act with democracy and freedom as the guiding principles of our thoughts and actions, and instead single-mindedly focus on the logic of imperialism and neoconservatism as our primary reality and target. In this context, this tribunal, I feel, inaugurates that moment, for we focus intently and sharply on the criminality of the American and British action. We must remember that, unlike freedom and democracy, the idea of international law and the criminality of wars of aggression were concepts fundamentally created as a bulwark against imperialism in the immediate context of the second global imperialist war that we call World War II. I would go so far as to say that democracy and freedom were mere handmaidens in the efforts of the antiwar movement of that time, whether they realized it or not. In this sense, this tribunal has already embarked on a historic task, which we all have to collectively see to completion. The tribunal's capacity to create a strategic discourse of criminality is core to our future work for the ways in which the idea of criminality has valence at multiple levels—social, political, and legal.

2. The second aspect of understanding our task as weakening the American state is that we should realize that the people doing the most effective job of that right now are the Iraqis themselves, and in that sense a specific part of the leadership of the antiwar movement belongs to them in particular and to the third world in general. What this means for the global antiwar movement is that our demonstrations and shows of strength can no longer be designed to fit a weekend of self-expression, but rather, if we understand Iraqi resistance as a different kind of self-expression born out of sheer necessity, then we must respond to it. And if we feel that our movements are not strong enough to do that, then we should get to the task of building it for such reasons.

In this context, I see the lull in the antiwar movement in the West—post–Republican National Convention in the US and pre-election in UK—as a really positive development, because I do firmly believe, at least in the case of the US, that the focus has begun to shift and the antiwar movement has moved to a new mode wherein the focus is on the sectors of society that are directly impacted by this war there—the families of soldiers, the parents of high-school students most susceptible to recruitment, etc.

But our vision has to expand even beyond this. This is what I meant when I said at the beginning that I cannot speak about this war by itself but only within the context of the social and economic logic it's embedded in.

The theater of the street is the ultimate arbitrator. The theater of the street is where hope is built and the possibility of the future is kept alive. And to the extent that this is true I want to begin with three images of the street:
—15 February 2003: 15 million across the world.
—The massive demonstrations against the coup that knocked Chavez out of office for 48 hours, and the enormous street presence of Chavez supporters in the days just preceding the referendum.
—The Bolivian struggle of the last several weeks, which was preceded by the water struggle in Cochabamba.

If we look at these three images we find that they are each of a different character.

The idea of sovereignty has a long history that begins with the body of the monarch, which is then split after the birth of bourgeois democracies into a process of transfer between the people and the state.

In this struggle over sovereignty, we learn from the people again that sovereignty is not a state of being but merely a process—where the split inaugurated by the bourgeois revolutions needs to be re-enacted often, wherein the people need to retake the aspect of sovereignty that they had handed to the state back again.

I am saying all this in the context of what I have already characterized as the period of the most significant consolidation of capitalist class power. It is a moment where there is a revolution in process, except it is in the direction that none of us wish to acknowledge. The last 30 years of hyper-consumerism have resulted in a condition where the very core of the human condition has been rewritten.

The WTI as an Alternative: An Experimental Assertion
WTI Istanbul Coordination

Ay e Berktay

The five people making this presentation now are certainly not *the* organizers of the World Tribunal on Iraq. Neither are they the leaders or coordinators of this work or the related process. This work as a whole is the outcome of the non-hierarchical, collective labor of thousands of people from all over the world and hundreds from Turkey, especially from Izmir and Istanbul. The work of many volunteers who have recently joined us, the help of our translators, and in fact, the support of all concerned, including yourselves, have made this accomplishment possible. It is, thus, necessary to begin this presentation by stressing this very important point.

We wanted to submit the process of the World Tribunal on Iraq for the evaluation of the Jury before this session was concluded. We thought that incorporating the process itself into the assessment and the recommendations of these hearings about the process concerning the war on Iraq would be suitable and constructive.

What we are doing is directly concerned with the act of reclaiming justice. At this point, we do not solely turn to some superior authorities for a judgment and action pertaining to justice. We believe that we have the power and the authority to do this. And to this end, as the "content committee" of the Istanbul session, we prepared a collective presentation about the WTI process.

Two years ago today, on 26 June 2003, the first meeting during which the World Tribunal on Iraq began to materialize was held in Brussels as part of a workshop at the Conference of European Peace and Human Rights Networks organized by the Bertrand Russell Peace Foundation.

They violated everything so flagrantly, they assaulted our futures so blatantly, and they continued their mean ways despite such global opposition from divergent groups and sectors that *it was impossible not to rise up in protest.*

It was, indeed, this naked injustice and outrageous violence that gathered together jurists and people who shrank from the word "tribunal" and whose relationship with "laws" consisted solely of appearing before courts on the occasion of breaking various laws. And this assemblage taught us all a lot.

What inspired us was the Russell Vietnam war crimes tribunal.

We believed in ourselves. We did not regard ourselves as inferior subjects who could only be expected to come up with evidence on the basis of which the superior authorities would run assessments and make judgments, but also as active subjects, capable of making evaluations and reaching a judgment to reclaim justice, as well as taking action to have these decisions implemented.

Our network expanded in a surprisingly rapid manner. Underlying the speed with which the idea of calling the criminals to account grew was our confidence in our ability to evaluate and to act as active subjects in reclaiming justice on the basis of this evaluation. The Jakarta Peace Conference, the Russell Foundation, and the antiwar assemblies of the European and World Social Forums supported this endeavor.

When we first embarked on this project we aimed, among other goals, to disclose the truth, to create a historical record, to emphasize that we do not accept the status quo imposed on us through military-economic force, to contribute to the prevention of future aggression, and to enable the current aggression to be brought to an end.

We wanted this tribunal to be more than a discussion among ourselves; we wanted it to be a strong voice that would reach out to the world and even beyond the circles of the antiwar movement.

We did not want this tribunal to be a show ornate with slogans, but a serious and veritable study based on testimonies, reports, and findings.

We wanted this tribunal to be not only a legal and academic study but also a dynamic piece of work that kept abreast of a campaign inter-connected with the antiwar movement.

Until the first coordination meeting, held in Istanbul on 26–29 October 2003, two important discussions took place among the members of the international team:

Would we try Saddam? If we did not try him, would we lose on our credibility?

What sort of operating bylaw would the tribunal have?

The issue of whether or not to try Saddam was resolved before the meeting. It was agreed that the US aggression against Iraq had no connection with Saddam's presence and that, consequently, putting the discussion of Saddam's doings as a pre-condition to a discussion of the actions of the United States was unacceptable.

The discussions as to what sort of bylaw the tribunal would have indicated that we had different approaches to law and the sense of justice. The Istanbul meeting was to provide the setting for these discussions and differences to be concluded and wrapped up in an inclusive way which did not call for the exclusion of differences and varying approaches.

Müge Gürsoy Sökmen
Some notes from the minutes of the International Coordination Meeting in Istanbul, 27–29 October 2003:
From the position statement read at the start of the meeting:

This is not a theatrical display of how the officially set up courts and tribunals should have acted and decided and operated if they had upheld international law as they are supposed to. This would belittle our endeavor and undermine it rather than strengthening it.

We should remain what we are, an initiative of global civil society, and reflect this in our forms and aims. We should rigorously uphold international law. But international law is not in essence a series of procedures and forms. It is the content. We should adopt a flexible form and at the same time rigorously seek to apply international law. We should also keep in mind that many bodies that in procedure and form claim to stick to international law are in effect condoning its violation.

Comments:
Lieven (from the Brussels Tribunal): If we say, the tribunal has the power to prosecute, we give ourselves a power we don't have, which is exactly what the state of exception, that Bush and others, do. So we mirror the state of exception. Very well voiced by Ken Coates, beware of mock tribunal. Very well voiced by Susan George, I don't like this idea of people's courts that are just "mock" in the worst sense of the word. So we have to watch that, because saying that we have the power to prosecute is not true.

Herbert (Philippines): Second important thing we have to address is, who do we get our legitimacy from? Who is our constituency? On whose behalf are we acting?

Eman (Iraq): I have the same question of legitimacy, in fact I am going to tell you a very short story. Before I came here on Thursday, I went to a human-rights organization, I told them about this tribunal. The first question a lawyer there asked me was what kind of legality you have, what kind of authority you have? And when we were talking, a woman came in the human-rights organization, she is very poor and very old and she has a file of documents. Her daughter was burned by the explosion of a car because of the hitting of a missile on it, on 14 April. She went to many places, to US bases, she wanted the body of her daughter, to bury her. Up to last Thursday they gave her no answer. So he asked, what can this tribunal do for this woman. In Baghdad now there are many human-rights organizations. Wherever you go, you find heaps of files about human-rights violations, about civilian casualties, compensation issues, injuries, damages, many... So what can this tribunal do to these people, to these issues?

Seishi (Japan): We are not doing just a political campaign; in order for the tribunal to be politically influential and have a greater political impact, we have to stick to the international law or legal procedure. International law is not perfect at the moment, so in order to raise the level of international law, and finally to illegalize war itself, the tribunal should issue, in addition to the final decision, we should issue some recommendations.

Jan (Sweden): I was in the UN human-rights mechanisms, they have put a lid on: "nothing must be discussed on any violations of human rights in Iraq after the US occupation." That was the formal decision by the Commission on Human Rights this summer. No examination of human-rights violations after the end of Saddam Hussein, only before. Maybe it should be one of the missions of this tribunal, to address the UN.

Sungur (Istanbul): Where do we get our legitimacy from? In Jakarta we talked about this a lot; there are people who think, as Jan does, that we should resurrect these international institutions, there are other people, who think, like myself, that we should perhaps look for other alternatives. Our language should be legal, poetic, and political.

Müge (the moderator): I had a chance to talk to each one of you during the break and you all agreed that we will be discussing these topics now. First we will start with discussing where we get our legitimacy from. Each one of you will have three minutes to tell your ideas about where you think we get our legitimacy from.

Leuren (a scientist): When we did the DU conference we had legal experts, scientists, medical doctors, activists, organizers, civilians, and veterans, and at first they didn't know how to work together, they knew different things. But we are all affected in different ways; that consensus also gives us legitimacy. But I am not a legal person, I'm a scientist, so I can't speak about that as well as other people.

Nicholas (Britain): Richard Falk emphasized what he called the promise of Nuremberg, that is, the idea that the individual has a right and a duty to say no to illegal state policy. Individuals have individual responsibility if their state is following criminal policy and there is some disagreement about the duty of every state.

John (Britain): We are legitimate because we are addressing a legitimate concern, doing it in a way which is responsible, and we are addressing ourselves to fellow citizens throughout the world to take this as an example of what needs to be done.

Jo (Brussels): I think that our legitimacy must be clearly based on the movements, the people who demonstrated against the war.

Lieven (Brussels): I think if official authorities fail, moral authorities have to intervene. So I think having top world authorities both as witnesses and jury members is really in a very concrete way reinforcing the moral authority of our endeavor.

Ayca (Turkey): For me the question of legitimacy is also temporal, because I see ourselves situated not only dispersed around globally, but also in a timeline, so I see myself at least operating in a tradition not only of the tribunals, but of, I would call it the tradition of oppressed people, who attempt to speak some kind of truth in the face of oppression. And since the question of legality and legitimacy are not necessarily the same thing, we do not need to leave it to experts of international law to decide whether we are legitimate or not.

Hilal-i Hulya (Izmir, Turkey): We could be legitimate on the basis of three factors. One, if we can be the common conscience of the world public opinion. Secondly, today there are no courts or tribunals who can judge the

US or UK; in the absence of such mechanisms, it is legitimate that we step forward and do this. And thirdly, we can base ourselves both on written humanitarian law and concepts which are established in the shared conscience of world public opinion but nonetheless have not yet been made into laws.

Gloria (US): I think the legitimacy comes from the people as a whole, the victims whose rights have been violated, and who are voiceless right now for that particular violation. But there are universal principles which have also been violated which can be used to give them voice. We are speaking also for the people to whom it might be happening in the future.

Daizo (Japan): This tribunal should employ ICC statute, Rome statute as criteria to try the war crimes. Since the ICC statute is not perfect, we have to supply by the international common law. Since the states do not observe the international law, it is the duty of us people to create a world based on the rule of law, not the rule of the jungle.

Eman: If we can tackle these crimes one by one and expose and talk and explain how it is a violation for the Iraqi people, I think for the Iraqi people we get legitimacy, because I am talking about legitimacy for the Iraqis. So I think we get our legitimacy from what we do, what we achieve.

Herbert: How do we concretize the people, that if we want to say that this is on behalf of the people, on behalf of all those opposed to war, this is on behalf of everyone who feels that their government did not do anything for them, how do we actually involve them in this process?

Ay e (from Istanbul): When we say legitimacy does legitimacy mean talking on behalf of others? I don't think so. We get our legitimacy from the fact that we, I participated in the protests, all of us participated. We are a part of it.

Jan: I agree that legitimacy of this tribunal movement comes from people of conscience who are upholding and defending the principles of international law in a situation where governments have failed to do so.

Müge (the moderator): If we go as broad as the antiwar movement, which I think we should, it will include all of us. Individualists, anti-globalization activists, anti-imperialists. I may feel I am acting only as a person, representing nobody but myself, because I feel personally attacked, that may be my reason for contributing to this tribunal, and you may be contributing because you believe this superpower should be stopped and only because of that. So I do believe we are not so far away from each other concerning legitimacy, so if you feel like me, I think we could put this matter in our pocket and continue with the next agenda.

Lieven: What should be done I think is that somebody tries to summarize main things.

Tonight. Lieven, Gloria, Paola, Sungur, Jan.
(Agreed!)

And the final outcome:

The legitimacy of the project
A war of aggression was launched despite the opposition of people and governments all over the world. However, there is no court or authority that will judge the acts of the US and its allies. If the official authorities fail, then authority derived from universal morals and human rights principles can speak for the world.

Our legitimacy derives from:
—the failure of official international institutions to hold accountable those who committed grave international crimes and constitute a continued menace to world peace
—being part of the worldwide antiwar movement which expressed its opposition to this invasion
—the Iraqi people resisting occupation
—the duty of all people of conscience to take action against wars of aggression, war crimes, crimes against humanity, and other breaches of international law
—the struggles of the past to develop systems of peaceful coexistence and prevent future aggression and breaches of the UN Charter
—giving voice to the voiceless victims of this war, articulating the concerns

of civil society as expressed by the worldwide social justice and peace movements

—the will to bring the principles of international law to the forefront

Further, our legitimacy will be earned as we proceed to achieve the aims stated in this document.

I would like to thank all of you here who have allowed us to show that it is possible to be powerful without exerting power on others, working non-hierarchically and in solidarity.

Thank you.

Hilal Küey

Dear members of the Jury, dear guests,

Was it a result of sheer coincidence that the tablets of the Khorasan Palace in Iraq, which survived through 26 centuries, were destroyed in the twenty-first century?

Or the question could be put forth as follows: Will the US be entitled to demolish these tablets with impunity on the basis of its declination to sign the Rome Statute?

If international law is to be reduced to statements of will between states and to previously signed conventions, as has been the case up to now, the work we are engaged in here will certainly seem pointless.

However, the right to judge, recognized as the exclusive domain of victors, provides them with an additional weapon: law.

Yet judgment is not something they need to resort to. Their rightfulness emanates from their military power. To be true to its word, law must build its interpretations on the rights of the vanquished.

Article 38 of the Statute of the International Court of Justice stipulates that, while the Court applies the prescribed documents, customs, rules, and principles in deciding disputes, this shall not prejudice the power of the Court to decide a case *ex aequo et bono*.

Article 38 also specifies general principles of law recognized by civilized nations among the instruments to be applied along with international conventions in making such judgment.

The antiwar movement that built up in the world before the war on Iraq declared its will pertaining to the illegality of this war and to the fact that the ambitions of the coalition did not coincide with the demands of the peoples of the world.

I remind those who defy this will, saying that peoples are neither nations, nor states, or official entities, that the United Nations Founding Charter opens with the words: "We, the peoples..." The UN charter does not say "we, the states" or "we, the governments" but it sets out saying "we, the peoples." In other words, the real willpower in safeguarding peace rests on human-to-human connection.

Thus, WTI aims to establish this genuine relationship both in its constitution process and during the hearings, while being aware that the act of holding a world tribunal, in itself, is an alternative method of putting forth opinions.

If world peace is to be constituted—and this is an absolute necessity for our world to continue to exist—we need to develop the bases for a different approach to justice, judgment, and institutions.

On this account, we demand that, while the Jury is making its decision, it take into consideration that this war, which has violated the collective conscience of the peoples of the world as well as international documents, in violating the law did not only breach some signed and stamped documents but also violated people's hopes and beliefs in the future, and that this, in fact, is the real atrocious crime and traumatic violation.

Otherwise, once again, we will be deprived of the human dignity that we have lost *en masse* in Iraq.

Properly speaking, the World Tribunal on Iraq is the story of the resistance to this shame. And resistance is, by all means, the guarantee of law.

Hülya Üçpınar

Honorable members of the Jury,

Similar to what Müge has just pointed out, the source of our legitimacy is not located in international law. But does that necessarily mean that we disclaim international law? Definitely, no.

International law and the sanctions mentioned in international codes of law have not been successfully used as solid arguments that could put a stop to the tragedy, to unlawful practices and illegitimacy in Iraq. The international organizations whose primary aims are to apply international documents, to implement customary law, and to guarantee that it is implemented failed to fulfill their duties. It must be underlined that the legitimacy of these organizations, which were incapable and powerless against the US and the occupying forces, is in fact based on international law. Thus, another point to be re-emphasized is that the balance of international powers that determine law also tries to determine the origins of legitimacy.

The WTI, whose legitimacy is not located in international law, does not claim to replace international mechanisms. We only demand that crimes be exposed and the criminals give account in the presence of the public for the crimes they have committed.

The fundamental principles of international law, written documents, the international customary law, and local laws are the legal means to have our demand evaluated.

However, we are of the opinion that these means are insufficient.

Even though the actions that are defined as crimes according to the common human conscience have not yet been defined by any written document of law, we are asking the Jury to evaluate them in the culminating decree.

You might ask whether taking the existent law as a basis is an act in defiance of law. Needless to say, our answer is "No."

Law is a dynamic social-political field, which is open for development. And we believe we can contribute to the development of international law by means of both the facts laid out by the prosecution and by the end decision of the jury. It is also obligatory to contribute to the improvement of law through the criticism of the existing jurisprudence.

It is of utmost benefit to take a look at the general structure of the hearings that have been going on for three days within the aforementioned scope.

Honorable Members of the Jury,

The below-mentioned presentations could be categorized totally differently by just arranging them in a different way than the prosecution has done. The prosecution based their arguments on the following basic categories and presented them accordingly.

The first one is called crimes against peace. Before all else, the essential issue of determining where the actions of the US and its allies can be placed within the general scope of international law was discussed.

Under this title, and within the scope of the crimes/war of aggression

defined below according to the frame set by international law
—the definition of aggression (1974 UN General Assembly Res.) and the definition of crime of aggression adopted by the ICC
—the destruction of the international legal and political system as a crime against peace
—people's right of self-determination (including post-war power transfer and the resistance in Iraq)
—PNAC and preemptive attack
—the illegality of the occupation
—the violation of the UN Charter on the use of force
   All this was taken up by qualified experts and through testimonies.

   However, we also demand that it be determined that the US and its allies have violated the will of the global antiwar movement in addition to the breach of positive law, as proven by means of the information, documents, and testimonials presented to you in the course of these last three days.

   The WTI prosecution has studied the acts of the US and its allies from 20 March to 1 May 2003 under a separate category. This time interval is the period during which the offense against Iraq was launched and then announced to have been "concluded" by the US. With regard to this clear-cut time period, the following subjects
—the use of weapons banned under international law and international humanitarian law
—the use of excessive/disproportionate force
—attacks against civilians
—the unaccountability of the mercenaries (UN convention, 1970)
were essentially considered and evaluated under the heading "war crimes."

   We demand that the actions of the US and its allies be discussed in the light of the evidence and the evaluations presented by witnesses and experts, and a final decision be made.

   After the invasion of Iraq and during the occupation, the US and its allies continued to breach the basic principles of law, the written laws and regulations as well as the international customary law, causing the wounds they have made in the human conscience to become mortal and deeper.

   In this respect, the operations after 1 May 2003 were evaluated under the heading "crimes against humanity" (pre-war sanctions, war, and occupation) and studied under the subheadings:

— the violation of national (Iraqi) law
—the use of weapons banned under international law and international humanitarian law
—the US and weapons of mass destruction
—depleted uranium weapons
—cluster bombs
—incendiary weapons (proportionality, legality)
—the use of excessive/disproportionate force
—attacks against civilians

Although the attacks against civilians were related to the intensive bombings that took place during the aggression against Iraq, neither the attacks nor the bombings were limited during the occupation and no boundaries of any sort were protected.

The attacks against the civilians were:
—general
—gender-based violence (rape, forced prostitution, and sexual slavery)
—attacks on non-military targets and vehicles of transportation (vs. collateral damage)
—use of cluster weapons on residential areas
—aerial attacks against the regime leaders
—indiscriminate missile attacks
—deliberate targeting of media outlets and journalists
—use of excessive force (proportionality)
—other human-rights violations (including torture and inhumane treatment of prisoners) in the form of "direct attacks by occupation forces," and they took place as a result of "failure to provide security"

In this section that dealt with the broad concept of "security," it was brought up that the occupying forces displayed
—failure to provide human security (gender security, security of movement, children's security, looting…)
—failure to provide access to health and education
—failure to secure a working infrastructure
—and that they limited the freedom of the Iraqi people at the checkpoints, exposed them to derogatory and malevolent treatment, and put restrictions on their freedom of movement

We demand that the Jury determine the aforementioned crimes of the US and its allies and also evaluate their actions with regard to "the impacts of militarization and culture of violence," "the impacts on the environment and natural heritage," and "the impacts on cultural heritage."

With their attacks and through the occupation of Iraq, the US and its allies did more than violate the Iraqi people and the natural, cultural, and historical heritage of Iraq. The consequences of their occupation and aggression are broad in scope and are also related to the future of humanity in its entirety.

In this respect, considering the issues pertaining to:

—the increasing gender violence in military families (US, UK, etc.)
—the global militarization and spreading of the culture of violence
—the privatization of war
—the creation of ethnic and religious hatred/intolerance
—the rise of political and religious extremisms (Christian fundamentalism in the US and Islamic fundamentalism)

As a whole, all the documents, opinions, evaluations, and testimonies put forth during the WTI process under the heading "global implications" will prove to be valuable.

As people from different regions and cultural environments of the world who have gathered here, we are aware that in addition to affecting the lives of Iraqi people, this aggression against Iraq and the country's occupation have deeply influenced our lives as well as our futures. Unfortunately, this effect will prove to last for many generations. However, we demand that the Jury take up the issues cited above in reaching their verdict to enable that at least the truth is restored and an accurate historical record is ensured at this specific point in time.

Ayça Çubukçu

In order to discuss the future actions and aspirations that the World Tribunal on Iraq may spark, it is necessary to put the global political field in which it was founded in perspective.

Within the last two years, one of the main aims of the World Tribunal on Iraq has been to register a counter-history so that what has happened in Iraq will never be forgotten. Shall we, however, be satisfied with this?

Since even before the war on Iraq had begun, millions of individuals and thousands of organizations and movements have participated in the numerous protests that have taken place around the world, while countless articles and petitions, chants, songs, and poems have circulated against the war on Iraq. The World Tribunal on Iraq has been a project arising from and aiming to organize this reaction—this rejection—in order to express and strengthen the antiwar resistance collectively and globally by embedding the opposition to this outrageous war in concrete evidence and testimony.

However, even if the WTI achieves its goal of strengthening the global antiwar movement, what can it hope to concretely accomplish now and in the future? After all, some say, neither the global antiwar movement, even as expressed on 15 February 2003, nor the World Tribunal on Iraq has any so-called enforcement power. At this point, it is possible to pose some further questions: where today is the global political field? Furthermore, within the global political field, except for that of (some) nation-states and the few international institutions that are nonetheless predicated on the consent of nation-states for their operation, whose "enforcement power," and under which conditions, can we talk about?

The records of the horrifying war and occupation that the Iraqi people have been bloodily forced into—these records that are kept with integrity, labor, and care—as well as the collective global subject keeping the records through the World Tribunal on Iraq have the potential to contribute to the perpetual metamorphosis of international law. However, regarding the potential and direction of this metamorphosis, the global tribunal network forms a broad and diverse political spectrum. Among the ones who support the World Tribunal on Iraq, there are those who find it sufficient that international law and its institutions be amended within its existing framework. On the other end of the spectrum, there are those who hold that as long as the international political field and international law are constituted on the basis of nation-states—at *this* historical juncture, operating through the presupposition of the legal impunity of the most powerful nation-states—it is mistaken to hold naïve expectations with regard to the potential transformation of international law and its institutions. Further still, it needs to be debated whether the so-called international community—often cited as the source of such legal transformations—is really effective and in which ways and by whom it is open to manipulation.

Having thus situated the global political field, it can be asserted that, perhaps, the political value of the World Tribunal on Iraq is not to be located in its potential "enforcement power," but in the fact that it constitutes, on the one hand, a civil global collective subject acting as a counterpart in the field of the force of nation-states, and on the other hand in the field of action and imagination that the World Tribunal on Iraq has created and will create in the future.

Without a doubt, Istanbul constitutes both an end and a beginning for the World Tribunal on Iraq. There are diverse hopes within the global world tribunal network on how the WTI process—and we may say, experiment—might take shape in the future. What is clear is that one of the next steps with utmost priority is the dissemination of the findings of the tribunal in such a way as to be employed in the service of strengthening the global antiwar movement. It is difficult to foresee precisely all of the ways in which the World Tribunal on Iraq will be drawn on—the ways in which it will be received as a call to further action and resistance against the illegal and illegitimate war on Iraq. To affirm a few, the persistent, organized will and the findings constituted through the World Tribunal on Iraq can be used in applications to the International Criminal Court; in the assertions of conscientious objectors around the world; in calls to boycott corporations profiting from the countless opportunities for exploitation created by the war on Iraq, as well as in local and global antiwar campaigns.

As long as our current predicament—namely, the legal impunity enjoyed by the United States and the paralysis of international institutions in the face of the invasion and occupation of Iraq, this predicament from which the World Tribunal on Iraq has emerged—does not change in revolutionary ways, it is possible to distinguish the World Tribunal on Iraq itself and similar initiatives it will inspire in the future as a new way of resistance expressing the desire for global peace and justice and the creativity to which this desire gives birth.

Finally, just as we have been inspired by the Russell Tribunal, it is our hope that others will find strength and inspiration in the work of the World Tribunal on Iraq. Compared to the world-historical time of 1967, when the Russell Tribunal was held, we believe that the age of heroes, even when they are Bertrand Russell and Jean Paul Sartre—the co-chairs of the Russell Tribunal—*that* age of heroes is over. As we celebrate the non-hierarchical network and the labor of ordinary persons that have made possible the World Tribunal on Iraq, Bertolt Brecht's famous words assume new meaning: unhappy is the *movement* that needs a hero.

Although in these shameful times, we may be especially reminded that, as Walter Benjamin observes, "the tradition of the oppressed teaches us that the state of emergency in which we live is not the exception but the rule," the future—we know—is as open as ever. Further, it is ours—in hope and solidarity.

Closing Speeches

Closing Speech on Behalf of the Panel of Advocates
Richard Falk

For all of us this has been a powerful and illuminating three days of intense testimony by the Panel of Advocates. I think we are especially thankful to our sisters and brothers from Iraq who took special risks to help us understand the terrible reality of the Iraq war and its oppressive occupation. I want also to take this opportunity to acknowledge the extraordinary work of Ay e Berktay and Müge Sökmen, and their talented and dedicated colleagues here in Turkey, who made such a great effort over the past two years, and managed to turn what started as a dream of such a tribunal into the truly extraordinary reality we have experienced. They, together with many others, overcame obstacles of all kinds along the way that would have discouraged most of us; please join me in expressing our thanks to these two exceptional Turkish women and their many devoted colleagues.

As we come to the end of these proceedings, we now look to our Jury of Conscience to instruct us and the world how to regard the Iraq war from legal, moral, and political perspectives. For those of us who have listened to the many serious questions raised by the jurors in response to testimony by the advocates, we have great confidence that the outcome of these deliberations will bring to a climax the vision and dedication of the WTI experience.

I intend these few remarks to be of some modest help to the Jury. They reflect my understanding, which reflects the benefit of consultation with members of the Panel of Advocates, especially those with a background in international law.

Of particular importance are two preliminary issues; first, whether to treat the occupation of Iraq as distinct from or part of the Iraq war. If separate from the invasion, the occupation clearly engages the Fourth Geneva Convention; if continuous with the Iraq war, then it reminds us that the combat phases of the war never ended, as George W. Bush pretended way back on 30 May 2003, when he stood on an American aircraft carrier in an appearance staged for TV with the infamous banner bearing the words "Mission Accomplished" visible as he spoke.

The second preliminary remark has to do with the identity of this tribunal. It is not a formal court of law in any conventional sense. At the same time, it is not a mere gathering of persons opposed to the Iraq war that is devoid of legal significance and lacking in moral and political weight. Indeed, it is a tribunal that endeavors to do what no court and no agency of the UN has yet dared to do: To tell the truth about the Iraq War as clearly, comprehensively, and unconditionally as possible, and to draw from this truth the legal consequences, including the personal and collective accountability of political and military leaders, of international civil servants and governments, of corporate officers, of soldiers in the field and businessmen who came to a devastated Iraq to reap tainted profits, of journalists who abused their role by helping to orchestrate the war. In essence, this tribunal should neither adopt a legalistic voice that mimics the style of a national court, nor should it be shy about its authority to declare the law, and attach legal, moral, and political consequences that should be implemented as a matter of urgency, to the extent possible, by the foot soldiers of civil society. At the same time, the WTI should repudiate what several of our advocates have properly called "empire's law," shaping legality by reference to power rather than in response to norms of justice. It is this interpretation of international law as a vehicle of global justice that is supported by the evidence and testimonies that we have heard these past two days. There are various types of implementation that need to be considered: to form a tribunal similar to this one in Iraq and in the United States, places where the pain and need is the greatest; to organize a boycott throughout the world on American products associated with companies that have profited from the war and warmaking—that is, for us in America to "buy foreign" whenever possible, while for those elsewhere to avoid American exports; to mount a campaign throughout the world around the slogan "US out of Iraq." These and other initiatives seem to follow from the evidence and testimonies, but it is up to the Jury of Conscience to provide guidance for persons of conscience throughout the world with respect to follow-up actions.

In approaching international law I would like to make several comments:

—While not mimicking regular courts that serve the state and are the province of lawyers, yet to show an awareness of the fundamental legal norms and express as strongly as possible the moral, political, and legal obligation to respect these norms, especially in matters of war and peace, and in relation to respect for the innocence of civilian society;

—And to exhibit responsiveness to the Nuremberg Obligation, which treats those who violate these norms as personally and criminally accountable, as individuals who should be indicted, prosecuted, and judged by a court with powers of direct penal enforcement;

—In fixing personal accountability, there should be lines drawn that distinguish degrees of responsibility based on levels of authority and clarity of criminal intent: I would suggest an inner circle of accountability to highlight the primary responsibility of Bush and Blair, and possibly their main partners in crime, including Donald Rumsfeld, Dick Cheney, Tommy Franks, Paul Wolfowitz, Alberto Gonzales;

—I would suggest a secondary level of accountability for officials and bureaucrats, for governments who actively and substantively supported the Iraq war either militarily, diplomatically, or economically, and for those of the corporate and financial world who pushed hard for a war that would bring their shareholders a windfall of profits;

—I would finally suggest a third level of legal accountability for policy planners who helped fabricate the lies, evidence, and arguments that produced the wars, the brain trust, so to speak, of American imperialism— inside and outside of government; and for journalists who willfully helped the US/UK with crucial misrepresentation that produced a climate of opinion made receptive to the war, or who are deliberately avoiding the awful and tragic truths about the occupation and distort in their dispatches and interpretative articles the true character of Iraqi national resistance;

—Beyond this legal accountability are degrees of moral and political accountability; journalists, bureaucrats, and soldiers who went along with criminal policies of the Iraq war deserve censure, but whose acts of participation may not rise to a level where criminal indictments seem justifiable.

Also, the Jury of Conscience is challenged to place this indictment of criminality and accountability in its larger geopolitical and historical setting. In this respect, the challenge is to repudiate as expressively as possible the American project to establish a global empire by mixing an exploitative ideology of neoliberalism with the weaponry of the Pentagon. It is also essential to link this imperial reality with a responsibility of peoples everywhere to resist this project, and by so doing, to stand in solidarity with those most severely victimized at the present historical moment—such as the Iraqi and Palestinian peoples.

We are confident that this Jury of Conscience will give the world a document that is at once persuasive, inspiring, and above all mobilizing; that it will draw unmistakable red lines that identify zones of criminal conduct, that it will offer political guidance and facilitate moral clarity. In effect, that despite not being a court of law in the familiar sense, that the judgment of this tribunal will help restore the authority of international law as a vehicle of global justice and as an instrument for truth telling. We all need to remember and celebrate the central reality: this tribunal—the WTI—was convened not to discover the truth about Iraq war, but to confirm the reality of its criminal nature; that this tribunal was not convened to debate whether "preventive war" was legal or not, but to repudiate the disgraceful efforts of the US/UK to rewrite "international law" so to as to legalize torture and validate aggressive war. We also must realize that this tribunal was not formed to celebrate the UN, but rather arose in part to express our grave disappointment that the organization, which supposedly represents the people of the world, nevertheless failed to lift a finger to protect the brave and long-abused people of Iraq against a war of aggression, nor to express support for the Iraqi resistance, which reflects the impulse of every national people to exercise their sacred right of self-determination. The convenors of the WTI were also vividly aware of the suffering caused to the people of Iraq resulting from sanctions administered under UN authority for twelve years, punishing the Iraqis in the aftermath of the Gulf War of 1991, which was undertaken with UN backing, thereby giving an unwarranted green light to war.

In closing, let me express the confidence of all of us gathered here in Istanbul that the Jury of Conscience will reach conclusions that accord with and reinforce precepts of global justice and truth telling, thereby reflecting the substance and assessments of the outstanding presentations made by our distinguished Panel of Advocates.

Closing Speech on Behalf of the Jury of Conscience
Arundhati Roy

W hen I was invited to be on the Jury by the WTI—yesterday, when they were making a film, they asked me, "Why did you agree? You must have had so many invitations; why did you choose this?" And I said, "You know, I feel so hurt that you are asking me this question. Because it's ours. Where else would I be? What other invitations would matter to me when we have to attend to this, this huge, enormous bloody thing?"

You know, since I'm not a lawyer, nor am I even much of an organizer, nor am I even somebody who has been particularly concerned about my legitimacy, I don't think in legal and bureaucratic terms. I didn't really go down the road of questioning who we are or who we represent, because to me it was a bit like somebody asking me whether I had the legitimacy to write a novel. I mean, we're just a group of human beings, whether we are five or ten or fifteen or ten million. Surely, we have the right to express an opinion, and surely, if that opinion is irrelevant, surely, if that opinion is full of false facts, surely, if that opinion is absurd, it will be treated as such, and if that opinion is, in fact, representative of the opinion of millions of people, it will become very huge.

So we don't need to really worry ourselves too much about defining ourselves. I think we need to worry about being very clear, being very honest, being very precise about what we think and express, that fearlessly and in solidarity with the values that all of us have so clearly expressed in so many ways here today, this last three days. Speaking as a writer, what I seek with complete greed, what I seek almost ruthlessly, is understanding. That is all I ever ask for, an understanding of the depth of this world we live in. And this was the gift that I received, and I will always be grateful for it.

To ask us why we are doing this, why is there a World Tribunal on Iraq, is like asking someone who stops at the site of an accident where people are dying on the road: Why did you stop? Why didn't you keep walking like everybody else?

While I listened to the testimonies yesterday, especially the testimonies of those who came from Iraq with the stories of the blood and the destruction and the brutality and the darkness of what is happening there, or the stories of that cold, calculated world where the business contracts are being made, where the laws are rewritten, where a country occupies another with no idea of how it's going to provide protection to people, but with such a sophisticated idea of how it's going to loot it of its resources. You know, the brutality or the contrast of those two things was so chilling.

There were times when I felt, I wish I wasn't on the Jury, because I want to say things. You know? I mean, I think that is the nature of this tribunal, that, in a way, one wants to be everything. You want to be on the Jury, you want to be on the other side, you want to say things. And I particularly wanted to talk a lot about—which I won't do now, so don't worry—but I wanted to talk a lot about my own, now several years of experience with issues of resistance, strategies of resistance, the fact that we actually tend to reach for easy justifications of violence and nonviolence, easy and not really very accurate historical examples. These are things we should worry about.

But at the end of it, today we do seem to live in a world where the United States of America has defined an enemy combatant, someone whom they can kidnap from any country, from anyplace in the world and take for trial to the US. An enemy combatant seems to be anybody who harbors thoughts of resistance. Well, if this is the definition, then I, for one, am an enemy combatant. Thank you.

Declaration of the Jury of Conscience of World Tribunal on Iraq—Istanbul, 23–27 June 2005

—27 June 2005, Istanbul

In February 2003, weeks before an illegal war was initiated against Iraq, millions of people protested in the streets of the world. That call went unheeded. No international institution had the courage or conscience to stand up to the threat of aggression of the US and UK governments. No one could stop them. It is two years later now. Iraq has been invaded, occupied, and devastated. The attack on Iraq is an attack on justice, on liberty, on our safety, on our future, on us all. We, people of conscience, decided to stand up. We formed the World Tribunal on Iraq (WTI) to demand justice and a peaceful future.

The legitimacy of the World Tribunal on Iraq is located in the collective conscience of humanity. This, the Istanbul session of the WTI, is the culmination of a series of twenty hearings held in different cities of the world focusing on the illegal invasion and occupation of Iraq. The conclusions of these sessions and/or inquiries held in Barcelona, Brussels, Copenhagen, Genoa, Hiroshima, Istanbul, Lisbon, London, Mumbai, New York, Östersund, Paris, Rome, Seoul, Stockholm, Tunis, various cities in Japan, and Germany are appended to this Declaration in a separate volume.

We, the Jury of Conscience, from ten different countries, met in Istanbul. We heard 54 testimonies from a Panel of Advocates and Witnesses who came from across the world, including from Iraq, the United States, and the United Kingdom.

The World Tribunal on Iraq met in Istanbul from 24 to 26 June 2005. The principal objective of the WTI is to tell and disseminate the truth about the Iraq war, underscoring the accountability of those responsible and underlining the significance of justice for the Iraqi people.

I. Overview of Findings

1. The invasion and occupation of Iraq was and is illegal. The reasons given by the US and UK governments for the invasion and occupation of Iraq in March 2003 have proven to be false. Much evidence supports the conclusion that a major motive for the war was to control and dominate

the Middle East and its vast reserves of oil as a part of the US drive for global hegemony.

2. Blatant falsehoods about the presence of weapons of mass destruction in Iraq and a link between al-Qaeda terrorism and the Saddam Hussein regime were manufactured in order to create public support for a "preemptive" assault upon a sovereign independent nation.

3. Iraq has been under siege for years. The imposition of severe, inhumane economic sanctions on 6 August 1990, the establishment of no-fly zones in the northern and southern parts of Iraq, and the concomitant bombing of the country were all aimed at degrading and weakening Iraq's human and material resources and capacities in order to facilitate its subsequent invasion and occupation. In this enterprise, the US and British leaderships had the benefit of a complicit UN Security Council.

4. In pursuit of their agenda of empire, the Bush and Blair governments blatantly ignored the massive opposition to the war expressed by millions of people around the world. They embarked upon one of the most unjust, immoral, and cowardly wars in history.

5. Established international political-legal mechanisms have failed to prevent this attack and to hold the perpetrators accountable. The impunity that the US government and its allies enjoy has created a serious international crisis that questions the import and significance of international law, of human-rights covenants, and of the ability of international institutions including the United Nations to address the crisis with any degree of authority or dignity.

6. The US/UK occupation of Iraq of the last 27 months has led to the destruction and devastation of the Iraqi state and society. Law and order have broken down, resulting in a pervasive lack of human security. The physical infrastructure is in shambles; the healthcare delivery system is in poor condition; the education system has virtually ceased to function; there is massive environmental and ecological devastation; and the cultural and archeological heritage of the Iraqi people has been desecrated.

7. The occupation has intentionally exacerbated ethnic, sectarian, and religious divisions in Iraqi society, with the aim of undermining Iraq's identity and integrity as a nation. This is in keeping with the familiar imperial policy of divide and rule. Moreover, it has facilitated rising levels of violence against women, increased gender oppression, and reinforced patriarchy.

8. The imposition of the UN sanctions in 1990 caused untold suffering and thousands of deaths. The situation has worsened after the occupation. At least 100,000 civilians have been killed; 60,000 are being held in US custody in inhumane conditions, without charges; thousands have disappeared; and torture has become routine.

9. The illegal privatization, deregulation, and liberalization of the Iraqi economy by the occupation regime has coerced the country into becoming a client economy that is controlled by the IMF and the World Bank, both of which are integral to the Washington Consensus. The occupying forces have also acquired control over Iraq's oil reserves.

10. Any law or institution created under the aegis of occupation is devoid of both legal and moral authority. The recently concluded election, the Constituent Assembly, the current government, and the drafting committee for the constitution are therefore all illegitimate.

11. There is widespread opposition to the occupation. Political, social, and civil resistance through peaceful means is subjected to repression by the occupying forces. It is the occupation and its brutality that has provoked a strong armed resistance and certain acts of desperation. By the principles embodied in the UN Charter and in international law, the popular national resistance to the occupation is legitimate and justified. It deserves the support of people everywhere who care for justice and freedom.

II. Charges

On the basis of the preceding findings and recalling the Charter of the United Nations and other legal documents indicated in the appendix, the Jury has established the following charges.

A. Against the Governments of the US and the UK

1. Planning, preparing, and waging the supreme crime of a war of aggression in contravention of the United Nations Charter and the Nuremberg Principles.

Evidence for this can be found in the leaked Downing Street memo of 23 July 2002, in which it was revealed: "Military action was now seen as inevitable. Bush wanted to remove Saddam through military action, justified by the conjunction of terrorism and WMD. But the intelligence and facts were being fixed around the policy." Intelligence was manufactured to willfully deceive the people of the US, the UK, and their elected representatives.

2. Targeting the civilian population of Iraq and civilian infrastructure by intentionally directing attacks upon civilians and hospitals, medical centers, residential neighborhoods, electricity stations, and water purification facilities. The complete destruction of the city of Falluja in itself constitutes a glaring example of such crimes.

3. Using disproportionate force and weapon systems with indiscriminate effects, such as cluster munitions, incendiary bombs, depleted uranium (DU), and chemical weapons. Detailed evidence was presented to the tribunal by expert witnesses that leukemia had risen sharply in children under the age of five residing in those areas that had been targeted by DU weapons.

4. Using DU munitions in spite of all the warnings presented by scientists and war veterans on their devastating long-term effects on human beings and the environment. The US administration, claiming lack of scientifically established proof of the harmful effects of DU, decided to risk the lives of millions for several generations rather than discontinue its use on account of the potential risks. This alone displays the administration's wanton disregard for human life. The tribunal heard testimony concerning the current obstruction by the US administration of the efforts of Iraqi universities to collect data and conduct research on the issue.

5. Failing to safeguard the lives of civilians during military activities and during the occupation period thereafter. This is evidenced, for example, by "shock and awe" bombing techniques and the conduct of occupying forces at checkpoints.

6. Actively creating conditions under which the status of Iraqi women has been seriously degraded, contrary to the repeated claims of the leaders of the coalition forces. Women's freedom of movement has been severely limited, restricting their access to the public sphere, to education, livelihood, political and social engagement. Testimony was provided that sexual violence and sex trafficking have increased since the occupation of Iraq began.

7. Using deadly violence against peaceful protestors, including the April 2003 killing of more than a dozen peaceful protestors in Falluja.

8. Imposing punishments without charge or trial, including collective

punishment, on the people of Iraq. Repeated testimonies pointed to "snatch and grab" operations, disappearances, and assassinations.

9. Subjecting Iraqi soldiers and civilians to torture and cruel, inhuman, or degrading treatment. Degrading treatment includes subjecting Iraqi soldiers and civilians to acts of racial, ethnic, religious, and gender discrimination, as well as denying Iraqi soldiers Prisoner of War status as required by the Geneva Conventions. Abundant testimony was provided of unlawful arrests and detentions, without due process of law. Well-known and egregious examples of torture and cruel and inhuman treatment occurred in Abu Ghraib prison as well as in Mosul, Camp Bucca, and Basra. The employment of mercenaries and private contractors to carry out torture has served to undermine accountability.

10. Rewriting the laws of a country that has been illegally invaded and occupied, in violation of international covenants on the responsibilities of occupying powers, in order to amass illegal profits (through such measures as Order 39, signed by L. Paul Bremer III for the Coalition Provisional Authority, which allows foreign investors to buy and takeover Iraq's state-owned enterprises and to repatriate 100 percent of their profits and assets at any point) and to control Iraq's oil. Evidence was presented of a number of corporations that had profited from such transactions.

11. Willfully devastating the environment, contaminating it by depleted uranium (DU) weapons, combined with the plumes from burning oil wells, as well as huge oil spills, and destroying agricultural lands. Deliberately disrupting the water and waste removal systems, in a manner verging on biological-chemical warfare. Failing to prevent the looting and dispersal of radioactive material from nuclear sites. Extensive documentation is available on air and water pollution, land degradation, and radioactive pollution.

12. Failing to protect humanity's rich archaeological and cultural heritage in Iraq by allowing the looting of museums and established historical sites and positioning military bases in culturally and archeologically sensitive locations. This took place despite prior warnings from UNESCO and Iraqi museum officials.

13. Obstructing the right to information, including the censoring of Iraqi media, such as newspapers (e.g., *Al-Hawza*, *Al-Mashriq*, and *Al-Mustaqila*) and radio stations (Baghdad Radio), the shutting down of the

Baghdad offices of Aljazeera Television, targeting international journalists, imprisoning and killing academics, intellectuals, and scientists.

14. Redefining torture in violation of international law, to allow use of torture and illegal detentions, including holding more than 500 people at Guantánamo Bay without charging them or allowing them any access to legal protection, and using "extraordinary renditions" to send people to be tortured in other countries known to commit human rights abuses and torture prisoners.

15. Committing a crime against peace by violating the will of the global antiwar movement. In an unprecedented display of public conscience, millions of people across the world stood in opposition to the imminent attack on Iraq. The attack rendered them effectively voiceless. This amounts to a declaration by the US government and its allies to millions of people that their voices can be ignored, suppressed, and silenced with complete impunity.

16. Engaging in policies to wage permanent war on sovereign nations. Syria and Iran have already been declared as potential targets. In declaring a "global war on terror," the US government has given itself the exclusive right to use aggressive military force against any target of its choosing. Ethnic and religious hostilities are being fueled in different parts of the world. The US occupation of Iraq has further emboldened the Israeli occupation in Palestine and increased the repression of the Palestinian people. The focus on state security and the escalation of militarization has caused a serious deterioration of human security and civil rights across the world.

B. Against the Security Council of the United Nations

1. Failing to protect the Iraqi people against the crime of aggression.

2. Imposing harsh economic sanctions on Iraq, despite knowledge that sanctions were directly contributing to the massive loss of civilian lives and harming innocent civilians.

3. Allowing the United States and United Kingdom to carry out illegal bombings in the no-fly zones, using false pretenses of enforcing UN resolutions, and at no point allowing discussion in the Security Council of this violation, and thereby being complicit and responsible for loss of civilian life and destruction of Iraqi infrastructure.

4. Allowing the United States to dominate the United Nations and hold itself above any accountability by other member nations.

5. Failure to stop war crimes and crimes against humanity by the United States and its coalition partners in Iraq.

6. Failure to hold the United States and its coalition partners accountable for violations of international law during the invasion and occupation, giving official sanction to the occupation and therefore, both by acts of commission and acts of omission, becoming a collaborator in an illegal occupation.

C. Against the Governments of the Coalition of the Willing
Collaborating in the invasion and occupation of Iraq, thus sharing responsibility in the crimes committed.

D. Against the Governments of Other Countries
Allowing the use of military bases and air space and providing other logistic support for the invasion and occupation, and hence being complicit in the crimes committed.

E. Against the Private Corporations which Have Won Contracts for the Reconstruction of Iraq and which Have Sued for and Received "Reparation Awards" from the Illegal Occupation Regime
Profiting from the war with complicity in the crimes described above of invasion and occupation.

F. Against the Major Corporate Media
1. Disseminating the deliberate falsehoods spread by the governments of the US and the UK and failing to adequately investigate this misinformation, even in the face of abundant evidence to the contrary. Among the corporate media houses that bear special responsibility for promoting the lies about Iraq's weapons of mass destruction, we name the *New York Times*, in particular their reporter Judith Miller, whose main source was on the payroll of the CIA. We also name Fox News, CNN, NBC, CBS, ABC, the BBC and ITN. This list also includes but is not limited to, the *Express*, the *Sun*, the *Observer*, and the *Washington Post*.

2. Failing to report the atrocities being committed against the Iraqi people by the occupying forces, neglecting the duty to give privilege and dignity to voices of suffering, and marginalizing the global voices for peace and justice.

3. Failing to report fairly on the ongoing occupation; silencing and discrediting dissenting voices and failing to adequately report on the full national costs and consequences of the invasion and occupation of Iraq; disseminating the propaganda of the occupation regime that seeks to justify the continuation of its presence in Iraq on false grounds.

4. Inciting an ideological climate of fear, racism, xenophobia, and Islamophobia, which is then used to justify and legitimize violence perpetrated by the armies of the occupying regime.

5. Disseminating an ideology that glorifies masculinity and combat, while normalizing war as a policy choice.

6. Complicity in the waging of an aggressive war and perpetuating a regime of occupation that is widely regarded as guilty of war crimes and crimes against humanity.

7. Enabling, through the validation and dissemination of disinformation, the fraudulent misappropriation of human and financial resources for an illegal war waged on false pretexts.

8. Promoting corporate-military perspectives on "security" which are counterproductive to the fundamental concerns and priorities of the global population and have seriously endangered civilian populations.

III. Recommendations

Recognizing the right of the Iraqi people to resist the illegal occupation of their country and to develop independent institutions, and affirming that the right to resist the occupation is the right to wage a struggle for self-determination, freedom, and independence as derived from the Charter of the United Nations, we the Jury of Conscience declare our solidarity with the people of Iraq.

We recommend:

1. The immediate and unconditional withdrawal of the coalition forces from Iraq.

2. That coalition governments make war reparations and pay compensation to Iraq for the humanitarian, economic, ecological, and cultural devastation they have caused by their illegal invasion and occupation.

3. That all laws, contracts, treaties, and institutions established under occupation which the Iraqi people deem inimical to their interests be considered null and void.

4. That the Guantánamo Bay prison and all other offshore US military prisons be closed immediately, that the names of the prisoners be disclosed, that they receive POW status, and receive due process.

5. That there be an exhaustive investigation of those responsible for the crime of aggression, war crimes, and crimes against humanity in Iraq, beginning with George W. Bush, president of the United States of America; Tony Blair, prime minister of the United Kingdom; those in key decision-making positions in these countries and in the coalition of the willing; those in the military chain-of-command who masterminded the strategy for and carried out this criminal war, starting from the very top and going down; as well as personalities in Iraq who helped prepare this illegal invasion and supported the occupiers.

We list some of the most obvious names to be included in such investigation:

—prime ministers of the coalition of the willing, such as Junichiro Koizumi of Japan, Jose Maria Anzar of Spain, Silvio Berlusconi of Italy, José Manuel Durão Barroso and Santana Lopes of Portugal, Roh Moo Hyun of South Korea, Anders Fogh Rasmussen of Denmark;

—public officials such as Dick Cheney, Donald H. Rumsfeld, Paul Wolfowitz, Colin L. Powell, Condoleezza Rice, Richard Perle, Douglas Feith, Alberto Gonzales, L. Paul Bremer from the US, and Jack Straw, Geoffrey Hoon, John Reid, Adam Ingram from the UK;

—military commanders beginning with Gen. Richard Myers, Gen. Tommy Franks, Gen. John P. Abizaid, Gen. Ricardo S. Sanchez, Gen. Thomas Metz, Gen. John R. Vines, Gen. George Casey from the US; Gen. Mike Jackson, Gen. John Kiszely, Air Marshal Brian Burridge, Gen. Peter Wall, Rear Admiral David Snelson, Gen. Robin Brims, Air Vice-Marshal Glenn Torpy from the UK, and chiefs of staff and commanding officers of all coalition countries with troops in Iraq;

—Iraqi collaborators such as Ahmed Chalabi, Iyad Allawi, Abdul Aziz al-Hakim, Gen. Abdul Qader Mohammed Jassem Mohan, among others.

6. That a process of accountability is initiated to hold those morally and personally responsible for their participation in this illegal war, such as journalists who deliberately lied, corporate media outlets that promoted racial, ethnic, and religious hatred, and CEOs of multinational corporations that profited from this war.

7. That people throughout the world launch nonviolent actions against US and UK corporations that directly profit from this war.

Examples of such corporations include Halliburton, Bechtel, the Carlyle Group, CACI Inc., Titan Corporation, Kellogg, Brown and Root (subsidiary of Halliburton), DynCorp, Boeing, ExxonMobil, Texaco, and British Petroleum. The following companies have sued Iraq and received "reparation awards": Toys 'R' Us, Kentucky Fried Chicken, Shell, Nestlé, Pepsi, Phillip Morris, Sheraton, Mobil. Such actions may take the form of direct actions such as shutting down their offices, consumer boycotts, and pressure on shareholders to divest.

8. That young people and soldiers act on conscientious objection and refuse to enlist and participate in an illegal war. Also, that countries provide conscientious objectors with political asylum.

9. That the international campaign for dismantling all US military bases abroad be reinforced.

10. That people around the world resist and reject any effort by any of their governments to provide material, logistic, or moral support to the occupation of Iraq.

We, the Jury of Conscience, hope that the scope and specificity of these recommendations will lay the groundwork for a world in which international institutions will be shaped and reshaped by the will of people and not by fear and self-interest, where journalists and intellectuals will not remain mute, where the will of the people of the world will be central, and human security will prevail over state security and corporate profits.

Arundhati Roy, India, Spokesperson of the Jury of Conscience
Ahmet Öztürk, Turkey
Ay e Erzan, Turkey
Chandra Muzaffar, Malaysia
David Krieger, US
Eve Ensler, US
François Houtart, Belgium
Jae-Bok Kim, South Korea
Mehmet Tarhan, Turkey
Miguel Angel de los Santos Cruz, Mexico
Murat Belge, Turkey
Rela Mazali, Israel
Salaam al-Jobourie, Iraq
Taty Almeida, Argentina

Appendix I: International Law

Explanatory Note

This international law appendix is intended to back up the Jury Statement that rests its assessments primarily on a moral and political appraisal of the Iraq war. The Statement relies upon the extensive testimony given in written and oral form by international law experts, who have world-class scholarly reputations, during the Istanbul culminating session of the World Tribunal on Iraq (WTI). It also reflects the testimony and submissions on related issues of war crimes and the failure of the United Nations to protect Iraq against aggression.

The Jury of Conscience was not a body composed of jurists or international law experts. It did not hear arguments supporting the legality of the invasion of Iraq as would have been made before a judicial body under the authority of either the state or an international institution acting on behalf of the international community. The World Tribunal on Iraq throughout all of its session proceeded from a sense of moral and political outrage of concerned citizens from all over the world with respect to the war. The tribunal was not interested in a debate solely as to legality. The legal issues were relevant to the extent that they added weight to the moral and political purpose of the tribunal, which was to expose the Iraq war as the crime it is, appealing to and drawing upon the deep bonds that link us all in our humanity. Therefore, the tribunal sought testimony and evidence to call into question the mantle of respectability thrown over the Iraq war by the aggressors, and the false impression disseminated by the mainstream media that the Iraq war was in any sense justified by political circumstances, moral considerations, or legal analysis.

The WTI is a worldwide process dedicated to reclaiming justice on behalf of the peoples of the world. It aims to record the severe wrongs, crimes, and violations that were committed in the process leading up to the aggression against Iraq, during the war, and throughout the ensuing occupation, continuing with unabated fury to this day. The role of international law is understood in light of these WTI goals.

The concerns of the WTI range much further than the demand for the implementation of international law, especially as much of this law currently serves the interests of wealth and power. Nevertheless, international law with respect to the use of force and recourse to war is important in relation to the work of the WTI. International law is useful for the WTI for the following reasons:

—International law grounds the political and moral demand for the criminal indictment and prosecution of those responsible for the Iraq war, and it clarifies the extent of criminal accountability as extending to corporate and media participation;

—International law rejects the dangerous imperialist claims of the United States and the United Kingdom to be exempt from international legal obligations.

In addition, the WTI makes use of international law to fulfill its mission:

—The WTI connects a call for global justice with the demand for the implementation of international law, but also for a rethinking of the premises and operations of international law so that it might be of greater relevance to the achievement of human security in the future;

—The WTI demands an interrogation as to why international institutions, particularly the United Nations, proved powerless against US unilateralism and aggression;

—The WTI insists that the United Nations exercise its constitutional responsibility to protect its members from aggression and illegal occupation;

—The WTI possesses the authority, as representing civil society, to declare and seek enforcement of international legal obligations when states and the United Nations fail to uphold international law in matters of war and peace.

It is important to distinguish:

—violations of international law, including the UN Charter, by a state;

—crimes associated with these violations committed by political and military leaders, government officials, corporations and their officers, soldiers and private contractors, journalists and media personnel.

Legal Analysis

—International law consists of (1) international treaties, including the UN Charter [see list of documents]; (2) international customary law [especially in relation to the conduct of states in war]; (3) international criminal law [a sub-category of (1) resting on treaties and agreements among states, based on the framework of the Nuremberg Judgment in

1945, unanimously affirmed by the UN General Assembly's adoption of the Nuremberg Principles in 1946, Res. 95(I)].

—In the war on Iraq, the three principles of customary international law have been violated: (1) Principle of Proportionality: force can only be used to attain permissible legal objectives, and then only to the extent required by "military necessity"; (2) Principle of Discrimination: force and weaponry can only be used if confined to military targets; indiscriminate weapons and tactics are prohibited; (3) Principle of Humanity: force must never be used to cause unnecessary suffering, and maximum care must be taken to protect civilian society, including its cultural heritage.

—The War on Iraq violates the Nuremberg Principles that set forth the following essential guidelines (as formulated by the International Law Commission of the UN in 1950 in response to request from General Assembly):

Principle I

Any person who commits an act which constitutes a crime under international law is responsible therefore and liable to punishment.

Principle II

The fact that local law does not impose a penalty for an act which constitutes a crime under international law does not relieve the person who committed the act from responsibility under international law.

Principle III

The fact that a person who committed an act which constitutes a crime under international law acted as head of state or responsible government official does not relieve him from responsibility under international law.

Principle IV

The fact that a person acted pursuant to order of his government or of a superior does not relieve him from responsibility under international law, provided a moral choice was in fact possible to him.

Principle V

Any person charged with a crime under international law has the right to a fair trial on the facts and law.

Principle VI

The crimes hereinafter set out are punishable as crimes under international law:

a) Crimes against peace:

i. Planning, preparation, initiation, or waging of a war of aggression or a war in violation of international treaties, agreements, or assurances;

ii. Participation in a common plan or conspiracy for the accomplishment of any of the acts mentioned under (i).

b) War crimes:

Violations of the laws or customs of war which include, but are not limited to, murder, ill treatment, or deportation to slave labor or for any other purpose of the civilian population of or in occupied territory, murder or ill treatment of prisoners of war, of persons on the seas, killing of hostages, plunder of public or private property, wanton destruction of cities, towns, or villages, or devastation not justified by military necessity.

c) Crimes against humanity:

Murder, extermination, enslavement, deportation and other inhuman acts done against any civilian population, or persecutions on political, racial or religious grounds, when such acts are done or such persecutions are carried on in execution of or in connection with any crime against peace or any war crime.

Principle VII

Complicity in the commission of a crime against peace, a war crime, or a crime against humanity as set forth in Principle VI is a crime under international law.

Violations and Crimes

I. The invasion of Iraq on 20 March 2003, together with the continuing occupation of Iraq, constitutes a violation of the core obligation of the United Nations Charter:

—resolving international conflicts by recourse to force or the threat of force is unconditionally prohibited by Article 2(4) of the Charter;

—the only exception to this probation is the right of states to act in self-defense against a prior armed attack as allowed by Article 51, but with the requirement that the defending state report its claim to the Security Council;

—the claims of the US/UK governments that are based on doctrines of "preemption" or "preventive war" have no standing in international law, and reliance on such specious arguments was in any event unsupported by facts; even if weapons of mass destruction had existed in Iraq it would not provide a legal justification for the invasion; nor would the claim that "regime change" would liberate the Iraqi people from dictatorial rule violative of human rights;

—with respect to Iraq there existed no basis for claiming self-defense or acting on the basis of a Security Council authorization; the invasion of Iraq and the subsequent occupation of the country constitutes a continuing aggression against a sovereign state and member of the UN in violation of international law;

—the cumulative effect of these violations is to create a strong factual and legal foundation for the indictment, prosecution, and punishment of the individuals responsible for planning, initiating, and waging a crime of aggression against Iraq.

II. The war on Iraq by the invading military forces, principally those of the United States and United Kingdom, and subsequent occupation, violated the law of war such as the Geneva Conventions on the Humanitarian Laws of War (1949), Additional Protocols to Geneva Conventions (1977), and Hague Conventions on the Laws of War (1899, 1907) in numerous respects, including the following:

—use of cluster bombs, napalm, depleted uranium;

—bombing of civilian targets and areas (e.g., markets, restaurants, media facilities, religious and cultural sites);

—intense and indiscriminate military operations against many cities and towns causing massive civilian casualties (e.g., Najaf, Falluja);

—repeated and systematic use of torture and degrading treatment of Iraqi civilian and military personnel detained in prison facilities or covertly transferred to foreign countries known for torture and severe prison conditions;

—overall failure to protect the civilian population and their property, cultural heritage sites (shootings at checkpoints; house raids; lootings of museums and other cultural sites; refusal to assess extent of civilian death and damage) [see especially common Article 3 of the Geneva Conventions, imposing duty to take special measures to protect civilian population to the

extent possible] (Also Geneva Convention IV specifies the obligations of the occupying power in Articles 47–78);
—the cumulative effect of this pattern of flagrant and extensive violations of the laws of war is to create the foundation for the indictment, prosecution, and punishment of those individuals responsible, as policy makers, leaders, and as implementers at various levels of command;
—Article 1 of the Geneva Conventions reads: "The High Contracting Parties, including US/UK, undertake to respect and ensure respect for the present Convention in all circumstances." The American legal specialists in the Office of the Legal Counsel in the White House, in the Justice Department, and Department of Defense who advised on the "legality" of torture and other behavior that violates the law of war are priority targets for indictment and prosecution.

III. The occupation of Iraq has fragrantly violated the right of self-determination of the people of Iraq:
—Article 1 of the International Covenant on Economic, Social, and Cultural Rights and of the International Covenant on Political and Civil Rights (1966): "(1) All peoples have the right of self-determination. By virtue of that right they freely determine their political status and freely pursue their economic, social and cultural development";
—It is evident that the occupation, by its decrees, practices, imposition of an interim government, managed elections, and administered constitution-making process has violated the right of self-determination of the Iraqi people, a fundamental element of international human rights law.

IV. The occupation of Iraq has included massive abuses of the Iraqi civilian population, including the widespread and pervasive reliance on torture, the practice of which is unconditionally prohibited by international law:
—Article 5 of the Universal Declaration of Human Rights: "No one shall be subjected to torture or cruel, inhuman or degrading treatment or punishment (repeated in Article 7 of International Covenant on Civil and Political Rights [1966], including Article 4(2) that affirms there are no exceptions, even in conditions of war or emergency) and further confirmed by the widely ratified treaty, the Convention Against Torture and Other Cruel, Inhuman or Degrading Treatment or Punishment (1984).

V. The United Nations has failed to uphold its obligations to protect sovereign states, especially its members, from violations of their legal rights to political independence and territorial integrity, passively allowing Iraq to be threatened and attacked for twelve years prior to the invasion of 2003:

—the UNSC maintained sanctions on Iraq that had a demonstrated genocidal effect on the civilian population during the period 1991–2003;

—the UNSC refrained from censuring and preventing repeated air strikes within Iraq territory during the period 1991 to 2003;

—the UNSC refrained from censuring and preventing overt calls for the subversion and replacement of the Iraqi government, as well as the financing and training of exiles dedicated to armed struggle;

—the UNSC failed to condemn or act to prevent aggressive threats or the actual initiation and conduct of an aggressive war against Iraq in 2003, and has to a limited extent cooperated in the illegal occupation of Iraq since the invasion.

Conclusions

1. The Jury Statement is consistent with an objective understanding of international law, including the United Nations Charter.

2. Members of the United Nations and governments of sovereign states have legal obligations to uphold the Charter and act to ensure respect for the laws of war.

3. All three categories of Nuremberg Crimes are associated with the invasion and occupation of Iraq.

4. The International Criminal Court should indict, prosecute, and punish the perpetrators and collaborators for this aggression against Iraq and the related international crimes arising from the subsequent occupation of the country.

5. The ICC should be supplemented by a specially constituted international tribunal with authority to indict, prosecute, and punish for crimes committed before 2002 when the ICC was established and to the extent that crimes associated with states not parties to the ICC are not addressed.

6. The UNGA should be encouraged to implement international law with respect to the Iraq war and occupation.

7. National courts relying on universal jurisdiction should be urged to investigate and prosecute individuals associated with Nuremberg Crimes in Iraq.

8. Organs of civil society, including the WTI, should act to ensure that the recommendations and conclusions of the Jury Statement are promptly and fairly implemented.

Appendix II: List of Legal Documents

—Hague Convention IV Respecting the Laws and Customs of War on Land (1907)
—Protocol for the Prohibition of the Use in War of Asphyxiating, Poisonous or Other Gases, and of Bacteriological Methods (1925)
—General Treaty ("Pact of Paris") for the Renunciation of War as an Instrument of National Policy (1928)
—Universal Declaration of Human Rights (1948)
—Geneva Conventions (I–IV) on International Humanitarian Law (1949)
—Nuremberg Principles Recognized in the Charter of the Tribunal and in the Nuremberg Judgment (1950)
—European Convention on Human Rights and Fundamental Freedoms (1950)
—Convention on the Prevention and Punishment of the Crime of Genocide (1948)
—Convention on the Political Rights of Women (1953)
—Code of Conduct for the Armed Forces of the United States of America (1963)
—International Convention on the Elimination of all Forms of Racial Discrimination (1965)
—International Covenant on Economic, Social and Cultural Rights (1966)
—International Covenant on Civil and Political Rights (1966)
—American Convention on Human Rights (1969)
—Convention on the Prohibition of the Development, Production and Stockpiling of Biological Weapons and Toxin Weapons (1972)
—Universal (or Algiers) Declaration of the Rights of Peoples (1976)
—Principles of Co-Operation in the Detection, Arrest, Extradition and Punishment of Persons Guilty of War Crimes or Crimes Against Humanity (1973)
—Protocol Additional (I–II) to the Geneva Conventions of 1949 (1977)
—Convention on the Elimination of All Forms of Discrimination Against Women (1979)
—African Charter on Human and Peoples' Rights (1981)
—Convention Against Torture and Other Cruel, Inhuman or Degrading

Treatment or Punishment (1984)
—International Convention Against the Recruitment, Use, Financing and Training of Mercenaries (1989)
—Convention on the Rights of the Child (1989)
—Convention on the Prohibition of the Development, Production, Stockpiling and Use of Chemical Weapons (1992)
—Declaration for the Protection of War Victims (1993)
—Rome Statute of the International Criminal Court (1998)

List of WTI Sessions Held Worldwide

London, November 2003
Have war crimes been committed during the military operation on and the occupation of Iraq?

Mumbai, January 2004
By El Taller
World Court of Women on US War Crimes held at the World Social Forum, Mumbai, India.

London, February 2004
By INLAP, Peacerights, and CND
A legal inquiry into the invasion and military occupation of Iraq.

Copenhagen, March 2004
The privatization of Iraqi public establishments and resources; the arbitrary detention of more than 20,000 civilians.

Brussels, April 2004
Project for a New American Century and the ideological background of the war on Iraq.

New York, May 2004
War crimes and crimes of occupation; the violation of international law, of the United Nations, and of the will of the global antiwar movement.

Germany, June 2004
The violation of international law and the complicity of the German government in the sanctions, the war, and occupation.

Istanbul, June 2004
by the Istanbul Initiative
The destruction of cultural heritage.

New York, August 2004
by International Action Center

The declaration of the WTI findings worldwide; testimonies from US soldiers who refuse to fight.

Japan, October 2004
by International Criminal Tribunal on Iraq
The use of depleted uranium and the complicity of the Japanese government.

Stockholm, November 2004
The social, economic, and cultural effects of the occupation on the Iraqi society.

Japan, 2004
Series of sessions held throughout the year in different cities.

Seoul, December 2004
The complicity of the South Korean government in the war and occupation.

Rome, December 2004
The illegality of the war on Iraq and the complicity of the Italian government.

Frankfurt, January 2005
Third session held in Germany.

Rome, February 2005
Media crimes against truth and humanity, politics of disinformation.

Lisboa, March 2005
The responsibility of the Portugese government, institutions and individuals on the uplead to the war on Iraq, during the war and during the occupation.

Genoa, March 2005
The role of the media in the war and occupation.

Barcelona, May 2005
The colonial domination project of the US and the Iraqi society: How to regain sovereignty?

Istanbul, June 2005
Culminating session.

The findings of the following have also been incorporated into the WTI process:
—International Uranium Weapons Conference, Hamburg, October 2003
—Spanish Tribunal against the Iraq War, May 2003
—Costa Rican Tribunal, September 2003

Notes

FALK: OPENING SPEECH

1 David Ray Griffin, *The New Pearl Harbor: Disturbing Questions about the Bush Administration and 9/11*, foreword by Richard Falk (Northampton, MA: Olive Branch Press, 2004).

FIRST SESSION: THE ROLE OF INTERNATIONAL LAW AND INSTITUTIONS
SHINER: THE ILLEGALITY OF PREVENTIVE ATTACK AND UNILATERAL USE OF FORCE

1 Lord Steyn, a Law Lord in Britain, accused the British and US governments of whipping up public fear of terrorism, and of being determined "to bend established international law to their will and to undermine its structures" (*Guardian*, 11 June 2005, 2). Tony Blair made this new policy explicit in a statement to his constituency on 5 March 2004. He said that

> our own self-interest is ultimately bound up with the fate of other nations. The doctrine of international community is no longer a vision of idealism. It is a practical recognition that just within a country, citizens who are free, well educated and prosperous tend to be responsible, to feel solidarity with a society with which they have a stake; so do nations that are free, democratic and benefiting from economic progress, tend to be stable and solid partners in the advance of Humankind. The best defense of our security lies in the spread of our values... I understand the worry the international community has over Iraq. It worries that the US and its allies will by sheer force of their military might, do whatever they want, unilaterally and without recourse as to any rule-based code or doctrine. But our worry is that if the UN—because of a political disagreement in its Councils—is paralysed, then a threat we believe is real will go unchallenged... this agenda [of justice and security] must be robust in tackling the security threat that this Islamic extremism poses; and fair to all peoples by promoting their human rights, wherever they are. It means tackling poverty in Africa and justice in Palestine as well as being utterly resolute in opposition to terrorism as a way of achieving political goals. It means an entirely different, more just and more modern self-interest. It means reforming the United Nations so its Security Council represents 21st-century reality; and giving the UN the capability to act effectively as well as debate. It means getting the UN to understand that faced with the threats that we have, we should do all we can to spread the values of freedom, democracy, the rule of law, religious tolerance and justice for the oppressed,

however painful for some nations that may be; but that at the
same time, we wage war relentlessly on those who would exploit
racial and religious division to bring catastrophe to the world…

2 It has to be recalled that war has, in effect, been abolished by the UN Charter
and replaced with the authorization of the use of force in limited circumstances by
the Security Council through Chapter VII or by member states using force in self-
defense as permitted by the limited circumstances of Article 51.

3 What is needed is a new creative network of academic and practicing lawyers
alongside civil society and activists who now push for a restructuring of international
law to make it stronger and more concerned with peace.

4 Nicaragua v United States, [1986] ICJ Report 14 at par. 190.

5 It is worth recalling the opening words of the UN Charter: "We, the Peoples
of the United Nations, determined to save succeeding generations from the scourge
of war, which twice in our lifetime has brought untold sorrow to mankind…"

6 i) There is no doctrine in international law of preventive attacks. What there
is are limited rights to use force in self-defense under Article 51 of the UN Charter.
ii) As far as the UK was concerned in March 2003 it had not been subject to a direct
attack which could even arguably be linked with Iraq. Thus, the right to self-defense
in response to an armed attack does not arise. iii) As for the US position, although
there had been an attack on 9/11, there was, and is, no evidence to link Iraq to those
attacks. Further, the US did not rely on its Article 51 rights in its justification of its
use of force. Indeed, it too felt it necessary to obtain a second UN Security Council
Resolution following the passing of Resolution 1441. It was only when it failed to
obtain one that it turned to the revival doctrine relying on the authorization from
Resolution 678. iv) Although neither state relied upon anticipatory self-defense for
the sake of completion it is worth noting the following from a skeleton argument on
behalf of Peacerights to the "Inquiry into the Legality of the Use of Force by the
United Kingdom against Iraq," 8 October 2002, from G. Farebrother and N.
Kollerstrom, eds., *The Case Against War; The Essential Legal Inquiries, Opinions and
Judgments Concerning War in Iraq* (Spokesman, 2004). There are numerous examples
of States claiming to have used force in anticipatory self-defense, and being
condemned by the international community. Examples of state practice are given by
Professor Antonio Cassese, former president of the International Criminal Tribunal
for the Former Yugoslavia, in *International Law* (Oxford: Oxford University Press,
2001), 309–331.

7 Recent occasions were: Security Council Resolution 678, authorizing the use
of "all necessary means" to liberate Kuwait; Security Council Resolution 794,
authorizing "all necessary means to establish as soon as possible a secure environment
for humanitarian relief operations in Somalia"; Security Council Resolution 940,
authorizing "all necessary means to facilitate the departure from Haiti of the military
leadership"; Security Council Resolution 929, authorizing France to use " all necessary
means" to protect civilians in Rwanda; and Security Council Resolutions 770,
authorizing states to take "all measures necessary" to facilitate humanitarian assistance

and enforce the no-fly zone in Bosnia.

8 See <www.guardian.co.uk/print/0,3858,4620124-103550,00.html>

9 Much of this is collected together in *The Case Against War*. See footnote 6.

10 Author of *Lawless World: America and the Making and Breaking of Global Rules* (London: Penguin, 2005).

11 <www.abc.net.au/lateline/content/2005/s1394137.htm>

12 <news.bbc.co.uk_news/politics/4377605.stm>

13 Memorandum from Sir David Manning, Tony Blair's chief foreign policy advisor, 14 March 2002. For more see Thomas Wagner, "British Memos: Iraq War Sounds More Like Mere 'Grudge'," *Chicago Sun-Times* <www.suntimes.com/output/news/cst-nws-blair19.html>; "Lawyers Warned Pre-War Iraq Strikes Illegal," Associated Press, 19 June 2005 <www.jpost.com/servlet/satellite?pagename—jpost/jpArticle/>. For all the memoranda, visit <www.afterdowningstreet.org>.

14 Trial of the major war criminals before the International Military Tribunal, Vol. II. Proceedings: 14 November 1945 to 30 November 1945.

15 While recognizing that this Tribunal is not bound by the same approach to jurisdiction as the ICC, it is clear that the possibility of the ICC prosecutor at least pursuing a formal investigation using his Article 15 ICC Statute powers is one to be taken seriously. It should be noted by the Panel that following the London inquiry, and subsequent Peacerights report (for more see below), the ICC prosecutor himself wrote to Peacerights on 10 December 2004 confirming that an initial pre-Article 15 investigation is underway. As a decision as to whether to proceed to a pre-trial chamber for authority to conduct an Article 15 investigation has not yet been made—the matter remains in the balance—it must be worth the Panel considering whether to refer these and other matters to him.

16 Example, paragraph 5 of Resolution 678 of 29 November 1990 resolved that the Security Council "decides to remain seized of the matter." Thus, when it decided that the threat to international peace and security in the region had been reduced sufficiently it passed Resolution 686 suspending the authorization of force on 2 March 1991.

17 The UK and US did not rely on humanitarian intervention as the justification for the war, nor could they have done. Further, as the UK's Attorney General noted on 7 March 2003, "Regime change cannot be the objective of military action," par. 36. <www.number-10.gov.uk/output/page7445.asap>

18 See Peacerights, "Report of the Inquiry into the Alleged Commission of War Crimes by Coalition Forces in the Iraq War during 2003," 2004: 2.1.1. The United Kingdom acknowledges that it has made use of both land-based and airborne cluster bombs. More specifically, RAF Harrier dropped approximately 70 RBL 755 cluster bombs, each containing 147 bomblets, mainly in the vicinity of Baghdad. On land, British Howitzers with a range of 30km fired over 2000 L20 cluster shells containing 49 bomblets, mostly around Basra (Ministry of Defense, *First Reflections*, par. 4.9 <www.mod.uk/linked_files/publications/Iraq2003operations>).

19 US Department of Defense press briefing, 25 April 2003.

20 This report followed the London inquiry into war crimes in the Iraq war, 8–9 November 2003: See <www.peacerights.org>

21 The ICC Statute came into force 1 July 2002. The UK gave effect to it by the International Criminal Court Act 2001.

22 Article 16 of the International Law Commission's Articles on State responsibility 2001 provides:

> A State which aids or assists another State in the commission of an internationally wrongful act by the latter is internationally responsible for doing so if: (a) that State does so with knowledge of the circumstances of the internationally wrongful act and; (b) the act would be internationally wrongful if committed by that State.

23 Professor Antonio Cassesse has assessed various kinds of joint actions, which can lead to liability for crime in international law (A. Cassesse, *International Criminal Law* [Oxford: Oxford University Press, 2000], 179–199). These include:
(a) Participation in a common purpose or design, where all the participants in a common criminal action are equally responsible if they (i) participate in the action, whatever their position and the extent of their contribution; and in addition (ii) intend to engage in the common criminal action. In this scenario all the participants are to be treated as principals;
(b) Participation in a common criminal design where although all participants share from the outset the common criminal design, one or more perpetrators commit a crime that had not been expressly or implicitly agreed upon or envisaged at the beginning and therefore was not part of the joint criminal enterprise. In *Prosecutor v. Tadi* the Appeals Chamber held that "responsibility for a crime other than the one agreed upon in the common plan arises only if, under the circumstances of the case (i) it was foreseeable that such a crime might be perpetrated by one or other members of the group and (ii) the accused willingly took that risk";
(c) Assistance (aiding or abetting) in the commission of the crime, by providing practical assistance, encouragement or moral support which has a substantial effect on the perpetration of the crime, knowing that the actions assist the perpetrator in the commission of the crime;
(d) Inducement or incitement of the commission of the crime, when the inducement actually has an effect on the commission of the crime. The ICTY held in *Prosecutor v Blaski* that "both positive acts and omissions may constitute instigation." The subjective element of the crime is that (i) the person intended to induce the commission of the crime by the other person; or (ii) the person was at least aware of the likelihood that commission of the crime would be a consequence of his action; (iii) the person must possess the *mens rea* concerning the crime he is instigating.

24 See par. 3.16.

25 Although the joint liability for any decisions to use cluster munitions in urban areas is a critically important issue too.

26 Par. 3.24 of the Peacerights Report. Note also Article 25(3)(d) of the ICC

Statute, which imposes liability upon a person who: "(d) In any other way contributes to the commission or attempted commission of such a crime by a group of persons acting with a common purpose. Such contribution shall be intentional and shall either: (i) Be made with the aim of furthering the criminal activity or criminal purpose of the group, where such activity or purpose involves the commission of a crime within the jurisdiction of the Court; or (ii) Be made in the knowledge of the intention of the group to commit the crime."

27 Peacerights Report, par. 2.1.1–2.1.11, 4.1–4.21.

28 However, this is not to deny the strength of the argument that as this was an aggressive war it must follow that the subsequent occupation was morally wrong and politically misguided. But the legal defects up to 22 May 2003 were remedied by Resolution 1483.

29 See, for example, Richard Norton-Taylor, "US Troops Face New Torture Claims," *Guardian*, 14 September 2004, 1; Peter Graff, "British Lawyer: US Torture in Iraq Spread to Mosul," 20 June 2005 <www.commondreams.org/headlines04/0914-20.htm>; Phil Shiner, "We Can Hold Our Military to Account," *Guardian*, 15 December 2004 <www.guardian.co.uk/print/0,3858,5085980-105744,00.html>; "Former Prisoner Calls US Center a 'Torture Camp'," *Knight Ridder Newspapers*, 8 May 2004 <www.showmenews.com/2004/may/20040508N026.asp>.

30 Memorandum for Alberto R. Gonzales, counsel to the president, Standard of Conduct for Interrogation under 18 U.S.C., 1 August 2002, reproduced in full in K. Greenberg and J. Dratel, eds., *The Torture Papers: The Road to Abu Ghraib* (Cambridge: Cambridge University Press, 2005), 172–217; Seymour M. Hersh, *The Chain of Command*, (London: Allen Lane, 2004).

31 See, for example, Jon Ronson, *The Men Who Stare at Goats* (New York: Simon and Schuster, 2005); D. Priest and B. Graham, "Guantánamo List Detail Approved Interrogation Methods," *Washington Post*, 10 June 2004; "Time Report Fuels Guantánamo Criticism," CNN, 13 June 2005 <www.cnn.com/2005/us/06/12/gitmo.time/>.

32 This was the name of the facility at the center of allegations in the court martial at Osnabruck, Germany, which concluded in February 2005. For more on the proceedings, see <www.guardian.co.uk/iraq/story/o,2763,1393116,00.html>; Richard Norton-Taylor, "Fresh Claims About Abuse of Iraqis by British Troops," *Guardian,* 19 May 2005, <www.guardian.co.uk/iraq/story/o,2763,1487238,00.html>; "New Basra Abuse Inquiries Sought By Iraqi Torture Victims" <www.al-jazeera.com/cgi-din/news_service/middle_east_full_story.asp?service_id=8219>.

33 They were asked to remember the names Van Basten, Gullit, and others.

34 <www.guardian.co.uk/iraq/0,2759,423009,00.html>

35 We are now acting for nine victims.

36 Michael Horsnel, "British Troops Face Fresh Prisoner Abuse Claims," *Times* (London) online, 19 May 2005 <www.timesonline.co.uk/article/0,,7379-1618082,00.html>; "Iraq Abuse Soldiers Have Sentences Reduced," *Guardian*, 1

June 2005 <www.guardian.co.uk/military/story/0,11816,1496887,00.html>.

37 Phil Shiner, "How Torture Falls Through the Legal Net," *European Lawyer* (Dec. 2004/Jan. 2005): 70–77.

38 Both refused to count the Iraq dead so the exact number is not known. Iraq Body Count estimates a minimum of 22,353 and a maximum of 25,341 of Iraqi civilian casualties but do not break these down into the periods of the war and subsequent occupation.

39 Geneva Convention (IV) relative to the Protection of Civilians and Persons in Time of War, 12 August 1949.

40 The date of Security Council Resolution 1483.

41 The date of the transfer of authority from the CPA to the Iraqi interim government.

42 Details of these cases can be obtained from the judgment of R (on the application of al-Skeini and others) v Secretary of State for Defence, [2004] EWHC 2911(Admin), obtainable at <www.publicinterestlawyers.co.uk>.

43 While UN Security Council Resolution 1483 gave de jure authority to the UK as an occupying power on 22 May 2003, it was not until 11 July 2003 that the ROE were amended.

44 This Panel will hear from witnesses and advocates on this issue in the third session today.

45 <english.aljazeera.net/NR/exeres>.

46 Naomi Klein, "You Asked for My Evidence, Mr. Ambassador. Here It Is," at <www.guardian.co.uk/Columnists/Column/0,5673,1366348,00.html>

47 Resolution 1482 (2003), adopted by the Security Council as its 4,761st meeting, on 22 May 2003.

48 The al-Skeini case (above) will decide the important issue of whether there was jurisdiction within the meaning of Article 1 ECHR during the occupation in SE Iraq, which was the particular responsibility of the UK Armed Forces. Another argument is that the UK, with the US, had effective control of all of Iraq through its senior partner membership of the CPA. As such, the UK would have a joint responsibility, with the US, of holding independent inquiries to examine the cause of deaths of civilians in incidents such as those in Falluja.

49 G.A.Res. 21/2200A, G.A.O.R, 21st Session, Supp., p. 52, UN Doc. A/6316 (1966), 999UNTS 171, entered into force 23 March 1976. Currently there are 147 contracting parties.

50 See R (on the application of al-Skeini) v Secretary of State for Defence, [2004] EWHC 2911(Admin), obtainable at <www.publicinterestlawyers.co.uk> and all the UK, European Court of Human Rights, UN committee on Human Rights, and Inter-American Commission on Human Rights case law referred to in that judgment.

51 Convention Against Torture and other Cruel, Inhuman or Degrading Treatment or Punishment (1994).

52 See the al-Skeini litigation, now in the Court of Appeal, ibid.

HARDING: THE DOCTRINE OF HUMANITARIAN INTERVENTION

1 Hans Kochler, *Global Justice or Global Revenge? International Criminal Justice at the Crossroads* (Wien/New York: Springer-Verlag, 2003). All quotes in this section from pp. 271–275.

2 Nicolaus Mills and Kira Brunnee, eds., *The New Killing Fields: Massacre and the Politics of Intervention* (New York Basic Books, 2002), xi.

3 The slaughter of the Armenians has become more contentious as Turkey enters talks over joining the EU.

4 See "Before the US Attacked Iraq" <www.informationclearinghouse.info/article9045.htm>

5 I discuss the dangers of American geo-fascism in *After Iraq: War, Imperialism and Democracy* (Black Point, Nova Scotia: Fernwood, 2004), 147–152.

6 The following documentation relies on Samantha Power, "Raising the Cost of Genocide," in Mills and Brunner, *The New Killing Fields*, 245–264.

7 See Gore Vidal, "Japanese Intentions in the Second World War," in *Dreaming War: Blood for Oil and the Cheney-Bush Junta* (New York: Thunder Mouth Press, 2002), 85–98.

8 See discussion in Power, "Raising the Cost," 255.

9 Canadian forces also contributed to the debacles in Somalia. The scandal resulting from the "racism" in the armed forces has led to the disbandment of one full regiment. The findings of the Commission of Inquiry into the Deployment of Canadian Forces to Somalia were so threatening to the Liberal government of the day that it disbanded the Commission before it completed its work. One commissioner has documented the cover-up. See Peter Desbarats, *Somalia Cover-Up* (Toronto: McClelland and Stewart, 1997).

10 See Hans Kochler, *Global Justice*. All quotes in this section are from 293–298.

11 See discussion of PNAC in Harding, *After Iraq*, 34–38.

12 The remaining quotes in this section, unless otherwise referenced, are from Kochler, *Global Justice,* 301–313.

13 See discussion of the two-track (Middle East and Caspian Sea) oil security strategy of the US in Harding, *After Iraq*, 47–57.

14 See George Melnyk (ed.), *Canada and the New American Empire: War and Anti-War* (Calgary: University of Calgary Press, 2004), especially Colleen Beaumier and Joyce Patel, "The Humanitarian Dimension of US-Iraq Relations," 67–82.

15 See discussion of this in Kochler, *Global Justice*, 310. Also see background on the US and ICC in Harding, *After Iraq*, 25–33.

16 I discuss this analogy in the forthcoming *Between Ages*.

17 Michael Ignatieff, *The Lesser Evil: Political Ethics in an Age of Terror* (Toronto: Penguin Canada, 2004), viii. All quotes in this section are from his preface, where he outlines the fundamentals of his argument.

18 Vidal, "Japanese Intentions," 69–84, 107–140.

19 I have critically examined these arguments in *After Iraq*, 67–71, 120–125.

20 Gwynne Dyer calls terrorism "a nuisance" rather than an international threat, and points out that in the 1,000 days after 9/11 there were 1,000 victims from terrorism worldwide. See his *Future:Tense: The Coming World Order?* (Toronto: McClelland and Stewart, 2004).

21 See the post-9/11 interview with Hitchens at <www.johannhari.com/archive/arcticle.php?id=450>.

22 In Christopher Hitchens, *A Long Short War: The Postponed Liberation of Iraq* (New York: Penguin, 2003), 52.

23 Hitchens, *A Long Short War*, 20.

24 I am aware that "jihad" has to do with personal struggle for good, and that the term has become a political football in the new geopolitics.

25 Hitchens, *A Long Short War*, 1–16.

26 "Amnesty: US Leads Global Human Rights Violations," al-Jazeera, 25 May 2005.

27 This has happened to a Canadian, Maher Arar. The public inquiry into this is investigating how the federal police and security agencies were complicit in Mr. Arar's rendering to and torture in Syria. See Michael Den Tandt and Brian Laghi, "CSIS Wanted Arar Kept in Syria, Memo Shows," *Globe and Mail*, 4 June 2005, A7, A4.

28 Wesley Wark, "Abu Ghraib: Much Worse than a Few 'Bad Apples,'" *Globe and Mail*, 12 March 2005, D10–11.

29 See Seymour Hersh, *Chain of Command: The Road from 9/11 to Abu Ghraib* (New York: Harper Collins, 2004); Karen J. Greenberg and Joshua L. Dratel, eds., *The Torture Papers: The Road to Abu Ghraib* (New York: Cambridge University Press, 2005); and Mark Danner, *Abu Ghraib: The Politics of Torture* (Berkeley, CA: North Atlantic Books, 2005).

30 Naomi Klein, "Torture's Dirty Secret: It Works," *Prairie Dog*, 26 May 2005.

31 All quotes in this section are from Tim Weiner, "Air Force Seeks Bush's Approval for Space Weapons Programs," *New York Times*, 18 May 2005. Also see Julian Borger, "Bush Likely to Back Weapons in Space," *Guardian*, 19 May 2005.

32 See Vidal, "Japanese Intentions," and David Ray Griffin, *The New Pearl Harbor: Disturbing Questions about the Bush Administration and 9/11* (Northampton: Olive Branch Press, 2004).

33 See Guy Anderson, "US Defence Budget Will Equal ROW Combined 'within 12 Months,'" *Jane's Defence Industry*, 4 May 2005.

34 But we shouldn't forget that all of this market-oriented, global economic growth is putting pressure on the world's ecosystems, which, in turn will create more dislocation, strife, and suffering, which the US MIC will try to turn into a more lucrative global police and security market.

35 John Ralston Saul, *The Collapse of Globalization: and the Reinvention of the World* (Toronto: Viking Canada, 2005).

36 Will Kymlicka, "Saul Tilts at the Market Windmills," *Globe and Mail*, 28 May 2005, D3.

37 For the workings of corporations within America and North America, see Joel Bakan, *The Corporation: The Pathological Pursuit of Profit and Power* (New York: Penguin, 2004).

BARTHOLEMEW: EMPIRE'S LAW AND HUMAN RIGHTS AS SWORDS OF EMPIRE

1 Draft comments. For the final version of this talk, see "Empire's Law and the Contradictory Politics of Human Rights," in Amy Bartholomew, ed., *Empire's Law: The American Imperial Project and the War to Remake the World* (London: Pluto, 2006).

2 Arthur Schlesinger Jr., "Eyeless in Iraq," *New York Review of Books*, no. 50, 23 October 2003 <www.nybooks.com/articles/article-preview?article_id=16677>. Perhaps the most succinct discussion of the Bush Doctrine has been provided by Jonathan Schell, whose description of it is worth quoting at length:

> Its aim, which many have properly called imperial, is to establish lasting American hegemony over the entire globe, and its ultimate means is to overthrow regimes of which the United States disapproves, pre-emptively if necessary. The Bush Doctrine indeed represents more than a revolution in American policy; if successful, it would amount to an overturn of the existing international order. In the new, imperial order, *the United States would be first among nations, and force would be first among its means of domination.* Other, weaker nations would be invited to take their place in shifting coalitions to support goals of America's choosing. The United States would be so strong, the President has suggested, that other countries would simply drop out of the business of military competition, "thereby making the destabilizing arms races of other eras pointless, and limiting rivalries to trade and other pursuits of peace." Much as in the early modern period, when nation-states were being born, absolutist kings, the masters of overwhelming military force within their countries, in effect said, "There is now a new thing called a nation; a nation must be orderly; we kings, we sovereigns, will assert a monopoly over the use of force, and thus supply that order," so now the United States seemed to be saying, "here now is a thing called globalization; the global sphere must be orderly; we, the sole superpower, will monopolize force throughout the globe, and thus supply international order." ("The Empire Backfires," *Znet*, 11 March 2004 <www.zmag.org/content/showarticle.cfm? SectionID=11&ItemID=5129>)

3 In the Kellogg-Briand Pact of 1928, reiterated at the Nuremberg Tribunal.

4 As stated in the Caroline case, preemptive war requires "a necessity of self-defense, instant, overwhelming, leaving no choice of means, and no moment of deliberation." See Nicholas S.J. Davies, "The Crime of War: From Nuremberg to

Fallujah," *Online Journal*, 31 December 2004 <www.onlinejournal.com>. At the United Nations, Colin Powell said that the United States had "the sovereign right to take military action." See Noam Chomsky, "Preventive War: The Supreme Crime," *Znet*, 11 August 2003. Available online at: <archives.econ.utah.edu/archives/ marxism/2003w32/msg00055.htm>

5 As is at least one interpretation of Giorgio Agamben's claims when he says, for example, that Guantánamo is a "camp" not a prison with the juridical/political significance that the camp is outside the law, a "black hole," or an "enclave beyond any juridical sphere" (Cauter 2) or a "normless exception" (Koskenniemi 3). But, when this is expanded to maintain that the US is acting beyond the law it risks, first, obscuring the instrumentalization of law (as can be seen in the way the US labels "problem states" as those that violate law and also in the "torture memos" produced by the US Justice Department which use and "interpret" the law, parse and squeeze it, to produce their desired result); second, underestimating the countercurrents that have been and are attempting to resist that move (such as the US Supreme Court in the Guantánamo cases and progressive lawyers like those at the Center for Constitutional Rights that have been central in those cases and other attempts to constrain the administration); and third (and what I really want to emphasize) obscuring the ways in which it is seeking to reconstitute law. See Lieven de Cauter, "The Bloody Mystifications of the New World Order," in *Ready for the New Imperial World Order?*, the Brussels Tribunal, 14–17 Apr. 2004, <www.brusselstribunal.org>; Martti Koskenniemi, "International Law as Political Theology: How to Read Nomos der Erde?" *Constellations* 11, no. 4 (2004): 493. Also see Giorgio Agamben, *Homo Sacer: Sovereign Power and Bare Life* (Stanford, CA: Stanford University Press, 1998).

6 Jürgen Habermas, "Interpreting the Fall of a Monument," in Bartholomew, *Empire's Law*.

7 Ulrich K. Preuss, "The Iraq War: Critical Reflections from 'Old Europe,'" in Bartholomew, *Empire's Law*.

8 Ibid.

9 Of course there is a long and productive literature on "the exception," starting with Schmitt. For Schmitt "sovereign power not only upholds the law, but also, and above all else maintains the right to suspend the law and to declare a state of exception." Lieven de Cauter, "The Bloody Mystifications of the New World Order."

10 Scholars like Nehal Bhuta worry that this new norm may become legal itself by virtue of customary international law. See Bhuta, "A Global State of Exception? The United States and World Order," *Constellations* 10, no. 3 (2003): 371–391. Also see the normally very staid *American Journal of International Law*, where, in the introduction to its "Agora: Future Implications of the Iraq Conflict," the editors note that: "The military action against Iraq in spring 2003 is one of the few events of the UN Charter period holding the potential for fundamental transformation, or possibly even destruction of the system of law governing the use of force that had evolved during the twentieth century." Lori Fisler Damrosch and Bernard H. Oxman, "Agora: Future Implication of the Iraq Conflict: Editors' Introduction," *American Journal of*

International Law no. 97 (2004): 553.

11 Bhuta, "A Global State," 380.

12 As Habermas has put it. See his unpublished paper, "Dispute on the Past and Future of International Law: Transition from a National to a Postnational Constellation," World Congress of Philosophy, Istanbul, Turkey, 2003.

13 Michael Ignatieff, "The Burden," *New York Times Magazine*, 5 January 2003, 22, at 26.

14 Teddy Roosevelt, quoted in Leo Panitch and Sam Gindin, "Theorising American Empire," in Bartholomew (ed.), *Empire's Law*.

15 Ignatieff, "The Burden," 54.

16 For the original formulation of "human rights as swords of empire," see Amy Bartholomew and Jennifer Breakspear, "Human Rights as Swords of Empire," in Leo Panitch and Colin Leys, eds., *The New Imperial Challenge: Socialist Register 2004* (London: Merlin Press, 2003), 125–145.

17 Norman Geras, "A Moral Failure," *Wall Street Journal Online Opinion Journal*, 4 August 2003 <www.opinionjournal.com/forms/printThis.html?id+110003834>. Also see his weblog, <normblog.typepad.com/normblog>. This analysis is rooted in his analysis of, and fierce and moving opposition to, the "contract of mutual indifference," that "brutal moral reality" that describes the "place of human suffering in an unnoticing cosmos" in *The Contract of Mutual Indifference: Political Philosophy after the Holocaust* (London: Verso, 1998).

18 Norman Geras, "The Reductions of the Left," *Dissent* magazine, winter 2005. 18 March 2005 <www.dissentmagazine.org/menutest/articles/wi05/geras.htm>.

19 Geras, "A Moral Failure." Similarly, in "The Reductions of the Left," Geras maintains that one of the reasons the left didn't support the war is due to a "lack of any genuine grasp of, or feeling for, the meaning of extreme forms of evil and oppression." In addressing Geras, I don't even address the palpable lack of solidarity with the Iraqi victims of the war and occupation evidenced by Ignatieff and Geras, especially with Ignatieff calling the resistance "despicable" just days before even the mainstream media began reporting on the obvious—that "the" resistance is not a monolithic block, but is, instead, composed of Iraqi nationalists opposed to occupation as well as Saddamists, Shiite religious figures, and a small proportion of "foreign fighters." On Geras, also see Maurice Chittenden, "Stormin' Marxist is Toast of the Neocons," *Sunday Times-Britain*, 6 February 2005. Chittenden reports that Geras began his "normblog" because "I was fed up with the prevailing left and liberal consensus that the war in Iraq was wrong."

20 See Ken Roth (for Human Rights Watch), "War in Iraq: Not a Humanitarian Intervention," 27 January 2004. 9 June 2004 <www.electronicIraq.net/news/printer1354.shtml>. Human Rights Watch refused the overly simple logic that "something must be done" and the far too quick leap of logic that that "something" needed to be or was justified as unilaterally decided upon, illegal war, implied by Geras's sort of humanitarianism, which argues that there is a "universal duty" to respond but avoids the question of who and under what conditions this should occur,

as well as Ignatieff's more straightforward support of American empire as the agency to be depended on.

21 The term is used in, United States of America, "The National Defense Strategy of the United States of America," 1 March 2005, issued by Secretary of Defense Donald H. Rumsfeld. Available online at: <www.globalsecurity.org/military/library/policy/dod/nds-usa_mar2005.htm>.

22 Amnesty International USA Executive Director William Schultz, "Guantánamo Bay: A 'Gulag Of Our Times' or a 'Model Facility'? A Debate on the U.S. Prison & Amnesty International," *Democracy Now*, 1 June 2005, hosted by Amy Goodman. Transcript available at: <www.democracynow.org/article.pl?sid= 05/06/01/1441204>.

23 Jürgen Habermas, original translation of "Interpreting the Fall of a Monument," as "What Does the Felling of the Monument Mean?" <slash.autonomedia.org/analysis/03/05/12/1342259.shtm>. This is a translation of "Was bedeutet der Denkmalsturz?," *Frankfurter Allgemeine Zeitung*, 17 April 2003, 33.

24 See Trevor Purvis, "Looking for Life Signs in an International Rule of Law," in Bartholomew, *Empire's Law*. Also see Naomi Klein, "Baghdad Year Zero" <www.informationclearinghouse.info/article6930.html>. Klein suggests that: "Iraq was to the neocons what Afghanistan was to the Taliban: the one place on Earth where they could force everyone to live by the most literal, unyielding interpretation of their sacred texts."

25 See Andrew Arato, "Empire's Democracy, Ours and Theirs," in Bartholomew, *Empire's Law*.

26 We should not accept, therefore, the position that Ignatieff has taken, for example, when he says in November 2004 that "The old questions about the war in Iraq—Was it legal? Was it necessary? Was it done as a last resort?—now seem beside the point." Ignatieff, "The Terrorist as Auteur," *New York Times Magazine*, 14 November 2004, 50, at 52.

27 Quoted in Marjorie Cohn, "Aggressive War: Supreme International Crime," *Truthout*, 9 November 2004 <www.truthout.org/docs_04/110904A.shtml>.

28 See Habermas, "Dispute on the Past and Future of International Law."

29 On the idea of "trustee," see Habermas, "Interpreting the Fall of a Monument."

30 Jean-Paul Sartre, "Inaugural Statement," Bertrand Russell Vietnam War Crimes Tribunal, available at: <web.archive.org/web/20041025164511/www.911review.org/Wget/www.homeusers>.

31 Ibid.

32 For this sort of orientation, one can turn to Hannah Arendt. See Robert Fine, "Crimes Against Humanity: Hannah Arendt and the Nuremberg Debates," *European Journal of Social Theory* 3, no. 3: 293–311. On page 306, Fine says, of Arendt, "Arendt leaves us with a sense of extreme equivocation: a vision of a new, cosmopolitan order as beautiful as it is necessary, but one beset by lost opportunities, tarnished by

competition between national memories, degraded by ideological servitude to particular powers and corralled into a moral dualism of good and evil which robs debate of political profundity." She avoids the illusion that cosmopolitan law "if only it could be compelled, will provide the key to perpetual peace and universal freedom." And so must we. Fine goes on to articulate the position that I think we need to adopt:

> Cosmopolitan law, like all law, remains a form of coercion; it cannot jump out of political life or political power, it presupposes a certain exercise of power. In relation to it, the great powers have a cautious and equivocal attitude. For many years they largely ignored it. Now that they are once again using it, they seek to put it into the service of their own interests, to restrict its sphere of operation, to forestall its capacity for independent initiative, to appropriate its means of enforcement, to prevent it from interfering with the political requirements of peace and security. This is not a reason to dismiss cosmopolitan law; but it is a reason to take further the rugged, tested, critical cosmopolitanism that Arendt did so much to initiate. (307)

Also see Pheng Cheah, "Pos(ition)ing Human Rights in the Current Global Conjuncture," *Public Culture* 9, (1997), 233–266, on the idea of "contaminated" human rights.

33 On "unconcealed" informal empire, see Leo Panitch and Sam Gindin, "Theorising American Empire."

SHIVJI: LAW'S EMPIRE AND EMPIRE'S LAWLESSNESS

1 This is the title of Ronald Dworkin's book, *Law's Empire* (London: Fontana, 1986).

2 Quoted in Frank Furredi, *The New Ideology of Imperialism* (London, Pluto, 1994).

ALESSANDRINI: THE VIOLATION OF THE WILL OF THE GLOBAL ANTIWAR MOVEMENT AS A CRIME AGAINST PEACE

1 "An Open Letter to the People of Iraq." See <www.citizen.org/documents/iraqletter.pdf>.

2 The slides that will accompany this presentation, by Ayça Çubukçu and Balam Kenter, can be viewed at <newyork.worldtribunal.org/Document/Case_1_B_cubukcu_slides.pdf>.

3 Ayça Çubukçu, "Presentation on the Violation of the Global Antiwar Movement" <newyork.worldtribunal.org/Document/Case_1_B_cubukcu.pdf>.

4 Çubukçu, ibid.

5 See <www.npr.org/programs/atc/transcripts/2003/feb/030218.gonyea.html>.

SECOND SESSION: THE RESPONSIBILITY OF GOVERNMENTS
ORAN: TURKEY'S SITUATION AND POLITICS IN THE US'S ASSAULT ON IRAQ

1 AKP is a right-wing, conservative party often portrayed as a moderate Muslim party. Other political organizations mentioned in the article include the CHP (Cumhuriyet Halk Partisi, or Republican People's Party) and the PKK (the Kurdistan Workers' Party, a militant separatist group).

2 "Sacking" was the term used in the Turkish press for an event in April 2003 in which Turkish soldiers were captured by the US on the Iraq border, and sacks were put over their heads.

THIRD SESSION: THE ACCOUNTABILITY OF THE MEDIA
LANDAU: ECONOMIC-POLITICAL CONNECTIONS OF MEDIA

1 In pluralist liberal models, the mass media or "fourth estate," become the guardians of democracy, defenders of the public interest. Edmund Burke said that there were "Three Estates in Parliament; but, in the Reporters' Gallery yonder, there sat a Fourth Estate more important than they all. .... Whoever can speak, speaking now to the whole nation, becomes a power, a branch of government, with inalienable weight in law-making, in all acts of authority. It matters not what rank he has, what revenues or garnitures: the requisite thing is that he have a tongue which others will listen to; this and nothing more is requisite."

Jürgen Habermas argued that a "public sphere" emerged in eighteenth-century England, one that "mediates between society and state." The press arose alongside of a culture including theater, book publishing, and libraries. As the wealthy public became more literate, the media allowed the elite to discuss politics in a different way.

2 "This is the second time in a month that UNSCOM has pulled out in the face of a possible U.S.-led attack. But this time there may be no turning back. Weapons inspectors packed up their personal belongings and loaded up equipment at U.N. headquarters after a predawn evacuation order. In a matter of hours, they were gone, more than 120 of them headed for a flight to Bahrain" (Jane Arraf, CNN, 16 December 1998).

"What Mr. Bush is being urged to do by many advisers is focus on the simple fact that Saddam Hussein signed a piece of paper at the end of the Persian Gulf War, promising that the United Nations could have unfettered weapons inspections in Iraq. It has now been several years since those inspectors were kicked out" (John King, CNN, 18 August 2002. See <www.fair.org>).

MILLER: MEDIA WRONGS AGAINST HUMANITY

1 David Miller, "Information Dominance: The Philosophy Of Total Propaganda Control?," 29 December 2003 <spinwatch.server101.com/modules.php?name= Content&pa=showpage&pid=292>.

2 In the UK case, see David Miller, "'They Were All Asylum Seekers': The Propaganda Campaign To Link Iraq To Terrorism At The expense Of Refugees," 27 March 2003 <spinwatch.server101.com/modules.php?name=Content&pa= showpage&pid=281>. On

the underlying philosophy of the threat, see Adam Curtis, "Fear Gives Politicians a Reason to Be," *Guardian*, 24 November 2004 <www.guardian.co.uk/comment/story/0,3604,1358277,00.html>; Andy Beckett, "The Making of the Terror Myth, *Guardian*, 15 October 2004 <www.guardian.co.uk/terrorism/story/0,12780,1327904,00.html>.

3 Sheldon Rampton and John Stauber, *Weapons of Mass Deception* (London: Constable and Robinson, 2003); Christopher Scheer, Robert Scheer, and Lakshmi Chaudhry, *The Five Biggest Lies Bush Told Us About Iraq* (New York: Seven Stories Press, 2003); Glen Rangwala, "Iraq's Weapons of Mass Destruction: The Assessment of the British Government, Problems, Contradictions, Falsehoods," 24 September 2002 <middleeastreference.org.uk/dossier030603.html>; Glen Rangwala, "Analysis of the Dossier of 30 January 2003," a paper produced at the request of the Foreign Affairs Committee of the House of Commons, 16 June 2003 <middleeastreference.org.uk/fac030616.html>; Glen Rangwala, "Claims in Secretary of State Colin Powell's UN Presentation concerning Iraq," 5 February 2003 <middleeastreference.org.uk/powell030205.html>; Glen Rangwala, "16 Discrepancies between Powell's Claims and the Evidence of Blix and ElBaradei," 14 February 2003 <middleeastreference.org.uk/un030214.html>; Sam Cowan, "Truth from These Podia" <www.usnews.com/usnews/politics/whispers/documents/truth.pdf>.

4 Justin Lewis and Rod Brookes, "Reporting the War on British Television," in *Tell me Lies: Propaganda and Media Distortion in the Attack on Iraq*, ed. David Miller (London: Pluto, 2004).

5 Justin Lewis, "Biased Broadcasting Corporation," *Guardian*, 4 July 2003 <media.guardian.co.uk/iraqandthemedia/story/0,12823,991215,00.html>.

6 Steve Rendall and Tara Broughel, "Amplifying Officials, Squelching Dissent," *Extra!* (May/June 2003) <www.fair.org/index.php?page=1145>.

7 John Theobald, *The Media and the Making of History* (Aldershot: Ashgate, 2004).

8 Justin Lewis and Rod Brookes, "British TV News and the Case for War in Iraq," in *Reporting War: Journalism in Wartime*, eds. S. Allan and B. Zelizer (London: Routledge, 2004); Howard Tumber and Jerry Palmer, *Media at War: The Iraq Crisis* (London; Sage, 2004).

9 Lewis and Brookes, "British TV," 290.

10 See "A Failure of Skepticism in Powell Coverage," FAIR press release, 2 October 2003, <www.fair.org/index.php?page=1846>.

11 See <www.fair.org/index.php?page=1167>.

12 *New York Post*, 17 December 1998.

13 Ahmed Janabi, "Iraqi Group: Civilian Toll now 37,000," 31 July 2004 <english.aljazeera.net/NR/exeres/66E32EAF-0E4E-4765-9339-594C323A777F.htm>.

14 Tariq Ali, "The Withdrawal of Foreign Troops is the Only Solution," *Guardian*, 12 August 2004. See "No Mea Culpa From the British Media, Part 1: Media Lens Challenges Senior Editors," Media Lens Media Alert, 2 September 2004

<www.medialens.org/alerts/2004/040902_No_Mea_Culpa.htm>.

15 "100,000 Iraqi Civilian Deaths—Part 1," Media Lens Media Alert, 2 November 2004 <www.medialens.org/alerts/2004/041102_Iraqi_Civilian_Deaths_1.HTM>.

16 "Iraqi Child Deaths: Media Indifferent as UNICEF Reports Worsening Catastrophe," Media Lens Media Alert, 19 October 2004 <www.medialens.org/alerts/2004/041019_Iraqi_Child_Deaths.HTM>.

17 "TV Not Concerned by Cluster Bombs, DU: 'That's Just the Way Life is in Iraq'," FAIR Action Alert, 5 June 2003 <www.fair.org/index.php?page=1611>.

18 See "Some Critical Media Voices Face Censorship," FAIR press release, 4 March 2003 <www.fair.org/index.php?page=1825>.

19 Angela Millar and David Miller, "Rose Gentle Censored by MoD," *SpinWatch Exclusive*, 22 September 2004 <spinwatch.org>.

20 Lewis and Brookes, "British TV."

21 See David Miller, "The propaganda machine" in *Tell Me Lies*.

22 Andy Beckett, "The Making of the Terror Myth"; Adam Curtis, "Fear Gives Politicians"; Adam Curtis, "Feign of Terror," *Village Voice*, 19 April 2005 <www.villagevoice.com/film/0516,curtis,63147,20.html>.

23 <www.pipa.org/OnlineReports/Iraq/Media_10_02_03_Report.pdf>.

24 Justin Lewis, "Changing Their Minds," *Guardian*, 30 September 2003 <www.guardian.co.uk/analysis/story/0,3604,1052233,00.html>.

25 Justin Lewis, "Television, Public Opinion and the War in Iraq: The Case of Britain," *International Journal of Public Opinion Research* 16, no. 3 (2004).

26 Murray Goot, "Public Opinion and the Democratic Deficit: Australia and the War Against Iraq," *Australian Humanities Review*, no. 29 (May/June 2003) <www.lib.latrobe.edu.au/AHR/archive/Issue-May-2003/goot.html>.

NAYAR: MEDIA WRONGS AGAINST TRUTH AND HUMANITY

1 Because Jayan Nayar was unable to attend the World Tribunal on Iraq Istanbul session, his presentation was delivered by Müge Gürsoy Sökmen.

FOURTH SESSION: THE INVASION AND OCCUPATION OF IRAQ
KHAMMAS: THE RUIN OF DAILY LIFE

1 The moderator of this session was Haifa Zangana.

DOCENA: "SHOCK AND AWE" THERAPY

1 Chip Cummins, Susan Warren, and Bhushan Bahree, "New Drill: Inside Giant Oil Industry, Maze Of Management Tensions," *Wall Street Journal*, 30 April 2003.

2 quoted in Naomi Klein, "Risky Business," *Nation*, 5 January 2004.

3 quoted in the *Ecologist* 29, no. 3 (May/June 1999).

4 quoted in Suleiman al-Khalidi, "Iraq's Businessmen Feel Left Out in the Cold," Reuters, 22 October 2003.

5 Dale Fuchs, "Companies Everywhere Seek Role in Iraq," *New York Times*, 24

October 2003.

6 Neil King Jr., "Bush Officials Devise a Broad Plan for a Free-Market Economy in Iraq," *Wall Street Journal*, 1 May 2003.

7 Ed Vulliamy and Faisal Islam, "And Now for the Really Big Guns," *Observer*, 29 June 2003.

8 For more on the project to overhaul Iraq economically, politically, and ideologically, see *Silent War: The US Economic and Ideological Occupation of Iraq* (Bangkok: Focus on the Global South, 2005), which can be downloaded from <www.focusweb.org/pdf/Iraq_Dossier.pdf>

9 For example, the occupation authorities preserved the Saddam-era law banning the formation of independent trade unions (Alan Maass, "Delegation of US Unionists Report Back: Rise of Iraq's New Labor Movement," Socialist Workers Online, 31 October 2003).

10 Rowan Scarborough, "US Rushed Post-Saddam Planning," *Washington Post*, 3 September 2003.

11 "Rumsfeld: Rebuilding Up to Iraqis," *Seattle Times*, 11 September 2003.

12 Address to World Economic Forum in Jordan, 22 June 2003 <usinfo.state.gov/regional/nea/summit/text2003/0623bremer.htm>.

13 Stephen J. Glain, "'Fast Track' Plan to Sell State-Owned Firms in Iraq is Put on Hold," *Boston Globe*, 18 September 2003.

14 Antonia Juhasz, "Ambitions of Empire: The Bush Administration Economic Plan for Iraq (and Beyond)," *LeftTurn* magazine, no. 12 (February/March 2004).

15 Reuters, September 21, 2003.

16 Marylou Malig, "War: Trade by Other Means" in *Silent War*.

17 USAID contract with Bearing Point, 84.

18 Ibid., 51

19 Steve Kretzman and Jim Vallette, "Operation Oily Immunity," CommonDreams.org, 23 July 2003; Andre Verloy, "Oil Immunity?: Government Denies Charges that Bushed Helped Oil Companies in Iraq," Center for Public Integrity, 30 October 2003 <www.publicintegrity.org>.

20 Focus on the Global South and GRAIN, "A Declaration of War against Farmers," in *Silent War*.

21 Jeff Madrick, "An Extreme Plan for Iraq," *New York Times*, 2 October 2003.

22 Joseph Stiglitz, "Iraq's Next Shock will be Shock Therapy," *Znet*, 17 March 2004 <www.zmag.org>.

23 Naomi Klein, "Downsizing in Disguise," *Nation*, 23 June 2003.

24 "Let's All Go to the Yard Sale: Iraq's Economic Liberalization," *Economist*, 27 September 2003.

25 US Department of Energy, Annual Energy Outlook 2004 (Washington DC, DOE/EIA: 2004).

26 International Monetary Fund Country Report No.4/325, September 2004.

27 According to the US government's Energy Information Administration, <www.eia.doe.gov>; see also David R. Becker, "Seeking Iraq's Oil Prize: Government

May Allow Foreign Firms to Invest," *San Francisco Chronicle,* 26 January 2005; Iain Boal, T.J. Clark, Joseph Matthews, and Michael Watts, "Blood for Oil?," *London Review of Books,* 21 April 2005.

28 Iain Boal, et al., "Blood for Oil?"

29 quoted in Gregg Muttitt, "Under the Surface: Iraqi Oil and Tony Blair's Absurd Conspiracy Theory," *Red Pepper,* January 2005.

30 Pratap Chatterjee, "To the Victors Go the Spoils of War," Inter Press Service, 22 May 2003.

31 Stephen J. Glain, "Projected Iraq Oil Costs Up Sharply," *Boston Globe,* 30 October 2003; Iain Boal, et al., "Blood for Oil?"

32 Ritt Goldstein, "'Oil War' Questions Surround Cheney Energy Caucus," Inter Press Service, 11 September 2003.

33 quoted in Michael Klare, "Bush-Cheney Energy Strategy: Procuring the Rest of the World's Oil," in *Petropolitics,* Institute for Policy Studies and Interhemispheric Resource Center, undated.

34 cited in Linda McQuaig, "History will Show US Lusted After Oil," *Toronto Star,* 26 December 2004.

35 "Commerce Secretary Evans Urges US Business to Deal with Iraq," CPA Press Release, 12 February 2004.

36 Commerce Secretary Don Evans' speech to the Iraq Business Council, 11 February 2003.

37 Human Rights Watch, "The War in Iraq and International Humanitarian Law," 16 May 2003; Thomas Catan, "Iraq Business Deals May Be Invalid, Law Experts Warn," *Financial Times,* 28 October 2003; Aaron Mate, "Pillage is Forbidden: Why the Privatisation of Iraq is Illegal," *Guardian,* 7 November 2003; Associated Press, "Experts: 'Shock-Restructuring of Iraq is on Shaky Ground,'" 17 November 2003; Daphne Eviatar, "Free Market Iraq? Not so Fast," *New York Times,* 10 January 2004.

38 14–23 May 2004, Coalition Provisional Authority survey, cited in Michael E. O'Hanlon and Adriana Lins de Albuquerque, "Iraq Index: Tracking Variables of Reconstruction & Security in Post-Saddam Iraq," Brookings Institution, 16 June 2005 <www.brookings.edu/iraqindex>.

39 Richard Burkholder, "Ousting Saddam Hussein Was Worth Hardships Endured Since Invasion, Say Citizens of Baghdad," Gallup Poll Organization, 24 September 2003.

40 Roula Khalaf, "Iraq's rebel cleric gains surge in popularity," *Financial Times,* 19 May 2004.

41 Ed Vulliamy and Faisal Islam, "And Now for the Really Big Guns," *Observer,* 29 June 2003; Seb Walker, "Corporate Takeover," *Baghdad Bulletin,* 31 August 2003.

42 Emad Mekay, "US on Track for Market Economy," Inter Press Service, 11 February 2004.

43 Naomi Klein, "Baghdad Year Zero," *Harper's* magazine, September 2004.

44 Carola Hoyos, "Oil Groups Snub US on Deals," *Financial Times,* 24 July 2003.

45 Donald Rumsfeld, "Core Principles for a Free Iraq," *Wall Street Journal*, 27 May 2003.

46 William Booth and Rajiv Chandrasekaran, "Occupation Forces Halt Elections Throughout Iraq," *Washington Post*, 28 June 2003.

47 Joel Brinkley, "US Rejects Iraqi Plan to Hold Census by Summer," *New York Times*, 4 December 2003; "UK Officials Say Iraq Elections by June Viable," *Financial Times*, 20 January 2004.

48 Herbert Docena, "Silent Battalions of Democracy," *Middle East Report*, fall 2004.

49 William Booth and Rajiv Chandrasekaran, "Occupation Forces Halt Elections Throughout Iraq," *Washington Post*, 28 June 2003.

50 Edward Wong, "US Tries to Give Moderates an Edge in Iraqi Elections," *New York Times*, 18 January 2004.

51 Tom Shanker and Steven R. Weisman, "US Tries to Define New Iraq Role: Goal for June—A Military Presence under Iraqi Sovereignty," *International Herald Tribune*, 20–21 December 2003.

52 cited by Bob Herbert, "Spoils of War," *New York Times*, 11 April 2003.

53 USAID contract with Bearing Point, 46.

54 Emad Mekay, "Free Marketeers Have a Plan in Iraq," Inter Press Service, 30 April 2003.

55 Ben Wootliff, "Bush Pals Hired to Rewrite Iraqi Law," *Observer*, 31 August 2003.

56 cited in Doug Lorimer, "Iraq: Globalisation at Gunpoint," *Green Left Weekly*, 10 September 2003.

57 Catherine Belton and Oksana Yablokova, "Gaidar Invited to Shock, Awe Iraq," *Moscow Times*, 9 September 2003; "Yegov Gaidar Brings his Heavy Bag of Instruments to Iraq," *New York Press* 16, no. 38 (17–23 September 2003).

58 USAID contract with Bearing Point, 5–6; in one of its reports, USAID said: "US experts in economic management helped Iraqi ministries examine and reform laws, regulations, and institutions, and they provided a framework for private sector trade, commerce, and investment." ("Reforms Pave the Way for Growth," USAID report)

59 USAID contract with Bearing Point, 46.

60 Ibid., 7

61 Jim Crane, "U.S. Wants Military Control in Iraq, Even After Sovereignty Handed Over," Associated Press, 13 March 2004.

62 USAID contract with Bearing Point, 41, 43.

63 Ibid., 11.

64 Ibid., 40.

65 Chris Toensing, "Another 'Historic Day' Looms in Iraq," *Middle East Report* online, 28 January 2005.

66 Thomas L. Friedman, "No Time to Lose in Iraq," *New York Times*, 20 August 2003.

67 USAID Center for Democracy and Governance, "Policy Implementation: What USAID Has Learned," (Washington, DC: USAID, 2001), 11.

68 Ibid.

69 Docena, "Silent Battalions."

70 USAID, "Foreign Aid in the National Interest," 48

71 Dilip Hiro, "Tipping Point in Iraq," MotherJones.com, 24 June 2004.

72 Elisabeth Bumiller, "Bush Lays Out Goals for Iraq: Self-rule and Stability," *New York Times*, 25 May 2004.

73 Josh White and Jonathan Weisman, "Limited Iraqi Sovereignty Planned," *Washington Post*, 22 April 2004.

74 Vicki Allen, "Negroponte Says Won't Command Iraqi Government," Reuters, 27 April 2004.

75 Vicki Allen, "US Senators Question Impact of Power Transfer," Reuters, 22 April 2004.

76 Vicki Allen and Donna Smith, "US Says June 30 Not a 'Magical Date' for Iraq," Reuters, 20 April 2004.

77 Associated Press, "US Will Help Draft Iraq Constitution," 16 November 2003; Barbara Slavin and Steven Komarow, "Iraq's Temporary Constitution To Resemble America's," *USA Today*, 17 November 2003; Jim Lobe, "US Lawmakers Warn of Brewing Crisis Over Women's Rights in Iraq," OneWorld, 3 February 2004; Rajiv Chandraekaran, "Kurds Reject Key Parts of Proposed Iraq Constitution," *Washington Post*, 21 February 2004; Rajiv Chandrasekaran and Walter Pincus, "US Edicts Curb Power of Iraq's Leadership," *Washington Post*, 27 June 2004.

78 Steven Weisman, "Iraq's New Government Faces Bargaining Over its Power," *New York Times*, 2 June 2004.

79 "Iraq Resolution Gives Wide Powers to US Forces," Reuters, 24 May 2004; Rory McCarthy, "US Will Override Baghdad in War on Terrorism," *Guardian*, 1 June 2004; Jim Krane, "US Will Retain Sovereign Power in Iraq," Associated Press, 21 March 2004; Yochi J. Dreazen and Christopher Cooper, "Behind the Scenes, US Tightens Grip on Iraq's Future," *Wall Street Journal*, 13 March 2004.

80 "Coalition Troops to Enjoy Immunity from Prosecution in Iraq," Agence France Press, 23 May 2004; Rory McCarthy, "US Will Override Baghdad"; Steven Weisman, "Iraq's New Government Faces Bargaining Over its Power," *New York Times*, 2 June 2004; Robin Wright, "US Immunity in Iraq Will Go beyond June 30," *Washington Post*, 24 June 2004.

81 Hannah Allam and Warren P. Strobel, "Amidst Doubts CIA Hangs on to Control of Iraqi Security Service," Knight Ridder, 8 May 2005.

82 Bradley Graham, "Duration of US Presence in Iraq 'Unknowable,' Myers Says," *Washington Post*, 20 February 2004.

83 "Powell: Iraq Will Have No Veto on US-led Force," Reuters, 3 June 2004.

84 Thom Shanker and Steven R. Weisman, "US Tries to Define New Iraq Role: Goal for June: A Military Presence under Iraqi Sovereignty," *International Herald Tribune*, 20–21 December 2003,

85 "Bremer to Appoint Iraq National Security Adviser," Reuters, 25 March 2004.

86 Dreazen and Cooper, "Behind the Scenes."

87 Ibid..; Phyllis Bennis, "Reading the Elections," Inter Press Service, 2 February 2005.

88 Krane, "US Will Retain Sovereign Power"; Chandrasekaran and Pincus, "US Edicts Curb Power."

89 Nicolas Pelham, "Iraqi Minister Unveils Proposal to Control Oil," *Financial Times*, 10 June 2004.

90 Steven Weisman, "Iraq's New Government Faces Bargaining Over its Power," *New York Times*, 2 June 2004; "USAID Activities Promote Trade and Open Markets in Iraq, Aim to Help Meet World Trade Organization Requirements," Portal Iraq, 10 February 2005.

91 T. Christian Miller, "Rules and Cash Flew Out the Window," *Los Angeles Times*, 20 May 2005.

92 One US official said: "The military commanders love that program [cash being given for US military teams to freely spend] because it buys them friends. You want to hire everybody on the street, put money in their pockets and make them like you. We have always spent Iraqi money on that" (Steven R. Weisman, "Iraqi Oil Cash Fuels Rebuilding Projects," *International Herald Tribune*, 22 June 2004).

93 "Fuelling Suspicion: the Coalition and Iraq's Billions," Christian Aid, June 2004; Emad Mekay, "'Staggering Amount' of Cash Missing in Iraq," Inter Press Service, 21 August 2004; Iraq Revenue Watch, "Audit Finds More Irregularities and Mismanagement of Iraq's Revenues," Revenue Watch Briefing no. 9 (December 2004); "Iraq Reconstruction 'Rife with Corruption,'" Agence France Press, 16 March 2005.

94 CPA Inspector General's Report to Congress, 30 July 2004, 63; David Usborne, Anne Penketh, and Colin Brown, "No Exit Date Set in Bush Handover Plan," *Independent*, 25 May 2004.

95 Chris Shumway, "Iraq's 'Sovereign' Government to Have Little Control over Oil Money," *New Standard*, 22 June 2004.

96 Republic of Iraq 2004 Budget, October 2003; transcript of news conference at National Press Club, Afternoon Newsmaker News Conference, Washington, DC, 21 December 2004 <www.state.gov>.

97 Krane, "US Will Retain Sovereign Power."

98 David E. Sanger, "America's Gamble: A Quick Exit Plan for Iraq," *New York Times*, 16 November 2003.

99 Rajiv Chandrasekaran, "Envoy Bowed to Pressure in Choosing Leaders," *Washington Post*, 2 June 2004; Anne Penketh and Justin Huggler, "UN Fury over Bush Attempts to Install PM," *Independent*, 27 May 2004; Rajiv Chandrasekaran, "Former Exile is Selected as Interim Iraqi Leader," *Washington Post*, 29 May 2004.

100 Associated Press, "Former Indian Envoy is Bush's Man Friday," 27 May 2004.

101 Christopher Adams and Roula Khalaf, "US and UK Close to Deal on Shape of Iraq's Government," *Financial Times*, 11 March 2004; Luke Baker, "Iraqi Governing Council Has Doubts About UN Role," Reuters, 14 March 2004; Jim Lobe, "Chalabi: From White House to Dog House in Just Five Months," Antiwar.com, 21 May 2004; Rajiv Chandrasekaran, "Former Exile is Selected as Interim Iraqi Leader," *Washington Post*, 29 May 2004; Monte Morin and Alissa J. Rubin, "U.S. Orders Iraqis to Delay Nomination," *Los Angeles Times*, 31 May 2004; Dexter Filkins, "A Worn Road for UN Aide," *New York Times*, 31 May 2004; Rajiv Chandrasekaran, "Envoy Bowed to Pressure in Choosing Leaders," *Washington Post*, 2 June 2004; Steven R. Weisman, "Iraq's New Government Faces Bargaining over Its Power," *New York Times*, 2 June 2004; Massimo Calabresi, "Our (Irascible) Man in Iraq," *Time*, 28 June 2004.

102 Filkins, "A Worn Road for UN Aide."

103 Warren Hoge and Steven R. Weisman, "Surprising Choice for Premier of Iraq Reflects US Influence," *New York Times*, 29 May 2004.

104 Filkins, "A Worn Road for UN Aide."

105 Chandrasekaran, "Envoy Bowed to Pressure."

106 Hoge and Weisman, "Surprising Choice."

107 Patrick Cockburn, "Exiled Allawi was Responsible for 45-minute WMD Claim," *Independent*, 29 May 2004.

108 Todd Zeranski, "Iraq's Al-Yawar Says U.S., Other Forces May Be Cut by Year End," Bloomberg.com, 2 February 2005.

109 Ian Fisher, "Early Steps, Maybe, Toward a Democracy in Iraq," *New York Times*, 27 July 2004.

110 Mark Turner, "Iraqis Doubt Move Towards Democracy," *Financial Times*, 25 July 2004; Dean Yates, "Mortars Mark Opening of Iraqi Political Conference," Reuters, 15 August 2004; Fiona Symon, "Financial Times Briefing on Iraq Elections," *Financial Times*, 17 August 2004; James Drummond, "Main Parties Maintain Hold on New Assembly," *Financial Times*, 18 August 2004; Lisa Ashkenaz Croke, "New Iraqi Council Chosen in Undemocratic Assembly," *New Standard*, 23 August 2004.

111 Christophe Boltanski, "The Baghdad National Conference Hubbub," *Liberation*, 18 August 2004.

112 Carolyn Skorneck, "White House Revises Details of Iraq Reconstruction," *Congressional Quarterly Weekly*, 10 January 2004.

113 Deborah Zabarenko, "US-Backed Iraqi Government Losing Support— Survey," Reuters, 22 October 2004.

114 Adam Entous, "Bush to Aid 'Moderate' Parties in Iraqi Election," Reuters, 8 October 2004.

115 For more on the US's "democracy promotion" activities, see William Robinson, *A Faustian Bargain: US Intervention in the Nicaraguan Elections and American Foreign Policy in the Post-Cold War Era* (Boulder: Westview, 1992). On Iraq, see Lisa Ashkenaz Croke and Brian Dominick, "Controversial US Groups Operate Behind Scenes on Iraq Vote," *New Standard*, 13 December 2004; Robin Wright and

Colum Lynch, "Limited UN Role Hinders Iraq Vote," *Washington Post*, 19 October 2004.

116 Timothy Burger and Douglas Waller, "How Much US Help?: The Bush Administration Takes Heat for a CIA Plan to Influence Iraq's Elections," *Time* 4 October 2004.

117 CPA Administrator's Weekly Governance Report, 13–19 March 2004.

118 CPA Administrator's Weekly Governance Report, 7–13 February 2004.

119 Robin Wright, "Religious Leaders Ahead in Iraq Poll," *Washington Post*, 22 October 2004.

120 Deborah Zabarenko, "US-Backed Iraqi Government Losing Support-Survey," Reuters, 22 October 2004.

121 Johanna McGeary, "Iraq's Shadow Ruler," *Time* magazine, 17 October 2004; Ashraf Khalil and Paul Richter, "US is Said to Urge its Iraqi Allies to Unite for Election," *Los Angeles Times*, 25 October 2004.

122 Rajiv Chandrasekaran and Walter Pincus, "US Edicts Curb Power of Iraq's Leadership," *Washington Post*, 27 June 2004.

123 Jonathan Steele and Patrick Wintour, "US Bans Cleric from Iraq Elections," *Guardian*, 8 June 2004; Seymour Hersh, "Plan B," *New Yorker*, 28 June 2004.

124 Adam Entous, "Bush to Aid 'Moderate' Parties in Iraqi Election," Reuters, 8 October 2004.

125 "Carl Conetta: The Iraq Election 'Bait and Switch': Faulty Poll will not Bring Peace or US Withdrawal," Project on Defense Alternatives Briefing Report #17, 25 January 2005.

126 Dahr Jamail, "Some Just Voted for Food," Inter Press Service, 31 January 2003; Bennis, "Reading the Elections."

127 "Shi'ite list Says Won Around 60 percent of Iraq Vote," Reuters, 13 February 2005; Michael Meacher, "America is Usurping the Democratic Will in Iraq," *Independent*, 5 April 2005.

128 Robin Wright and Colum Lynch, "Limited UN Role Hinders Iraq Vote," *Washington Post*, 19 October 2004; "Iraq Presses UN for More Help on Elections," Alertnet, 13 December 2004; "Carl Conetta: The Iraq Election 'Bait and Switch': Faulty Poll will not Bring Peace or US Withdrawal," Project on Defense Alternatives Briefing Report #17, 25 January 2005.

129 Nicolas Pelham, "Iraqi Minister Sees Oil Privatization Obstacles," *Financial Times*, 5 September 2003.

130 Gregg Muttitt, "Under the Surface: Iraqi Oil and Tony Blair's Absurd Conspiracy Theory," *Red Pepper*, January 2005.

131 Chip Cummins, "State-run Oil Company is Being Weighed for Iraq," *Wall Street Journal*, 7 January 2004.

132 Dan Morgan and David B. Ottaway, "In Iraqi War Scenario, Oil Key Issue," *Washington Post*, 15 September 2002.

133 T. Christian Miller, "Firms Fear Iraq Contracts Won't Survive Transfer of Power," *Los Angeles Times*, 11 February 2004.

134 Chris Toensing, "Another 'Historic Day' Looms in Iraq," *Middle East Report* online, 28 January 2005.

135 John F. Burns, "At Iraqi Request, the UN Extends Approval for US-Led Forces to Stay," *New York Times*, 1 June 2005.

136 Emad Mekay, "US to Take Bigger Bite of Iraq's Economic Pie," Inter Press Service, 23 December 2004.

137 International Crisis Group, "Iraq: Don't Rush the Constitution," *International Crisis Group Middle East Report* no. 42, 8 June 2005.

138 Azzaman, "No Foreign Hand in Drafting Constitution," in *Institute for War and Peace Reporting: Iraqi Press Monitor* no. 248, 25 May 2005.

139 Robin Wright, "US has Big Plans for Embassy in Iraq," *Washington Post*, 2 January 2004.

140 David Salman, "Iraq Draws up Plan to Privatize State-owned Firms," *Daily Star* (Lebanon), 17 May 2005.

141 Gregg Muttitt, "Under the Surface: Iraqi Oil and Tony Blair's Absurd Conspiracy Theory," *Red Pepper,* January 2005; David R. Becker, "Seeking Iraq's Oil Prize: Government May Allow Foreign Firms to Invest," *San Francisco Chronicle*, 26 January 2005.

142 Bryan Bender, "Seeking Political Solution in Iraq: With Conflict Unabated, Allies Hope for Alternative to Battle," *International Herald Tribune*, 11–12 June 2005.

143 Naomi Klein, "Baghdad: Year Zero," *Harper's*, September 2004.

144 Brian Dominick, "US Forgives Iraq Debt to Clear Way for IMF Reforms," *New Standard*, 19 December 2004.

145 IMF Country Report no. 4/325, September 2004.

146 IMF Press Statement, 13 October 2004.

147 IMF Country Report no. 4/325, September 2004.

148 George Wright, "Wolfowitz: Iraq War Was about Oil," *Guardian*, 4 June 2003.

149 World Bank, "Building a Sustainable Investment Climate in Iraq," World Bank Reconstructing Iraq Working Paper Series no. 1 (27 September 2004), 4.

150 Zaid al-Ali, "The IMF and the Future of Iraq," *Middle East Report* online, 7 December 2004.

151 IMF Country Report no. 4/325, September 2004; Borzou Daragahi, "Iraqis Look at Cuts in Payroll," *Los Angeles Times*, 6 June 2005.

152 Klein, "Baghdad: Year Zero."

153 Todd Eastham, "Powell: US to Command Post-July 1 Iraqi Troops," Reuters, 16 May 2004.

154 Julian Borger, "Iraq Elections: US Debate Focuses on Plan B—to Stay on or to Go?," *Guardian*, 29 January 2005; Christine Spolar, "14 'Enduring' Bases Set in Iraq; Long-term Military Presence Planned," *Chicago Tribune*, 23 March 2004.

155 Amy Svitak Klamper, "Garner Sees Iraq as Long-Term Military Outpost in the Middle East," *National Journal's Congress Daily*, 6 February 2004.

156 Eli Lake, "Broad Latitude is Recommended for US Military's Stay in Iraq," *New York Sun*, 3 February 2005.

157 Walter Pincus, "Limited Sovereignty for Iraq is Described," *Washington Post*, 23 April 2004.

158 Paul Richter and Ashraf Khalil, "US Moves to Reassert Itself in Iraq Affairs," *Los Angeles Times*, 20 May 2005.

BHAGWAT: THE PRIVATIZATION OF WAR

1 Kevin Zeese, "How Much Proof Needed Before the Truth Comes Out? Now Seven British Leaked Documents Raise Questions," <Globalresearch.ca>.

2 Reported by Jeremy Scahill on the *Nation's* website.

3 Sukumaran Muralidharan, "The Need to Safeguard Oil Resources," *Economic and Political Weekly*, 30 March 1991, 838.

4 Thomas Friedman, *The Lexus and the Olive Tree: Understanding Globalization* (New York: Farrar, Straus and Giroux, 1999).

5 Documents available at www.JudicialWatch.org.

6 Reported by the Center for Public Integrity International Consortium of Investigative Journalists.

GALTUNG: HUMAN RIGHTS AND THE US/UK ILLEGAL ATTACK ON IRAQ

1 From Susan George, "The Corporate Utopian Dream," *The WTO and the Global War System* (Seattle, November 1999). He is missing the political dimension and might have added "a fair amount of bullying" or "arm-twisting" after killing.

2 Barbara W. Tuchman, *The March of Folly: From Troy to Vietnam* (New York: Knopf, 1984).

3 Visitors today to the ruins of Troy (in Turkey, near the Dardanelles, on the Asian side) will find a model of the famous wooden horse, and can judge for themselves the wisdom of letting such a thing within their walls. In the other three cases, a little patience, flexibility, willingness to listen, and real dialogue might have come a far way. But then we might have had neither economic growth and individualizing democracy as we know them, if we accept that both are related to the worldview of Protestantism, nor the end of the beginning of the US republic, nor the beginning of the end of the US empire.

4 Tuchman, *The March of Folly*, 5.

FIFTH SESSION: CULTURAL HERITAGE, THE ENVIRONMENT, AND WORLD RESOURCES

PULHAN: THE DESTRUCTION OF CULTURAL HERITAGE

1 Neil Brodie, "Introduction," in *Illicit Antiquities: The Theft of Culture.*, ed. Neil Brodie and Kathryn Walker Tubb (London: Routledge, 2001), 1–22.

2 Andrew Lawler, "News Focus Special Report, A Museum Looted: Mayhem in Mesopotamia," *Science*, 1 August 2003, 583.

3 Benjamin R. Foster, (2003), "Missing in Action: The Iraq Museum and the Human Past," in *The Iraq War and its Consequences: Thoughts of Nobel Peace Laureates and Eminent Scholars*, eds. Irwin Abrams and Wang Gungwu (New Jersey: World

Scientific, 2003), 304.

4 Lawler, 583.

5 Ibid.

6 Ibid.

7 Robert Fisk, "A Civilization Torn to Pieces," *Independent*, 13 April 2003.

8 Angela M.H. Schuster, "Theft of Time," in *The Looting of the Iraq Museum, Baghdad: The Lost Legacy of Ancient Mesopotamia*, eds. Milbry Polk and Angela M.H. Schuster (New York: Harry N. Abrams, 2005), 10.

9 James A.R. Nafziger, "Protection of Cultural Heritage in Time of War and Its Aftermath," *IFAR Journal* 6, nos. 1 and 2 (2003), 2.

10 Ibid., 5–6.

11 Jeff Spurr, "Indispensable yet Vulnerable: The Library in Dangerous Times: Preface to a Report on the Status of Iraqi Academic Libraries and a Survey of Efforts to Assist Them," *Report of the Middle East Librarians Association Committee on Iraqi Libraries* (2005), 10 and 41–42. Also see <oi.uchicago.edu/OI/IRAQ/mela/indispensable.html>.

KOVEL: THE ECOLOGICAL IMPLICATIONS OF THE WAR

1 DOE report <www.eia.doe.gov/emeu/cabs/iraq.html>

2 There were 123 documented attacks on the 4,359 miles of the Iraqi pipeline system between April 2003 and September 2004. As a result of this and other problems such as lack of reliable energy and water supplies, the production of oil, which was 3.0 million barrels/day in 1989, fell to 0.7 million bpd after the first Gulf war and rose again to 2.6 by 2001, was only 2.0 million bpd after a year and a half of US occupation (DOE report, op. cit; United Nations Environmental Program report on Iraq, May 2003).

3 In Vietnam, owing to the inconvenient fact that the United States lost the war, this kind of brutal transformation could not be imposed. Instead, normal market mechanisms were brought into play, which left the victorious country in some control of its fate.

4 Joel Kovel, *The Enemy of Nature* (London: Zed, 2002).

5 Focus on the Global South and GRAIN, "Iraq's New Patent Law: A Declaration of War against Farmers," October 2004 <www.grain.org/articles/?id=6>.

6 Sonja Ann Jozef Boelaert-Suominen, "International Environmental Law and Naval War: The Effect of Marine Safety and Pollution Conventions during International Armed Conflict," Naval War College Newport, Rhode Island Center for Naval Warfare Studies, Newport, Paper Number Fifteen, December 2000.

7 Brad Knickerbocker, "Military Gets Break from Environmental Rules," *Christian Science Monitor*, 24 November 2003 <www.csmonitor.com/2003/1124/p02s02-usmi.html>.

8 The actual troops in the latest United States war have ended up very poorly trained, in any case, in large part because they are National Guard members and reservists who never figured on going to Iraq, and often receive only the most cursory

training. This is related to the colossal error of failing to realize that the war and occupation would provoke resistance, along with the political need to rely on a volunteer army at all costs, in order to avoid a military draft that would provoke extreme resistance.

9 United Nations Environmental Program, "Desk Study on the Environment in Iraq," Switzerland, 2003. Khaled Yacoub Oweis, "Postwar Iraq Paying Heavy Environmental Price," Reuters, 2 June 2005.

10 The supreme industrial disaster that was the explosion of the methyl isocyanate factory in Bhopal, India, in December 1984 is the paradigmatic example of this. See Kovel, *Enemy*.

11 Long associated with George Schultz, secretary of state under Reagan, as Halliburton is associated with Vice President Dick Cheney—remarkable coincidences, these.

12 Chiefly from the *San Francisco Chronicle* of March 29 and the *Los Angeles Times* of April 10, as summarized in Doug Lorimer, "Iraq: Making a Killing: The Big Business of War," *GreenLeft Weekly* online, <www.greenleft.org.au/back/2005/625/625p20.htm>.

13 For detailed and vivid accounts of the disaster comprised by the electricity-water-sewage nexus, see Dahr Jamail (primary contributor), "Bechtel's Dry Run: Iraqis Suffer Water Crisis," Public Citizen, spring 2004 <www.dahrjamailiraq.com/reports/>; and Christian Parenti, "The Rough Guide to Baghdad," *Nation*, 19 July 2004 <www.thenation.com/doc.mhtml?i= 20040719&s=parenti>. For the most recent survey, see UNDP, *Iraq Living Condition Survey 2004*, vol. 2, Analytic Report, 1 April 2005.

14 As well as 90 tons in Bosnia and Kosovo, against Serbia.

15 See, for example, the 2004 German-made video by Frieder Wagner and Valentin Thurn, "The Doctor, the Depleted Uranium, and the Dying Children," (Telepool; available in the US through www.traprockpeace.org). The video shows research testing water and dust samples around areas of the invasion, with positive results, not just for U-238, but also plutonium and U-236.

16 See, for example, Juan Gonzalez, "Poisoned? Shocking Report Reveals Local Troops May Be Victims of America's High-tech Weapons," *New York Daily News*, 3 April 2004; Juan Gonzalez, "The War's Littlest Victim," *New York Daily News*, 29 September 2004.

AL-AZZAWI: ENVIRONMENTAL DAMAGE OF MILITARY OPERATIONS DURING THE INVASION OF IRAQ (2003–2005)

1 "War in Iraq, Forces: Weapons" <cnn.com/specials/2003/iraq/weapons/index.html>; Simon Helweg-Larson, *Znet*, 7 April 2003; United States Naval Forces, Central Command and Fifth Fleet, <www.cusnc.navy.mil>; "Bunker Buster Bombs Used Against Baghdad," Associated Press, 27 March 2003 <www.azcentral.com/12news/news/articles /03272003iraqpm-cr.html>; "B-2 Successfully Drops Improved Bunker Buster Bomb," Air Force News Service, 26 March 1998, Global

Politics; "Factfile: Bunker Buster Bombs," BBC News <news.bbc.co.uk/1/ hilworld/americas/289508.stm>; Jay Shaft, "US Colonel Admits 500 Tons of DU were Used in Iraq," *Scoop: Independent News* (New Zealand), 5 May 2003, <www.scoop.co.nz/stories/HL0305/500050.html>; Marshal Brain, "How Bunker Busters Work," <science.howstuffworks.com/bunker-buster.html>; Frida Berrigan, "Weapons of Mass Deception," *In These Times*, 20 June 2003, <www.inthesetimes.com/ comments>; Sara Flounders, "Iraq: A Depleted Uranium Nightmare," Portland Independent Media Center, 18 August 2003, <portland.indymedia.org/ en/2003/269974.shtml>; BLU–118/B Thermobaric Weapon <www.globalsecurity.org>; "Toxic Radioactive Uranium Weapons: Did You Know, Abolish DU," <www.nukewatch.com/du/factsheet.html>; Scott Peterson, "Remains of Toxic Bullets Litter Iraq," *Christian Science Monitor*, 18 May 2003; Larry Johnson, "Use of Depleted Uranium Weapons Lingers as Health Concern," 4 August 2003, <www.seattlepi.com>; March W. Herold, "Uranium Wars: The Pentagon Steps Up its Use of Radioactive Munition," 13 November 2002 <www.cursor.org/stories/ uranium.htm>; Admiral Vishnu Bhagwat, "Silent WMD, Effects of DU," 29 February 2004 <www.xs4all.nl/~stgvisie/ VISIEsilentwmds.html>; Amy Worthington, "Death by Slow Burn—How American Nukes Its Own Troops," *Idaho Observer*, 13 August 2003, *Sierra Times*, <www.sierratimes.com/03/05/02article>; Christian Scherrer, "Depleted Uranium and the 'Liberation of Iraq': A Report from Hiroshima," <www.japanfocus.org>; "Coalition Forces Employ DU—A Weapon of Mass Destruction," *The Light Party*; Dai Williams, "Hazards of Uranium Weapons in the Proposed War on Iraq," 22 September 2002.

2 "Deadly Waste Returned to US Forces," Greenpeace, 24 June 2003 <www.greenpeace.org/usa/news/deadly-waste-returned-to-us>.

3 R. Aaren Vesilined, et al., *Environmental Pollution and Control* (Woburn: Butterworth-Heinemann, 1990).

4 Muthana al-Omar, "Aggression and Economical Sanctions," *Umm al-Maarik* (Baghdad), 2000; David Smith-Ferri, "Iraq Health and Infrastructure," *Voices in the Wilderness* no. 7, 15 April 2005.

5 Helweg-Larson, *Znet*; Berrigan, "Weapons"; Johnson, "Use of Depleted Uranium"; Herold, "Uranium Wars"; Scherrer, "Depleted Uranium."

6 MEDACT News and Analysis, *The Health and Environmental Costs of War on Iraq*, 11 November 2003 <electroniciraq.net/news>; Smith-Ferri, "Iraq Health."

7 Institute of Analysis for Global Security, "Iraq Pipeline Watch," *Energy Security* <www.iags.org/iraqpipelinewatch.htm>.

8 Al-Omar, "Aggression."

9 Scott Peterson, "Remains"; Johnson, "Use of Depleted Uranium"; Herold, "Uranium Wars"; Bhagwat, "Silent WMD"; "Coalition Forces Employ DU"; Williams, "Hazards of Uranium Weapons."

10 Williams, "Hazards of Uranium Weapons."

11 J. Magwar, *Effects of Radiological Weapons on Human and the Environment in Iraq*, M.Sc. Thesis in Environmental Engineering, Baghdad University, 1998.

12 United States Naval Forces, Central Command and Fifth Fleet <www.cusnc.navy.mil>.

13 "Deadly Waste Returned to US Forces."

14 Ibid.

SIXTH SESSION: THE GLOBAL SECURITY ENVIRONMENT AND FUTURE ALTERNATIVES
ALTINAY: MILITARISM AND THE CULTURE OF VIOLENCE

1 Leo Tolstoy, "Patriotism and Government" [1905], in *Classics of International Relations*, 2nd ed., ed. John A. Vasquez (New Jersey: Prentice Hall, 1990), 41.

2 Elaine Scarry, *The Body in Pain: The Making and Unmaking of the World* (Oxford: Oxford University Press, 1985).

3 Alfred Vagts, *A History of Militarism: Civilian and Military* (Meridian Books, Inc., 1959 [1937]), 134.

4 Eugen Weber, *Peasants Into Frenchmen: The Modernization Of Rural France, 1870–1914* (Stanford: Stanford University Press, 1976).

5. John Dewey, "On Military Training in Schools" in *John Dewey: The Later Works, 1925–1953,* ed. Jo Ann Boydston (Carbondale: Southern Illinois University Press, 1990), 124.

6 John Langdon-Davies, *Militarism in Education: A Contribution to Educational Reconstruction* (London: The Swarthmore Press, 1919), 149.

7 I think it is noteworthy that feminist scholarship on militarism has been particularly vibrant and profilic in recent decades. For pioneering works in this field, see Betty Reardon, *Sexism and the War System* (New York: Columbia University, Teacher's College Press, 1985); Cynthia Enloe, *Bananas, Beaches and Bases: Making Feminist Sense of International Politics* (Berkeley: University of California Press, 1989); Cynthia Enloe, *Maneuvers: The International Politics of Militarizing Women's Lives* (Berkeley: University of California Press, 2000); Jean Bethke Elshtain and Sheila Tobias, eds. *Women, Militarism, and War* (Savage, Maryland: Rowman and Littlefield Publishers, 1990); Lois Ann Lorentzen and Jennifer Turpin, *The Women and War Reader* (New York: New York University Press, 1998); Catherine Lutz, *Homefront: A Military City and the American 20th Century* (Boston: Beacon Press, 2001).

8 Ay e Gül Altınay, *The Myth of the Military-Nation: Militarism, Gender, and Education in Turkey* (New York: Palgrave Macmillan, 2004).

9 Anuradha M. Chenoy, "Militarization, Conflict, and Women in South Asia," in *The Women and War Reader,* eds. Lois Ann Lorentzen and Jennifer Turpin (New York: New York University Press 1998), 101–110.

10 Celal Sıtkı, "Askerlikten Dönü," *Ülkü,* 1(3) [1933]:250–254.

11 Cynthia Enloe, *The Curious Feminist: Searching for Women in a New Age of Empire* (Berkeley: University of California Press, 2004).

AL-ALI: GENDER AND WAR: THE PLIGHT OF IRAQI WOMEN

1 A later version of this paper was published as "Reconstructing Gender: Iraqi

Women Between Dictatorship, War, Sanctions and Occupation," *Third World Quarterly* 26, no. 4/5 (2005).

2 Cynthia Cockburn, "Background Paper: Gender, Armed Conflict and Political Violence," World Bank Conference on Gender, Armed Conflict and Political Development (Washington, DC, 1999), 3.

3 Nira Yuval-Davis and Floya Anthias, *Woman-Nation-State* (New York: Palgrave Macmillan, 1989), 7.

4 Nira Yuval-Davis, *Gender and Nation* (London: Sage Publications, 1997), 66.

5 Ibid., 76.

6 Cockburn, "Background Paper," 8.

7 Women Watch, Fact Sheet 5, 2005.

8 Silvia Meznaric, "Gender as an Ethno-Marker: Rape, War and Identity Politics in the Former Yugoslavia," in *Identity, Politics and Women: Cultural Reassertions and Feminisms in International Perspective*, ed. Valentine Moghadam (Oxford: Westview Press, 1994); see also Cockburn, "Background."

9 Johan Galtung, *Essays in Peace Research*, vols. 1–5 (Copenhagen: Christian Ejlers, 1975–1980); Cockburn, 6.

10 Maja Korac, *Linking Arms: Women and War in Post-Yugoslav States* (Uppsala: Life and Peace Institute 1998).

11 Liz Kelly, "Wars against Women: Sexual Violence, Sexual Politics and the Militarized State," in Susie Jacobs, et al., *States of Conflict: Gender, Violence, and Resistance* (London and New York: Zed Books, 2000).

12 Marianne Hester, Liz Kelly, and Jill Radford, "Introduction" in *Women, Violence and Male Power*, eds. M. Hester, et al. (Milton Keynes: Open University Press, 1996), 3.

13 Jacobs, et. al., 2.

14 Chris Corrin, "Introduction," in *Women in a Violent World: Feminist Analyses and Resistance Across "Europe,"* ed. Chris Corrin (Edinburgh: Edinburgh University Press, 1996), 1.

15 Ronit Lentin, *Gender and Catastrophe* (London: Zed Books, 1997), 12.

16 Recognizing that patriarchy is a contested concept, I have adopted the definition as "a set of social relations which has a material base and in which there are hierarchical relations between men, and solidarity between them, which enable them to control women. Patriarchy is thus the system of male oppression of women" (Heidi Hartmann, "Capitalism, Patriarchy, and Job Segregation by Sex", in *Capitalist Patriarchy and the Case for Socialist Feminism*, ed. Zillah Eisenstein [New York: Monthly Review, 1979], 232). It is important to stress, however, that forms of patriarchy vary historically, cross-culturally, and according to class standing.

17 Cynthia Cockburn and Dubravka Zarkov, eds., *The Postwar Moment: Militaries, Masculinities and International Peacekeeping* (London: Lawrence & Wishart, 2002); Cynthia Enloe, "All the Men Are in the Militias, All the Women Are Victims," *Women and War Reader*, eds. L. Lorentzen and J. Turpin, (New York: New York University Press, 1998), 50–62.

18 Cockburn and Zarkov, 12.

19 Robert Connell, *Gender and Power* (Cambridge: Polity Press, 1987).

20 Cynthia Enloe, "Demilitarization—or More of the Same? Feminist Questions to Ask in the Postwar Moment," in *The Postwar Moment*, 23–24.

21 Cockburn and Zarkov.

22 Robert Connell, *Masculinities* (Cambridge: Polity Press, 1995); Robert Connell, "Masculinities, the Reduction of Violence and the Pursuit of Peace," in Cockburn and Zarkov, *The Postwar Moment*.

23 Cockburn, "Background Paper," 8; Cockburn and Zarkov; Judy El-Bushra, "Transforming Conflict: Some Thoughts on a Gendered Understanding of Conflict Dynamics," in Jacobs et al., *States of Conflict*; H. Afshar and D. Eade, eds., *Development, Women, and War: Feminist Perspectives* (Oxford: Oxfam, 2004), 40.

24 Francine D'Amico, "Citizen-Soldier? Class, Gender, Sexuality and the US Military," in Jacobs et al., *States of Conflict*.

25 Myriam Gervais, "Human Security and Reconstruction Efforts in Rwanda: Impact on the Lives of Women," in Afshar and Eade, *Development, Women, and War.*

26 Cynthia Enloe, "All the Men Are in the Militias," 538.

27 Kelly, 48.

28 Donna Pankhurst, "The 'Sex War' and Other Wars: Towards a Feminist Approach to Peace Building," in Afshar and Eade, *Development, Women, and War*, 19.

29 Birgitte Sorenson, "Women and Post-Conflict Reconstruction," War-torn Societies Project, article 3, United Nations Research Institute for Social Development (Geneva), 1998.

30 Cockburn, "Background Paper."

31 Ferris, in Sorenson 1998.

32 Ricardo Grassi, "Iraq: Everyone Needs Food Aid," UNICEF, 2003 <www.globalpolicy.org/security/issues/iraq/attack/crisis/2003/0630foodaid.htm>.

33 Nadje al-Ali and Yasmin Hussein, "Between Dreams and Sanctions: Teenage Lives in Iraq," in *Teenagers in the Middle East*, ed. Akbar Mahdi (Westport: Greenwood Publishing Group, 2003).

34 *Abbayah* is the traditional black garment worn by Iraqi women. Najaf, a holy city south of Baghdad, is the location of the main Shi'a cemetery in Iraq.

35 Nadje al-Ali, "Women, Gender Relations, and Sanctions in Iraq," in *Iraq: Its History, People, and Politics*, ed. Shams Inati (New York: Humanity Books, 2003), 233–250.

36 Press Release, Human Rights Watch, November 2003.

FEKETE: CREATING RACISM AND INTOLERANCE

1 Further examples can be found in Human Rights Watch, "In the Name of Counter-Terrorism: Human Rights Abuses Worldwide" (New York, 2003).

2 The US Anti-Terrorism and Effective Death Penalty Act (AEDPA) appears to be the model for deciding what groups constitute "foreign terrorist organizations." This empowered the US secretary of state to create a list of designated foreign terrorist

organizations, defined as those engaged in any activity which threatens "the national defense, foreign relations or economic interests of the United States." The names of organizations and individuals in the EU deemed terrorist have already been proscribed by the US Treasury Department's Office of Foreign Assets Control. See Liz Fekete, "Anti-Terrorism and Human Rights," *European Race Bulletin* no. 47 (2004).

3 Nancy Murray, "Profiled: Arabs, Muslims, and the Post-9/11 Hunt for the 'Enemy Within,'" in *Civil Rights in Peril: The Targeting of Arabs and Muslims*, ed. Elaine C. Hagopian (London: Pluto Press, 2004).

4 David Cole, "The Missing Patriot Debate," *Nation*, 30 May 2005.

5 See A. Sivanandan and Liz Fekete, "The Three Faces of British Racism: A Special Report," *Race & Class* 43, no. 2 (October–December 2001).

6 Murray, "Profiled."

7 A. Sivanandan, as quoted in "Speech Crimes and Deportations," *European Race Bulletin* (forthcoming).

AL-JARADAT: THE RELATIONSHIP BETWEEN IRAQ, PALESTINE, AND ISRAEL

1 Ahmad Mohamed al-Jaradat was unable to attend the World Tribunal on Iraq Istanbul Session because Israeli authorities did not allow him to leave. His paper was presented by Ay e Berktay.

NADHMI: POLARIZATION AND THE NARROWING SCOPE OF POLITICAL ALTERNATIVES

1 Wamid Nadmi was unable to attend the WTI Istanbul session due to illness. His paper was presented by Ay e Gül Altınay.

COATES: NEXT STEPS FOR THE PEACE MOVEMENT

1 To follow the attempt to develop the work of the World Tribunal on Iraq, please go to <www.worldtribunal.org.>

2 Various campaigns have devoted their efforts to tracing and documenting the consequences of this development. The surge in military preparations is highlighted in the development of nuclear weaponry, and the evolution of advanced plans to site offensive weapons in space. The campaign against Star Wars can be visited at <www.space4peace.org.> The extensive spawning of military bases by the United States now spreads all around the world, and includes numerous emplacements in the territories of States belonging to the former Soviet Union <http://lists.riseup.net/www/info/nousbases>.

3 The war on terror has produced a whole series of setbacks for human rights, although real terrorists, we are told, have done nothing but thrive since the occupation of Iraq. Civil liberties have not been so fortunate. This problem will be one of the themes of the next meeting of the Bertrand Russell Network for Peace and Human Rights, in Brussels on 20–21 October 2005. More information can be found at <www.russfound.org>, and also at <www.statewatch.org}.

4 See the remarkable series of leaked documents which reveal the advice given to Tony Blair by his officials, during the covert preparations for the coming war on Iraq <www.afterdowningstreet.org>.

5 Go to <www.forumsocialmundial.org.br.> The campaign for the removal of American nuclear weapons from Europe can be found at <www.abolition2000 europe.org.> The overall campaign against new nuclear weapons in the context of the failure of the Review Conference of the Non-Proliferation Treaty is at <www.acronym.org.>

KUMAR: TOWARDS A NEW POLITICAL IMAGINARY

1 Mazisi Kunene, "Congregation of the Storytellers at the Festival of the Children of Soweto," *Ancestors and the Sacred Mountains.*

2 Ivan Illich, *Shadow Work: Vernacular Values Examined* (London: Marion Boyars, Inc., 1981).

3 Corinne Kumar, "A South Wind, Towards A New Political Imaginary," in *Dialogue and Difference: Feminisms Challenge Globalization*, eds. Marguerite Waller and Sylvia Marcos (London: Palgrave Macmillan, 2005).

4 Maya Angelou, "These Yet to Be United States," in *I Shall Not Be Moved* (New York: Bantam, 1991), 21.

Biographies of the Contributors

Anthony Alessandrini (US)
Anthony Alessandrini is a lecturer at Rutgers University on comparative literature and an active member of Students for Justice in Palestine. He worked as an organizer of the WTI-New York session and is a member of WTI International Coordination Team.

Nadje al-Ali (Iraq/UK)
Nadje al-Ali is a social anthropologist of Iraqi origin and a senior lecturer at the University of Exeter's Institute of Arab and Islamic Studies. She specializes in women's and gender issues in the Middle East and has been working on the impact of war and economic sanctions on women in Iraq. She is also a founding member of Act Together: Women's Action on Iraq and a member of Women in Black UK. Her book on the history of Iraqi women from the 1950s to today is forthcoming from Zed Books.

Ay e Gül Altınay (Turkey)
Ay e Gül Altınay is a doctor of cultural anthropology at Sabancı University. She works on militarism, nationalism, and gender, and has been active in the antiwar and anti-militarist movement in Turkey. She has two books to her name: *Homeland, Nation, Women* (ed.) and *The Myth of the Military Nation*.

Samir Amin (Egypt/Senegal)
Born in Egypt and trained in Paris, Samir Amin is one of the better-known thinkers of his generation, both in development theory as well as in the relativistic-cultural critique of social sciences. Amin currently occupies the post of director of the Third World Forum in Dakar, Senegal, an international pool of academics from Africa, Asia, and South America. Being a promoter of the conscious self-reliance of developing countries, he has written extensively on economics, development, and international affairs.

Souad Naji al-Azzawi (Iraq)
Souad Naji al-Azzawi directs a doctoral program in environmental engineering. She studied geological and environmental engineering in the

US. After graduating in 1991, she returned home to Baghdad in the midst of the Gulf War. In 1996, together with six researchers, she was able to do a survey on the radiation in the soil, air, and water of southern Iraq.

Amy Bartholomew (Canada)

Amy Bartholomew is a professor in the department of law, Carleton University, Ottawa, Canada. She is a contributor to and the editor of *Empire's Law: The American Imperial Project and the War to Remake the World* and has written on the Iraq war, international law, and the "human-rights hawks" in *The New Imperial Challenge: The Socialist Register 2004* (edited by Leo Panitch and Colin Leys). She has written widely on legal and political theory, particularly with regard to human rights. She was a witness at the Brussells Tribunal, is currently on the advisory committee to that tribunal, and was on the international advisory board of the conference "International Humanitarian Law and Impunity of Powerful States: The Case of the United States," held in Paris, September 2005.

Abdul Ilah al-Bayaty (Iraq/France)

Abdul Ilah al-Bayaty began his political life as a Ba'athist when he was fifteen years old, in 1955, becoming one of the party's leaders in 1961. He led a leftist schism in the Ba'ath Party in 1962 and was imprisoned by the Ba'athists in 1963. He has lived under all the dictatorships which have ruled Iraq since 1940 and has been imprisoned by all the regimes. He left Iraq in 1970 because the regime wanted to arrest him. In Iraqi political circles, he is considered a democratic leftist personality who has never compromised with the governments. A member of the Arab National Congress, he is now part of the redaction of the Al-Wifaq al-Democrati and writes from time to time in *Al-Ahram Weekly*.

Fadhil al-Bedrani (Iraq)

Fadhil al-Bedrani works as a correspondent for al-Jazeera in Iraq and also works for Reuters. He stayed inside Falluja during the last major assault on the city.

Walden Bello (Philippines)

Walden Bello is the director of Focus on the Global South in Bangkok, a project of Chulalongkorn University's Social Research Institute, and a professor of public administration and sociology at the University of the Philippines. His interest areas are regionalism and globalization, international financial institutions, the WTO, and alternative security in the Asia-Pacific. He is also chairman of the board of Greenpeace Southeast Asia.

Niloufer Bhagwat (India)

Professor Bhagwat is a judge from India and the vice president of Mumbai-based Indian Lawyers' Association. She wrote the final opinion of the International Criminal Tribunal for Afghanistan at Tokyo in March 2004.

Guglielmo Carchedi (Netherlands)

Guglielmo Carchedi is a retired professor from the University of Amsterdam. He is the author of many articles and books including *Frontiers of Political Economy*, *Marx and Non-Equilibrium Economics* (edited with Alan Freeman), and *For Another Europe, a Class Analysis of European Economic Integration*.

Christine Chinkin (UK)

Christine Chinkin is an advisor to the Office of the UN High Commissioner for Human Rights and a professor of international law at the London School of Economics. She is a member of the London Commission of Inquiry that submitted an appeal to the International Criminal Court (ICC) against Tony Blair and members of the UK government, which led to the decision that there was sufficient grounds for the ICC to launch an investigation of Blair and his cabinet members for breaches of the ICC statute in relation to crimes against humanity and/or war crimes committed during the Iraq conflict and occupation in 2003.

Ken Coates (UK)

Ken Coates is the chairman of the Bertrand Russell Peace Foundation and editor of the *Spokesman*. A special professor at the University of Nottingham until 2004, he served as a Member of the European Parliament between 1989 and 1999, and was president of its Human Rights Subcommittee from 1989 to 1994.

Mete Çubukçu (Turkey)

A journalist who has been to Palestine and Iraq several times, Çubukçu has published two books, entitled *Our Palestine* and *Journalism under Fire*.

Herbert Docena (Thailand)

Herbert Docena is one of the consulting assistants of Focus on Global South, a project of Chulalongkorn University's Social Research Institute that concentrates on international policy studies. He was in Iraq for International Occupation Watch and observed the reconstruction and political transition period.

Hilal Elver (Turkey/US)

Professor Elver received both a degree in law and a Ph.D. from the University of Ankara Law School in Turkey. She teaches environmental policy as a visiting professor in the global studies program at the University of California, Santa Barbara. She was a legal advisor to Turkey's Ministry of Environment and has a book entitled *Peaceful Uses of International Rivers: The Euphrates and Tigris Rivers Dispute*.

Larry Everest (US)

Author of *Oil, Power and Empire: Iraq and the US Global Agenda*, Everest has covered the Middle East and Central Asia for over 20 years for the *Revolutionary Worker* newspaper and other publications. In 1991, shortly after the end of the Persian Gulf War, Everest went to Iraq to document the impact of the war on the Iraqi people and filmed the award-winning video *Iraq: War Against the People*. He is also the author of *Behind the Poison Cloud: Union Carbide's Bhopal Massacre*.

Khaled Fahmy (Egypt/US)

Khaled Fahmy is an associate professor of modern Middle Eastern history in the department of Middle Eastern and Islamic studies at New York University. He is the author of numerous studies on the social and cultural history of nineteenth-century Egypt. Fahmy also continues working on contemporary Middle Eastern politics, particularly on Israel, Palestine, and Iraq.

Richard Falk (US)

Richard Falk is a professor of international law at the University of California, Santa Barbara, and has published over 30 books on international law and human rights, most recently *The Declining World Order: America's Imperial Geopolitics* (2004).

Thomas Fasy (US)

Dr. Fasy is an associate clinical professor of pathology at the Mount Sinai School of Medicine in New York City. He has longstanding interests in carcinogenesis and environmental toxicology. In the past two years, he has lectured at conferences and university campuses on the toxic effects of inhaling uranium oxide dusts derived from depleted uranium weapons. He is collaborating in a research project designed to assess the extent to which Iraqi children have been contaminated with uranium derived from DU weapons.

Liz Fekete (UK)

Liz Fekete is the vice president of the London Race Relations Institute. She has conducted research on the effects of the politics of the "war on terror" on civil rights and liberties and racism in Europe. She is also the co-editor of *Race & Class*, a journal on racism, empire, and globalization.

Johan Galtung (Norway/Spain)

Johan Galtung is a peace studies and general social science professor at the Universidad de Alicante in Spain and an advisor to the UN. He won the Right Livelihood Award, also known as the alternative peace prize, in 1987. Galtung is currently the director of Transcend, a network for peace and development. He has many books to his name, including *Human Rights in Another Key*.

Tim Goodrich (US)

Coming from a family with a tradition of military service, in his childhood Tim Goodrich always dreamed of becoming an Air Force pilot. During his deployment in Saudi Arabia in October 2002, around the time the Bush administration started talking about going into war, he started to research, and later question, the legitimacy of this war. On the return home from his tour of duty two weeks after the US invasion of Iraq, he joined the ranks of antiwar demonstrations in the US and co-founded Iraq Veterans Against the War in 2004.

Denis Halliday (Ireland)

Halliday served between 1994 and 1998 as assistant secretary-general of the United Nations, and was appointed by Secretary-General Kofi Annan to the post of UN humanitarian coordinator in Iraq and administrator of the oil-for-food program as of 1 September 1997. He resigned from his post in Iraq and from the United Nations as a whole in September 1998, protesting the economic sanctions and the inefficiency of the program.

Jim Harding (Canada)

Jim Harding is a retired professor in the School of Human Justice at the University of Regina in Canada. He is a peace activist and former city councilor and author of *After Iraq: War, Imperialism and Democracy*. Since the 1970s he has worked as a researcher and activist for an end to uranium mining in his home province of Saskatchewan, which now houses the largest operating uranium mines in the world.

Hana Ibrahim (Iraq)

A writer and journalist, Ibrahim worked in the Palestinian camps in Jordan and Lebanon during 1970–1973. She was the manager of the Women's Cultural Center in Baghdad and edited and wrote for many feminist journals. She worked in the Occupation Watch Center in 2004, and is currently the chair of the Women's Will Organization and edits its journal.

Dahr Jamail (US)

Dahr Jamail is an independent American journalist who went to Iraq after the invasion to bring attention to how the Iraqi people and US soldiers were being affected, through his internet journal DahrJamailIraq.com. His articles have appeared in the *Guardian*, the *Nation*, and the *Sunday Herald*, and he is a regular contributor to Inter Press Service.

Ahmad Mohamed al-Jaradat (Palestine)

Ahmad Mohamed al-Jaradat is a veteran political activist and coordinator of the AIC Settler Violence project.

Eman Khammas (Iraq)

Eman Khammas is an Iraqi human-rights activist based in Baghdad. She is the former co-director of the International Occupation Watch Center. During the war and the occupation, she has been writing articles for the alternative media, an invaluable effort to let the world outside Iraq comprehend the realities of occupation.

Amal al-Khedairy (Iraq)

Amal al-Khedairy is the founder and director of al-Beit al-Iraqi, or Iraqi House, an arts and cultural center in Baghdad since 1988, which was bombed and destroyed by US forces on 4 April 2003. She is also a widely traveled expert in Iraqi history, regional culture, arts, archeology, and music.

Joel Kovel (US)

Joel Kovel is a professor of social studies at Bard College in New York. He is the founder and editor of *Capitalism, Nature, Socialism* magazine. He was the Green Party candidate for the US presidency in the 2000 elections. His most recent book is *The Enemy of Nature: The End of Capitalism or the End of the World?*

Corrine Kumar (India/Tunisia)

Corinne Kumar is a storyteller, weaver, dreamer, and also sociologist/political philosopher. She works with El Taller International, an NGO based in Tunisia focusing on the global south. She also works with the Asian Women's Human Rights Council, and in partnership with networks and women's human-rights organizations prepares and holds Courts of Women, creating public spaces with new political visions. Her writings challenge the dominant discourses particularly on human rights, drawing the contours of a new political imaginary, often titled "a South wind."

Saul Landau (US)

Saul Landau is a film producer and academic and has produced more than 40 films on social, political, and historical issues. He has received the Letelier-Moffitt Human Rights Prize, the George Polk Investigative Journalism Prize, the Edgar Allen Poe Prize, and an Emmy Award. His latest film is *Syria: Between Iraq and a Hard Place*, and his latest book is *The*

Business of America: How Consumers Have Replaced Citizens and How We Can Reverse the Trend?

Akira Maeda (Japan)

Akira Maeda is a professor of law at Tokyo Zokei University, as well as the director of Japanese Association of Democratic Lawyers and a representative of the International Criminal Tribunal for Afghanistan and the International Criminal Tribunal for Iraq (ICTI-Japan).

Ömer Madra (Turkey)

Ömer Madra is the co-founder, editor in chief, and programmer of Açık Radyo, an independent radio station in Istanbul. He has also been a lecturer in the department of international relations at Istanbul Bilgi University since 1996. Beside his published academic works, essays, and a novel, Madra has taken editorial posts at several Turkish newspapers and magazines.

Mark Manning (US)

Mark Manning was among the rare unembedded American journalists inside Falluja during the two sieges of April and November 2004. He spent one week inside Falluja with a video camera interviewing survivors of the November siege and edited a film from these interviews, which will make its world premiere at the WTI.

Biju Matthew (US)

Biju Matthew is the assistant professor of business at Rider University. His main areas of interest are migration, diaspora, and international labor market. Matthew is one of the organizers of New York Taxi Workers Alliance. He has participated in NY Brecht Forum, Revolutionary Leftists Forum, Campaign to Stop Funding Hate. His latest book is, *Taxi! Cabs and Capitalism in New York.*

David Miller (Scotland)

As a faculty member of the sociology and geography department at Strathclyde University in Glasgow, Miller's current research interests include propaganda and the "war on terror," corporate communications, corporate power, lobbying, the strategic use of science, corporate influences on academic work, spin, and the decline of democratic governance. He is editor of *Tell Me Lies: Propaganda and Media Distortion in the Attack on Iraq*.

Nermin al-Mufti (Iraqi Turkoman)

Nermin al-Mufti is a writer, journalist, activist, and former co-director of Occupation Watch Center who lives in Baghdad.

Rana M. Mustafa (Iraq)

Rana Mustafa is a filmmaker and human-rights activist.

Jayan Nayar (Malaysia/Italy)

Dr. Nayar is a professor of law at Warwick University. He was also the coordinator of the Peoples' Law Program at the Lelio Basso International Foundation. He has written extensively on peoples' tribunals, peoples' law, and the relationship between legal processes and transnational corporations.

Abdul Wahab al-Obeidi (Iraq)

Abdul Wahab al-Obeidi is a member of the executive board of "Freedom Voice for Human Rights," a human-rights organization in Baghdad, mostly constituted of lawyers, that keeps records of human-rights violations, especially the cases of missing people in Iraq.

Barbara Olshansky (US)

Barbara Olshansky has been the assistant legal director of the Center for Constitutional Rights since 1995. She is one of the lawyers who prepared the case concerning the illegality of the US detention activities in Guantánamo. She is the author of *Secret Trials and Executions: Military Tribunals and the Threat to Democracy* (2002), co-author of *Against War in Iraq: An Anti-War Primer* (2003), and also co-author of *America's Disappeared: Secret Imprisonment, Detainees, and the "War on Terror"* (2004).

Baskın Oran (Turkey)

Baskın Oran is a professor of international relations. He works on issues of nationalism, minorities, and Turkish foreign policy. A columnist in the daily *Agos*, he has written many articles and books, and was a member of the recently abolished Advisory Board on Human Rights.

Gül Pulhan (Turkey)

Gül Pulhan is an assistant professor in the department of history at Koç University. She is a specialist in ancient Near Eastern archeology and has excavated extensively in Anatolia. She recently organized an international symposium, "A Future for Our Past," which was devoted to the subject of redefining cultural heritage and its protection.

Mohammed al-Rahoo (Iraq)

Mohammed al-Rahoo is a professor of law at Mosul University.

John Ross (US)

A long-time antiwar activist and one of the first US resisters to be imprisoned for opposing the Vietnam draft, Ross is a long-time Latin America correspondent with four decades on the ground covering social movements in the region, from Peru's Sendero Luminoso to the Zapatista Army of National Liberation in Chiapas, Mexico. He is a frequent lecturer on university campuses from Harvard to Berkeley. In addition to his latest publication, *Murdered by Capitalism: A Memoir of 150 Years of Life and Death on the American Left*, Ross has published six titles of fiction and nonfiction.

Arundhati Roy (India)

Renowned author and activist Arundhati Roy received the Booker Prize for literature in 1997 for *The God of Small Things*. Presently one of the most eloquent voices for the global justice and antiwar movement, her many awards include the Sydney Peace Prize in 2004 and the Lannan Cultural Freedom Prize in 2002.

Amal Sawadi (Iraq)

Amal Sawadi is a lawyer in Iraq who represents and defends the rights of detainees and prisoners of war.

Phil Shiner (UK)

Phil Shiner leads the team at Public Interest Lawyers (PIL) in the UK. He is a lawyer with an international and national reputation for his work on issues concerning international, environmental, and human-rights law. He has dealt with international law issues, including a judicial review challenging the UK government's decision to go to war and instructing barristers on the legality of the Mutual Defense Agreement between the US and UK.

Issa Shivji (Tanzania)
Issa Shivji is a professor of international law at the University of Dar es Salaam in Tanzania and was the founder and former director of the Institute for Research on Land Rights and Resources. He has written extensively on democracy and law in Africa, "law's empire and empire's lawlessness," and related subjects.

Hans von Sponeck (Germany/Switzerland)
Former United Nations Assistant Secretary-General Hans von Sponeck joined the UN Development Program in 1968, and worked in Ghana, Turkey, Botswana, Pakistan, and India, before becoming director of European Affairs. Serving 36 years with the organization, his last post succeeded Denis Halliday as UN humanitarian coordinator for Iraq and administrator of the oil-for-food program in October 1998. Sponeck resigned in February 2000, in protest of the international policy toward Iraq, including sanctions.

WTI Istanbul Coordination–Content Committee (Turkey)
The Content Committee of the WTI Istanbul Coordination was composed of Ayça Çubukçu, Ay e Berktay, Hilal Küey, Hülya Üçpınar, and Müge Gürsoy Sökmen.

Biographies of the Jury of Conscience

Taty Almeida (Argentina)
Taty Almeida is a representative of Madres de la Plaza de Mayo (Linea Fundadora), an NGO dedicated to peace and human rights formed by mothers looking for justice after their children were kidnapped and, in most cases, killed during the dictatorship in Argentina named the "Dirty War" (1976–1983).

Murat Belge (Turkey)
Murat Belge is an editor, political scientist, and writer. He resigned from his position as an associate professor in the Faculty of English Language and Literature of Istanbul University and co-founded Iletisim Publishers. In addition to criticism and commentaries published in literary and political magazines, he is known for his translations of authors such as Faulkner, James Joyce, Patrick White, and Dickens. He was the editor in chief of monthly socialist cultural magazine *Birikim* and *Yeni Gündem*. He is currently teaching at Bilgi University and has a column in *Radikal* newspaper.

Eve Ensler (US)
Eve Ensler's Obie Award–winning play *The Vagina Monologues*, which has been translated into over 35 languages and run in theaters all over the world, initiated V-Day, a global movement to stop violence against women and girls. Ensler is also chair of the Women's Committee of PEN American Center and is an executive producer of "What I Want my Words to Do to You," a documentary about the writing group she has led since 1998 at the Bedford Hills Correctional Facility for Women.

Ay e Erzan (Turkey)
A professor of physics at the Istanbul Technical University, Ay e Erzan has been active in the Peace Initiative of Turkey. She was the L'Oreal-UNESCO Women in Science 2003 Laureate for Europe.

François Houtart (Belgium)
François Houtart participated in the Bertrand Russell War Crimes Tribunal on US crimes in Vietnam in 1967. He is a spiritual father and a

member of the International Committee of the World Social Forum of
Porto Alegre, director of the Tricontinental Center (Cetri) for research on
alternative globalization, executive secretary of the Alternative World
Forum, and president of the International League for rights and liberation
of people. He participated as an expert in the works of the Vatican Council
II (1962–1965). He has written numerous works on globalization and
social stuggles, and regularly collaborates with *Le Monde Diplomatique*.

Salaam al-Jobourie (Iraq)

Salaam al-Jobourie comes from a village which was harmed during the
war in Iraq, in which many of his relatives were killed. He is currently
working as a journalist in Baghdad.

Jae-Bok Kim (South Korea)

Jae-Bok Kim is a South Korean priest and an Iraq Peace Team member
who went on a 58-day hunger strike to protest the Korean government's
decision to send troops to Iraq.

David Krieger (US)

Dr. Krieger is the founder and president of the Nuclear Age Peace
Foundation, an international organization dedicated to the abolition of
nuclear weapons, the strengthening of international law, and the
empowerment of a new generation of peace leaders. He has lectured
throughout the world on issues of peace, international law, and the
elimination of nuclear weapons, and is the author and editor of many
books on these subjects, including *Nuclear Weapons and the World Court*
and, most recently, the poetry collection *Today Is Not a Good Day for War*.
He is the recipient of the 2005 Global Green Millennium Award
for International Environmental Leadership.

Rela Mazali (Israel)

Rela Mazali is an Israeli writer and feminist peace activist. A founder of the
New Profile movement to de-militarize Israeli civil society, Mazali has
worked for many years to end the occupation of the Palestinian territories.
She is the author of numerous short stories, articles, and essays, including
WhaNever: A Novel (1987); *Playbie Sitter*, a children's book co-authored
with No'a Mazali, her daughter (1997); and educational curricula. Her

first book in English, *Maps of Women's Goings and Stayings* (2001) was published by Stanford University Press.

Chandra Muzaffar (Malaysia)

Chandra Muzaffar is one of Malaysia's most prominent human-rights activists. Founder of *Aliron*, a multiethnic Malaysian reform movement dedicated to justice, freedom, and solidarity, he was its president from 1977 to 1991. Professor Muzaffar, who used to teach at the Center for Civilizational Dialogue at the University of Malaysia in Kuala Lumpur, is now the president of the International Movement for a Just World. He is a board member of the International Movement Against All Forms of Discrimination and Racism, based in Belgium. He is the author of many books including *Human Rights and the New World Order* and *Muslims, Dialogue, Terror*.

Ahmet Öztürk (Turkey)

Ahmet Öztürk as been active in many NGOs. He is a member of the Board of Zonguldak Cultural and Education Foundation and is a columnist for a local newspaper. He is working as a mine worker.

Arundhati Roy (India)

Renowned author and activist Arundhati Roy received the Booker Prize for literature in 1997 for *The God of Small Things*. Presently one of the most eloquent voices for the global justice and antiwar movement, her many awards include the Sydney Peace Prize in 2004 and the Lannan Cultural Freedom Prize in 2002.

Miguel Angel de los Santos Cruz (Mexico)

In 1994, de los Santos became the lawyer for the Non-Governmental Organizations' Coordinator for Peace, or CONPAZ, a human-rights group founded to end the unrest in Chiapas. He has defended more than 100 indigenous Mexicans accused of membership in the guerrilla Zapatista army. When tensions in Chiapas boiled over in 1996, de los Santos was targeted by right-wing extremists, but the young attorney refused to keep silent.

Mehmet Tarhan (Turkey)

Anti-militarist and gay-rights activist Mehmet Tarhan declared his conscientious objection in October 2001, for which he was arrested 8 April 8 2005. He has currently been transferred to his unit without his consent.